Exploring
Sport and Exercise
Psychology

Exploring
Sport and Exercise
Psychology

Edited by

Judy L. Van Raalte
Britton W. Brewer

AMERICAN PSYCHOLOGICAL ASSOCIATION

WASHINGTON, DC

First printing June 1996
Second printing January 1997
Third printing July 1998

Published by the
American Psychological Association
750 First Street, NE
Washington, DC 20002

Copies may be ordered from
APA Order Department
P.O. Box 92984
Washington, DC 20090-2984

In the UK and Europe, copies may be ordered from
American Psychological Association
3 Henrietta Street
Covent Garden
London WC2E 8LU
England

Typeset in Futura and New Baskerville by EPS Group Inc., Easton, MD

Printer: Kirby Lithographic Company, Inc., Arlington, VA
Cover designer: Minker Design, Bethesda, MD
Technical/production editor: Sarah J. Trembath

Library of Congress Cataloging-in-Publication Data
Exploring sport and exercise psychology / edited by Judy L. Van Raalte and Britton W. Brewer.
    p. cm.
  Includes bibliographical references and index.
  ISBN 1-55798-355-0 (acid-free paper)
  1. Sports—Psychological aspects. 2. Exercise—Psychological aspects.
I. Van Raalte, Judy L. II. Brewer, Britton W.
GV706.4.E96 1996
796′.01—dc20   96-11811
                                                  CIP

British Library Cataloguing-in-Publication Data
A CIP record is available from the British Library.

Printed in the United States of America

To Steven R. Heyman, PhD (1946–1993), a pioneer scholar and practitioner of sport and exercise psychology.

Contents

Contributors

Mark B. Andersen, Victoria University of Technology, Melbourne, Australia
Partick H. F. Baillie, Calgary General Hospital, Alberta, Canada
Beth C. Bock, The Miriam Hospital, Providence, Rhode Island
Britton W. Brewer, Springfield College
Matthew M. Clark, The Miriam Hospital, Providence, Rhode Island
Karen D. Cogan, University of North Texas
Nicole Damarjian, University of North Carolina
Steven J. Danish, Virginia Commonwealth University
T. David Elkin, University of Memphis
Daniel Gould, University of North Carolina
Kate F. Hays, The Performing Edge, Concord, New Hampshire
John Heil, Lewis-Gale Clinic, Roanoake, Virginia
Keith Henschen, University of Utah
Thad R. Leffingwell, University of Washington
Bess H. Marcus, The Miriam Hospital, Providence, Rhode Island
Penny McCullagh, University of Colorado
Andrew W. Meyers, University of Memphis
William P. Morgan, University of Wisconsin, Madison
Valerie C. Nellen, Virginia Commonwealth University
John M. Noble, University of Colorado
Bruce C. Ogilvie, San Jose State University
Susanna S. Owens, Virginia Commonwealth University
Frank Perna, West Virginia University
Albert J. Petitpas, Springfield College
Trent A. Petrie, University of North Texas
Bernardine M. Pinto, The Miriam Hospital, Providence, Rhode Island
Wes Sime, University of Nebraska
Robert N. Singer, University of Florida
Robert J. Smith, Creative Problem-Solving, Wellesley, Massachusetts
Ronald E. Smith, University of Washington
Frank L. Smoll, University of Washington
Jim Taylor, Alpine/Taylor Consulting, Aspen, Colorado
Judy L. Van Raalte, Springfield College
Robert S. Weinberg, Miami University, Oxford, Ohio
James P. Whelan, University of Memphis
Jean M. Williams, University of Arizona
Leonard Zaichkowsky, Boston University

Foreword

Future historians of psychology are likely to view the twentieth century as a formative period during which some of the major themes in the profession were first developed. One of those themes has been the relationship between the mind and the body. That relationship has been a central issue in psychology ever since its emergence as a separate discipline. Indeed, it is not coincidental that psychology's conceptual parents—philosophy and physiology—represented the polar extremes of this contrast. The mind–body dichotomy became a problem primarily because of the difficulties in conceptualizing an interaction between metaphysical and physical realms. This separation, technically termed *dualism*, has been prevalent in Western civilization since the times of Pythagoras, and became formalized and enshrined by René Descartes. Dualism became an intractable problem. How was it possible for a nonmaterial mind to influence the material substance of the body? And how did the experiences of that body make their way from the physical to the mental realm? Proposed answers to questions like these have taken a variety of forms, all of which have clustered around a handful of positions: there is no mind (*materialistic monism*); there is no physical body (*idealistic monism*); mind and body interact by means of [fill in this blank] (*interactionism*); mind and body interact, but only occasionally (*occasionalism*); mind and body do not interact; and mind and body do not interact but are parallel (*psychophysical parallelism*). Each of these positions has had its share of adherents and detractors in the history of psychology.

In the second half of the nineteenth century, influential pioneers in psychology defined their work and the field itself as studies of consciousness. The pendulum of focus, so to speak, was on the mind's side of the dichotomy. As Wilhelm Wundt's voluntarism and E. B. Titchener's structuralism gave way to the post-Darwinian tradition of functionalism, however, the pendulum moved toward the bodily side. The rise of behaviorism marked the beginning of an anti-mind era, and this was the dominant position in North American psychology for the first half of this century. Private events were largely banished from experimental psychology, and the "black box" of mental life was deemed unimportant to the allegedly "real science" of studying functional relations between stimulus (*input*) and response (*output*). The pendulum began its return journey around 1955 and, in the 1970s, psychology and other disciplines were in the throes of a sweeping "cognitive revolution." Beginning with studies in cybernetics and information processing, the cognitive sciences gained momentum and voice. The paradigms of connectionism and constructivism became second and third waves in the cognitive revolution, and the pendulum seemed destined toward the mind side again.

But something else happened. It was an unexpected and, in many ways, unprecedented something. The pendulum of focus broke out of its fixed path of alternations between mind and body. Instead of swinging in a straight line of separation between these two poles, the pendulum began swinging toward a circle that connected mind and body in an integrative way. Signs of this new development were popping up everywhere. The "dry look" in neurobiology, which had likened the brain and nervous system to an electronic circuit board, began to give way to the "wet look" of a nervous system literally bathed in fluids that connected it with the body. Respected brain scientists like Roger Sperry, who had previously endorsed an interactionist position on mind–body relations, began to encourage a new position that moved beyond the Cartesian assumption of dualism. The tradition of *rationalist supremacy*, which had placed reason above and in control of the body and its passions, was challenged by research emphasizing the power and pervasiveness of emotionality in attention, perception, learning, and memory. George Lakoff, Mark Johnson, and Antonio Damasio were among a creative group of theorists and researchers who documented that the body is in the mind no less than the mind is in the body. Developmental psychologists showed that infants used their bodily movements to establish communicative channels with their caregivers long before their development of language. Esther Thelen introduced the "new look" in motor development, showing how children display complex and dynamic self-organizing processes that defy any meaningful segregation of brain and body. The doctrine of *cerebral primacy*, which assumed that development and evolution were led by the head, receded in the face of evidence that body and brain development are integrated phenomena. Health psychology and sport psychology came to be recognized as legitimate and promising specializations that reflected this more integrative view.

The body is back, and so is the mind. They are not separate realms. They never were. It may be a long time before people develop a more adequate vocabulary and language habits to address the complexity of bodybrain processes, but I believe it is promising that steps have recently been taken toward liberating ourselves from the chains of dualism that have enslaved philosophy for more than two millenia and psychology for more than a century. There is still a long way to go, of course, but this should be an inspiring rather than daunting realization. Psychology is at the beginning of a new era, which promises to be filled with exciting insights that cannot now be anticipated. To use the terminology now popular in the sciences of complexity, psychology is in the midst of a *phase transition*, in which old patterns of order are in the process of being incorporated (literally, *embodied*) into new patterns.

Dualistic notions about mind and body will not go away quickly or easily, and it is important that we realize the likelihood that dualistic conceptualizations probably served valuable functions in the early stages of reflective inquiry and psychological science. As tempting and popular as it may be to engage in "Descartes-bashing," it is wise to respect the roles that traditions play in all evolutions of our thinking. Philosopher Thomas Kuhn is best known for his work on the structure of scientific revolutions, but he was equally emphatic about the role of *essential tensions* in the development of knowledge. Revolutions require traditions as the targets of their revolts. Changes require enduring stabilities to define them. Recognizing this is central to the appreciation that all development is fundamentally *dialectical*—that is, that it emerges out of the interaction of contrasts. The embodiment of mind and the return of the body to psychology are developments that have emerged out of a series of longstanding contrasts regarding mind, body, and their possible relationships. New paradigms are now appearing that integrate and elaborate in ways that will break new ground in theory, research, and practice. And one of the areas where such integrations and elaborations are particularly apparent is that of exercise and sport psychology. This volume represents a major contribution to that area, and I am honored to be a contributor to it.

To appreciate the significance of this volume one must realize what it represents in the context of the emerging specializations of exercise and sport psychology. And one does not have to go too far back to see why the range and depth of this volume are a welcome and timely contribution. The pioneering works of Norman Triplett in the 1890s and of Coleman Roberts Griffith in and after the 1920s have been around for close to a century, and yet the field of sport psychology has remained—until very recently—an undernourished specialization. For the first three quarters of the twentieth century, psychological studies of exercise and sport were rarely undertaken and even less frequently reported. Things began to change in the 1970s, however, and have continued accelerating since then. A popular rise in health consciousness among the public has encouraged that development. The "movement movement" placed new demands on psychologists interested in incorporating the body into their services.

It is interesting to reflect back upon exercise and sport psychology only a quarter of a century ago. Exercise was the domain of exercise scientists, and it was considered an esoteric interest. Neighborhood health clubs were rare and little used. Those gyms that did exist were neither high-tech nor fashionable, and their clientele were few and predominantly male. Bicycle lanes, running and walking paths, and fitness equipment were very difficult to find. Shopping malls did not abound with stores selling athletic apparel, running shoes, and home gyms. In North America, at least, sport was largely ignored by psychology. There were no trained specialists in sport psychology, no training programs, and relatively few researchers or practitioners. There were a few, however, who found themselves focusing more and more on sport. They began to write about the multiple roles of sport in society and the impact of an audience or competitor on athletic performance, the contributions of sports involvement to children's personality development, the existence of biases and preconceptions about women's involvement in exercise and sport, and the effects of hypnosis on athletic training and sports performance. In those days there was precious little literature—either experimental or case study—to inform and assist practitioners interested in offering psychological services to athletes or in recommending exercise or movement to their clients. Practitioners were essentially on their own in shaping their services. Many important lessons were learned and, fortunately, many were conveyed in forms that eventually made them more accessible to the growing numbers of practicing exercise and sport psychologists.

Even today, of course, there are relatively few training programs that incorporate exercise and sport psychology as a possible emphasis, let alone a primary specialization. And there are even fewer training opportunities for experienced practitioners who would like to expand their competencies to include exercise and sport applications. Unfortunately, those interested in becoming exercise and sport psychologists are still somewhat on their own in finding experiences that will adequately prepare them for the range of challenges presented by athletes and by clients in professional counseling. At a recent conference one of the participants asked, "But *how* do you bring the body into psychotherapy?" My response, with a smile, was "It usually comes in underneath the head, but it's always *there*." The point I was trying to make was that "talking heads" therapy must be transformed into a service that reflects a deep and working appreciation of embodiment in all human experiencing.

How does the practitioner do this? How do psychologists help their clients to appreciate the significance of their bodies in their psychological lives? How do we assess their attitudes toward their bodies, eating, exercise, dance, touch, and so on? How do we individualize recommendations for healthy activities that bring joy as well as fitness into their lives? How do we teach children to develop a relationship with sports, movement, and themselves that sings with a sense of sublime delight at their capacities for "being bodily?" How do we help athletes to enjoy and optimally express their gifts and their hard work in their performances? What are the needs of special populations that may be challenged? And how do we encourage and participate in research and the training of psychologists who are interested in questions such as these?

These are among the issues addressed in the present volume. Here the reader has a well-balanced range of chapters on basic themes and contemporary issues in exercise and sport psychology. The authors are highly respected specialists, including some of the pioneers in the field, and all share invaluable knowledge and experience. The topics addressed are core themes, such as motivation, imagery, cognitive strategies, intensity regulation, hypnosis, exercise therapy, assessment, psychological problems, referral practices, work with children and special populations, professional training, certification, clinical practice, and ethics. This volume represents a wealth of expertise and information that will be invaluable to anyone interested in serving athletes or clients who choose to explore exercise as a path toward well-being. This is a contemporary classic, and it deserves wide readership and practical application.

Michael J. Mahoney

Acknowledgments

We undertook the editing of this book with ambitious goals and tight time lines. There are many people whose dedication, hard work, moral support, sage advice, and assistance made this project possible.

We gratefully acknowledge the diligence, perseverence, and tolerance of the chapter authors, who willingly met deadlines, made revisions, made additional revisions, and produced outstanding chapters. The entire publication process was simplified by words of wisdom from several experienced authors and colleagues who had written or edited books and gave us invaluable advice. Thanks to John Heil, Mike Mahoney, Bill Morgan, Ron Smith, Steve West, and Jean Williams.

We would also like to thank our mentors: Darwyn Linder, who taught us that you can fit one more thing into your schedule if it is something that you really want to do, and Paul Karoly, who taught us that editing a book can be a rewarding activity. Our appreciation extends to our colleagues and students at Springfield College: Al Petitpas, who taught us to affiliate with intelligent people and served as a sounding board throughout the preparation of this book; Molly Rau and Gretchen Brockmeyer, who enthusiastically supported this project; and Antoinette Minitti and David Kleinschuster, who provided technical support.

We salute the professionals at APA Books who made this book possible. Ron Wilder nurtured the project from its earliest stages and, when difficulties were encountered, assured us that all would be "hunky dunky." We appreciate the thoughtful reviews of Diane Gill and Sean

McCann, whose insightful comments helped to improve the quality of the book. We gratefully acknowledge the contributions of APA Books editors Paula Whyman and Sarah Trembath, and Steve Remer, APA marketing specialist.

Finally, we would like to thank our families, who remained interested and excited about the progress of the book throughout the entire process.

Preface

Psychology is a diverse and ever expanding field of research and practice. Given this diversity and expansion, it is not surprising that the domains of sport and exercise, both of which receive regular media attention and occupy important roles in daily living, have served as arenas for scientific scrutiny and applied work of a psychological nature.

Our interest in sport and exercise psychology evolved naturally from our experiences as undergraduate psychology majors and varsity athletes. Graduate training in the area brought the realization that there was much to learn and confirmed our initial favorable impression of the field. We became actively involved in sport and exercise psychology by joining professional organizations, conducting research, teaching, and coaching.

As committee chairs in Division 47 (Exercise and Sport Psychology) of the American Psychological Association, we often received telephone calls and responded to inquiries about the field. There were those who asked, "I'm thinking of expanding my psychology practice. Is there a course I could take or a book I could read about sport and exercise psychology?" There were some practitioners who found themselves working with an athlete and asked, "Do you have any suggestions for me that I can use to help my client, who is going through a slump (or not getting along with the coach, or lacking confidence, or having problems concentrating, and so on)?" Students often contacted us, wanting to find out more about graduate training, career opportunities, and the field in general.

This book reflects our attempt to gather together experts in sport and exercise psychology to answer the questions most commonly raised by professionals and students interested in the field. As researchers, practitioners, and educators in sport and exercise psychology, we believe that it is important to include thoroughly referenced material with a strong scientific foundation and to address applied issues in the field. We tried to create a book that combines current research findings with the latest applied approaches to bridge the gap between the scientific and popular literatures.

Exploring Sport and Exercise Psychology provides an overview of the field of sport and exercise psychology, connects theory and practice, and discusses important practical issues related to credentialing and training. We hope that this book will serve as a resource for people interested in sport and exercise psychology and will be a springboard for further exploration of the field.

Introduction to Sport and Exercise Psychology

Britton W. Brewer and Judy L. Van Raalte

Physical activity is a salient aspect of human experience across the life span. There are competitive and recreational sport leagues for children, adolescents, adults, and seniors. Exercise has been identified as an important part of a healthy lifestyle for the young and old alike. Given the centrality of physical activity to contemporary living, it is not surprising that psychologists have become interested in sport and exercise behavior. This interest has given rise to sport and exercise psychology—an emerging field that offers an abundance of exciting opportunities for research and practice in an inherently interesting domain of human behavior (Cox, Qiu, & Liu, 1993; Hays, 1995; Taylor, 1991).

As is the case with many subfields of psychology, sport and exercise psychology encompasses a wide variety of clinical, educational, and research activities. A sport and exercise psychologist might work with athletes at the United States Olympic Training Center, use exercise therapeutically with clients, or conduct workshops for parents and youth sport coaches. Although there may be no typical sport and exercise psychologist, there are a number of issues and content areas with which all practicing sport and exercise psychologists should be familiar. This book is designed to acquaint psychologists, psychologists-in-training (i.e., students), and other mental health practitioners interested in sport and exercise psychology with basic interventions, clinical issues, special populations, and professional issues in the field.

The primary purpose of this chapter is to provide an introduction to the growing field of sport and exercise psychology. The chapter describes the historical foundations, research trends, current controversies, client populations, and applied settings of the field. After the history and current status of the field are summarized, an overview of the book is presented.

A Brief History of Sport and Exercise Psychology in the United States

Despite the popular misconception of the field as a novel area of inquiry, sport and exercise psychology has a rich history. Although investigation of psychological factors associated with exercise is a relatively recent phenomenon (Gill, 1986, 1987), scientists have been studying psychological aspects of sport for more than 100 years (Wiggins, 1984). Examination of the evolution of sport and exercise psychology contributes to an understanding of the field as it stands today.

At the end of the 19th and beginning of the 20th century, a number of theoretical and empirical works addressing sport-related topics appeared in the psychological literature (Wiggins, 1984). Notable among these writings were Norman Triplett's (1897) study of audience effects on cycling performance, which is also considered the first experiment in social psychology (West & Wicklund, 1980), and American Psychological Association (APA) founding president G. Stanley Hall's (1908) report extolling the psychological benefits of physical education.

On the heels of these early developments, Coleman Griffith established what is regarded as the first sport-psychology laboratory in North America in 1925 at the University of Illinois. Griffith conducted research on psychological aspects of sport performance, such as psychomotor learning, personality, and motivation. He also developed coursework in sport psychology and later served as sport psychologist for the Chicago Cubs (Kroll & Lewis, 1970).

Despite Griffith's advances in the 1920s and 1930s, interest in sport psychology was restricted primarily to a growing core of motor-learning researchers in physical education departments in the 1940s and 1950s. It was not until the 1960s and 1970s that sport psychology began to flourish as a discipline, as evidenced by the emergence of textbooks, professional organizations, and scholarly journals devoted to sport psychology (Wiggins, 1984; Williams & Straub, 1993). Popular sport-specific research topics during this period included personality, arousal/anxiety, performance-enhancement interventions (e.g., relaxation, imagery), achievement motivation, causal attributions, aggression, and team cohesion (Cox et al., 1993).

Building upon the developments of the 1960s and 1970s, the field expanded further in the 1980s. During this decade, there were major trends toward investigation of psychological aspects of exercise (Browne & Mahoney, 1984; Rejeski & Thompson, 1993) and application of the growing knowledge-base to assist sport participants in achieving maximal athletic performance (Browne & Mahoney, 1984). Reflecting these trends, the *Journal of Sport Psychology* became the *Journal of Sport and Exercise Psychology* (Gill, 1986, 1987) in 1988 and the Association for the Advancement of Applied Sport Psychology (AAASP) was founded in 1985 (Williams & Straub, 1993). The first recognition of sport and exercise psychology by mainstream psychology occurred in 1987 with the formation of Division 47 (Exercise and Sport Psychology) of the APA (Williams & Straub, 1993).

Current Status of Sport and Exercise Psychology

Its early history was dominated by the efforts of physical educators, but sport and exercise psychology has evolved into an interdisciplinary field, involving both sport scientists and psychologists. From an initial focus on sport performance as the primary outcome of interest, sport and exercise psychology has broadened considerably. Performance enhancement remains an important area of research and applied work, but improvement of the quality of participant involvement in physical activity has emerged as an emphasis of researchers and practitioners (Hays, 1995; Williams & Straub, 1993). Although collegiate, professional, and elite-amateur athletes have traditionally been the main recipients of interventions, professionals have expanded the horizon to include youth competitors, adult recreational participants, masters athletes, and underserved populations (Murphy, 1995). In keeping with the widening range of populations targeted for intervention, sport and exercise psychology research and practice has extended beyond the playing field and the laboratory to a host of other venues, including schools, health clubs, sports medicine clinics, counseling centers, and private practice offices.

As a result of continued expansion over the past three decades, sport and exercise psychology has experienced growing pains. In particular, because the field encompasses professionals of varying educational background, issues of training, credentials, and ethics have come to the fore. Current debates are centered on the training needed to become a sport and exercise psychologist, competencies required to be labeled a sport and exercise psychologist, and standards of ethical professional conduct (Hays, 1995; Murphy, 1995; Taylor, 1991).

Overview of the Book

As was previously mentioned, this book is intended to present an overview of the wide array of issues of potential interest to prospective sport and exercise psychology practitioners. The book is designed to serve as a resource with theoretical and practical suggestions related to the practice of sport and exercise psychology. The sections of the book are organized around three questions frequently asked about the field: What specifically do sport and exercise psychologists do? With whom do sport and exercise psychologists work? What do I need to do to become a sport and exercise psychologist? Chapter authors have adopted a practical approach in answering these critical questions. Where available empirical data are limited or nonexistent, gaps in the knowledge base are acknowledged and sound recommendations for practice based on professional experience are provided.

The first three sections of the book, Performance Enhancement, Promoting Well-Being, and Clinical Issues, pertain primarily to what practitioners in sport and exercise psychology do. The section on Performance Enhancement addresses various cognitive–behavioral interventions designed to facilitate optimal sport-performance. Interventions such as goal-setting, imagery, cognitive strategies, intensity regulation, and hypnosis are commonly considered the "meat and potatoes" of this aspect of sport and exercise psychology. For each intervention, a theoretical rationale for use is provided, empirical support for the intervention is reviewed, and practical suggestions for implementation are given. Although the interventions featured in this section are presented individually in chapters, professionals most likely would combine them in an integrated psychological skills-training program. This section is most appropriate for practitioners primarily interested in assisting athletes to achieve favorable outcomes in sport tasks.

The section Promoting Well-Being reflects the current breadth of sport and exercise psychology and deals with psychological applications intended to enhance the physical and mental health of athletic and general populations alike. A chapter titled "Exercise Initiation, Adoption, and Maintenance" describes interventions designed to increase exercise behavior in the general population, an issue with enormous public health ramifications. In a chapter that demonstrates the versatility of physical activity as a medium for promoting well-being, the author of "Guidelines for Clinical Applications of Exercise Therapy for Mental Health" considers the use of exercise to treat psychological problems. In the remaining chapters in this section, authors of "Counseling Interventions in Applied Sport Psychology" and "Teaching Life Skills Through Sport: Community-Based Programs for Adolescents" use developmental perspectives to examine ways in which sport participation can produce favorable psychosocial consequences. Both chapters provide additional evidence of how practitioners of sport and exercise psychology are concerned with outcomes beyond sport performance.

The third section of the book, Clinical Issues, addresses aspects of practice that have been largely ignored in the sport and exercise psychology literature. That there has been little coverage of clinical issues such as assessment, psychopathology, and referral may seem surprising to practitioners with clinical training, but this knowledge gap is probably attributable to the fact that the field traditionally has been a subdiscipline of physical education rather than psychology. A chapter titled "Assessment in Sport and Exercise Psychology" serves as a logical point of departure for this section, because consultation with sport and exercise participants often begins with assessment. In addition to reviewing assessment instruments specific to this field, the chapter examines issues in applying traditional methods of psychological assessment to the sport and exercise milieu. "Psychopathology in Sport and Exercise" and "Referral Processes in Sport Psychology" follow the chapter on assessment, highlighting two possible outcomes of assessment: identification of pathological behavior in sport and exercise participants and recognition of the need to refer some clients to other professionals. The chapters in this section are especially relevant to practitioners who lack clinical training or professional experience with sport and exercise populations.

The fourth section of the book, Working with Specific Populations, focuses on the individuals with whom sport and exercise psychology practitioners work. The chapters in this section present detailed information on several typical client populations in the field (see Murphy, 1995). Special considerations for working with children ("Psychosocial Interventions in Youth Sport"), intercollegiate sport participants ("Working with College Student-Athletes"), and professional or elite amateur athletes ("Working with Elite Athletes") are outlined. The last chapter in this section, "Diversity in Sport," addresses possible influences of selected individual-difference factors (i.e., gender, race/ethnicity, sexual orientation, and physical disability status) on sport and exercise psychology consultation.

The fifth and final section of the book, Professional Issues, addresses what individuals aspiring to become a sport and exercise psychologist need to know and do. In particular, issues central to the professionalization of sport and exercise psychology are explored. Chapters in this section tackle the controversial issues that confront the field (see Hays, 1995; Murphy, 1995): training ("Education and Training in Sport and Exercise Psychology"), credentialing ("Certification in Sport and Exercise Psychology"), and ethics ("Ethics in Sport and Exercise Psychology"). Readers may be surprised to learn that the majority of training programs in sport and exercise psychology are in departments of physical education, that certification procedures in the field currently are in place, and that there are a number of unique ethical challenges that can occur in practice. Helpful "nuts-and-bolts" suggestions for diversifying any practice to include work with sport and exercise participants are given in "Incorporating Sport and Exercise Psychology into Clinical Practice." In "The Future of Sport and Exercise Psychology" —the chapter that concludes both the section and the book—anticipated trends in the field are examined.

Conclusion

Sport and exercise psychology is a growing field with a rich history. As a domain of research and practice, sport and exercise psychology is becoming increasingly diversified. *Exploring Sport and Exercise Psychology* is designed to reflect this diversity and serve as a resource for professionals and students interested in the field.

References

Browne, M. A., & Mahoney, M. J. (1984). Sport psychology. *Annual Review of Psychology, 35,* 605–625.

Cox, P. H., Qiu, Y., & Liu, Z. (1993). Overview of sport psychology. In R. N. Singer, M. Murphey, & L. K. Tennant (Eds.), *Handbook of research on sport psychology* (pp. 3–31). New York: Macmillan.

Gill, D. L. (1986). A prospective view of the *Journal of Sport (and Exercise) Psychology. Journal of Sport Psychology, 8,* 164–173.

Gill, D. L. (1987). Journal of Sport and Exercise Psychology. *Journal of Sport Psychology, 9,* 1–2.

Hall, G. S. (1908). *Physical education in colleges: Report of the National Education Association.* Chicago: University of Chicago Press.

Hays, K. F. (1995). Putting sport psychology into (your) practice. *Professional Psychology: Research and Practice, 26,* 33–40.

Kroll, W., & Lewis, G. (1970). America's first sport psychologist. *Quest, 13,* 1–4.

Murphy, S. M. (1995). Introduction to sport psychology interventions. In S. M. Murphy (Ed.), *Sport psychology interventions* (pp. 1–15). Champaign, IL: Human Kinetics.

Rejeski, W. J., & Thompson, A. (1993). Historical and conceptual roots of exercise psychology. In P. Seraganian (Ed.), *Exercise psychology: The influence of physical exercise on psychological processes* (pp. 3–35). New York: Wiley.

Taylor, J. (1991). Career direction, development, and opportunities in applied sport psychology. *The Sport Psychologist, 5,* 226–280.

Triplett, N. (1897). The dynamogenic factors in pacemaking and competition. *American Journal of Psychology, 9,* 507–553.

West, S. G. & Wicklund, R. A. (1980). *A primer of social psychology theories.* Monterey, CA: Brooks/Cole.

Wiggins, D. K. (1984). The history of sport psychology in North American. In J. Silva & R. Weinberg (Eds.), *Psychological foundations of sport* (pp. 9–22). Champaign, IL: Human Kinetics.

Williams, J. M. & Straub, W. F. (1993). Sport psychology: Past, present, and future. In J. M. Williams (Ed.), *Applied sport psychology: Personal growth to peak performance* (2nd ed., pp. 1–10). Mountain View, CA: Mayfield.

Part One

Performance Enhancement

Goal Setting in Sport and Exercise: Research to Practice

Robert S. Weinberg

My goal is to improve my first serve percentage to 65%. My objective is to make the starting lineup when the season starts. Our goal is to win the state championship. I want to be able to bench press my own weight.

The above are just a few examples of different types of goals that athletes set in an attempt to improve their performance. Unlike some other mental health care workers helping their clients improve psychological skills, sport psychologists do not typically have a problem getting athletes to set goals. Rather, they have difficulty getting athletes to set the right kind of goals—goals that enhance motivation. Athletes do not need to be convinced that goals are important; athletes need to be instructed concerning the most effective types of goals to set and to develop a goal-setting program that works.

This chapter is designed specifically to have individuals involved in sport and exercise learn more about effective goal setting. A research-to-practice orientation is taken. I begin by defining the different types of goals and discussing goal-setting theory and the latest goal-setting research. From this research, principles of effective goal-setting will be identified, methods of designing a goal-setting program will be presented, and common problems and ways to overcome these problems will be discussed.

The Concept of Goal Setting

By definition, a goal is that which an individual is trying to accomplish; it is the objective or aim of an action. For example, in most goal-setting studies, the term *goal* refers to a specific level of proficiency on a task, usually within a specified time limit (Locke, Shaw, Saari, & Latham, 1981). From a practical point of view, goals focus on standards of excellence such as improving free-throw percentage by 5 points, losing 10 pounds, lowering one's time in the mile run by 3 seconds, or improving one's batting average by 10 points. In addition, these goals would have to be reached within a given time frame, such as by the end of the season or within a certain number of days, weeks, or months.

In sport and exercise settings, the type of goals set by participants and coaches vary in their degree of specificity and difficulty in measuring whether the goal was accomplished. This has led sport psychologists to distinguish between subjective goals and objective goals. Subjective goals include things such as having fun, trying one's best, "hustling" more, and becoming more fit. Examples of objective goals include improving first-serve percentage in tennis to 65%, winning the state championship, or knocking three strokes off a golf score. Clearly, although subjective goals are important, it is often difficult to accurately assess how much an athlete has improved in hustling. Therefore, the focus of goals in sport and exercise settings has been on objective rather than subjective goals.

Goal Setting Theory

Much of the early work on goal setting originated from two major sources—one academic and one organizational. The academic source extends back to the early 1960s and focuses on the associated concepts of intention, task set, and level of aspiration (see Ryan, 1970 for a review). The organizational line of research can be traced to the work of Taylor (1967) in which the concept of *task* (a specific assignment or goal given to a worker each day) eventually led to the application of goal setting in the form of management-by-objectives programs now widely used in industrial settings (Ordiorne, 1978).

Using these early sources as building blocks, Locke and his colleagues (Locke, 1966, 1968, 1978; Locke, Shaw, Saari, & Latham, 1981; Locke & Latham, 1990) developed a theory of goal setting that has served as the stimulus for literally hundreds of studies in industrial and organizational settings, and, more recently, in sport and exercise settings. The basic assumption of goal setting theory is that task performance is regulated directly by the conscious goals that individuals are trying for on a task. In essence, goals are immediate regulators of human action. Goals operate largely through internal comparison processes and require internal standards against which to evaluate ongoing performance.

According to the theory, hard goals result in a higher level of performance and effort than easy goals, and specific hard goals result in a higher level of performance than no goals or generalized goals of "do your best." In addition, the theory states that a person's goals mediate how performance is affected by monetary incentives, time limits, knowledge of results, participation in decision making, degree of commitment, and competition. Locke argued that although goals can influence behavior, no simple correlation can be assumed because people make errors, lack the ability to attain their objectives, or subconsciously subvert their conscious goals. It should be noted that although most research investigating the goal setting–performance relationship has set out to test the propositions put forth by Locke, other theories have recently been developed. These include cognitive mediation theory (Garland, 1985), goal orientation theory (Nicholls, 1984a, 1984b; Maehr & Braskamp, 1986), and the competitive goal setting model (Burton, 1992), which will be discussed later in the chapter. Although these relatively new approaches to goal-setting have potential for enhancing our understanding of the goal setting process, to date, most of the research testing the goal–performance relationship has tested Locke's original theory and thus this will be the focus of the ensuing review.

Goal Setting and Task Performance in Industrial Settings

Research on goal setting as a motivational strategy has been proliferating so rapidly in the past 20 years that reviews such as that by Locke et al. (1981) become quickly outdated. This has necessitated more updated reviews that have often used the statistical technique of meta-analysis, which enables the reviewer to aggregate findings across studies using both inferential and descriptive statistics (e.g., Locke & Latham, 1990; Mento, Steel, & Karren, 1987; Tubbs, 1991).

The most tested aspect of Locke's theory revolves around the relationship of goal difficulty/specificity and performance. As previously mentioned, Locke (1966, 1968) has argued that specific, difficult, challenging goals lead to higher levels of task performance than easy goals, no goals, or vague "do your best" goals. Locke and Latham (1990) reviewed 201 studies (over 40,000 subjects). Of these studies, 183, or 91%, supported Locke's initial hypothesis. These results were found using approximately 90 different tasks in both laboratory and field settings, which demonstrates the robustness and generalizability of these findings.

A second core aspect of Locke's goal-setting theory is that there is a linear relationship between degree of goal difficulty and performance. The only exception is when subjects reach the limits of their ability at high goal-difficulty levels; in such cases performance levels off. Three separate metaanalyses have reviewed the empirical studies testing the goal difficulty–performance relationship (Chidester & Grigsby, 1984; Mento, Steel & Karren, 1989; Tubbs, 1991). Results from these meta-analyses have revealed effect sizes ranging from 0.52–0.82. In addition, of the 192 studies reviewed, 175 (91%) provided support for harder goals producing higher levels of task performance than easy goals. Thus, the goal difficulty/specificity relationships found in industrial settings provide one of the most consistent and robust patterns of findings in the social science literature.

Goal Setting in Sport and Exercise

Whereas considerable research has been conducted on goal setting in industrial and organizational settings, sport and exercise psychology researchers have begun to examine the topic only in the last 10 years. A systematic and concerted effort to study this relationship began with the publication of Locke and Latham's (1985) article on the application of goal setting to sports. Locke and Latham suggested that goal setting could work even better in sports than in business because the measurement of an individual's performance is typically more objective in sports than in organizational settings. Following the emphasis in industrial psychology, goal setting research in sport and exercise settings has focused on the areas of goal specificity, goal difficulty, and goal proximity.

These areas have been investigated using a variety of skilled and physical fitness tasks such as number of sit-ups in 3 minutes, and basketball, lacrosse, circuit training, and swimming skills. However, results have been somewhat equivocal, with some studies finding support for goal setting effectiveness and others not (see Burton, 1992; Weinberg, 1994 for detailed reviews). An example of the inconsistent findings is to be found in a study by Burton (1989), which investigated the effects of specific or general goals on a variety of fundamental basketball skills (e.g., dribbling, shooting, footwork) varying in complexity. Results indicated that setting specific as compared to general goals enhanced performance. However, performance was not enhanced on all tasks, and in fact, higher performance was evidenced on tasks of low complexity rather than those of high complexity.

Despite the somewhat mixed results in sport and exercise settings, it would be premature and inappropriate to conclude that goal setting is a less powerful technique than has been suggested by the industrial and organizational psychology literatures. For example, Weinberg (1994) argued that the inconsistent findings are at least in part due to the different methodologies employed in sport and exercise settings along with moderator variables that mediate the goal setting-performance relationship. Some of the methodological and design considerations include spontaneous goal setting in control groups, subject motivation and commitment, task characteristics, and competition among subjects. Furthermore, athletes and exercise participants are simply different in their motivations and perform under different task conditions than subjects in other goal setting studies. Thus, it is incumbent on sport and exercise researchers to investigate the conditions under which goal setting techniques are most effective.

Overall, it seems that goal setting is an extremely powerful technique for enhancing performance. For example, in one of the few studies investigating goal setting across an entire athletic season (Weinberg, Stitcher, & Richardson, 1994), it was found that lacrosse players using goal setting improved in a variety of performance measures (e.g., goals, assists, defensive and offensive ground balls) when compared to a control group of players not using goals. The perceived effectiveness of goal setting was also demonstrated in a survey conducted with leading sport psychology consultants working with U.S. Olympic athletes (Gould, Tammen, Murphy, & May, 1989). Results revealed that goal setting was the most often used psychological intervention in both one-on-one athlete–coach and group consultations. Results from Orlick and Partington's (1988) extensive study of Canadian Olympic athletes also demonstrated the use of goal setting because athletes reported daily goal setting as part of their regular training regimen. Thus, it is clear from research and professional practice literature that, as with most sport psychology techniques, goal setting can be effective in enhancing performance. However goal setting is not a fool-proof method that can be easily implemented without some careful thought and planning. Thus, individuals who attempt to implement goal-setting programs in sport and exercise settings should be knowledgeable professionals with a firm understanding of the goal-setting process. It is especially important that each practitioner possess a keen understanding of his or her individual situation (e.g., type of sport, individual personalities of participants) in order to implement goal-setting programs most effectively.

Explanations for the Effectiveness of Goal Setting

As noted above, it is important for practitioners to understand how and why goal setting influences performance. Two general categories of explanations have been advanced to explain the ways that goals influence performance. These explanations are known as the *mechanistic view* and the *cognitive view*.

Mechanistic Explanation

The mechanistic explanation for the effectiveness of goals on enhancing performance was put forth by Locke and his colleagues (Locke et al., 1981). They argued that goals influence performance in four distinct ways: (a) directing attention, (b) mobilizing effort, (c) enhancing persistence, and (d) developing new learning strategies. These are briefly discussed below.

One way that goals can influence performance is through directing an individual's attention to the task at hand and focusing on the relevant cues in the athletic or exercise environment. In fact, recent research (Weinberg, Burton, Yukelson, & Weigand, 1993) found that college athletes felt that the most important reason they set goals was to focus attention to the task at hand. For example, if a basketball player set goals to improve his field-goal percentage, foul-shot percentage, or number of rebounds and assists, then he would focus his attention in these specific game areas. In essence, the basketball player's attention is focused on important elements of his game that need to be improved.

In addition to focusing attention, goals also increase effort and persistence by providing feedback in relation to one's progress. For example, a long-distance runner may not feel like putting in the required mileage day after day or may feel bored with the repetitive routine of training. But by setting short-term goals and seeing progress toward her long term goal, she can maintain motivation on a day-by-day basis as well as over time. Similarly, losing 60 pounds might seem like an impossible task for an obese person who has been overweight much of his life. However, by setting a goal to lose two pounds a week and charting this subgoal accomplishment, the individual can stay motivated and persist with the weight-loss program for the time required.

A good example of the effectiveness of goals as a means of feedback was demonstrated in a season-long study on collegiate lacrosse players mentioned previously (Weinberg et al., 1994). Collegiate lacrosse players were evaluated by the head and assistant coaches and matched on their lacrosse-playing ability. The matched pairs were then randomly assigned to either a goal-setting condition or control condition. It should be noted that coaches did not know which players were assigned to the goal-setting and control conditions. Players set short-term goals each week and had a long-term seasonal goal. Feedback was provided weekly concerning goal attainment. Compared to players in the control group, players in the goal-setting condition had consistently higher levels of both offensive and defensive measures of performance throughout the season.

The final mechanism by which goals can influence performance is development of relevant learning strategies. That is, when goals are set, strategies to help reach the goal should be put in place by coaches or athletes. For example, if a basketball player had a goal to improve her free-throw percentage from 70% to 75%, then she might invoke the strategy of shooting an extra 100 free throws each day, changing her pre-shot routine, or even changing her mechanics of shooting. In any case, new strategies are developed to help the player to obtain her free-throw shooting goal.

Cognitive Explanations

A more recent explanation of how goals influence performance comes from the work of Garland (1985) and Burton (1989, 1992). Both of these researchers argued that such psychological states as anxiety, confidence, and satisfaction affect one's goal setting and subsequent performance. For example, Burton (1989) claimed that athletes who set outcome goals based on winning and losing will experience more anxiety and less confidence in competitive settings because their goals are really not under their control. That is, if a swimmer sets a goal to come in first in a race and breaks her personal best by two seconds but only places third in the race, then she would not be satisfied with her performance. This could result in increased anxiety and decreased confidence because the swimmer has little control over the outcome. Conversely, a swimmer who sets a goal to reduce his swimming time by two seconds can feel confident about his performance if he reaches this goal even if he came in third place.

This cognitive explanation for the effects of goal setting on performance was supported in a study of intercollegiate swimmers (Burton, 1989). Specifically, swimmers participated in a five-month goal-setting program that emphasized the setting of performance goals (referenced against one's own self-improvement) versus outcome goals focused on winning or place of finish. Results indicated that swimmers who were high, as compared to low, in their ability to set performance goals were less anxious and exhibited better performance. These results demonstrate not only the importance of setting performance goals, but that proper goal setting is a psychological skill to be learned and practiced.

Another cognitive explanation of how goals relate to behavior and performance, known as *goal orientation theory*, has been championed by several different psychologists (Dweck, 1986; Maehr & Braskamp, 1986; Nicholls, 1984a, 1984b) as well as sport and exercise psychologists (Duda, 1992; Roberts, 1992). Goal orientation theory predicts that an individual's achievement goals and perceived ability interact to affect achievement-related behaviors. Specifically, it is suggested that an individual's goal perspective will affect self-evaluations of demonstrated ability, expended effort, and attributions for success and failure. In turn, these cognitions are assumed to influence achievement-related affect, strategies, and subsequent behaviors such as performance, task choice, and persistence.

Research has indicated two major goal perspectives: ego orientation and task orientation (Duda, 1992). Individuals with *ego orientations* derive their notions of ability from success and failure. In essence, their competence is other-referenced with the goal being to outdo others, rather than simply improving. Conversely, individuals with *task orientations* derive their perceptions of ability and competence from improvements from their own performance. That is, competence is seen as self-referenced, with personal improvement and effort viewed as critical to the individual's perception of ability. Thus, task-oriented individuals will tend to set goals that are realistic because they are focused on self improvement rather than the performance of others. Finally, it is important to note that these two goal perspectives are not seen as independent. For example, research has indicated that elite athletes are high in both task and ego orientations (White & Duda, 1991). In summary, research on goal perspectives underscores the notion that individuals' perceptions of ability depend largely on their subjective interpretation of success and failure. This, in turn, affects goal-directed behavior in sport and exercise environments.

Goal Setting Principles

It is apparent from the theoretical and empirical research reviewed previously, that goal setting can enhance performance and personal growth in sport and exercise environments. It is misleading to think, however, that all types of goals are equally effective in achieving these ends. The key is to structure goal-setting programs so that they are consistent with the basic principles derived from the organizational and sport psychology literatures as well as from professional practice knowledge of sport and exercise psychologists working in field settings. It is important to keep in mind, however, that the effectiveness of any motivational technique is dependent on the interaction of the individuals and the situation in which the individuals are placed; the goal-setting principles listed in Exhibit 1 and discussed subsequently should be considered within this context.

Exhibit 1

Goal Setting Principles

1. Set specific goals.
2. Set realistic but challenging goals.
3. Set both long- and short-term goals.
4. Set goals for practice and competition.
5. "Ink it, don't think it."
6. Develop goal-achievement strategies.
7. Set performance goals.
8. Set individual and team goals.
9. Provide support for goals.
10. Provide for goal evaluation.

Set Specific Goals

One of the most consistent findings from the goal-setting literature is that specific goals produce higher levels of task performance than no goals or general "do your best" goals (Weinberg & Weigand, 1993). Athletes often hear coaches and teachers tell participants simply to "go out and do your best." Although this type of instruction can be motivating, it is not as powerful in enhancing motivation and performance as encouraging participants to go out and achieve a specific goal. Furthermore, when giving performers specific goals, it is important that they be measurable and be explained in behavioral terms. For example, telling a tennis player to improve her first serve percentage would not be as helpful as telling her that you want her to improve her percentage from 50% to 60% by tossing the ball out in front more. This gives the player a specific goal to shoot for and a way to measure whether she achieved the goal. To take an exercise example, it does not help much to tell an individual taking a weight training class that the goal is to become stronger. Rather, a specific goal of increasing the amount he can bench press by 25% over the next 3 months would be more useful. Exhibit 2 provides a format for getting started setting specific goals and developing strategies to reach these goals.

Set Realistic But Challenging Goals

Another consistent finding from the research literature is that goals should be challenging and difficult, yet attainable (Locke & Latham,

---

Exhibit 2

Setting Specific Goals

1. Dream goal
2. Dream goal can be broken down into the following:
   a. Short-term goals (weekly and daily)
   b. Intermediate goals (monthly)
   c. Goals for this year or season
3. Target dates
   a. Short-term goals
   b. Intermediate goals
   c. Long-term goals
4. Strategies for achieving goals
   a. Daily practices
   b. Match competition
   c. Seasonal plans

1990). Goals that are too easy do not present a challenge to the individual, which leads to less than maximum effort. This, in turn, might result in being satisfied with a mediocre performance instead of extending oneself to reach one's potential. Conversely, setting goals that are too difficult and unrealistic often result in failure. This can lead to frustration, lowered self-confidence and motivation, and decreased performance. For example, many high school and college athletes have goals and aspirations of becoming professional athletes. Unfortunately, less than 1 percent will ever reach this goal and thus the vast majority of these athletes are doomed to failure and possible motivational problems. This is not to say that athletes should not strive to do their best or aspire for a professional career. Rather, a realistic look at one's abilities and chances of success are needed within the context of that dream goal of becoming a professional athlete. Thus, the secret is to find a balance between setting oneself up for failure and pushing oneself to strive for success. In this middle ground reside challenging, realistic, attainable goals.

Those who have been athletes, coaches, and teachers understand that striking this balance between goal difficulty and achievability is no easy task. For example, it is critical for sport psychologists to know the capabilities and motivation of the athletes when attempting to help them set realistic goals. Sometimes this is a trial-and-error process. Sport and exercise professionals can help athletes in goal setting by offering concrete suggestions for challenging goals. If professionals do not have extensive experience with the activity or individuals involved in the program they are working with, it is suggested that they err on the side of setting goals too easy rather than too hard. In this way, the participant can at least experience some success and will not become frustrated with a string of failures. If it becomes apparent that the goals are too easy, then immediately begin to set more difficult and challenging goals.

Set Both Long- and Short-Term Goals

When working with sport and exercise participants, the focus tends to be on some long-term or seasonal goal such as winning the state championship or losing 30 pounds in six months. However, research has shown that both short- and long-term goals are necessary to keep motivation and performance high over time (Weinberg et al., 1993). Short-term goals are important because they can provide feedback concerning progress toward the long-term goal. This feedback can serve a motivational function and allow adjustment of goals either upward or downward, depending on the situation.

By their nature, short-term goals also allow sport and exercise participants to focus on improvement in smaller increments, which may make goals seem more attainable than otherwise seemingly impossible long-term or dream goals. For example, a swimmer getting ready for the Olympic Games calculated that he would have to cut 2 seconds off his time in the 200 meter backstroke if he was to win a medal. In a short race, 2 seconds is an enormous amount of time, and the swimmer felt that this seemed impossible. Thus, instead of focusing on this long-term goal, he figured out how to break this up into manageable short-terms goals. Specifically, the Olympics was 2 years away, so he figured that he would have to knock off 1 second per year. Furthermore, since there are 12 months in a year, he figured he would have to knock off .08 seconds each month. Finally, because there are 4 weeks in a month, he would have to shave off .02 seconds each week. The swimmer felt he could do this; thus, achieving short-term weekly goals of reducing his time by .02 seconds became his goal. The result was a gold medal in the backstroke for John Nabor.

Although short-term goals are obviously important, long-term goals are also necessary. Long-term goals provide the direction and final destination for sport and exercise participants and sometimes act as a dream goal. In essence, they keep the focus on where to end up. If progress toward this goal is not fast enough or if it is ahead of schedule, then the long-term goal can be adjusted so that it is in tune with the new short-term goals. A good way to envision the interaction of short-term and long-term goals is to think of a staircase with the long-term goal at the top, the present level of performance at the bottom, and a sequence of progressively linked short-term goals connecting the top and bottom of the stairs.

Set Goals For Practice and Competition

One of the mistakes that is often made in setting goals is focusing solely or predominantly on competition goals. This does not imply that setting competitive goals is inappropriate; rather, it suggests that practice goals should not be forgotten (Bell, 1983). With the emphasis placed on winning in most competitive sports, it is no wonder that competition goals that focus on competitive outcomes are predominant. However, for most sports, daily practices encompass much more time commitment than do competitions. This is especially the case in sports such as gymnastics, figure skating, and track and field where there are usually only a few important meets; the rest of the time is spent on practice, practice, practice. Moreover, most athletes report that it is easier to "get up" and get motivated for a game or match, whereas additional motivation is needed for daily practice (Weinberg & Gould, 1995)

Practice goals could focus on both performance and nonperformance outcomes. Some typical practice goals could include getting to practice on time, giving teammates positive reinforcement and encouragement, displaying leadership behaviors, and achieving certain performance standards for specific drills. For example, a basketball player might set a goal of hitting 10 consecutive free throws at the end of practice. This practice goal can serve several purposes. First, it will help the player focus on his free-throw shooting and possibly developing different strategies to improve his free throw percentage (e.g., pre-shot routine). In addition, as the player gets closer to hitting 10 in a row, the pressure starts to build because he certainly does not want to miss after making 8 or 9 in a row and then have to start all over. This creates a sense of pressure that is analogous to the pressure of real-game situations.

"Ink It, Don't Think It"

Several sport psychologists (e.g., Gould, 1992; Harris & Harris, 1984) have emphasized the importance of writing down and recording goals. Not only should goals be written down, they also should be recorded in a place where they can be easily seen. This can be done in a number of different ways such as putting goals (as well as goal progress) on a bulletin board outside a swimming pool with a graph recording the number of miles that each swimmer has completed each week. Or athletes can write their goals on a 3" by 5" card before each practice. The key is not simply that the goals are written down, but rather that the goals are available and remain salient to each individual. Often coaches will go through elaborate goal-setting procedures with their athletes at the beginning of the season, writing down all sorts of goals that then are placed in a drawer, never to be looked at again. Coaches or sport and exercise psychologists should record goals and find a highly visible spot to keep them fresh in the participant's mind. (Some athletes post them in their locker or on their bedroom mirror at home.)

Develop Goal-Achievement Strategies

In Locke's (1968) seminal work, the author proposed that one of the mechanisms underlying the effectiveness of goals in enhancing performance is the development of relevant learning strategies. Unfortunately, this aspect of goal setting is often neglected as goals are set without a solid series of strategies identified to achieve these goals. Setting goals without also setting appropriate strategies for achieving these goals is like setting a goal to drive from New York to Los Angeles in four days, but forgetting to bring a map.

A sport example highlighting the importance of goal-achievement strategies begins with a softball player setting a goal to improve her batting average 25 points from last season. The question now becomes, how is she going to accomplish this goal? At this point, the setting of relevant learning strategies comes into play. The player might decide to change her stance and move further back in the batter's box to get a better look at the ball. She may change her routine while in the on-deck circle and employ some imagery before she gets up to bat. Or she may decide she needs to lift more weights to build up her upper body strength. The key is that some learning strategy (or strategies) needs to be identified and incorporated into the daily training regimen so that the player can actively pursue the goal of improving her batting average by 25 points.

Set Performance Goals

As noted previously, it is extremely important for individuals to set goals that are based on their own levels of performance rather than on the outcome of winning and losing. Unfortunately, given the emphasis society places on competition and winning, it is often difficult not to focus on the final score and outcome of the competition. Socialization into this competitive ethic begins at an early age, and it is often hard to change this focus on winning. The irony of this focus on outcome goals is that sport psychologists working with elite athletes have found that the best way to win a championship or gold medal is to focus on performance goals (Orlick & Partington, 1988). These sport psychology consultants found that too much emphasis placed on outcome goals (i.e., winning) at the time of the competition can result in increases in competitive anxiety. This can result in athletes focusing on the consequences of their success or failure—"What will my coach and friends think about me if I lose?"—instead of remaining focused on the task at hand.

Once again, the key point is not that outcome goals are inappropriate; rather, problems arise when individuals focus on outcome goals to the exclusion of performance goals. In fact, as most coaches will confirm, if athletes meet performance goals, the outcome goal of winning will usually take care of itself. For example, if a basketball team meets its goals in the areas of assists, field-goal percentage, rebounds, and foul-shooting percentage, their chances of winning will go up dramatically. Setting performance goals keep goals under the individual's control, and satisfaction can be derived by simply improving against one's past performance rather than comparing oneself against an opponent. Finally, some recent research (Weinberg et al., 1993) has indicated that fun (along with performance and outcome goals) was given by collegiate athletes as one of their top three goals. Mixing in some fun in the practices and games can help keep motivation high and enhance persistence over the long haul.

Set Individual and Team Goals

Coaches of team sports often ask, "Should I have my players set individual goals in addition to team goals?" My answer is that it depends on the nature of the individual goals. That is, there is a place for individual goals within a team sport, as long as the individual goals do not conflict with team goals. Thus, if a hockey player sets a goal to score 30 goals throughout the season, this has the potential to be in conflict with team goals if the player becomes more concerned with scoring goals than helping the team win. In basketball, even a point guard's goal to increase her assists per game could backfire if she starts to exclusively look to pass the ball and turns down good opportunities for her own shots. But if athletes meet individual goals that are not in conflict with team goals, this should theoretically help ensure success as a team. Thus, sport psychology consultants should be cautious when athletes set individual goals, making sure they contribute to overall team goals.

Provide Support For Goals

The psychological literature has provided strong evidence for the notion that social support is an important factor in keeping people motivated and persistent, especially when there are obstacles preventing goal attainment (Albrecht & Adelman, 1984; Cohen, 1988). Similarly, recent research in sport and exercise psychology (Hardy, Richman, & Rosenfeld, 1991), has reinforced the critical role that significant others can play in helping individuals achieve their goals. For example, in fitness settings, it has been shown that spouse support is an important factor affecting exercise adherence (Dishman, 1988). As a result, exercise programs aimed at increasing fitness and losing weight now try to involve spouses in the program by informing them of the goals of the participant and ways in which a spouse can support the participant's achievement of these goals. Similarly, a volleyball coach who is trying to emphasize performance goals with her athletes may enlist the help of parents, teachers, and friends to provide support for these performance goals rather than focusing on winning and losing.

Finally, one of the most important (yet easy and effective) ways to provide goal support is to show a genuine concern and interest to athletes, students, and exercisers. First, it is important to be aware of the goals of each individual and to ask them about the progress they are making. Moreover, encouraging them to strive toward their goals but also being sympathetic and concerned as a listener when participants are struggling to meet their goals will go a long way to keep spirits and motivation high.

Provide For Goal Evaluation

One of the most overlooked aspects of formal goal-setting programs is the evaluation component. As Locke et al. (1981) found, evaluative feedback is essential if goals are going to be effective in enhancing performance. Therefore, it is critical to provide individuals with feedback concerning the effectiveness of their goals, and goal-evaluation strategies should be continuously implemented throughout the goal-setting process. Many performance goals based on statistics such as batting average, runs batted in, steals, and runs scored are readily available, for example, to a baseball player. But these are not always used throughout the season to make changes in goals that were set up at the start of the season. Therefore, periodic goal-evaluation meetings should be set up between the players and the coach or the players and the sport psychologist to evaluate current performance in relation to the player's goals. In this way, goals can be reevaluated and adjusted to new motivation and commitment for the players. In addition, there are a number of areas besides performance in which goals could be set that are often harder to monitor and evaluate. Gould (1995) provided a number of examples of how to provide for goal evaluation in these areas. For instance, an athlete may have a goal to improve concentration during practice. To evaluate this goal, the coach could give the player a weekly report card rating his practice concentration on a 1 (*poor*) to 10 (*excellent*) scale. Similarly, an injured player might have a goal to go to the rehabilitation clinic three times a week and do range-of-motion exercises and light lifting for 1 hour each time. Attendance could be posted at the rehabilitation center and the athletic trainer could note how long the athlete performed the prescribed exercises each session. Exhibit 3 presents a sample goal-evaluation card that is designed for tennis but can be modified for other activities and used to evaluate progress in reaching both short-term and long-term goals.

Exhibit 3

Goal Evaluation Card: Tennis Serve Improvement

Stroke	Specific goal	Strategy	Short-term goal	Target date
Serve	Improve 1st serve percentage from 50% to 60%	Hit an extra 50 serves in practice	Improve 1st serve percentage to 55% over the next 3 matches	Achieve 60% 1st serve by end of the season

Common Problems When Setting Goals

This chapter so far has focused on the research and practice concerning the effectiveness of goal setting strategies. Although goals can help improve performance and change behavior, it is not always easy to implement goal setting programs in sport and exercise settings. In fact, there appear to be some common problems that athletes, coaches, exercise leaders, and applied sport psychologists have faced when attempting to employ goal setting programs. By understanding and anticipating these problems, their potential negative effects can be softened or even circumvented.

Failing to Monitor Goal Progress and Readjust Goals

Often, individuals are excited about setting goals and go ab[...] lots of goals at the start of a program. But as time passes or [...]

moves along, these goals are often forgotten or at least put "on the back burner." Sometimes the goals are not forgotten, but they are not reevaluated on a regular or periodic basis. Reevaluating goals is important because goals can help to keep people motivated over long periods of time. Furthermore, situations that can limit athletic performance and exercise participation, such as an injury, "throw people off-course" in meeting their goals.

It is therefore critical that regularly scheduled meetings or times be set up specifically for goal evaluation. For example, a marathon runner may have the goals of running 50 miles a week for 4 months in training for a marathon and then knocking 5 minutes off her personal best time in the marathon. But after 6 weeks, due to some illness and business obligations, it becomes obvious to the runner that she will not be able to meet these goals. Instead of losing motivation and possibly even quitting, new goals could be established based on her current level of fitness and performance. For example, the weekly training mileage goal could be reduced to 30 miles for the next 2 weeks and then increased back up to 40 to 50 miles for the remainder of the training. The competitive goal also could be reevaluated and changed to simply equaling her best time.

Failing to Recognize Individual Differences

One of the most common errors in any psychological intervention in sport and exercise settings is not recognizing individual differences. As noted earlier, for example, individuals may differ in their goal orientations (i.e., task vs. ego), which could make a significant difference in the specific goals that are effective for them. Research (Giannini, Weinberg, & Jackson, 1988) has indicated that goal effectiveness is maximized when goal orientations and specific types of goals are matched. Thus, task-oriented individuals are most motivated by goals focusing on self-improvement, whereas ego-oriented individual are most motivated by goals that focus on winning and losing.

Failing to Set Specific Measurable Goals

Probably the most frequent problem when helping participants in sport and exercise settings is their failure to set specific and measurable goals. Individuals seem to have a propensity for simply setting general goals like "improving my passing in soccer" or "improving my overall fitness level." Applied sport psychology consultants need to assist individuals in identifying specific goals and to provide feedback throughout the goal-setting program to ensure that the goals remain specific. Coaches can also help out in these instances by providing subjective assessments of performance, example, if a baseball pitcher has a goal to improve his "pick off" move to first base, the coach could rate the pitcher in practice and game situations using a 1 (*not at all improved*) to 5 (*much improved*) scale. This helps the pitcher not only to have a specific goal, but also to focus on his "pick off" move because he knows the coach will be carefully evaluating him.

Setting Too Many Goals at the Start

As noted earlier, individuals get excited at the start of goal-setting programs and often "bite off more than they can chew." This is especially the case for individuals with little experience in goal-setting techniques. In their enthusiasm to change their behavior or improve their performance, participants sometimes get carried away setting up a large number of goals. It is not the number of goals per se that causes the problem; rather it is monitoring and tracking these goals across time that becomes extremely difficult and time consuming.

Therefore, particularly when working with individuals with little goal setting experience, it is useful to set only a couple of goals by choosing those goals that are the highest priority. For example, for a person just starting an exercise program, a simple goal of exercising 3 to 4 times a week for 20 to 30 minutes each time would be sufficient. Also, in setting these initial goals, it is usually better to focus on short-term rather than long-term goals because this keeps the salience of the goals high and provides feedback that can serve as a motivator to the individual.

Summary

This chapter focused on the effectiveness of setting goals in sport and exercise environments. A goal was defined as a specific level of proficiency on a task, usually attained within a specified period of time and a distinction was made between subjective and objective goals. Locke's theory of goal setting, which indicates that specific, difficult, challenging goals lead to higher levels of task performance, was presented. More recent research investigating the goal-performance relationship in sport and exercise settings also has found support for the effectiveness of goals although the findings are not as robust as those in the industrial/ organizational literature.

It has been hypothesized that goals directly influence behavior by orienting performer attention to important elements of the task, increasing effort and persistence, and facilitating the development of relevant learning strategies. Goals also can influence behavior more indirectly through changes in cognitions such as self-confidence, and anxiety, and can be mediated by goal orientation (i.e., task orientation vs. ego orientation). Basic goal-setting principles based on the literature were presented, including setting specific goals, setting realistic and challenging goals, setting both short- and long-term goals, setting performance goals, writing goals down, providing support for goals, and providing for goal evaluation. It should be remembered that the effectiveness of any goal-setting program will in large part rely on the interaction of the coach, exercise leader, or sport psychologist and the motivations of the specific participants. In essence, individual differences and environmental considerations should always be taken into account.

References

Albrecht, J. L., & Adelman, M. B. (1984). Social support and life stress: New directions for communication research. *Human Communications Research, 2,* 3–22.

Bell, K. F. (1983). *Championship thinking: The athlete's guide to winning performance in all sports.* Englewood Cliffs, NJ: Prentice-Hall.

Burton, D. (1989). Winning isn't everything: Examining the impact of performance goals on collegiate swimmers' cognitions and performance. *The Sport Psychologist, 32,* 105–132.

Burton, D. (1992). The Jekyll/Hyde nature of goals: Reconceptualizing goal setting in sport. In T. Horn (Ed.), *Advances in Sport Psychology* (pp. 267–297). Champaign, IL: Human Kinetics.

Chidester, J. S., & Grigsby, W. C. (1984). A meta-analysis of the goal setting performance literature. In A. Pearce and R. B. Robinson (Eds.), *Proceedings of the 44th annual meeting of the academy of management* (pp. 202–206).

Cohen, S. (1988). Psychosocial models of the role of social support in the etiology of physical disease. *Health Psychology, 7,* 269–297.

Dishman, R. K. (1988). *Exercise adherence: Its impact on public health.* Champaign, IL: Human Kinetics.

Duda, J. L. (1992). Motivation in sport settings: A goal perspective approach. In G. C. Roberts (Ed.), *Motivation in sport and exercise* (pp. 57–92). Champaign, IL: Human Kinetics.

Dweck, C. S. (1986). Motivational processes affecting learning. *American Psychologist, 41,* 1040–1048.

Garland, H. (1985). A cognitive mediation theory of task goals and human performance. *Motivation and Emotion, 9,* 345–367.

Giannini, J., Weinberg, R. S., & Jackson, A. (1988). The effects of master, competitive and cooperative goals on the performance of simple and complex basketball skills. *Journal of Sport & Exercise Psychology, 10,* 408–417.

Gould, D. (1992). Goal setting for peak performance. In J. Williams (Ed.), *Applied sport psychology: Personal growth to peak performance* (2nd ed.) (pp. 158–169). Mountain View, CA: Mayfield.

Gould, D., Tammen, V., Murphy, S., & May, J. (1989). An examination of U.S. Olympic sport psychology consultants and the services they provide. *The Sport Psychologist, 3,* 300–312.

Hardy, C. V., Richman, J. M., & Rosenfeld, L. B. (1991). The role of social support in the life stress/injury relationship. *The Sport Psychologist, 5,* 128–139.

Harris, D. V., & Harris, B. L. (1984). *The athlete's guide to sports psychology: Mental skills for physical people.* New York: Leisure Press.

Locke, E. A. (1968). Toward a theory of task motivation incentives. *Organizational Behavior and Human Performance, 3,* 157–189.

Locke, E. A. (1966). The relationship of intentions to level of performance. *Journal of Applied Psychology, 50,* 60–66.

Locke, E. A. (1978). The ubiquity of the technique of goal setting in theories of and approaches to employee motivation. *Academy of Management Review, 31,* 594–601.

Locke, E. A., Shaw, K. N., Saari, L. M., & Latham, G. P. (1981). Goal setting and task performance. *Psychological Bulletin, 90,* 125–152.

Locke, E. A., & Latham, G. P. (1985). The application of goal setting to sports. *Journal of Sport Psychology, 7,* 205–222.

Locke, E. A., & Latham, G. P. (1990). *A theory of goal setting and task performance.* Englewood Cliffs, NJ: Prentice Hall.

Maehr, M. L., & Braskamp, L. (1986) *The motivation factor: A theory of personal development.* Lexington, MA: Health.

Mento, A. J., Steel, R. P., & Karren, R. J. (1987). A meta-analytic study of the effects of goal setting on task performance: 1966–1984. *Organizational Behavior and Human Decision Processes, 39,* 52–83.

Nicholls, J. G. (1984a). Achievement motivation: Conception of ability, subjective experience, task choice and performance. *Psychological Review, 91,* 328–346.

Nicholls, J. G. (1984b). Conception of ability and achievement motivation. In R. Ames & C. Ames (Eds.), *Research on motivation in education: Vol. 1. Student motivation* (pp. 39–73). New York: Academic Press.

Odiorne, G. S. (1978, Oct.) MBO: A backward glance. *Business Horizons, 21(5),* 14–24.

Orlick, T., & Partington, J. (1988). Mental links to excellence. *The Sport Psychologist, 2,* 105–130.

Roberts, G. C. (1992). Motivation in sport and exercise: Conceptual constraints and consequence. In G. C. Roberts (Ed.), *Motivation in sport and exercise* (pp. 3–30). Champaign, IL: Human Kinetics.

Ryan, T. A. (1970). *Intentional behavior: An approach to human motivation.* New York: Ronald Press.

Taylor, F. W. (1967). *The principles of scientific management.* New York: Norton (Original work published 1911).

Tubbs, M. E. (1991). Goal setting: A meta–analytic examination of the empirical evidence. *Journal of Applied Psychology, 71,* 474–483.

Weinberg, R. S. (1992). Goal setting and motor performance: A review and critique.

In G. C. Roberts (Ed.), *Motivation in sport and exercise* (pp. 177–198). Champaign, IL: Human Kinetics.

Weinberg, R. S. (1994). Goal setting and performance in sport and exercise settings: A synthesis and critique. *Medicine and Science in Sport and Exercise, 26,* 469–477.

Weinberg, R. S., Burton, D., Yukelson, D., & Weigand, D. (1993). Goal setting in competitive sport: An exploratory investigation of practices of collegiate athletes. *The Sport Psychologist, 7,* 275–289.

Weinberg, R. S. & Gould, D. (Eds.), *Foundations of sport and exercise psychology.* Champaign, IL: Human Kinetics.

Weinberg, R. S., Stitcher, T., & Richardson, P. (1994). Effects of a seasonal goal setting program on lacrosse performance. *The Sport Psychologist, 8,* 166–175.

Weinberg, R. S., & Weigand, D. (1993). Goal setting in sport and exercise. A reaction to Locke. *Journal of Sport & Exercise Psychology, 15,* 88–95.

White, S. A., & Duda, J. L. (1991, October). *The interdependence between goal perspectives, psychological skill, and cognitive interference among elite skiers.* Paper presented at the annual meeting of the Association for the Advancement of Applied Sport Psychology, Savannah, GA.

Imagery Training for Peak Performance

Daniel Gould and Nicole Damarjian

Carolyn is a highly talented professional golfer. She plays well during the practice rounds, but does not seem to be able to play up to her potential during the actual tournaments. In an effort to enhance her confidence, her coach recommends that she imagine herself executing each shot perfectly before she actually swings. Although skeptical, Carolyn tries this in her next tournament. She finds it difficult to control the "pictures" in her mind and sees little immediate improvement in her game. Frustrated, Carolyn decides that she is not a good imager and retreats to the driving range to hit balls.

Alan is the new basketball coach at Bacon Academy and decides that he will develop an imagery training program for his team. Every day, after 2 hours of hard practice, Alan has his team lie down and imagine themselves going through the various plays outlined in practice. As the season progresses, Alan notices more and more resistance with some of his players with regard to the imagery training. He overhears them complain that after a workout they want to go home and eat supper, not sit in the dark and daydream. Besides, they do not know why they are doing all this "mental stuff" anyway. The team never did imagery last year with Coach Shea, and he led them to a conference championship. Concerned about losing credibility with his team, Alan decides to drop the imagery program.

Lauren is an elite gymnast. Six weeks prior to the Olympic tryouts, she sprains her ankle during a dismount. The athletic trainer assures both Lauren and her coach that the injury is minor and that, with proper rest and rehabilitation, she should be completely recovered in time for the tryouts. Two weeks later, Lauren returns to her normal practice schedule, but she continues to hesitate before her dismounts. Her sport psychologist and coach both encourage her to replay past successful performances in her mind to overcome the fear she has developed as a result of her recent fall. Lauren halfheartedly does as they suggest, but is not truly committed to imagery training. She feels foolish and self-conscious in front of her teammates and insists that her ankle is still not fully recovered

"Wait a minute," you say, "Everything I have ever heard or read about sport psychology says that imagery works." After all, Hank Aaron used it to become the all-time home run leader in major league baseball, golf great Jack Nicklaus religiously does it before every shot, and what about all those Olympic athletes who report how useful imagery is in enhancing their performance? How can it be suggested that imagery does not work?

To begin with, it should be made clear that we believe in the power of imagery and its importance as a psychological skill for enhancing athletic performance. As we convey in this chapter, research has clearly demonstrated the efficacy of imagery as a sport psychological change mechanism. However, stories like those above are not uncommon. Many well-meaning athletes, like Carolyn, assume that psychological skills such as imagery can be developed overnight to produce immediate performance improvements. When they do not achieve the results they had expected, they falsely conclude that imagery does not work. Still other athletes, like Lauren, do not fully understand what imagery is or how it can help them achieve their goals. They never truly commit to an imagery training program and, as a result, they fail to gain any performance benefit. This is why it is important for coaches like Alan to ensure that their teams understand what imagery is and how it can be used to enhance athletic performance.

This chapter is designed to provide sport psychologists and coaches with a comprehensive and practical overview of imagery research, theory, and intervention. Specifically, we address five areas:

1. The nature of imagery and how it can enhance athletic performance;
2. Evidence examining the importance and utility of imagery training programs;
3. General guidelines for using imagery;
4. Recommendations on how to implement an imagery training program; and

5. Problems and pitfalls often made in imagery training programs, as well as ways in which they can be avoided.

What Is Imagery, and How Can It Enhance Athletic Performance?

What is imagery, and how does it help athletes to perform better? *Imagery* can be defined as a process by which sensory experiences are stored in memory and internally recalled and performed in the absence of external stimuli (Murphy, 1994). It is important to understand from this definition that imagery involves the use of all the senses. Although imagery is often associated with visualization, it can and should include senses other than sight. This is especially true in sports where the feel of the movement is so important.

Assume, for example, that a swimmer is using imagery to prepare herself mentally for a conference meet in the next month. She imagines herself swimming confidently, while leading her team to their first conference victory. She smells the chlorine of the pool as she waits for the race to begin. She sees herself dive into the water. She feels the power in her kick as she pushes herself past her competitors. She hears water splashing and her teammates cheering her on. By incorporating all of the appropriate senses, this athlete is able to more vividly imagine her upcoming race.

With an appropriate training program, imagery skills can increase self-awareness, facilitate skill acquisition and maintenance, build self-confidence, control emotions, relieve pain, regulate arousal, and enhance preparation strategies (Murphy & Jowdy, 1992). However, before outlining specific guidelines for setting up an imagery training program, it is important that we summarize the research examining the relationship between imagery and performance, as well as the theories that explain why imagery works.

Imagery Research

The research studies examining the relationship between imagery and athletic performance can be categorized into four main areas (Murphy, 1994; Murphy & Jowdy, 1992): (a) mental practice studies, (b) precompetition imagery intervention research, (c) studies comparing the psychological characteristics of successful and unsuccessful competitors, and (d) mediating variables studies.

Mental Practice Studies

The majority of the mental practice studies are concerned with the effects of mental practice on learning and performance of motor skills. In these studies, *mental practice* is typically defined as mental rehearsal of a given task or performance without any associated overt actions. Although mental practice may or may not include the use of imagery, the overlap between the two areas warrants a discussion of the findings.

The standard methodology used in the mental practice studies involves a between-subjects, pretest–posttest design with four groups: physical practice only, mental practice only, both physical and mental practice, and no practice. Performance changes in each condition are typically expressed in terms of percentage gains and losses. For example, Rawlings, Rawlings, Chen, and Yilk (1972) examined the effects of mental practice on a pursuit rotor task. At the onset of the study, all participants were introduced to the task and received 25 practice trials. Following these trials, participants differed in their practice methods. Group 1 received physical practice only, Group 2 received no practice, and Group 3 received mental practice only (imagery and visualization). After an 8-day training period, all participants were retested on the pursuit rotor task for 25 more trials. The results showed that the mental practice group improved considerably over the course of the experiment, almost to the extent that the physical practice group did. In contrast, the no-practice group showed little if any improvement.

On the basis of a meta-analysis of 60 mental practice studies, Feltz and Landers (1983) suggested that mental practice is better than no practice at all. Furthermore, in a comprehensive review of the literature, Weinberg (1981) stated that

> mental practice combined and alternated with physical practice is more effective than either physical or mental practice alone. In addition, physical practice is superior to mental practice. Mental practice should not replace physical practice, but rather it can be used as a valuable addition to physical practice. (p. 203)

This literature supports the belief that the ideal training program combines both physical and mental practice.

Precompetition Imagery Interventions

Unlike mental practice studies, imagery intervention studies involve the use of imagery or mental rehearsal immediately prior to performance. They examine the effectiveness of imagery to prepare an athlete who is about to perform. Unfortunately, however, studies in this area have generated more questions than answers.

For example, several studies have suggested that imagery rehearsal prior to performance can benefit performance on some tasks in comparison with a condition where no imagery rehearsal is used (see Murphy & Jowdy, 1992, for a detailed review). Shelton and Mahoney (1978) found that 15 male weight lifters asked to use their favorite "psyching-up" strategy before a test of hand strength showed significantly greater improvement over baseline than did 15 male weight lifters asked to improve their performance but given a distracting cognitive task during preperformance. Unfortunately, this type of research is problematic, for two reasons. First, such designs do not specify the type of mental rehearsal that facilitates performance. Although each athlete may report having used imagery, this may mean different things to different athletes. Second, this research does little to improve understanding of how imagery interventions influence performance. It fails to address the important and often elusive question about what mechanisms underlie the imagery–performance relationship.

In addition to these problems, several studies have failed to find a positive relationship between imagery and performance. For example, Weinberg, Gould, Jackson, and Barnes (1980) examined three mental preparation strategies and their effects on a tennis serve task. Participants were divided into one of four conditions: (a) using imagery to prepare for serving, (b) making positive self-efficacy statements, (c) using attentional focus, and (d) a control condition in which participants were asked to prepare as they normally would. The results showed that none of the cognitive strategies used increased performance over the control condition.

Murphy and Jowdy (1992) have suggested that these mixed results may be due to a number of variables, including task, individual difference, and physiology. With regard to task variables, it is possible that imagery rehearsal may be a more effective strategy for particular types of tasks than for others. Perhaps imagery rehearsal is more effective with predominantly cognitive as opposed to motor tasks, for example. It is also important to examine individual difference variables. Some individuals may, for example, have a higher quality of imagery and thus experience greater improvements in performance. Finally, how does imagery influence certain physiological variables (e.g., electromyogram, electroencephalogram, and heart rate), and how does this help to explain changes in performance? Overall, although showing that an imagery–performance relationship often exists, the preperformance imagery intervention studies have been methodologically weak. Future research in this area needs to include better intervention descriptions and manipulation checks.

Psychological Comparisons of Successful and Unsuccessful Competitors

Another area of imagery research has examined the psychological characteristics of successful versus unsuccessful athletes. For example, Mahoney and Avener (1977) administered a questionnaire to the 13 male finalists for selection to the 1976 U.S. Olympic gymnastic team. When comparing the responses from those gymnasts who qualified for the Olympic team and those gymnasts who did not qualify, Mahoney and Avener found that the qualifiers had greater self-confidence, a higher frequency of gymnastic dreams, thought more about gymnastics in everyday life, and had a higher frequency of internal performance imagery than nonqualifiers.

Although these results are encouraging, like the preperformance imagery intervention studies, several problems exist with this type of research design. The first is the obvious methodological limitations of a correlational study. Although results can conclude an association between imagery and enhanced performance, a causal relationship cannot be established. Also, this type of research fails to contribute to the understanding of how imagery processes affect performance.

Mediating Variables Studies

The final area of research to be discussed focuses on a variety of possible mediating variables and their influence on the imagery–performance relationship. For example, some researchers have examined the influence of imagery ability on performance. Primarily imagery ability has been defined by the level of vividness and controllability that an athlete has over his or her imagery. *Vividness* refers to the clarity and reality in an athlete's image, whereas *controllability* refers to the athlete's ability to influence the content of the image. Several correlational studies have found that more successful performers have a higher quality of imagery

(Highlen & Bennett, 1983; Meyers, Cooke, Cullen, & Liles, 1979). As we stated earlier, it is important to consider individual differences in imagery ability when conducting this type of research.

Another possible mediating variable relates to the correctness of an athlete's imagery. For example, Woolfolk, Parrish, and Murphy (1985) used a putting task to determine the effects of imagery correctness on performance. The results showed that participants in the negative imagery condition performed significantly worse than participants in the positive imagery and control conditions.

A final mediating variable relates to imagery perspective. Some athletes imagine themselves from the perspective that they are inside their body actually experiencing the imagined sensations, whereas others imagine themselves from the perspective of a spectator watching the performance. Although some researchers have found an internal perspective to be associated with higher levels of performance (Mahoney & Avener, 1977), others have found no difference in performance for those with internal versus external imagery perspectives (Mumford & Hall, 1985). It is possible that these mixed results may relate to the purpose of the intervention. For example, internal imagery may serve to enhance skill learning through kinesthetic feedback. However, it is also possible that external imagery can enhance performance, but that it does so through a different process. That is, external imagery may help an athlete see himself or herself performing successfully in an important competition and, thus, may enhance self-confidence.

Our brief review of the sport and motor performance imagery research shows that this area of investigation is not without problems. More carefully controlled and methodologically sound research is certainly needed. On a more positive note, when combined with physical practice, imagery has been shown to facilitate athletic performance. However, this research also demonstrates that imagery does not work for all tasks, with all people, in all situations. Although improved research will clarify on what tasks, with whom, and in what situations imagery works best, it is clear that simply asking athletes to imagine themselves performing better will not guarantee beneficial effects. Sport psychologists and coaches must make informed imagery prescriptions that are guided by an understanding of imagery research and theory as well as those sport psychological guidelines identified for the effective use of imagery.

Theoretical Explanations for the Relationship Between Imagery and Performance

To effectively use imagery, sport psychologists and coaches must have an understanding of the mechanisms underlying the imagery–performance relationship. Traditionally, two main theories have been forwarded within the sport psychology literature: the psychoneuromuscular theory, and the symbolic learning theory.

Psychoneuromuscular Theory

The psychoneuromuscular theory proposes that imagery rehearsal duplicates the actual motor pattern being rehearsed, although the neuromuscular activation is of smaller magnitude when compared with actual physical practice. This neuromuscular activation is thought to be sufficient enough to enhance the motor schema in the motor cortex. For example, Suinn (1972) monitored muscle activity in the legs of skiers as they imagined a downhill run. He found that the electrical patterns in the muscles closely approximated those expected if the person had actually been skiing.

Unfortunately, not all research has been able to replicate Suinn's (1972) results or to show support for the psychoneuromuscular theory. In the previously discussed meta-analysis of the literature, Feltz and Landers (1983) concluded that it is doubtful that imagery effects result in low-level muscular-impulse activity. Furthermore, research in experimental psychology has suggested that the effects of imagery are more a function of operations within the central nervous system than muscular activity during imagery (Kohl & Roenker, 1983). In other words, imagery may function more at the higher levels of information processing than at the lower muscular levels. The muscular responses found may merely be an effect mechanism rather than a cause of performance changes.

Symbolic Learning Theory

In contrast to psychoneuromuscular theory, symbolic learning theory contends that imagery rehearsal gains are more often due to the opportunity to practice symbolic elements of a specific motor task than to the muscle activation itself. In other words, imagery functions by helping athletes develop a "mental blueprint" to guide overt performance. Support for the symbolic learning theory has come from two areas of research. First, a number of studies have shown that imagery is more effective for tasks that have a high cognitive component as opposed to a high motor component (Ryan & Simons, 1981). Second, motor learning theories contending that early stages of learning are primarily cognitive are compatible with the notion that imagery will have its greatest effects during the early stages of learning.

Informational and Motor Process Theories of Imagery

Although much of the imagery research in the sport psychology literature has examined the psychoneuromuscular and symbolic learning theories, Murphy and Jowdy (1992) suggested that researchers look beyond traditional theories and investigate the relevance of imagery theories developed in other areas, such as cognitive and clinical psychology. Two such theories are Lang's (1977, 1979) psychophysiological information-processing theory and Ahsen's (1984) triple-code model of imagery.

Lang's (1977, 1979) psychophysiological information-processing theory is based on the assumption that an image is a functionally organized, finite set of propositions regarding the relationship and description of stimulus and response characteristics. The stimulus proposition describes the content of the scenario to be imagined. For example, this may include the weather conditions of a particular tennis match or the pin position of a particularly difficult golf hole. The response proposition describes the imager's response to the imagined scenario. This may include, for example, a kinesthetic awareness of any muscular changes while performing.

It is important to note that, according to Lang's (1977, 1979) theory, for imagery rehearsal to influence athletic performance, both stimulus and response propositions must be activated. Rather than conceptualizing an image as merely a stimulus in the athlete's mind to which he or she responds, this theory suggests that images also contain "response scenarios" that enable athletes to access the appropriate motor program and effectively alter athletic performance.

Similar to Lang's (1977, 1979) information-processing theory, Ahsen's (1984) triple-code model of imagery also recognizes the primary importance of psychophysiological processes in the imagery process. However, Ahsen's theory goes one step further, to incorporate the meaning that an image has for an individual. According to the triple-code model, then, there are three essential parts of imagery that must be described by both theorists and clinicians. These include the image itself, the somatic response to the image, and the meaning of the image. For example, a sprinter imagines herself successfully qualifying for the 100 m race in the 1996 Olympics. Her arousal level increases with the image of running in this event and having achieved her life-long dream. In addition, she attaches a great sense of personal pride and satisfaction to the image of this accomplishment. Both the image itself and the somatic response to the image are analogous to Lang's (1977, 1979) stimulus and response propositions. However, no other theory or model of imagery has addressed the importance of the meaning that an individual attaches to a particular image. (See Murphy & Jowdy, 1992, and Suinn, 1993, for a more detailed review of imagery theories.)

Psychological State Notions

Although most imagery theories focus on improving performance through information-processing and motor control processes, it is important to recognize that imagery is also thought to influence athletic performance through its effect on other psychological states, such as self-efficacy or confidence and anxiety. For example, in his classic theory of self-efficacy, Bandura (1977) proposed that an important source of efficacy information is the modeling of vicarious experiences and that imagery is thought to be an excellent way to reinforce modeled acts and mentally learn from others' experiences. Similarly, widely used multimodal stress management techniques—such as Meichenbaum's (1985) stress inoculation training, Smith's (1980) cognitive–affective stress management training, and Suinn's (1972) visuomotor behavioral rehearsal—all involve imagery as a critical variable in their programs to reduce anxiety. Moreover, a review of these programs shows that they have been successful in helping athletes control anxiety and enhance athletic performance (Gould & Udry, 1994). Imagery thus influences important psychological states such as confidence and anxiety, which in turn influence athletic performance.

Although research is needed to further develop and test imagery theories, given the current state of knowledge, imagery is thought to influence athletic performance in several ways. First, although newer theories and most sport psychologists who design imagery programs for athletes still recommend emphasizing kinesthetic feelings of movement, it is doubtful that imagery works through neuromuscular activation. It is more likely that yet unexplored, higher levels of information processing are involved. Second, it is clear that imagery facilitates performance by providing extra opportunities for an athlete to develop symbolic elements of motor tasks. Third, more recent theories of imagery stress the importance of emphasizing stimulus propositions (e.g., the task of making a foul shot), response propositions (e.g., the feel of executing the shot), and the meaning of the image to the performer. Finally, imagery influences important psychological states, such as confidence and anxiety.

Guidelines for Using Imagery

From the research conducted thus far, many practical applications have been suggested to help coaches and athletes use imagery as a performance enhancement tool. Similarly, some sport psychologists (Harris & Harris, 1984; Martens, 1987; Orlick, 1986, 1990; Vealey & Walter, 1992) who have had extensive experience in using imagery rehearsal with athletes have been able to derive a number of useful guidelines for those practitioners or athletes interested in implementing such techniques, the most important of which are discussed below.

Practice Imagery on a Regular Basis

Unfortunately, many coaches and athletes believe that psychological skills such as imagery do not require the same practice that physical skills require. For example, consider the story of Carolyn at the beginning of this chapter. She half-heartedly attempts to use imagery to enhance her golf game. She never truly commits to practicing imagery and becomes frustrated when she fails to realize immediate performance gains. Mental skills are like physical skills. To become proficient with the use of imagery requires a commitment throughout the training season. It is unrealistic to think that either a physical or mental skill will be effective in a competitive situation when it is never practiced at any other time. Ideally then, imagery training should become an integral part of daily practice.

Use All Senses to Enhance Image Vividness

The more senses incorporated into imagery, the more vivid and effective it will be (Harris & Harris, 1984; Orlick, 1986). Many athletes assume that imagery is synonymous with visualization. Although visualization can be an important component of imagery rehearsal, it is important to draw from senses other than sight to increase the quality of imagery, especially in physical activities like sports. For example, a skier may wish to familiarize herself with an upcoming race course. In addition to "seeing" the course, she also needs to experience the kinesthetic feeling of passing through a particularly tough gate, feeling the wind, and hearing the ski edges slash through the snow. This helps the athlete develop positive feelings as well as a sense of confidence when entering the upcoming event.

Develop Imagery Control

In addition to improving image clarity, it is also important that athletes be able to control the content of their images. Is an athlete's image positive and self-enhancing or negative and self-defeating? As previously discussed, negative imagery can have a detrimental effect on performance. As a sport psychologist or coach, it is important to know the extent to which the individual athletes you are working with are able to influence the content of their imagery. For example, if a tennis player consistently imagines his serves going into the net, then it may be important to provide specific exercises to strengthen his ability to control his imagery. Fortunately, with practice, most athletes can learn to control the content of their imagery.

Use Both Internal and External Perspectives

As stated earlier, some athletes imagine themselves from the perspective that they are inside their bodies actually experiencing the imagined sensations, whereas others imagine themselves from the perspective of watching their performance on a movie screen. Some researchers have suggested that an internal imagery perspective is superior to an external imagery perspective because of the importance of kinesthetic awareness in sport performance (Mahoney & Avener, 1977). However, this research is currently inconclusive. It is possible, for example, that external imagery enhances athletic performance by building athletes' self-confidence or allowing them to see patterns of play. As a sport psychologist or coach, you may suggest an internal or an external perspective, or both, depending on the needs of the individual athlete.

Facilitate Imagery Through Relaxation

Research suggests that imagery combined with relaxation is more effective than imagery alone (Weinberg, Seabourne, & Jackson, 1981). It is thought that relaxation strategies (e.g., passive progressive relaxation or deep breathing) prior to imagery rehearsal clear athletes' minds of possible distractions and, therefore, allow them to better concentrate on their imagery. The combination of relaxation and imagery training is especially helpful with athletes who are just developing their imagery skills. Unlike athletes who are highly proficient with imagery, less skilled imagers tend to be more easily distracted because their imagery skills are not yet automatic. The purpose of this chapter is not to review various relaxation techniques; however, readers can refer to Taylor's chapter on arousal regulation (chap. 4) in this book for more specific relaxation strategies that may be used with imagery.

Develop Coping Strategies Through Imagery

Although positive imagery is generally preferred over negative imagery, there are occasions when negative imagery can also be helpful. If athletes always imagine themselves performing perfectly, then they are almost assured to set themselves up for failure. Therefore, it is important that athletes learn to cope with adversity as well as success. For example, a baseball player may wish to imagine himself striking out the first few times at bat, only to come back with a critical hit in the late innings. Coping imagery can help athletes turn a poor performance around. However, such imagery is not recommended for use just prior to a competitive event. Coping imagery may be best used in the off-season and should not be done too frequently. When athletes are preparing for an important competitive event, it is best to have them imagine themselves performing successfully rather than unsuccessfully.

Use Imagery in Practice as well as for Competition

Imagery rehearsal should be used in practice sessions as well as before competition. Imagery can help an athlete to get in the right zone both mentally and physically to optimize training. As an example, imagery can help direct an athlete's attention to specific practice goals. It can also help an athlete who may not be motivated to practice on a given day. Many athletes find it difficult to get up for practice in the off-season. By calling forth arousal-producing situations (e.g., losing to a rival), imagery can be used to help motivate athletes to train hard for competitions that may be months away. Finally, the quality of imagery will improve if it is used daily in practice, and, thus, it will serve to better help athletes during the pressures of competition.

Imagery is not only helpful in mentally preparing for practice, but should be used frequently during practice. For example, after a mistake, coaches could instruct athletes to correct the problem in their heads through imagery before making their next attempt. Likewise, after performing correctly, athletes can take a moment to imagine the look and feel of the correct response. Similarly, when demonstrating, coaches should ask athletes to imagine the skill that was demonstrated before they execute a response. Finally, when teaching new offensive or defensive plays to team-sport athletes, coaches should instruct athletes to visualize the correct flow of movement of the team's play. It should be noted, however, that the effective use of imagery during practices does not typically mean that one stops play or instruction for a special 5- or 10-minute imagery session. Rather, coaches should repeatedly ask athletes to "image" for very short times (3 to 10 seconds) as a part of the normal coaching and instructional procedures.

Use Video- or Audiotapes to Enhance Imagery Skills

Some athletes find videotapes or audiotapes helpful to develop and reinforce constructive imagery. Although several audiotapes exist on the market, athletes can also make their own tapes to help guide them through an imagery session. If the athlete or sport psychologist records the tape, then it is important that he or she incorporate the same cues in the tape that are used during physical practice. For example, if a swimmer uses the cue word *punch* to instruct herself to explode off the turn, then this same cue should be used during imagery rehearsal.

Videotapes can also be used to help athletes develop their imagery skills. "Success tapes" can be made with clips of athletes' actual practices or competitions in which they have performed well. An athlete's favorite music can be dubbed onto the tape to serve as a cue or trigger in the future. For example, a field hockey player may use a success tape to reinforce specific techniques that she has been working on in practice as well as to create positive feelings of confidence. In situations where it is not practical for her to watch the videotape (e.g., traveling on the bus), she can listen to the same music on a portable stereo headset to help trigger feelings of success.

Use Triggers or Cues to Facilitate Imagery Quality

As mentioned above, triggers or cues are important components of imagery rehearsal. For some athletes, triggers are words or phrases that help them to focus on appropriate cues during imagery. However, it is important to note that triggers may also include a specific sensory experience, such as how a given technique or movement feels kinesthetically. Triggers can involve any of the five senses. The key point is that whatever trigger or cue an athlete uses, it must be able to conjure up the appropriate image.

Emphasize Dynamic Kinesthetic Imagery

Another way to enhance the quality of imagery is to have athletes focus particular attention on the kinesthetic feel of the movement. Some athletes also find it useful to actually move during imagery rehearsal. For example, a sprinter may assume a starting position and then imagine blasting from the blocks en route to a record time. A golfer may stand at address and actually swing a golf club while imagining the ball traveling through the air and landing close to the hole. With dynamic imagery the actual movement of the activity often helps athletes to recall more clearly the sensations associated with their performance.

Imagine in Real Time

At times, athletes find it helpful to slow play down during imagery, which helps in analyzing techniques or patterns of play. Sometimes they may even find it useful to speed images up. It is important to emphasize, however, that because an athlete does not execute techniques in slow motion or in a faster-than-normal speed, the bulk of imagery should be done in real time (the speed at which athletes actually perform). In this way, imagery practice will replicate the actual conditions of play.

Use Imagery Logs

Imagery logs or notebooks can serve a variety of purposes. For instance, they can assist athletes in monitoring imagery practice and progress. Different imagery exercises can be recorded along with the extent to which the athlete feels that each exercise was helpful. Imagery logs can also be used to describe previous best performances in an effort to identify better triggers or cues for imagery rehearsal. Overall, imagery logs increase athletes' awareness with regard to the practice they devote to imagery as well as the effectiveness of this practice.

Developing an Imagery Training Program

Having established specific guidelines for using imagery, we now address how to best implement an imagery training program with athletes. Although no two imagery programs are alike, it is important to incorporate the four phases depicted in Figure 1, each of which we discuss in detail below.

Phase 1: Awareness, Realistic Expectations, and Basic Education

Many coaches are eager to try all that imagery training has to offer. Unfortunately, their efforts are often undermined because of the lack

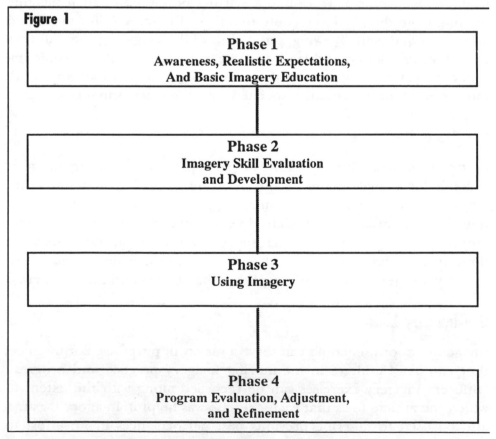

Figure 1

Phase 1
Awareness, Realistic Expectations, And Basic Imagery Education

Phase 2
Imagery Skill Evaluation and Development

Phase 3
Using Imagery

Phase 4
Program Evaluation, Adjustment, and Refinement

Phases of imagery training and utilization.

of understanding that many athletes have regarding what imagery is as well as how it can enhance performance. Consider the story of Alan at the beginning of this chapter. After attending a coaching education seminar, he decided to implement an imagery training program with his high school boys basketball team. Although his intentions were good, he failed to educate his team with regard to basic imagery principles and to convince them of the importance of imagery training to their basketball success. As a result, his players questioned the purpose of all this "mental stuff" and never truly made a commitment to it during practice.

Before implementing any imagery training program, it is critical that sport psychologists and coaches explain what imagery is and address any possible misconceptions that athletes may have. For example, some athletes may look to imagery training as a quick-and-easy solution to complex performance problems. This thinking is consistent with the desire for instant gratification so prevalent in Western society today. In reality, however, developing and refining imagery skills requires the same systematic practice that physical skills require.

Another common misconception that many athletes hold with regard to imagery training is that it is not useful. It is evident both from the claims of athletes in the popular press (which should be conveyed to athletes) and from a growing body of research that imagery training can have a positive influence in helping athletes achieve their potential. Although imagery training certainly cannot solve all problems, it has helped many athletes reach higher levels of performance.

Finally, because the media attention surrounding sport psychology is often associated with elite performers, many falsely assume that mental skills such as imagery are only for top-ranked amateur or professional athletes. In reality, imagery training can help athletes of all ability levels to achieve their potential. Imagery rehearsal can be used in conjunction with physical training to enhance skill acquisition in any less experienced athlete.

Overall, athletes must be aware of the importance of imagery for performance success if they are to develop a commitment to a training program (Martens, 1987). However, sport psychologists and coaches must be cautious to avoid unrealistic expectations about the effectiveness of imagery. Promises of dramatic performance improvements will set even the best designed program up for failure and undermine the credibility of imagery training.

Therefore, before actually implementing a program, it is important that sport psychologists and coaches hold a brief introductory meeting to explain to athletes what imagery is as well as how it has helped other athletes in the past. If possible, sport psychologists and coaches should provide examples of successful athletes who have used imagery in the same sport that the athletes are training for. For example, Alan could have conveyed to his basketball team how Bill Russell, one of the best all-time basketball players and winner of 11 National Basketball Association championships, used imagery to execute new plays and build self-confidence (Russell & Branch, 1979). Stories such as this help to establish credibility and respect in the minds of the athletes you are working with. It lets the athletes know you can speak their language and relate imagery skills to their specific individual needs (Orlick & Partington, 1987; Partington & Orlick, 1987; Ravizza, 1988).

In addition to explaining how imagery can enhance athletic performance (e.g., building self-confidence or, learning a particular play or strategy), it is also important to stress in the introductory meeting the need to practice imagery on a regular basis. During preseason, many coaches and athletes are enthusiastic about the prospects of an imagery training program. Unfortunately, as the season progresses and time demands and pressures increase, imagery training is often reduced to a handful of brief meetings added on to an already demanding practice schedule. Coaches and athletes must view imagery training as an integral part of practice. Sport psychologists should emphasize that imagery training will not take away from physical practice, but will instead enhance it.

Phase 2: Imagery Skill Evaluation and Development

Once athletes are aware of the value of imagery training, have realistic expectations, and have received basic education, their specific imagery skills should be evaluated and developed. There are several methods for evaluating imagery ability. One is to administer a psychological skills inventory, such as the Sport Imagery Questionnaire discussed by Vealey and Walter (1993). This questionnaire was originally created by Martens (1982) to measure an athlete's ability to experience each of the five senses as well as various emotional or mood states. Another way to evaluate imagery ability is to guide an athlete through an imagery exercise and, afterward, discuss the quality of the images. One should consider several aspects of the athlete's images in such an evaluation:

- Were the images vivid and controllable?
- Were they experienced from an internal or external perspective?

- Were images seen in color or in black and white?
- Were images under the athlete's control?

It is important to remember that, just as individual athletes differ in physical ability, they will also differ in their ability to image.

Once a sport psychologist or coach recognizes an athlete's strengths and weaknesses with regard to imagery, he or she can determine what specific practice strategies are most appropriate. In general, imagery training is designed to enhance the vividness and controllability of an athlete's imagery. Martens (1987) recommended that a sport imagery training program consist of these three steps: (a) sensory awareness training, (b) vividness training, and (c) controllability training.

Sensory Awareness Training

The first step in Martens's (1987) sport imagery training program is to have athletes become more aware of their sport experiences. The more athletes are consciously aware of what they see, hear, and feel, the more likely that they will be able to mentally re-create these experiences through imagery. For example, following a successful practice or competition, an athlete may wish to make note of the various sensations associated with that performance in an effort to identify specific cues that will enhance the quality of imagery in the future.

Vividness Training

After athletes have gained a greater sense of awareness with regard to their sport experiences, Martens (1987) suggested they should work to develop and refine the vividness of their images. This can be accomplished with a variety of exercises. For example, if athletes have very poor imagery skills, then the sport psychologist or coach might recommend that they start with a simple exercise, such as imagining the details of their bedroom or a piece of equipment associated with their sport (e.g., a football or running shoes). As their imagery skills develop, they can begin to imagine more complex skills associated with their sport performance. Also, athletes may find it helpful to practice in a relaxed environment, free of any possible distractions. As discussed earlier, many athletes use relaxation techniques prior to imagery rehearsal to better focus their attention. There is no limit to the exercises that athletes can do to enhance the vividness of their images. It requires only a little imagination and creativity.

Controllability Training

The final step of Martens's (1987) sport imagery training program involves learning to control and manipulate images. Similar to Phase 2, if athletes have poor imagery skills, it is important to begin with a simple exercise in a quiet setting before moving to a more complex, sport-specific exercise. Assume, for example, that a basketball player has difficulty controlling the content of his images. When he tries to imagine himself hitting a 3-point shot, he is unable to visualize the ball going into the basket. In this situation, a sport psychologist or coach may want to suggest that the athlete try a more simple exercise, such as simply imagining that he is dribbling the ball from a stationary position. As he becomes more proficient with this exercise, he can gradually work toward controlling images of more complex basketball skills (e.g., layups, 8-foot jumpshots, 16-foot jumpshots, and then 3-point shots).

It is important to remind athletes to be patient with themselves at first and not expect too much too soon. This is apparent from comments by Sylvie Bernier, former Olympic champion in springboard diving:

> It took me a long time to control my images and perfect my imagery, maybe a year, doing it every day. At first I couldn't see myself, I always saw everyone else, or I would see my dives wrong all the time. I would get an image of hurting myself, or tripping on the board, or I would "see" something done really bad. As I continued to work at it, I got to the point where I could feel myself doing a perfect dive and hear the crowd yelling at the Olympics. But it took me a long time. (quoted in Orlick, 1990, p. 68)

Regardless of whether an athlete is working on sensory awareness, image vividness, or image control, imagery is a skill like any other, requiring consistent effort to attain a high level of proficiency.

Overall, it is important to remember that individuals differ in their ability to image. Therefore it is important that within any training program, athletes are evaluated with regard to their imagery ability. Once athletes' strengths and weaknesses are recognized, an imagery program can be tailored to fit the individual needs of a team or athlete.

Phase 3: Using Imagery

Once athletes have evaluated and developed their imagery skills, it is important that they be reminded to continue to use them on a regular basis. Coaches are in the best position to remind athletes to use imagery and can do so with any number of strategies. For example, Mike White, former University of Illinois football coach, made a large meeting room available to his team in the hotel on the nights before games. This "imagery room" was used on a voluntary basis and players went to this dark, quiet place to mentally prepare themselves. As previously emphasized, coaches should also incorporate the use of imagery in instructional settings by having athletes visualize demonstrations, correct mistakes, and learn new offensive and defensive strategies. Finally, players should spend time visualizing themselves performing successfully and achieving their goals.

Phase 4: Imagery Evaluation, Adjustment, and Refinement

The final step in any successful imagery training program involves evaluating whether or not the program is meeting its established objectives (Weinberg & Williams, 1993) as well as determining what further adjustments and refinements are needed. For example, assume that you have designed a 12-week training program to help a high school soccer team develop and refine their imagery skills. Prior to implementing the program, you would evaluate current ability levels and assign appropriate exercises for each player. Midway through the season, you would reevaluate the athletes' imagery ability (e.g., with Martens's [1982] sport imagery questionnaire) to determine what, if any, progress has been made. For those athletes who have shown little improvement, individual meetings would be set up to identify possible problems. Depending on the individual situation, a new strategy may be suggested for future practice. Those athletes that are improving would simply be encouraged to continue with their current strategies, to log imagery effectiveness, and to explore new ways of using imagery.

If an imagery training program is meeting its established objectives, then the sport psychologist or coach can continue with confidence. However, if the program is not meeting its objectives, it is critical to examine the situation to determine why. What obstacles are preventing the program from reaching its goals, and how can these obstacles be overcome? Without critically examining an imagery training program, some athletes may falsely conclude that they are poor imagers when, in fact, they were using inappropriate strategies to develop their imagery skills. Program evaluations provide important feedback as to what strategies are effective and for whom they are effective. In addition, they provide an opportunity to alter strategies that may not be effective.

In summary, no two imagery training programs are identical. Each is designed to meet the unique characteristics and needs of the athlete or team it is intended for. However, within an individual training program it is important to include each of the four phases outlined above. For any training program to be effective, the athletes must understand that imagery is a skill that requires consistent effort over time to develop. Furthermore, during the training process, it is necessary to evaluate progress and make whatever adjustments are necessary to ensure that the program is meeting its desired objectives.

Problems and Pitfalls in Imagery Training

Even the best planned imagery training programs are not immune to difficulties. Although each situation presents its own unique set of challenges, a number of common problems have been identified by coaches, athletes, and consultants involving the actual implementation of an imagery training program. These obstacles include (a) unrealistic expectations, (b) lack of commitment to practicing imagery skills, and (c) lack of coach support and follow-up. Next, we briefly address each of these consulting issues and make specific suggestions about how to handle potential problems.

Unrealistic Expectations

Some coaches and athletes turn to imagery training for a quick performance fix. Although imagery can enhance athletic performance, it will not make up for poor physical skills or techniques. Also, imagery skills require the same time and patience to develop that physical skills do. Therefore, it is important that sport psychologists carefully plan a brief introductory meeting to address any possible misconceptions that may potentially undermine the realistic expectations of an imagery training program.

Lack of Commitment to Practicing Imagery Skills

Throughout this chapter, we have emphasized that imagery is a skill that requires systematic practice to develop and refine. Unfortunately, many athletes quickly lose interest in imagery training when they fail to realize immediate performance improvements. Such athletes often mistakenly assume that imagery does not work. One way to foster a commitment to imagery rehearsal is to integrate it into daily practice. As discussed earlier, this does not imply periodically stopping practice for, say, a 10-minute imagery session. Instead, coaches can suggest that athletes use imagery for brief periods throughout instruction and practice. For example, immediately following a mistake, athletes can take 5 seconds to replay a correct version of their performance in their mind. Also, following a successful performance, athletes can take a few moments to reinforce what they did well. Sport psychologists should emphasize that imagery training will not take away from physical practice, but will instead enhance it.

Lack of Coach Support and Follow-Up

In addition to the challenges discussed thus far, sport psychologists must also find ways to maintain coach support throughout the season. Unlike coaches, sport psychologists are rarely able to meet with a team or athlete on a daily basis. It is therefore critical that coaches reinforce the importance of imagery training in the sport psychologist's absence. Coaches must be encouraged to make imagery training as much a priority as physical training. This can be accomplished by integrating imagery training into practice. As discussed, this will help foster a commitment to imagery training. Athletes will perceive imagery to be valuable when their coaches designate practice time to it. Sport psychologists must emphasize that an imagery training program's success is dependent on the support and involvement of the coaches.

Summary

Imagery can be defined as a process by which sensory experiences are stored in memory and internally recalled and performed in the absence of external stimuli. Although current imagery research is not without problems, sufficient evidence exists to suggest that, when combined with physical practice, imagery can enhance athletic performance. A number of theories exist to explain the mechanisms underlying this imagery–performance relationship. These include the more well known psychoneuromuscular and symbolic learning theories as well as psychophysiological information-processing theory and the triple-code model of imagery. Although future research is needed to further develop and test imagery theories, the current state of knowledge suggests that imagery can influence athletic performance in several ways. These include developing higher levels of information processing for the symbolic elements of a given skill, providing added opportunities to rehearse stimulus and response propositions, and positively influencing other psychological states, such as confidence and anxiety.

Several guidelines were suggested to help those practitioners or athletes interested in implementing imagery rehearsal to enhance athletic performance:

1. Practice imagery on a regular basis.
2. Use all senses to enhance image vividness.
3. Develop imagery control.
4. Use both internal and external perspectives.
5. Facilitate imagery through relaxation.
6. Develop coping strategies through imagery.
7. Use imagery in practice as well as in competition.
8. Use videotapes or audiotapes to enhance imagery skills.
9. Use triggers or cues to facilitate imagery quality.
10. Emphasize dynamic kinesthetic imagery.
11. Imagine in real time.
12. Use imagery logs.

When implementing an imagery training program, it is important to incorporate the four specific phases we have outlined here. These include (a) educating coaches and athletes about what imagery is and how it can realistically enhance athletic performance, (b) evaluating current imagery ability and outlining appropriate practice strategies for individual athletes, (c) using imagery skills on a regular basis during practice, and (d) evaluating whether or not the training program is meeting its established objectives and determining what future adjustments are needed.

Finally, we have addressed several common problems involving the actual implementation of an imagery training program and made specific suggestions about how to best handle these potential obstacles. Problems include unrealistic coach and athlete expectations, lack of commitment to practice imagery skills, and lack of coach support and follow-up.

Overall, it is important to remember that imagery is like any physical skill in that it requires systematic practice to develop and refine. Individual athletes will differ in their ability to image and, therefore, must be encouraged to remain patient. Imagery is not a magical cure for performance woes. It is, however, an effective tool that—when combined with practice and commitment—can help athletes reach their personal and athletic potentials.

References

Ahsen, A. (1984). ISM: The triple code model for imagery and psychophysiology. *Journal of Mental Imagery, 8,* 15–42.

Bandura, A. (1977). Self-efficacy: Toward a unifying theory of behavioral change. *Psychological Review, 84,* 191–215.

Feltz, D. L., & Landers, D. M. (1983). The effects of mental practice on motor skill learning and performance: A meta-analysis. *Journal of Sport Psychology, 5,* 25–57.

Gould, D., & Udry, E. (1994). Psychological skills for enhancing performance: Arousal regulation strategies. *Medicine and Science in Sports and Exercise, 26,* 478–485.

Harris, D. V., & Harris, B. L. (1984). *The athlete's guide to sport psychology: Mental training for physical people.* New York: Leisure Press.

Highlen, P. S., & Bennett, B. B. (1983). Elite divers and wrestlers: A comparison between open and closed-skilled athletes. *Journal of Sport Psychology, 5,* 390–409.

Kohl, R. M., & Roenker, D. L. (1983). Mechanism involvement during skill imagery. *Journal of Motor Behavior, 15,* 179–190.

Lang, P. J. (1977). Imagery in therapy: An information processing analysis of fear. *Behavior Therapy, 8,* 862–886.

Lang, P. J. (1979). A bio-information theory of emotional imagery. *Psychophysiology, 16,* 495–512.

Mahoney, M. J., & Avener, M. (1977). Psychology of the elite athlete: An exploratory study. *Cognitive Therapy and Research, 3,* 361–366.

Martens, R. (1982, September). *Imagery in sport.* Paper presented at the Medical and Scientific Aspects of Elitism in Sport Conference, Brisbane, Australia.

Martens, R. (1987). *Coaches guide to sport psychology.* Champaign, IL: Human Kinetics.

Meichenbaum, D. (1985). *Stress inoculation training.* Elmsford, NY: Pergamon Press.

Meyers, A. W., Cooke, C. J., Cullen, J., & Liles, L. (1979). Psychological aspects of athletic competitors: A replication across sports. *Cognitive Therapy and Research, 3,* 361–366.

Mumford, P., & Hall, C. (1985). The effects of internal and external imagery on performing figures in figure skating. *Canadian Journal of Applied Sport Sciences, 10,* 171–177.

Murphy, S. M. (1994). Imagery interventions in sport. *Medicine and Science in Sports and Exercise, 26,* 486–494.

Murphy, S., & Jowdy, D. (1992). Imagery and mental rehearsal. In T. Horn (Ed.), *Advances in sport psychology* (pp. 221–250). Champaign, IL: Human Kinetics.

Orlick, T. (1986). *Psyching for sport: mental training for athletes.* Champaign, IL: Leisure Press.

Orlick, T. (1990). *In pursuit of excellence: How to win in sport and life through mental training.* Champaign, IL: Leisure Press.

Orlick, T., & Partington, J. (1987). The sport psychology consultant: Analysis of critical components as viewed by Canadian athletes. *Sport Psychologist, 1,* 4–7.

Partington, J., & Orlick, T. (1987). The sport psychology consultant: Olympic coaches' views. *Sport Psychologist, 1,* 95–102.

Ravizza, K. (1988). Gaining entry with athletic personnel for season-long consulting. *Sport Psychologist, 2,* 243–254.

Rawlings, E. I., Rawlings, I. L., Chen, C. S., & Yilk, M. D. (1972). The facilitating effects of mental rehearsal in the acquisition of rotary pursuit tracking. *Psychonomic Science, 26,* 71–73.

Russell, B., & Branch, T. (1979). *Second wind.* New York: Ballantine Books.

Ryan, E. D., & Simons, J. (1981). Cognitive demand imagery and frequency of mental practice as factors influencing the acquisition of mental skills. *Journal of Sport Psychology, 15,* 1–15.

Shelton, T. O., & Mahoney, M. J. (1978). The content and effect of "psyching-up" strategies in weight lifters. *Cognitive Therapy and Research, 2,* 275–284.

Smith, R. E. (1980). A cognitive–affective approach to stress management training for athletes. In C. Nadeau, W. Halliwell, K. Newell, & G. C. Roberts (Eds.), *Psychology of motor behavior and sport: 1979* (pp. 54–72). Champaign, IL: Human Kinetics.

Suinn, R. (1972). Removing emotional obstacles to learning and performance by visuomotor behavioral rehearsal. *Behavior Therapy, 3,* 308–310.

Suinn, R. (1993). Imagery. In R. N. Singer, M. Murphey, & L. K. Tennant (Eds.), *Handbook of research on sports psychology* (pp. 492–510). New York: Macmillan.

Vealey, R., & Walter, S. (1993). Imagery training for performance enhancement. In J. M. Williams (Ed.), *Applied sport psychology: Personal growth to peak performance* (2nd ed., pp. 200–224). Mountain View, CA: Mayfield.

Weinberg, R. S. (1981). The relationship between mental preparation strategies and motor performance: A review and critique. *Quest, 33,* 195–213.

Weinberg, R. S., Gould, D., Jackson, A., & Barnes, P. (1980). Influence of cognitive strategies on tennis serves of players of high and low ability. *Perceptual and Motor Skills, 50,* 663–666.

Weinberg, R. S., Seabourne, T. G., & Jackson, A. (1981). Effects of visuo-motor behavior rehearsal, relaxation, and imagery on karate performance. *Journal of Sport Psychology, 3,* 228–238.

Weinberg, R. S., & Williams, J. M. (1993). Integrating and implementing a psychological skills training program. In J. M. Williams (Ed.), *Applied sport psychology: Personal growth to peak performance* (2nd ed., pp. 274–298). Mountain View, CA: Mayfield.

Woolfolk, R., Parrish, W., & Murphy, S. M. (1985). The effects of positive and negative imagery on motor skill performance. *Cognitive Therapy and Research, 9,* 235–241.

Cognitive Strategies in Sport and Exercise Psychology

Jean M. Williams and Thad R. Leffingwell

"Change your thoughts and you change your world."
—Norman Vincent Peale

Over 10 years have passed since Straub and Williams (1984) heralded the emergence of the field of cognitive sport psychology, and it has been over 15 years since Mahoney's (1977) landmark paper advocating a cognitive skills approach to the understanding and improvement of athletic performance. Today, cognitive approaches to enhancing athletic performance dominate sport psychologists' research and intervention strategies (Strean & Roberts, 1992; Whelan, Mahoney, & Meyers, 1991).

Cognitive approaches in sport psychology have been broadly and loosely defined, and include techniques such as goal setting, imagery and mental rehearsal, attention control, and cognitive anxiety management. Other chapters in this text deal with many of these topics. This chapter primarily focuses on the relationship of one's thoughts to athletic performance and on approaches to altering thinking for the enhancement of sport performance and enjoyment. The chapter begins with a discussion of cognitive–behavioral strategies that can be used to combat problematic thinking. Next a discussion of self-talk is presented. The chapter concludes with a brief discussion of the relationship of cognitions to exercise behavior, attention, and anxiety.

The authors would like to acknowledge an earlier chapter written by Bunker, Williams, and Zinsser (1993), in J. M. Williams (Ed). *Applied sport psychology: Personal growth to peak performance,* Mountain View, CA: Mayfield. Their chapter very much influenced the content in this chapter.

Cognitions and Athletic Performance

What athletes think about themselves, their performance, specific situations, and so forth directly affects their feelings and behaviors. Unfortunately, what athletes say to themselves is not always conducive to good performance, and all too often is at the root of poor performance. Although many athletes and sport psychologists believe best performances occur with no conscious thinking—*automatic performance*—it is probably unrealistic to expect athletes to shut off all thinking during every performance (Bunker, Williams, & Zinsser, 1993). However, thinking itself should not be blamed for poor performance, but rather inappropriate or misguided thinking (Bell, 1983). The critical question to answer for improved performance is not whether to think, but what, when, and how to think.

A number of research studies have supported the notion of successful athletes using different cognitive strategies than less successful athletes (see Greenspan & Feltz, 1989 or Williams & Krane, 1993 for a more thorough review). Highlen and Bennett (1979) found that wrestlers who qualified for an elite national team reported fewer negative thoughts about themselves than did wrestlers who did not qualify, but qualifying and nonqualifying wrestlers did not differ in terms of positive thoughts about themselves or in terms of rationalizations. Similarly, Gould, Weiss, and Weinberg (1981) found that more successful collegiate wrestlers had fewer self-doubts and more match-related thoughts prior to competition than less successful wrestlers. All of the researchers reported higher self-confidence for their more successful athletes. These results indicate that more successful athletes use more appropriate thoughts and experience less negativity and self-doubt as compared to even slightly less successful athletes (e.g., Olympic qualifiers vs. nonqualifiers).

Recent qualitative studies have looked at the differences in cognitions and affect before and during best versus worst performance for elite Olympic wrestlers. Gould, Eklund, and Jackson (1992a, 1992b) found that the wrestlers reported positive expectancies and heightened commitment prior to their best performances. In contrast, prior to their worst performances, the athletes reported negative, irrelevant, or irregular thought patterns. In terms of their thoughts during competition, the wrestlers reported task-focused thinking, which included task-specific self-talk during their best performances and a number of ineffective thoughts during their worst performances, including task irrelevant and negative thoughts. In another qualitative study, Gould, Finch, and Jackson (1993) investigated the stress-coping strategies of U.S. national champion figure skaters. The two most common coping strategies employed by these highly successful athletes included (a) rational thinking and self-talk, and (b) positive focus and orientation. Although causality cannot be inferred from these studies, results suggest that successful athletes employ more effective cognitive strategies than less successful athletes, indicating that interventions to enhance effective cognitions (e.g., make cognitions more positive, rational, task focused, etc.) may prove effective at enhancing performance.

Cognitive–Behavioral Interventions

The high-pressure situations of competitive sport may represent an ideal environment for fostering irrational or distorted thinking styles. Irrational, self-defeating beliefs are roadblocks to self-direction and achievement in sport and exercise settings. In addition to interfering with good, consistent performance, these self-defeating beliefs can interfere with motivation to participate and may result in individuals avoiding the competitive arena (Ellis, 1982). Sport psychologists use a number of cognitive–behavioral techniques (e.g., Beck, 1970; Ellis & Harper, 1975; Meichenbaum, 1977) to help athletes become aware of irrational or inappropriate thinking styles and to combat or counter this thinking, ultimately creating habits of effective thinking. According to Dobson and Block (1988), three important assumptions underlie cognitive–behavioral interventions:

1. Cognitive activity can affect behavior (including athletic performance).
2. Cognitive activity can be altered.
3. Cognitive change can facilitate desired behavioral change.

This section of the chapter will discuss common types of distorted thinking and how to identify and refute irrational or distorted thinking in sport.

Irrational and Distorted Thinking

Ellis (1982) identified four general irrational beliefs that may interfere with athletes reaching their potential. These four beliefs are (a) "I must

do well in sport and if I don't I am an incompetent, worthless person";
(b) "I must do well to gain the love and approval of others, and if I
don't it is horrible"; (c) "Everyone must treat me with respect and
fairness at all times"; and (d) "The conditions of my life must be arranged so that I get what I want easily and quickly." These four general
beliefs may contribute to a great deal of emotional distress for athletes
and clearly do contribute to the pressure already present in achievement situations.

In addition to these irrational beliefs, athletes may employ a number of cognitive distortions that can interfere with effective performance (Gauron, 1984). Distorted thinking patterns interfere with performance by providing the athlete with faulty information about the
competitive environment, resulting in misdirected attention, emotional
distress such as excessive anxiety, or lowered self-concept. Gauron
(1984) identified the following list of distorted thinking styles that athletes commonly employ:

1. *Perfectionism.* Athletes and coaches often get caught up in demanding perfection. This unrealistic expectation leads to excessive pressure and undermines effective coping. Ellis (1982) dif-
   ferentiated between perfectionist *desires*, which may lead to
   championship performance, and perfectionist *demands* and *com-
   mands*, which have "probably wrecked more athletic attempts
   than any other self-sabotaging factor" (p. 30). Perfectionistic
   attitudes can also lead to a negative self-concept and a fear-of-
   failure syndrome due to self-imposed negative consequences
   when less-than-perfect performances occur.
2. *Catastrophizing.* When athletes hold beliefs that include horrible
   consequences when beliefs are not met, they often exaggerate
   potential consequences of imagined or real negative events. Ca-
   tastrophizers may expect the worst in every situation—often
   worse than reality or previous experience would suggest. This
   expectation can contribute to actual negative outcomes.
3. *Self-worth depends on achievement.* Many athletes view their value
   as individuals relative to their degree of athletic success. This
   perception is particularly damaging for young athletes who perceive their self-worth and worth to others, particularly their parents, as depending upon their participation and success in
   sports. This perception clearly increases the pressure to per-

form, contributes to low and unstable self-worth, and can interfere with the fun of participation in sport.

4. *Personalization.* Closely related to the self-worth and achievement belief, athletes sometimes exhibit a self-defeating tendency to personalize everything. These athletes tend to overestimate their personal responsibility for every failure and mistake. For example, a missed free throw in the final seconds of the game "caused the team to lose." Over time, this misperception clearly contributes to a low self-concept, elevated performance anxiety, and even decreased motivation and commitment.

5. *Fallacy of fairness.* Unfortunately, often times *fairness* translates simply to wanting one's own way versus what someone else (e.g., the coach) thinks is fair, or best for the group. This perception of unfair treatment may interfere with interpersonal relations, appropriate focus of attention, and coping with adversity.

6. *Blaming.* Although some athletes may over-personalize—that is, they internally attribute all failure—others excessively attribute failure externally, to coaches, conditions, officials, and so on. This type of thinking allows athletes relief from all responsibility, which is counter to good performance and effective coping. Athletes need to be taught to realistically and rationally evaluate performance outcomes and to accept responsibility when appropriate to do so.

7. *Polarized thinking.* Athletes are often tempted to view things and people in absolute terms, in black and white. This type of distorted thinking often represents itself as labeling selves or others in simple, unidimensional terms—*losers*, *cheaters*, or *unbeatable opponents*. These irrational labels contribute to performance expectancies and can directly influence performance.

8. *One-trial generalizations.* Similar to polarized thinking, athletes may sometimes use a single incident to define expectancies for future performances. For example, a college basketball player stated, "We are a second-half basketball team" after his team played its first two games of the season. This kind of irrational generalization interferes with good performance, proper preparation, and appropriate focus. In the example above, that team may now underemphasize the importance of its play in the first half of a game and thus fail during that half to make adjustments and take advantage of opportunities.

Identifying and Modifying Irrational and Distorted Thinking

Athletes are often unaware of the irrational beliefs or distorted thinking underlying emotional conflicts and performance difficulties. Identifying these distortions is the first and most important step toward modifying maladaptive thinking styles and enjoying the benefits of rational thinking. Coaches and sport psychologists can help identify ineffective thinking by paying close attention to the athlete's attributions and evaluations following performances, particularly poor performances. Often, teachable moments occur just after important competitions, when the athlete has a greater awareness of cognitions before and during competition and may be more open to learning. Also, because athletes often learn distorted thinking patterns from their coaches, coaches in particular must be aware of their own irrational beliefs and the way they model distorted thinking for the athletes.

Silva (1982) identified three phases for implementing cognitive restructuring interventions with athletes: *identification, cognitive restructuring,* and *pairing*. In the identification phase, the sport psychologist and the athlete attempt to define the boundaries of the effected behavior and the irrational beliefs or self-defeating verbalizations present in the situation. This identification can be accomplished through conversation, journal writing, or actual performance of the skill and verbalization of thoughts in the presence of the sport psychologist. During the restructuring phase, the athlete is convinced of the inappropriateness of the present thoughts and more effective replacement thoughts are created. Silva (1982) emphasized that the effectiveness of the intervention depends on getting the athlete to recognize the need to change. Finally, in the pairing phase, the athlete uses self-instructional imagery and verbal cues to facilitate the application of new thinking patterns into actual performance. The athletes should practice the imagery several times a day to make the new thoughts automatic.

Ellis and Harper (1975), Beck (1970), and Meichenbaum (1977) all emphasized the importance of underlying beliefs in maintaining automatic thoughts. These authors recommended challenging underlying beliefs as a vehicle for long-term change in thinking patterns. Beck (1970) suggested purposefully acting counter to identified irrational beliefs as a way of experiencing new thinking and feeling. For example, an athlete who employs excessive criticism and self-abuse after every mistake may try to smile and be overtly self-complimentary after a few mistakes to experience the positive consequences (i.e., thoughts, feelings, and performance) associated with this new behavior.

Athletes, coaches, sport psychologists, and parents must make an effort to substitute rational for irrational thinking during all phases of training and competition. If athletes have a particularly difficult irrational belief to rid themselves of, they may benefit from daily affirmation statements counter to the belief. For example, an athlete may use the affirmation "I want to be a successful athlete, but my worth does not depend on that success." Physically relaxing may increase the effectiveness of attempts to counter irrational beliefs. As mentioned previously, most irrational beliefs create anxiety and tension, thus decreasing receptivity to more effective, rational thoughts.

If doubt exists about whether a belief is irrational or ineffective, Steinmetz, Blankenship, Brown, Hall, and Miller (1980) suggested the following criteria to evaluate the belief:

1. Are the beliefs based on objective reality?
2. Are they helpful to you?
3. Are they useful in reducing interpersonal conflicts?
4. Do they help you reach your goals?
5. Do they reduce emotional conflict?

If the athlete answers "no" to any of the above questions, the belief is likely to be irrational or counterproductive, and the individual will benefit from modifying it.

Irrational beliefs are well entrenched in sport: "No pain, no gain." "Give 110% all the time." "Practice makes perfect." "Winning isn't everything, it's the only thing." Sometimes athletes or coaches believe that modifying some types of irrational thinking (e.g., perfectionism, self-worth depends on achievement) threatens competitiveness or drive. More likely, modifying irrational beliefs enhances performance by helping athletes stay relaxed, task-focused, positive, and motivated (Bunker et al., 1993).

Metaanalytic reviews of sport psychology intervention research have concluded that cognitive interventions such as cognitive restructuring do, in fact, improve the performance of athletes (Greenspan & Feltz, 1989; Meyers, Whelan, & Murphy, in press). Greenspan and Feltz (1989) found that researchers reported positive results in 11 studies using cognitive-restructuring interventions. Greenspan and Feltz (1989) cautioned that causality could be inferred from only a few of these studies and expressed concern that perhaps journals only publish studies with positive results, thus causing an overestimation of the effectiveness of sport psychology interventions, including cognitive restructuring. The metaanalysis by Meyers, Whelan, and Murphy (in press) calculated a greater effect size for cognitive restructuring interventions ($n = 4$, $d = .79$, $SD = .36$) than that found for goal setting ($n = 3$, $d = .54$, $SD = .15$); mental rehearsal ($n = 28$, $d = .57$, $SD = .75$); and relaxation interventions ($n = 25$, $d = .73$, $SD = 1.65$). These authors also concluded that cognitive-restructuring interventions improve performance. Although published studies of the effectiveness of cognitive-restructuring interventions are limited in number and practically nonexistent with elite athletes, they have reliably demonstrated effectiveness at improving athletic performance.

Self-Talk

Broadly defined, *self-talk* occurs whenever an individual thinks, whether that individual is making statements internally or externally. Sport and exercise psychologists are most concerned with athletes' self-statements that direct attention ("focus"), label the self or others ("I am a choker."), judge performances ("great shot"), and contribute to or undermine good performance. The irrational beliefs and cognitive distortions discussed previously are manifested in self-talk. Self-talk serves as the vehicle for making perceptions and beliefs conscious, thereby providing the key to gaining cognitive control (Bunker et al., 1993).

A number of studies have documented the usefulness of self-talk in competitive sport. Highlen and Bennett (1983) found divers qualifying for the Pan American Games used more positive self-instruction self-talk and less praising self-talk during competition than nonqualifiers. More successful divers also reported using self-talk more during training and competition. Orlick and Partington (1988) found that successful Olympic athletes often used positive self-statements as part of a well-developed precompetition plan. In contrast, athletes with an ineffective focus of attention were characterized by self-doubt. Similarly, the Gould et al. (1992a, 1992b) studies of Olympic wrestlers indicated that self-talk was a common technique for fostering positive expectancies and appropriately focusing attention on the task.

A study of observed self-talk and behavioral assessments with junior tennis players found that negative self-talk was associated with losing (Van Raalte, Brewer, Rivera, & Petitpas, 1994). These results implicated negative self-talk as a contributor to poorer performance, but failed to show a relationship of positive self-talk to better performance. The authors concluded that the tennis players may have internalized their positive self-talk and thus the researchers could not observe it as readily as negative self-talk.

An experimental investigation of three different types of positive self-talk—*task-relevant statements, mood words*, and *positive self-statements*—demonstrated positive performance effects with cross country skiers for all three experimental conditions compared to a control condition that employed the self-talk normally used by the skiers (Rushall, Hall, Roux, Sasseville, & Rushall, 1988). Other experimental studies investigating the effects of positive self-monitoring have suggested that positive self-statements may be more effective than negative ones at improving both golfing and bowling performance (Johnston-O'Conner & Kirschenbaum, 1986; Kirschenbaum, Ordman, Tomarken, & Holtzbauer, 1982). A number of studies have found positive self-talk led to better performance than negative self-talk for subjects completing fairly simple tasks (Dagrou, Gauvin, & Halliwell, 1992; Schill, Monroe, Evans, & Ramanaiah, 1978; Van Raalte et al., 1995).

Some descriptive studies using self-report of self-talk content found no difference in the content of self-talk between more and less successful athletes (Rotella, Gansneder, Ojala, & Billings, 1980) or between an athlete's best and worst performances (Dagrou, Gauvin, & Halliwell, 1991). Overall, however, the preponderance of studies provide evidence in support of the hypothesis that both positive self-talk and self-confidence are associated with better or at least "no-worse" performances. It appears that, in general, a positive self-concept, high self-confidence, a task-relevant focus of attention, and less self-doubt relate to better performance. Self-talk that detracts from any of these conditions probably inhibits performance. This section will offer suggestions for identifying and modifying self-talk.

Uses for Self-Talk

Self-talk serves a variety of different uses in sport and exercise. For example, individuals can use self-talk to correct habits, focus attention, modify activation, build and maintain self-confidence, and encourage and maintain exercise participation.

Correcting Bad Habits

Athletes can use self-talk when trying to correct well-learned skills or habits. Often, bad habits are "automatic" in technique, and self-talk can help consciously override this automaticity. The content of the self-talk may range from a description of an entire motion (e.g., "swing back, step, hit, follow through") to a single cue word for minor changes (e.g., "turn" or "push"). When using self-talk for changing technique, the self-talk must focus on desirable movements, and not on unwanted movements. For example, if a golfer wants to shift weight on the down-swing, appropriate self-talk would be "shift" not "don't hang back." This type of self-talk is appropriate for the learning or corrective stage, but may not be necessary once skills are learned or during actual competitive performance if the correct actions occur automatically, that is, without prompting.

Self-Talk for Focusing Attention

Athletes can use self-talk for effectively focusing attention during practice or competition. Athletes can use self statements or cue words to focus attention in the present moment ("right now," or "be here") and on task-specific cues ("Track the ball." or "Pick your target."). These cues are used to maintain focus and to refocus when an athlete has lost appropriate focus.

Self-Talk for Modifying Activation

Athletes who perceive a need to modify activation level can use self-statements to decrease or increase their physical activation. These self statements may include relaxing cues ("easy," "quiet," "relax") or energizing cues ("go," "get up," "pumped"). For greater effectiveness, athletes should pick cues that have the best emotional content for them. These cues can help to establish optimal activation prior to and during competition or can help modify it when not appropriate.

Self-Talk for Self-Confidence

Self-statements affect self-confidence either positively or negatively. Self-talk that reflects negative expectancies and excessive self-doubt ("Once again you're a loser." or "You have no chance at all.") undermines self-confidence. Although some situations warrant self-criticism, this criticism must remain restricted to performance or behavior, and not extend to the self. Many perceived sources of self-confidence, such as performance outcomes, expectations of others, or talent exist outside of an athlete's control. The athlete alone, however, controls self-talk, which is another major source of self-confidence and motivation. Development of positive self-statements ("You can do it." You're good enough to challenge anyone.) can be facilitated by the sport psychologist. Occasionally, self-statements about negative expectancies ("Don't choke again, stupid!") can self-motivate and mobilize effort, but problems with self-confidence can arise if this theme of self-statements dominates the athlete's self-talk content. Other methods of enhancing motivation and mobilizing effort would probably prove more effective with fewer negative consequences.

Self-Talk for Increasing Efficacy and Maintaining Exercise Behavior

Recent studies in the area of exercise behavior have implicated self-efficacy cognitions as a significant factor in predicting adoption and adherence to an exercise program (Armstrong, Sallis, Hovell, & Hofsetter, 1993; Marcus, Selby, Niaura, & Rossi, 1992; McAuley, 1992).[1] Self-efficacy cognitions may also serve as potential mediators in the relationship of social support to exercise adherence (Duncan & McAuley, 1993). These preliminary findings suggest that modifying self-efficacy cognitions toward exercise contribute to exercise adoption or adherence.

Although cognitive interventions hold promise for fostering exercise behaviors, these interventions have received little attention or research support. For example, Buffone, Sachs, and Dowd (1984) recommended modifying self-talk as a potential cognitive strategy for maintaining exercise behavior, but did not provide any research support for its use. Gauvin (1990) hypothesized that persistent exercisers use positive and motivational self-talk while drop-outs and sedentaries use self-defeating negative self-talk. Based on these recommendations and the preliminary research findings, a need exists for more thorough study of the role of cognitions and the effectiveness of different cognitive-intervention strategies for fostering exercise adoption and adherence.

Identifying Self-Talk

In order to determine if self-talk needs changing, athletes first must have an awareness of the content of their self-statements and the effect the self-talk has on performance (Meichenbaum, 1977). Athletes must become aware of not only negative and self-defeating self-talk, but also positive and facilitating self-talk. A simple paper-clip exercise can help many athletes increase awareness of the frequency of their negative self-talk. Have the athlete carry a number of paper clips in a pocket and then transfer a paper clip to a different pocket each time a negative

---

1. See Chapter 6 for a discussion of exercise adherence.

self-statement occurs. Often, athletes become motivated to change because of their amazement at the number of paper clips shifted and the adverse consequences of the self-talk. Sport psychologists can use a number of other techniques to help athletes identify self-talk. These techniques include retrospection, imagery, observation, and use of self-talk logs.

Retrospection

When athletes use the retrospection technique, they reflect upon performances in which they performed particularly well or poorly in an effort to recall thoughts and feelings prior to and during these performances. For maximal effectiveness, athletes should use this technique as soon after a performance as possible in order to not forget important aspects of the performance. Often, watching a videotape of the performance can aid more accurate and thorough recall. If sport psychologists observe the performance, they can give specific prompts to help athletes to recall significant moments before, during, or after a performance. For athletes who have little awareness of their self-talk, retrospection may not work.

Imagery

Athletes skilled in imagery can vividly recreate past performances to help recall thoughts and feelings. The reliving of the performance through imagery helps athletes become more aware of the self-talk they had and the effects of the self statements upon their emotions and performance.

Observation

For athletes who frequently say their self-talk out loud, the sport psychologist can help raise the awareness of self-talk by observing and recording verbalized self-talk during performance. Ideally, sport psychologists should collect information about athletes' verbalizations, the situations in which they occurred, and, if possible, the performance consequences. Armed with these data, sport psychologists more effectively can raise athletes' awareness of the content and frequency of their self-talk. Also, this technique provides sport psychologists with data about the actual effects of self-talk on performance. For example, if a tennis player wins most points following negative verbalizations, the sport psychologist may reconsider altering those self-statements. If the observed self-statements improve performance but may damage self-esteem or self-confidence, the sport psychologist may choose different strategies for altering that self-talk to help the athlete get the same performance effects without long-term consequences to self-concept. This technique has the major drawback of only including verbalized, observable self-statements.

Self-Talk Logs

Often, athletes claim to be unaware of the content or frequency of verbalizations during performance. These athletes typically cannot recall accurately self-talk through retrospection or imagery. Daily record keeping in a self-talk log can effectively increase awareness. The log should include the situation in which the self-talk occurred (e.g., in the locker room, after a foul was called against the athlete, just before a big point); the content of the self-statements (e.g., "Don't choke;" "I can't believe you did that."); and the consequence of the self-talk, expressed in terms of performance consequences (*double fault*), emotional consequences (*frustration, anger*), or both. The self-talk log has a number of advantages. It usually creates the greatest awareness of self-talk by providing the most accurate and thorough identification of self-talk. It also provides for the best identification of the situations triggering the self-talk and the consequences of the self-talk. If convenient, athletes should occasionally carry a small tape recorder during practice to provide immediate documentation of verbalizations, whether said out-loud or merely thought. The sport psychologist should also encourage the athlete to record the situation triggering the self-talk and the behavioral and emotional consequences of the self-talk.

Modifying Self-Talk

Once the preceding techniques raise awareness of self-talk and identify potentially facilitating or self-defeating thoughts, the athlete and sport psychologist can use a number of techniques to modify self-talk. Assuming the athletes have an appropriate awareness of their self-talk and sufficient motivation to make changes, the sport psychologist can use the following techniques—thought stoppage, changing negative thoughts to positive thoughts, countering, and reframing—to facilitate modification. Without commitment to change by the athlete, attempts at using the techniques to modify self-talk probably will prove futile.

Even with commitment to change and appropriate practice, some athletes may not have success with the cognitive techniques. When this problem occurs, the sport psychologist may need to look for underlying factors that contribute to the athlete's difficulty at altering ineffective self-talk. For example, athletes with low self-esteem and negative self-concepts may lack sufficient confidence to believe constructive self-talk or to believe that they deserve to succeed and to have good things happen to them. When this type of situation exists, sport psychologists may need to intervene at the level of trying to improve self-esteem and self-concept or may need to make a referral. For athletes without these difficulties, the following self-talk modification techniques may be helpful.

Thought Stoppage

After the athlete has identified specific self-statements or patterns of self-talk that need elimination, the technique of thought stoppage can help minimize this self-talk (Meyers & Schleser, 1980). Thought stoppage involves the use of a trigger or cue to interrupt unwanted thoughts when they occur. This trigger can be verbal (e.g., the word *stop*), visual (e.g., a piece of tape on a tennis racquet or visualizing a red stop light), or physical (e.g., snapping of the fingers). Athletes can use almost any trigger they choose, as long as it does not interfere with performance and it gets applied consistently. This technique immediately interrupts the unwanted thoughts and, with practice, may effectively control negative self-talk. By stopping negative self-statements before they lead to negative feelings and behaviors, athletes experience relief from self-imposed negativity. It is hoped that with consistent use of thought stoppage, the need for the technique would decrease because the frequency of the unwanted negative self-talk decreases.

Sport psychologists may not want to use thought stoppage exclusively in their attempt to suppress unwanted thoughts. Recent laboratory experiments by Wegner and colleagues (Wegner & Erber, 1992; Wegner, Schneider, Carter, & White, 1987; Wegner, Schneider, Knutson, & McMahon, 1991; Wegner, Shortt, Blake, & Page, 1990) have demonstrated that merely attempting to suppress unwanted thoughts can have the paradoxical effect of making unwanted thoughts hyperaccessible during and after suppression and can result in greater effects on mood than when no attempt is made to suppress the thought. This effect may be even greater in stressful situations, such as athletic competition. Although these studies were not conducted in field situations such as sport settings, their results suggest that a more lasting change might come from augmenting thought stoppage with one of the following techniques.

Changing Negative Thoughts to Positive Thoughts

For maximum effectiveness, the athlete initially may want not only to stop negative or counterproductive thoughts, but to follow them with a positive thought that encourages or appropriately directs attention. For example, if the athlete says, "I hate playing for this coach," she might follow the statement with "I may not enjoy this coach as much as my high-school coach, but I can learn a lot from him."

Supplementing thought stoppage with this technique has several advantages. Athletes who doubt their ability to stop negative thoughts from occurring may accept that at least they can replace that thought with a more constructive one. If athletes experience more early success in using the cognitive techniques, they might persevere longer in trying to change faulty thinking habits. Finally, substituting a positive thought may negate, or at least minimize, the effect of the negative thought.

One way to help athletes successfully implement this technique is to have them list their typical negative self-statements on one side of a sheet of paper and then opposite each write an appropriate positive self-statement that they might immediately substitute the next time they make the statement. Because negative thoughts often occur when an individual is under stress and over-activated physiologically (Bunker et al., 1993), the sport psychologist may want to suggest that the athlete say the positive self-statement after the exhalation of a deep breath.

Countering

Changing negative self-statements to positive ones likely will not change behavior as long as the athlete still believes in the negative statements (Bell, 1983). If athletes are encouraged only to "be nicer to themselves," more than superficial and short-term effects cannot be expected. Countering is a useful technique for challenging the athlete's belief in the negative statement, thereby facilitating the acceptance of the constructive self-statement.

Countering is a process of internal debate—using facts, reason, and rational thinking to counter self-defeating thoughts. Bell (1983) suggested that when athletes believe in negative self-statements, they need to build a case against that belief in order to effectively make changes in self-talk and performance. When using countering, the athlete gathers evidence from a variety of sources to refute the negative belief. For example, an athlete may perceive heightened activation during competition as a sign of fear and weakness. "My heart is pounding so hard. I'm going to choke. I'm such a wimp," athletes may tell themselves. The athlete can counter these self-defeating statements by using evidence from past experiences with heightened activation. An athlete may say, "My heart is pounding hard, but that's natural, happens to everybody. It is a sign that this is important and exciting. I have come through in these situations before and I can do it now." In this situation, encouraging athletes to say "I am not nervous" or "I am calm" would not be sufficient, particularly when athletes have evidence available that they are nervous (e.g., a pounding heart).

Reframing

Individuals, athletes included, tend to view the world in narrow, rigid terms. Consistent with Peale's quote at the start of this chapter— "Change your thoughts and you change your world"—Gauron (1984) recommended the technique of reframing for changing an athlete's frame of reference or view of the world. Often times, athletes can change negative self-statements to positive by changing their perspective. For example, athletes concerned about competing against a much higher ranked opponent may think "I'm going to really embarrass myself," they can reframe this concern as an opportunity to assess their skill—"I'm going to see how good I've gotten and where I need improvement." Similarly, an athlete who has the self-talk "I'm feeling tense and nervous" can reframe the statement to "I'm excited and ready."

Reframing can help maintain a proper perspective on competition. Coaches often use reframing to focus their teams or to affect morale. For example, if a team loses a number of games successively, the coach may emphasize the value of the learning experience. After a big win, coaches often say, "That game is behind us; we have to focus on the next one."

Bell's (1983) caution regarding the importance of knowing the beliefs underlying negative statements bears repeating. If an athlete reframes the situation and thus changes the self-talk, but the belief that caused the negative statement remains, behavior change is unlikely. For the greatest effectiveness, the sport psychologist and athlete should employ a combination of thought stoppage, changing negative thoughts to positive thoughts, reframing, and countering when attempting to modify negative, unwanted, or self-defeating self-talk.

Cognitions and Endurance Performance

Investigations of optimal cognitions for enhancing endurance performance have focused on attentional focus, specifically *associative* and *dissociative* cognitive strategies (Brewer & Sachs, 1996). Associative cognitions direct attention toward task-related cues (e.g., strategy, pace) and physical sensations that result from the exercise (e.g., breathing, leg muscle fatigue). Dissociative cognitions refer to thoughts that have nothing to do with exercising (e.g., relationships, spiritual matters, doing math problems).

Since Morgan and Pollock's (1977) original work in this area, a number of studies have investigated the effect associative and dissociative strategies have on endurance performance. In general, researchers have found that experienced endurance athletes, such as elite marathoners, choose associative strategies as their dominant attentional focus (Masters & Lambert, 1989; Morgan & Pollock, 1977; Silva & Appelbaum, 1989) and most effective strategy for improving performance (Clingman & Hilliard, 1990; Spink & Longhurst, 1986). The opposite occurred for inexperienced individuals. They used dissociative strategies the most and found them the most effective at improving performance (Fillingim & Fine, 1986; Gill & Strom, 1985; Pennebaker & Lightner, 1980; Rejeski & Kenney, 1987; Spink, 1988).

Brewer and Sachs (1996) explained these findings with a parallel processing perspective. Experienced athletes interpret signs of the physical distress encountered during endurance performance (e.g., pounding heart, muscle fatigue) in an objective, nonemotional manner. Thus, they can benefit from the task-relevant cognitions by using the information to evaluate their performance and decide whether they should increase or decrease their pace. Inexperienced athletes, on the other hand, interpret physical distress emotionally and thus benefit from distracting dissociative strategies as a method of coping with the distress.

In terms of the application of these findings, Brewer and Sachs (1996) recommended that sport and exercise psychologists determine the *boundary conditions* (e.g., skill level, length of event) for using either attentional strategy. Previously, Morgan (1984) recommended that association should be the method of choice because it is more efficient and entails less risk for injury, but dissociative strategies can be selectively used to cope with a particularly stressful portion of an endurance performance. Since Morgan's recommendation, one intervention study demonstrated that a mental training program can be used to increase associative thought content for marathoners (Schomer, 1987).

Cognitions, Anxiety, and Attentional Focus

Cognitive techniques can provide important interventions for dealing with anxiety and maintaining appropriate attentional focus. Cognitions play an important role in the experience of stress and anxiety (Lazarus & Folkman, 1984; Smith, 1980). The cognitive appraisals of the demands of the situation, the importance of meeting the demands, and the individual's ability to meet the demands of a situation mediate the athlete's anxiety responses. For example, Mahoney and Avener (1977) found that more successful gymnasts tended to constructively use their elevated activation (i.e., physiological arousal), and less successful gymnasts approached near panic states by combining activation with self-defeating thoughts. Clearly, much of the distorted thinking habits discussed earlier in the chapter can create excess anxiety in practice and competition. When an athlete experiences excess stress and anxiety, maintaining a proper attentional focus becomes more difficult, with attention often becoming narrow and internally directed towards worry, self-doubt, and other task-irrelevant thoughts (Nideffer, 1993). Thus, ineffective thinking can hinder good performance in two ways: (a) creating excess anxiety and accompanying physiological changes, possibly moving activation out of the athletes optimal level; and (b) misdirecting attention away from an effective attentional focus, inhibiting good concentration.

Many of the techniques discussed previously in the chapter can be useful for dealing with anxiety and maintaining appropriate attentional focus. Thought stoppage, countering, changing negative thoughts to positive thoughts, and reframing can be used to intervene effectively when anxiety-provoking thoughts occur. Self-talk in the form of cue-words can be used effectively to both modify activation (e.g., *relax, easy*) and focus attention (e.g., *see the ball, be here now*). Sport psychologists, coaches, and athletes must become aware of situations in which thoughts create anxiety or misdirect attention and use the appropriate techniques to intervene when necessary.

Conclusion

Cognitive–behavioral techniques will continue to dominate sport psychology performance-enhancement interventions in the future (Meyers et al., in press). After interviewing four leading sport psychology practitioners, Newburg (1992) concluded that a primary goal in applied sport psychology is to teach *effective thinking*—the use of good thoughts—during competition. This recommendation points to a worthy and challenging goal.

The popularity and usefulness of cognitive–behavioral techniques is not limited to the field of sport psychology and enhancement of sport performance (Dobson & Block, 1988). Once individuals learn to use the techniques discussed in this chapter to modify ineffective thinking, techniques can be applied in a variety of situations to enhance the personal growth of athletes and their performance in academic and other nonsport situations. For example, cognitive-behavioral techniques can be effectively used for enhancing and maintaining self-esteem (Branden, 1994; McKay & Fanning, 1994). By fostering healthy self-esteem, sport psychologists can enhance the personal growth and development of athletes as well as their performance.

In conclusion, we must caution that thought-control techniques often challenge the sport psychologist who attempts to teach them and the athlete who tries to use them. Thought patterns frequently resist change. Prior to implementing any changes, practitioners should emphasize an awareness of ineffective thoughts, and their consequences and, when appropriate, the underlying beliefs that contribute to the thoughts. Cognitive techniques such as those described in this chapter require skill, practice, and patience by both the sport psychologist and the athlete for maximal effectiveness.

Although we believe that sufficient support exists for the concepts and interventions addressed in this chapter, we concur with individuals who challenge sport psychology researchers and practitioners to continue testing the efficacy of these interventions, particularly when used with elite athletes (Greenspan & Feltz, 1989; Meyers et al., in press; Morgan, 1994; Smith, 1989). Only through careful, theory-based intervention and testing will the field of applied sport psychology advance as a profession and a science.

References

Armstrong, C. A., Sallis, J. F., Hovell, M. F., & Hofsetter, C. R. (1993). Stages of change, self-efficacy, and the adoption of vigorous exercise: A prospective analysis. *Journal of Sport & Exercise Psychology, 15,* 390–402.

Beck, A. T. (1970). Cognitive therapy. *Behavior Modification, 1,* 184–200.

Bell, K. F. (1983). *Championship thinking: The athlete's guide to winning performance in all sports.* Englewood Cliffs, NJ: Prentice-Hall.

Branden, N. (1994). *The six pillars of self-esteem.* New York: Bantam.

Brewer, B. W., & Sachs, M. L. (1996). The mind of the runner: Attentional focus and endurance performance. Unpublished manuscript, Springfield College, Springfield, MA.

Buffone, G. W., Sachs, M. L., & Dowd, E. T. (1984). Cognitive–behavioral strategies for promoting adherence to exercise. In M. L. Sachs & G. W. Buffone (Eds.), *Running as therapy: An integrated approach* (pp. 198–214). Lincoln, NE: University of Nebraska.

Bunker, L. K., Williams, J. M., & Zinsser, N. (1993). Cognitive techniques for improving performance and building confidence. In J. M. Williams (Ed.), *Applied sport psychology: Personal growth to peak performance* (pp. 225–242). Mountain View, CA: Mayfield.

Clingman, J. M., & Hilliard, D. V. (1990). Race walkers quicken their pace by tuning in, not stepping out. *The Sport Psychologist, 4,* 25–32.

Dagrou, E., Gauvin, L., & Halliwell, W. (1991). La préparation mentale des athlètes invoiriens: Pratiques courantes et perspectives de recherche. [Mental preparation of Ivory Coast athletes: Current Practices and Research Perspectives.] *International Journal of Sport Psychology, 22,* 15–34.

Dagrou, E., Gauvin, L., & Halliwell, W. (1992). Effets du langage positif, négatif, et neutre sur la performance motrice. [Effects of positive, negative, and neutral language on motor performance.] *Canadian Journal of Sport Sciences, 17,* 145–147.

Dobson, K. S., & Block, L. (1988). Historical and philosophical bases of the cognitive–behavioral therapies. In K. S. Dobson (Ed.), *Handbook of cognitive behavioral therapies* (pp. 3–34). New York: Guilford.

Duncan, T. E., & McAuley, E. (1993). Social support and efficacy cognitions in exercise adherence: A latent growth curve analysis. *Journal of Behavioral Medicine, 16,* 199–218.

Ellis, A. (1982). Self-direction in sport and life. *Rational Living, 17,* 27–33.

Ellis, A. E., & Harper, R. A. (1975). *A new guide to rational living.* Englewood Cliffs, NJ: Prentice-Hall.

Fillingim, R. B., & Fine, M. A. (1986). The effects of internal versus external information processing on symptom perception in an exercise setting. *Health Psychology, 5,* 115–123.

Gauron, E. F. (1984). *Mental training for peak performance.* Lansing, NY: Sport Science Associates.

Gauvin, L. (1990). An experiential perspective on the motivational features of exercise and lifestyle. *Canadian Journal of Sport Sciences, 15,* 51–58.

Gill, D. L., & Strom, E. H. (1985). The effect of attentional focus on performance of an endurance task. *International Journal of Sport Psychology, 16,* 217–223.

Gould, D., Eklund, R. C., & Jackson, S. A. (1992a). 1988 U.S. Olympic wrestling excellence: I. Mental preparation, precompetitive cognition, and affect. *The Sport Psychologist, 6,* 358–382.

Gould, D., Eklund. R. C., & Jackson, S. A. (1992b). 1988 U.S. Olympic wrestling excellence: II. Thoughts and affect occurring during competition. *The Sport Psychologist, 6,* 383–402.

Gould, D., Finch, L. M., & Jackson, S. A. (1993). Coping strategies used by national champion figure skaters. *Research Quarterly for Exercise and Sport, 64,* 453–468.

Gould, D., Weiss, M., & Weinberg, R. (1981). Psychological characteristics of successful and nonsuccessful Big Ten wrestlers. *Journal of Sport Psychology, 3,* 69–81.

Greenspan, M. J., & Feltz, D. L. (1989). Psychological interventions with athletes in competitive situations: A review. *The Sport Psychologist, 3,* 219–236.

Heyman, S. R. (1984). Cognitive interventions. In W. F. Straub & J. M. Williams (Eds.), *Cognitive sport psychology* (pp. 289–303). Lansing, NY: Sport Science Associates.

Highlen, P. S., & Bennett, B. B. (1979). Psychological characteristics of successful and nonsuccessful elite wrestlers: An exploratory study. *Journal of Sport Psychology, 1,* 123–137.

Highlen, P. S., & Bennett, B. B. (1983). Elite divers and wrestlers: A comparison between open- and closed-skill athletes. *Journal of Sport Psychology, 5,* 390–409.

Johnston-O'Conner, E. J., & Kirschenbaum, D. S. (1986). Something succeeds like success: Positive self-monitoring for unskilled golfers. *Cognitive Therapy and Research, 6,* 335–342.

Kirschenbaum, D. S., Ordman, A. M., Tomarken, A. J., & Holtzbauer, R. (1982). Effects of differential self-monitoring and level of mastery on sports performance: Brain power bowling. *Cognitive Therapy and Research, 6,* 335–342.

Lazarus, R. S., & Folkman, S. (1984). *Stress, appraisal, and coping.* New York: Springer.

Mahoney, M. J. (1977, October). Cognitive skills and athletic performance. Paper presented at the annual meeting of the Association for the Advancement of Behavior Therapy, Atlanta, GA.

Mahoney, M. J., & Avener, M. (1977). Psychology of the elite athlete: An exploratory study. *Cognitive Therapy and Research, 1,* 135–141.

Marcus, B. H., Selby, V. C., Niaura, R. S., & Rossi, J. S. (1992). Self-efficacy and the stage of exercise behavior change. *Research Quarterly for Exercise and Sport, 63,* 60–66.

Masters, K. S., & Lambert, M. J. (1989). The relations between cognitive coping strategies, reasons for running, injury, and performance of marathon runners. *Journal of Sport & Exercise Psychology, 11,* 161–170.

McAuley, E. (1992). The role of efficacy cognitions in the prediction of exercise behavior in middle-aged adults. *Journal of Behavioral Medicine, 15,* 65–88.

McKay, M., & Fanning, P. (1994). *Self-esteem* (2nd ed.). Oakland, CA: New Harbinger.

Meichenbaum, D. (1977). *Cognitive-behavior modification.* New York: Plenum.

Meyers, A. W., & Schleser, R. A. (1980). A cognitive–behavioral intervention for improving basketball performance. *Journal of Sport Psychology, 3,* 69–73.

Meyers, A. W., Whelan, J. P., & Murphy, S. M. (in press). Cognitive behavioral strategies in athletic performance enhancement. In M. Hersen & A. S. Belack (Eds.), *Handbook of behavior modification.*

Morgan, W. P. (1984). Mind over matter. In W. F. Straub & J. M. Williams (Eds.), *Cognitive sport psychology* (pp. 311–316). New York: Sport Science Associates.

Morgan, W. P. (1994). Forty years of progress: Sport psychology in exercise and sports medicine. *American College of Sports Medicine—40th Anniversary lectures* (pp. 81–92). Indianapolis, IN: American College of Sports Medicine.

Morgan, W. P., & Pollock, M. L. (1977). Psychologic characterization of the elite distance runner. *Annals of the New York Academy of Sciences, 301,* 382–403.

Newburg, D. (1992). Performance enhancement: Toward a working definition. *Contemporary Thought on Performance Enhancement, 1,* 10–25.

Nideffer, R. M. (1993). Concentration and attention control training. In J. M. Williams (Ed.), *Applied sport psychology: Personal growth to peak performance,* (pp. 243–261). Mountain View, CA: Mayfield.

Orlick, T., & Partington, J. (1988). Mental links to excellence. *The Sport Psychologist, 2,* 105–130.

Pennebaker, J. W., & Lightner, J. M. (1980). Competition of internal and external information in an exercise setting. *Journal of Personality and Social Psychology, 39,* 165–174.

Rejeski, W. J., & Kenney, E. (1987). Distracting attentional focus from fatigue: Does task complexity make a difference? *Journal of Sport Psychology, 9,* 66–73.

Rotella, R. J., Gansneder, B., Ojala, D., & Billings, J. (1980). Cognitions and coping strategies of elite skiers: An exploratory study of young developing athletes. *Journal of Sport Psychology, 2,* 350–354.

Rushall, B. S., Hall, M., Roux, L., Sasseville, J., & Rushall, A. C. (1988). Effects of three types of thought content instructions on skiing performance. *The Sport Psychologist, 2,* 283–297.

Schill, T., Monroe, S., Evans, R., & Ramanaiah, N. (1978). The effects of self-verbalizations on performance: A test of the rational–emotive position. *Psychotherapy: Theory, Research, and Practice, 15,* 2–7.

Schomer, H. H. (1987). Mental strategy training programme for marathon runners. *International Journal of Sport Psychology, 18,* 133–151.

Silva, J. M., & Appelbaum, M. E. (1989). Association–dissociation patterns of United States Olympic marathon trial contestants. *Cognitive Therapy and Research, 13,* 185–192.

Silva, J. S. (1982). Competitive sport environments: Performance enhancement through cognitive intervention. *Behavior Modification, 6,* 443–463.

Smith, R. E. (1980). A cognitive–affective approach to stress management training for athletes. In C. H. Nadeau, W. R. Halliwell, K. M. Newell, and G. C. Roberts (Eds.), *Psychology of motor behavior and sport* (pp. 54–72). Champaign, IL: Human Kinetics.

Smith, R. E. (1989). Applied sport psychology in an age of accountability. *Journal of Applied Sport Psychology, 1,* 166—180.

Spink, K. S. (1988). Facilitating endurance performance: The effect of cognitive strategies and analgesic suggestions. *The Sport Psychologist, 2,* 97–104.

Spink, K. S., & Longhurst, K. (1986). Cognitive strategies and swimming performance: An exploratory study. *Australian Journal of Science and Medicine in Sport, 18,* 9–13.

Steinmetz, J., Blankenship, J., Brown, L., Hall, D., & Miller, G. (1980). *Managing stress before it manages you.* Palo Alto, CA: Bull.

Straub, W. F. & Williams, J. M. (1984). *Cognitive sport psychology.* Lansing, NY: Sport Science Associates.

Strean, W. B., & Roberts, G. C. (1992). Future directions in applied sport psychology research. *The Sport Psychologist, 6,* 55–65.

Van Raalte, J. L., Brewer, B. W., Lewis, B. P., Linder, D. E., Wildman, G., & Kozimor, J. (1995). Cork! The effects of positive and negative self-talk on dart throwing performance. *Journal of Sport Behavior, 18,* 50–57.

Van Raalte, J. L., Brewer, B. W., Rivera, P. M., & Petitpas, A. J. (1994). The relationship between observable self-talk and competitive junior tennis players' match performance. *Journal of Sport and Exercise Psychology, 16,* 400–415.

Wegner, D. M. & Erber, R. (1992). The hyperaccessibility of suppressed thoughts. *Journal of Personality and Social Psychology, 63,* 903–912.

Wegner, D. M., Schneider, D. J., Carter, S. R., & White, T. L. (1987). Paradoxical effects of thought suppression. *Journal of Personality and Social Psychology, 53,* 5–13.

Wegner, D. M., Schneider, D. J., Knutson, B., & McMahon, S. R. (1991). Polluting the stream of consciousness: The effect of thought suppression on the mind's environment. *Cognitive Therapy and Research, 15,* 141–152.

Wegner, D. M., Shortt, J. W., Blake, A. W., & Page, M. S. (1990). The suppression of exciting thoughts. *Journal of Personality and Social Psychology, 58,* 409–418.

Wenzlaff, E. M., Wegner, D. M., & Klein, S. B. (1991). The role of thought suppression in the bonding of thought and mood. *Journal of Personality and Social Psychology, 60,* 500–508.

Whelan, J. P., Mahoney, M. J., & Meyers, A. W. (1991). Performance enhancement in sport: A cognitive behavioral domain. *Behavior Therapy, 22,* 307–327.

Williams, J. M., & Krane, V. (1993). Psychological characteristics of peak performance. In J. M. Williams (Ed.), *Applied sport psychology: Personal growth to peak performance* (pp. 137–147). Mountain View, CA: Mayfield.

Intensity Regulation and Athletic Performance

Jim Taylor

As the day of a competition arrives and an event approaches, intensity assumes the central role in precompetitive preparation. Intensity is the most critical factor prior to competitive performance because, no matter how confident, motivated, or technically or physically prepared athletes are to perform, they will simply not be able to perform their best if their bodies are not at an optimal level of intensity, accompanied by the requisite physiological and psychological changes. As such, an essential responsibility of athletes before competition is to attain a level of intensity that will enable them to perform at their highest level; the applied practitioner can play a significant role in this process.

This chapter is organized to lead the reader to an in-depth understanding of intensity, how it impacts athletic performance, and what applied practitioners can do with athletes to help them attain ideal intensity for competition. First, a clarification of the definition of intensity is offered, as is an explanation of why this particular term is used in place of more commonly referred to terms such as arousal or anxiety. Second, the chapter provides a discussion of the theoretical and empirical foundation of intensity, and presents several conceptualizations of intensity and a review of relevant literature. Third, an understanding of the nature of intensity is presented with attention placed upon symptoms and causes of over- and underintensity. Fourth, the issue of identifying ideal intensity is delineated to show practitioners how to assist athletes in specifying a variety of cognitive, physiological, and general interventions that can be used to regulate intensity prior to competition.

What is Intensity?

In previous research and applied writings, other terms that have been used synonymously with intensity include *arousal, anxiety,* and *nervousness* (Landers & Boutcher, 1986; Silva & Hardy, 1984; Spielberger, 1972). The term *intensity* is used here for several reasons. First, the term *arousal* has sexual connotations associated with it. Using this term with athletes, particularly with youthful competitors, often produces a comical or anxious reaction that interferes with the appreciation and understanding of importance of the concept to competitive preparation. Second, the terms *anxiety* and *nervousness* are typically perceived negatively, as something to be avoided when, in fact, athletes need some level of this attribute. Finally, the term *intensity* does not carry these limitations. Rather, intensity is viewed by athletes as a positive and important contributor to optimal competitive performance.

The issue of defining intensity has been a point of contention for decades (Borkovec, 1976; Cannon, 1928; Neiss, 1988; Spielberger, 1966). For the purposes of the applied practitioner, Zaichkowsky and Takenaka (1993) provide the most detailed and parsimonious conceptualization of intensity. They view *intensity* as a multidimensional construct that performs an energizing function of the mind and body. They suggest that intensity has three critical responses that impact performance: There is a physiological activation that includes heart rate, glandular and cortical activity, and blood flow (Landers & Boutcher, 1986; Zaichkowsky & Takenaka, 1993). Additionally, behavioral responses are evident in terms of motor activity including changes in coordination, pace, and idiosyncratic behavioral reactions to the physiological alterations. Cognitive and emotional responses are also exhibited in terms of evaluations of the physiological and behavioral manifestations of intensity and the accompanying emotional reactions to those evaluations.

Athletes will experience intensity in a range from very low, as in a deep sleep, to very high, as in extreme fear (Sonstroem, 1984). Intensity may be experienced by athletes positively as increased confidence, motivation, strength, stamina, agility, and heightened sensory acuity. It may also be perceived negatively by athletes as fear, dread, muscle tension, breathing difficulty, loss of coordination, and other inhibiting manifestations.

Theoretical and Empirical Perspectives on Intensity

Three primary theoretical explanations for the relationship between intensity and athletic performance have been offered: *inverted-U* theory (Yerkes & Dodson, 1908), the *zone of optimal functioning* hypothesis (Hanin, 1980), and most recently, *catastrophe* theory (Hardy & Fazey, 1987).

Inverted-U Theory

Yerkes and Dodson (1908) suggested a curvilinear relationship between intensity and performance. Specifically, they posited that increases in intensity produce commensurate improvement in performance, but only to a point, after which greater intensity inhibits performance (see Figure 1).

Considerable research has provided support for the inverted-U theory in a variety of settings. Laboratory studies examining reaction time (Levitt & Gutin, 1971), balance (Martens & Landers, 1970), and motor coordination (Beuter & Duda, 1985) as well as field studies in the sports of baseball (Lowe, 1971), basketball (Klavora, 1979; Sonstroem & Bernardo, 1982), pistol shooting (Gould, Petlichkoff, Simons, & Vevera, 1987), and swimming (Burton, 1988) have produced confirmatory evidence for the inverted-U theory. It should be pointed out, however, that support has not been unanimous in either the laboratory or the field (Bergstrom, 1970; Carron, 1968; Cox, 1983; Giabrone, 1973). Additionally, a significant criticism of the inverted-U theory is that it implies that there is one ideal level of intensity for all individuals in all activities.

Zone of Optimal Functioning (ZOF)

The ZOF, presented by Hanin (1980), is an extension of the inverted-U theory that incorporates individual differences into its framework. Hanin (1989) defined *optimal intensity* as the level of intensity "that enables a particular athlete to perform his/her personal best" (p. 22). Hanin (1980) further suggested that this ideal level of intensity is an individual response; it is different for everyone. That is, there is not

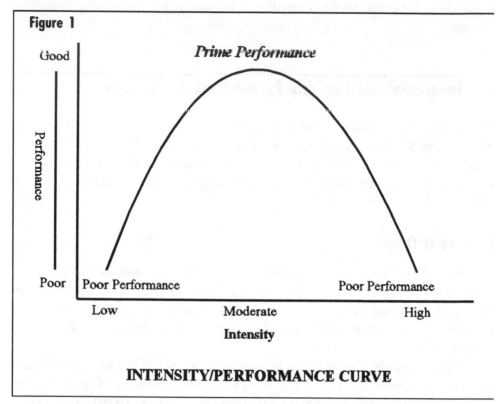

Figure 1

Good

Prime Performance

Performance

Poor | Poor Performance | | Poor Performance

Low | Moderate | High

Intensity

INTENSITY/PERFORMANCE CURVE

Inverted-U theory of intensity and athletic performance.

one ideal level of intensity for all athletes. For example, some athletes may perform at their best when they are at a very low level of intensity (i.e., totally relaxed). Others may perform their best at a very high level of intensity (i.e., extremely energized). Moreover, Hanin (1980) has argued that the only way that the ZOF can be identified in athletes is through multiple assessments of individual athletes' intensity and corresponding performances.

Hanin's theory, originating from his work conducted in the former Soviet Union, has been considered as the framework for only a limited number of empirical investigations by Western researchers. A study by Raglin and Turner (1993) using swimmers and track and field athletes indicated that the ZOF theory best explained the relationship between anxiety and performance. Some additional tentative support for ZOF theory was reported by Morgan and his colleagues in their studies of elite distance runners (Morgan, O'Connor, Ellickson, & Bradley, 1988; Morgan, O'Connor, Sparling, & Pate, 1987). These studies were criticized, however, for using group rather than individual means in determining the ZOF and for using retrospective rather than real-time assessment. More recently, Krane (1993) demonstrated partial support for the ZOF hypothesis among collegiate soccer players. Overall, a significant criticism of the ZOF hypothesis is that it conceptualizes intensity as a unidimensional construct instead of one comprised of several related dimensions.

Catastrophe Theory

In response to the multidimensional theory of anxiety developed by Martens, Vealey, and Burton (1990), Hardy and Fazey (1987) applied the mathematically derived catastrophe theory (Thom, 1975) to the intensity–performance relationship. Hardy and Fazey suggested that there are two subcomponents to intensity: physiological arousal and cognitive anxiety. They further indicated that cognitive anxiety mediates the effects of physiological arousal on performance. In other words, the impact of physiological arousal on performance will depend on the level of cognitive anxiety. From an applied perspective, this model suggests that athletes' perceptions of their intensity (whether positive or negative) will determine how their level of intensity affects their performance.

Due to the recent development of catastrophe theory, little research has been conducted examining it. Two studies by Hardy and his colleagues (Hardy, Parfitt, & Pates, 1989, cited in Hardy, 1990; Hardy & Parfitt, 1992) demonstrated support for several predictions made by the theory. Additionally, Krane, Joyce, and Rafeld (1994) reported findings consistent with the catastrophe model. However, support for the theory was not found by Krane (1993).

Additional Theoretical and Empirical Considerations

Oxendine (1970) posited that task complexity is another factor that affects the intensity–performance relationship. He suggested that different sports require different levels of intensity for optimal performance. For example, golf and baseball pitching require low intensity, gymnastics and boxing involve moderate intensity, and weight lifting and sprinting demand high intensity (Zaichkowsky & Takenaka, 1993).

Billing (1980) helped clarify the notion of task complexity by suggesting that it is based on the information processing that is needed for the activity and the complexity of the required motor responses. More specifically, he indicated that activities that are accomplished best at low to moderate levels of intensity involve focus, decision-making, multiple cue discrimination, and fine motor control. Conversely, activities best performed at high levels of intensity involve power, strength, endurance, and speed.

Though the concept of task complexity has considerable intuitive appeal and has received much anecdotal support, empirical findings in the area have been limited and equivocal. Brewer, Van Raalte, and Linder (1990) found a significant inverse relationship between arousal (operationalized as pain) and performance on three tasks of increasing complexity. Levitt and Gutin (1971) and Shelton and Mahoney (1978) also reported findings consistent with this notion in regards to reaction time and strength, respectively. However, Weinberg, Gould, and Jackson (1980) did not find support for the proposed task complexity–intensity relationship with balance and speed tasks.

Individual differences between athletes on similar tasks also must be considered by the applied practitioner (Ebbeck & Weiss, 1988). Individual psychological differences that have been suggested in the literature as relevant to intensity and athletic performance include trait anxiety (Spielberger, 1989); attentional processes (Nideffer, 1989); confidence, motivation, and investment in the activity (Taylor, 1993); and cognitive appraisal (Landers & Boutcher, 1986; Passer, 1982). Physical individual differences that should be considered include level of physical conditioning, general health, fatigue, and injuries.

The setting in which athletes perform may also influence their level of intensity and, as a consequence, must be addressed by the applied practitioner (Taylor, 1993). Factors related to the competitive setting may include the event being contested. For example, a gymnast may experience higher intensity on the balance beam than the floor exercise. The level of competition should also be considered. This notion is particularly relevant to athletes moving up to new and higher levels of competition. The specific site may also affect intensity (Kroll, 1979; Passer, 1981). For instance, a small-town, high school star football player will likely experience increased intensity in his first game in a stadium with a capacity of 70,000 people. Other environmental variables include competing internationally (unfamiliar culture or playing conditions) and competing under different conditions (e.g., field surface, different rules). The composition of the audience may also be influential, for example, friendly versus hostile crowds and the presence or absence of family and friends (Zajonc, 1965).

Understanding the Nature of Intensity

A primary goal of the applied practitioner should be to assist the athletes with whom they work in identifying and attaining the athletes' optimal level of intensity. First, it is necessary to gain a greater awareness of the symptoms and causes of over- and underintensity.

Symptoms of Overintensity

As alluded to in the theoretical discussion above, intensity can be manifested in three ways: physically, behaviorally, and psychologically. The most apparent symptoms are physical reactions that include extreme muscle tension, shaking muscles, breathing difficulty, and excessive perspiration (Landers & Boutcher, 1986). Other more subtle physical symptoms include stomach butterflies, fatigue, and a decrease in motor coordination. Behaviorally, symptoms include an increase in pace during competition, generalized agitation, an increase in performance-irrelevant or superstitious behaviors, tense body-language, and a decrease in competitive performance (e.g., "choking" under pressure). Psychological symptoms of overintensity include negative self-talk (e.g., "I know I will screw up."); irrational thinking (e.g., "If I perform poorly, everyone will hate me."); decline in motivation; an over-narrowing of concentration (Nideffer, 1993); and emotional feelings of fear and dread (Elko & Ostrow, 1991; Hamilton & Fremouw, 1985).

It is important for the applied practitioner to educate the athletes with whom they work to recognize the less overt indications of overintensity. Some relevant symptoms include stomach butterflies, mistakes during precompetitive preparation, an extreme narrowing of concentration, and a shift from performance-relevant thoughts to negative or performance-irrelevant thoughts.

Causes of Overintensity

Causes of overintensity may be characterized as either psychological, social, or situational. Landers and Boutcher (1986) provided a conceptual framework for important psychological influences on intensity. They specify five areas of cognitive appraisal that lead to a negative intensity reaction: (a) the demands of the situation, (b) the individual's resources to effectively manage the demands, (c) the consequences of the situation, (d) the meaning that is placed on the consequences, and (e) recognition of bodily reactions. For example, Richard, a talented

18-year-old freshman pitcher for a highly ranked NCAA Division I base-ball team, was named the starter for the final game of the College World Series. Richard perceived that the requirements of his starting role in such an important game (demands) were greater than his ability (re-sources) to perform successfully. He believed that he was going to fail in his performance (consequences) and it would disappoint his family and ruin his chances for a professional career (meaning).

Lack of confidence may also contribute to overintensity. Athletes who do not believe they will be successful but are required to perform will feel threatened and experience this in terms of overintensity. A severe manifestation of lack of confidence is *irrational thinking*, in which athletes develop extreme and often harmful cognitions about their per-formance. For example, a downhill ski racer inspecting the course comes to a difficult high-speed turn that she doubts she can negotiate. She sees a tree that would be in her path if she is unable to make the turn and thinks, "That tree has my name on it." Another intrapersonal cause of overintensity involves focusing on the outcome of the compe-tition rather than its process. Whether the outcome is positive (e.g., "If I win, people will expect me to always win.") or negative (e.g., "If I lose, I will let the whole town down."), considering the consequences of a performance adds unnecessary pressure and detracts from a proper competitive focus that allows for optimal performance.

Social causes of overintensity are derived primarily from expecta-tions of significant others in the lives of athletes including parents, coaches, friends, community, and media. Overintensity results from the perception that if athletes do not live up to the socially derived expec-tations, they will not be loved and supported, which is a direct threat to their self-esteem (Krohne, 1980; Passer, 1982; Smith, Smoll, & Curtis, 1978).

Environmental variables may also exacerbate the overintensity re-action. Factors such as unfamiliarity with a situation, the occurrence of unexpected events, and worry over uncontrollable aspects of the com-petitive situation can cause overintensity by producing feelings of un-certainty and helplessness. For instance, Richard, the baseball pitcher just described, was a freshman unfamiliar with the competitive level of the College World Series and the size of the stadium. In addition, less than an hour before he was to take the mound, he could not find his spikes. Finally, instead of focusing on what he needed to do in order to pitch his best, he was thinking about the importance of the game and how his entire family drove 20 hours to see him play. These events and the associated perceptions added to his feelings of uncertainty, thereby increasing his level of intensity.

Symptoms of Underintensity

Because of the inherent pressures associated with competition, underintensity is not a common occurrence (Harris, 1986). However, it may be evident in some athletes and in some competitive situations. As with overintensity, underintensity can manifest itself physically, behaviorally, and psychologically.

Physical symptoms of underintensity include low levels of heart rate, respiration, and adrenaline. These changes are exhibited in the form of low energy and feelings of lethargy. Behaviorally, underintensity can be seen as a decrease in pace during competition, generalized lethargy, "let-down" body language, a reduction in performance-relevant behaviors (e.g., routines), increase in reaction to distractions, and a decline in competitive performance. Psychological symptoms include a loss of motivation to compete, difficulty narrowing concentration, and a generalized feeling of "not being all there."

Causes of Underintensity

Unlike overintensity, underintensity is less influenced by social and situational factors and may be characterized primarily as having psychological and physical causes. Overconfidence is a significant psychological causes of underintensity. Athletes who are over confident believe that they will win easily with little effort. As a result, they do not activate their physiological systems (e.g., heart rate, respiration, adrenaline) that will enable them to perform optimally. A lack of interest in competing or motivation to compete will also produce underintensity. Athletes who lack the desire to perform will not feel the need to activate themselves physiologically.

Csikszentmihalyi (1975) suggested that athletes who perceive that their ability exceeds the demands of the competitive situation will experience boredom, which is a form of underintensity. For example, in contrast to Richard described above, Marilyn, a 28-year-old world-class high jumper for the past 10 years, found that, she could reach optimal intensity for important competitions against other top athletes. However, she often lacked intensity when she competed in less important competitions in which she was clearly the best. Because of her experience, Marilyn was very confident in her ability to perform well, but she found that she was not motivated to prepare for and perform in lesser meets, and wished she could sit them out. Also, since she is such a gifted athlete, she was not challenged by the demands of less rigorous competition. This lack of intensity results in unnecessary mistakes and periodic upset losses to less talented athletes.

Fatigue from overtraining or overcompeting, sleeping difficulties, and competitive stress are physical causes of underintensity. Other physical causes of underintensity include nutritional deficiencies and injuries. In all cases, athletes suffering from these physical causes will simply not have the physiological resources to activate their bodies when needed.

Identifying Prime Intensity

With a clear understanding of intensity provided, it is now time to consider the practical implications and approaches to intensity regulation. The term *prime intensity* will be used to describe ideal intensity and its key components.

What is Prime Intensity?

Prime intensity refers to the ideal level of physiological and cognitive intensity that will enable athletes to perform their best (Taylor, 1993). The term, *prime*, is chosen for several reasons. First, the term, *peak*, which is most commonly used to describe ideal performance and its subcomponents, has two difficulties associated with it. An obvious aspect of a peak is that the apex is small. Also, an inevitable feature of a peak is the valleys that must accompany it. Both of these concerns are in sharp contrast to the primary goal for athletes, namely, consistently high performance with a minimum of vacillation. Second, the dictionary defines prime as "being of highest quality or value" (Woolf, 1992; 914), which is the level of performance to which athletes aspire.

As suggested previously, there is no one prime intensity for all athletes. Rather, prime intensity is personal. It involves ideal levels of physiological and cognitive activity. Additionally, prime intensity is not something that athletes will automatically reach in all competitions. Rather, intensity is often felt by athletes to be determined by numerous psychological, social, and situational variables over which they have little awareness and even less control. The goal then of the applied practitioner in working with athletes on intensity regulation is first, to teach them to monitor their level of intensity and, second, to show them how they can effectively attain and maintain their prime intensity.

Determining Prime Intensity

As the ZOF and catastrophe theories indicate, all athletes have a level of intensity at which they are able to perform their best. Moreover, as the latter theory suggests, there are two types of intensity that impact the intensity-performance relationship: physiological and cognitive. Though catastrophe theory has not yet received empirical support, it provides a broad base for intervention, has strong intuitive appeal, and is consistent with the experience of applied practitioners. Consequently, keeping in mind the unproved nature of catastrophe theory, it can be used to assist athletes in identifying their prime and nonprime levels of intensity (Taylor, 1993; Weinberg, 1988).

Using a form such as the Intensity Identification Form (see Exhibit 1), applied practitioners can ask the following questions about athletes' prime intensity: (a) Prior to and during a successful competition, how did their body feel? For example, was their heart pounding and sweating or calm and at ease? The athletes should be very specific in describing their physiological condition. (b) What were their thoughts and emotions at the time? For example, were they very positive and excited, or neutral-thinking and low-key? (c) What social influences—for example, family, coaches, friends—were present or absent during successful performances? The same questions should then be asked for poor performances. What typically emerges is a consistent pattern of physiological, cognitive, and social activity that is associated with prime and nonprime intensity and the corresponding quality of competitive performance. At the bottom of Exhibit 1, the athletes can summarize the factors that are associated with successful and unsuccessful performance.

The purpose of this exercise is to create in athletes an understanding of what their body feels like, what they are thinking and feeling, and with whom they are interacting when they perform well or poorly. The goal of intensity identification is to make athletes aware of these differences before they compete so they can then take active steps to reproduce those factors that are associated with good performance through the use of intensity regulation.

Exhibit 1

Intensity Identification Form

Directions: In the space below, indicate the psychological and situational factors that impact your intensity and the quality of your competitive performances. At the bottom, summarize the positive and negative performance factors that distinguish your best and worst performances.

	Best Performances	Worst Performances
Physical Feelings		
Thoughts		
Emotions		
Social Influences		
Competition Site		
Event		
Competitive Level		
Positive Performance Factors		
Negative Performance Factors		

Intensity Regulation

Once athletes have identified their prime and nonprime levels of intensity, they must learn how to regulate their intensity so, when the time of competition arrives, they will have the ability to actively alter their intensity to its prime level. Intensity can be addressed at cognitive, physiological, and situational levels, and at various times as the competition approaches (e.g., during training and precompetitive preparation). It should be noted that the cognitive interventions are most effectively used as preventive measures, whereas the physiological and situational interventions are most often used immediately prior to competition.

Cognitive Interventions for Intensity Regulation

This section will address a variety of cognitive techniques that may be used to regulate intensity. These techniques can be used during practice sessions and at times prior to the competition as a means of preventing nonprime intensity. They can also be applied immediately before the competition to attain prime intensity. This section will be divided into two segments: regulation of overintensity and regulation of underintensity.

Overintensity

Cognitive Reappraisal. As the model presented by Landers and Boutcher (1986) indicates, overintensity most often is caused by negative, inaccurate, or extreme cognitive appraisal of a situation. Consequently, a good place to begin controlling overintensity is at its source, that is, by altering that appraisal process. A fundamental aspect of the faulty appraisal process that leads to overintensity is the athletes' perception that they do not have the ability to cope effectively with the five areas of appraisal (i.e., demands, resources, consequences, meaning, and recognition of bodily reactions). This evaluation indicates a basic lack of confidence in their ability. Thus, by developing their confidence and evaluating the situation positively and accurately, athletes may inhibit overintensity at its source.

Applied practitioners also can assist athletes in rationally assessing the upcoming competition by discussing the five appraisal areas with athletes individually and as a group. Often athletes, particularly those who are young or less experienced, become so overwhelmed by an approaching competition that they lose perspective and simply are not able to perceive the situation objectively. As mentioned previously, this may lead to irrational thinking that further increases intensity (Ellis, 1962). Typically, by being shown another way of viewing the situation, athletes are able to recognize the extremity of their thinking and accept a more realistic perspective, which then results in a decline in their intensity (Heyman, 1984). Applied practitioners can also use this approach in addressing the social causes of overintensity. Assessing athletes' perceptions of others' expectations and intervening when appropriate can effectively diminish the negative effects of social influences, thus reducing overintensity and improving competitive performance.

As mentioned previously, three factors may exacerbate the negative cognitive appraisal process: unfamiliarity with the competitive situation, the occurrence of unexpected events, and focus on uncontrollable events. The applied practitioner may significantly attenuate these three areas by addressing them before the competition.

Self-Talk. At a more direct level, negative, worrying, or irrational self-talk such as "I know I will fail," "I am so scared," or "I am going to break every bone in my body" typically are found in athletes suffering from overintensity. The applied practitioner can intervene with self-talk by using cognitive restructuring techniques including thought-stopping and positive litanies. For example, athletes can be taught to say "positive" when a negative thought occurs. Negative thoughts can then be replaced by positive statements such as "I will try my hardest and play my best." Developing a series of positive self-statements (e.g., "I love to compete. I am a great athlete. I always think and talk positively.") can help athletes to train themselves to be more positive. These strategies increase athletes' awareness of unproductive thinking and show them how to develop more positive and constructive ways of thinking about situations.

Unfamiliarity. Unfamiliarity may occur in several ways. Lack of knowledge of the physical environment in which athletes compete may cause stress. The best solution for this particular problem is to give athletes an opportunity to familiarize themselves with the competitive setting, ideally through practice or preliminary competition in the competitive arena. In the absence of direct experience practicing or competing in that setting, enabling athletes to attend another competition at that site or simply allowing them to walk around the setting may be helpful. Athletes may then combine this observational experience of the setting with mental imagery to see themselves competing there in the days before the actual competition. In addition to any first-hand experience at the setting, it can be useful for coaches or some of the athletes who have been there previously to describe to newcomers some of the critical physical aspects of the setting.

These same strategies may also be used to assist athletes in familiarizing themselves with other aspects of the competitive setting. For example, perhaps the upcoming competition is the first for several new members of a track and field team. These athletes have never competed in such a large stadium. Important factors with which the applied practitioner should familiarize these athletes include media coverage before the game, typical activity on the infield, audience responses, access to the locker rooms, and the location of the warmup areas. Developing a mentoring system with more experienced athletes would be beneficial for less experienced athletes.

Unexpected Events. Another difficulty that causes overintensity is the occurrence of unexpected events prior to and during competitions. The most effective means of handling this problem is to prevent or minimize unexpected incidences from occurring. This does not mean that all problems can be prevented from arising during a competition. Rather, the goal is to prevent these problems from being unexpected, thereby causing overintensity. This may be achieved in two steps. First, in a meeting with athletes, the applied practitioner can have them identify all of the things that can go wrong at a competition. Then, have the athletes propose solutions to these occurrences (see Exhibit 2). Even though difficulties will still arise, instead of panicking and raising intensity to a debilitating level, athletes will recognize that a problem has occurred and will have a plan for solving the problem, thus stress is not generated and intensity remains at a healthy level.

Uncontrollable Events. Finally, athletes, like other people, spend considerable time worrying about things over which they have little control (Bandura, 1986). This is a fruitless endeavor because not only can they not influence a given thing, but they put significant stress on themselves over it. Much of what occurs in the competitive sports world is outside of the control of athletes. Moreover, there is only one thing that is truly within their control: themselves. As such, they should only focus on themselves, and, specifically, on what they need to do to perform their best (see Exhibit 3).

Exhibit 2

Expect the Unexpected Form

Directions: A variety of unexpected situations and how to deal with them have been provided. In the space below, identify specific unexpected situations that you may encounter and how to deal with them.

Unexpected	Plan
Late arrival to competition.	Have shortened precompetitive routine.
Forget clothing or accessory.	Pack extra gear.
Broken equipment.	Have backup equipment properly prepared.
No place to practice.	Have alternative physical warm-up routine.
Bad weather or conditions.	Stay relaxed and focused; stay warmed up.
Change in schedule.	Repeat precompetitive routine.
Different opponent.	Stay calm; reassess strategy.

Exhibit 3

Control or Not-to-Control Form

Directions: A variety of controllable and uncontrollable factors have been provided. In the space below, identify specific controllable and uncontrollable factors that you may encounter.

Controllable	Uncontrollable
Your behavior	Others' attitudes, thoughts, emotions, behavior
Physical condition	Competitors' performances
Motivation/effort	Coaches
Attitude	Family
Thoughts	Officials
Emotions	Opponent Selection
Equipment	Competition Conditions
Preparation	Weather
Performance	

The applied practitioner can play a meaningful role in helping athletes to maintain that focus on controllable things. When applied practitioners hear athletes worrying about things outside of their control, athletes should be asked several questions: First, they should be asked if it is something that is within their control. If it is, the athletes should be asked what they can do to relieve the problem and should be helped to develop a plan to do so. If it is not within their control, athletes should be asked what in the situation they can control; the practitioner should have them focus on what is in their control, and should assist them in finding a way to alleviate the problem.

Underintensity

Underintensity, though less likely to occur, can have dramatic negative effects on competitive performance. As a result, applied practitioners should create an awareness of underintensity and teach athletes how to address this phenomenon when it occurs (Caudill, Weinberg, & Jackson, 1983; Harris, 1986).

High-Energy Self-Talk. Let-down self-talk such as "I have this competition won" and "I quit" are commonly associated with feelings of underintensity (Caudill, Weinberg, & Jackson, 1983; Harris, 1986). These types of self-talk produce a physiological decline in intensity that directly interferes with effective performance. This self-talk needs to be replaced with high-energy self-talk that will raise physiological intensity to a prime level. For example, the statements described above should be replaced with "Finish strong" and "Keep at it."

Physiological Interventions for Intensity Regulation

Despite the best efforts to achieve prime intensity by cognitive means, nonprime intensity will still be experienced by many athletes due to the situational and social aspects of competition. Consequently, it is important for the applied practitioner to provide athletes with simple and practical techniques they may use prior to competition that will enable them to attain prime physiological intensity.

Overintensity

Breathing. Perhaps the simplest, but most important technique that may reduce intensity is breathing (Harris, 1986). It is common to see athletes taking short, choppy breaths before a competition. When athletes are under stress and experiencing overintensity, the breathing system contracts so that they are getting an inadequate supply of oxygen. Breathing serves several essential functions. Physically, athletes' bodies cannot function without oxygen. They fatigue and lose coordination, and their muscles become tense—all of which seriously impair performance. Taking some deep, rhythmic breaths allows athletes to replenish their oxygen supply and reduce overintensity, thus enabling them to perform their best.

Breathing also has psychological ramifications. A significant problem with overintensity is that athletes tend to become focused on the negative symptoms such as muscle tension and stomach butterflies. By taking slow, deep breaths, athletes alleviate some of these symptoms, thereby increasing self-confidence and feelings of well-being. Additionally, focusing on breathing takes the focus off some of the negative feelings associated with overintensity.

Muscle Relaxation. One of the most uncomfortable manifestations of overintensity is extreme muscle tension (Landers & Boutcher, 1986). A common sight before a competition is athletes who look like they are made of stone. Tight muscles inhibit coordination, interfere with quality performance, and increase the likelihood of injury. As a result, the applied practitioner can teach athletes several techniques to relax muscles.

Initially, athletes who experience muscle tension should try a basic muscle relaxation scenario such as the one described in Exhibit 4. This procedure will work effectively with all but the most overintense athletes. It involves deep breathing and a *tension draining* process.

Exhibit 4

Deep Muscle Relaxation Script

Imagine there are drain plugs on the bottom of your feet. You will undo these plugs and all the tension will drain out of your body and you'll become very, very relaxed. Take a long, slow, deep breath.

Now, undo those plugs. You can feel the tension begin to drain out of your body. Down from the top of your head, past your forehead, your face and neck; you are becoming more and more relaxed. And the tension drains out of your jaw and down past your neck, and now your face and your neck are warm and relaxed and comfortable. Take a long, slow, deep breath.

The tension continues to drain out of your upper body, out of your hands and forearms and upper arms and shoulders. Now your hands, arms and shoulders are warm and relaxed and comfortable. Take a long, slow, deep breath.

The tension continues to drain out of your upper body, past your chest and upper back, down past your stomach and lower back, and your upper body is becoming more and more relaxed. Now there is no more tension in your upper body. Your entire upper body is warm and relaxed and comfortable. Take a long, slow, deep breath.

The tension continues to drain out of your body, past your buttocks and down past your thighs and your knees. And your lower body is becoming more and more relaxed. The tension drains out of your calves. Now, there is almost no tension left in your body and the last bit of tension drains past your ankles, the balls of your feet, and your toes. Now there is no more tension left in your body. Your entire body is warm and relaxed and comfortable. Now, replace the plugs so that no tension gets back in. Take a long, slow, deep breath.

This relaxation method may not work with athletes who are experiencing extreme muscle tension. These athletes will try to get their muscles to relax by shaking them and wishing them to relax, but the tension is so great that this does not work. A technique that directly affects this symptom of overintensity is called *progressive relaxation* (Jacobson, 1938). This procedure involves tightening and relaxing major muscle groups (see Exhibit 5).

To illustrate this process, consider Rob, a 24-year-old pistol shooter in his first world championship. At approximately 15 minutes before the start of his event, Rob was very nervous and tense. But no matter what he did, he couldn't get himself to relax. Fortunately, several weeks earlier, the team's sport psychologist taught him progressive relaxation. She told him that to relax the muscles he must first do just the opposite, that is, tighten them up. So he tightened each of the four major muscle groups (legs and buttocks, chest and back, arms and shoulders, face

---

Exhibit 5

Progressive Relaxation

Progressive relaxation involves tightening and relaxing major muscle groups. You will focus on four major muscle groups: legs and buttocks, chest and back, arms and shoulders, face and neck. To start, tense the muscles in your legs and buttocks for 5 seconds, then release. Take a long, slow, deep breath. Feel the difference between the tension and relaxation. Repeat this process in your legs and buttocks.

Tense the muscles in your chest and back for 5 seconds, then release. Take a long, slow, deep breath. Feel the difference between the tension and relaxation. Repeat this process in your chest and back.

Tense the muscles in your arms and shoulders for 5 seconds, then release. Take a long, slow, deep breath. Feel the difference between the tension and relaxation. Repeat this process in your arms and shoulders.

Tense the muscles in your face and neck for 5 seconds, then release. Take a long, slow, deep breath. Feel the difference between the tension and the relaxation. Repeat this process in your face and neck.

Tense the muscles in your entire body for 5 seconds, then release. Take a long, slow, deep breath. Feel the difference between the tension and the relaxation. Repeat this process in your entire body.

---

and neck) for 5 seconds, relaxed them for 5 seconds, and repeated this, taking a deep breath between each phase of the exercise. Almost immediately he noticed that his muscles were more relaxed and comfortable, and he went on to have a strong competition.

This somewhat counterintuitive approach is effective because muscles work on an opponent-principle process (Jacobson, 1938). Returning to the example of Rob, consider a scale of 1 to 10 representing the extent of intensity Rob feels prior to the competition, where 1 is *completely relaxed* and 10 is *totally tense*. Rob was at about 8, but he needed to be near 4 in his intensity to shoot his best. By tightening his muscles to a 10, the natural reaction of the muscles is to rebound past 8 down to a more relaxed state near 4.

Progressive relaxation has value for athletes on two levels. First, athletes are often so accustomed to being tense that they are simply not aware of their level of muscle tension and how it affects their competitive performances. Thus, the process of tightening and relaxing teaches athletes to discriminate between the states of tension and relaxation. Once this recognition occurs, athletes become more sensitive to their bodies' signals and, thus, better able to respond effectively to nonprime levels of intensity. As with any technique, the muscle awareness and control that develops from progressive relaxation takes practice. As a result, the applied practitioner or coach can facilitate this process by making progressive relaxation a part of practice. For example, it can be an enjoyable and beneficial part of the cool-down at the end of each training session. Additionally, a useful tool in teaching relaxation is using a personalized or commercially available relaxation audiotape.

Smiling. The final physiological intervention to be discussed is so basic it is surprising that it is so effective. This technique is smiling; that is, athletes whose intensity levels are too high should simply smile. This technique was described several years ago by a sport psychologist who was working with a professional tennis player who became very angry and frustrated during an on-court practice session as she struggled to improve a weak part of her game. She became so tense that she could not perform at all. Purely on a whim, the sport psychologist told her to smile. As you can imagine, smiling was the last thing she wanted to do and she expressed those feelings quite emphatically. However, and simply to appease her sport psychologist, with persistence she formed a big, though forced smile. The sport psychologist told her to hold it for 60 seconds. Within 30 seconds a remarkable change began to occur. As she held the smile, the tension in her shoulders disappeared, the wrinkle in her brow went away, and her body, which had been hunched and closed, began to rise and open up. Within 2 minutes, the tension dissipated. She went on to have a productive practice during which she was able to overcome her earlier difficulties.

The sport psychologist was curious as to why smiling had such a dramatic effect. By examining research on the effects of smiling, he discovered several causes of this phenomenon. First, people are conditioned to associate certain types of smiling with happiness and feeling good (Ekman, Davidson, & Friesen, 1990). Also, research has shown that smiling changes blood flow through the brain and causes the release of neurochemicals that have a relaxing effect (Zajonc, 1985). Finally, it is difficult to think and feel in a way that is contrary to what the body is expressing. As such, it is difficult to be angry, frustrated, and tense when smiling.

Underintensity

Physical Activity. Fundamentally, intensity is the amount of physiological activity experienced by an athlete. As a result, the most direct way to increase intensity is through vigorous physical activity. The type of physical activity will depend on the particular sport, but any form of running, jumping, or active movement will be sufficient. The bottom line involves getting the heart pumping and the blood flowing.

High-Energy Body Language. Internal physiological activity can be effectively activated with external physiological activity, that is, *high-energy body language.* Athletes who pump their fist, slap their thighs, and give high-fives to their teammates are all using this technique to increase their intensity. Athletes in many sports such as Shaquille O'Neal in basketball, Dennis Mitchell in track, Steffi Graf in tennis, and Pernell Whitaker in boxing use high-energy body language to maintain prime intensity.

General Interventions for Intensity Regulation

In addition to the cognitive and physiological techniques described in this chapter, there are a number of general performance-enhancement strategies that are beneficial to many aspects of mental preparation for athletes. Some of these interventions are discussed in the following sections in terms of how they can be used to regulate intensity. These techniques impact athletes both cognitively and physiologically.

Mental Imagery

Considerable research has indicated that mental imagery can have a distinct physiological effect on athletes (for a review, see Feltz & Landers, 1983). Consequently, athletes can use mental imagery to adjust intensity before a competition (Caudill, Weinberg, & Jackson, 1983). High-energy images of intense competition, strong effort, and success will raise physiological activity. Calming images of relaxing scenes, peace, and tranquility will reduce intensity. Additional discussion on the use of imagery in sport and exercise psychology is presented in chapter 2 of this volume.

Keywords

A common trap that athletes fall into is that they get so absorbed in the heat of competition that they forget to do the things necessary for performing their best. In particular, athletes forget to monitor and adjust their intensity. A useful tool to maintain an awareness of intensity is with the development of meaningful keywords (see Exhibit 6).

Applied practitioners can encourage the athletes with whom they work to identify keywords and place them in visible settings such as their bedroom, locker room, and weight room. Also, athletes can place the

Exhibit 6	
Intensity Keywords	
Directions: A variety of intensity keywords have been provided. In the space below, identify other intensity keywords you can use.	
Psych Down	Psych Up
Breathe	Go For It
Loose	Charge
Relax	Attack
Calm	Positive
Easy	Hustle
Focus	Punch It
Trust	Commit
Cool down	Fire up

keywords on their equipment so, during competition, they will see the keywords and remember to monitor and adjust their intensity.

Music

Music has a profound emotional and physical effect on people. Music can cause people to feel happy, sad, inspired, or angry. Music can also excite or relax people. Although this relationship has not been studied empirically in the sports world, many well-known athletes including Greg Louganis (diving), Kristie Phillips (gymnastics), and Kristi Yamaguchi (figure skating) have used music to help them regulate their intensity before competition.

Applied practitioners can assist athletes in selecting the style of music that is most appropriate for their intensity needs. For example, athletes who need to increase their intensity should listen to high energy music. In contrast, those who need to lower intensity should listen to relaxing music. In fact, some athletes combine music with relaxation audiotapes.

Precompetition Management

On the day of a competition, the time that athletes spend before they compete is the most crucial period of competitive preparation. What athletes think, feel, and do before they compete will dictate how they perform. This precompetitive time can ensure prime intensity that leads to quality performance. Athletes should have three goals before they compete: Their equipment should be ideally prepared. Their bodies

Exhibit 7

Precompetitive Management Plan

Directions: Respond to each question below as it relates to your precompetitive preparation. Then apply this information to your precompetitive routine.

Where should you stay in the competition site?

What do you need to do to be totally prepared?

Who can assist you with your preparation?

Who and what can interfere with your preparation?

should be properly warmed up and should be at prime intensity. Finally, they should be mentally prepared, most notably with prime levels of confidence and focus. Applied practitioners can ensure this total preparation by asking athletes four questions (see Exhibit 7) about their precompetitive environment.

Where to Stay in the Competition Site. Where athletes can best accomplish their precompetitive preparation depends largely on their attentional style. Athletes who have an external focus (i.e., are overly sensitive to external distractions) should isolate themselves from the typical activity of the competition site. This will reduce the likelihood that environmental distractions such as other competitors, coaches, and officials will interfere with their precompetitive preparations. In contrast, athletes with an internal focus (i.e., overly sensitive to internal distractions) should stay around the activity of the competition site. By doing so, these athletes will be drawn out of their internal focus by the activity and will be less likely to think negative or irrelevant thoughts that will inhibit their precompetitive preparation.

What They Need to Do to be Totally Prepared. Three primary areas for preparation need to be considered: equipment, physical preparation, and mental preparation. For each of these areas, specific methods should be developed to ensure total preparation. Then, athletes should develop precompetitive routines in order to combine the many preparation strategies into a cohesive plan that is most effective for the particular competition site.

Who Can Assist in Their Preparation. There are many people at the competition site with whom athletes may interact during precompetitive preparation, including coaches, teammates, family, friends, and fans. Some of these people are important to athletes' precompetitive preparation and others are not. The applied practitioner can assist athletes in identifying those individuals who will facilitate their precompetitive preparation.

Who and What Can Interfere with Their Preparation. There are also people or things that are either irrelevant to or will interfere with athletes' precompetitive preparation, such as chatty teammates, family, unwanted competition information, and results of earlier competitions. These people and things need to be identified and actively avoided so as not to inhibit precompetitive preparation. Plans to deal with these people and situations if they are encountered should also be developed.

Precompetitive Routines

Considerable research has demonstrated that precompetitive routines are an effective means of controlling intensity and enhancing the consistency and quality of performances (Boutcher & Crews, 1987; Cohn, Rotella, & Lloyd, 1990; Ravizza & Osborne, 1991). As a result, routines are an important part of precompetitive preparation and are useful to athletes in attaining and maintaining prime intensity.

Routines are valuable for many reasons. They ensure completion of every key aspect of precompetitive preparation. They enhance familiarity of situations because the routines become familiar to the athletes. They decrease the likelihood of unexpected events occurring by giving athletes greater control over precompetitive events. Routines develop consistency of thought, feeling, and behavior. They increase feelings of control over the competitive environment. Routines raise self-confidence and reduce intensity due to the reasons just described. By developing and implementing an effective precompetitive routine, regardless of the importance of the competition, athletes will condition their minds and bodies into thinking and feeling that this is just another competition in which they will perform their best.

Performance Funnel. All precompetitive routines should involve a consistent narrowing of focus, intensity, and effort as athletes approach the start of the competition. Each step closer to the competition should lead athletes to that unique state of readiness in which they are physi-

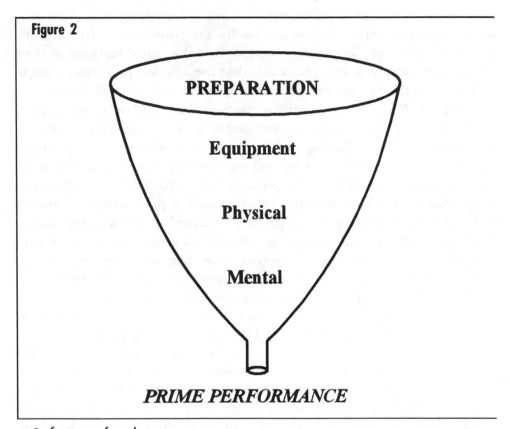

Figure 2

PREPARATION

Equipment

Physical

Mental

PRIME PERFORMANCE

Performance funnel.

cally and psychologically prepared to play their best. This notion is conceptualized nicely as the performance funnel, in which all preparation flows down the funnel and what emerges is quality performance (Taylor, 1993; see Figure 2).

Routines versus Rituals. Superstitious behavior is a common phenomenon among athletes. Superstitious rituals are the rigid adherence to precompetitive behavior that serves no practical function in preparation for the competition. Often, athletes develop a series of steps that appear to be routines, but are, in fact, superstitious rituals. It is important for the applied practitioner to be able to distinguish between the two in order to assist athletes with whom they work in developing effective routines.

The goal of routines is to totally prepare athletes for competition. As such, everything done in precompetitive routines serves a specific and necessary function in the preparation for competition. Also, routines are flexible and can be adapted to unique aspects of each competitive situation. In contrast, rituals involve anything that does not serve a specific purpose in preparation for the competition. In addition, rituals are inflexible and athletes believe that they must be done or they will not perform well. It is important that the applied practitioner show athletes that they control their routines, but rituals control them.

What to Put in a Precompetitive Routine. Each athlete's precompetitive routine should comprise every factor that influences competitive performance. The following factors can be included in every routine: (a) meals, (b) physical warm-up, (c) equipment preparation, (d) technical warm-up, and (e) mental preparation. A useful means of identifying what those elements are is for the applied practitioner to discuss with athletes what they do to prepare themselves for a competition. Team-sport athletes must deal with the added dimension of team precompetitive routines (e.g., a football offensive unit running plays). These athletes must manage their precompetitive time effectively in order to meet their individual and team precompetitive needs.

Early-Morning Routine. Precompetitive preparation begins as soon as athletes awake in the morning. This early-morning preparation sets the tone for the day and ensures that the athletes are physically and mentally ready for later preparation. Before athletes get out of bed, they should use mental imagery to rehearse their performance in the upcoming competition. Athletes can also use some of the previously discussed intensity regulation techniques to begin the movement to prime intensity. These techniques set the stage for the competitive performance by generating positive feelings and focus.

Physical preparation, in the form of vigorous warm-up, is important for athletes who participate in morning competitions. When people wake up in the morning, their core body temperature is 3 to 5 degrees below normal, and it takes up to 5 hours for it to return to normal. If athletes get up at 7 am and competition begins at 10 am, their bodies may not be ready to perform and their performances will suffer. The morning warm-up may involve any exercises that result in the athletes working up a sweat, for example, running or jumping rope, and stretching. If they are sweating, they know their body is warming up and will be ready for the competition. Also, this early morning warm-up will reduce the likelihood of injury.

Arrival at Competition Site. A similar preparation process should be conducted upon arrival at the competition site several hours before the event. Similar to the early morning routine that involves mental and physical preparation, this procedure is aimed at further readying athletes for the upcoming competition. Athletes should again use mental imagery to produce the feelings associated with good competitive performance. The imagery, keywords, and other intensity regulation techniques also may be used to focus concentration and to begin the move toward prime intensity.

A more vigorous physical warm-up is also necessary with the emphasis on the shift toward prime intensity. For technical sports such as tennis, golf, and baseball, this phase should be accompanied by technical warm-up in which proper technique is reviewed and reinforced. Initial physical and technical warm-up should be slow and gentle as the body warms up. Once the initial warm-up is completed, the preparation should be rehearsed with increasing focus and intensity aimed at sim-

Exhibit 8

Precompetitive Routine

Directions: List the precompetition activities that will help you prepare to perform your very best.

During Early Morning
    1. Physical:

    2. Mental:

At Competition Site
    1. Physical:

    2. Mental:

Prior to Competition
    1. Equipment:

    2. Physical:

    3. Mental:

ulating competitive conditions. This *priming* effect makes it easier for athletes to attain their prime focus and intensity when the competition begins.

Final Preparation Routine. This last stage of the athletes' precompetitive routine ensures that complete readiness is attained just prior to the competition. First, any adjustments to equipment should be made. As with the previous routines, emphasis is placed on mentally and physically fine tuning the athletes to their optimal state of readiness. Final mental preparation involves using mental imagery to review their performance, repeating keywords to narrow and maintain focus on the competition, and using intensity-regulation exercises that will enable the athletes to reach prime intensity. Final physical preparation also include last minute physical warm-up and technical fine tuning.

The goal of the three levels of precompetitive preparation is that when athletes begin competition, they are optimally ready both mentally and physically to perform their very best. How each of these factors is accomplished is what makes a routine personal to every athlete. Once athletes have established the necessary components of the routine, the applied practitioner can assist each athlete in establishing their own personalized precompetitive routine that satisfies their individual needs and style (see Exhibit 8).

Summary

When the time of the competition arrives, intensity becomes the most important factor because if the body is not optimally prepared, athletes will not be able to perform their best. Some level of intensity is necessary for optimal performance, but too much or too little intensity will hurt performance. Moreover, there is no one ideal intensity level for every athlete. Some athletes perform best at low intensity, others perform best at moderate intensity, while still others perform best at high intensity.

Overintensity is caused by lack of confidence, extreme or inaccurate cognitive appraisals of the competition, and unfamiliar, unexpected, or uncontrollable events before the competition. Overintensity is characterized by muscle tension, breathing difficulty, negative self-talk, loss of coordination, and feelings of fear and dread. Underintensity is caused by overconfidence, lack of motivation, fatigue, and high ability combined with low demands. Athletes experience underintensity as feelings of lethargy and low energy, an absence of alertness and interest, and problems narrowing concentration prior to and during a competition.

Applied practitioners should assess athletes' intensity levels when they are performing well vs. poorly in order to help them understand and attain their prime intensity. Overintensity may be lessened cognitively by building self-confidence, countering inaccurate or extreme thinking, and rationally assessing the upcoming competition. Overintensity may be reduced by making familiar unfamiliar situations, planning for unexpected events, and helping athletes to focus only on controllable events. Overintensity may be regulated physiologically with the use of breathing, progressive relaxation, and smiling.

Underintensity may be increased through the use of exercise to raise physiological activity, stopping let-down thinking, and using high-energy thinking and talking. General techniques to regulate intensity include mental imagery, keywords, music, precompetition management, and precompetitive routines.

References

Bandura, A. (1986). *Social foundations of thought and action.* Englewood Cliffs, NJ: Prentice-Hall.

Bergstrom, B. (1970). Tracking performance under threat-induced stress. *Scandinavian Journal of Psychology, 11,* 109–114.

Beuter, A., & Duda, J. L. (1985). Analysis of the arousal/motor performance relationship in children using movement kinematics. *Journal of Sport Psychology, 7,* 229–243.

Billing, J. (1980). An overview of task complexity. *Motor skills: Theory into practice, 4,* 18–23.

Borkovec, T. D. (1976). Physiological and cognitive processes in the regulation of arousal. In G. E. Schwartz & D. Shapiro (Eds.), *Consciousness and self-regulation: Advances in research (Vol. 1)* (pp. 261–312). New York: Plenum.

Brewer, B. W., Van Raalte, J. L., & Linder, D. E. (1990). Effects of pain on motor performance. *Journal of Sport & Exercise Psychology, 12,* 353–365.

Burton, D. (1988). Do anxious swimmers swim slower? Reexamining the elusive anxiety–performance relationship. *Journal of Sport & Exercise Psychology, 10,* 45–61.

Butcher, S. H., & Crews, D. J. (1987). The effect of a preshot attentional routine on a well-learned skill. *International Journal of Sport Psychology, 18,* 30–39.

Cannon, W. B. (1928). The mechanism of emotional disturbance of bodily function. *New England Journal of Medicine, 198,* 877–884.

Carron, R. B. (1968). Motor performance under stress. *Research Quarterly, 39,* 463–469.

Caudill, D., Weinberg, R., & Jackson, A. (1983). Psyching-up and track athletes. A preliminary investigation. *Journal of Sport Psychology, 5,* 231–235.

Cohn, P. J., Rotella, R. J., & Lloyd, J. W. (1990). Effects of a cognitive behavioral intervention on the preshot routine and performance in golf. *The Sport Psychologist, 4,* 33–47.

Cox, R. H. (1983). Consolidation of pursuit rotor learning under conditions of induced arousal. *Research Quarterly for Exercise and Sport, 54,* 223–228.

Csikszentmihalyi, M. (1975). *Beyond boredom and anxiety.* San Francisco. Jossey-Bass.

Ebbeck, V., & Weiss, M. R. (1988). The arousal–performance relationship: Task characteristics and performance measures in track and field athletics. *The Sport Psychologist, 2,* 13–27.

Ekman, P., Davidson, R. J., & Friesen, W. V. (1990). The Duchenne smile. Emotional expression and brain physiology: II. *Journal of Personality and Social Psychology, 58,* 342–353.

Elko, P. K., & Ostrow, A. C. (1991). Effects of a rational-emotive education program on heightened anxiety levels of female collegiate gymnasts. *Sport Psychologist, 5,* 235–255.

Ellis, A. (1962). *Reason and emotion in psychotherapy.* New York: Lyle Stuart.

Feltz, D. L., & Landers, D. M. (1983). The effects of mental practice on motor skill learning and performance: A meta-analysis. *Journal of Sport Psychology, 5,* 25–57.

Giabrone, C. P. (1973). *Effect of situation criticality on foul shooting.* Unpublished master's thesis, University of Illinois, Urbana.

Gould, D., Horn, T., & Spreemann, J. (1983). Sources of stress in junior elite wrestlers. *Journal of Sport Psychology, 5,* 159–171.

Gould, D., Petlichkoff, L., Simons, H., & Vevera, M. (1987). The relationship between Competitive State Anxiety Inventory - 2 subscale scores and pistol shooting performance. *Journal of Sport & Exercise Psychology, 9,* 33–42.

Hamilton, S. A., & Fremouw, W. J. (1985). Cognitive–behavioral training for college basketball free–throw performance. *Cognitive Therapy and Research, 9,* 479–483.

Hanin, Y. L. (1980). A study of anxiety in sports. In W. F. Straub (Ed.), *Sport psychology: An analysis of athlete behavior* (pp. 236–249). Ithaca, NY: Mouvement.

Hanin, Y. L. (1989). Interpersonal and intergroup anxiety: Conceptual and methodological issues. In C. D. Speilberger & D. Hackfort (Eds.), *Anxiety in sports: An international perspective* (pp. 19–28). Washington, DC: Hemisphere.

Hardy, L. (1990). A catastrophe model of performance in sport. In J. G. Jones & L. Hardy (Eds.), *Stress and performance in sport* (pp. 81–106). Chichester, England: Wiley.

Hardy, L., & Fazey, J. (1987, June). *The inverted-U hypothesis: A catastrophe for sport psychology.* Paper presented at the annual meetings of the North American Society for the Psychology of Sport and Physical Activity, Vancouver, British Columbia, Canada.

Hardy, L., & Parfitt, G. (1992, October). *Different approaches to the study of the anxiety–performance relationship.* Paper presented at the annual meetings of the Association for the Advancement of Applied Sport Psychology, Colorado Springs, CO.

Harris, D. V. (1986). Relaxation and energizing techniques for regulation of arousal. In J. M. Williams (Ed.), *Applied sport psychology: Personal growth to peak performance* (pp. 185–207). Palo Alto, CA: Mayfield.

Heyman, S. R. (1984). Cognitive interventions: Theories, applications, and cautions. In W. F. Straub & J. M. Williams (Eds.), *Cognitive sport psychology* (pp. 289–303). Lansing, NY: Sport Science Associates.

Jacobson, E. (1938). *Progressive relaxation.* Chicago: University of Chicago.

Klavora, P. (1979). Customary arousal for peak athletic performance. In P. Klavora & J. V. Daniel (Eds.), *Coach, athlete, and the sport psychologist* (pp. 155–169). Toronto, Ontario: University of Toronto.

Krane, V. (1993). *Anxiety and athletic performance: A test of the multidimensional anxiety and catastrophe theories.* Unpublished doctoral dissertation, University of North Carolina, Greensboro.

Krane, V., Joyce, D., & Rafeld, J. (1994). Competitive anxiety, situation criticality, and softball performance. *The Sport Psychologist, 8,* 58–72.

Krohne, J. W. (1980). Parental child-rearing behavior and the development of anxiety and coping strategies in children. In I. G. Sarason & C. D. Spielberger (Eds.), *Stress and anxiety (Vol. 7).* Washington, DC: Hemisphere.

Kroll, W. (1979). The stress of high performance athletes. In P. Klavora & J. V. Daniel (Eds.), *Coach, athlete, and the sport psychologist* (pp. 211–219). Toronto, Ontario: University of Toronto.

Landers, D. M., & Boutcher, S. H. (1986). Arousal–performance relationships. In J. M. Williams (Ed.), Applied sport psychology: Personal growth to peak performance (pp. 163–184). Palo Alto, CA: Mayfield.

Levitt, S., & Gutin, B. (1971). Multiple choice reaction time and movement time during physical exertion. *Research Quarterly, 42,* 405–410.

Lowe, R. (1971). Stress, arousal, and task performance of little league baseball players. Unpublished doctoral dissertation. University of Illinois, Urbana-Champaign.

Martens, R., & Landers, D. M. (1970). Motor performance under stress: A test of the inverted-U hypothesis. *Journal of Personality and Social Psychology, 16,* 29–37.

Martens, R., Vealey, R. S., & Burton, D. (1990). Competitive anxiety in sport. Champaign, IL: Human Kinetics.

Morgan, W. P., O'Connor, P. J., Ellickson, K. A., & Bradley, P. W. (1988). Personality structure, mood states, and performance in elite male distance runners. *International Journal of Sport Psychology, 19,* 247–263.

Morgan, W. P., O'Connor, P. J., Sparling, P. B., & Pate, R. R. (1987). Psychological characteristics of elite female distance runners. *International Journal of Sports Medicine, 8,* 124–131.

Neiss, R. (1988). Reconceptualizing arousal: Psychological states in motor performance. *Psychological Bulletin, 103,* 345–366.

Nideffer, R. M. (1989). Anxiety, attention, and performance in sports: Theoretical and practical considerations. In D. Hackfort & C. D. Spielberger (Eds.), *Anxiety in sports: An international perspective* (pp. 117–136). New York: Hemisphere.

Nideffer, R. M. (1993). Concentration and attentional control training. In J. M. Williams (Ed.), *Applied sport psychology: Personal growth to peak performance* (2nd ed., pp. 257–269). Palo Alto, CA: Mayfield.

Oxendine, J. B. (1970). Emotional arousal and motor performance. *Quest, 13,* 23–32.

Passer, M. W. (1981). Children in sport: Participation motives and psychological stress. *Quest, 33,* 231–244.

Passer, M. W. (1982). Psychological stress in youth sports. In R. A. Magill, M. J. Ash, & F. L. Smoll (Eds.), *Children in sport* (2nd ed., pp. 153–177). Champaign, IL: Human Kinetics.

Raglin, J. S., & Turner, P. E. (1993). Anxiety and performance in track and field athletes: A comparison of the inverted U hypothesis with zone of optimal function theory. *Personality and Individual Differences, 14,* 163–171.

Ravizza, K., & Osborne, T. (1991). Nebraska's 3 R's: One-play-at-a-time preperformance routine for collegiate football. *The Sport Psychologist, 5,* 256–265.

Shelton, T. O., & Mahoney, M. J. (1978). The content and effect of "psyching-up" strategies in weight lifters. *Cognitive Therapy and Research, 2,* 275–284.

Silva, J. M., & Hardy, C. J. (1984). Precompetitive affect and athletic performance. In

W. F. Straub & J. M. Williams (Eds.), *Cognitive sport psychology* (pp. 79–88). Lansing, NY: Sport Science Associates.

Smith, R. E., Smoll, F. L., & Curtis, B. (1978). Coaching behaviors in Little League baseball. In F. L. Smoll & R. E. Smith (Eds.), *Psychological perspectives in youth sports.* Washington, DC: Hemisphere.

Sonstroem, R. J. (1984). An overview of anxiety in sport. In J. M. Silva, III & R. S. Weinberg (Eds.), *Psychological foundations of sport* (pp. 104–117). Champaign, IL: Human Kinetics.

Sonstroem, R. J., & Bernardo, P. (1982). Intraindividual pregame state anxiety and basketball performance: A re-examination of the inverted-U curve. *Journal of Sport Psychology, 4,* 235–245.

Spielberger, C. D. (1966). Theory and research on anxiety. In C. D. Spielberger (Ed.), *Anxiety and behavior* (pp. 3–22). New York: Academic.

Spielberger, C. D. (1972). *Anxiety: Current trends in theory and research (Vol. 1),* New York: Academic.

Spielberger, C. D. (1989). Stress and anxiety in sports. In D. Hackfort & C. D. Spielberger (Eds.), *Anxiety in sports: An international perspective* (pp. 3–17). New York: Hemisphere.

Taylor, J. (1993). *The mental edge for competitive sports* (3rd ed.). Denver, CO: Minuteman.

Thom, R. (1975). *Structural stability and morphogenesis* (D. H. Fowler, Trans.). New York: Benjamin-Addison Wesley.

Weinberg, R. S. (1988). *The mental advantage: Developing your psychological skills in tennis.* Champaign, IL: Leisure.

Weinberg, R. S., Gould, D., & Jackson, A. (1980). Cognition and motor performance effect of psyching-up strategies on three motor tasks. *Cognitive Therapy and Research, 4,* 239–245.

Woolf, H. B. (1992). *Webster's new collegiate dictionary.* Springfield, MA: G & C Merriam.

Yerkes, R. M., & Dodson, J. D. (1908). The relation of strength of stimulus to rapidity of habit formation. *Journal of Comparative Neurology of Psychology, 18,* 459–482.

Zaichkowsky, L., & Takenaka, K. (1993). Optimizing arousal level. In R. N. Singer, M. Murphey, & L. K. Tennant (Eds.), *Handbook of research on sport psychology* (p. 511–527). New York: MacMillan.

Zajonc, R. B. (1965). Social facilitation. *Science, 149,* 269–274.

Zajonc, R. B. (1985). Emotion and facial efference: A theory reclaimed. *Science, 228,* 15–21.

Hypnosis in Sport and Exercise Psychology

William P. Morgan

Hypnosis in Sport and Exercise Psychology

I t is remarkable that hypnosis has not been used more frequently by workers in the field of sport and exercise psychology because the difference between success and failure is often minuscule. Indeed, the difference between a gold medal in Olympic competition and failure to even qualify for the final event is sometimes less than a hundredth of a second. Hence, any ergogenic procedure that might enhance performance by even a small margin (e.g., 0.001%), providing it is legal, would have potential value.

At this point in time, the use of hypnosis has not bccn banned by the United States Olympic Committee (USOC) or the International Olympic Committee (IOC), nor are there any regulations against the use of hypnosis by other sport governing bodies, such as the National Collegiate Athletic Association (NCAA) or professional organizations, such as the American Psychological Association (APA) or the American College of Sports Medicine (ACSM). There are, however, many instances in which the use of hypnosis in the practice of sport psychology or sports medicine would be questionable from both an ethical and a moral standpoint, and although not in direct violation of existing rules and codes, such actions would potentially violate the "spirit of the law." It is inappropriate, for example, to use drugs such as morphine or no-

Adapted from *The Handbook of Clinical Hypnosis* (pp. 649–670). J. Rhue, S. J. Lynn, & I. Kirsch (Eds.). Copyright 1993 by the American Psychological Association.

vocaine to manage an athlete's pain so that she or he might compete; hence, the use of hypnosis for the same purpose would certainly be questionable. Adherence to the American Psychological Association's (1992) ethical code of conduct should be viewed as necessary but not sufficient in such a case. It is imperative that psychologists who elect to use hypnosis in the treatment of athletes also become familiar with established ethical and legal guidelines adopted by sport governing bodies (e.g., the NCAA, the IOC, and the USOC) and sport science organizations (e.g., the ACSM).

Theoretical Formulations

In this chapter, a review of selected theoretical formulations is presented, and this is followed by an overview of empirical research involving the application of hypnosis in sport and exercise psychology. The qualifications of practitioners is then reviewed, along with a discussion of published clinical applications. This is followed by a section dealing with case material in which three case studies are described.

The rationale for the clinical applications described in this chapter is based on theoretical formulations advanced by Hanin (1978) and Unestáhl (1981), together with the empirical case studies described by Johnson (1961a, 1961b). Although the theoretical views of Hanin and Unestáhl represent independent proposals, these formulations converge in terms of hypnotic application.

Hanin (1978) presented a theory of performance that maintains that each individual athlete possesses a *zone of optimal function* (ZOF), and this zone is based on the individual's optimal state anxiety level in precompetitive settings. Hanin empirically demonstrated that athletes have their best performances when they fall within this ZOF, and he has operationalized this zone as a given point plus or minus 4 raw-score units on the state anxiety scale developed by Spielberger (1983). Although Hanin's theory is based on work carried out with elite Soviet athletes and with the Russian translation of the State-Trait Anxiety Inventory (STAI; Spielberger, 1983), his research has been replicated with elite and nonelite American athletes (Raglin, 1992). The theory advanced by Hanin incorporates retrospective recall of precompetitive state anxiety levels obtained in the nonhypnotic state. There is no mention of hypnotic procedures in this theoretical formulation, but the potential for hypnotic intervention is obvious.

The theoretical views of Uneståhl (1981) are related to those of Hanin (1978) in that both believe that athletes experience unique affective states when having peak performances. Uneståhl has chosen to label this the *ideal performing state* (IPS). Although the theoretical views of Uneståhl are in agreement with those of Hanin with respect to the existence of an ideal or optimal affective state, these theories of performance differ in one respect: Whereas Hanin believes that these states can be accurately recalled, Uneståhl has emphasized that athletes often have selective or even total amnesia after perfect performance, which makes it difficult for them to describe or analyze the IPS afterwards. Therefore, Uneståhl has used hypnosis in defining the IPS, and this theory has been applied with several thousand Swedish athletes (Railo & Uneståhl, 1979).

Research and Appraisal

Research involving hypnosis and sport and exercise psychology has been restricted to laboratory experimentation in which attempts have been made to elucidate the effectiveness of hypnotic suggestion on the transcendence of baseline measures of physical capacity. There have been two principal methodological problems associated with the published literature that warrant mention from the outset. First, investigators have used laboratory tasks (e.g., grip strength and weight-holding endurance) under controlled conditions, and it is unlikely that any of this work possesses ecological validity. In other words, the results of research involving simple motor tasks performed in the laboratory setting with nonathletes cannot be easily generalized to complex sport skills performed by athletes in emotionally charged competitive settings. Second, there has been a tendency to contrast performances in the laboratory following hypnotic suggestion with control or baseline performances in which suggestion has not been used (e.g., Ikai & Steinhaus, 1961). This traditional research paradigm has been characterized by the confounding of state (hypnosis vs. control) and suggestion. With very few exceptions, it has been difficult to delineate the effects due to hypnosis versus those due to suggestion, because hypnosis with suggestion typically has been contrasted with nonhypnotic interventions without suggestion. Furthermore, the influence of demand characteristics has been largely ignored in this research literature.

The first comprehensive review of this topic was prepared by Hull

(1933), who focused on hypnotic suggestibility and transcendence of voluntary capacity. Hull's principal conclusion was that existing evidence bearing on this question was contradictory. Furthermore, Hull explained the equivocal nature of this experimentation as being due to design flaws. Later reviews by Gorton (1959), Johnson (1961b), Weitzenhoffer (1953), Barber (1966), Morgan (1972b, 1980a, 1993), and Morgan and Brown (1983) were inconsistent regarding the ability of hypnotic suggestion to enhance physical performance.

Historically, the most critical review of research in this area was presented by Barber (1966), who concluded that hypnosis, without suggestions for enhanced performance, did not influence muscular strength or endurance. Furthermore, Barber reported that motivational suggestions are generally capable of augmenting muscular strength and endurance in both nonhypnotic and hypnotic conditions. Barber presented a compelling argument in that review and related writings regarding the necessity of not confounding hypnosis and suggestion. Typical experimental paradigms have involved the comparison of muscular performance following suggestions of enhanced or decreased capacity under hypnosis, on the one hand, with no suggestions under control or nonhypnotic conditions, on the other. There have been exceptions to this generalization; one of the earliest examples was the finding by Nicholson (1920) that suggestions given during hypnosis were much more effective than the same suggestions given without hypnosis. Another exception to this generalization is the report by Eysenck (1941) that hypnosis per se resulted in facilitation of muscular endurance. On the other hand, there is evidence that suggestion without hypnosis can lead to enhanced muscular performance (Barber, 1966; Morgan, 1981). Therefore, it is imperative that experimental designs not confound suggestion and procedure.

The reviews presented by Barber (1966), Gorton (1959), Hull (1933), Johnson (1961b), and Weitzenhoffer (1953) dealt primarily with the influence of hypnotic suggestion on muscular strength and endurance. More recent research has focused on the extent to which the hypnotic suggestion of an altered workload can influence the perception of effort (Morgan, 1994), as well as the extent to which perturbation of effort sense is associated with corresponding changes in metabolism. It has been reported, for example, that hypnotic suggestion can influence cardiac output, heart rate, blood pressure, forearm blood flow, respiratory rate, ventilatory minute volume, oxygen uptake, and carbon dioxide production, at rest and during exercise (Morgan, 1985).

It has also been shown that perception of effort can be systematically increased and decreased during exercise with hypnotic suggestion (Morgan, 1970; Morgan, 1981; Morgan, Hirota, Weitz, & Balke, 1976; Morgan, Raven, Drinkwater, & Horvath, 1973). Also, when exercise intensity is perceived as being more effortful, there is a corresponding elevation in physiological responses even though the actual workload remains unchanged. A summary of recent reviews by Morgan (1980a, 1985, 1993) and Morgan and Brown (1983) follows:

1. Although some investigators have reported that hypnosis per se has no influence on muscular strength and endurance, an equal number have found that hypnosis (without suggestion) can lead to both increments and decrements in muscular performance. The evidence in this area is equivocal.

2. Hypnotic suggestions designed to enhance muscular performance generally have not been effective, whereas suggestions designed to impair strength and endurance have been consistently successful.

3. Individuals who are not accustomed to performing at maximal levels usually experience gains in muscular strength and endurance when administered *involving* suggestions in the hypnotic state. However, suggestions of a *noninvolving* nature are not effective when administered to individuals who are accustomed to performing at maximal levels.

4. Efforts to modify performance on various psychomotor tasks (e.g., choice reaction time) have effects similar to those observed in research involving muscular strength and endurance. That is, efforts to slow reaction time are usually effective, whereas attempts to raise reaction time are not.

5. Case studies involving efforts to enhance performance in athletes by means of hypnosis appear to be universally successful. However, this observation should probably be viewed with caution because therapists and journals are not known for emphasizing case material depicting failures.

6. Hypnotic suggestion of exercise in the nonexercise state is associated with increased cardiac frequency, respiratory rate, ventilatory minute volume, oxygen uptake, carbon dioxide production, forearm blood flow, and cardiac output. These metabolic changes often approximate responses noted during actual exercise conditions.

7. Perception of effort during exercise can be systematically in-

creased and decreased with hypnotic suggestion even though the actual physical workload is maintained at a constant level. Furthermore, alterations in effort sense (i.e., perceived exertion) are associated with significant changes in physiological responses (e.g., ventilation).

Qualifications of Practitioners

The question of who is qualified to use hypnosis has been discussed for many years, and the issue involves a rather complex matter. Hilgard (1979) offered an interesting perspective on this issue in stating that "Lack of advanced degrees does not necessarily mean incompetence and society memberships do not guarantee competence either" (p. 5). Hilgard (1979) has also pointed out that broader professional training extending beyond hypnosis has various advantages, the principal one being "that the true professional will know much more that is relevant about personality and individual differences than is implied by hypnosis" (p. 5). This is an important point because a person who lacks training in fields such as psychology or psychiatry can easily learn how to perform hypnotic inductions.

It is reasonable to expect that an individual using hypnosis has advanced training in fields such as psychology or psychiatry, and it is equally reasonable to expect that such a person would hold membership in hypnosis organizations such as the Society for Clinical and Experimental Hypnosis, Division 30 (Psychological Hypnosis) of the American Psychological Association (APA), or the American Society of Clinical Hypnosis. However, affiliation with such professional groups should be regarded as necessary, rather than sufficient evidence for the reasons pointed out by Hilgard (1979).

There was a time when Division 30 of APA was regarded as a quasi-licensing group in that applicants for membership in the division were required to provide letters of recommendation, evidence of training in hypnosis, and documented evidence of experience in the use of hypnosis. Today, however, membership in Division 30 of APA merely requires application and payment of dues. Membership in this division can no longer be viewed as a sign that an individual has competence in the use of hypnosis. Division 30 is now merely an interest group within APA. Since the leading scientific and professional societies historically have not licensed or certified individuals in the use of hypnosis, it has been proposed by Levitt (1981) that certification by the American Board of Psychological Hypnosis (ABPH) is the only realistic testimony of an individual's ability as a hypnotist.

It is difficult to answer to everyone's satisfaction the question of who is qualified to use hypnosis. However, it is possible to provide some guidelines and principles to which workers in the field of sport and exercise psychology can adhere. For instance, all professional organizations concerned with the use of hypnosis make a clear distinction between its use in research and in clinical practice. Manipulation of an independent variable in an experimental setting with hypnotic suggestion is quite different than employing hypnotherapy in the treatment of clinical problems such as anxiety disorder or depression. In other words, although the use of hypnosis in research and clinical practice may have a number of procedural and methodological similarities in technical terms, these applications require different competencies.

It also seems reasonable to expect that workers in sport and exercise psychology who use hypnotic procedures as an experimental tool possess an advanced degree with a primary focus in psychology, and that these individuals have affiliations with appropriate hypnosis organizations such as Division 30 of APA, ASCH, or SCEH. Although affiliation with professional organizations does not ensure that individuals will stay within their areas of competence, such affiliations may increase the likelihood that a hypnotist will comply with existing ethical codes. All 50 states and the District of Columbia have enacted laws regulating the practice of psychology, and certification laws regulate the use of the title *psychologist,* and limit the scope of practice to those areas in which individuals possess competence and training. Sport and exercise psychologists who use hypnosis for clinical purposes should possess the appropriate certification or licensure. A longstanding principle in the area of hypnosis, and one that applies to both clinical and research applications, is that individuals not use hypnosis to perform manipulations or treatments that they are not qualified to perform without hypnosis. It is simply imperative that sport psychologists who use hypnosis in their research and clinical practice be qualified to use this intervention.

Clinical Applications

The selected cases described in this section are based on the assumption that important information associated with athletic competition is sometimes repressed and that this information can be retrieved by means of hypnotic age-regression. It is also assumed that efforts to retrieve this repressed material should be of a nondirective nature, and the decision to use this approach is based primarily on the successful results described in the clinical reports by Johnson (1961a, 1961b). Finally, these applications are based on a multidisciplinary approach that includes medical, physiological, and psychological components. Hypnotic applications should not be attempted in sport settings unless it can be shown that pathology does not exist and that the requisite physiological capacity is present.

One of the most widely cited cases involved a report by Johnson (1961a), who successfully used hypnosis to treat a baseball player. The player had requested that hypnosis be used to resolve his batting slump. The athlete played for a professional baseball team, and his batting average normally exceeded .300. However, he had not had a hit for the last 20 times at bat, and neither he nor any of his coaches could detect any problems with his swing, stance, and so on. The player had become quite frustrated about his inability to return to his prior performance level. Although the player was unaware of the basis for his performance decrement and although he was initially unable to offer any explanation for his slump under hypnosis, he eventually provided a detailed analysis of his swing that included the identification of specific problems throughout the analysis. Johnson (1961a) reported that he initially asked the batter under hypnosis to explain the nature of his problem, and the athlete replied that he had no idea why he was in a slump. Johnson then informed the batter that he would gradually count from 1 to 10, and with each number he would become more and more aware of why he could no longer hit effectively. He also informed the player that at the count of 10 he would have complete awareness of why he was in the slump. Johnson reported that at the count of 10 a look of incredulity came across the player's face, and he then proceeded to present a detailed analysis of his swing. This self-analysis under hypnosis included elaboration of specific problems that the player was unaware of in the nonhypnotic state. Johnson asked the batter if he wished to have immediate, conscious recall of his analysis, or simply have the information "just come to him gradually" over time. The player replied that he would prefer to have this information come back to him in time rather than all at once. The player's slump ended at once, and he went on to complete the season with an impressive batting average of .400.

This particular case is instructive in several ways, and sport psychologists who elect to use hypnosis in the treatment of such problems should first consider each of the following points. First, it is widely recognized that players in various sports often have spontaneous remission of problems such as slumps, and it would be difficult to argue that a hypnotic intervention was responsible for the resolution of a given problem. Second, the information gained in the hypnoanalysis done by Johnson (1961a) was not available in the nonhypnotic state. Third, the batter demonstrated unusual insight, according to Johnson, because he chose to have the wealth of biomechanical information return gradually. Once a complex motor skill has been learned, athletes are encouraged by coaches to "do it" rather than "think about it." In some ways, the situation is analogous to the problem of "paralysis through analysis," which occurred when the mythical frog asked the centipede, "Pray tell, which foot do you move first?" As the story goes, the centipede was unable to resume normal locomotion once the question was considered. Fourth, at the completion of the season, the player returned and thanked Johnson for the hypnoanalysis that led to his improved performance. The player was unable to accept the fact that he, not the hypnotist, had performed the analysis.

The efficacy of hypnosis in the treatment of pain has been widely documented, and there is at least one comprehensive report dealing with the use of hypnosis in the management of various problems in sports medicine. Ryde (1964) used hypnosis in the treatment of 35 individual cases involving problems such as tennis elbow, shin splints, chronic Achilles tendon sprain, bruised heels, arch sprains, and other common ailments involving minor trauma. As a matter of fact, Ryde reported that hypnosis was so effective in the treatment of minor trauma resulting from injuries in sports that he offers "to treat these disabilities initially by hypnosis and only proceed with conventional methods, should hypnosis fail or be refused" (p. 244). Although Ryde's report appears to support the value of hypnosis in the treatment of sports injuries, there is no evidence presented to suggest that it is any more effective than a placebo. This is an important consideration because it is known that placebo treatments can be just as effective as morphine in the treatment of moderate pain in anxious patients (Morgan, 1972a). However, the use of hypnosis in the treatment of medical problems associated with sport injuries should only be attempted by, or under the supervision of, an appropriately trained physician.

There has not been a great deal written about the use of psychodynamic approaches involving the use of hypnosis in sport and exercise psychology. However, in the review by Johnson (1961b), a number of case studies were summarized dealing with performance decrements in sports as a consequence of aggression blockage. In each of these cases hypnotic age-regression was used in an effort to retrieve repressed material, and this was followed by psychoanalytic interpretation and treatment. Also, posthypnotic suggestion was used to resolve the aggression conflicts. In one case, for example, a cycle of aggression–guilt–aggression was identified, and this cycle was directly associated with performance. The athlete, a pitcher in baseball, performed well when characterized by aggressive affect, but his performance fell when he felt guilty and lacked aggression. This transitory affect was found to be governed by feelings of guilt associated with repressed childhood incidents of aggression. When the athlete felt guilty, his performance declined, and his performance improved as the guilt passed and he became aggressive. The therapy in this case focused on resolution of the repressed guilt. Once this was achieved, the aggression–guilt–aggression cycle was broken and the pitcher's performance became more consistent. This general theme is repeated in the related cases described by Johnson (1961b).

It has been shown by Hanin (1978) that some athletes experience their best performances when precompetition anxiety is low, in others when anxiety is high, and in other athletes when anxiety is intermediate. This theoretical view is supported by empirical research involving athletes from various sports (Morgan & Ellickson, 1989; Morgan, O'Connor, Ellickson, & Bradley, 1988; Morgan, O'Connor, Sparling, & Pate, 1987; Raglin, 1992). Hence, it would be inappropriate to use psychological interventions designed to either reduce or increase anxiety in *groups* of athletes. In other words, an intervention such as autogenic training or progressive relaxation with athletes in a precompetitive setting would not only be ineffective, it would have the effect of placing a large number of athletes outside of their individual zone of optimal anxiety (ZOA).

The concept of a ZOA for athletes has now been well established (Hanin, 1978; Morgan & Ellickson, 1989; Raglin, 1992). It is imperative that efforts designed to manipulate precompetition anxiety be carried out on an individual basis, but the difficulty, of course, involves the determination of an athlete's ZOA, because it is necessary to evaluate an athlete's anxiety level prior to many competitions in order to arrive at his or her ZOA. Alternatively, one might use hypnotic age regression in an effort to ascertain anxiety levels prior to an athlete's best, usual, and worst performances. Once the individual's ZOA was determined, it then would be possible to strive, with autohypnosis or posthypnotic suggestion, for precompetition anxiety that falls within the athlete's optimal range (i.e., ZOA). Although this view is speculative, it is based on a sound theoretical rationale (Hanin, 1978) and extensive empirical evidence of an indirect nature (Morgan & Ellickson, 1989; Raglin, 1992).

Despite the compelling support for ZOA theory, it is apparent that sport psychologists are more likely to be consulted about problems involving elevations in precompetition anxiety. Indeed, athletes have been reported to be almost incapacitated at times prior to competition, and these anxiety attacks often prevent customary levels of performance. Although an equal number of athletes may experience inadequately low levels of anxiety, this problem tends to be less apparent. One of the best discussions of how hypnosis can be used with athletes in the precompetitive setting was presented by Naruse (1965). Intense anxiety in the precompetitive setting was labeled as *stage fright* by Naruse, who summarized the use of (a) direct hypnotic suggestions, (b) posthypnotically produced autohypnosis, and (c) self-hypnosis in conjunction with autogenic training and progressive relaxation in the treatment of anxiety states in athletes.

There are two important points to be made about Naruse's (1965) report. First, the athletes used in this study consisted of elite performers, and the results may not generalize to pre-elite or nonelite athletes. Second, the actual procedure used with a given athlete in Naruse's study was determined on an individual basis. Furthermore, the unique nature of the athlete's stage fright was considered together with the individual's personality structure in deciding on the procedure to be used in a given case. The report by Naruse should prove to be particularly useful to hypnotherapists involved in the treatment of precompetition anxiety in athletes competing at the national or international levels.

It has been emphasized by Vanek (1970) that attempts to manipulate anxiety levels prior to competition must be pursued with caution and that the psychologist should have a complete appreciation for the athlete's psychodynamic nature. Furthermore, Vanek described the case of a heavyweight boxer who experienced an anxiety attack prior to an Olympic contest. The boxer's anxiety was controlled effectively with the administration of a nonhypnotic (autogenic method) procedure. The boxer then proceeded to lose his match to an opponent he had previously beaten. Vanek reported that follow-up study revealed that the boxer typically experienced anxiety attacks prior to important competitions, but he apparently performed well in this state. Anxiety reduction, in retrospect, was judged by Vanek to be contraindicated. This is an interesting case, and it serves to confirm the ZOA theory described earlier. At any rate, it is apparent that indiscriminant use of psychological procedures designed to relax athletes prior to competition is not appropriate.

A novel approach to performance enhancement using hypnotic control of arousal levels has been described by Garver (1977). This method requires that athletes establish a personal arousal scale ranging from 0 (*low*) to 10 (*high*) while in the hypnotic state. The number 10 represents the highest possible level of arousal an athlete might experience, whereas the zero anchor represents the lowest. The athlete is moved up and down this arousal scale in an attempt to experience how different arousal-intensities feel. Furthermore, the athlete's optimal level of arousal is defined as the sensations associated with the number 5 on the scale. An effort is made to have the athlete develop for each intensity level, with the idea that these arousal levels can be used posthypnotically during competition. Garver described cases of a gymnast and a golfer who experienced performance problems associated with elevated anxiety and anger, respectively. In these cases, posthypnotic cues and cognitive rehearsal were used to produce preferred arousal levels, and this approach led to enhanced performance.

Case Material

The cases reviewed in this section involve athletes from the sports of distance running, baseball, and cycling. The overall approach used in these cases relied on insight training through hypnotic age regression. The hypnotic procedure can be viewed as nondirective, and it built on the earlier case reports of Johnson (1961a; 1961b). Also, the theoretical formulations of Hanin (1978) and Unestähl (1981) specified that optimal or ideal affective states characterize peak performance and maintained that information of this nature can be retrieved. Therefore, efforts were made in these cases to retrieve repressed material by means of hypnotic age regression. A multidisciplinary approach was used in each situation, and these case studies demonstrate that performance decrements in sports are sufficiently complex to rule out simplistic, unidimensional solutions.

In the first two cases, hypnosis was employed in an effort to help a distance runner and baseball player gain insights about problems they were experiencing during competition. In the third case, it was decided that hypnosis was contraindicated. In all three cases, the athletes were patients under the care of a sports medicine physician who participated in the hypnoanalysis. The author assumed responsibility in these cases for the hypnotic inductions.

Case 1: Distance Runner

This case represents a common problem in which an athlete is no longer able to perform at his or her customary level. This type of situation is considerably different from the case of an athlete performing at a given level who wishes to enhance his or her performance. In other words, the present case involved a situation in which an athlete previously performed at an elite level but was now unable to do so.

The case involved a 21-year-old distance runner who had previously established a school and conference record but was unable to replicate the performance. Indeed, the runner was not able to even complete many of his races, much less dominate a given competition. Problems of this nature are usually diagnosed as *staleness* in the field of sports medicine, and the only effective treatment appears to be rest (Morgan, Brown, Raglin, O'Connor, & Ellickson, 1987). However, this was not the problem in the present case. The runner's inability to perform at his previous level was judged by the coach simply to reflect inadequate motivation and unwillingness to tolerate the distress and discomfort associated with high-level performance. On the other hand, the athlete reported that he was willing to do anything to perform at his previous level, and he felt that his principal problem stemmed from inadequate coaching. Although the athlete and the coach were both interested in the restoration of the runner's previous performance ability, they were clearly at odds with one another. Indeed, the conflict had reached the point where the two were unable to discuss the matter, and the runner had turned to his team physician for support. However, a thorough physical examination, including blood and urine chemistries routinely used in sports medicine, failed to reveal any medical problems.

The physician proposed that hypnosis be used in an effort to resolve this problem, and the athlete was eager to try such an approach. However, it seemed appropriate to first evaluate the runner's physical capacity in order to ensure that he was actually capable of performing at the desired level. Aerobic power is an important factor in successful distance running, so the runner was administered a test of maximal aerobic power on a treadmill. This required that he run at a pace of 12 miles per hour on the treadmill, and the grade was increased by 2% every minute until he could no longer continue. This test revealed that he achieved a peak or maximal VO_2 of 70 ml/kg·min by the 5th minute of exercise, and his ability to uptake oxygen fell during the 6th minute. In other words, a true physiological maximum, as opposed to a volitional or symptomatic maximum, was achieved. The recorded value of 70 ml/kg·min represents the average reported for elite distance runners, and the runner was therefore physiologically capable of achieving the desired performance level. However, our calculations revealed that it would have been necessary for him to average 96% of his maximum throughout the event to replicate his record performance. This could be problematic because exercise metabolites such as lactic acid begin to accumulate and to limit performance during prolonged exercise, at 60% to 80% of maximum in most trained individuals. In other words, it would have been possible for this runner to perform at the desired level, but such an effort would be associated with considerable discomfort (pain).

The runner was observed to score within the normal range on anxiety, depression, and neuroticism as measured by the State-Trait Anxiety Inventory (STAI), Depression Adjective Check List (DACL), and Eysenck Personality Inventory (EPI), respectively. He scored significantly higher than the population norms on extroversion (EPI), but this has been a common finding for many athletes (Morgan, 1980b). He was found to be hypnotizable following preliminary induction and deepening sessions, and he was eager to pursue "insight training" through hypnosis and deep relaxation. The runner was viewed as a good candidate for hypnosis for the following reasons: (a) There were no medical contraindications detected; (b) he possessed the necessary physiological capacity to achieve the desired goal; (c) there were no apparent psychological contraindications; and (d) he was able to enter into a deep trance.

Next, the athlete was age-regressed to the day of his championship performance, and he was instructed to describe the competition as well as any related events that he judged to be relevant. However, rather than telling him that the race was about to begin or instructing him in the customary "on your marks" command, he was asked to recall all events leading up to the race on that day. He was instructed, "For example, try to remember how you felt when you awakened that morning; your breakfast or any foods or liquids you consumed; the temperature before and during the race; the nature and condition of the course; interactions with your coach, teammates, and opponents; your general frame of mind; and then proceed to the starting line *when you are ready*." The athlete's team physician and the author had previously asked the runner if it would be acceptable for either or both of them to ask questions during the session, and the athlete had no objections. The athlete had a somewhat serious or pensive look, but within a few minutes he began to smile and chuckle, saying that he had false-started. When asked why this was so amusing, he replied that it was "ridiculous since there is no advantage to a fast start in a distance race." This event can be viewed as a critical incident because runners and swimmers will intentionally false start at times in an effort to reduce tension. Others will do this in an effort to upset or "unnerve" their opponents. At any rate, his facial expression became serious once again, and his motor behavior (e.g., grimacing and limb movements) suggested the race had begun. The verbatim narrative follows:

The pace is really fast. I'm at the front of the pack. I don't think I can hold this pace much longer, but I feel pretty good. The pace is picking up...I don't think I can hold it...my side is beginning to ache...I have had a pain in the side many times. It will go away if I continue to press. There...it feels good now. The pain is gone, but I'm having trouble breathing. I'm beginning to *suck air*...the pain is unbearable...I'm going to drop out of the race as soon as I find a soft spot. There's a soft, grassy spot up ahead...I'm going to stop and lay in the soft grassy spot...wait, I can't, three of my teammates are up on top of the next grade...they are yelling at me to *kick* ...I can't let them down. I will keep going. I'm over the hill now ...on level grade...it feels ok...I'm alright. There's another hill up ahead. I don't like hills...It is starting to hurt again...I can't keep this up...I'm going to find a soft spot again and stop. There's a spot ahead...I'm going to quit...I'm slowing down...this is it. Wait, there...I see a television set about 10 feet off the ground at the top of the hill...hey, I'm on the TV, but this race isn't televised ...but I can see myself clearly on the TV...I'm not here anymore ...I'm on the TV. Now there's another TV, but to the right of the first one. My parents are on that TV, and they are watching me run this race on the other TV. I can't stop now. I can't let them down. Got to keep going. I'm not here...I'm on TV. It's starting to feel better. I feel like I'm in a vacuum now. I can't feel anything. My feet aren't hitting the ground anymore...I can't feel the wind hitting me. Hey, I'm a Yankee Clipper...I'm on the high seas...I'm flying ...the sails are full...the wind is pushing me...I'm going to *blow out*...I'm going to *kick*...I don't feel pain anymore...This is going to be a PB, maybe a record, I'm flying now, there is no one in sight, this is my race, there's the tape, I'm almost there, the tape hit my chest, it feels weird...weird...weird...the tape feels weird...that's the end...the end...the end...the end.

The runner appeared to be deeply relaxed at this point, and he had previously agreed to answer any questions we might have following his recall of the race. He was asked, "You almost dropped out of the race twice. Why didn't you simply slow your pace? Would that not have been better than quitting?" The runner replied without any hesitation that "Oh, no, you really have to take pride in yourself to quit. You have to be a *real* man...it takes guts to quit. Anybody can continue and turn in a lousy performance. I have too much pride to do that. I would rather quit." Although this view can be judged as somewhat unusual, it is noteworthy that he had dropped out of more races than he had completed during the present season.

The runner was asked to clarify the meaning of selected terms or phrases he had used, and then he was asked the following question: "Would you like to have complete recall for all of this information, or would you prefer to forget about it, or perhaps, have it come back to you gradually?" The decision to ask this question was based on the earlier demonstration by Johnson (1961a) that athletes sometimes do not wish to become aware of repressed material in the posthypnotic state. The decision to ask whether he would prefer that this information gradually return was also based on Johnson's case study, and it was intended to prevent the athlete from becoming overwhelmed or further confused as a result of this previously repressed material. At any rate, the runner responded that he would like to have complete recall following the session. Hence, no effort was made to produce posthypnotic amnesia.

The runner was also asked in the hypnotic state whether he wished to continue with this program of insight training, and he replied that he would like to give this some thought. For this reason, posthypnotic suggestions designed to ensure adherence to future hypnotic sessions were not administered. In other words, motivating instructions designed to ensure continuation could have been, but were not, administered to the runner. This decision was based on our belief in the efficacy of nondirected approaches in such cases, as well as on an a priori contingency agreements with the runner. These agreements were of a generic nature, and they were decided on prior to intervention with hypnosis.

This case serves to illustrate several points that practitioners in sport psychology or sports medicine might wish to consider prior to using hypnosis with an athlete. First, efforts designed to enhance physical performance with hypnosis should not be carried out within a unidimensional context. It is important first to obtain relevant information concerning the athlete's physiological, psychological, and medical state. Second, the decision to proceed with hypnosis should be made after obvious contraindications (i.e., pathophysiology and psychopathology) have been ruled out. Third, peak performances involving the transcendence of usual or customary levels can be associated with cognitive–

perceptual processes of a remarkable nature. The record-setting performance of this athlete was found to be associated with considerable pain, but the sensation of pain had been repressed; that is, the runner was unaware of this pain experience in the nonhypnotic state. However, the cognitive–perceptual experience was "replayed" during hypnotic age-regression, and the runner elected to have awareness of this experience in the posthypnotic state. It is possible that conscious awareness of this previously repressed material may have provided the runner with insights he previously lacked.

The runner subsequently elected to terminate insight training, and this decision was not congruent with his initial statement that he would do anything to return to his previous level of performance. It should be kept in mind that although he did possess the physiological capacity necessary to perform at a high level, to do so would have been associated with considerable pain. Also, despite the fact that his subsequent performance did not improve, our subjective impression was that he had "come to terms" with the situation. In a sense, then, he did not terminate the insight training we were providing, but rather, the insight he gained resolved the problem—at least from his perspective.

It is also noteworthy that the athlete's record performance was characterized by the cognitive strategy known as *dissociation* (Morgan, 1984). Runners who use this strategy attempt to ignore sensory input (e.g., muscle pain and breathing distress) by thinking about other activities (i.e., distraction). Other runners have reported that they initiate out-of-body experiences by entering the body's shadow cast on the ground in front of them. These cognitive strategies have been labeled as dissociation. Although this strategy can clearly facilitate endurance performance (Morgan, Horstman, Cymerman, & Stokes, 1983), it is not the preferred strategy of elite distance runners (Morgan & Pollock, 1977). Indeed, elite runners have been found to use a cognitive strategy known as *association,* which is based on systematic monitoring of physical sensations, rather than ignoring such input (Morgan & Pollock, 1977; Morgan et al., 1987, 1988).

There is a possibility that this athlete could have been taught to use dissociation (Morgan, 1984), in either the hypnotic or the nonhypnotic state, in an effort to help him cope with the perception of pain during competition. It is also possible that such an approach would have led to enhanced performance because (a) laboratory research has shown that such an approach is ergogenic (Morgan et al., 1983) and (b) the runner had actually experienced a form of dissociation during his record-setting performance. However, ignoring sensory input while performing at a high metabolic level in a sport contest is not without risk, and such an approach can lead to heatstroke, muscle sprains or strains, and stress fractures (Morgan, 1984). Cognitive strategies designed to minimize or eliminate the sensation of pain and discomfort during athletic competition and training should be used judiciously and with caution.

Case 2: Baseball Player

Hypnotic age-regression was used in an effort to resolve a periodic problem experienced by a college baseball player who was an outfielder on a Division I team.

> The player was introduced to the author by his team physician in the hope that hypnosis might be used to improve the player's batting performance. He was regarded as a strong hitter, with the exception that he would "bail out" of (jump back from) the batter's box at times when he was not in apparent danger of being hit by a pitched ball. He had been examined and treated by the team physician and found to be in good physical health, including unimpaired vision. The player was highly regarded by a number of professional baseball teams, and he stood a good chance of earning a professional contract following his graduation in 2 months' time. He was highly motivated to solve his batting problem because several professional scouts had arranged visits to campus to observe him play. The coach was somewhat frustrated about the situation, and his only approach had been to instruct the player to "hang in with the pitch." This instruction was of no help to the batter, and the exhortation seemed to exacerbate the problem.
>
> The player was deeply concerned about the possibility that he would bail out of the batter's box during the forthcoming visits by pro scouts. Because the batter had a .315 batting average despite bailing out of the batter's box periodically, it was decided that he would be a possible candidate for hypnoanalysis. A battery of psychological questionnaires was administered to the athlete, and he was found to score within the normal range on measures of state and trait anxiety (STAI); aggression (Thematic Apperception Test and a Sentence Completion Test); tension, depression, anger, vigor, and confusion (Profile of Mood States); and neuroticism-stability and extroversion-introversion (EPI). Also, his lie score on the EPI was not remarkable. This screening was followed on separate days by administration of the Harvard and Stanford C Scales of hypnotizability. He was quite responsive, scoring high on both the Harvard Group Scale and the Stanford C Scale (i.e., raw scores of 9 and 10 respectively).

On the basis of the earlier example described by Johnson (1961a), the athlete was initially age-regressed to a recent game in which the problem occurred, and he was asked to describe the situation. He previously had agreed that he did not object to the team physician or author asking him questions as the analysis proceeded. Although the author assumed responsibility for the hypnoinduction, it was agreed by the athlete, physician, and author that the physician would be responsible for the clinical dimensions of the process. The athlete was unable to provide any detail during this age regression that was not available previously in the waking state. The author indicated that he would count from 1 to 10 and that the player would have recall for relevant information that was not previously available when the number 10 was reached. This, too, was based on the earlier approach successfully used by Johnson. At the count of 10, the athlete began to shake his head from side to side, and he apologized for not remembering additional material. He was assured that such a response was not unusual, and he was given posthypnotic suggestions to the effect that he would feel relaxed and refreshed following the session. It was also emphasized that he would look forward to next week's session.

The player returned a week later, at which time a second age regression was used, but on this occasion he was asked to drop back in time and try to recall any events in his baseball career that were of particular importance to him. Within a brief period of time he described an occasion during his first year at the university in which he was hit on the back as he turned in an attempt to avoid a pitched ball. He thought the ball was going to "break," but it did not, and as he turned away from the ball his left scapula was hit and broken. It is remarkable that he had apparently repressed this event, because it was quite significant. At any rate, he had never mentioned this incident to us during the waking state. He then proceeded to describe a situation in high school when, as a pitcher, he had attempted to "dust off" a batter (i.e., throw at the batter rather than the plate) to distract the batter and increase his apprehension about succeeding pitches. Unfortunately, he hit the batter in the head (helmets were not worn at that time). Although the injury was not serious, the batter did not return to the game, and the athlete reported that he felt bad about the event.

It would have been possible to administer various posthypnotic suggestions, but we decided not to do so for several reasons. The case resembled an earlier one described by Johnson (1961b) in which a pitcher regularly cycled through a guilt–rage–guilt cycle, with performance decrements during the guilt phase and enhanced performance during periods of rage. In the present case, there may have been a fear–guilt–repression cycle in which the batter, presumably at an unconscious level, experienced the fear of being hit, or guilt associated with the injury of his opponent, and these states could have created sufficient psychomotor perturbation to provoke the present problem. Additionally, these affective states may have been repressed periodically, during which time performance was increased. These explanations are purely speculative, and we elected not to build on these hypotheses. We also felt that it would be inappropriate to administer suggestions designed to restrain him in the batter's box, because of the potential for injury from a pitched ball. Rather, we elected to ask the batter if he wanted to have conscious recall of this previously repressed material in the posthypnotic state. He indicated that he would like to recall all of the information, and he was then given the same concluding suggestions administered in the previous session.

In the next and final session, following the induction the athlete was asked to once again drop back in time and recall events in his baseball career that possessed particular meaning to him. He responded to this request by saying,

Okay, but I want to tell you something first. I think I have solved my bailing out problem. I have been using a closed stance, and I crowd the plate as much as possible in order to control the plate and reduce the pitcher's strike zone. All good batters do this, but you always run the chance of being "beaned." Therefore, I'm changing to an open stance with my left foot dropped back so I will have a wide open view of all pitches. I'm a good enough hitter that I can do that without hurting my average.

Because the athlete seemed to have gained insight and resolved the problem, we elected not to proceed with further age regression. We talked with him briefly about his decision, and he was encouraged to review this plan with his coach. He was then given posthypnotic suggestion that he would feel relaxed, rested, and confident about his decision following the session. He was also encouraged to contact us if he had any further problems.

This case can be judged as representing a successful resolution of a presenting symptom, because the batter's performance improved. He was no longer plagued with the problem of bailing out, he completed the remainder of the season with a .515 average, and his overall average ranked near the top for all Division I players that year.

Case 3: Cyclist

A 27-year-old male, competitive cyclist approached the author with the request that hypnosis be used to resolve a problem he was experiencing with his training.

The cyclist was unable to complete routine training rides of 50 to 75 km, and he was concerned that he would not be able to compete effectively in a forthcoming national race. He completed a standard battery of psychological questionnaires, and the results were remarkable in that he was found to be depressed and anxious. Because of the elevated scores on these measures, it was felt that his performance problem should not be addressed with hypnoanalysis. He was referred to a clinical psychologist for evaluation and possible treatment. This assessment revealed that he was not only clinically depressed, but it was felt that crisis intervention was warranted. Therefore, he was referred to an outpatient psychiatry clinic where he was treated for several months. Treatment consisted of time-limited psychotherapy in concert with antidepressant drug therapy.

During the course of his psychotherapy, the cyclist continued to visit our physiology-of-exercise laboratory where he had previously completed a test of maximal aerobic power on the bicycle ergometer. His earlier test revealed that he possessed a peak $\dot{V}O_{2max}$ of 66 ml/kg·min. In other words, maximal capacity was defined in terms of physiological capacity, rather than a symptom-limited or subjective maximum. The retest consisted of the same protocol and the test was performed by the same laboratory technician, who performed the earlier assessment. The cyclist's maximal capacity had fallen to 53 ml/kg·min. Since a reduction of 20% in actual physiological capacity is both atypical and remarkable, the cyclist was retested a week later in order to confirm the test results. The second test yielded identical results, and these data served to confirm that the decision to use hypnosis in such a case was contraindicated. That is, he could no longer perform at his customary level, because he no longer possessed the physiological capacity to do so! The unexplained reduction in $\dot{V}O_{2max}$ warranted further assessment, and he was referred for a complete physical examination to include routine blood and urine chemistries employed in our sports medicine clinic. All results were negative with the exception that he seemed to have some suspicious chest sounds. For this reason, he was next referred to the pulmonary function laboratory, where all test results were found to be negative.

The psychotherapy and drug therapy led to a reduction in this cyclist's anxiety and depression, and he was eventually able to resume customary levels of training. However, the 20% decrement in physical capacity was not restored, and he was unable to return to competitive cycling at the national level. The purpose of elaborating on this case study is threefold. First, the motivational problem was based upon a profound and difficult to explain reduction in the cyclist's physiological capacity. Second, the use of hypnosis to treat this problem was contraindicated owing to the demonstration of both psychopathology (anxiety and depression) and pathophysiology (reduced $\dot{V}O_{2max}$). Third, it is apparent in retrospect, as well as on theoretical grounds, that a multidisciplinary approach to performance problems is the only defensible course of action.

Conclusion

Hypnosis has been used in the field of sport and exercise psychology for a number of years as a research tool in efforts designed to elucidate the mechanisms underlying physical performance. Also, there have been numerous clinical applications designed to enhance performance in sport settings, and these interventions have been based largely on theoretical formulations as opposed to empirical research evidence. These clinical applications have generally been successful, but there has been little attention paid to behavioral artifacts such as expectancy effects, placebo effects, and demand characteristics in this work. Furthermore, there is no evidence that effects obtained with these clinical applications exceed those that one might achieve with the same or comparable approaches in the absence of hypnosis.

Efforts to enhance athletic performance by increasing or decreasing precompetitive anxiety usually have not been effective. This can be explained by the observation that most athletes perform best within a narrow ZOA. Hence, efforts to decrease or increase anxiety in athletes should be discouraged unless the athlete's ZOA is known. It is noteworthy that hypnotic age-regression offers considerable promise in defining an individual's ZOA. Furthermore, once this anxiety zone has been established, it can be reproduced with various hypnotic procedures (e.g., autohypnosis and posthypnotic suggestion).

An additional area in which hypnosis has proven to be effective in sport and exercise psychology involves the interpretation of decreased performance levels (i.e., slumps and failure) in previously successful individuals. Examples of nondirective hypnotic age regression are presented in this chapter, and these cases emphasize the importance of multidisciplinary approaches. In conclusion, direct hypnotic suggestions of enhanced performance are not likely to be successful, but there are a number of ways in which the hypnotic tool can be used effectively in sport and exercise psychology.

References

American Psychological Association (1992). Ethical principles of psychologists and code of conduct. *American Psychologist, 47,* 1597–1611.

Barber, T. X. (1966). The effects of hypnosis and suggestions on strength and endurance: A critical review of research studies. *British Journal of Social and Clinical Psychology, 5,* 42–50.

Eysenck, H. J. (1941). An experimental study of the improvement of mental and physical functions in the hypnotic state. *British Journal of Medical Psychology, 18,* 304–316.

Garver, R. B. (1977). The enhancement of human performance with hypnosis through neuromotor facilitation and control of arousal level. *American Journal of Clinical Hypnosis, 19,* 177–181.

Gorton, B. E. (1959). Physiologic aspects of hypnosis. In J. M. Schneck (Ed.), *Hypnosis in modern medicine* (pp. 246–280). Springfield, IL: Charles C. Thomas.

Hanin, Y. L. (1978). A study of anxiety in sports. In W. F. Straub (Ed.), *Sport psychology: An analysis of athlete behavior* (pp. 236–249). Ithaca, NY: Movement.

Hilgard, E. R. (1979, April). More about forensic hypnosis. *Division 30 Newsletter,* p. 5.

Hull, C. L. (1933). *Hypnosis and suggestibility.* New York: Appleton-Century-Crofts.

Ikai, M., & Steinhaus, A. H. (1961). Some factors modifying the expression of human strength. *Journal of Applied Psychology, 16,* 157–163.

Johnson, W. R. (1961a). Body movement awareness in the non-hypnotic and hypnotic states. *Research Quarterly, 32,* 263–264.

Johnson, W. R. (1961b). Hypnosis and muscular performance. *Journal of Sports Medicine and Physical Fitness, 1,* 71–79.

Levitt, E. E. (1981, August). Presidential Address. *Division 30 Newsletter,* p. 2.

Morgan, W. P. (1970). Oxygen uptake following hypnotic suggestion. In G. S. Kenyon (Ed.), *Contemporary psychology of sport* (pp. 283–286). Chicago, IL: Athletic Institute.

Morgan, W. P. (1972a). Basic considerations. In W. P. Morgan (Ed.), *Ergogenic aids and muscular performance* (pp. 3–31). New York: Academic Press.

Morgan, W. P. (1972b). Hypnosis and muscular performance. In W. P. Morgan (Ed.), *Ergogenic aids and muscular performance* (pp. 193–233). New York: Academic Press.

Morgan, W. P. (1980a). Hypnosis and sports medicine. In G. D. Burrows & L. Dennerstein (Eds.), *Handbook of hypnosis and psychosomatic medicine* (pp. 359–375). Amsterdam: Elsevier/North-Holland Biomedical Press.

Morgan, W. P. (1980b). The trait psychology controversy. *Research Quarterly for Exercise and Sport, 51,* 50–76.

Morgan, W. P. (1981). Psychophysiology of self-awareness during vigorous physical activity. *Research Quarterly for Exercise and Sports, 52,* 385–427.

Morgan, W. P. (1984). Mind over matter. In W. F. Straub & J. M. Williams (Eds.), *Cognitive sport psychology* (pp. 311–316). Lansing, NY: Sport Science Associates.

Morgan, W. P. (1985). Psychogenic factors and exercise metabolism. *Medicine and Science in Sports and Exercise, 17,* 309–316.

Morgan, W. P. (1993). Hypnosis and sport psychology. In J. Rhue, S. J. Lynn & I. Kirsch (Eds.), *Handbook of clinical hypnosis* (pp. 649–670). Washington, DC: American Psychological Association.

Morgan, W. P. (1994). Psychological components of effort sense. *Medicine and Science in Sports and Exercise, 26,* 1071–1077.

Morgan, W. P., & Brown, D. R. (1983). Hypnosis. In M. L. Williams (Ed.), *Ergogenic aids and sports* (pp. 223–252). Champaign, IL: Human Kinetics.

Morgan, W. P., Brown, D. R., Raglin, J. S., O'Connor, P. J., & Ellickson, K. A. (1987). Psychological monitoring of overtraining and staleness. *British Journal of Sports Medicine, 21,* 107–114.

Morgan, W. P., & Ellickson, K. A. (1989). Health, anxiety, and physical exercise. In C. D. Spielberger & D. Hackbart (Eds.), *Anxiety in sports: An international perspective* (pp. 165–182). Washington, DC: Hemisphere.

Morgan, W. P., Hirota, K., Weitz, G. A., & Balke, B. (1976). Hypnotic perturbation of perceived exertion: Ventilatory consequences. *American Journal of Clinical Hypnosis, 18,* 182–190.

Morgan, W. P., Horstman, D. H., Cymerman, A., & Stokes, J. (1983). Facilitation of physical performance by means of a cognitive strategy. *Cognitive Therapy and Research, 7,* 251–264.

Morgan, W. P., O'Connor, P. J., Ellickson, K. A., & Bradley, P. W. (1988). Personality structure, mood states, and performance in elite male distance runners. *International Journal of Sport Psychology, 19,* 247–263.

Morgan, W. P., O'Connor, P. J., Sparling, B. P., & Pate, R. R. (1987). Psychological characterization of the elite female distance runner. *International Journal of Sports Medicine, 8,* 124–131.

Morgan, W. P., & Pollock, M. L. (1977). Psychologic characterization of the elite distance runner. *Annals of the New York Academy of Science, 301,* 382–403.

Morgan, W. P., Raven, P. B., Drinkwater, B. L., & Horvath, S. M. (1973). Perceptual and metabolic responsivity to standard bicycle ergometry following various hypnotic suggestions. *International Journal of Clinical and Experimental Hypnosis, 31,* 86–101.

Naruse, G. (1965). The hypnotic treatment of stage fright in champion athletes. *International Journal of Clinical and Experimental Hypnosis, 13,* 63–70.

Nicholson, N. C. (1920). Notes on muscular work during hypnosis. *Johns Hopkins Hospital Bulletin, 31,* 89–91.

Raglin, J. S. (1992). Anxiety and sport performance. In J. O. Holloszy (Ed.), *Exercise and sport sciences reviews* (Vol. 20, pp. 243–274), Baltimore, MD: Williams & Wilkins.

Railo, W. S., & Unestähl, L.-E. V. (1979). The Scandinavian practice of sport psychology. In P. Klavora (Ed.), *Coach, athlete, and the sport psychologist* (pp. 248–271). Champaign, IL: Human Kinetics.

Ryde, D. (1964). A personal study of some uses of hypnosis in sports and sports injuries. *Journal of Sports Medicine and Physical Fitness, 4,* 241–246.

Spielberger, C. D. (1983). *Manual for the State Trait Anxiety Inventory.* Palo Alto, CA: Consulting Psychologists Press.

Unestähl, L.-E. V. (1981). *New paths of sport learning and excellence* [Monograph]. Orebro, Sweden: Orebro University, Department of Sport Psychology.

Vanek, M. (1970). Psychological problems of superior athletes: Some experiences from the Olympic Games in Mexico City, 1968. In G. S. Kenyon (Ed.), *Contemporary psychology of sport* (pp. 183–185). Chicago, IL: Athletic Institute.

Weitzenhoffer, A. M. (1953). *Hypnotism: An objective study in suggestibility.* New York: John Wiley.

Part Two

Promoting Well-Being

Exercise Initiation, Adoption, and Maintenance

Bess H. Marcus, Beth C. Bock, Bernardine M. Pinto, and Matthew M. Clark

This chapter focuses on the promotion of exercise behavior in the general population. The health benefits of regular exercise are presented, followed by data on the prevalence of sedentary lifestyles in the U.S. population. The lack of theory-driven interventions has been a limitation in exercise promotion efforts. We present a summary of several potentially useful theoretical models for exercise adoption and adherence. For the practitioner, we provide information on exercise interventions based on some of these theories. Finally, we identify several important issues that need to be addressed in exercise promotion.

Benefits of Exercise and Physical Activity

Physical activity has been identified as a health behavior with potential benefits for improved physical and psychological health in men and women of all ages. Inactivity has been established as a risk factor for coronary heart disease (Paffenbarger et al., 1993) and acute myocardial infarction (Lakka et al., 1994), and increased physical activity is significantly correlated with changes in other major cardiovascular risk factors such as HDL cholesterol and body mass index (Bovens et al., 1993; Young, King, Oka, & Haskell, in press). Besides showing that exercise increases protection against coronary heart disease (Blair et al., 1989), epidemiological studies suggest that increased activity appears to provide protective benefits against colon cancer in men (e.g., Kohl, LaPorte, & Blair, 1988) and certain reproductive cancers in women (Bernstein, Henderson, Hanisch, Sullivan-Halley, & Ross, 1994; Frisch et al., 1985; see review by Pinto & Marcus, 1994). Exercise is recommended as an adjunctive treatment to diet for control of noninsulin dependent diabetes mellitus (NIDDM) and perhaps helps to prevent onset of NIDDM (Helmrich, Ragland, Leung, & Paffenbarger, 1991). Additionally, physical activity is recommended in the prevention and treatment of obesity and facilitates weight maintenance in men (King, Frey-Hewitt, Dreon, & Wood, 1989) and women (Craighead & Blum, 1989). Finally, physical activity can help prevent other chronic diseases such as osteoporosis in postmenopausal women (R. Marcus et al., 1992).

The health benefits cited above have been demonstrated among middle-aged adults (< 60 years of age). Improvements in cardiovascular fitness, strength, and flexibility have also been reported among older adults following exercise adoption (e.g., Morey et al., 1989; Posner et al., 1990). In addition, there is recent evidence that participation in resistance exercise training can counteract muscle weakness and frailty in nursing home residents (Fiatarone et al., 1994).

Apart from the promising improvements in health, exercise is believed to offer psychological benefits for adults that include improvements in anxiety, depression, and self-concept (Raglin, 1990). Improvements in mood have been found to occur following aerobic exercise, although a few recent studies claim similar benefit from nonaerobic activity such as yoga (Berger & Owen, 1992) and weight lifting (Doyne et al., 1987; Ossip-Klein et al., 1989). With adoption of regular exercise regimens, significant improvements in anxiety, depression, and self-esteem have been found with clinical samples (Ossip-Klein et al., 1989; Pappas, Golin, & Meyer, 1990), but such significant changes have not been reported for individuals within the normal range on these dimensions (Hughes, 1984; Lennox, Bedell, & Stone, 1990). In community-based interventions among retirees, regular exercise participation has been found to produce significant reductions in anxiety and depression compared to assessment-only controls (King, Haskell, Taylor, Kraemer, & Debusk, 1991). Mood benefits such as decreases in tension/anxiety can be obtained following moderate intensity aerobic training (Moses, Steptoe, Mathews, & Edwards, 1989) and with home-based exercise programs (either low or high intensity), suggesting that exercise need not be vigorous or uncomfortable to achieve positive mental health effects (King, Taylor, & Haskell, 1993). Available evidence suggests that participation in physical activity, rather than increased cardiovascular fitness, may be the factor associated with better health and mood (see review by LaFontaine et al., 1992).

In sum, exercise can help modify risk factors for chronic disease (primary prevention) and assist in the treatment of some chronic diseases in men and women. The significance of physical activity in disease prevention is reflected in Healthy People 2000 in which promotion of physical activity has been identified as the first of 22 priority areas. Although the causal role of exercise in improving psychological well-being is less clear, there is a consensus that exercise and depression are inversely related, and that adoption of exercise among sedentary individuals is associated with attenuation of affective distress.

Current Status of Exercise Participation

The U.S. Centers for Disease Control and Prevention (USCDCP) and the American College of Sports Medicine (ACSM; Pate et al., 1995) have recommended that every American adult should accumulate at least 30 minutes of moderate physical activity (e.g., brisk walking, gardening) over the course of most, and ideally all, days of the week. Despite increasing evidence of the benefits of physical activity, data from the Behavioral Risk Factor Surveillance System (BRFSS) showed that 58% of the United States population is *sedentary* (engaging in irregular or no leisure-time activity; USCDCP, 1993). Prevalence of sedentary lifestyle does not differ by sex; however, sedentary behavior is more prevalent among minority groups (64%) than non-Hispanic Whites (57%). Income and education appear to be inversely related to sedentary lifestyle. Of those earning less than $15,000 annually, 65% are inactive as compared to 48% of those whose earnings exceed $50,000. Of those with less than a high school education, 72% are sedentary as compared to 50% of college educated individuals (USCDCP, 1993).

Reviews of determinants of exercise adoption have concluded that demographic factors associated with sedentary lifestyle include being older, African American, female, poorly educated, overweight, or having a history of being physically inactive (Blair et al., 1993). More recent data from the 1991 and 1992 BRFSS reveal that among women, a sedentary lifestyle is reported most frequently by African Americans (68%) and least frequently by non-Hispanic Whites (56%). Among men, the prevalence of a sedentary lifestyle was highest for both African Americans (63%) and Hispanics (62%) and lowest for American Indians/Alaskan Natives (51%; USCDCP, 1994).

Both national samples and community studies of participants beyond adolescence and early adulthood reveal a decrease in participation in regular activity (Gartside, Khoury, & Glueck, 1984; Schoenborn, 1986). Limited data in older adults suggest that this decline continues through age 80 with progressively larger proportions of men and women reporting that they get no leisure-time physical activity (Caspersen & DiPietro, 1991; Caspersen, Merritt, Heath, & Yeager, 1990). Even among adults who take up exercise, 50% of men and women are likely to drop out within 6 months (Dishman, 1990; Sallis et al., 1986). The decline in activity with age is particularly disappointing, given the evidence suggesting that people who increase their activity during adulthood can reduce their risk for cardiovascular disease to the level of those who have been active for many years (Paffenbarger et al., 1993).

When type of activity is examined, there is a trend for women to report lower participation in vigorous activity compared with men (Hovell et al., 1989; Sallis et al., 1986; Sidney et al., 1991). In a community sample of California adults, Sallis and colleagues (1986) found that 5% of women adopted vigorous activity versus 11% of men, but 34% of women adopted moderate activity versus 26% of men. Traditionally, assessments of physical activity were developed for male samples, and this bias may account partially for the gender differences favoring greater vigorous activity in men (Young, King, Oka, & Haskell, in press). When light and moderate activities are considered in the determination of regular leisure-time physical activity levels, the gender difference diminishes or disappears. Besides sex differences related to intensity of exercise, women show a greater preference for aerobic dance and videotaped exercise programs than men (King, Taylor, Haskell, & DeBusk, 1990). If the intensity of the activity is standardized for declining cardiovascular fitness, the proportion of men reporting regular and intense activity increases around retirement and remains relatively stable through age 80 (Caspersen et al., 1990; Caspersen, Pollard, & Pratt, 1987). In contrast, the proportion of women reporting regular and intense activity continues to decline in older age groups. The USCDCP (1993) report that 64.9% of older women are sedentary versus 59.1% of older men. Hence, although participation in regular activity could improve cardiovascular status in older men and women, and perhaps reduce risk of osteoporosis in older women, older Americans are less likely to be active and have also been neglected in public health interventions to improve activity levels.

To conclude, although physical inactivity has been identified as a major risk factor for chronic disease, the adoption of an active lifestyle across all age groups remains a major challenge to health educators, health promotion experts, and health care professionals. The higher prevalence of inactivity among the economically disadvantaged, minorities, women, and older adults makes it clear that exercise promotion in these groups is a public health necessity that cannot be neglected.

Theoretical Models in Exercise Research

The exercise-adherence literature frequently has focused on providing descriptions of nonmodifiable factors such as gender, age, and educational level associated with increased attrition from exercise programs. Although an understanding of the epidemiology of exercise adherence is useful, psychological theory can guide the development of new interventions.

Theoretical models of exercise adoption and maintenance are helpful in order to investigate the usefulness of interventions. Researchers define their questions based upon their theoretical frame of reference (Dzewaltowski, 1994). In the past, many sport and exercise psychology researchers sought to identify an *exercise personality* (Feltz, 1992). Researchers examined profiles of athletes on standard personality profiles. These researchers generally lacked a theoretical rationale for their projects, and few conclusive results were drawn from these atheoretical approaches (Feltz, 1992). More recently, researchers have examined cognitive models in exercise research, which has yielded more consistent results. In this section, we will describe several potentially useful models of exercise adoption and adherence.

The Health Belief Model

The Health Belief Model was developed by Rosenstock (1966) and Becker and Maiman (1975). This model stipulates that the likelihood that an individual will engage in preventive health behaviors (such as exercise) depends upon the outcome of two assessments. The first assessment involves the individual's perception of the severity of the potential illness and his or her perceived susceptibility to that illness. In the second appraisal, the individual weighs the benefits (pros) against the costs (cons) related to taking action. If an individual believes the potential illness is serious and he or she is at risk, and the pros of taking action outweigh the cons, the individual is likely to adopt the target health behavior.

It is important to note that other factors such as demographic characteristics (e.g., age, ethnicity, gender), social psychological variables (e.g., social class, peer influence), and cues in the environment (e.g., media campaigns, physician counseling) can also influence these assessments. For example, a younger person may feel less vulnerable to the types of diseases linked to inactivity, such as cardiovascular disease (Blair et al., 1989), which tend to occur later in life. Interventions targeted to a younger audience should therefore focus on states to which there may already be a perceived vulnerability (such as body-image issues), or target other aspects of the health belief equation.

Theory of Reasoned Action

This theory developed by Ajzen and Fishbein (1980) rests upon the notion that people generally do those behaviors that they intend to do. Therefore, to predict whether individuals are going to exercise, one should ask what they intend to do. According to this model, intentions are the product of individuals' attitudes toward a particular behavior and their perceptions of what is normative regarding the behavior (subjective norm). The *subjective norm* is a product of beliefs about others' opinions and the individual's motivation to comply with others' opinions. Attitudes are determined by beliefs about the outcome of the behavior and the value placed on that outcome. For example, Susan, a nonexerciser, may believe that other people think she should exercise and she may wish to do what others want her to do. This results in a positive subjective norm for exercising. In addition, Susan may also believe that she will lose weight and feel less tired if she exercises regularly (*outcome beliefs*). Because Susan values these results highly, a positive attitude toward exercise is formed. The combination of this subjective norm and attitude should create a positive intention for Susan to exercise.

Ajzen and Fishbein (1980) observed that the theory of reasoned action was particularly useful when predicting behaviors that were entirely subject to volitional control. However, most behaviors involve a degree of practical constraint and are not entirely subject to volitional control. For example, the adoption of exercise requires opportunities, resources, and skills that many individuals currently lack.

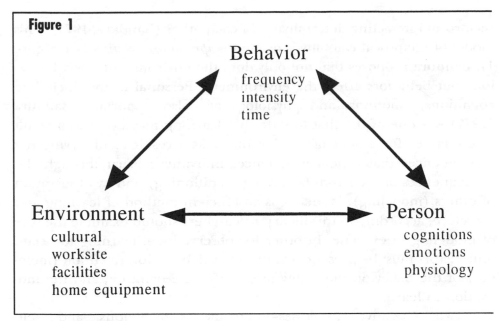

Figure 1

Behavior
frequency
intensity
time

Environment
cultural
worksite
facilities
home equipment

Person
cognitions
emotions
physiology

Reciprocal determinism.

Theory of Planned Behavior

Subsequent to the development of the theory of reasoned action, Ajzen (1985) argued that intention could not be the sole predictor of behavior in situations in which people's control over the behavior might be incomplete. The theory of planned behavior incorporates notions of the subjective norm and attitudes similar to the theory of reasoned action (Ajzen & Madden, 1986). However, in the theory of planned behavior, *perceived behavioral control,* that is people's perception of their ability to perform the behavior, will also affect behavioral outcomes. (The notion of perceived behavioral control in this model is similar to Bandura's construct of self-efficacy [Bandura, 1986], which is discussed in the following section.) The theory of planned behavior postulates that the intention to perform a behavior may not be strong—even when attitudes and subjective norms are positive—if people believe that they do not have the resources or opportunities to perform that behavior.

Social Cognitive Theory

Social cognitive theory is an integration of operant conditioning, social learning theory, and cognitive psychology. Social cognitive theory proposes that personal, behavioral, and environmental factors operate as reciprocal interacting determinants of each other (Bandura, 1977). This model of reciprocal causality is termed *reciprocal determinism* (see Figure 1). Bandura proposes that not only does the environment affect behaviors, but behaviors affect the environment. Personal factors including cognitions, emotions, and physiology are also important. Bandura (1977) was one of the first to state that learning may occur as a result of direct reinforcement of a behavior, or as a result of observing the consequences that others experience. Individuals learn through the consequences of their own behavior (conditioning) and by observation of others (modeling). Modeling is an efficient method of learning and therefore, according to this theory, researchers should examine the role of modeling in exercise. In order for observational learning to occur, four factors must be present: attention to the behavior, retention (memory) of the behavior, the ability to perform the behavior, and the motivation to learn.

Two cognitive processes—outcome expectations and self-efficacy—have been identified as important components in social cognitive theory. *Outcome expectations* are beliefs about the effects of a behavior. Individuals may expect improvement in health status, to receive social approval, or to experience self-satisfaction as an outcome of exercising (Dzewaltowski, 1994). Outcomes can be classified as immediate benefits, such as a lower stress level, or long-term benefits, such as improvements in body composition.

Self-efficacy is judgment of the ability to successfully perform a behavior (Bandura, 1977). People's perception that they can perform a behavior successfully increases the likelihood that they will engage in the behavior. Self-efficacy judgments have predicted behaviors in a number of studies (Annis & Davis, 1988; Bernier & Avard, 1986; Condiotte & Lichtenstein, 1981). Self-efficacy is behavior-specific. Therefore, self-efficacy for exercise is different from self-efficacy for smoking cessation or weight management. In looking across a range of behaviors, researchers have demonstrated that for each behavior there is a global level of self-efficacy with underlying situational factors. In smoking cessation, negative affect, social situations, and habit/addictive situations have been identified as situational factors (Velicer, DiClemente, Rossi, & Prochaska, 1990). In weight management, negative emotions, physical discomfort, social pressure, positive activities, and availability have been identified as situational factors (Clark, Abrams, Niaura, Eaton, & Rossi, 1991). A five-item self-efficacy measure for exercise includes negative affect, resisting relapse, and making time for exercise as situational factors (Marcus, Selby, Niaura, & Rossi, 1992).

Decision Theory

Decisional balance, which is based on the theoretical model of decision making developed by Janis and Mann (1977), is an individual's perception and evaluation of the relative costs (cons) and benefits (pros) associated with exercise participation. Several procedures have been developed to help individuals understand how they are making decisions about exercise. Clients generate responses both to short- and long-term consequences of making a behavioral change and of failing to make the behavioral change. This procedure can be used to better understand the benefits of and barriers to change and to help devise ways to avoid or cope with the negative consequences of behavior change. These procedures were first developed to help individuals attempting to change health-related behaviors such as smoking (Marlatt & Gordon, 1985; Velicer, DiClemente, Prochaska, & Brandenburg, 1985). Recently, these procedures have been adapted and applied to exercise adoption (Marcus, Rakowski, & Rossi, 1992) by using a decisional balance sheet, in which the individual writes down anticipated consequences of exercise participation in terms of gains and losses to self and others, and approval or disapproval from others and from the self. This procedure may promote an awareness of the benefits and costs of exercise participation (Hoyt & Janis, 1975; Wankel, 1984).

Transtheoretical Model

According to the transtheoretical model of behavior change (Prochaska & DiClemente, 1983), individuals progress through a series of stages of change: precontemplation, contemplation, preparation, action, and maintenance. *Precontemplators* do not exercise and do not intend to start in the next 6 months. *Contemplators* do not currently exercise but intend to start in the next 6 months. *Preparers* are exercising some but not regularly (3 or more times per week for 20 minutes or longer, or accumulating 30 or more minutes per day 5 or more days per week; ACSM, 1990; Pate et al., 1995). Individuals in the *action* stage exercise regularly but have been doing so for less than 6 months. Individuals in *maintenance* exercise regularly and have done so for 6 months or longer (Marcus, Rossi, Selby, Niaura, & Abrams, 1992). Movement across the stages is thought to be cyclic (see Figure 2), not linear, because many

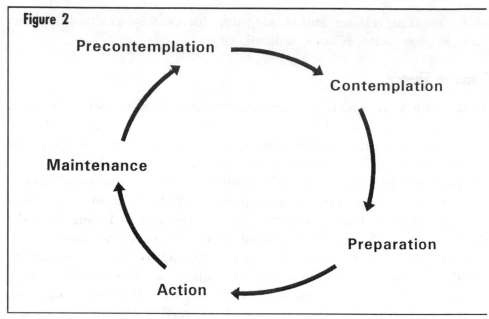

Figure 2

Precontemplation

Contemplation

Maintenance

Preparation

Action

Cyclic pattern of stages of change.

do not succeed in their efforts at establishing and maintaining lifestyle changes (Prochaska, DiClemente, & Norcross, 1992). Most intervention programs are designed for individuals in the action stage. However, most individuals are not in the action stage. Marcus and colleagues (Marcus, Rossi, et al., 1992), in a sample of 1,172 participants in a work-site health promotion project, classified 24.4% in *precontemplation*, 33.4% in *contemplation*, 9.5% in *preparation*, 10.6% in *action*, and 22.0% in *maintenance*. This pattern of distribution is similar to the distribution of stages of change for other behaviors. Research has demonstrated that when there is a mismatch between stage of change and intervention strategy, attrition is high. Therefore, matching treatment strategies to an individual's stage of change is one strategy to improve adherence and reduce attrition.

The stages of change document when people change, and the processes of change describe how people change (Prochaska, Velicer, DiClemente, & Fava, 1988). People use a range of strategies and techniques to change behaviors and these strategies are the *processes of change*. Use of the specific processes of change depends on the individual's stage of change. Processes are divided into two categories: cognitive and behavioral. The *cognitive processes* for exercise are consciousness raising, dramatic relief, environmental reevaluation, self-

Table 1

Exercise Processes of Change

Processes	Examples
Cognitive Processes	
Consciousness raising	I recall information people have personally given me on the benefits of exercise.
Dramatic relief	Warnings about health hazards of inactivity move me emotionally.
Environmental reevaluation	I feel I would be a better role model for others if I exercised regularly.
Self-reevaluation	I am considering the idea that regular exercise would make me a healthier, happier person to be around.
Social liberation	I find society changing in ways that make it easier for the exerciser.
Behavioral Processes	
Counterconditioning	Instead of remaining inactive, I engage in some physical activity.
Helping relationships	I have someone on whom I can depend when I am having problems with exercising.
Reinforcement management	I reward myself when I exercise.
Self-liberation	I tell myself I am able to keep exercising if I want to.
Stimulus control	I put things around my home to remind me of exercising.

Items From: Marcus, B. H., Rossi, J. S., Selby, V. C., Niaura, R. S., & Abrams, D. B. (1992). The stages and processes of exercise adoption and maintenance in a worksite sample. From *Health Psychology, 11*, pg. 389. Adapted with permission of the author and publisher.

reevaluation, and social liberation. The *behavioral processes* for exercise are counterconditioning, helping relationships, reinforcement management, self-liberation, and stimulus control. Use of the cognitive processes tends to peak in the preparation stage and use of the behavioral processes tends to peak in the action stage. The Processes of Change Questionnaire is a 40-item measure of these processes for exercise (Marcus, Rossi, et al., 1992). A sample item from each process is listed in Table 1.

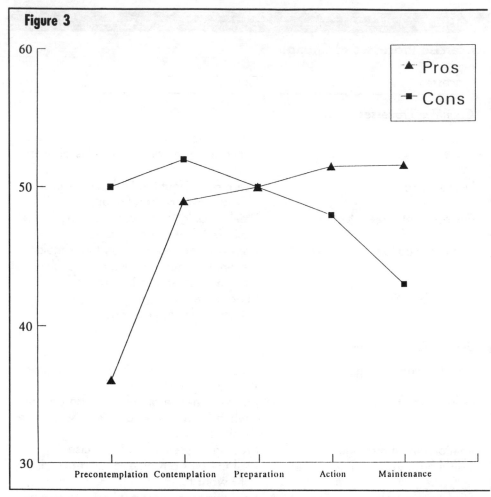

T-score means for the pros and cons scales by stage of exercise adoption. From Marcus, Rakowski, and Rossi, 1992. Reprinted with permission of the author and publisher.

Also related to stage-of-change is a cost–benefit analysis called *decisional balance,* which was discussed in the decision theory section. When people are considering a lifestyle change, they weigh the pros of that behavior against the cons. In a study of 12 problem behaviors, researchers found that usually in the precontemplation and contemplation stages, the cons are greater than the pros (Prochaska et al., 1994). Usually, the crossover occurs in the preparation stage, and then the pros are greater than the cons in the action and maintenance stages (Prochaska et al., 1994). (See Figure 3.) The 16-item Decisional Balance Measure for Exercise has 10 pros (e.g., "I would sleep more soundly if I exercised regularly.'') and 6 cons (e.g., "I would have less time for my family and friends if I exercised regularly.'') (see Figure 3) Marcus, Rakowski, & Rossi, 1992.

Self-efficacy, which was discussed in the social cognitive section, has been shown to be related to stage-of-change for exercise in both cross-sectional (Marcus & Owen, 1992; Marcus, Pinto, Simkin, Audrain, & Taylor, 1994; Marcus, Selby, Niaura, & Rossi, 1992) and longitudinal studies (Marcus, Eaton, Rossi, & Harlow, 1994). The relationship between stage-of-change and self-efficacy is positive and linear, with enhanced self-efficacy being associated with higher levels of readiness for change.

Relapse Prevention Model

The problem of relapse is an important challenge in health behaviors (Brownell, Marlatt, Lichtenstein, & Wilson, 1986). Relapse rates in exercise programs are high. Approximately 50% of exercise program participants drop out during the first 3 to 6 months (Dishman, 1982). In a community sample of 562 current exercisers, Sallis and colleagues (1990) found that 40% of the sample had experienced an exercise relapse (stopping exercise for at least 3 months) and 20% had experienced three or more relapses. The most frequent reason for relapse was injury, which was followed by work demands, lack of interest, lack of time, family demands, end of sport season, bad weather, and stress. Unfortunately, relapse is a problem for a range of behaviors including alcoholism, drug addiction, obesity, and smoking (Brownell et al., 1986). The goal of relapse prevention is to help individuals anticipate problems and cope effectively in high-risk situations. Researchers have been able to identify only a few factors that may contribute to relapse. Negative emotions, physiologic factors, limited coping skills, limited social support, low motivation, high-risk situations, and stress appear to all be factors in relapse (Brownell et al., 1986).

The principles of the relapse prevention model (see Figure 4) include identifying high-risk situations for relapse (e.g., change in season, change in work hours, end of organized team) and then identifying problem-solving solutions for these high-risk situations (e.g., "When it starts to snow, I'll shift from outdoor walks to walking in the mall;" "I'll find other times for my aerobic classes;" "When tennis season ends, I'll join a soccer club;" Dishman, 1991). When individuals do experience a *lapse* (a few days of not participating in their planned activity) they

Figure 4

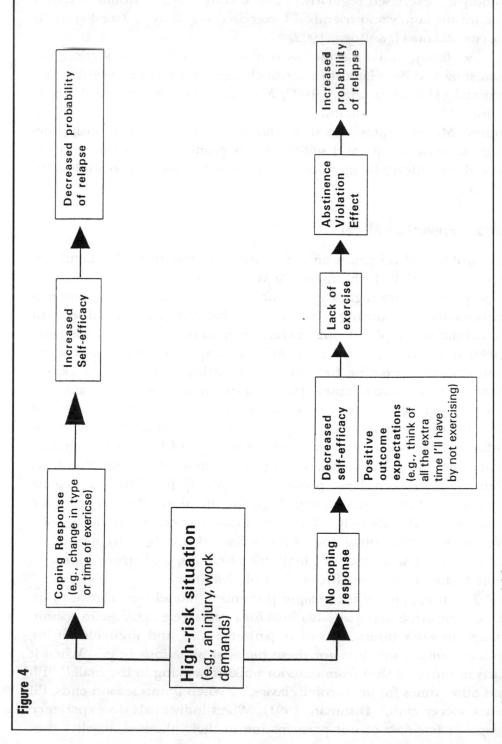

Relapse prevention model for exercise.

need to challenge the *abstinence violation effect* (AVE). The AVE applies to a range of behaviors, and simply stated, the AVE is the belief that once one has slipped, one is doomed. For dieters, it is the belief that one cookie terminates a diet. For ex-smokers, it is the belief that, following 6 months of abstinence, one cigarette makes them a smoker again. For exercisers, it is the belief that one missed exercise class means that they are no longer exercisers. In the obesity literature, Brownell (1989) hypothesizes that individuals may experience a lapse, a relapse, or a collapse. A lapse is a slip, a *relapse* is a string of lapses, and a *collapse* is when the person gives up and returns to past behaviors. Having individuals become aware of the AVE effect and teaching them about the differences between lapse, relapse, and collapse may help reduce recidivism. Clinically, we have found this model helpful, and during past winter storms, have used the terms *slip, slide,* and *fall* to help people remain aware of lapse, relapse, and collapse. In areas where total abstinence (or perfection) is not possible, such as in exercise, where at times individuals may not be capable of exercise due to medical problems, researchers have suggested that individuals have a planned lapse, in order to practice challenging the AVE. Our clinical experience and research findings (Marcus & Stanton, 1993), however, has not shown a planned lapse to be beneficial. Therefore, it is currently not known how to effectively prevent the AVE in exercise, and future research is warranted.

Interpretation

Recently, exercise researchers have used theoretical models to guide their investigations and this has been beneficial. However, there are still numerous questions to be addressed. For instance, most of the theoretical models that have been applied to exercise behavior were developed or first applied to other behaviors. How exercise may differ from other behaviors currently is unclear. Also, most of the research has used upper socioeconomic-status populations, and how these models apply to other demographic groups is unclear. Finally, research has only examined the application of each model to exercise, and has yet to compare the different models (King et al., 1992).

Many of the models reviewed contain common theoretical elements or share similar constructs with other models. The health belief model examines the individual's perception of his or her risks associated with a sedentary lifestyle and the perceived benefits of engaging in exercise. This appears similar to the comparisons made within social cognitive theory, which examines the interactions of social, exercise-related and personal factors like beliefs, emotions, and physiology. In decision theory, these comparisons can be reduced to a simpler two-factor structure comparing the benefits to the costs of exercising. The theory of planned behavior incorporates the individual's beliefs about exercise and confidence in his or her ability to exercise. The relapse prevention model focuses on cognitive processes that enhance (e.g., problem-solving strategies for high-risk situations) or prevent (e.g., the AVE) a long-term active lifestyle. The transtheoretical model of behavior change incorporates many components of the other models, including perceived benefits and costs, self-confidence, and strategies for change to a model of a series of stages of change. Multifactorial models may be superior to less complex models. However, research has yet to compare these different models (King et al., 1992) and therefore comparisons of the strengths and weaknesses across models is not yet possible. Additional research is needed to highlight differences between these models.

Intervention Applications

In the previous section we described some of the theoretical models in exercise research. In this section we describe some practical strategies for interventions based on some of these theories, particularly the transtheoretical or stages of change model.

One concept that has been popular for years in the psychotherapy literature is patient–treatment matching. This notion that treatments should be matched to the specific characteristics and needs of the given patient has also gained much popularity in the realms of smoking cessation and obesity treatment. Part of the reason why this concept has been slow to reach the exercise arena may be that lack of exercise only recently has been recognized as a problem in and of itself, worthy of treatment. After all, it was only recently (Fletcher et al., 1992) that the American Heart Association recognized physical inactivity as one of the top five causes of heart disease. Similarly, it was not until 1991 (King et al., 1992) that the National Heart, Lung, and Blood Institute held a major consensus conference on physical activity. Furthermore, it was in 1993 that the USCDCP and ACSM held their consensus conference on the health benefits of physical activity and the risks of physical inactivity

(Pate et al., 1995). When one looks at the large percentage of sedentary people in the population, the large number of health clubs and YMCA-type programs, and the high dropout rate from programmed exercise (Dishman, 1982), one might conclude that the time is right to consider patient–treatment matching for the promotion of physical activity.

The underlying theme of the transtheoretical model is that people are at different levels of readiness to change their behavior and thus different interventions using differing levels of different strategies and techniques are needed to bring about the desired change (see Prochaska, DiClemente, & Norcross). To illustrate the usefulness of this model for exercise behavior, we will describe a few different studies. The impetus for conducting these studies came from the lack of success in prior interventions. That is, prior community- and worksite-based interventions were not able to recruit and retain contemplator-type individuals in their programs.

The Imagine Action campaign was a community-wide program designed to increase physical activity behavior (Marcus, Banspach et al., 1992). Participants were 610 adults who enrolled through their worksites (53%) or in response to posted or mass-circulated announcements in the community. Potential participants received a description of the program with a brief letter explaining that if they were inactive or having difficulty staying active, this was a program designed for them. People who responded provided information about their activity level, name, address, gender, and birthdate. They also were told that they would receive a free t-shirt for enrolling. The participants had an average age of 42, and 77% were women. At baseline, 39% were in *contemplation*, 37% were in *preparation*, and 24% were in *action*.

A 6-week intervention consisting of stage-matched self-help materials, a resource manual, and weekly "fun walks" and "activity nights" was delivered. The content for the stage-matched manuals was based on key issues in the exercise adherence literature and was informed by the transtheoretical model, social cognitive theory, and decision theory. The manual for contemplators was called *What's In It For You*, because this is the critical question a contemplator must address. This manual included information on increasing lifestyle activity (e.g., taking the stairs instead of the elevator, parking the car at the end of the parking lot); considering the benefits (e.g., weight control) and barriers (e.g., takes too much time) of becoming more active; considering the social benefits of activity (e.g., meet people in a class, walk with significant other);

and learning how to reward oneself for increasing activity (e.g., buying self flowers as a reward for increasing from one to two walks per week).

The manual for those in *preparation* was called *Ready for Action* because this group had been participating in some activity, and the goal was to get these folks into action (daily accumulation of 30 minutes of moderate activity or 3 to 5 times per week of vigorous activity performed for at least 20 minutes each time). This manual focused on helping people to overcome the barriers and experience benefits of physical activity; setting short-term goals (e.g., walking for 10 minutes 2 times per week); setting longer-term goals (e.g., walking for 30 minutes 5 times per week); rewarding oneself for activity; applying time-management skills to fit activity into a busy schedule (e.g., going dancing with significant other or kids instead of going to a movie, riding exercise bicycle or walking on treadmill while watching the news or other television); and exploring details of developing a walking program.

The manual for those in *action* was called *Keeping It Going* because these individuals were performing activity at the goal level, but had been doing so only for a short period of time and thus were at great risk for lapsing or relapsing. The greatest risk for these folks was that they would slide back to *preparation* where they would only exercise occasionally. This manual focused on troubleshooting situations that might lead to lapse or relapse (e.g., illness, injury, boredom); goal setting; rewarding oneself (giving both internal rewards like praise, and external rewards like flowers); cross-training to prevent boredom (e.g., walk one day and bicycle the next); avoiding injury; and gaining social support (e.g., finding people to be active with or people supportive of one's active lifestyle). The resource manual described a wide variety of free and low-cost light, moderate, and vigorous physical activity options in the local community. The organized physical activity options included fun walks and free and appropriate classes at local facilities such as very low-impact aerobics and volleyball for people who had never played.

Following the intervention, 30% of those in *contemplation* at baseline and 61% of those in *preparation* at baseline progressed to *action*, and an additional 31% in *contemplation* progressed to *preparation*. Only 4% of those in *preparation* and 9% of those in *action* regressed. These findings demonstrate that a low-cost, relatively low-intensity intervention can produce significant improvement in stage of exercise adoption.

The study just described was not a controlled trial, and thus a randomized-design study was conducted to examine a similar question;

this study investigated the efficacy of a stage-matched physical activity intervention at the workplace (Marcus, Emmons, et al., 1994). In this second study, employees were randomized to a stage-matched self-help intervention or a standard-care self-help intervention. The interventions consisted of print materials delivered at baseline and 1 month.

At baseline, individuals in the stage-matched group received manuals specifically tailored to their stage of readiness for exercise. At 1 month, individuals received the manual matched to their stage plus the next manual in the series. The manual written for precontemplators was entitled *Do I Need This?* and focused on increasing awareness of the benefits of activity and encouraging participants to think about the barriers preventing them from being active. Specific suggestions for starting an exercise routine were not provided in this manual. The contemplator's manual, entitled *Try It You'll Like It,* included a discussion of the reasons to stay inactive versus the reasons to become more active, learning to reward oneself, and setting realistic goals. For those in *preparation, I'm On My Way* reviewed the benefits of activity, goal setting, and tips on safe and enjoyable activities, and addressed obstacles to regular activity. *Keep It Going* provided information for those in *action* on topics such as the benefits of regular activity, staying motivated, rewarding oneself, enhancing confidence about being active, and overcoming obstacles. For those in *maintenance, I Won't Stop Now* emphasized the benefits of regular activity, avoiding injuries, goal setting, varying activities, rewarding oneself, and planning ahead. Those individuals in the standard-care group received American Heart Association print materials (e.g., *Walking for a Healthy Heart, Swimming for a Healthy Heart*) because these are excellent and readily available and thus the best proxy of standard care. Comparison of the results from baseline to the 3-month follow-up revealed that more subjects in the stage-matched group demonstrated stage progression; in contrast, more subjects in the standard-care group displayed stage stability or stage regression.

A study that is currently underway addresses whether the stages-of-change model can be applied in a more comprehensive, yet low-cost manner. In this study, stages-of-change concepts are being used to develop a computerized "expert" system (Marcus, Bock, Rossi, & Redding, 1994). This system makes use of normative data (comparing an individual to an already established group norm) about stages of change, processes of change, self-efficacy, and decisional balance as well as subjects' actual responses to these various questionnaires. The goal is to provide tailored messages for the subject that give both comparisons to what other successful individuals have done and feedback on how the subject is doing at reaching his or her exercise goals. This is a randomized controlled trial in which individuals either receive the expert-system feedback along with stage-matched manuals or American Heart Association manuals. Two hundred individuals in the precontemplation, contemplation, and preparation stages are being recruited into this trial.

Summary of Studies

The studies reviewed indicate that using psychological models and theories enhances both the assessment and treatment process for individuals striving to start or continue participation in physical activity. Theoretically grounded and psychometrically sound assessment instruments seem critical to the development of effective treatment programs. Many opportunities remain for using the approaches just described for a variety of clinical and community populations.

Future Directions

In earlier sections of this chapter, we highlighted issues that merit further investigation. However, there are some specific challenges that confront the clinician working in the realm of exercise promotion.

The new CDC/ACSM recommendations (Pate et al., 1995) regarding accumulating moderate bouts of activity need to be used in programs for individuals, groups, worksites, and communities. Many of the barriers to the initiation and early adoption of physical activity may no longer be as potent now that individuals have a variety of ways to get their "doses" of exercise.

Physical activity opportunities and programs should be tailored to individuals' level of readiness to consider, prepare for, initiate, and maintain increases in physical activity. In particular, creative efforts to establish programs that appeal to the large (65%) sedentary and underactive segments of the population are needed. Additional tailoring of programs to meet the diverse needs of various racial, ethnic, and socioeconomic groups is also critical.

The developmental stages through which individuals progress during their lives have a great deal to do with their ability to succeed at lifelong practices of regular physical activity. Potentially important transitional periods that deserve special programs include adolescence, entry into college or the workforce, pregnancy and postpartum, menopause, and retirement.

Many people prefer to exercise on their own or with friends but not in a formal class-based program. However, these same people may need guidance and support from professional and or lay individuals to initiate and maintain an active lifestyle. Therefore, there seems to be a need for instruction in how to be physically active on one's own in one's own home or community. This approach may be particularly desirable for older adults, parents of young children, and individuals who have difficulty with transportation due to disabilities or finances or other difficulties. Worksite health promotion and educational programs can be successful. However, these programs could be enhanced by offering a variety of physical activities, maximizing convenience, permitting employees to exercise on company time or allowing flexible time schedules, and using incentives judiciously.

References

Ajzen, I. (1985). From intentions to actions: A theory of focus on these important subgroups. In J. Kuhl & J. Beckman (Eds.), *Action-control: From cognition to behavior* (pp. 11–39). Heidelberg: Springer.

Ajzen, I., & Fishbein, M. (1980). *Understanding attitudes and predicting social behavior.* Englewood Cliffs, NJ: Prentice-Hall.

Ajzen, I., & Madden, T. J. (1986). Prediction of goal-directed behavior: Attitudes, intentions, and perceived behavioral control. *Journal of Experimental Social Psychology, 22,* 453–474.

American College of Sports Medicine. (1990). Position statement on the recommended quantity and quality of exercise for developing and maintaining cardiorespiratory and muscular fitness in healthy adults. *Medicine and Science in Sports and Exercise, 22,* 265–274.

Annis, H. M., & Davis, C. S. (1988). Assessment of expectancies. In D. M. Donovan & G. A. Marlatt (Eds.), *Assessment of addictive behaviors* (pp. 84–111). New York: Guilford.

Bandura, A. (1977). Self–efficacy: Toward a unifying theory of behavior change. *Psychological Review, 84,* 191–215.

Bandura, A. (1986). *Social foundations of thought and action. A social cognitive theory.* Englewood Cliffs, NJ: Prentice Hall.

Becker, M. H., & Maiman, L. A. (1975). Sociobehavioral determinants of compliance with health care and medical care recommendations. *Medical Care, 13,* 10–24.

Berger, B. G., & Owen, D. R. (1992). Mood alteration with yoga and swimming: Aerobic exercise may not be necessary. *Perceptual and Motor Skills, 75,* 1331–1343.

Bernier, M., & Avard, J. (1986). Self–efficacy, outcome and attrition in a weight–reduction program. *Cognitive Therapy and Research, 10,* 319–338.

Bernstein, L., Henderson, B. E., Hanisch, R., Sullivan-Halley, J., & Ross, R. K. (1994).

Physical exercise and reduced risk of breast cancer in young women. *Journal of the National Cancer Institute, 86,* 1403–1408.

Blair, S. N., Jacobs, D. R., & Powell, K. E. (1985). Relationships between exercise or physical activity and other health behaviors. *Public Health Reports, 100,* 172–180.

Blair, S. N., Kohl, H.W., III, Pattenbarger, R. S., Jr., Clark, D. G., Cooper, K. II., & Gibbons, L. W. (1989). Physical fitness and all cause mortality: A prospective study of healthy men and women. *Journal of the American Medical Association, 262,* 2395–2401.

Blair, S. N., Powell, K. E., Bazzarre, T. L., Early, J. L., Epstein, L. II., Green, L. W., Harris, S. S., Haskell, W. L., King, A. C., Kaplan, J., Marcus, B., Paffenbarger, R. S., & Yeager, K. C. (1993). Physical inactivity, Workshop V. *Circulation, 88,* 1402–1405.

Bovens, A. M., Van Baak, M. A., Vrencken, J. G., Wijnen, J. A., Saris, W. H., & Verstappen, F. T. (1993). Physical activity, fitness, and selected risk factors for CHD in active men and women. *Medicine and Science in Sports and Exercise, 25,* 572–576.

Brownell, K. D. (1989). *The LEARN Program for Weight Control.* Dallas, TX: Brownell & Hager.

Brownell, K. D., Marlatt, G. A., Lichtenstein, E., & Wilson, G. T. (1986). Understanding and preventing relapse. *American Psychologist, 41,* 765–782.

Caspersen, C. J., & DiPietro, L. (1991). National estimates of physical activity among older adults (Abstract). *Medicine and Science in Sports and Exercise, 23* (Suppl), S106.

Caspersen, C. J., Merritt, R. K., Heath, G. W., & Yeager, K. K. (1990). Physical activity patterns of adults aged 60 years and older. *Medicine and Science in Sports and Exercise, 22* (Suppl), S79.

Caspersen, C. J., Pollard, R. A., & Pratt, S. O. (1987). Scoring physical activity data with special consideration for elderly populations. *Proceedings of the 1987 Public Health Conference on Records and Statistics: Data for an aging population.* (DHHS pub. no. PHS 88–1214; pp. 30–34). Washington, DC.

Centers for Disease Control and Prevention. (1993). Prevalence of sedentary lifestyle—Behavioral Risk Factor Surveillance System, United States, 1991. *Morbidity and Mortality Weekly Report, 42,* 576–579.

Clark, M. M., Abrams, D. B., Niaura, R. S., Eaton, C. A., & Rossi, J. S. (1991). Self-efficacy in weight management. *Journal of Consulting and Clinical Psychology, 59,* 739–744.

Condiotte, M. M., & Lichtenstein, E. (1981). Self-efficacy and relapse in smoking cessation programs. *Journal of Consulting and Clinical Psychology, 49,* 648–658.

Craighead, L. W., & Blum, M. D. (1989). Supervised exercise in behavioral treatment for moderate obesity. *Behavior Therapy, 20,* 49–59.

Desharnais, R., Bouillon, J., & Godin, G. (1986). Self-efficacy and outcome expectations as determinants of exercise adherence. *Psychological Reports, 59,* 1155–1159.

Dishman, R. K. (1982). Compliance/adherence in health-related exercise. *Health Psychology, 1,* 237–267.

Dishman, R. K. (1990). Determinants of participation in physical activity. In C. Bouchard, R. J. Shephard, T. Stephens, J. R. Sutton, & B. D. McPherson (Eds.), *Exercise, fitness and health* (75–102). Champaign, IL: Human Kinetics.

Dishman, R. K. (1991). Increasing and maintaining exercise and physical activity. *Behavior Therapy, 22,* 345–378.

Doyne, E. J., Ossip-Klein, D. J., Bowman, E. D., Osborn, K. M., McDougall-Wilson, I. B., & Neimeyer, R. A. (1987). Running versus weight lifting in the treatment of depression. *Journal of Consulting and Clinical Psychology, 55,* 748–754.

Dzewaltowski, D. A. (1994). Physical activity determinants: A social approach. *Medicine and Science in Sports and Exercise, 26,* 1395–1399.

Feltz, D. L. (1992). The nature of sport psychology. In T. S. Horn (Ed.), *Advances in sport psychology* (pp. 3–11). Champaign, IL: Human Kinetics.

Fiatarone, M. A., O'Neill, E. F., Ryan, N. D., Clements, K. M., Solares, G. R., Nelson, M. E., Roberts, S. B., Kehayias, J. J., Lipsitz, L. L., & Evans, W. J. (1994). Exercise training and nutritional supplementation for physical frailty in very elderly people. *New England Journal of Medicine, 330,* 1769–1775.

Fletcher, G. F., Blair, S. N., Blumenthal, J., Caspersen, C., Chaitman, B., Epstein, S., Falls, H., Froelicher, E. S., Froelicher, V. F., & Pina, I. L. (1992). Statement on exercise: Benefits and recommendations for physical activity programs for all Americans: A statement for health professionals by the Committee on Exercise and Cardiac Rehabilitation of the Council on Clinical Cardiology, American Heart Association. *Circulation, 86,* 340–344.

Frisch, R. E., Wyshak, G., Albright, N. L., Albright, T. E., Schiff, I., Jones, K. P., Witschi, J., Shian, E., Koff, E., & Marguglio, M. (1985). Lower prevalence of breast cancer and cancers of the reproductive system among former college athletes compared to non-athletes. *British Journal of Cancer, 52,* 885–891.

Gartside, P. S., Khoury, P., & Glueck, C. J. (1984). Determinants of high-density lipoprotein cholesterol in blacks and whites: The second National Health and Nutrition Examination Survey. *American Heart Journal, 108,* 641.

United States Department of Health and Human Services, Public Health Service. Author: *Healthy People 2000.* National Health Promotion and Disease Prevention Objectives. (1990). Washington, DC.

Helmrich, S. P., Ragland, D. R., Leung, R. W., & Paffenbarger, R. S. (1991). Physical activity and reduced occurrence of non-insulin-dependent diabetes mellitus. *New England Journal of Medicine, 325,* 147–152.

Hovell, M. F., Sallis, J. F., Hofstetter, C. R., Spry, V. M., Faucher, P., & Casperson, C. J. (1989). Identifying correlates of walking for exercise: An epidemiologic prerequisite for physical activity promotion. *Preventive Medicine, 18,* 856–866.

Hoyt, M. F., & Janis, I. L. (1975). Increasing adherence to a stressful decision via a motivational balance-sheet procedure: A field experiment. *Journal of Personality and Social Psychology, 31,* 833–839.

Hughes, J. R. (1984). Psychological effects of habitual aerobic exercise: A critical review. *Preventive Medicine, 13,* 66–78.

Iverson, D., Fielding, J., Crown, R., & Christenson, G. (1985). The promotion of physical activity in the United States population: The status of programs in medical, worksite, community, and school settings. *Public Health Reports, 100,* 212–224.

Janis, I. L., & Mann, L. (1977). *Decision making: A psychological analysis of conflict, choice and commitment.* New York: Free Press.

King, A. C., Blair, S. N., Bild, D. E., Dishman, R. K., Dubbert, P. M., Marcus, B. H., Oldridge, N. B., Paffenbarger, R. S., Powell, K. E., & Yeager, K. K. (1992). Determinants of physical activity and interventions in adults. *Medicine and Science in Sports and Exercise, 24,* S221–S236.

King, A. C., Frey-Hewitt, B., Dreon, D. M., & Wood, P. D. (1989). Diet vs. exercise in weight maintenance: The effects of minimal intervention strategies on long-term outcomes in men. *Archives of Internal Medicine, 149,* 2741–2746.

King, A. C., Haskell, W. L., Taylor, C. B., Kraemer, H. C., & DeBusk, R. F. (1991). Group- vs. home-based exercise training in healthy older men and women. *Journal of the American Medical Association, 266,* 1535–1542.

King, A. C., Taylor, C. B., & Haskell, W. L. (1993). Effects of differing intensities and formats of 12 months of exercise training on physical outcomes in older adults. *Health Psychology, 12,* 292–300.

King, A. C., Taylor, C. B., Haskell, W. L., & DeBusk, R. F. (1990). Identifying strategies for increasing employee physical activity levels: Findings from the Stanford/Lock-heed exercise survey. *Health Education Quarterly, 17,* 269–285.

Kohl, H. W., LaPorte, R. E., & Blair, S. N. (1988). Physical activity and cancer. *Sports Medicine, 6,* 222–237.

LaFontaine, T. P., DiLorenzo, T. M., Frensch, P. A., Stucky–Ropp, R. C., Bargman, E. P., & McDonald, D. G. (1992). Aerobic exercise and mood. A brief review, 1985–1990. *Sports Medicine, 13,* 160–170.

Lakka, T. A., Venalaninen, J. H., Rauramaa, R., Salonen, R., Tuomilehto, J., & Salonen, J. (1994). Relation of leisure-time physical activity and cardiorespiratory fitness to the risk of acute myocardial infarction in men. *New England Journal of Medicine, 330,* 1549–1554.

Lennox, S. S., Bedell, J. R., & Stone, A. A. (1990). The effect of exercise upon normal mood. *Journal of Psychosomatic Research, 34,* 629–636.

Marcus, B. H., Banspach, S. W., Lefebvre, R. C., Rossi, J. S., Carleton, R. A., & Abrams, D. A. (1992). Using the change model to increase the adoption of physical activity among community participants. *American Journal of Health Promotion, 6,* 424–429.

Marcus, B. H., Bock, B. C., Rossi, J. S., & Redding, C. A. (1994). *Development and evaluation of an exercise expert system for cardiovascular risk reduction.* American Heart Association, Rhode Island Affiliate.

Marcus, B. H., Eaton, C. A., Rossi, J. S., & Harlow, L. L. (1994). Self-efficacy, decision making and stages of change: An integrative model of physical exercise. *Journal of Applied Social Psychology, 24,* 489–508.

Marcus, B. H., Emmons, K. M., Simkin, L. R., Taylor, E. R., Linnan, L., Rossi, J. S., & Abrams, D. B. (1994). Comparison of stage-matched versus standard care physical activity interventions at the workplace. *Annals of Behavioral Medicine, 16,* S035.

Marcus, B. H., & Owen, N. (1992). Motivational readiness, self-efficacy and decision-making for exercise. *Journal of Applied Social Psychology, 22,* 3–16.

Marcus, B. H., Pinto, B. M., Simkin, L. R., Audrain, J. E., & Taylor, E. R. (1994). Application of theoretical models to exercise behavior among employed women. *American Journal of Health Promotion, 9,* 49–55.

Marcus, B. H., Rakowski, W., & Rossi, J. S. (1992). Assessing motivational readiness and decision-making for exercise. *Health Psychology, 11,* 257–261.

Marcus, B. H., Rossi, J. S., Selby, V. C., Niaura, R. S., & Abrams, D. B. (1992). The stages and processes of exercise adoption and maintenance in a worksite sample. *Health Psychology, 11,* 386–395.

Marcus, B. H., Selby, V. C., Niaura, R. S., & Rossi, J. S. (1992). Self-efficacy and the stages of exercise behavior change. *Research Quarterly for Exercise and Sport, 63,* 60–66.

Marcus, B. H., & Stanton, A. L. (1993). Evaluation of relapse prevention and reinforce-ment interventions to promote exercise adherence in sedentary females. *Research Quarterly for Exercise and Sport, 64,* 447–452.

Marcus, R., Drinkwater, B., Dalsky, G., Dufek, J., Raab, D., Slemenda, C., & Snow-Harter, C. (1992). Osteoporosis and exercise in women. *Medicine and Science in Sports and Exercise, 24,* S301–307.

Marlatt, G. A., & Gordon, J. R. (1985). *Relapse prevention: Maintenance strategies in ad-dictive behavior change.* New York: Guilford.

Morey, M. C., Cowper, P. A., Feussner, J. R., DiPasquale, R. C., Crowley, G. M., Kitzman,

D. W., & Sullivan, R. J. (1989). Evaluation of a supervised exercise program in a geriatric population. *Journal of the American Geriatric Society, 37,* 348–354.

Moses, J., Steptoe, A., Mathews, A., & Edwards, S. (1989). The effects of exercise training on mental well-being in the normal population: A controlled trial. *Journal of Psychosomatic Research, 33,* 47–61.

Ossip-Klein, D. J., Doyne, E. J., Bowman, E. D., Osborn, K. M., McDougall-Wilson, J. B., & Neimeyer, R. A. (1989). Effects of running or weight lifting on self-concept in clinically depressed women. *Journal of Consulting and Clinical Psychology, 57,* 158–161.

Paffenbarger, R. S., Hyde, R. T., Wing, A. L., Lee, I. M., Jung, D. L., & Kambert, J. B. (1993). The association of changes in physical-activity level and other lifestyle characteristics with mortality among men. *New England Journal of Medicine, 328,* 538–545.

Pappas, G. P., Golin, S., & Meyer, D. L. (1990). Reducing symptoms of depression with exercise. *Psychosomatics, 31,* 112–113.

Pate, R. R., Pratt, M., Blair, S. N., Haskell, W. L., Macera, C. A., Bouchard, C., Buchner, D., Caspersen, C. J., Ettinger, W., Heath, G. W., King, A. C., Kriska, A., Leon, A. S., Marcus, B. H., Morris, J., Paffenbarger, R. S., Patrick, K., Pollock, M. L., Rippe, J. M., Sallis, J., & Wilmore, J. H. (1995). Physical activity and public health: A recommendation from the Centers for Disease Control and Prevention and the American College of Sports Medicine. *Journal of the American Medical Association, 273,* 402–407.

Pinto, B. M., & Marcus, B. H. (1994). Physical activity, exercise and cancer in women. *Medicine, Exercise, Nutrition and Health, 3,* 102–111.

Posner, J. D., Gorman, K. M., Gitlin, L. N., Sands, L. P., Kleban, M., Windsor, L., & Shaw, C. (1990). Effects of exercise training in the elderly on the occurrence and time to onset of cardiovascular diagnoses. *Journal of the American Geriatrics Society, 38,* 205–210.

Prochaska, J. O., & DiClemente, C. C. (1983). Stages and processes of self change of smoking: Toward an integrative model. *Journal of Consulting and Clinical Psychology, 51,* 390–395.

Prochaska, J. O., DiClemente, C. C., & Norcross, J. C. (1992). In search of how people change. *American Psychologist, 47,* 1102–1114.

Prochaska, J. O., Velicer, W. F., DiClemente, C. C., & Fava, J. (1988). Measuring processes of change: Applications to the cessation of smoking. *Journal of Consulting and Clinical Psychology, 56,* 520–528.

Prochaska, J. O., Velicer, W. F., Rossi, J. S., Goldstein, M. G., Marcus, B. H., Rakowski, W., Fiore, C., Harlow, L. L., Redding, C. A., Rosenbloom, D., & Rossi, S. R. (1994). Stages of change and decisional balance for twelve problem behaviors. *Health Psychology, 13,* 39–46.

Raglin, J. S. (1990). Exercise and mental health: Beneficial and detrimental effects. *Sports Medicine, 9,* 323–329.

Rosenstock, I. M. (1966). Historical origins of the health belief model. *Health Education Monographs, 2,* 328–335.

Sallis, J. F., Haskell, W. L., Fortmann, S. P., Vranizan, K. M., Taylor, C. B., & Solomon, D. S. (1986). Predictors of adoption and maintenance of physical activity in a community sample. *Preventive Medicine, 15,* 331–341.

Sallis, J. F., Hovell, M. F., Hofstetter, C. R., Elder, J. P., Faucher, P., Spry, V. M., Barrington, E., & Hackley, M. (1990). Lifetime history of relapse from exercise. *Addictive Behaviors, 15,* 573–579.

Sallis, J. F., Hovell, M. F., Hofstetter, C. R., Elder, J. P., Hackley, M., Caspersen, C. J., &

Powell, K. E. (1990). Distance between homes and exercise facilities related to frequency of exercise among San Diego residents. *Public Health Reports, 105,* 179–180.

Schoenborn, C. A. (1986). Health habits of U.S. adults: The "Alameda 7" revisited. *Public Health Reports, 101,* 571–580.

Sidney, S., Jacobs, D. R., Haskell, W. L., Armstrong, M. A., Dimicco, A., Oberman, A., Savage, P. J., Slattery, M. L., Sternfeld, B., & Van Horn, L. (1991). Comparison of two methods of assessing physical activity in the Coronary Artery Risk Development in Young Adults (CARDIA) Study. *American Journal of Epidemiology, 133,* 1231–1245.

United States Centers for Disease Control and Prevention. (1993). Prevalence of sedentary lifestyle—behavioral risk factor surveillance system, United States, 1991. *Morbidity and Mortality Weekly Report, 42,* 576–579.

United States Centers for Disease Control and Prevention. (1994). Prevalence of selected risk factors for chronic disease by education level in racial/ethnic population—United States, 1991–1992. *Morbidity and Mortality Weekly Report, 43,* 894–889.

United States Centers for Disease Control and Prevention and American College of Sports Medicine. (1993). Summary statement: Workshop on physical activity and public health. *Sports Medicine Bulletin, 28,* 7.

Velicer, W. F., DiClemente, C. C., Prochaska, J., & Brandenburg, N. (1985). A decisional balance measure for assessing and predicting smoking status. *Journal of Personality and Social Psychology, 48,* 1279–1289.

Velicer, W. F., DiClemente, C. C., Rossi, J. S., & Prochaska, J. O. (1990). Relapse situations and self-efficacy: An integrative model. *Addictive Behaviors, 15,* 271–283.

Wankel, L. M. (1984). Decision-making and social support strategies for increasing exercise involvement. *Journal of Cardiac Rehabilitation, 4,* 124–135.

Young, D. R., King, A. C., Oka, R. K., & Haskell, W. L. (in press). Patterns of physical activity in older men and women: Are women really less active than men? *Medicine, Exercise, Nutrition, & Health.*

Guidelines for Clinical Applications of Exercise Therapy for Mental Health

Wes Sime

Case #1

Sheila is a 30-year-old nurse in a small-town hospital in a cold-weather region. She is the mother of five children under the age of 8, and she is the primary source of income in a family with financial problems. Overwhelmed by job, parenting, strained marital relations, and impending bankruptcy, she is definitely stressed out and depressed on occasion. Simply stated, Sheila feels she has no time or opportunity for exercise even though she knows it would be beneficial for her. Sheila does not have access to a health club or community exercise facility, and she cannot afford home exercise equipment. She does not feel safe walking to or from work.

Case #2

Abigail is a 40-year-old single woman who works an evening shift at a radio station. She has difficulty getting to sleep before 5 a.m. and usually sleeps until 2 p.m. the next afternoon. She is 60 lbs. overweight, which she blames on the psychotropic medication she is taking. She is very uncomfortable in crowds; she fears that bad things will happen and she feels "down" much of the time. Medication and counseling serve to keep her functional. She has no social life and prefers isolation in her work. She is a "nutrition junkie" (health foods and vitamins) but lapses into junk food when depressed, which causes guilt feelings. She likes yoga but hates any form of aerobic exercise. She has participated in three walk and talk therapy sessions, but can't motivate herself to walk or do yoga between therapy sessions.

Case #3

John is a 28-year-old single man recovering from drug and alcohol abuse. He is intelligent and very well educated. John is taking medication for anxiety and depression in addition to undergoing counseling and biofeedback for coping with social stress. Recently he had a *manic attack* (an unrestrained bout of euphoria) that nearly forced him to be hospitalized. John enjoys exercise, especially commuting by bicycle. His current avocation is turning an abandoned railroad track into a bicycle trail. He fluctuates between periods of excitement (mania) and lows (depression), the latter of which is relieved quite well by exercise. However, John has great difficulty starting to exercise when he is depressed.

Case #4

Richard is a 68-year-old retired man who lives with his wife in a high-rise apartment. He is extremely anxious, sometimes depressed, and routinely has difficulty making decisions. Richard is not willing to take medication and is very resistant to psychotherapy. He has hearing loss in one ear and has an old foot injury that occurred when he dropped a dumbbell on his foot while trying to exercise. He is self-conscious in social situations; he is very dependent on his wife and, because he did try to exercise in the past when the foot injury occurred, currently does not value exercise. Ironically, his wife has been exercising regularly for the treatment of hypertension. Richard has a good location for exercise (indoors and outdoors), plenty of time to do the exercise, and the social support of his wife. However, he cannot decide whether to engage in exercise and/or psychotherapy.

Everyone has heard or read about the psychological benefits of exercise. Those who do exercise regularly enthusiastically report that they feel better and show evidence of improved mental health status. Some people who are deprived of exercise due to injury or workload experience psychological problems much like the withdrawal from a drug. There is scientific evidence showing that exercise is effective both in the treatment and prevention of various psychological disorders among clients similar to those described in the preceding examples (Folkins & Sime, 1981; Petruzzello, Landers, & Salazar, 1993). If all of this is true, then why should these four clients have such a difficult time using exercise effectively for improvement in psychological function?

These case descriptions are not fictitious examples. They are fairly typical cases involving difficult clients in situations in which exercise is a logical adjunctive treatment. These circumstances, and perhaps the personalities of the clients, however, are not conducive to an easy course of therapy with either exercise or psychotherapy.

There are many physicians and mental health professionals who routinely recommend exercise for their patients (Lehofer, Klebel, Gersdorf, & Zapatoczke, 1992; Rooney, 1993). Unfortunately, if a therapist or a physician was to prescribe exercise for these four patients without providing either supervision or proper guidance, it would likely have either no impact or be counterproductive (e.g., upon failure to achieve success in an exercise prescription, the client may feel more guilt, remorse, and a depressing sense of worthlessness than had been previously experienced). Therefore, it is critical for the therapist to understand the scientific and therapeutic basis for exercise and to approach the prescription process with knowledge derived from the success and failures of others as described herein. Furthermore, it should be noted that among the four clinical cases, exercise therapy may be contraindicated in at least one instance.

The purpose of this chapter is to provide guidelines for the clinical application of exercise therapy for mental health. The chapter will begin with a discussion of what exercise therapy is and how it has been used effectively. Theory and research explaining the relationship between exercise and mental health will be presented. Specific information indicating for whom exercise therapy is effective will be described. Finally, the chapter will conclude with practical guidelines for clinical application of exercise therapy.

What is Exercise Therapy, and How Has It Been Used Effectively?

Providing a definition for exercise therapy requires a separation of the concepts of *exercise* and *therapy*. Therapy involves a set of procedures aimed at facilitating return to normal functioning in a patient or client who has experienced some form of injury, temporary disorder, or permanent disability. Exercise consists of either passive or active muscle exertion involving small or large areas of body muscle mass sometimes taxing either or both anaerobic and aerobic metabolism systems. Exercise may be purely functional in the form of daily activities of living (DAL) such as walking, lifting, pushing, or climbing stairs. It may also include a wide variety of enjoyable, play-type, recreational or leisure activities in which the inherent satisfaction of an activity may be sufficient to maintain the behavior indefinitely. For example, such activities as hiking, biking, and cross-country skiing may create the opportunity to enjoy scenic vistas while enduring the physical challenge of both the exertion and the weather conditions, which have been shown to develop psychological hardiness (Dienstbier, LaGuardia, & Wilcox, 1987). To isolate the exclusive psychological benefits of exercise, it is necessary to first review the parameters of treatment success found in clinical applications that include some form of exercise as therapy.

Clinical Applications of Exercise as Therapy

Exercise therapy has a broad variety of treatment applications. It has become a common practice in such rehabilitation settings as cardiac, respiratory, occupational, recreational, and stroke therapy. In cardiac rehabilitation, exercise prescriptions are intended to stimulate improvement in cardiopulmonary function, and the physiological benefits therein are well established (Froelicher, 1990). However, it is the psychological benefits of exercise with cardiac patients that piques our interest here, especially because depression has been shown to be a predictor of reinfarction in this population (Denollet, 1993). Furthermore, there is evidence showing that exercise in cardiac rehabilitation has potential to decrease anger and hostility (Tennant et al., 1994); depression (Herrmann, Buss, Buecker, Gonska, & Kreuzer, 1994); and anxiety/emotional disturbances (Kugler, Seelbach, & Kruskemper, 1994). Therefore, it seems that exercise therapy in cardiac rehabilitation is beneficial through psychological as well as physiological mechanisms. That does not mean, however, that exercise should be prescribed as a substitute for a psychological evaluation and psychotherapy as needed in a prudent and conservative treatment plan.

Exercise therapy also is an essential element in physical therapy for the purpose of regaining strength, range of motion, and endurance following injury, burn, stroke, or some other form of chronic disability (e.g., arthritis, diabetes, respiratory disorders; Sluijs, Kok, & van der Zee, 1993). The essential element in all of these exercise applications is that the patient–client has a certain level of dysfunction or disability that has been shown by clinical research to progress toward normal functioning over an extended period by gradually increasing the exertional challenge or physical demand of the patient.

How Exercise Therapy Is Different From Other Therapies: Active Versus Passive and Potency Versus Risk

It should be noted that exercise therapy is distinctly different from other forms of rehabilitation in which the active ingredient is an external agent such as a drug, a form of radiation therapy, or palliative physical therapy interventions including heat, massage, and ultrasound. These are passive interventions in which the client is merely a recipient in the process. Treatment applications using exercise require the participant to be quite active in the process of therapy, as evidenced by effort, strain, pain, and increased metabolism. To follow the exercise prescription, the client must (a) overcome inertia to start motion; (b) make a choice of activity including location, time, etc.; and (c) continue what some describe to be the effortful, sometimes painful process of movement.

In the analysis of exercise therapy for mental health applications it is important to consider not only the active-versus-passive dimensions but also the potency-versus-risk dimensions. The active process of exercise therapy has the potential to be quite potent therapeutically with the possibility of some notable risk to the client depending upon the intensity and type of exercise chosen (aerobic, anaerobic, or leisure). Other treatments, notably drug treatments, probably have greater po-

Figure 1

	Passive Therapy Low Demands	Active Therapy High Demands
High Risk of Side Effects and Quick Acting, Potent	Drug Therapy Electroconvulsive Therapy	Exercise Therapy (Aerobic/Anaerobic)
Low Risk of Side Effects and Slow Acting, Less Potent	Group Therapy Relaxation Therapy	Exercise Therapy (Walking, Recreation) Psychotherapy Recreational Therapy

Exercise and Other Therapies Categorized According to Active Versus Passive Roles and High Versus Low Potency and Risk.

tency as well as greater risk of side effects. Figure 1 depicts exercise and parallel forms of therapy along two descriptive dimensions—active or passive and high or low risk and potency.

It should be noted that all of these types of therapy share a similar problem with adherence, compliance, and recidivism. Although exercise programs in healthy and clinical populations show 50% losses after 6 months (Dishman, 1991), patient compliance with other psychological treatment (psychotherapy and drug therapy) can be equally compromised by client resistance to therapy or by the side effects of drug therapy. Even exercise prescriptions given in physical therapy for rehabilitation of injury are poorly adhered to (Sluijs et al., 1993). By following proper guidelines for clinical applications, it is possible to improve upon the recidivism rate to achieve the desired psychological benefits. However, before outlining specific guidelines for setting up an exercise therapy program, it is important to present both the epidemiological and clinical literature supporting the association between exercise and mental health in prevention as well as treatment applications.

Theory and Research

Large Scale Epidemiological Studies

Numerous studies on large populations have shown a significant association between exercise and several psychological measures of mental health. In a psychosocial rehabilitation setting, a series of studies using intensive interview techniques determined that level of fitness was inversely related to depression (Pelham, Campagna, Ritvo, & Birnie, 1993). In several large-scale studies of older adults who had successfully completed an organized exercise program, the degree to which participants maintained a continuous program of exercise at follow-up was related to the level of anxiety reduction achieved (Emery, Hauck, & Blumenthal, 1992; Ruuskanen & Parkatti, 1994). Similar studies conducted in a field setting (community) found that level of exercise was negatively related to self-reports of depression in a noninstitutionalized population of healthy middle-aged adults (Rajala, Uusimaki, Keinanen-Kiukaanniemi, & Kivela, 1994; Weyerer, 1992). By contrast, in a cross-sectional study of 147 adolescents, level of exercise was related to anxiety, depression, hostility, and stress; however, in a follow-up experimental study there was no difference between high and low intensity of exercise effecting change in these variables (Norris, Carroll, & Cochrane, 1992).

In the larger and longer epidemiological studies, there are two remarkable examples of the relationship between exercise and psychological variables. In the Alameda County study (Camacho, Roberts, Lazarus, Kaplan, & Cohen, 1991), which monitored inhabitants from 1965–1983, there was a greater risk of developing problems with depression at a later date among those individuals who had been less active at baseline. In a study of Harvard University alumni, the incidence of physician-diagnosed depression rates was lower among the more physically active, but activity level did not predict rate of suicide as well as the level of depression in this population did (Paffenbarger, Lee, & Leung, 1994). It seems clear that physically active populations are also psychologically more stable and perhaps healthier than those who are not active. Obviously, before drawing conclusions about this issue, however, it is necessary to examine the experimental studies on clinical populations to assess the cause and effect relationship.

Experimental Studies Using Exercise as Clinical Therapy

Early studies using clinical populations demonstrated substantial benefits for aerobic exercise in comparison with other psychological interventions (Greist et al., 1979; Klein et al., 1985). Similar support is shown by a long series of studies in Norway by Martinsen (1993, 1994), whose institutionalized patients were very satisfied with exercise in addition to having shown improvements in mood and affect. In another study with psychiatric patients randomized into aerobic and nonaerobic groups, running was more effective than other less intense exercise in reducing depression (Bosscher, 1993). In a younger population of institutionalized patients (adolescents), the level of depression was decreased significantly by just three sessions per week of exercise (Brown, Welsh, Labbe, Gitulli, & Kulkarni, 1992). Others have found that the combination of exercise and talk therapy was more effective than an equivalent experience in cognitive therapy alone (i.e., the exercise was determined to be an essential element in the improvement of psychological functioning; McNeil, LeBlanc, & Joyner, 1991; Sime, 1987).

In other clinical studies featuring highly anxious patients, exercise treatment has been shown to reduce both anxiety and depression significantly more than a placebo treatment (Steptoe, Kearsley, & Walters, 1993). Others have demonstrated similar results, notably a reduction of anxiety in nonclinical populations (Brown, Morgan, & Raglin, 1993). In general, the psychiatric community has come to view exercise as a valuable adjunct to mental health therapy and has advocated its use across many psychological diagnoses, but in particular for depression (Lehofer et al., 1992). A number of review articles also support the effectiveness of exercise as a part of a comprehensive treatment program although there is some criticism of experimental design and other factors such as controlling for expectancy, especially when viewed by meta-analyses (Byrne & Byrne, 1993; Hinkle, 1992; North, McCullaugh, & Tran, 1990; Petruzzello, Landers, Hatfield, Kubitz, & Salazar, 1991; Rabins, 1992). On the other hand, it should be noted that not all of the literature is supportive of exercise therapy, as demonstrated in the following section.

Studies Not Supporting the Role of Exercise in Mental Health

One study evaluating the comparative benefits of exercise and stress management in the work site revealed no significant reductions in anxiety after 10 weeks and at 6-month follow-up in spite of physiological changes in fitness levels (Gronningsaeter, Hyten, Skauli, & Christensen, 1992). In a correlational study of 330 unemployed migrants from East Germany, it was hypothesized that exercise would serve a stress-buffering role, thus reducing levels of dispositional anxiety (Fuchs & Hahn, 1992). In this study, trait anxiety levels were related to stress–illness measures, but the level of exercise was not found to be associated with either anxiety or illness. Another cross-sectional study focused on long-term habitual exercisers compared to those who had recently embarked upon an exercise program and those who were sedentary (Dua & Hargreaves, 1992). The results showed that long-term exercisers reported less overall stress and more positive affect than the other two groups; however, they did not show lower levels of negative affect or depression. Another study showed that exercise was not effective, after 14 months of training on an elderly population, in producing a significant improvement in cognitive function (Hill, Storandt, & Malley, 1993).

It is important to note that among these studies reporting negative results on the effects of the exercise intervention, there are similar problems with design and experimental controls. Dishman (1991) has concluded that adherence is usually poor in these exercise studies and that many of the earlier studies were not well designed. Therefore, caution must be used in drawing conclusions either positively or negatively from the accumulated data that are available. Clearly, however, there appears to be more potential benefit than risk associated with exercise therapy in these populations.

Given the fact that there appears to be ample evidence supporting the use of exercise for psychological benefit, the next step is for the therapist and the client to examine what possible mechanisms account for these benefits, thus addressing the logical question, "why does it work?" Following is a review of the literature linking exercise to mental health.

Theories of Physiological Mechanisms

There are several previously published reviews and books that have documented substantial evidence suggesting possible physiological mechanisms (Johnsgaard, 1989; Leith & Taylor, 1990; Seraganian, 1993) linking exercise to mental health. These mechanisms include thermogenic effects, endorphin release, and changes in several neurotransmitters and/or receptors in the autonomic nervous system.

The Thermogenic Theory

It is of interest to note that exercise has been shown to increase heat tolerance and cold tolerance thereby having an influence on emotional stability (Dienstbier et al., 1987). However, the specific thermogenic hypothesis presented here was originated years ago by researchers who surmised that the elevation in core temperature during and after moderate to intense exercise was related to simultaneous decreases in muscle tension (deVries, Beckman, Huber, & Dieckmeir, 1968). This theory is supported by the fact that the physiological process of modulating core temperature is known to influence emotions substantially (Koltyn & Morgan, 1993). It has been suggested that a reduction in gamma motor activity is a key physiological mechanism accounting for the reductions in muscle tension and state anxiety that occur following exercise and passive heating (Morgan, 1988). A review of other recent studies indicates that temperature may be related to changes in brainwave laterality, which links exercise to mental health (Petruzzello et al., 1993). Although temperature accounts for a small percentage of variance in anxiety and for the changes in EEG laterality, the differences in anxiety levels across temperature levels are not large. Though the thermogenic hypothesis appears to be related to a reduction in anxiety, there is no data available regarding effects on depression and there is no explanation for why the temperature change during exercise makes a difference.

The Endorphin "Exercise High" Theory

The other more common theory regarding exercise and mental health involves endorphins. Lobstein and Rasmussen (1991) found that endurance training changed resting plasma beta-endorphins and improved nonclinical depression in healthy middle-aged men. Some have argued that the endorphin response is so small and elusive in the body cells, that a placebo effect is a better explanation. However, Daniels, Martin, and Carter (1992) used naltrexone, the opiate receptor antagonist, and a placebo in a randomized double-blind crossover design to study the effects of exercise. Following high-intensity exercise, the subjects showed reduced levels of depression. When they were administered the drug naltrexone before the exercise, however, there was no change in level of depression, thus supporting the endorphin theory. Others have shown clearly that exercise is associated with an increase the endorphin levels and with a reduction in the stress reactivity effects (McCubbin, Cheung, Montgomery, Bulbulian, & Wilson, 1992) and in reduced sensitivity to pain (Haier, Quaid, & Mills, 1981). Although this theory is quite an interesting explanation for exercise beneficence, there remains considerable controversy on the issue.

The Monoamine Neurotransmitter Theory

A review of research suggests that deficiencies in norepinephrine and serotonin systems are associated with onset of depression (Johnsgaard, 1989). Several carefully controlled animal studies have elucidated the unique biochemical outcome of exercise that links it to depression and mood state. In the initial phase of these studies (Dey, 1994; Dey, Singh, & Dey, 1992), it was determined that adaptive changes in serotonin receptor functioning appears to play an important role in mediating the action of various antidepressant medications. In effect, exercise serves to increase the sensitivity of serotonin receptors, making these naturally produced chemicals more potent in the process of reducing depression. Additional evidence supporting this theory is provided by a study showing that electroconvulsive therapy (ECT), a common treatment for severe depression, seems to achieve an antidepressant effect through the release of serotonin, dopamine, and norepinephrine (Grahame-Smith, Green, & Costain, 1978). Because common medical treatments for depression (drugs and ECT) also produce this neurotransmitter receptor effect, it is assumed that the serotonin uptake theory is one of the more important mechanisms linking exercise to psychological benefits.

Wurtman (1993) provided more evidence supporting the role of serotonin. This study, however, focused on the relationships among exercise, appetite, weight gain, and mood state. Results indicated that the ability to control food intake was related to perturbations in mood which resulted in an excessive intake of carbohydrate and resistance to exercise. With exercise, brain serotonin was increased, followed by a reduction in food intake and some relief from depression. Other studies have postulated that another viable mechanism involves the role of exercise in decreasing sympathetic and increasing parasympathetic activity followed by simultaneous improvement in emotional stability (Kubitz & Landers, 1993). Among the various mechanisms studied, there remains one other potential cause of exercise benefits—that is, the role of various cognitive factors.

Cognitive Theories

Studies have demonstrated that exercise influences several personality variables, all of which may be related to mood, affect, and depression. Individuals who exercise regularly are more quiet and reserved, emotionally stable, assertive, forthright, expedient, imaginative, self-sufficient, "happy-go-lucky," placid, and relaxed (Leith & Taylor, 1990). Two cognitive theories have gained prominence in accounting for the cognitive association between exercise and mental health. These theories attribute the mental health benefits of exercise to an increase in self-esteem, self-concept, mastery, and achievement, and to the distraction from other worries and stresses.

Self-Esteem, Self-Concept, Mastery, and Achievement

Both acute and long-term exercise have been causally linked to improvement in self-esteem (McAuley, Corneya, & Lettunich, 1991). One study comparing exercise to a cognitive–behavioral intervention showed that exercise was significantly more effective in increasing positive body image (Fisher & Thompson, 1994). Another study showed that exercise participants who were not able to achieve their fitness goals actually had lower self-efficacy following training than those who did achieve their goals (Dzewaltowski, Acevedo, & Pettay, 1992). Thus, involvement in exercise does not necessarily result in enhanced self-esteem. Rather, these results show that expectancy (placebo effect) may be as important as the exercise itself. Indeed, other reviews have concluded that a sense of mastery and control that occurs as an outcome of exercise accounts for much of the psychological benefits (Norris et al., 1992).

The Distraction/"Time-Out" Theory

Initial research by Bahrke and Morgan (1978) suggested that taking "time out" was sufficient to relieve anxiety and that exercise is not the critical variable of exercise-based anxiety reduction interventions. More recently, however, Morgan and colleagues have concluded from the overview of additional research that the distraction theory does not contradict other psychological mechanisms; rather it is possible that exercise may be one of many possible factors that occupy one's thought processes to temporarily postpone immediate emotional concerns in a positive way (Morgan, 1988; Morgan & O'Connor, 1989). More recent studies (Roth, 1989; Roth, Bachtler, & Fillingim, 1990) using the same research paradigm have shown that exercise produces greater reduction in anxiety than quiet rest periods. Thus, it can be concluded that the overall impact of exercise as time out is meaningful, but likely does not account for a large portion of the exercise benefits.

Some critics have suggested that because exercise is so prominent in the media, there may be a strong placebo effect that accounts for the psychological changes we observe. For example, one study showed that when patients were led to believe that they were getting exercise designed to improve well-being, their self-esteem levels increased as much as those involved in exercise with strong expectancy for psychological benefits (Desharnais, Jobin, Cote, Levesque, & Godin, 1993). However, another study focused specifically upon the placebo (expectancy) factor found more favorable results for exercise (McCann & Holmes, 1984). It appears that exercise does engender an expectancy effect, but it is not substantial compared to other cognitive and physiological mechanisms.

Exercise Type and Dose–Response Effect Studies

In the past, the majority of studies of exercise type and dose–response effects on mental health status have featured aerobic activities such as running and swimming compared to anaerobic (e.g., strength training) exercise (Berger & Owen, 1992; Folkins & Sime, 1981). Norvell and Belles (1993) demonstrated remarkable benefits from weight training in reducing anxiety, depression, and hostility among law-enforcement personnel. However, another study found equally significant reductions in depression from aerobic versus strength training in comparison to a self-selected control group (Johnston, Petlichkoff, & Hoeger, 1993). By contrast, Bosscher (1993) compared running with a combination of low-level exercise and relaxation. He found a substantial advantage for the running group in a clinical population of middle-aged depressed adults. McMurdo and Rennie (1993) found similar results with a population of older adults. Although some research advocates the benefits of one or another type of exercise, personal preference and enjoyment of the activity may be more important for mental health benefits than any single modality of exertion.

Recently there has been great emphasis on discerning the level of intensity in combination with the type of exercise that might be optimal for achieving psychological benefits. The vast majority of recent studies seem to suggest that high-intensity aerobic activity is not necessary for achieving the mental health benefits of exercise (Blumenthal et al., 1991; Doyne, Schambless, & Beutler, 1983; Martinsen, 1993). More specifically, Hobson and Rejeski (1993) found no dose–response interaction associated with higher or lower stress responses to cognitive challenge. Stein and Motta (1992) tested the effects of aerobic and nonaerobic exercise on depression and self-concept in 89 college students. Both treatment groups showed significant reduction in depression compared to a control group and, interestingly, the nonaerobic group was superior to the aerobic condition for enhancing self-concept. Berger and Owen (1992) compared aerobic swimming with low-intensity yoga and found an improvement in mood state in both groups. In addition, for men, yoga produced greater reductions in tension, fatigue, and anger than did the swimming intervention.

Summary of Research on Psychological Benefits and Mechanisms

In conclusion, it appears that a preponderance of literature supports the use of exercise therapy with clinical populations, though a substantial number of patients (up to 50% or more) are not able or willing to continue exercise on a long-term basis (Dishman, 1991). Understanding the acute and long-term mechanism of exercise beneficence may serve to improve the efficacy of treatment. However, amid the confusion of trying to isolate single mechanisms (physiological or cognitive), we may have overlooked the most logical explanation for the exercise effects, that is, the *interaction effect*. That some of the physiological theories may be interrelated or overlapping seems obvious perhaps. For example, temperature elevation may influence the release, synthesis, or uptake of certain brain monoamines or they might interact in a synergistic manner (Morgan, 1988). Further, it has been suggested that there may be an interaction between endorphins and monoamines (Hamachek, 1987).

Interactive cognitive effects are also likely. For example, exercise has been shown to produce a hardiness effect overlapping with feelings of self-worth mediated by social support (Oman & Haskel, 1993). It is also possible that both physiological and cognitive interactions are present; for instance, exercise has been shown to develop overall hardiness by attenuating sympathetic nervous system responses (Dienstbier, 1991). Although the exact mechanism by which exercise promotes mental health is not known, the value of exercise therapy is clear. Next, the populations most likely to benefit from therapy are examined.

For Whom Is Exercise Therapy Appropriate?

Depression, Anxiety, and Low Self-Esteem

People with mild to moderate depression are a clinical population that should be treated with exercise independently or adjunctively. The evidence is clear that exercise can be therapeutically effective in this population, although many patients have difficulty overcoming the captivating inertness associated with depression. Exercise therapy also can be used for patients suffering from various forms of anxiety disorders (test anxiety, social phobia, panic attack, etc.). Many patients are plagued by a combination of depression and some form of anxiety. In these cases, the conventional treatment is more complicated, usually involving pharmacological therapy and psychotherapy. In these cases, the addition of exercise to the regime can be difficult.

Those who suffer with low self-esteem also may benefit from an exercise program. Those whose body image contributes to self-esteem problems should especially be considered for exercise therapy because exercise habits have been shown to differentiate the effectiveness of weight-loss strategies (Schwartz, 1993). Both exercise and cognitive therapy are effective in improving overall body image. Caution is urged, however, regarding the use of exercise therapy for eating disorders because depressive symptoms are prevalent in this population and exercise is over-used by some bulimia patients in an effort to purge (Prussin & Harvey, 1991).

Somatopsychic Aspects of Medical Disorders

I include this discussion on other clinical applications because medical problems often cause anxiety, depression, and low self-esteem; the effects of exercise upon mental health are *somatopsychic*, which is the polar opposite of the more common term *psychosomatic*, used to explain physical symptoms caused by emotional distress. Specifically, there may be synergistic, conjoint physical and psychological benefits of exercise as therapy when combined with conventional medical treatment in a behavioral medicine setting. For example, psychological benefits of exercise have been documented for the following medical disorders: heart disease (Duivenvoorden & van Dixhooren, 1991); chronic obstructive pulmonary disease (Emery, Leatherman, Burker, & MacIntyre, 1991); irritable bowel syndrome (Jones, 1989); arthritis (Minor & Brown, 1993); menstrual cramps (Choi, 1992); back pain (Sluijs et al., 1993); sleep disorders (Bliwise, King, Harris, & Haskell, 1992); substance abuse (Kivella & Pahkala, 1991); hyperactivity and attentional deficit disorders (Shipman, 1984); and migraine headaches (Lockett & Campbell, 1992). Lastly, it should be noted that exercise has been used effectively in the care and treatment of patients with AIDS symptoms (MacArthur, Levine, & Birk, 1993). Specifically, exercise was associated with increased sense of well-being (lower anxiety/depression) as well as with improvements in immunocompetence.

Special Populations

There are three other populations that deserve special attention in regard to exercise therapy. Two of these are delimited by age. Given the developmental adaptations that young adults face, many are especially vulnerable to anxiety, depression, and low self-esteem. It has been shown that aerobic exercise (e.g., running) is an efficacious treatment with psychiatric institutionalized adolescents (Brown et al., 1992) as well as outpatient clients (Norris et al., 1992). Reductions were seen in depression, anxiety, hostility, confused thinking, and fatigue. Those adolescents and adults with the diagnosis hyperactivity or attentional deficit disorder should also be good candidates for exercise therapy (Shipman, 1984).

Elderly clients also can benefit greatly from exercise therapy. Geriatric specialists have advocated and documented the benefits of physical activity for, in particular, depression (Rooney, 1993). Another carefully controlled experimental study showed benefits for depression in a cross-over design comparing high and low intensity exercise; both groups showed reduced psychiatric symptoms (McMurdo & Rennie, 1993).

Lastly it should be noted that special-need populations also benefit psychologically from exercise programs (Shephard, 1991). In particular, wheelchair-bound students who were able to exercise on an arm-crank bicycle ergometer showed that anxiety was significantly decreased by the exercise (Brown et al., 1993).

Because the populations that might benefit the most from exercise therapy have now been identified, the practical applications of exercise therapy in a clinical setting are now considered.

Guidelines for Clinical Application of Exercise Therapy

Therapists working with clients in the process of exercise therapy are advised to follow the general guidelines outlined in Exhibit 1 and detailed below.

    1. In taking the client's history, include questions about current exercise habits. Find out what the client does regularly in work

---

Exhibit 1

Guidelines for Clinical Application of Exercise Therapy in Conjunction with Counseling or Psychotherapy

  1. Explore the client's exercise history (good and bad experiences).
  2. Engage in a walk/talk counseling session.
  3. Explain the potential benefits of exercise.
  4. Evaluate impact of walk/talk on catharsis and cognitive orientation.
  5. Recognize differences in physical ability, motivation, etc.
  6. Recommend desirable setting and comfortable clothing for exercise.
  7. Make exercise practical and functional (e.g., commuting to work).
  8. Include a variety of activities from circuit training to social dance.
  9. Use exercise prescription for duration, intensity, and frequency of exercise.
10. Evaluate the influence of family and friends (facilitate support).
11. Develop a self-behavior modification system to reinforce activity.
12. Develop a plan for recidivism and irregular patterns of activity.
13. Evaluate progress using well-accepted, standardized psychological tests.
14. Follow ethical guidelines for professional practice.

or leisure that might be conducive to the addition of more vigorous activity (e.g., if the job requires trips to different floors in the building, consider taking the stairs instead of elevator). Then begin to explore past experiences (both good and bad outcomes) to identify opportunities for positive experiences with exercise. Research shows that finding "enjoyable" exercise is critical to the long-term continuity of an exercise program (Wankel, 1993). In case #4, the practitioner found that Richard had extremely negative experiences with exercise in the past. As a result he was very resistant to exercise.

2. During an early counseling session, suggest to the client that it might be interesting and enjoyable to continue talking while going for a walk in the nearby vicinity. For clients who are interested, this could occur in the hallway, if there is not much traffic, or on the sidewalks outside the building, if the weather permits. The duration of this walk/talk might be 10 to 20 minutes depending upon the condition of the client and upon the attractiveness versus the distraction of the environment. If walking in this setting tends to facilitate the client's interaction, then continue as long as possible. However, if the walk seems to be intimidating to the client, then return to the counseling office after a short while. In case #2, Abigail was willing to try exercise as long as it was a part of the counseling therapy.

3. Explain to the client that the purpose of the walk/talk is to demonstrate the invigorating aspects of exercise and the refreshing aspects of recovery from exercise. Give the client a brief explanation of the reasons (theories) underlying the potential benefits of exercise, noting the aesthetic and kinesthetic experiences associated with movement. The client should know, by first-hand observation, that the therapist uses exercise for preventive purposes in addition to the rehabilitative applications being prescribed. In case #1, Sheila only had time for exercise during her counseling sessions.

4. Use the walking experience as an opportunity for greater cognitive catharsis on the part of the client. Be observant of how the client responds to questions or volunteers comments in the midst of walking conversation. For some clients, the side-by-side conversation (in contrast to face-to-face therapy) seems to elicit more candor as though the movement together with the informal nature of the activity seems to break down barriers

and facilitate greater emotional release (Kendzierski & Johnson, 1993). For other clients, the exercise may impede communication (see case #4). If this happens, the therapist should return to the office setting immediately. It is important to note that extended exercise (e.g., marathon running) is associated with catharsis and more dramatic changes in cognitive orientation (Acevedo, Dzewaltowski, Gill, & Noble, 1992).

5. Recognize individual differences in ability, motivation, and so on. Some clients may be unwilling to try this approach. Not every client is endowed with the burning desire to stay involved in exercise. Give examples of other persons who have overcome similar problems with exercise. Kenneth Cooper, the author of *Aerobics* (1968), tells the story of a man with heart disease who was so despondent that he wanted to die. Because his heart was weak, he thought the best way to commit suicide without embarrassing his family was to run around the block as fast as he could until he killed himself. After several futile attempts at causing a fatal heart attack in this manner, he discovered to his surprise that he began to feel better and eventually chose to live instead of to die.

6. Take advantage of environmental factors such as water, beach, hills, wooded areas, stairs, streets, malls (in cold weather), and home exercise to find secondary advantages to the exercise and to eliminate excuses for not being active. Dealing with excuses is a critical issue (Kendzierski & Johnson, 1993). Encourage the client to obtain comfortable and attractive clothing (shorts, sweats, shoes) gradually as rewards or added incentives for accomplishment in continuing the exercise program. Demonstrate to the client that wearing more comfortable, casual clothing (e.g., bright-colored warm-ups) for work or leisure tends to make it feasible to include exercise as a natural part of daily activities of living, which can be important existentially (Fahlberg, Fahlberg, & Gates, 1992).

7. Consider options to make exercise functional, especially when the client cannot afford home-exercise equipment or health-club membership fees. Cost-effective exercise options include commuting to work by walking, jogging, or biking; hiking to get to a remote scenic area; or doing hard physical work (shoveling snow or dirt, moving boxes, and lawn or gardening work). Commuting exercise is perhaps the most functional in

that it an have the inherent rewards of saving money for bus fare, parking, or gas. In case #3, John has discovered great satisfaction in commuting by bicycle even during inclement weather. If the commuting distance is not reasonable for biking or jogging, find a compromise by getting a ride or taking a bus one way or by driving part way, thus saving on parking and avoiding traffic congestion.

8. Consider a broad spectrum of activities, some that involve socializing and others that are merely conditioning necessary to be able to enjoy a favored activity (e.g., older adults may be inclined to walk or climb stairs in order to be capable of maintaining the physical demands of social or square dancing). If clients complain that one form of exercise is uncomfortable, urge them to switch to other parallel activities. The multiple station work-out (e.g., stationary bicycle, rowing machine, minitramp, stair climber) is helpful to avoid boredom and local fatigue in one muscle area. During home exercise, suggest using radio, television, or tapes to relieve boredom or as reinforcement for having started the exercise program for that day. Note that the music in aerobic dance or in recreational dancing may be an essential ingredient for motivating some clients. In case #1, Sheila was willing to consider dancing as an exercise because it also met her social needs. But for John, in case #3, the dancing would have been too threatening because he struggles with social phobia.

9. Set the standards for duration, intensity, and frequency based upon level of conditioning, tolerance for discomfort, and length of time since beginning the exercise program. Set reasonable goals and be prepared to adjust the workload (i.e., to increase the duration, intensity or total time of activity as needed). For those not trained or experienced in exercise physiology, it is advisable to seek the assistance of a local specialist who can supervise the on-going prescription process. Above all, be aware of the risks of too much activity at one extreme and the lack of benefits with too little exercise at the other extreme.

10. Evaluate the influence of family and friends. If there is no support or if there is a sense of disdain for exercise, the client will have a bigger hurdle to overcome in maintaining exercise. Initially, try to facilitate activities that bring the clients into

positive interaction with others while they are gaining benefits from exercise. Also consider encouraging the client to exercise as a role model for their children or some other family member. Sheila, in case #1, may respond to this rationale, particularly if it also gives her some relief from the pressure of parenting.

11. Help the client set up self-behavior modification strategies to reinforce the activity. For example, clients might set up a pact with you whereby they will only watch television when simultaneously exercising on a bicycle ergometer, mini-tramp, stair-stepper, or treadmill. Alternatively, they might agree not to watch more than 1 hour of television without engaging in at least 10 to 20 minutes of exercise. In this latter example, the TV becomes the reinforcer for the exercise behavior. Set up a log and a system of accountability for the clients such that they can review their progress in accomplishments (e.g., distanced walked; number of consecutive days participated; change in mood; alertness and fatigue; relief from nagging joint or muscle pain) and so that you can provide reinforcement for the success and the resulting psychological changes. John, in case #3, was conscientious about record keeping, but Sheila in case #1 could not find the time to do so and failure to keep records simply added to her guilt feelings about not exercising enough.

12. Plan for the first bout of recidivism and let the client know that it will happen sometime. Nearly everyone who engages in exercise will also experience periodic lapses from exercise due to job, family, illness, injury, and so on. Planning ahead to accommodate serves to defuse the potentially devastating effects of failure (i.e., guilt, remorse, low self-esteem). Help clients to anticipate the problem, plan for the adjustment, and welcome the return to activity following a lapse. To prevent future lapses, seek to identify the client's immediate rewards for exercise, which may include (a) the break from the hassles of the day, (b) an opportunity to enjoy the fresh air out-of-doors, (c) the chance to talk with you or with a friend about problems, (d) the refreshing sensation of the cool air or warm shower, depending upon the existing weather conditions, and (e) the pleasant culinary satisfaction of a good meal or the fluid replacement with a favorite nonalcoholic drink.

13. Evaluate progress using the one or more well-accepted, standardized psychological tests. Examples of tests for several of the important domains include the following: (a) Profile of Mood States (McNair, Lorr, & Droppleman, 1971); (b) Beck Depression Inventory (Beck, Ward, Mendelson, Mock, & Erbaugh, 1961); (c) State-Trait Anxiety Scale (Spielberger, 1983); and (d) Tennessee Self-Concept Scale (Fitts, 1964). Also evaluate sleep habits and appetite control. It is possible that clients will notice serendipitously that they have more rapid sleep onset and more restful, night-long sleep patterns (Bliwise et al., 1992), and that healthy foods like fruits and vegetables taste much better following a vigorous bout of exercise with shower and extended recovery period. These aesthetic rewards of exercise can be very powerful immediate reinforcers. Plan to revise the exercise program based upon client feedback at 2 to 4 week intervals.

14. Follow ethical practices involving responsibility to and communication with other health-care professionals. It is important to get medical approval for the exercise and to establish regular communication with other health-care professionals (e.g., primary physician, physical therapist, psychiatrist, social worker, counselor) regarding progress and concerns. Observe other ethical guidelines per medical or psychological licensing requirements. Maintain clearly established boundaries. For example, in case #2, Abigail had difficulty understanding that the walk/talk sessions constituted serious therapeutic interventions. She wanted to make the content of the conversations more informal and social. Obviously, there will be some additional information conversation because of the circumstances (e.g., change in scenery). Remember, the therapist's responsibility is to get the clients started exercising with well-founded goals, to participate with them on occasion during the counseling session while maintaining strict ethical boundaries, and to highlight the potential benefits of exercise to the client (Sime, 1987). The therapist is not, however, personally responsible for clients' motivation or their personal social agenda.

Contraindications and Pitfalls to be Avoided in Exercise Therapy

The following areas of concern outlined in Exhibit 2 and detailed below should be seriously considered in order to avoid frustration and disap-

---

Exhibit 2

Contraindicators and Pitfalls to be Avoided in the Conduct of Exercise Therapy with Counseling or Psychotherapy

1. Don't expect all clients to be receptive to or enthusiastic about exercise as therapy.
2. Don't expect clients to make substantial changes in lifestyle to accommodate a structured exercise program.
3. Be aware that some clients may expect too much change in affect too soon following onset of activity.
4. Be aware that some clients are prone to extreme behaviors (e.g., workaholic, alcoholic) and, thus, may overdo exercise, too.
5. Don't allow exercise therapy to be a substitute for counseling or psychotherapy where needed.
6. Remember that exercise can create a potent risk in spite of the therapeutic intention.

---

pointment with difficult client problems and to aid in the prevention of unwarranted lawsuits.

1. Don't expect everyone to get benefits from exercise. It should be noted that there are many very happy, healthy, functioning individuals with no mental health problems who are not exercising in a manner that fits the definition of vigorous exercise, and there are some individuals who seem to be allergic to activity and may never develop an appreciation for the benefits of exercise. Richard, in case #4, never did start either a counseling or an exercise program. His wife and his physician could have made the exercise prescription obligatory for his personal well-being, but the risk of falling or having some other tragic outcome was too great given his attitude. Exercise is contraindicated for this client.

2. Don't expect the program to supersede other lifestyle patterns. Abigail, in case #2, who works nights at the station would not be a good candidate for a regularly scheduled aerobics or yoga class. The demands of her night job and the social phobia she harbors would make it difficult for her to fit into such a structured group class, resulting in more bad feelings supporting her view that exercise is just too much trouble (time-consuming, difficult to schedule, etc.) in addition to the fact that she finds it to be very uncomfortable. Being overweight makes exercise

uncomfortable and she has no previous history of good experiences with exercise.

3. Some clients may expect too much change in how they feel too soon following onset of activity. Get them to appreciate the aesthetic aspects of the activity at the beginning and gradually increase the prescriptive workload to achieve a reasonable physiological training effect, which is especially important for treating depression. Be aware that the antianxiety effects of exercise last about 2 to 4 hours and the anti-depressant effects of exercise last about 12 to 24 hours (Johnsgaard, 1989). Knowing this, one should recommend exercise (of shorter duration and lower intensity) for anxiety at frequent intervals throughout the day. For depression, exercising at daily intervals but with somewhat greater intensity should be effective.

4. Some clients will take the exercise to extreme the same way that they have abused substances or life experiences (e.g., workaholic, alcoholic). In the case of John, in case #3, who is recovering from drug abuse, the practitioner found that his tendency was to take exercise to extreme in the manic phase. Other personality variables such as a Type A behavior pattern have been associated with overdoing it on the exercise prescription due to poor perception of appropriate exercise intensity (Hassm'en, Ståhl, & Borg, 1993). Also, be cautious in the use of exercise for clients with eating disorders. Exercise may produce more opiate-like endorphins than the client can handle, which can be addictive. There are some who are bulimic and use exercise as a means of purging, thus avoiding the need to deal with the cause of the depression (Prussin & Harvey, 1991). Even though the clients who exercise regularly have less depression, they still may be purging in addition to the exercise and therefore need careful psychological evaluation and therapy.

5. Don't let the exercise prescription preclude the option for psychotherapy. Some clients tend to avoid their real problem, and exercise can be a risky substitute for necessary counseling about other issues not resolved by exercise (Sime, 1987). Remember that exercise, like medication, is generally a method of getting immediate (and temporary) symptom relief. As such, medication and exercise are similar in that they allow the person to get through a particularly difficult period of pain or discomfort (either physical or emotional) after which time, insight-oriented

counseling may be needed for prevention of escalating problems.

6. Remember that treatment with exercise can create a potent risk
in spite of the therapeutic intention. For example, clients with
bipolar disorder fluctuate through periods of euphoric highs
followed by polar-opposite lows of depression. In the early stages
of the euphoric highs, exercise can have widely varying responses: Exercise can either exacerbate the mood symptoms to
an extreme or it can help to dissipate the responses dramatically.
John, in case #3, has to be very careful in carrying out his exercise prescription during the manic phase. In one instance of
euphoric high, he found himself working carelessly near the
roof's edge on a three-story building without protective supports. Use caution in conducting exercise therapy with these
clients.

Summary and Conclusions

In this chapter, exercise has been considered as a viable, adjunctive
therapy in the treatment of a broad array of psychological disorders and
medical disorders with underlying psychological etiology. Evidence has
been presented supporting the effectiveness of various modalities of
exercise treatment among numerous divergent populations across a
wide range of disorders. Although most of the evidence is positive in
regard to exercise, the exact mechanism of beneficence (cognitive or
physiological) is not yet known. The dosage of exercise needed to
achieve benefits may differ greatly across individuals, and the type of
exercise should include personal preference and accessibility as the primary determinants.

In conclusion, the benefits of exercise will occur only if clients find
a way to become actively involved in vigorous motion as often as possible
with as much enjoyment and satisfaction as possible. In addition it seems
desirable for some parts of an exercise program to be functional; that
is, the product of the activity is rewarding (commuting to work, chop-
ping wood, dancing, hiking in a scenic area, etc.). Numerous guidelines,
contraindications, and pitfalls also have been provided. The exercise
therapist is encouraged to be bold in the use of innovative strategies,
but cautious where there are extenuating circumstances that might be
risky for the client.

References

Acevedo, E., Dzewaltowski, D., Gill, D., & Noble, J. (1992). Cognitive orientations of ultramarathoners. *The Sport Psychologist, 6,* 242–252.

Bahrke, M. S., & Morgan, W. P. (1978). Anxiety reduction following exercise and meditation. *Cognitive Therapy and Research, 2,* 323–333.

Beck, A. T., Ward, C. H., Mendelson, M., Mock, J., & Erbaugh, J. (1961). An inventory for measuring depression. *Archives of General Psychiatry, 4,* 561–571.

Berger, B., & Owen, D. (1992). Mood alteration with yoga and swimming: Aerobic exercise may not be necessary. *Perceptual and Motor Skills, 75,* 1331–43.

Bliwise, D., King, A., Harris, R., & Haskell, W. (1992). Prevelance of self-reported parsleep in a healthy population aged 50 to 65. *Social Science in Medicine, 34,* 49–55.

Blumenthal, J., Emery, C., Madden, D., Schmiebolk, S., Walsh-Riddle, M., George, L., McKee, D., Higginbothan, N., Cobb, F., & Coleman, R. (1991). Long-term effects of exercise on psychological functioning in older men and women. *Journal of Gerontology, 46,* 352–361.

Bosscher, R. J. (1993). Running and mixed physical exercises with depressed psychiatric patients: Exercise and psychological well being. *International Journal of Sport Psychology, 24,* 170–184.

Brown, D., Morgan, W., & Raglin, J. (1993). Effects of exercise and rest on the state anxiety and blood pressure of physically challenged college students. *Journal of Sports Medicine and Phsyical Fitness, 33,* 300–305.

Brown, S., Welsh, M., Labbe, E., Gitulli, W., & Kulkarni, P. (1992). Aerobic exercise and the psychological treatment of adolescents. *Perceptual and Motor Skills, 74,* 555–560.

Byrne, A., & Byrne, D. (1993). The effect of exercise on depression, anxiety and other mood states: A review. *Journal of Psychosomatic Research, 37,* 565–574.

Camacho, T. C., Roberts, R. E., Lazarus, N. B., Kaplan, G. A., & Cohen, R. D. (1991). Physical activity and depression: Evidence from the Alameda County study. *American Journal of Epidemiology, 134,* 220–231.

Choi, P. (1992). The psychological benefits of physical exercise: Implications for women and the menstrual cycle [Special issue: The menstrual cycle]. *Journal of Reproductive and Infant Psychology, 10,* 111–115.

Cooper, K. H. (1968). *Aerobics.* New York: Evans.

Daniels, M., Martin, A., & Carter, J. (1992). Opiate receptor blockade by naltrexone and mood state after acute physical activity. *British Journal of Sports Medicine, 26,* 111–115.

Denollet, J. (1993). Emotional distress and fatigue in coronary heart disease: The Global Mood Scale (GMS). *Psychological Medicine, 23,* 111–121.

Desharnais, R., Jobin, J., Cote, C., Levesque, L., & Godin, G. (1993). Aerobic exercise and the placebo effect: A controlled study. *Psychosomatic Medicine, 55,* 149–154.

DeVries, H., Beckman, P., Huber, H., & Dieckmeir, L. (1968). Electromyographic evaluation of the effects of sauna on the neuromuscular system. *Journal of Sports Medicine and Physical Fitness, 8,* 61–69.

Dey, S. (1994). Physical exercise as novel anti-depressant agent: Possible role of serotonin receptor subtypes. *Psychological Behavior, 55,* 323–329.

Dey, S., Singh, R., & Dey, P. (1992). Exercise training: Significance of regional alterations in serotonin metabolism of rat brain in relation to anti-depressant effect of exercise. *Psychological Behavior, 52,* 1095–1099.

Dienstbier, R. (1991). Behavioral correlates of sympathoadrenal reactivity: The toughness model. *Medicine and Science in Sports and Exercise, 23,* 846–852.

Dienstbier, R. A., LaGuardia, R. L., & Wilcox, N. S. (1987). The tolerance of cold and heat: Beyond (cold hands–warm heart). *Motivation and Emotion, 11,* 269–295.

Dishman, R. K. (1991). Increasing and maintaining exercise and physical activity. *Behavior Therapy, 22,* 345–378.

Doyne, E., Schambless, D., & Beutler, L. (1983). Aerobic exercise as a treatment for depression in women. *Behavior Therapy, 41,* 434–440.

Dua, J., & Hargreaves, L. (1992). Effects of aerobic exercise on negative affect, positive affect, stress, and depression. *Perceptual and Motor Skills, 75,* 355–361.

Duivenvoorden, H. J., & van Dixhooren, J. (1991). Predictability of psychic outcome for exercise training and exercise training including relaxation therapy after myocardial infarction. *Journal of Psychosomatic Research, 35,* 569–578.

Dzewaltowski, D., Acevedo, E., & Pettay, R. (1992). Influence of cardiorespiratory fitness information on cognitions and physical activity. *Medicine and Science in Sports and Exercise, 24,* S-24.

Emery, C., Hauck, E., & Blumenthal, J. (1992). Exercise adherence and maintenance among older adults: One year follow-up study. *Psychology and Aging, 7,* 466–470.

Emery, C., Leatherman, N., Burker, E., & MacIntyre, N. (1991). Psychological outcomes of a pulmonary rehabilitation program. *Journal of Chest, 100,* 613–617.

Fahlberg, L. L., Fahlberg, L. A., & Gates, W. K. (1992). Exercise and existence: Exercise behavior from an existential-phenomenological perspective. *The Sport Psychologist, 6,* 172–191.

Fisher, E., & Thompson, J. (1994). A comparative evaluation of cognitive-behavioral therapy (CBT) versus exercise therapy (ET) for the treatment of body image disturbance. Preliminary findings. *Behavioral Modification, 18,* 171–185.

Fitts, W. H. (1964). *Tennessee Self-Concept Scale.* Nashville, TN: Counselor Recordings and Tests.

Folkins, C. H., & Sime, W. E. (1981). Physical fitness training and mental health. *American Psychologist, 36,* 373–389.

Froelicher, V. (1990). Exercise, fitness, and coronary heart disease. In C. Bouchard, R. Shephard, T. Stephens, J. Sutton, & B. McPherson (Eds.), *Exercise, fitness and health* (pp. 429–447). Champaign, IL: Human Kinetics.

Fuchs, R., & Hahn, A. (1992). Physical exercise and anxiety as moderators of the stress-illness relationship. *Anxiety, Stress and Coping, 5,* 139–149.

Grahame-Smith, D. G., Green, A. R., & Costain, D. W. (1978). Mechanism of anti-depressant action of ECT therapy. *Lancet, 1,* 254–257.

Greist, J., Klein, M., Eischens, R., Faris, J., Gurman, A., & Morgan, W. (1979). Running as a treatment for depression. *Comprehensive Psychiatry, 20,* 41–54.

Gronningsaeter, H., Hyten, K., Skauli, G., & Christensen, C. (1992). Improved health and coping by physical exercise or cognitive behavioral stress management training in a work environment. *Psychology and Health, 7,* 147–163.

Haier, R. J., Quaid, B. A., & Mills, J. S. (1981). Naloxone alters pain perceptions after jogging. *Psychiatric Research, 5,* 231–232.

Hamachek, D. E. (1987). *Encounters with the self.* New York: Holt, Rinehart, and Winston.

Hassm'en, P., Stähl, & Borg, G. (1993). Psychophysiological responses to exercise in Type A/B men. *Psychosomatic Medicine, 55,* 178–184.

Herrmann, C., Buss, U., Buecker, A., Gonska, B., & Kreuzer, H. (1994). Relationship of cardiologic findings and standardized psychological scales to clinical symptoms in 3,705 ergometrically studied patients. *Zeitschrift Kardiology, 83,* 264–272.

Hill, R. D., Storandt, M., & Malley, M. (1993). The impact of long-term exercise training on psychological function on older adults. *Journal of Gerontology, 48,* P12–P17.

Hinkle, J. (1992). Aerobic running behavior and psycho-teutices: Implications for sport counseling and psychology. *Journal of Sport Behavior, 15,* 163–177.

Hobson, M. L., & Rejeski, W. J. (1993). Does the dose of acute exercise mediate psychophysiological responses to mental stress? *Journal of Sport & Exercise Psychology, 15,* 77–87.

Johnsgaard, K. W. (1989). *The exercise prescription for depression and anxiety.* New York: Plenum.

Johnston, J. N. L., Petlichkoff, L. M., & Hoeger, W. W. K. (1993). Effects of aerobic and strength training exercise participation on depression. *Medicine and Science in Sports and Exercise, 25,* S-135.

Jones, M. M. (1989). Multimodal treatment of irritable bowel syndrome: A preview and proposal. *Medical Psychotherapy: An International Journal, 2,* 11–20.

Kendzierski, D., & Johnson, W. (1993). Excuses, excuses, excuses: A cognitive behavioral approach to exercise implementation. *Journal of Sport & Exercise Psychology, 15,* 207–219.

Kivella, S., & Pahkala, K. (1991). Relationships between healthy behavior and depression in the aged. *Aging Milano, 3,* 153–159.

Klein, M., Greist, J., Gurman, A., Neimeyer, R., Lesser, D., Bushnell, N., & Smith, R. (1985). Comparative outcome study of group psychotherapy versus exercise treatments for depression. *International Journal of Mental Health, 13,* 148–177.

Koltyn, K., & Morgan, W. P. (1993). The influence of wearing a wet suit on core temperature and anxiety responses during underwater exercise. *Medicine and Science in Sports and Exercise, 25,* S-45.

Kubitz, K., & Landers, D. (1993). The effects of aerobic training on cardiovascular responses to mental stress: An examination of underlying mechanisms. *Journal of Sport & Exercise Psychology, 15,* 326–337.

Kugler, J., Seelbach, H., & Kruskemper, G. (1994). Effects of rehabilitation exercise programmes on exercise and depression in coronary patients: A meta-analysis. *The British Journal of Clinical Psychology, 33,* 401–410.

Lehofer, M., Klebel, H., Gersdorf, C. H., & Zapotoczke, H. G. (1992). Running in motion therapy for depression. *Psychiatria-Danubina, 4,* 149–152.

Leith, L., & Taylor, A. (1990). *Psychological aspects of exercise: A decade literature review. Journal of Sport Behavior, 13,* 1–22.

Lobstein, D., & Rasmussen, C. (1991). Decreases in resting plasma beta-endorphine and depression scores after endurance training. *Journal of Sports Medicine and Physical Fitness, 31,* 543–551.

Lockett, D-M. C., & Campbell, J. F. (1992). The effects of aerobic exercise on migraine. *Headache, 32,* 50–54.

MacArthur, R., Levine, S., & Birk, T. (1993). Supervised exercise training improves cardiopulmonary fitness in HIV-infected persons. *Medicine and Science in Sports and Exercise, 25,* 684–688.

Martinsen, E. W. (1993). Therapeutic implications of exercise for clinically anxious and depressed patients: Exercise and psychological well being. *International Journal of Sport Psychology, 24,* 185–199.

Martinsen, E. (1994). Physical activity and depression: Clinical experience. *Acta-Psychiatrica Scandanavia Supplement, 377,* 23–27.

McAuley, E., Courneya, K., & Lettunich, J. (1991). Effects of acute and long term exercise on self-efficacy responses in sedentary middle aged males and females. *The Gerontologist, 31,* 534–542.

McCann, I., & Holmes, D. (1984). The influence of aerobic exercise on depression. *Journal of Personality and Social Psychology, 46,* 1142–1147.

McCubbin, J. A., Cheung, R., Montgomery, T. B., Bulbulian, R., & Wilson, J. F. (1992). *Aerobic fitness and opiodergic inhibition of cardiovascular stress reactivity. Psychophysiology, 19,* 687–697.

McMurdo, M., & Rennie, L. (1993). The controlled trial of exercise by residence of old people's homes. *Age and Aging, 22*(1), 11–15.

McNair, D. M., Lorr, N., & Droppleman, L. F. (1971). *Manual for the Profile of Mood States.* San Diego, CA: Educational and Industrial Testing Service.

McNeil, J., LeBlanc, E., & Joyner. (1991). The effect of exercise on depressive symptoms in the moderately depressed elderly. *Psychology and Aging, 6,* 187–188.

Minor, M. A., & Brown, J. D. (1993). Exercise maintenance of persons with arthritis after participation in a class experience. *Health Education Quarterly, 20,* 83–95.

Morgan, W. P. (1988). *Exercise and mental health.* In R. K. Dishman (Ed.), *Exercise adherence: Its impact on public health* (pp. 9–121). Champaign, IL: Human Kinetics.

Morgan, W. P., & O'Connor, P. J. (1989). Psychological effects of exercise and sports. In E. Ryan & Allman (Eds.), *Sports medicine* (pp. 671–689). New York: Academic Press.

Norris, R., Carroll, D., & Cochrane, R. (1992). The effects of physical activity and exercise training on psychological stress and well-being in an adolescent population. *Journal of Psychosomatic Research, 36,* 55–65.

North, T. C., McCullaugh, P., & Tran, Z. V. (1990). Effective exercise on depression. *Exercise and Sports Sciences Review, 18,* 379–415.

Norvell, N., & Belles, D. (1993). Psychological and physical benefits of circuit weight training and law enforcement personnel. *Journal of Consulting and Clinical Psychology, 61,* 520–527.

Oman, R. F., & Haskel, W. L. (1993). The relationships among heartiness, efficacy, cognition, social support and exercise behavior. *Medicine and Science in Sports and Exercise, 25,* S-135.

Paffenbarger, R., Jr., Lee, I., & Leung, R. (1994). Physical activity and personal characteristics associated with depression and suicide in American college men. *Acta-Psychiatrica Scandanavia Supplement, 377,* 16–22.

Pelham, T. W., Campagna, P. D., Ritvo, P. G., & Birnie, W. A. (1993). The effects of exercise therapy on clients in a psychiatric rehabilitation program. *The Psychosocial Rehabilitation Journal, 16,* 75–84.

Petruzzello, S., Landers, D., Hatfield, P., Kubitz, K., & Salazar, W. (1991). A meta-analysis on the anxiety-reducing effects of acute and chronic exercise. Outcomes and mechanisms. *Sports Medicine, 11,* 143–182.

Petruzzello, S. J., Landers, D. M., & Salazar, W. (1993). Exercise and anxiety reduction: Examination of temperature as an explanation for effective change. *Journal of Sport and Exercise Psychology, 15,* 63–76.

Prussin, R., & Harvey, P. (1991). Depression, dietary restraint, and binge eating in female runners. *Addictive Behaviors, 16,* 295–301.

Rabins, P. (1992). Prevention of mental disorder in the elderly: Current perspective and future prospects. *Journal of the American Geriatrics Society, 70,* 727–733.

Rajala, U., Uusimaki, A., Keinanen-Kiukaanniemi, F., & Kivela, F. (1994). Prevalence of depression in a 55-year-old Finnish population. *Social Psychiatry and Psychiatric Epidemiology, 29,* 126–130.

Rooney, E. M. (1993). Exercise for older patients: Why it's worth your effort. *Geriatrics, 48,* 68–77.

Roth, D. L. (1989). Acute emotional and psychophysiological effects of aerobic exercise. *Psychophysiology, 26,* 593–602.

Roth, D. L., Bachtler, S. D., & Fillingim, R. (1990). Acute emotional and cardiovascular effects of stressful mental work during aerobic exercise. *Psychophysiology, 27,* 694–701.

Ruuskanen, J., & Parkatti, T. (1994). Physical activity and related factors among nursing home residents. *Journal of the American Geriatric Society, 42,* 987–991.

Schwartz, F. (1993). Obesity in adult females: The relationship among personality characteristics, dieting, and weight. *AAOHN-J, 41,* 504–509.

Seraganian, P. (1993). Current status and future directions in the field of exercise psychology. In P. Seraganian (Ed.), *Exercise psychology: The influence of physical exercise on psychological processes* (pp. 383–390). New York: John Wiley & Sons.

Shephard, R. (1991). Benefits of sports and physical activity for the disabled: Implications for the individual and for society. *Scandanavian Journal of Rehabilitation Medicine, 23*(2), 51–59.

Shipman, W. M. (1984). Emotional and behavioral effects of long-distance running on children. In M. Sachs & G. Buffone (Eds.), *Running as therapy: An integrated approach* (pp. 125–137). Lincoln: University of Nebraska Press.

Sime, W. E. (1987). Exercise in the prevention and treatment of depression. In W. P. Morgan & S. E. Goldston (Eds.), *Exercise and mental health* (pp. 145–152). Washington, DC: Hemisphere.

Sluijs, E., Kok, G., & van der Zee, J. J. (1993). Correlates of exercise compliance in physical therapy. *Physical Therapy, 73,* 41–53.

Sonstroem, R., & Morgan, W. (1989). Exercise and self-esteem: Rationale and model. *Medicine and Science in Sports and Exercise, 21,* 329–337.

Spielberger, C. D. (1983). *Manual for the State-Trait Anxiety Inventory* (Form Y). Palo Alto, CA: Consulting Psychologists Press.

Stein, P., & Motta, R. (1992). Effects of aerobic and nonaerobic exercise on depression and self concept. *Perceptual and Motor Skills, 74,* 79–89.

Steptoe, A., Kearsley, M., & Walters, N. (1993). Acute mood responses to maximal and sub-maximal exercise in active and inactive men. *Psychology and Health, 8,* 89–99.

Tennant, C., Mihailidou, A., Scott, A., Smith, R., Kellow, J., Jones, M., Hunyor, S., Lorang, M., & Hoschel, R. (1994). Psychological symptom profiles in patients with chest pain. *Journal of Psychosomatic Research, 38,* 365–371.

Wankel, L. M. (1993). The importance of enjoyment to adherence and psychological benefits from physical activity: Exercise and psychological well being. *International Journal of Sports Psychology, 24,* 151–169.

Weyerer, S. (1992). Physical inactivity and depression in the community. Evidence from the Upper Bavaria Field Study. *International Journal of Sports Medicine, 13,* 492–496.

Wurtman, J. (1993). Depression and weight gain: The serotonin connection. *Journal of Affective Disorders, 29,* 183–192.

8 Counseling Interventions in Applied Sport Psychology

Albert J. Petitpas

Sport psychology interventions have evolved from focusing on improving sport skills to being more broadly concerned with the impact of sport on human development and the use of sport to enhance personal competence (Danish, Petitpas, & Hale, 1993; Murphy, 1995). Within this broader view of sport psychology there exist several types of interventions. The first group of interventions consists of the traditional sport performance enhancement skills, such as imagery, arousal regulation, and goal setting. The second group of interventions focuses on remediating various clinical problems such as eating disorders or adjustment reactions. The final group of interventions consists of counseling strategies that assist athletes with various developmental concerns as they progress through the life cycle.

The purpose of this chapter is to examine counseling interventions with athletes. Following a discussion of the differences between counseling and clinical interventions, the role of sport in human development will be explored, several examples of counseling strategies will be outlined, and suggestions for working with athletes will be offered.

Defining Counseling Interventions

Although the differences between clinical and counseling psychology training have become less clear over recent years (Davis, Alcorn, Brooks, & Meara, 1992), traditional views suggest that counseling psychology is psychoeducational and developmental, whereas clinical approaches are more remedial and pathology oriented (Danish et al., 1993). Unlike the clinical model's focus on illness, diagnosis, and therapy, counseling approaches emphasize enhancement and growth in normal populations.

Counseling psychologists have been described as career development or life-work planning specialists, system change agents, psychoeducators, and primary prevention specialists (Hansen, 1981). These work roles are consistent with Shertzer and Stone's (1966) definition of counseling as "an interaction process which facilitates meaningful understanding of self and environment and results in the establishment and/or clarification of goals and values for future behavior" (p. 26). For the purpose of this chapter, counseling interventions with athletes are those that focus on development, decision making, and life-work planning across the life span.

Sport and Human Development

If counseling interventions are based on developmental factors, then an understanding of the role of sport in human development is important in planning interventions for athletes. The legitimacy of sport as a cocurricular activity is based on the premise that sport participation prepares students for later adult roles. Sport teaches young people how to live by rules, work hard to achieve goals, and play and interact with others.

Over the years, the efficacy of sport as a vehicle to enhance development and "build character" has spawned considerable debate. Several authors have argued that the increased competitive nature of sport and the emphasis on winning can have a deleterious effect on the psychosocial development of youth sport athletes (Martens, 1978; Ogilvie & Tutko, 1971; Orlick & Botterill, 1975). Unfortunately, only a handful of empirical investigations have been reported and these have questionable designs and inconsistent findings (Danish, Petitpas, & Hale, 1990).

Erikson's (1959) life-span developmental theory suggests that latency-aged children (6 to 10 years old) need to develop a sense of industry or be subject to feelings of inferiority. It has been argued that youth sport involvement, unimpeded by an exclusive emphasis on winning, provides numerous opportunities for participants to acquire and master skills (Martens, 1983). Being a successful athlete, even at youth levels, is highly valued by children and adults, and may result in increased feelings of self-efficacy and a sense of industry (Danish et al.,

1993). If this is the case, then youth sport participation can have a positive influence on children's psychosocial development. This notion has received some empirical support, as shown in Iso-Aloha and Hatfield's (1986) review of the youth sport literature. They concluded that early participation in sport is correlated with positive psychosocial characteristics, but cautioned that no direct causal relationships had been identified.

If sport is structured in a manner that allows young people to master skills and have fun, it is quite likely that they will continue to participate and accrue psychosocial benefits (Gould, 1987). Unfortunately, the nature of the sport system weeds out less physically gifted individuals at each progressive level of competition. The most gifted performers may continue to benefit from sport participation, while many others drop out or are deselected because of a lack of ability.

As students reach late adolescence, their primary developmental task shifts from an emphasis on developing a sense of industry to a need to establish a personal identity (Erikson, 1959). The quest for an identity involves two primary activities (Erikson, 1959; Marcia, Waterman, Matteson, Archer & Orlofsky, 1993). First, individuals must engage in exploratory behavior by which they experiment with various adult roles. Second, these individuals must then make commitments to those ideological and occupational options that appear most consistent with their values, needs, interests, and skills.

Exploratory behavior has been identified as a critical activity for subsequent personal and career development (Jordaan, 1963; Super, 1957). Ironically, the same sport system that provides opportunities to enhance personal competence for youth sport participants may preclude opportunities for exploratory behavior for college-aged adults (Hurley & Cunningham, 1984). It has been suggested that the physical and time demands of intercollegiate sport participation, coupled with the restrictiveness of the sport environment, may discourage student-athletes from exploring nonsport roles or alternative identities (Chartrand & Lent, 1987; Nelson, 1983; Petitpas & Champagne, 1988). This may be particularly true for student-athletes who are Black (Leach & Conners, 1984; Sellers, 1993).

Whereas sport involvement is related to positive psychosocial factors for youth sport participants, the same does not hold true for college athletes. In fact, several empirical investigations have shown that college student-athletes lag behind their age mates on several markers of psychosocial maturity (Blann, 1985; Good, Brewer, Petitpas, Van Raalte, &

Mahar, 1993; Kennedy & Dimick, 1987; Murphy, 1994; Sowa & Gressard, 1983).

Danish (1983) has suggested that athletes may use *selective optimization,* a process in which they give exclusive attention to their sport at the expense of all other interests. This concept is closely linked to a developmental status called *identity foreclosure* (Marcia, 1966). Foreclosure occurs when individuals make commitments to roles without engaging in exploratory behavior. On the surface, identity-foreclosed individuals appear to be psychosocially mature (Marcia et al., 1993). They have low levels of anxiety and confusion, and are clearly committed to a role. However, this seemingly healthy presentation may mask a lack of self-awareness and a failure to develop adequate coping resources (Marcia et al., 1993; Petitpas, 1978). Problems associated with foreclosed commitments to sport roles are most likely to surface when the athletic identity is threatened (Baillie & Danish, 1992; Pearson & Petitpas, 1990).

Several studies have shown that the strength and exclusivity of an athletic identity is related to negative consequences when athletes disengage from sport roles because of retirement, injury, or the selection process (Brewer, 1993; Hinitz, 1988; Kleiber & Brock, 1992). Unfortunately, the sport system does little to assist athletes in preparing for threats to their identities, and often promotes an attitude that only a 110% level of commitment to sport is acceptable (Danish et al., 1993).

There is little written on the impact of athletic participation on later developmental tasks. Heyman (1987) suggested that athletes may not be experienced in developing meaningful interpersonal relationships and therefore would have difficulty resolving the *intimacy-versus-isolation* crisis of young adulthood. Although there is no empirical support for this notion with athlete samples, foreclosed men have been shown to engage in stereotyped or pseudointimate dating relationships (Marcia et al., 1993)

Most formal athletic careers end before individuals reach middle or later adulthood and are faced with the *generativity-versus-stagnation* crisis of this stage. Heyman (1987) suggested that retired athletes, who have not developed another source of meaning or enjoyment in life, would be prone to stagnation, but there is no empirical validation of this hypothesis. Assisting athletes in expanding their self-concepts and identities beyond athletics may be helpful in preparing for later adult transitions (Pearson & Petitpas, 1990).

From this developmental perspective, counseling interventions should be geared toward creating an environment where athletes can learn about themselves through exploratory behavior, develop coping skills, prepare for future events, and have fun. To accomplish these goals, counseling interventions need to target not only athletes, but all components of the athletic system, including coaches, parents, and athletic administrators.

Counseling Interventions

An examination of athletes' transitions provides a useful framework for understanding developmental processes that underlie counseling interventions with this population (Pearson & Petitpas, 1990). Athletes go through a series of normative transitions as they move through their athletic life cycle. For example, National Basketball Association (NBA) players typically progress from youth sport, to high school, to college, to the NBA, before they retire from sport. Each of these transitions can be anticipated and counseling services can be provided. In addition, athletes may also experience unexpected events (e.g., injury) or nonevents (e.g., not making the starting team) that may require attention (Danish et al., 1993; Pearson & Petitpas, 1990).

Although it may be possible to extrapolate from transitional theory and predict those athletes who might be most susceptible to problems during transitions, it is often quite difficult to get at-risk athletes to participate in prevention programs (Pearson & Petitpas, 1990). Therefore, a well designed counseling program should contain several types of interventions.

In designing counseling programs for athletes, it is helpful to link the timing of the transitional experience to an appropriate intervention (Danish et al., 1993). These interventions can occur before, during, or after a transition. Interventions that assist athletes in preparing for upcoming events by identifying transferable skills or developing new coping or life skills are called *enhancement strategies*. During a transition, interventions can buffer the impact of a transition by assisting athletes in mobilizing their personal and support resources. Other counseling related strategies can be used to assist athletes in coping with the aftermath of a transition (Danish, Petitpas, & Hale, 1992).

An examination of counseling programs in two areas, namely career development and athletic injury, may help to clarify the link between developmental theory and the selection of counseling interventions. More information about other expected and unexpected transitions of athletes is available elsewhere (Baillie & Danish, 1992; Petitpas, Brewer, & Van Raalte, in press; Taylor & Ogilvie, 1994).

Career Development

One of the major tasks of career development is exploratory behavior (Crites, 1969; Super, 1957; Tiedeman & O'Hara, 1963). If the athletic system creates an environment that precludes opportunities for exploratory behavior, then it is not surprising that college student-athletes tend to exhibit unrealistic educational and career goals (Blann, 1985; Sowa & Gressard, 1983) and low levels of career maturity (Kennedy & Dimick, 1987).

There is evidence suggesting that as the level of athletic involvement increases, so does both the level of identity foreclosure and the strength and exclusivity of the athletic identity (Brewer, Van Raalte, & Linder, 1993; Good et al., 1993; Murphy, 1994). Chartrand and Lent (1987) suggested that this exclusive commitment to sport roles restricts career decision-making and biases information interpretation, making athletes less likely to accept information that is contrary to their position (e.g., "I'm going to be a professional or Olympic athlete.").

In planning career-development programs for athletes, it is important to design strategies that do not directly challenge or interfere with athletes' sport dreams (Chartrand & Lent, 1987). These programs must be clearly supported by coaches and elite athletes. One example of this type of program is the United States Olympic Committee's Career Assistance Program for Athletes (CAPA). The CAPA Program was designed to assist elite amateur athletes in preparing for and coping with their transition out of sport and to introduce these athletes to the career-development process (Petitpas, Danish, McKelvain, & Murphy, 1992). To accomplish these goals, regional one-day workshops were offered in major cities throughout the United States.

Although CAPA workshops were organized to introduce participants to common career-development themes, they were structured to avoid any direct challenges to participants' athletic dreams. To add additional credibility to the importance of learning these skills, high-visibility athletes who had demonstrated leadership, had been trained, and were willing to self-disclose served as workshop presenters. Workshops included the components shown in Exhibit 1 and detailed subsequently. A typical workshop began with athletes and workshop leaders

---

Exhibit 1

A Career Assistance Program for Athletes

Presenters:	Career development specialists with knowledge of sport environment
	High visibility athletes
Workshop activities:	Managing transitions
	Self exploration
	Career exploration
	Career implementation
Strategies to enhance long-term impact:	Commitment to action
	Follow-up
	Ongoing support groups

---

introducing themselves and sharing their expectations for the day. After summarizing the main expectations for the workshop, one of the leaders would briefly introduce the three main aspects of the career development process: self-exploration, career exploration, and career implementation.

The athlete-spokespersons typically set a tone of openness and trust that carried over into small-group discussions about feelings associated with retirement from sport. Quite often these groups discussed fear of not having any work skills, frustration at not feeling understood, anger about the politics of elite-level sports, confusion about an uncertain future, and sadness about missing teammates and others associated with the sports world.

The small-group discussions revealed that many athletes felt inadequate and lacked confidence in their abilities outside their sport roles. In order to increase participants' self-efficacy in nonsport areas, a series of self-exploration activities that focused on understanding and identifying transferable skills were introduced (Danish et al., 1993; Petitpas & Schwartz, 1989). For example, when participants were asked how they would prepare for a job search, they typically answered, "I don't know." Yet when these same athletes were asked how they might prepare for a major competition, they answered with activities such as scouting the opposition, checking out the playing surface, matching their strengths against an opponent's weaknesses, learning the opponent's plays or tendencies, preparing themselves, getting teammates ready, and developing goals and a competition plan. The group leaders then showed the athletes how these activities paralleled the skills needed for learning about jobs, preparing for interviews, and using their support system. The familiarity of competition planning enabled many of the participants to feel more comfortable with the career planning process.

As the workshop continued, career exploration was introduced and participants learned how to identify clusters of careers that might best match critical components of their personal profile. In addition, several career implementation skills such as writing effective cover letters and resumes, job-interview preparation, and job-hunt strategies were outlined.

The final segment of the CAPA workshop addressed three important issues: a commitment to action, follow-up, and continued support. Goal setting served as participants' initial commitment to action. Participants identified specific activities related to their stage in the career-development process that they believed they could complete in a 2-month period. These specific activities were sequenced along a goal ladder with target completion dates and strategies to overcome any roadblocks that they anticipated might interfere with goal attainment.

Follow-up occurred in two ways. First, letters were sent to all CAPA participants soliciting additional feedback about their workshop experience. This letter contained a copy of their goal ladder and a reminder of their commitment to accomplish several career goals. Second, participants were invited to become involved with local Olympic alumni groups that provided shared experience programs, in which former Olympians provided names of business contacts and information about career possibilities in that area.

Participants also were encouraged to develop support groups of CAPA participants and other elite athletes in the local area. These support groups provided the continued feedback and encouragement that assisted individuals in reaching their career-development objectives. In addition, various sources of continued support were identified and made available to elite athletes through the establishment of a national support network of professional counselors and career-development specialists.[1]

As shown, the CAPA program dealt with common career-development themes, but did so in a manner that addressed several developmental concerns. It also provided enhancement, support, and counsel-

---

1. The specifics of the CAPA workshops have been described elsewhere (Petitpas et al., 1992) and a participant's workbook is available through the Job Opportunity Program of the United States Olympic Committee in Colorado Springs, Colorado.

ing components that served individuals at different stages in their athletic life cycle.

Counseling Injured Athletes

Incurring a physical injury can be a stressor for most individuals. For athletes, who derive significant portions of their self-worth from sports, a serious injury can be a threat to their basic identity (Brewer et al., 1993; Elkind, 1981; Little, 1969).

Several studies have shown a relationship between the strength and exclusivity of athletic identity and negative reactions in athletes who experience injury (Brewer, 1993; Kleiber & Brock, 1992). However, attempts to equate reactions to athletic injury to stage models of grief and loss have received little empirical support (Brewer, 1994). It may be that severe injury presents a threat to the athletic identity, causing emotional distress that continues until the individual believes that full recovery is possible. Two longitudinal studies revealed that athletes experienced mood disturbance following severe injury, but that emotional distress diminished when athletes perceived they were making progress toward recovery (McDonald & Hardy, 1990; Smith, Scott, O'Fallon, & Young, 1990).

In planning counseling interventions for injured athletes, it is important to consider commitment to sport roles as one of several factors that can affect psychological adjustment. If this commitment suggests identity foreclosure, differentiating between situational and psychological types of foreclosure will facilitate treatment planning. As described by Henry and Renaud (1972), *psychological foreclosure* is an intrapsychic defense mechanism whereby individuals ward off threats to their self-worth by avoiding any situations that might challenge their identity. This contrasts markedly with *situationally foreclosed* individuals, whose commitment to an athletic identity is due to a lack of exposure to new options or possibilities, but is not the athlete's main defensive structure. Psychologically foreclosed athletes typically will require more intense treatment options.

Other factors to be considered include coping skills, life stress, family life-cycle dynamics, secondary gain, sources and types of support, characteristics of the injury, and a range of situational variables (Hardy & Crace, 1993; Petitpas & Danish, 1995; Smith, Scott, & Wiese, 1990; Wiese-Bjornstal & Smith, 1993). The complexity of the athletic injury situation requires counselors to put considerable time and energy into understanding athletes and their injury experience.

The goal in counseling injured athletes is to assist them in identifying and developing resources to more effectively cope with the injury process. Although several counseling models for injured athletes offer suggestions for what to do (e.g., Etzel & Ferrante, 1993; Smith et al., 1990; Wiese-Bjornstal & Smith, 1993), there is little attention given to how to intervene with injured athletes (Petitpas & Danish, 1995). Some guidelines for *how* to intervene with injured athletes are outlined below and described subsequently.

1. Build rapport
2. Understand what sports and the injury means to the athletes
3. Insure that athletes understand both the injury and the rehabilitation process
4. Help athletes identify coping resources
5. Use goal setting for rehabilitation
6. Mobilize athletes' social support networks

The first step in the counseling process with injured athletes is to build rapport. This is accomplished by using basic listening skills to learn what the injury means to the athlete. Many athletes display confusion, anxiety, and doubt during the initial time period following a serious injury, so it is important to be patient and avoid the urge to offer a quick "fix." Some athletes may use potentially harmful strategies in coping with the injury (e.g., withdrawing from teammates or abusing alcohol). It is helpful to examine what these strategies are doing for the athlete and then explore other options that might give the athlete the same benefits without the potential costs. Premature confrontations may cause athletes to lose face and may jeopardize the therapeutic relationship (Petitpas & Danish, 1995).

Counselors should insure that injured athletes are provided with specific information about the nature of the injury, the medical procedures to be used, any possible side effects, and the goals of rehabilitation (Danish, 1986). This type of information helps prepare injured athletes for possible plateaus or setbacks in rehabilitation and eliminates some of the potential surprises that could happen during rehabilitation.

Collaborating with injured athletes in identifying coping resources can help them feel more in control and more responsible for rehabilitation outcomes. Using coping skills that injured athletes are already familiar with may help them feel more confident in their ability to influence their recovery. If injured athletes lack appropriate coping resources, counselors can teach them new skills (see Danish & Hale, 1981; Meichenbaum, 1985).

Once coping skills are identified or learned, counselors and injured athletes should collaborate to develop goal ladders for the rehabilitation process and strategies to address any roadblocks to goal attainment. Counselors also typically are involved in working with injured athletes' support systems (e.g., family, sports medicine personnel, coaches) to insure a good rehabilitation and smooth return to competition. A more detailed description of these suggested techniques is provided elsewhere (Petitpas & Danish, 1995).

Although the interventions described above take place after an injury has occurred, it should be noted that the focus of these counseling strategies is on coping-skill identification and acquisition, not pathology. This psychoeducational approach may be familiar to counseling oriented psychologists, but there are several unique considerations in working with this population.

Special Considerations in Counseling Athletes

Psychologists who are accustomed to working with clients in clinical settings often find that consultation work with athletes is quite different from their traditional practice (Danish et al., 1993). Special considerations that must be taken into account when counseling athletes are identified in the following list and described subsequently:

- Knowing sport and the sport system
- Balancing relationship expectations with appropriate boundaries
- Maintaining confidentiality
- Interacting with the media
- Working with coaches and sport administrators
- Maintaining an action orientation

As described earlier, the athletic system can be so narrowly focused that it becomes a closed system, where nonparticipants are seen as outsiders. For example, athletes and coaches have reservations about working with "shrinks," whose lack of understanding of the sport environment can result in behaviors that are intrusive and potentially harmful to performance (Orlick & Partington, 1987).

To gain access to the athletic system, sport and exercise psychology consultants must demonstrate a general understanding of the sport environment and an appreciation for what athletes go through during practices and competitions (Danish et al., 1993). Psychology-trained consultants with a basic understanding of the sport sciences and experience as an athlete have clear advantages over their nonsport oriented colleagues in gaining entry to the sports world. In lieu of this background, experience can be acquired by volunteering to coach youth sport teams or participating in personal fitness programs. It is critical to become familiar with the rules and language of sport. Even with all of the above experiences, it is still necessary for sport and exercise psychologists to demonstrate their interest by attending practices and competitions.

Once sport and exercise psychology consultants gain entry into a sport system, they soon realize that boundaries are not as clearly defined as they are in traditional clinical practice. Contacts with clients are more extensive, and attendance at practices and games is often an expectation (Orlick & Partington, 1987). Although this extended contact is helpful in giving consultants opportunities to observe their clients perform, it is also very time consuming. In addition, consultants may be expected to travel with teams, have meals and share lodging with team members, and participate in team social functions. For psychologists, balancing relationship expectations with appropriate clinical boundaries is often a difficult challenge.

Confidentiality is another common concern in working with athletes. Most often, the initial contact for consultation services will come from a coach, parent, or sport administrator who wants help for a team or an individual athlete. These individuals often assume that because they are responsible for athletes, they should have access to records and be informed about what happens during counseling. It is important to address confidentiality and the nature of the counseling relationship before consultations begin. In cases where a sport administrator hires a sport and exercise psychologist to work with a team, the sport and exercise psychologist must clearly define the nature of the consultation with the coach and the sport administrator.

When working with high-visibility sports, it is quite common to have more exposure to the media. Sport and exercise psychology consultants in these situations are often under increased pressure to disclose information about athlete clients. This is particularly the case when athlete-clients identify the consultant they are working with. Aggressive media personnel often assume that because athletes have publicly named their sport and exercise psychologists, confidentiality is no longer applicable.

Athletes have been shown to be highly influenced by the expectations of significant others, most particularly their coach (LeUnes &

Nation, 1983). Consultants working with athletes must acknowledge this influence and work diligently to build a cooperative working relationship with the coach. Sport and exercise psychologists who claim credit for athlete clients' successes will often create an adversarial relationship with coaches. The most effective consultants appear to be those who work through coaches, and who know when to assist and when to stay in the background (Orlick & Partington, 1987).

Athletes tend to be action oriented. Consultants who provide concrete information that is sport specific are likely to be more effective than those who employ more abstract, insight-oriented interventions (Danish et al., 1993).

Summary

The purpose of this chapter has been to examine counseling interventions with athletes. Sport and exercise psychologists who understand the unique world of athletics are in a better position to gain access to consulting with this unique population. Employing an educational, developmental approach to interventions can enhance athletes' ability to transfer skills that they acquired through sport to enhance their functioning in other life domains and better prepare for future events.

References

Baillie, P. H. F., & Danish, S. J. (1992). Understanding the career transition of athletes. *The Sport Psychologist, 6,* 77–98.

Blann, W. (1985). Intercollegiate athletic competition and students' educational and career plans. *Journal of College Student Personnel, 26,* 115–118.

Brewer, B. W. (1993). Self-identity and specific vulnerability to depressed mood. *Journal of Personality, 61,* 343–364.

Brewer, B. W. (1994). Review and critique of models of psychological adjustment to athletic injury. *Journal of Applied Sport Psychology, 6,* 87–100.

Brewer, B. W., Van Raalte, J. L., & Linder, D. E. (1993). Athletic identity: Hercules' muscles or Achilles heel? *International Journal of Sport Psychology, 24,* 237–254.

Chartrand, J., & Lent, R. (1987). Sports counseling: Enhancing the development of the student-athlete. *Journal of Counseling and Development, 66,* 164–167.

Crites, J. O. (1969). *Vocational psychology.* New York: McGraw-Hill.

Danish, S. J. (1983). Musings about personal competence: The contributions of sport, health, and fitness. *American Journal of Community Psychology, 11,* 221–240.

Danish, S. J. (1986). Psychological aspects in the care and treatment of injured athletes. In P. E. Vinger & E. F. Hoerner (Eds.), *Sports injuries: The unthwarted epidemic* (2nd ed., pp. 345–353). Boston: John Wright.

Danish, S. J., & Hale, B. D. (1981). Toward an understanding of the practice of sport psychology. *Journal of Sport Psychology, 3*, 90–99.

Danish, S. J., Petitpas, A. J., & Hale, B. D. (1990). Sport as a context for developing competence. In T. Gullota, G. Adams, & R. Montemayor (Eds.), *Developing social competency in adolescence* (Vol. 3, pp. 169–191). Newbury Park, CA: Sage

Danish, S. J., Petitpas, A. J., & Hale, B. D. (1992). A developmental-educational intervention model of sport psychology. *The Sport Psychologist, 6*, 403–415.

Danish, S. J., Petitpas, A. J., & Hale, B. D. (1993). Life development interventions for athletes. Life skills through sports. *The Counseling Psychologist, 21*, 352–385.

Davis, K. L., Alcorn, J. D., Brooks, L., & Meara, N. M. (1992). Crystal ball gazing: Training and accreditation in 2000 A.D. *The Counseling Psychologist, 20*, 352–371.

Elkind, D. (1981). *The hurried child*. Reading, MA: Addison Wesley.

Erikson, E. H. (1959). Identity and the life cycle. *Psychological Issues, 1*, 1–171.

Etzel, E. F., & Ferrante, A. P. (1993). Providing psychological assistance to injured and disabled college student-athletes. In D. Pargman (Ed.), *Psychological bases of sport injuries* (pp. 265–283). Morgantown, WV: Fitness Information Technology.

Good, A. J., Brewer, B. W., Petitpas, A. J., Van Raalte, J. L., & Mahar, M. T. (1993). Identity foreclosure, athletic identity, and college sport participation. *The Academic Athletic Journal*, Spring, 1–12.

Gould, D. (1987). Promoting positive sport experiences in children. In J. R. May, & M. J. Askens (Eds.), *Sport psychology: The psychological health of the athlete* (pp. 77–98). New York: PMA.

Hansen, F. K. (1981). Primary prevention and counseling psychology: Rhetoric or reality? *The Counseling Psychologist, 9*, 57–60.

Hardy, C. J., & Crace, R. K. (1993). The dimensions of social support when dealing with sport injuries. In D. Pargman (Ed.), *Psychological bases of sport injuries* (pp. 121–144). Morgantown, WV: Fitness Information Technology.

Henry, M., & Renaud, H. (1972). Examined and unexamined lives. *Research reporter, 7*(1), 5

Heyman, S. R. (1987). Counseling and psychotherapy with athletes: Special considerations. In J. R. May & M. J. Asken (Eds.), *Sport psychology: The psychological health of the athlete* (pp. 135–156). New York: PMA.

Hinitz, D. R. (1988). *Role theory and the retirement of collegiate gymnasts*. Unpublished doctoral dissertation, University of Nevada, Reno.

Hurley, R. B., & Cunningham, R. L. (1984). Providing academic and psychological services for the college athlete. In A. Shriberg, & F. R. Brodzinski (Eds.), *Rethinking services for college athletes* (New Directions for Student Services, No. 28; pp. 51–58). San Francisco: Jossey-Bass.

Iso-Aloha, S., & Hatfield, B. (1986). *Psychology of sports: A social psychological approach*. Dubuque, IA: William C. Brown.

Jordaan, J. P. (1963). Exploratory behavior: The formulation of self and occupational concepts. In D. E. Super, R. Starishevsky, N. Matlin, & J. P. Jordaan (Eds.), *Career development: Self-concept theory* (pp. 46–57). New York: CEEB Research Monographs.

Kennedy, S. R., & Dimick, K. M. (1987). Career maturity and professional expectations of college football and basketball players. *Journal of College Student Personnel, 28*, 293–297.

Kleiber, D. A., & Brock, S. C. (1992). The effect of career-ending injuries on the subsequent well-being of elite college athletes. *Sociology of Sport Journal, 9*, 70–75.

Leach, B., & Conners, B. (1984). Pygmalian on the gridiron: The Black student-athlete at the White university. In A. Shriberg & F. R. Brodzinski (Eds.), *Rethinking services for college athletes* (New Directions for Student Services, No. 28; pp. 31–49). San Francisco: Jossey-Bass.

LeUnes, A., & Nation, J. R. (1983). Saturday's heroes: A psychological portrait of college football players. *Journal of Sport Behavior, 5,* 139–149.

Little, J. C. (1969). The athletic neurosis: A deprivation crisis. *Acta Psychiatrica Scandinavia, 45,* 187–197.

Marcia, J. E. (1966). Development and validation of ego-identity status. *Journal of Personality and Social Psychology, 3,* 551–558.

Marcia, J. E., Waterman, A. S., Matteson, D. R., Archer, S. L., & Orlofsky, J. L. (1993). *Ego identity: A handbook for psychosocial research.* New York: Springer-Verlag.

Martens, R. (Ed.). (1978). *Joy and sadness in children's sports.* Champaign, IL: Human Kinetics.

Martens, R. (1983). Coaching to enhance self-worth. In T. Orlick, J. Partington, & J. Salmela (Eds.), *Mental training for coaches and athletes.* Ottawa, Ontario: Coaching Association of Canada.

McDonald, S. A., & Hardy, C. J. (1990). Affective response patterns of the injured athlete: An exploratory analysis. *The Sport Psychologist, 4,* 261–274.

Meichenbaum, D. (1985). *Stress inoculation training.* Elmford, NY: Pergamon Press.

Murphy, G. M. (1994). *Athletic identity, identity foreclosed thinking, and career maturity of student athletes.* Unpublished master's thesis, Springfield College, MA.

Murphy, S. (Ed.). (1995). *Sport psychology interventions.* Champaign, IL: Human Kinetics.

Nelson, E. S. (1983). How the myth of the dumb jock becomes fact: A developmental view for counselors. *Counseling and Values, 27,* 176–185.

Ogilvie, B., & Tutko, T. (1971). Sport: If you want to build character, try something else. *Psychology Today, 5,* 61–63.

Orlick, T. D., & Botterill, C. (1975). *Every kid can win.* Chicago: Nelson-Hall.

Orlick, T., & Partington, J. (1987). The sport psychology consultant: Analysis of critical components as viewed by Canadian Olympic athletes. *The Sport Psychologist, 1,* 4–17.

Pearson, R., & Petitpas, A. (1990). Transitions of athletes: Developmental and preventive perspectives. *Journal of Counseling and Development, 69,* 7–10.

Petitpas, A. (1978). Identity foreclosure: A unique challenge. *Personnel and Guidance Journal, 56,* 558–561.

Petitpas, A. J., Brewer, B. W., & Van Raalte, J. L. (in press). Transitions of student-athletes: Theoretical, empirical, and practical perspectives. In E. F. Etzel, A. P. Ferrante, & J. W. Pinkney (Eds.), *Counseling college student-athletes: Issues and interventions* (2nd ed.). Morgantown, WV: Fitness Information Technology.

Petitpas, A., & Champagne, D. E. (1988). Developmental programming for intercollegiate athletes. *Journal of College Student Development, 29,* 454–460.

Petitpas, A., & Danish, S. (1995). Psychological care for injured athletes. In S. M. Murphy (Ed.), *Sport psychology interventions* (pp. 255–281). Champaign, IL: Human Kinetics.

Petitpas, A., Danish, S., McKelvain, R., & Murphy, S. (1992). A career assistance program for elite athletes. *Journal of Counseling and Development, 70,* 383–386.

Petitpas, A., & Schwartz, H. (1989, Fall). Assisting student-athletes in understanding and identifying transferable skills. *The Academic Athletic Journal,* 37–42.

Sellers, R. M. (1993). Black student-athletes: Reaping the benefits or recovering from the exploitation. In D. D. Brooks & R. C. Althouse (Eds.), *Racism in college athletics: The African-American athlete's experience* (pp. 143–174). Morgantown, WV: Fitness Information Technology.

Shertzer, B., & Stone, S. (1966). *Fundamentals of Counseling.* Boston: Houghton Mifflin.

Smith, A. M., Scott, S. G., O'Fallon, W. M., & Young, M. L. (1990). Emotional responses of athletes to injury. *Mayo Clinic Proceedings, 65,* 38–50.

Smith, A. M., Scott, S. G., & Wiese, D. M. (1990). The psychological effects of sports injuries: Coping. *Sports Medicine, 9,* 352–369.

Sowa, C. J., & Gressard, C. F. (1983). Athletic participation: Its relationship to student development. *Journal of College Student Personnel, 24,* 236–239.

Super, D. E. (1957). *The psychology of careers.* New York: Harper & Row.

Taylor, J., & Ogilvie, B. C. (1994). A conceptual model of adaptation to retirement among athletes. *Journal of Applied Sport Psychology, 6,* 1–20.

Tiedeman, D. V., & O'Hara, R. P. (1963). *Career development: Choice and adjustment.* New York: College Entrance Examination Board.

Wiese-Bjornstal, D. M., & Smith, A. M. (1993). Counseling strategies for enhanced recovery of injured athletes within a team approach. In D. Pargman (Ed.), *Psychological bases of sport injuries* (pp. 149–182). Morgantown, WV: Fitness Information Technology.

Teaching Life Skills Through Sport: Community-Based Programs for Adolescents

Steven J. Danish, Valerie C. Nellen, and
Susanna S. Owens

We consider sport psychology to be the use of sport to enhance competence and promote development throughout the life span (Danish, Petitpas, & Hale, 1993). Given this definition, sport psychologists are as concerned about life development as they are athletic development. Sport is so closely tied to other life domains that the value of sport psychology interventions extends well beyond the domain of sport. Using sport as a basis for an intervention can serve as a metaphor for a variety of other life situations (Danish et al., 1993).

In this chapter we will describe a community-based intervention using sport as a means of teaching life skills to adolescents. We begin with a definition of adolescence and a discussion of how life experiences influence adolescent behavior and of the value of sport in adolescence. We then address the particular characteristics of sport and their relationship to life skills. Following this, a description of the Sports United to Promote Education and Recreation (SUPER) program, a sport-based life skill intervention program designed to teach sport and life skills, is presented. As part of the description, the Going for the Goal (GOAL) program (Danish et al., 1992a, 1992b) will be discussed, as it is the GOAL component that focuses on the teaching of the life skills. The value and rationale of implementing these sport-based interventions in the community is then introduced. Finally, we outline a process whereby the reader can develop, implement, and evaluate sport-based, community-oriented, life skills programs.

A Perspective on Adolescent Development

We begin by defining adolescence because our perspective on this period of the life span has influenced the intervention program we have developed. The decision as to what kind of intervention to develop is based in large measure on our understanding of individual development and societal functioning. This understanding enables us to differentiate normative, dysfunctional, and optimal development of a target population and thus to discriminate normal from abnormal behavior (Baltes & Danish, 1980; Danish, 1990).

What constitutes adolescence has become increasingly confusing. For many, adolescence simply is considered the period between childhood and adulthood. However, the difficult question to answer always has been, "When is that?" Generally adolescence has been divided into three periods: early (ages 11–14); middle (ages 15–18); and late (ages 18–21) (Steinberg, 1993). Rather than use age as the variable for determining these boundaries, we prefer to consider adolescence a time when an individual is faced with an increasingly complex set of new roles and, at the same time, needs to reject or modify previously held roles.

Havighurst (1953) proposed that there are developmental tasks associated with each phase of the life-span. Among the tasks identified for adolescence and expanded upon by Chickering (1969) are achieving competence, managing emotions, becoming autonomous, establishing relationships, developing more mature interpersonal relationships, clarifying purpose, and developing integrity. The focus, then, during adolescence is on broadening one's horizons.

Hill (1983) organized his perspective of adolescence around three components: the fundamental changes associated with adolescence, the contexts of adolescence, and the psychosocial developments of adolescence. Some of the fundamental changes are the onset of puberty (biological), the beginning of detachment from parents and the attainment of a separate identity (emotional), the development of advanced reasoning (cognitive), a focus on peer as opposed to parental relations (interpersonal), and a transition to adult work and family roles (social). The four main contexts that affect the development of adolescents are families, peer groups, schools, and work and leisure groups. Finally, there are five major psychosocial issues that accompany adolescent development: identity, autonomy, intimacy, sexuality, and achievement (Steinberg, 1993).

The intervention we will be describing is directed at teaching life skills to adolescents, ages 10 to 14. Because of the changes these adolescents are undergoing, developing an effective intervention provides a number of unique challenges. An adolescent's well-being can be viewed as encompassing four domains of health: physical, psychological, social, and personal. Within each of these domains, adolescents may engage in *health-compromising behaviors* (Jessor, 1982), that is, behaviors that threaten the well-being of the individual; or in *health-enhancing behaviors*, behaviors that tend to improve an individual's well-being (Perry & Jessor, 1985).

Among the health-compromising behaviors that researchers have targeted are drug and alcohol abuse, violent and delinquent behaviors, engaging in premature and unsafe sexual activity that may result in pregnancy or sexually transmitted diseases such as AIDS, and dropping out of school (Johnston & O'Malley, 1986; Perry & Jessor, 1985). Researchers have found that youth who have problems in one of these areas are likely to experience problems in other areas (Johnston & O'Malley, 1986). The result is a lifestyle syndrome of health-compromising behaviors.

In a study of middle-school students started at Virginia Commonwealth University's Life Skills Center (Farrell, Danish, & Howard, 1992), researchers found the existence of a lifestyle syndrome of health-compromising behaviors. As a result of this research, two important conclusions were drawn. First, there is a strong relationship among substance abuse, unsafe sexual activity, violent behavior, a lack of school attendance, and school disciplinary problems. Second, students involved in one behavior are likely to be involved in one or more of the other behaviors, but it is unclear which behavior occurs first and how the cycle develops.

In addition to knowing what adolescents do that compromises their health, it is important to understand why they engage in these behaviors. Researchers who have studied several of the health-compromising behaviors among adolescents have identified three reasons why adolescents become involved in these behaviors (Johnston & O'Malley, 1986): (a) a social–recreational and peer factor ("to be part of the group"); (b) a factor related to coping with negative affect ("getting away from problems and frustrations" or "to relax and relieve tensions"); and (c) a lack of optimism about the future.

We believe that adolescents would be able to avoid unhealthy behaviors if they learned healthy options—the life skills associated with future success. However, focusing on a single health-compromising behavior or trying to develop interventions for each behavior individually would be ineffective and time consuming. Instead, we have examined what is needed to become a "successful" adolescent and emphasized the positive side—the learning of health-enhancing behaviors. The core of our interventions is teaching "what to say yes to" rather than "just say no."

To help teach adolescents how to succeed, it is necessary to operationalize success. The definition of *success* will differ across different individuals. However, in this chapter, a successful adolescent is viewed as one who has attained the life skills necessary for effective functioning in the family, high school, and community. These skills are similar to those described by the Task Force on Education of Young Adolescents (1989) as the five desired outcomes or characteristics for every young adolescent. These characteristics are (a) to process information from multiple sources and communicate clearly, (b) to be en route to a lifetime of meaningful work by learning how to learn and therefore being able to adapt to different educational and working environments, (c) to be a good citizen by participating in community activities and feeling concern for, and connection to, the well-being of others, (d) to be a caring and ethical individual by acting on one's convictions about right and wrong, and (e) to be a healthy person (Task Force on Education of Young Adolescents, 1989). Our rationale, then, is to teach adolescents how to think about and develop confidence about their future, and to acquire a sense of personal control over themselves and their environment so that they can make better decisions and ultimately become better citizens.

The Rationale for Sport-Based Programming for Adolescents

Understanding adolescent development and the life events that adolescents experience provides an indication of why using an ecological intervention such as sport has value when targeting these youth. Sport has the participation level necessary for practitioners to reach many, if not most, of the youth in a given community. The demographics are undeniable—only family, school, and television involve children's and adolescents' time more than sport (Institute for Social Research, 1985). As of 1984, about 20 million of the 45 million youth ages 6 to 18 participated in nonschool sports and over 5 million youth participated in interscholastic high school sports (Martens, 1978).

The qualities intrinsic to participation in sport also make it an excellent metaphor for virtually anything that one would wish to teach in an intervention. For many adolescents, as their interest and involvement in sport increases, so does their concern about their performance and competency. Sport then becomes a readily accessible metaphor and example of personal competence and, as a result, an effective analogy for teaching skills for successful living (Danish, Petitpas, & Hale, 1990). All skills regardless of their purpose require practice to master. Basic goal-setting skills can enhance sport performance by clarifying an athlete's training and competition objectives. Furthermore, goal setting can help athletes gain self-efficacy and competence as they master progressive steps in reaching goals they set.

It is this connection between sport skills and skills for successful living that makes coaches, athletes, and sport administrators believe that participation in sport can have a beneficial effect on the psychosocial development of participants far beyond the immediacy of what is learned on the field or in the pool (Danish et al., 1990). It is generally believed that what is learned in sport is directly transferable to the classroom and the boardroom. For example, Kleiber and Roberts (1981) observed that sport has been advocated as "a forum for learning responsibility, conformity, subordination to the greater good, persistence, delay of gratification, and even a degree of risk taking" (p. 114). Kleiber (1983) also suggested that "the sporting contest itself is a deliberately structured test of strength, courage, endurance, and self-control—attributes that may seem elusive to the developing adolescent" (p. 87).

A recent review of the research on the effects of sport on development concluded that sport can have a positive impact on youth's development (Danish, Petitpas, & Hale, 1990). Danish et al. (1990) also concluded that to fully understand the role sport plays in the development of adolescents, it is preferable to examine the topic across the life-span rather than to focus on a single specific developmental period.

Most of the research about the value of sport on adolescents has focused on the impact of sport on the development of identity and feelings of competence among youth (Danish, 1983; Danish, Kleiber, & Hall, 1987; Danish et al., 1990; Kleiber & Kirshnit, 1991). Sport is an arena in which the adolescent searches for personal identity and dreams about what he or she might become. This identity, a product of past experiences and the feedback of significant others, is defined by Waterman (1985) as "a self-definition comprised of those goals, values and beliefs which a person finds personally expressive and to which he or she is unequivocally committed" (p. 6). For most adolescent athletes, sport is an area in which they can clearly define themselves, a welcome respite from the confusion usually associated with the "no-longer-a-child-but-not-yet-an-adult" years.

Sport has the potential to enhance development and to enable people to enjoy themselves in the process. However, enhancing development is not an unplanned outcome of sports participation. It occurs when athletes compete against themselves and, more specifically, against their own potential and goals. As Danish noted in the Athletic Footwear Association (AFA, 1990) report, "When knowing oneself becomes as important as proving oneself, sport becomes an essential element in personal growth and self expression" (p. 6).

Having discussed the potential for positive impact that sport has, it is important to point out that the beneficial aspects of sport need to be cultivated. They do not occur unintentionally. Without careful guidance, those elements of sport that build identity and character can be taken to an extreme and lead to identity foreclosure. As described by Marcia (1966), *identity foreclosure* occurs when a decision is made to invest all of one's energies in one activity such as sport (for further discussion of identity foreclosure see Chapter 8, this volume). For the adolescent who is significantly rewarded for athletic endeavor, the choice not to commit to seeking success in other activities such as school or career may be due to the sense of security associated with sport.

Baltes and Baltes (1980) referred to an individual's decision to select a pathway based on his or her assessment of the environmental demands, motivation, skills, and biological capacities as *selective optimization.* This decision, whether it is called identity foreclosure or selective optimization, is not necessarily harmful; many professions require early and relatively complete commitments. However, if such a decision impedes the individual from seeding a personal identity and thwarts career exploration, it can be harmful (Petitpas & Champagne, 1988). For it is through the process of exploration that individuals learn more about themselves. They acquire additional social competencies through their interaction with others. They receive feedback about their strengths and weaknesses by testing themselves in a variety of situations. Without such exploration, it is likely that a person's self-concept may be too narrowly defined and subject to severe threat in the face of possible loss (Petitpas, 1978).

Sport-Related Life Skills for Adolescents

To use sport to promote personal growth we first must recognize that the activity is a metaphor for enhancing competence, not an end in itself. In other words, the lasting value of a sport experience lies in the application of the principles learned through participation to other areas. Of the millions of children who play sports, only a tiny fraction of a percentage will parlay those activities directly into a career. For the rest, growing up means further defining their identity, discovering other skills and interests, and, it is hoped, applying some of the valuable principles learned during sport participation to their adult pursuits. These transferable behaviors and attitudes are called *life skills.*

Life skills enable individuals to succeed in the environments in which they live. Examples of these environments include families, schools, workplaces, neighborhoods, and communities. Life skills are both behavioral (e.g., effective communication with peers and adults) and cognitive (e.g., effective decision-making). As people age, the number of environments in which they must be successful increases. Environments vary from individual to individual, just as the definition of what it means to succeed differs across individuals and across environments.

Individuals in the same environment are likely to be dissimilar from each other as a result of the life skills they have already mastered, their other resources, and their opportunities, real or perceived. For this reason, those who teach life skills must be sensitive to developmental, environmental, and individual differences and the possibility that the needed life skills may not be the same for individuals of different ages, ethnic or racial groups, or socioeconomic groups (Danish, in press).

Although it is necessary to be sensitive to individual differences, it is also important to recognize that individuals can often effectively apply life skills learned in one environment to other environments. Sport is a particularly appropriate environment to learn skills that can be transferred to other environments. First, physical skills are similar to life skills in the way they are learned—through demonstration and practice (Danish & Hale, 1981; Whiting, 1969). Second, many of the skills learned in sport, including such abilities as performing under pressure, solving problems, meeting deadlines and challenges, setting goals, communicating, handling both success and failure, working with a team and within a system, and receiving and benefitting from feedback are transferable to other life domains.

In transferring skills from one domain to another (e.g., from sport to nonsport areas), it is important to recognize that abilities acquired in one area do not automatically transfer to another area. Understanding what is necessary for skills to be transferable and learning to transfer them are critical life skills in themselves (Danish et al., 1992). To this end, programs using sport as their metaphor need to be aware of this, and to realize that the teaching of skills needs to be accompanied by explanations of how and why these skills will be useful later in life and in other domains.

To accomplish this, adolescents must first believe that they have skills and qualities that are of value in other settings. Individuals of all ages often do not recognize that many of the skills that they have acquired in order to excel in one domain such as sport are transferable to other life areas. Petitpas, Danish, McKelvain, and Murphy (1992) found that elite athletes had a number of insecurities and doubts about their ability to embark on new careers. Generally, these athletes felt that they possessed only sport-related skills and lacked the skills to succeed in a new career. These athletes, who had demonstrated the ability to learn one set of skills to an elite level and were not able to transfer them to another setting, provide an object lesson for the importance of assuring that adolescents learn about transferable skills.

Second, adolescents participating in sports must learn that they possess both physical and cognitive skills. There is more to sport than just throwing a ball or running fast. Athletes plan, set goals, make decisions, seek out instruction, and manage their arousal levels as a routine part of their athletic participation. Some of these same skills are necessary for success in other domains. Without these cognitive skills, it is unlikely that an individual can succeed in any domain. When adolescents are able to recognize that the cognitive skills they possess are critical to their success in sport, they improve their performance in sport and can transfer these skills to other domains.

Third, adolescents must know how physical and cognitive skills were learned and in what context they were learned. Both types of skills are learned in the same fashion. Skills can be acquired both through formal instruction and trial and error. When learned through formal instruction, the skill is named and described and a rationale for its use is given. Then the skill is demonstrated so that the individual can observe correct and incorrect use of the skill. Finally, the individual is given numerous opportunities to practice the skill under supervision to insure continuous feedback. Skills can also be learned by trial and error.

Adolescents practice skills they observe in the playground or on television. They attempt to imitate these skills on their own and, with continual trial and error, they acquire their own version of the skill.

Fourth, adolescents must understand the rationale for learning a skill for sport and nonsport environments. Adolescents may lack confidence in their ability to apply skills in nonsport-settings. They may fear failure or "looking bad." They also may fear the unknowns of new settings, which may add to their hesitancy in attempting to apply the skill.

Fifth, some adolescents have so much of their personal identity tied up in sport that they have little motivation to explore nonsport-roles (Petitpas & Champagne, 1988). They view themselves as successful athletes, not successful people. This mind-set can rob them of their confidence and prevent them from exploring nonsport roles. If they do not think they can be successful in other settings, they may choose not to explore other options.

For many, their interest and involvement in sport and their concern about their performance and competency increases during adolescence. Sport then becomes a readily accessible metaphor and example of personal competence and, as a result, an effective analogy for teaching life skills. Sport skills, like life skills, require practice to master. Basic goal-setting skills can enhance sport performance by clarifying an athlete's training and competition objectives. Goal setting also can help athletes gain self-efficacy and competence as they master progressive steps in reaching goals they set. Through programs such as the one to be described in the next section, adolescents can master and refine basic skill-building by learning how to break objectives into smaller steps, focus on features that are under their control, and build on personal strengths.

The SUPER Program

SUPER (Sports United to Promote Education and Recreation) is a sports-based program that takes advantage of the clearly defined, contingency-dependent, closed environment of sport and uses it as a training ground for life. Participants are taught to use a variety of skills to improve their athletic performance, some physical and some mental, to recognize situations both in and out of sports requiring these skills, and then to apply them in sport and nonsport settings.

The goals of the SUPER Program are for each participant to leave the program with the understanding that (a) there are effective and accessible student-athlete role models; (b) physical and mental skills are important for both sport and life; (c) it is important to set and attain goals in sport; (d) it is important to set and attain goals in life; and (e) roadblocks to goals can be overcome.

In SUPER, older student-athletes, generally well-trained high school student-athletes, are chosen to teach the program to younger adolescents. When peers teach other peers, they become part of what Seidman and Rappaport (1974) called an *educational pyramid.* Such a pyramid starts with the Life Skills Center staff members, who develop the intervention and then train the SUPER student-athlete leaders how to implement the intervention. The SUPER leaders then teach SUPER and GOAL programs to the target audience, the younger peers. The training for the leaders ranges from between 10 and 20 hours. The ultimate training goal is to extend the pyramid by training on-site, community professionals to select and train SUPER leaders.

There are a number of advantages to this implementation strategy. First, by using older peers there is a potential for choosing natural, indigenous leaders to serve as role models. Successful high school students serve as concrete images of what younger adolescents can become. Because these high school students have grown up in the same neighborhoods, attended the same schools, and confronted similar roadblocks, they serve as important role models and thus are in an ideal position to be effective teachers (Danish, 1993). Second, there has been an increasing awareness of the mutual benefits to the peer leaders and the younger students. Riessman (1976) identified what he called the *helper therapy principle.* He noted that the "helper" gains a sense of power, control, and being needed through the helping process. More recently, Lindstrom and Meyer (1994) found similar benefits among senior-level U.S. Diving Federation high school divers when they taught the core component of the SUPER Program to younger divers.

What has not been well examined is the effect on the cognitive development of the peer teacher. Teaching may be one of the best ways of learning. Peer teaching can provide the peer teacher with benefits of both a psychological and content nature: By teaching others how to succeed, the peer teacher's ability to succeed is enhanced.

The core of the SUPER training for the leaders is to learn how to teach the GOAL program (Danish et al., 1992a, 1992b), which consists of 10 1-hour skill-based workshops focusing on teaching goal setting.[1] The skills include (a) the identification of positive life goals, (b) the importance of focusing on the process (not the outcome) of goal attainment, (c) the use of a general problem-solving model, (d) the identification of health-compromising behaviors that can impede goal attainment, (e) the identification of health-promoting behaviors that can facilitate goal attainment, (f) the importance of seeking and creating social support, and (g) ways to transfer these skills from one life situation to another.

SUPER leaders are involved in three sets of activities with their younger peers. They teach sport skills related to specific sports, coach them to improve their sport performance, and teach GOAL. To assist them in the teaching and coaching of sport skills, the leaders are taught how skills are learned, how to teach sport skills to athletes who are less able and experienced, and how to use sport observation strategies. They are told that when they instruct, demonstrate, and conduct practices they must focus on how the youth are participating as opposed to only how well they are performing and participating. Attending to *how* provides information on the mental skills that the youth employ in dealing with coaching and teaching and may be indicative of the manner in which the youths will respond to other forms of instruction, such as school and job training. Observing how participants react entails answering such questions as the following: (a) Are participants attentive when given instructions or observing demonstration? (b) Do they become frustrated with themselves when they cannot perform the activity to their expectations, and does this frustration impede or enhance later efforts? (c) Are they first to initiate questions when they do not understand something being taught or do they wait quietly for someone else to talk first? (d) Are they first to initiate conversation with group members or do they wait for someone else to talk to them first? (e) How do they react when they have a good performance? A bad performance? (f) How do they react when others have a good performance? A bad performance? (g) How do they react when someone gives them praise? Criticism? (h) Do they give up when they can't do as well as they would like or as well as others, or do they continue to practice in a determined manner to learn the skill? (i) Do they compete or cooperate with the other youth?

---

1. GOAL has been taught by itself in schools (Danish, 1993; in press), and as part of a number of sport-based life skills programs in addition to SUPER.

SUPER leaders are asked to speak to the youth about what they have observed. Leaders are asked to explain what they have learned by observing the participants' activities and help them explore what this means to them. Leaders spend at least 1 minute with each youth to discuss the *hows* of their performance (separate from the *how wells*) during each session of the sport clinics.

Other Applications of SUPER

SUPER has served as the basis of a summer camp conducted in conjunction with a school system. It has also been conducted at a neighborhood youth center during the summer. Two other noncommunity-based applications of the SUPER program deserve brief mention.

Since 1993, the Life Skills Center has collaborated with the U.S. Diving Federation to offer GOAL nationally to junior-level divers. The U.S. Diving-GOAL Program involved 55 Junior Olympic (JO) Zone Championships qualifiers being trained to teach GOAL following the championships and then teaching it to younger divers during regional clinics. Rather than conducting the program 1 hour per day, six of the sessions were conducted as part of a one-day workshop. The specifics of how this program was implemented and the results of the program are presented elsewhere (Lindstrom & Meyer, 1994).

The second program deserving mention is a Mentoring Clinic in Golf and Tennis sponsored by the Black Women in Sports Foundation under the direction of Tina Sloan Green, who serves as the Foundation's President/Executive Director. In each of the 10 cities in which the clinics were implemented, 50 to 75 African American mentors and an equal number of mentees were identified. As part of the program, four individual clinics were held in which mentors and mentees learned beginning golf and tennis skills and some segments of the GOAL Program, especially how to set a goal and how to develop a plan to reach the goal. These goal-setting and goal-attainment activities were applied to both the sport skills and to life skills.

The Community as a Setting for Sport-Based Interventions

We believe that the most effective and efficient way to implement sport-based life skills programs such as SUPER is through the community. As defined by the *Random House Dictionary of the English Language* a community is ''a social group sharing common characteristics or interests and perceived or perceiving itself as distinct in some respect from the larger society within which it exists'' (p. 298).

The rationale for the belief that these programs can best be delivered in a community setting is based on several factors. First, as Eitzen (1984) has noted, the significance of sport in America[2]:

> Sport is such a pervasive activity in contemporary America that to ignore it is to overlook one of the most significant aspects of society. It is a social phenomenon which extends into education, politics, economics, art, the mass media, and even international diplomatic relations. Involvement in sport, either as a participant or in more indirect ways, is almost considered a public duty by many Americans.
> (p. 9)

Second, involvement in sport is a community activity. Although individual athletes compete in sport, sports are often group activities played with or against others and may be viewed by large numbers of interested fans and spectators. Third, participation in sport creates and defines new and unique communities (e.g., master's level participants in such sports as swimming and track) and generates identification with community, professional, college, and high school teams. Fourth, use of the community may be the best way to meet program goals.

Rappaport (1977) delineated several models for the delivery of mental health services. He identified two factors that constitute his model: a *conceptual component* and a *style of delivery*. There are a number of different possible conceptual components upon which an intervention can be based. The framework of SUPER and GOAL is a cognitive–behavioral one; it involves the teaching of life skills to enable youth to learn health-enhancing behaviors, to assist them in developing resources and resiliency to overcome the effects of past health-compromising behaviors, and to prevent them from engaging in health-compromising behaviors. However, the style of delivery is often overlooked, and is so critical. Rappaport (1977) identifies two styles: a *waiting-mode* and a *seeking-mode*. The creators of the community-based programs discussed in this chapter have adopted a seeking-mode for the purpose of teaching life skills because we are trying to reach adolescents in their everyday environments and with an educational rather than a clinically-oriented approach.

---

2. Sport has attracted the hearts and minds of the public, and it has also attracted their wallets and pocketbooks. In 1993, the wholesale cost of the sports equipment, apparel, and footwear alone, excluding any program costs such as salaries, medical expenses, insurance, or the rental/building of sport venues, was estimated at over $34 billion (Riddle, 1994).

Developing and Evaluating Community-Based Programs

Effective community-based sport programming requires careful design, implementation, and evaluation. Although the specifics of the programs vary, there are seven essential steps that should be followed in developing all programs. These steps are described in the following sections. (For a more complete discussion of this process, see Danish, 1990.)

Step 1. Determine the Objectives of the Intervention

The goals of the intervention should be based on a needs assessment. Needs can be determined by surveying the community and ascertaining community members' expressed needs, through a demographic study of the community, or by reviewing research reports and literature on the community. Often, more than one of these procedures is used.

In developing the sport-related life skills program for adolescents, needs to help youth develop more optimism about their future, to reduce their involvement in behaviors that compromise their health, and to help them understand that skills learned and applied in sport could be transferred from sport to other life domains were found. The program goals, then, were to teach sport skills and life skills related to sport. In identifying goals for the program being developed, questions asked were "why?" and "for what purpose?"

Step 2. Determine the Target(s) of the Intervention

When designing interventions the questions of *who, where,* and *when* are critical. Rappaport (1977) identified six potential targets for interventions: the individual, the group, an organization, an institution, a community, or society. The SUPER Program intervened at the individual level using a group format. SUPER focused on individuals because program developers believed that they must first teach adolescents new skills before trying to intervene at a larger level.

A separate target issue relates to the timing of the intervention. A recent report by the Institute of Medicine (IOM; 1994) divided mental health interventions into prevention, treatment, and maintenance. Three types of preventive interventions were identified: *universal* interventions, such as prenatal care or parenting training, that focus on the entire population rather than an at-risk segment of the population; *selective* interventions focused on subgroups, such as children of divorced parents or widows, that are at higher than average risk for developing mental health problems; and *indicated* interventions that target individuals or subgroups, such as families who have children with demonstrated behavioral problems, and who are at high risk because they present minimal but detectable signs of mental health problems. The prevention categories in the IOM report refer to interventions that occur before the onset of problems. What was not considered are preventive interventions that have a mental health promotion or enhancement of competence focus. Danish et al. (1993) developed an alternative set of categories related to the timing of intervention. Their system related the timing of the intervention to the experiencing of critical life events such as injury, desertion, and retirement (Danish, Smyer, & Nowak, 1980). Interventions occurring before an event are considered *enhancement* strategies; those occurring during an event are *supportive* strategies; and once an event has occurred, interventions are considered *counseling* strategies. From the life-development intervention perspective developed by Danish and his colleagues (Danish, Petitpas, & Hale, 1992; 1993; 1995), the SUPER and GOAL programs clearly represent *enhancement* strategies.

Step 3. Develop the Technology to Be Used in Implementing the Intervention

Implementation involves assessing both *what* the intervention is and *how* it is being delivered. What is being delivered should be closely related to the goals of the intervention. SUPER, GOAL, and other programs developed at the Life Skills Center teach skills. Therefore, specific life and sport skills, especially ones that transfer from one setting or domain to another, have been identified. A skill-based approach is taken to teach the identified life and sport skills.

Unfortunately, how an intervention is implemented is often overlooked or taken for granted. In the development of technology to be used in program implementation, the program developer becomes an instructional technologist. The developers of SUPER and GOAL believe that a program curriculum should be developed, printed, and made available for dissemination because programs that depend exclusively on the charisma of a leader are less likely to be successful and clearly cannot be replicated. An operations manual describing how to design, train staff, implement, and evaluate the program is also very useful (see Danish et al. 1992a, 1992b). Issues such as how to disseminate the program from one site to another and how to work with various organizations to implement the intervention should be included.

Step 4. Determine the Most Effective Means of Carrying Out the Intervention

When deciding where to deliver the intervention, it is critical that a credible local person assist in developing contacts and serve as a champion for the program. Discussions about implementing the program should be organized so that people in the community believe that the program is being done *with* them not *to* or *for* them. One way to ensure this atmosphere is to hire staff who are or have been employed in the setting, and are indigenous to the community where the program is to be implemented. For example, in one of the SUPER programs taught in conjunction with the schools, program developers have arranged with Richmond City Public Schools to pay for a teacher to be "on loan" to the Life Skills Center. This arrangement helped the Life Skills Center staff better understand the school environment. As a result, implementation of the program in the schools was less disruptive and evaluation was less intrusive.

Step 5. Determine the Reason(s) Evaluation is Being Done

There are three purposes for evaluation. The first purpose is to prove that the intervention was effective or valuable, or did what it was intended to do. In an age of accountability, decision-makers and funding sources want this kind of evidence as a means of determining whether a program should be continued. Too often this kind of evaluation is confused with research. Evaluators must be sensitive to the needs and expectations of those wanting the evaluation and provide it in a format that meets these needs. The second reason is to improve the intervention. The emphasis is on gathering information and making judgements to change any aspect of the intervention for the purpose of bettering it. These two purposes should be interactive. The third purpose of evaluation is to advance scientific knowledge. Interventions serve both a knowledge-application and a knowledge-generation role (Baltes & Willis, 1977).

Step 6. Determine the Types of Evaluation to Be Conducted and the Most Effective Means of Carrying Them Out

For an evaluation to be effective, it must be a part of the intervention, not a process applied after its implementation (Danish & Conter, 1978). There are two types of evaluation: process or formative evaluation; and outcome or summative evaluation (Scriven, 1980). Whereas the goals of the two types of evaluations are different, they are generally inter-related in that they often go on at the same time. *Process evaluations* are conducted for a number of reasons, including monitoring the progress of the intervention, determining how it is being received, assessing the cost-effectiveness of the activity, and assisting in making replication possible (Price & Smith, 1985). The overall question being asked in process evaluations is whether the target population learned what was taught and why or why not (Danish, 1990). The failure of the target population to learn what is being taught may have nothing to do with the goals of the intervention but may be related to the process of the implementation. Problems can stem from the participants, the instructors, the topic area, and the setting. In *outcome evaluations*, the question asked is whether the intervention goal was attained.[3]

A number of the programs described herein have been, and are presently, undergoing evaluation. Readers interested in the results of the evaluation should consult Lindstrom and Meyer (1994) and Meyer (1994a, 1994b).

Step 7. Develop Intervention Programs That Can Be Disseminated at More Than One Site

Interventions are often developed and implemented for one site. However, the test of the effectiveness of a program is how well it can be disseminated to more than one site. If a program cannot be implemented in more than one site, the intervention, regardless of how effective it is in the original site, has limited usefulness. First, to facilitate program development and diffusion, it is important to ensure that the cost of dissemination is reasonable so that the program can become an ongoing part of a setting. Dissemination then cannot be dependent on ongoing federal or state funding, but should be able to be sponsored by a school district, an agency, or a private business. To keep the cost manageable at other sites, program developers at the Life Skills Center focus on conducting training sessions for trainers identified by the site. These trainers may be school or organizational staff or personnel such as graduate students from participating universities. These trainers then train the high school student-leaders and serve as on-site coaches and supervisors. As a result, there is a cadre of individuals familiar with the

---

3. Research by McCaul and Glasgow (1985) provides a particularly good representation of the difficulties of evaluation as it relates to preventing adolescent smoking.

programs in every site, so that the need for Life Skills Center staff to be at a site more than two or three times—including setting up the program—is limited. Second, by focusing on life skills or some generic concept rather than an individual health-compromising behavior, the attractiveness of the programs significantly increases. In some cities, violence prevention has become the "hot" topic; in other cities, it is pregnancy prevention or drug abuse prevention. Having a life- and sport-skills focus enables the Life Skills Center to meet a number of needs and to complement other, often state-mandated programs. A life-skills program also is less controversial in terms of its content. Third, programs that have the potential to enhance life skills are much more likely to be supported by private businesses because they see these skills as essential for future employees. Fourth, for a program that is compact, relatively easy to implement, and has a well-developed technology (see step 3), dissemination problems are minimized.

Closing Comments

In this chapter we have described a community-based intervention using sport as a means of teaching life skills to adolescents. We have also presented a rationale for such a program based on an understanding of developmental issues faced by adolescents, adolescents' commitment to sport, and the value of using the community as a setting to deliver such an intervention. Finally, we have outlined a process that can be used by others to develop, implement, and evaluate sport-based, community-oriented, life-skills program.

Psychologists have few opportunities to observe adolescents intent on optimizing their development in any area and assist them in this process. Because of the importance of sport for youth, psychologists are in a unique position to help young people enhance their sport performance and, at the same time, teach them how to transfer skills learned in sport to other life domains. Programs such as the ones described in this chapter enable psychologists interested in sport to combine some of their vocational and avocational interests—something professionals rarely have the opportunity to do.

References

Athletic Footwear Association (1990). *American youth and sports participation*. North Palm Beach, FL: Author.

Baltes, P. B., & Baltes, M. M. (1980). Plasticity and variability in psychological aging: Methodological and theoretical issues. In G. Gurski (Ed.), *Determining the effects of aging on the central nervous system.* Berlin, Germany: Shering.

Baltes, P. B., & Danish, S. J. (1980). Intervention in life-span development and aging: Issues and concepts. In R. R. Turner & H. W. Reese (Eds.), *Life-span developmental psychology: Intervention* (pp. 49–78). New York: Academic Press.

Baltes, P. B., & Willis, S. L. (1977). Toward psychological theories of aging and development. In J. E. Birren & K. W. Schaie (Eds.), *Handbook of the psychology of aging.* New York: Reinhold-Van Nostrand.

Chickering, A. W. (1969). *Education and identity.* San Francisco: Jossey-Bass.

Danish, S. J. (1983). Musings about personal competence: The contributions of sport, health, and fitness. *American Journal of Community Psychology, 11,* 221–240.

Danish, S. J. (1990). Ethical considerations in the design, implementation and evaluation of developmental interventions. In C. B. Fisher & W. W. Tryon (Eds.), *Ethics in applied developmental psychology: Emerging issues in an emerging field* (Vol. 4, pp. 93–112). New York: Ablex.

Danish, S. J. (1993). A life-skills, multi-site intervention program for adolescents. *NMHA Prevention Update, 4,* 8–9.

Danish, S. J. (1995). Reflections on the status and future of community psychology. *Community Psychologist, 28,* 16–18.

Danish, S. J., & Conter, K. R. (1978). Intervention and evaluation: Two sides of the same community coin. In L. Goldman (Ed.), *Research Methods for Counselors* (pp. 343–359). New York: Wiley.

Danish, S. J., & Hale, B. D. (1981). Toward an understanding of the practice of sport psychology. *Journal of Sport Psychology, 3,* 90–99.

Danish, S., Kleiber, D., & Hall, H. (1987). Developmental intervention and motivation enhancement in the context of sport. In *Advances in motivation and achievement: Enhancing motivation (Vol. 5,* pp. 211–238). Greenwich, CT: JAI Press.

Danish, S. J., Mash, J. M., Howard, C. W., Curl, S. J., Meyer, A. L., Owens, S. S., & Kendall, K. (1992a). *Going for the Goal Leader Manual.* Virginia Commonwealth University: Department of Psychology.

Danish, S. J., Mash, J. M., Howard, C. W., Curl, S. J., Meyer, A. L., Owens, S. S., & Kendall, K. (1992b). *Going for the Goal Student Activity Manual.* Virginia Commonwealth University: Department of Psychology.

Danish, S. J., Petitpas, A. J., & Hale, B. D. (1990). Sport as a context for developing competence. In T. Gullotta, G. Adams, & R. Monteymar (Eds.), *Developing social competency in adolescence* (Vol. 3, pp. 169–194). Newbury Park, CA: Sage.

Danish, S., Petitpas, A., & Hale, B. (1992). A developmental-educational intervention model of sport psychology. *The Sport Psychologist, 6,* 403–415.

Danish, S., Petitpas, A., & Hale, B. (1993). Life development intervention for athletes: Life skills through sports. *Counseling Psychologist, 21,* 352–385.

Danish, S., Petitpas, A., & Hale, B. (1995). Psychological interventions with athletes: A life development model. In S. Murphy (Ed.), *Clinical Sport Psychology.* Champaign, IL: Human Kinetics.

Danish, S. J., Smyer, M. A., & Nowak, C. A. (1980). Developmental intervention: Enhancing life-event processes. In P. B. Baltes & O. G. Brim, Jr. (Eds.), *Life-span development and behavior* (Vol. 3, pp. 339–366). New York: Academic Press.

Eitzen, D. S. (1984). *Sport in contemporary society.* New York: St. Martin's Press.

Farrell, A. D., Danish, S. J., & Howard, C. W. (1992). Risk factors for drug use in urban adolescents: Identification and cross-validation. *American Journal of Community Psychology, 20,* 263–286.

Havighurst, R. J. (1953). *Human development and education*. New York: Longmans.

Hill, J. (1983). Early adolescence: A research agenda. *Journal of Early Adolescence, 3,* 1–21.

Institute of Medicine (1994). *Reducing risks for mental disorders: Frontiers for preventive intervention research*. Washington, DC: National Academy Press.

Institute for Social Research. (1985). *Time, goods & well-being*. Ann Arbor: University of Michigan.

Jessor, R. (1982). Critical issues in research on adolescent health promotion. In T. J. Coates, A. C. Petersen, & C. Perry (Eds.), *Promoting adolescent health: A dialogue on research and practice* (pp. 447–465). New York: Academic Press.

Johnston, L., & O'Malley, P. (1986). Why do the nation's students use drugs and alcohol: Self-reported reasons from nine national surveys. *Journal of Drug Issues, 16,* 29–66.

Kleiber, D. A. (1983). Sport and human development: A dialectical interpretation. *Journal of Humanistic Psychology, 23,* 76–95.

Kleiber, D. A., & Kirshnit, C. E. (1991). Sport involvement and identity formation. In L. Diamant (Ed.), *Mind-body maturity: Psychological approaches to sports, exercise, and fitness* (193–211). New York: Hemisphere.

Kleiber, D. A., & Roberts, G. C. (1981). The effects of sport experience in the development of social character: An exploratory investigation. *Journal of Sport Psychology, 3,* 114–122.

Lindstrom, K. K., & Meyer, A. L. (1994). *The United States diving 1993 GOAL program clinics* (Report No. 3 of the Life Skills Center). Virginia Commonwealth University: Department of Psychology.

Marcia, J. E. (1966). Development and validation of ego-identity status. *Journal of Personality and Social Psychology, 3,* 551–558.

Martens, R. (1978). *Joy and sadness in children's sports*. Champaign, IL: Human Kinetics.

McCaul, K. D., & Glasgow, R. E. (1985). Preventing adolescent smoking: Have we learned about treatment construct validity? *Health Psychology, 4,* 361–387.

Meyer, A. L. (1994a). *Assessing the effectiveness of the goal program* (Report No. 5 of the Life Skills Center). Virginia Commonwealth University: Department of Psychology.

Meyer, A. L. (1994b). The effectiveness of a peer-led health promotion program for sixth graders. Unpublished doctoral dissertation, Pennsylvania State University, University Park.

Perry, C. L., & Jessor, R. (1985). The concept of health promotion and the prevention of adolescent drug abuse. *Health Education Quarterly, 12,* 169–184.

Petitpas, A. (1978). Identity foreclosure: A unique challenge. *Personnel and Guidance Journal, 56,* 55–561.

Petitpas, A. L., & Champagne, D. E. (1988). Developmental programming for intercollegiate athletes. *Journal of College Student Development, 29,* 454–460.

Petitpas, A., Danish, S., McKelvain, R., & Murphy, S. (1992). A career assistance program for elite athletes. *Journal of Counseling and Development, 70,* 383–386.

Price, R., & Smith, S. (1985). A guide to evaluating prevention programs in mental health. *Monograph of the National Institute of Mental Health, 6* (DHHS Publication No. ADM 85-1365). Washington, DC: U.S. Government Printing Office.

Rappaport, J. (1977). *Community psychology: Values, research, and action*. Chicago: Holt, Rinehart & Winston.

Riddle, J. (1994). *1994 State of the Industry Report*. North Palm Beach, FL: Sporting Goods Manufacturing Association.

Riessman, (1976). How does self-help work? *Social Psychology, 7,* 41–45.

Scriven, M. (1980). *The Logic of Evaluation*. Inverness, CA: Edgepress.

Seidman, E., & Rappaport, J. (1974). The educational pyramid: A paradigm for training, research, and manpower utilization in community psychology. *American Journal of Community Psychology, 2*, 119–130.

Steinberg, L. (1993). *Adolescence* (3rd ed.). New York: McGraw-Hill.

Task Force on Education of Young Adolescents (1989). *Turning points: Preparing American youth for the 21st century*. New York: Carnegie.

Waterman, A. S. (1985). *Identity in adolescence: Processes and contents*. San Francisco: Jossey-Bass.

Whiting, H. T. A. (1969). *Acquiring ball skill: A psychological interpretation*. London: G. Bell & Sons.

Part Three

Clinical Issues

10 Assessment in Sport and Exercise Psychology

John Heil and Keith Henschen

Measurement is at the heart of sport, wherein competitive excellence is quantified in exquisite detail—objectively by time and distance and subjectively by the evaluation of form or in the quality of performance. The Olympic motto—*citius, altius, fortius*[1]—underscores the fundamental role of measurement in sport. Psychological assessment in sport, simply stated, includes any systematic attempts at measurement of psychological attributes relevant to athletes. It includes the use of formal assessment devices, behavior analysis, and the structured interview. Although this chapter focuses on formal assessment instruments, the authors recognize the structured interview as the most versatile of assessment methods.

The purpose of this chapter is to provide a brief history of assessment in sport and exercise psychology and then to describe four major areas of sport-related assessment. These areas include *traditional clinical* (e.g., assessment of an athlete with an eating disorder or substance abuse problem); *health and exercise* (e.g., assessment of an individual's motivation to exercise); *performance enhancement* (e.g., assessment of individual athletes' performance-related mental skills); and special assessment topics (e.g., selection testing, polygraph testing, head injury assessment, and psychophysiological assessment). The chapter concludes with two case studies designed to highlight application of assessment principles.

---

1. Faster, higher, stronger.

Milestones and Controversies

The first significant milestone in psychological testing in sport is the work of the "grandfather" of sport psychology, Coleman Griffith (Kroll & Lewis, 1970), in the 1930s. He developed psychological questionnaires and surveys assessing attitudes, perceptions, and personality characteristics of coaches and athletes. Although his instruments would fail to meet the rigor of contemporary psychometric standards, Griffith's work was an interesting beginning that was fairly well accepted by the athletic establishment, and that paved the way for future work. The second major milestone was the formulation of the Athletic Motivation Inventory by Tutko, Lyon & Ogilvie (1969). This instrument measured several variables including aggressiveness, coachability, and trust in ability. In part because of validity issues, an emotionally charged controversy regarding whether the Athletic Motivation Inventory (AMI) was being used inappropriately for selection followed. Nevertheless, the AMI was an innovative attempt to bring psychological testing into a sport specific framework.

The 1960s and 1970s saw the emergence of the sport personology debate. At the center of the debate was the question of whether there was, in fact, an ideal sport personality. This controversy was resolved when it became apparent that using standardized personality assessment devices was not a viable method of developing a typology of the successful athlete. For a more detailed treatment of the sport personology debate, see Mahoney and Epstein (1981) and Straub (1978).

In 1976, the National Football League Players Union voted to not allow psychological testing of their members. This action was sparked by a number of incidences of the misuse of psychological testing and its results. Players were being selected, deselected, and stereotyped by psychological measures not formulated for that purpose. In retrospect, it appears that the behavior of psychologists hired by professional teams was questionable at best and perhaps unethical, and the players of the National Football League in essence said "no more."

A major breakthrough in sport psychology testing was the work of Morgan and his colleagues (e.g., Morgan, Brown, Raglin, O'Connor, & Ellickson, 1987; Morgan & Pollock, 1977) using the Profile of Mood States (POMS; McNair, Lorr, & Droppleman, 1971). It was determined that high-level performers normally manifested mood states above the mean in vigor, and below the mean in tension, anger, depression, fatigue, and confusion. In graphic presentation, this yielded a distinctive

Figure 1

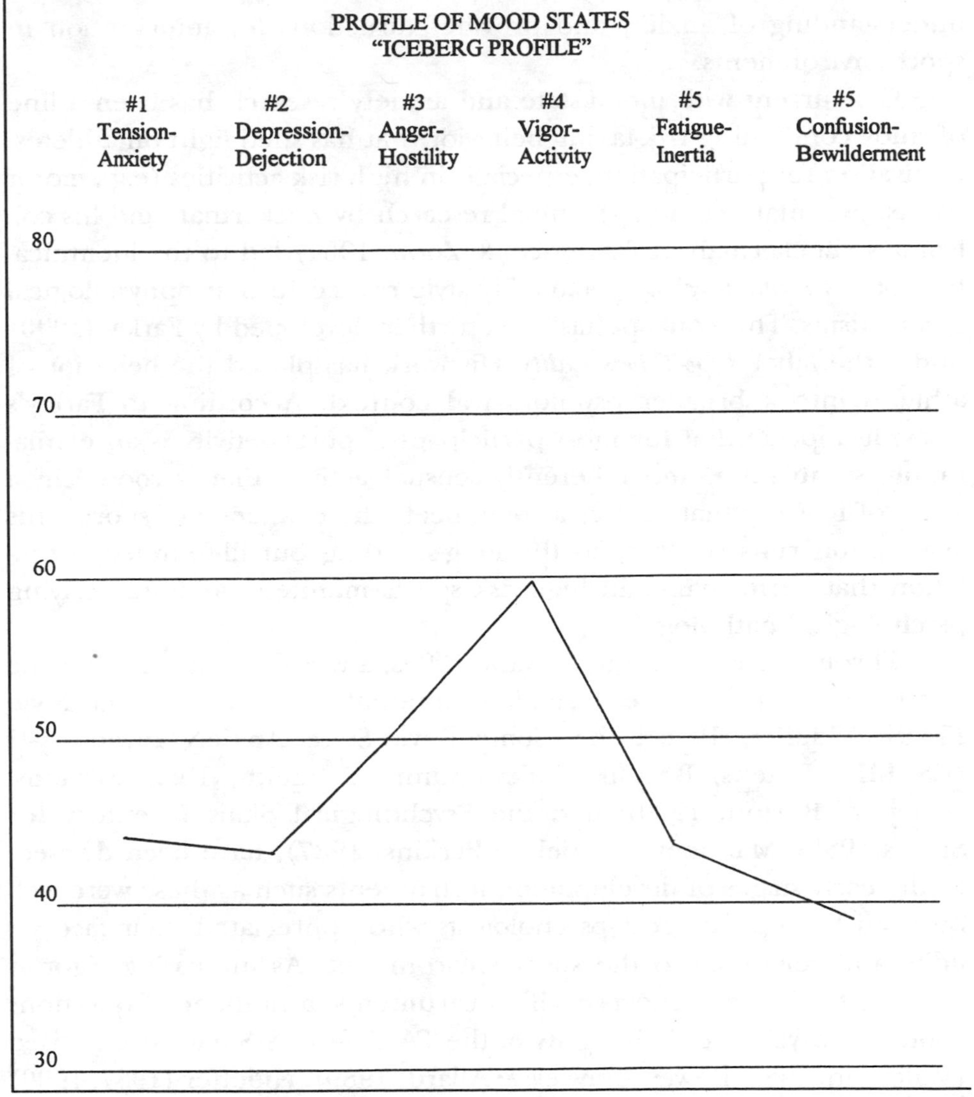

PROFILE OF MOOD STATES
"ICEBERG PROFILE"

#1 Tension- Anxiety	#2 Depression- Dejection	#3 Anger- Hostility	#4 Vigor- Activity	#5 Fatigue- Inertia	#5 Confusion- Bewilderment

The Profile of Mood States "Iceberg Profile".

shape that has been called the *iceberg profile* (see Figure 1). The fundamental value of this work was its shift in emphasis from stable personality traits to mood profiles. An independent but related line of research focused on the role of anxiety and its relationship to sport performance. The State Trait Anxiety Inventory (STAI; Spielberger, Gorsuch, & Luchene, 1970) proved to be a valuable instrument sensitive to the variations in anxiety experienced by athletes. This work has been extended by

Hanin (1986, 1993). His *individual zones of optimal functioning* (IZOF) has provided a firm grounding in sport-relevant theory that facilitates understanding of anxiety and provides directions for intervention in sport environments.

Concurrent with mood-state and anxiety research has been a line of study concerning risk-taking behavior that has shed light on athletes' motivation for participation, especially in high-risk activities (e.g., motor sports, mountain climbing). Initial research by Zuckerman and his colleagues (Zuckerman, Kolin, Price, & Zoob, 1964) led to the identification of a *sensation-seeking* personality style rooted in neurophysiological mechanisms. This concept has been further developed by Farley (1990) under the label *Type-T personality*. His work has placed the behavior of athletes into a broader psychological context. According to Farley's work, it appears that for most participants, sports activity is an exhilarating, stimulating, and inherently sensual activity that is rooted in a sense of mastery that evolves as one meets the challenge of sport. This assumption runs contrary to the long-standing but ill-founded speculation that performance in high-risk sports manifests some underlying psychological pathology.

Through the 1980s and into the 1990s, a vast array of sport-specific instruments, such as the Test of Attentional and Interpersonal Style (TAIS; Nideffer, 1976); the Competitive State Anxiety Inventory-II (CSAI-II; Martens, Burton, Vealey, Bump, & Smith, 1982; Martens, Vealey, & Burton, 1990); and the Psychological Skills Inventory for Sports (PSIS; Mahoney, Gabriel, & Perkins, 1987), have been devised. In the early stages of development, instruments such as these were well received by applied sport psychologists who appreciated their face validity and relevance to the sport environment. As increasing rigor is brought to the early sport-specific instruments, a number of questions about the psychometric integrity of the TAIS and PSIS have been raised (Vallerand, 1983; Dewey, Brawley, & Allard, 1989). Nideffer (1987, 1990) has rebutted criticisms that the TAIS lacks psychometric integrity and should not be used for research purposes by noting the different objectives and priorities of the researcher and the applied practitioner.

Current Assessment Tools

Currently, there is a broad range of assessment instruments available to the practitioner (Gauvin & Russell, 1993; Ostrow, 1990). The *Directory of Psychological Tests in the Sport and Exercise Sciences* (Ostrow,

1990) identifies 175 tests organized into 20 different categories. The topics include achievement orientation, aggression, anxiety, attention, attitudes toward sport and exercise, attributions, body image, cognitive strategies, cohesion, confidence, imagery, leadership, life adjustment, locus of control, motivation, and sex roles. Today, the early historical emphasis on stable multidimensional measures of athletic personality has broadened to include measures of mood and cognitive skills (e.g., attention control, imagery). Multidimensional measures of personality style continue to play an important role in athlete selection and in the assessment of sport-related adjustment problems (such as failure to rehabilitate from injury and poor adjustment to retirement).

Because there are so many types of psychological assessment instruments available, it is of little wonder that there are such widely varying testing practices among sport psychology professionals. Depending upon their training, sport psychologists may be comfortable with certain types of psychological testing but not others. It is the rare sport psychologist who can competently use clinical instruments, performance measures, and behavioral assessment. Most clinical assessment instruments require that the practitioner have advanced psychology training to administer and interpret the tests. This requirement may preclude exercise/kinesiology-trained performance-enhancement sport psychologists from using clinical instruments. Clinical sport psychologists are not usually trained in the use of sport-specific instrumentation. Therefore, clinical sport psychologists may also be limited in the assessment techniques available to them. This situation is further confounded by emerging trends in psychological testing that require specialized expertise not routinely a part of the training of either clinical psychologists or performance-enhancement sport psychologists. These trends, discussed in the final section of this chapter, include head injury assessment, psychophysiological assessment, polygraph testing, and selection testing.

Assessment Guidelines

At its best, psychological testing offers a relatively concise, time-efficient, and objective approach to assessing athlete behavior. Individual differences in type of practice and philosophy regarding testing will determine the approach taken. As a general rule, clinical sport psychologists appear to be more testing oriented than performance-enhancement

---

Exhibit 1

Assessment Guidelines for Sport Psychologists

1. Share your personal philosophy concerning testing with the athlete along with an explanation of the limitations inherent in testing.
2. Be sensitive to preconceptions that the athlete may carry into the testing situation.
3. Wherever possible, use assessment instruments that have a readily apparent relationship to what is being investigated; use sport-specific, validated, reliable instruments when available.
4. Provide results in the language of the athlete or coach, and avoid the use of psychological jargon.
5. Use sport examples, preferably from the athlete's sport, when interpreting test results.
6. Offer the athlete the opportunity to ask follow-up questions at a later date.
7. Be sure to clarify confidentiality issues with the athlete; the athlete should know with whom and under what circumstances information will be shared.
8. Let your overall approach to assessment provide a system of checks and balances whereby triangulation of information enhances confidence in interpretation; behavioral analysis is an excellent complement to the use of formal assessment measures in this regard.

---

sport psychologists. As the context of testing moves away from an individual office-based clinical setting to a team-based performance-enhancement setting, caution is urged. Simply put, expectations and receptivity to testing in the sport environment are manifested in a way distinct from that noted in the clinical settings.

Sport can be considered a subculture in which behavior is guided by a unique set of principles with subtleties of language and behavior that distinguish the insider from the outsider. One should approach a particular sport environment with the same sensitivity that one brings to work with culturally diverse populations. Even as the sport psychologist takes steps to better understand the behavior of the athlete, the athlete is assessing the sport psychologist. Where testing or any intervention is conducted in a way that conveys respect, trust, and efficacy, the intervention is well begun (Ravizza, 1988). (See Exhibit 1 for assessment guidelines for sport psychologists.)

Sensitivity to *response sets* (e.g., fake good, fake bad, conservative) is as important in the sport environment as it is in the clinical setting (Nideffer, 1981). A strong emphasis on a positive attitude in sport and a reluctance to show vulnerability may result in a fake good response. This is most likely to be found with selection testing. Ultimately, the fake bad response is less likely to be seen in the performance situation than in the clinical one. When encountered, it may well be a reflection of athlete hostility or a rejection of the test situation. However, this should be relatively easy to distinguish with appropriate follow-up. Emphases on being tough minded and playing with pain may encourage athletes to underreport both pain and injury. In fact, athletes may be explicitly deceitful in this regard.

Assessment in Practice

In this section, four contexts for testing are reviewed: clinical, focused on the assessment of disorder; health and exercise, focused on the use of exercise for rehabilitation and a healthy lifestyle; performance enhancement, focused on the evaluation of mental skills; and special topics, including selection testing, polygraph testing, head-injury assessment, and psychophysiological assessment. In practice, the distinctions between these four categories blur. Regardless of the context of assessment, sport psychologists should be sensitive to the presence of *subclinical syndromes*, which are behaviors not severe enough to meet a diagnosis, but sufficiently disruptive to impair health or performance.

Clinical

The clinical presentation of an athlete with a psychological disorder will be tempered by elements unique to sport such as pressures related to training and competition and expectations of strong performance despite personal adversity. Athletes may be reluctant participants in therapy out of fear that they may be withheld from competition or because of resistance to disclose attitudes or feelings that might be interpreted as signs of psychological weakness. In addition, athletes appear to be at increased risk for certain disorders (e.g., problems of adjustment to injury and retirement, eating disorders, alcohol and drug use disorders) as a consequence of the nature and demands of athletic participation (for further discussion of psychopathology in athletes, see chapter 11, this volume).

Injury
Injury is a commonplace occurrence in sport. Success at coping with injury is ultimately linked to success as an athlete. Injury assessment

should identify the level of stress and coping in the athlete to determine an appropriate level of intervention (Heil, 1993; Pargman, 1993).

Of greatest concern are severe injuries, which threaten athletes' sense of well being and their sport careers. As such, psychological intervention with severely injured athletes is a formidable challenge. Where significant adjustment problems are noted, a traditional clinical approach to assessment is warranted using instruments such as the Minnesota Multiphasic Personality Inventory-2 (MMPI-2), which has been well studied with injured populations (Fordyce, 1979; Wise, Jackson, & Rocchio, 1979). Structured interviews such as the Emotional Responses of Athletes to Injury Questionnaire (ERAIQ; Smith, Scott, & Wiese, 1990) can identify subclinical adjustment problems. This allows early intervention for minor mood disturbances, compliance problems, conflict with treatment providers, secondary gain behaviors, and fear of reinjury.

In otherwise well adjusted athletes, fear of reinjury may occur with return to play. Fear of reinjury can also be assessed by undertaking behavior analyses assessing pain and emotional response across a variety of conditions including athlete practice, rehabilitation, and day-to-day activities. Because the physician and sports medicine specialist provide a first line of intervention, they play an important role in the identification of problems of adjustment to injury. The Sports Medicine Injury Checklist (Heil, 1993) has been devised for medical specialists to facilitate early identification of psychological adjustment problems (see Figure 2).

Eating Disorders

Athletes appear to be at increased risk relative to the general population for eating disorders like anorexia nervosa and bulimia (Thompson & Sherman, 1993). This is largely a reflection of the sport environment, which emphasizes ideal body size, shape, and weight and which may, at times, emphasize athletic performance over health. Female athletes in sports that emphasize subjective evaluation of form (e.g., gymnastics, dance, figure skating) appear to be at greatest risk (Thompson & Sherman, 1993). However, eating disorders are found among male and female athletes in other sports also. Disordered patterns of eating among male athletes appear most commonly in sports such as boxing, wrestling, and the martial arts in which competitions occur in specific weight classes (Thompson & Sherman, 1993).

Widespread concern regarding the prevalence of eating disorders

Figure 2

SPORTSMEDICINE INJURY CHECKLIST

ACUTE PHASE

_____ Pain fails to respond to routine management strategies
_____ Failure to comply with recommended rehabilitation program
_____ Emotional (depression, irritability, confusion, guilt, withdrawal)
_____ Irritational fear or anxiety in specific situations in the otherwise well-adjusted athlete
(may be seen as avoidance of feared situation)
_____ Overly optimistic attitude toward injury and recovery
_____ Persistent fatigue
_____ Sleep problems
_____ Gross overestimate or underestimate rehab progress by athlete

CHRONIC PHASE

Current Factors

_____ Pain persists beyond natural healing
_____ "Odd" descriptions of pain
_____ Inconsistency in "painful" behavior or reports of pain
_____ Failed attempt(s) at return to play
_____ Performance problems following return to play
_____ Inability to identify realistic goals for recovery
_____ Recent stressful changes in sport situation
_____ Stressful life circumstances (within the last year)
_____ Depression (including changes in sleep, appetite, energy, and libido)
_____ Strained relationships with coaches, teammates, or friends
_____ Personality conflicts between treatment providers and the athlete
_____ Poor compliance with scheduled visits, medication usage, etc.
_____ Seeks additional medical treatment with consultation to current treatment providers
(including emergency room visits)
_____ Iatrogenic problems
_____ Repeated pain (especially psychoactive) medication requests
_____ Evidence of illicit drug use (recreational or ergogenic)

HISTORY

_____ Multiple surgeries at pain site
_____ Chronic pain in the same or another physiologic system (may be resolved)
_____ Family member(s) with chronic pain
_____ Problematic psychosocial history (behavior problems in school; vocational, marital
or legal problems, history of physical or sexual abuse)
_____ Problematic psychological history (repeated or prolonged psychological adjustment
problems; alcohol/drug problems; eating disorder)

The Sports Medicine Injury Checklist.

in sport is reflected in special publications by the American College of Physicians, the Association for the Advancement of Behavior Therapy, the Committee on Sports Medicine of the American Academy of Pediatrics, the American College of Sports Medicine, and the United States Olympic Committee. Because of the severity of eating disorders and their resistance to treatment, early identification is essential. Therefore, effective assessment methods should focus on identification of subclinical patterns of disordered eating. Routine monitoring of body weight in high-risk sports, preventive education programs that include nutritional education, and sensitivity to the diagnostic signs are the best approaches to early identification and intervention. Self-report measures are available that allow routine screening (e.g., Eating Attitudes Test, Garner & Garfinkel, 1979). When an individual athlete is seen and there is suspicion of an eating disorder, a more formalized approach to assessment is warranted. This begins with structured interview. Various measures are available for assessing body image (e.g., the Body-Self Relations Questionnaire, Winstead & Cash, 1984; Body Image Assessment; Williamson, Kelley, Davis, Ruggiero, & Blouin, 1985); these tests generally include three essential elements: body-size distortion, body-size dissatisfaction, and preference for thinness/fear of weight gain. Because there can be a high degree of secondary psychopathology, including substance use disorder, additional use of traditional clinical psychometric instruments is also warranted (Williamson, 1990).

Alcohol and Drug Use

As in society at large, alcohol and drug use is a deeply ingrained and complex problem in sport (see Tricker & Cook, 1990; Wadler & Hainline, 1989). Recreational drug use patterns seen in society are mimicked in the competitive environment. At times, the athlete may rely on alcohol or drugs to manage the emotional ups and down of athletic competition. This may also be related to the prevalence of sensation seeking and risk taking seen in certain sports. Also, the use of ergogenic or performance-enhancing drugs can be prompted by the desire to excel, which is at the heart of sport. This includes the use of illicit substances such as black-market hormonal preparations and the illicit use of legal substances (e.g., the use of narcotic analgesics to mask pain and injury). Because of sanctions on alcohol and drug use in the athletic environment and the potential for a remarkable degree of denial, both emerging and established patterns of drug use are difficult to identify.

Many of the instruments used in the assessment of alcohol and drug related behaviors are face valid in nature and, therefore, easily faked. The need to control drug use in sport has led athletic government bodies to establish strict guidelines and to rely on drug testing to enforce these guidelines (Wadler & Hainline, 1989). A substance-abusing athlete may have to see a psychologist after having a positive drug screen. There is a danger that such forced referral can set up an adversarial relationship between the athlete and the treatment provider. Nonetheless, this does provide an opportunity for treatment that might not otherwise be available.

Effective assessment begins with an awareness of the symptoms of recreational and ergogenic drug use as demonstrated in every day behavior, and specific knowledge of drug use patterns typical to certain sports. For instance, blood doping and erythropoetin use are seen in cycling and other endurance sports; beta-blockers may be used by shooters to manage anxiety and to steady aim; and diuretics and laxatives can become drugs of abuse in weight loss sports (Wadler & Hainline, 1989). Early identification is greatly enhanced when the psychologist works in a team setting with coaching staff and members of the sports medicine team. For instance, in the case of anabolic steroid use, the coach may observe rapid changes in muscle mass or definition, the athletic trainer may notice acute soft tissue injuries that are of atypical etiology (and suggest steroid use), or the physician may become suspicious of athletes who offer unusual symptomatic complaints and request specific medications in an attempt to manage the side effects of illicit substance use. Once a problem is identified, a traditional clinical approach to assessment is appropriate. This should include screening for concurrent psychological disorders with attempts to differentiate premorbid conditions from those developing subsequent to both drug use and its detection.

Health and Exercise

The relationship between exercise and both physical and psychological health is being increasingly recognized. As wellness emerges as a mainstream concept, a growing array of exercise programs are available to those who show interest. Recently, a great deal of attention has focused on the benefits of exercise for aging populations and people who are obese. A maladaptive response to exercise has been observed in some enthusiastic recreational athletes whose inability to set sensible limits on physical activity ultimately undermines their health and well being.

Compliance with regular exercise regimens is a critical element of success, assessment of motivation is important. Ostrow (1990) listed 17 instruments that may be used to assess motivation for exercise. Although motivation assessment plays an important role in health and exercise interventions, a pragmatic approach will include examination of both *person* and *situation* variables. Instruments particularly useful for assessing person-related variables include the Self-Motivation Inventory (Dishman, Ickes, & Morgan, 1980) and the Personal Incentives for Exercise Questionnaire (Duda & Tappe, 1989). Knowledge of what is unique to the situation of specific exerciser populations helps place psychometrically identified motivational variables in context. Attending to both the person and the situation will likely optimize compliance and enhance benefits from exercise. Increasingly sophisticated approaches to managing activity in the general population are available. For instance, project PACE (Physician-Based Assessment and Counseling for Exercise; Patrick et al., 1994) guides physicians in counseling patients regarding physical activity. This approach uses self-assessment instruments and related educational materials to facilitate both initiation and maintenance of regular exercise. Special recommendations for selected patient populations are also described.

Aging Populations

The later stages of adulthood are marked by the loss of physical expertise and fitness. There is also increasing prevalence of chronic medical conditions. Nevertheless, increased leisure time offers a greater opportunity for participation in physical activity. Fitness programs may meet a wide variety of social, emotional, cognitive, and medical needs for this group (Van Camp & Boyer, 1989). Although cognitive decline may place constraints on the activity program in which selected late age adults may engage, it is noteworthy that regular exercise programs tends to enhance cognitive function overall (Spirduso, 1995). Regular adherence to a well designed activity program reduces the impact of chronic diseases due to age related decline (Spirduso, 1995). Pragmatic assessment of the needs, interests, and physical abilities of this population is warranted as a part of the exercise prescription process in order to maximize adherence. This may include assessment of physical functional abilities by a physician or other health professional. (See Dishman

(1988, 1994) for recommendations regarding exercise prescription and maintenance.)

General Medical Patients

Among nonathletes having difficulty rehabilitating from acute injury, problems of adapting to physical rigors of rehabilitation are often the root cause. When injuries fail to rehabilitate with appropriate measures over a reasonable time course, the individual's motivation may be called into question. In these cases, the psychologist has an important role to play in differentiating those who are directly resistant because of secondary gain issues (e.g., getting sympathy, reduced responsibilities) from those who simply fail to overcome barriers to rehabilitation. Use of behavioral assessment may be the most pragmatic approach to assessment (Heil, 1993). This begins with a careful analysis of barriers to rehabilitation as part of a structured interview. Standard clinical assessment measures such as the MMPI-2 are quite useful.

Those who adapt most poorly to the limits of the medical condition they suffer are typically plagued by a disability mind-set. This is a formidable barrier to exercise adherence. However, once overcome, a host of benefits are noted as the disability mind-set is directly challenged by the progressive gains in physical ability and mental state that exercise programs offer. An approach to assessment of chronic conditions similar to that previously described for acute conditions is recommended.

Obesity

Obesity is a widespread health problem that is highly resistant to change. Pervasive societal pressure for a trim appearance and an exceptionally high failure rate at weight loss have created a billion dollar industry focused primarily on reduction of caloric intake. However, research suggests that obesity is maintained more by inactivity than by overeating (Williamson, 1990). It also has been noted that as weight increases activity decreases. Regular exercise not only offers potential for weight reduction, but also helps ameliorate certain of the risk factors linked to obesity, such as heart disease. Hence, the importance of exercise in this population is difficult to underestimate. Accurate assessment of weight and body composition is essential for both accurate identification of the magnitude of obesity and for marking change. Among the factors complicating exercise adherence in this population is anxiety regarding appearance. Although it has broader application than with clinically obese populations, the Social Physique Anxiety Scale (Hart, Leary, & Rejeski, 1989) is a useful tool for assessing body anxiety.

The "Addicted" Athlete

The so-called addicted athlete demonstrates a reverse compliance problem—failing to restrict activity when it is appropriate or necessary to do so. This is typically seen in recreational athletes whose enthusiasm for their sport grows beyond the capability of their lifestyle to support it. The athlete appears to need to perform relatively intensive exercise on a regular basis in order to maintain emotional equilibrium and will do so in spite of significant adverse consequences. Withdrawal-like symptoms have been described with cessation of activity (Morgan, 1979). The Exercise Salience Scale (TESS; Morrow & Harvey, 1990) is useful for the identifying recreational athlete for whom over-reliance on otherwise health-enhancing behaviors can come to have negative psychological, interpersonal, or medical effects. A similar pattern of compulsive adherence to exercise may be seen in individuals with disordered patterns of eating including anorexia nervosa and bulimia. Consequently, when dealing with compulsive exercisers, one should use assessment measures designed to explore the possibility of eating disorders.

Performance Enhancement

Psychological testing can be beneficial in a number of areas concerning performance. Individual athletes, sport teams, and coaches are all connected with performance, and various tests can be used to guide intervention.

Individual Athletes

Testing of athletes can provide crucial information concerning strengths and weaknesses of mental skills and motivation strategies that might be successful for particular individuals, and can suggest the use of particular performance-enhancement interventions. Commonly used assessment instruments currently include CSAI-II (Martens et al., 1982, 1990); POMS (McNair et al., 1971); STAI (Spielberger et al., 1970); Tennessee Self Concept Scale (TSCS; Fitts, 1965); and TAIS (Nideffer, 1976).

Team Testing

Testing of an entire team can provide a general group profile that can be useful to the sport psychologist, coaches, and athletes themselves. Appropriate testing will indicate (a) cohesion levels, (b) stage of group development, (c) relationships of team members, and (d) communication channels within the team. Team-based psychometric testing also has a number of special applications related to identification of over-training, burnout, and other performance problems. Frequently used instruments in team testing include sociometric tests (Moreno, 1935) and the Group Environment Questionnaire (GEQ) (Carron, Widmeyer, & Brawley, 1985).

Coach Testing

If a team is to be assessed as part of a sport psychology program, then the coaches should also be tested. It is virtually impossible to be a successful sport psychologist of a team if the coaches are not totally involved and behind the psychological program. Further, coaches might benefit from testing of their personality, leadership styles, and proneness to burnout. Assessment approaches commonly used to these ends include the Maslach Burnout Inventory (Maslach, 1982), the Least Preferred Coworker (Fiedler, 1954), and the POMS.

Special Topics

Selection testing, polygraph testing, head injury assessment, and psychophysiological assessment are reviewed because of their timeliness and unique fit in sport. Selection testing and the use of the polygraph are controversial issues in sport, but deserve special attention because of their emerging role in addressing specific sport-related concerns. Head injury assessment reflects growing concern for the well-being of athletes experiencing minor head injuries that traditionally have been overlooked. Evidence from the medical neurosciences has clarified the potential risks and offers guidelines for head injury assessment with which all applied sport science practitioners should be acquainted. Psychophysiological assessment is an underused but potentially fruitful approach to the integration of mind and body in sport performance. It is included because of its relatively untapped potential.

Selection Testing

The use of psychological assessment for selection purposes is most sensible and defensible for positions requiring great responsibility. Such testing practices are now commonplace among police and public safety workers. The significant level of responsibility that such professionals bear justifies the extraordinary level of scrutiny to which police officers are exposed as well as the high costs for training them. Similarly, high-level athletes are subject to intensive scrutiny that ranges from detailed performance statistics during competition to fan- and media-based focus on "off-court" behaviors of high-profile athletes. The costs in selecting and retaining high level athletes through successful careers are also substantial. Those who make decisions about athlete selection may therefore want to include the results of physical examinations, drug tests, and psychological tests among the factors that they consider. Including psychological testing as a part of this selection procedure appears to be well reasoned to the extent that it guides a sport organization in the judicious use of the training funds. When such testing is administered, the psychologist bears the burden of informing the athlete and the team of the nature and limits of testing. In such cases, it is understood that the results of psychological testing are most useful when considered in conjunction with the broad range of information gathered in the selection process. Wherever possible, psychological testing should be complemented by a direct face-to-face interview with the psychologist. This precaution adds depth and clarity to the psychological evaluation and minimizes the limitations and potential pitfalls of blind testing. Further investigation is needed to establish the validity of various instruments and strategies that guide selection testing. The ready availability of objective markers of performance in sport offers potential for quality research.

Polygraph Testing

In polygraph testing psychophysiologic reactions (respiration, cardio-vascular activity, skin resistance) are examined in conjunction with skilled interrogation to assess deception. The polygraph is the most frequently used of individual psychological tests, having seen widespread application for over 70 years (Iacono & Patrick, 1988). Typically, it is administered by a polygraph specialist trained in psychophysiology and interrogation.

The polygraph has gained entry into sport as a method to assess deception. For example, it is commonly used by the American Drug Free Power Lifting Association to assess the drug use history of medal winners. In this setting, it is seen as a cost-efficient alternative to drug testing that offers the advantage of immediate feedback. The polygraph has also been used to assess the fair play of competitors in professional bass fishing tournaments where lucrative financial prizes are awarded. Both the polygraph and drug testing elicit ethical concerns regarding invasion of privacy.

Controversy regarding the polygraph is based on both questionable scientific status and ethical objections to the deception often used in its administration (Iacono & Patrick, 1988). First of all, there is no autonomic response pattern uniquely associated with lying. It is also known that counter-measures designed to "beat the test" can be successful. Frequently, the administration of the test itself involves deception. For instance, polygraphers have been observed to overstate the accuracy of testing. Finally, the athlete's due process in the case of a failed test (Iacono & Patrick, 1988) is an important ethical concern. If the use of the polygraph in sport is accepted as a given, then one must insure that the test is administered in an ethical manner.

Head Injury Assessment

Traditionally, concern has been focused on single incidents of severe head injury and cumulative trauma over years of exposure. However, more recently, attention has been focused on relatively minor head injuries, which occur more frequently. Because an estimated 250,000 injuries occur yearly in contact sports, head injury has been labeled a *silent epidemic* (Kelly et al., 1991). In a given season, 20% of high school football athletes will suffer at least one concussion. Equally compelling is the realization that the effect of even mild head injury is cumulative, that is, head injuries increase in severity and duration with each incident. In rare cases, a potentially fatal second-impact syndrome can occur with a second minor head injury in individuals who are symptomatic from a prior concussion (Kelly et al., 1991).

Guidelines for the Management of Concussion in Sports (Colorado Medical Society, 1991) identifies three levels of concussion in sports:

> Grade I: Confusion without amnesia; no loss of consciousness
> Grade II: Confusion with amnesia; no loss of consciousness
> Grade III: Loss of consciousness

Head injury assessment immediately following injury generally focuses on rapid resumption of mental and sensory–motor abilities as a condition for return to play. Problems seen in the immediate post-injury period variably persist for 1 week. Symptoms include headaches, dizziness, posttraumatic memory loss, nausea, double or blurred vision, light sensitivity, unsteadiness, and poor coordination as well as confusion, postconcussive amnesia, and other information-processing deficits. Athlete-reported symptoms (headache, memory loss, nausea, dizziness, weakness) and cognitive status as assessed by neuropsychological instruments typically resolve simultaneously (Barth et al., 1989). Evaluation of head injury and related neuropsychological assessment are areas of expertise requiring specialized training. However, sport psychologists should be sensitive to reported or observed symptoms of head injury in conjunction with casual reference by the athlete to "getting dinged" or having his or her "bell rung," and may have to refer the athlete to a physician.

Psychophysiological Assessment

The value in psychophysiological monitoring rests in the critical role that physiological variables play in athlete health and performance. Mental training techniques influence a variety of physiological parameters (Dishman, 1987; Druckman & Bjork, 1991). Multimodal assessment, including psychological and psychophysiological variables, offers a view of the interplay of mind and body in sport.

Biofeedback is a self-regulation procedure in which detailed information about biological functions not readily available to ordinary awareness is provided to the participant. Biofeedback is implemented in a user-friendly format that includes auditory or visual channels. Measures may include muscular activity, joint range of motion, respiration rate, heart rate, and brain-wave activity. Feedback methods vary from the simple to the complex and may be immediate or delayed. Timely and precise feedback about variation in biological parameters enhances the athlete's awareness of the specific circumstances and behaviors that improve performance. Sandweiss and Wolf (1985) described a variety of potential applications of biofeedback to sport performance. Muscular biofeedback can facilitate injury rehabilitation. For example, EMG-assisted muscular relaxation training can help eliminate muscular bracing or guarding, which is commonly seen in injury and which may result in poor technique and increased injury risk upon return to play. *Discrimination training*—relaxing one muscle or muscle group while another is worked optimally—can be used to enhance body awareness and fine-tune muscular response, guiding safe and efficient biomechanical response.

Not all biofeedback necessarily relies on sophisticated electronic instrumentation. A simple self-assessment procedure, whereby the athlete rates perceived level of exertion and correlates this with heart rate, can be used to regulate training intensity. For instance, a scale of 15 points, ranging from 6 to 20, has been developed (Borg & Ottoson, 1986) as a simple but effective tool for rating effort.

Careful modulation of training intensity is of critical importance in highly competitive sports, especially those that require intensive aerobic conditioning. Sport training is designed to induce a physiological overload that results in adaptive changes in the organism and ultimately in improved athletic performance. However, if the delicate balance between training load and coping capacity is not maintained, the athlete is in danger of developing *overtraining syndrome* (Froehlich, 1993). Overtraining syndrome symptoms include decreased performance, rapid onset of fatigue during exercise, loss of motivation, problems with concentration, and disturbed regulation of the central nervous system, the autonomic nervous system, and the endocrine system. Overtraining is identified through a multimodal assessment including immune function parameters, heart rate, body weight, self-reported mood states, and routine psychological behaviors (e.g. digestion, sleep).

In an overview of sport psychology worldwide, Singer (1992) called attention to the development of sport-simulation training devices that simultaneously evaluate situation-specific physical and psychological parameters. Examples of such equipment include visual search and movement timing devices. Currently, psychophysiological monitoring is a relatively unexplored and underused assessment tool in the sport setting.

The wide array of assessment tools available to sport and exercise psychologists provide a rich opportunity for careful assessment of athletes and exercisers. Two case studies are presented below to highlight some of the ways in which these assessment tools may be used.

Case Studies

The following two scenarios illustrate the use of assessment in sport psychology. The first is a physician referral of a young athlete with multiple physical and psychological symptoms. A multifaceted approach, including structured interview, psychological testing, behavior analysis, and interview with significant others, is used by the clinical psychologist facing this diagnostic dilemma. The approach recognizes the unique role of sport in the athlete's life, and thus incorporates a coach interview into the diagnostic assessment and mental training into treatment. The second scenario involves an athlete whose difficulties become apparent during a routine, performance-based psychological screening conducted by a sport psychologist who has an ongoing consulting relationship with a university team. It demonstrates the benefit of the routine use of assessment tools in the identification of performance and potential adjustment problems. This routine testing allows early intervention by the sport psychologist, whose ongoing relationship with the team facilitates a timely and minimally intrusive approach to management of problems. The data provided by psychological testing not only serve a diagnostic purpose, but also facilitate intervention.

Case Study #1

Tina is a 15-year-old competitive swimmer referred by her physician for mood disturbance and chronic shoulder pain as well as a possible eating disorder. In the initial interview, she appeared anxious and socially awkward. Affect was restricted, and suggested possible depression. Shoulder pain was apparently an overuse injury that responded well to rest, but limited training and competition. Tina conveyed a sense of loss about swimming because she convincingly presented her desire to return to regular swim training and competition. Four diagnostic issues arose from initial contact: reactive depression to injury and loss of competition and training; premorbid anxiety; chronic pain; and possible eating disorder.

Initially, Tina completed a Beck Depression Inventory (BDI; Beck, Ward, Mendelson, Mock, & Erbaugh, 1961) and a pain drawing (in which she drew the pain she was experiencing within the outline of a human figure). The BDI failed to show significant mood disturbance. However, because of the face valid nature of this instrument, results were considered equivocal. The pain drawing showed pain in both shoulders although the primary problem was in the left shoulder. A brief structured interview regarding eating disorders showed a pronounced preference for thinness or fear of being fat, accurate assessment of body image, and satisfaction with current weight although, by objective medical opinion, Tina was 5 to 10 pounds under a minimum satisfactory body weight. Orthopedic and gynecologic work-ups reported in the medical record indicated no objective physical limitations nor any apparent underlying organic pain process. There were no changes in bone that would suggest poor nutrition. Gynecologic function was normal.

With Tina's permission, her parents and coach were interviewed. The parents expressed concern regarding Tina's relatively recent mild depression and more long-standing anxiety. They described her as perfectionistic and inflexible. They have observed no signs of binging or purging. Tina had very specific food preferences and elected to prepare her own meals separate from the family. Tina's parents believed their daughter was highly motivated to return to swimming. The coach was somewhat critical of Tina and had doubts regarding her true desire to swim competitively. He felt that she was, however, capable of making a significant contribution to the team. He described Tina as tense and quiet and noted that the quality of the biomechanics of her stroke varied considerably for reasons that are not apparent to him. Speaking with the coach at the pool provided an opportunity to observe Tina participate in practice on a limited basis. Slight shoulder guarding noted in initial interview clearly was more pronounced in the swimming environment—in and out of the water. Tina was instructed in a self-monitoring task in order to allow behavioral analysis of pain across situations. She self-rated pain during light swim training, 1 hour after swimming, at bedtime, and upon awakening. The pain predictably was most problematic during work-outs and gradually subsided thereafter until it was at a minimum, and was sometimes absent, by the following morning at awakening.

Interpretation

The results of this multifaceted assessment led to the following conclusions: There clearly was a disordered pattern of eating, but no actual anorexia or bulimia. Chronic pain was both without active underlying structural pathology and without obvious evidence of secondary gain. There was a mild degree of dysphoria, primarily a sense of loss regarding competition, that was complicated by diminished social contact that was due to decreased attendance at practice. Anxiety was seen as characterlogical and was believed to be the primary problem. Anxiety was assumed to have a significant somatic component, evidenced by chronic muscle tension and guarding of the shoulder, especially in stressful circumstances. The obsessive component of the anxiety led to rumination regarding chronic pain, which further exacerbated the psychosomatic symptoms. Obsessiveness and perfectionism were seen to be factors underlying the disordered eating pattern. This impression was confirmed by a subsequent administration of the MMPI. Scale 7 (*psychosthemia*) showed significant elevation, signaling anxiety with obsessive–compulsive features. Scale 1 (*hypochondriasis*) showed a moderate elevation, indicating somatic preoccupation. Scales 2 (*depression*), 3 (*hysteria*), and 0 (*social introversion*) showed slight elevations (T = approximately 65), signaling that other symptomatic and characterlogical factors were playing a contributing but relatively minor role.

Interventions

Tina went through nutritional counseling with a focus on proper food selection and accurate calorie counting, and accepted a daily calorie goal. This led to slow gradual weight gain. Tina was instructed in a mental training program, which began with general stress management training to help her deal with chronic anxiety and reactive depression. It also involved lengthy evening sessions during which Tina practiced imagery of relaxed, pain-free swimming. Additional mental training focused on body awareness and relaxation in the recovery portion of her stroke. A gradual and progressive goal-oriented approach to returning to swimming was implemented. Tina was initially slow to comply with recommended treatment measures, but began to show slow, steady gains over time, and eventually returned to swimming.

Case Study #2

Eschelle, a 20-year-old elite competitive gymnast, trains at a gym that recently hired a sport psychologist to work with the athletes. After meeting the athletes and the coaches and observing some practices and competitions, the sport psychologist decided to administer a battery of instruments to a group of athletes that included Eschelle. Eschelle completed the POMS (McNair et al., 1971), the STAI (Spielberger et al., 1970), the Scale of Sporting Environments (SSE; Rushall & Fry, 1980), and the TAIS (Nideffer, 1976).

Interpretation

The sport psychologist evaluated Eschelle's responses on the POMS and noted that her *tension* and *depression* scores were elevated relative to her *vigor* score. Her scores were not in line with the typical iceberg profile demonstrated by athletes on the POMS. Thus, the sport psychologist suspected that Eschelle may have been suffering from staleness related to her gymnastics involvement.

The STAI indicated that Eschelle had an average state anxiety level, but was high in trait anxiety. Scores of this nature frequently mean that an athlete is a "worrier." The high trait anxiety indicated that Eschelle may have been finding it difficult to concentrate appropriately in pressure situations.

The high scores on the SSE characterized Eschelle as a person who was sometimes success oriented, but also frequently was just trying to avoid failure. The sport psychologist concluded that Eschelle probably could be intimidated by competitors and was affected by the *expectancy theory*; that is, she may have been developing expectancies of how she was going to perform even before the competition began.

The final psychological test, the short form of the TAIS, indicated to the sport psychologist that Eschelle had difficulty in some of the areas of concentration. She may have been distracted when a number of things were happening concurrently; and she may have been confusing herself by thinking too much.

Interventions

Based on the results of the questionnaires administered, the sport psychologist found Eschelle to be typical of collegiate athletes. She had a number of psychological strengths, but performance-enhancement techniques seemed like they would be of great benefit to her. The sport psychologist met individually with her to discuss the testing results. After some discussion, a program of realistic short-term goals was formulated with Eschelle to reduce her tension and depression related to gymnastics and to increase her vigor. Eschelle's goals included allowing herself to have fun during practice and enjoying the emotional support of her teammates. Eschelle made smaller goals to help in reaching her main goals. As each of these small goals was accomplished, Eschelle decided to reward herself with a rented movie video. It was important for Eschelle's motivation that a reward followed a success. Eschelle was then taught *autogenic training* (a method of relaxation) and practiced this technique for four weeks in order to lower her anxiety. She seemed to respond and expressed that she felt less pressure and handled stressful situations much better. Eschelle expressed concerns about her ability to focus and subsequently was trained in a number of concentration exercises that taught her how to control her attention. She was able to think less during performance and to be less easily distracted. She was taught how to think of certain positive phrases instead of letting negative, downgrading thoughts prevail.

These interventions were not quick fixes, but they seemed to provide Eschelle with the direction to change her psychological weaknesses. After approximately 6 months, Eschelle had acquired a number of new mental skills that allowed her to slowly progress in gymnastics skills and perform at a more proficient level.

Conclusion

The uses of psychological testing with athletes are many and varied. Psychological testing reflects all the issues and controversies that arise out of the use of assessment in clinical psychology, organizational behavior, and performance-enhancement sport psychology. The practice of assessment in sport has grown and matured considerably since its controversial beginnings. Because of the inherent and inescapable emphasis on the measurement of ability and performance in sport, psychological testing in sport will continue to gain acceptance and grow in scope and effectiveness.

The future of psychological testing in sport and exercise is increasingly bright. Sport psychologists will continue to use a broad array of assessment devices ranging from brief sport-specific self-report measures, such as those presented by Orlick (1990) in *In Pursuit of Excellence*, to standardized clinical instruments such as the MMPI-2. The development of brief psychological inventories suitable for use in the athletic environment will continue. The advantages of these instruments include diminished intrusiveness, suitability for repeat testing over time, and opportunity for use in close conjunction with training and competition. These advantages balance their disadvantages, which include less information per testing and reduced psychometric stability. The development of sport (and team) norms will enhance the applicability and meaningfulness of test results. This approach offers an elegant compromise to the otherwise conflicting priorities of the trait and situationist philosophies. Psychological assessment will continue to become increasingly user friendly. Computer and communication technology will allow increasingly quick feedback. The face valid nature of sport specific tests facilitates feedback that is immediately relevant to sport performance. These same features also allow the development of understandable feedback reports that can be offered to the athlete as an adjunct to interpretation by the sport psychologist. Ongoing research will also lead to a better understanding of the relevance of standardized clinical instruments for use with athletes. From the perspective of professional practice, there likely will be a greater emphasis on psychological testing in the training of psychologists who work with athletes. It will be increasingly important for all sport psychologists to become familiar with the assessment instruments used for clinical applications as well as those for selection purposes and performance-enhancement applications.

References

Anastasi, A. (1988). *Psychological testing*. New York: Macmillan.

Barth, J. T., Alves, W. M., Ryan, T. V., Macciocchi, S. N., Rimel, R. W., Jane, J. A., & Nelson, W. E. (1989). Mild head injury in sports: Neuropsychological sequelae and recovery of function. In H. S. Levin, H. M. Eisenberg, & A. L. Benton (Eds.), *Mild head injury* (pp. 257–275). New York: Oxford University Press.

Beck, A. T., Ward, C. H., Mendelson, M., Mock, J., & Erbaugh, J. K. (1961). An inventory for measuring depression. *Archives of General Psychiatry, 4,* 561–571.

Borg, G. A. V., & Ottoson, D. (Eds.). (1986). *The perception of exertion and physical work*. New York: Macmillan.

Carron, A. V., Widmeyer, W. N., & Brawley, L. R. (1985). The development of an instrument to assess cohesion in sport teams: The Group Environment Questionnaire. *Journal of Sport Psychology, 7,* 244–266.

Colorado Medical Society. (1991). Guidelines for the management of concussion in sports (revised). Denver, CO: Author.

Dewey, D., Brawley, L., & Allard, F. (1989). Do the TAIS attentional-style scales predict how information is processed? *Journal of Sport & Exercise Psychology, 11,* 171–186.

Dishman, R. K. (1987). Psychological aids to performance. In R. H. Strauss (Ed.), *Drugs and performance in sports* (pp. 121–146). Philadelphia: Saunders.

Dishman, R. K. (Ed.). (1988). *Exercise adherence: Its impact on public health.* Champaign, IL: Human Kinetics.

Dishman, R. K. (1994). *Advances in exercise adherence.* Champaign, IL: Human Kinetics.

Dishman, R. K., Ickes, W., & Morgan, W. P. (1980). Self-motivation and adherence to habitual physical activity. *Journal of Applied Social Psychology, 10,* 115–132.

Druckman, D., & Bjork, R. A. (Eds.). (1991). *In the mind's eye: Enhancing human performance.* Washington, DC: National Academy Press.

Duda, J. L., & Tappe, M. K. (1989). The personal incentives for exercise questionnaire: Preliminary development. *Perceptual and Motor Skills, 68,* 1122.

Farley, F. (1990, May). The Type T personality with some implications for practice. *The California Psychologist,* p. 29.

Fiedler, F. E. (1954). Assumed similarity measures as predictors of team effectiveness. *Journal of Abnormal Social Psychology, 49,* 381–388.

Fiedler, F. (1967). *A theory of leadership effectiveness.* New York: McGraw-Hill.

Fitts, S. W. (1965). *Tennessee self-concept scale. Manual.* Nashville, TN: Counselor Recordings and Tests.

Fordyce, W. E. (1976). *Behavioral methods for chronic pain and illness.* St. Louis: Mosby.

Fordyce, W. E. (1979). Use of the MMPI-2 in the assessment of chronic pain. In J. Butcher, G. Dahlstrom, M. Gynther, & W. Schofield (Eds.), *Clinical notes on the MMPI* (pp. 2–13). Nutley, NJ: Roche Psychiatric Service Institutes.

Froehlich, J. (1993). Overtraining syndrome. In J. Heil (Ed.), *Psychology of sport injury* (pp. 59–72). Champaign, IL: Human Kinetics

Garner, D. M., & Garfinkel, P. E. (1979). The eating attitude test: An index of symptoms of anorexia nervosa. *Psychological Medicine, 9,* 273–279.

Gauvin, L., & Russell, S. J. (1993). Sport-specific and culturally adopted measures in sport and exercise psychology research: Issues and strategies. In R. N. Singer, M. Murphey, J. K. Tennant (Eds.), *Handbook on research in sport psychology* (pp. 891–900). New York: Macmillian.

Hanin, Y. L. (1986). The state-trait anxiety research on sports in USSR. In C. D. Spielberger & R. Diaz-Guerrero (Eds.), *Cross-cultural anxiety, Vol. 3* (pp. 45–61). New York: Hemisphere.

Hanin, Y. L. (1993). Temporal patterning in performance anxiety. *Medicine and Science in Sports and Exercise, 25,* (Suppl. 5), 860.

Hart, E. A., Leary, M. R., & Rejeski, W. J. (1989). The measurement of social physique anxiety. *Journal of Sport & Exercise Psychology, 11,* 94–104.

Hathaway, S. R., & McKinley, S. C. (1989). *Minnesota Multiphasic Personality Inventory-2* [Manual]. Minneapolis: University of Minnesota Press.

Heil, J. (1993). *Psychology of sport injury.* Champaign, IL: Human Kinetics.

Iacono, W. G., & Patrick, C. J. (1988). Assessing deception: Polygraph techniques. In R. Rogers (Ed.), *Clinical assessment of malingering and deception* (pp. 205–233). New York: Guilford.

Kelly, S. P., Nichols, J. S., Filley, C. M., Lilleher, K. O., Rubenstein, D., & Kleinschmidt-

DeMasters, B. K. (1991). Concession in sports: Guidelines for the prevention of catastrophic outcome. *Journal of the American Medical Association, 266,* 2867–2869.

Kroll, W., & Lewis, G. (1970, winter). America's first sport psychologist. *Quest, Monograph VIII,* 1–4.

Mahoney, M. J., & Epstein, M. L. (1981). The assessment of cognition in athletes. In T. V. Merluzzi, C. R. Glass, & M. Genest (Eds.), *Cognitive assessment* (pp. 435–451). New York: Guilford.

Mahoney, M. J., Gabriel, T. J., & Perkins, T. S. (1987). Psychological skills and exceptional athletic performance. *The Sport Psychologist, 1,* 181–199.

Martens, R., Burton, D., Vealey, R. S., Bump, L. A., & Smith, D. (1982, May). *Cognitive and somatic dimensions of competitive anxiety.* Paper presented at the annual meeting of the North American Society for the Psychology of Sport and Physical Activity, University of Maryland, College Park.

Martens, R., Vealey, R. S., & Burton, D. (1990). *Competitive anxiety in sport.* Champaign, IL: Human Kinetics.

Maslach, C. (1982). Understanding burnout: Definitional issues in analyzing a complex phenomenon. In W. S. Paine (Ed.), *Job stress and burnout: Research, theory, and intervention perspectives* (pp. 29–40). Beverly Hills, CA: Sage.

McNair, D. N., Lorr, M., & Droppleman, L. F. (1971). *Profile of Mood States.* San Diego, CA: Educational and Industrial Testing Services.

Morgan, W. P. (1979). Negative addiction in runners. *The physician and sports medicine, 7*(2), 56–63, 67–69.

Morgan, W. P., Brown, D. R., Raglin, J. S., O'Connor, P. J., & Ellickson, K. A. (1987). Psychological monitoring of overtraining and staleness. *British Journal of Sports Medicine, 21,* 107–114.

Morgan, W. P., & Pollock, M. L. (1977). Psychological characterization of the elite distance runner. *Annals of the New York Academy of Science, 301,* 382–403.

Moreno, J. (1935). *Who shall survive.* Beacon, NY: Beacon House.

Morrow, J., & Harvey, P. (1990). Fitness report: The Exercise Salience Scale. *American Health, 9,* 31–32.

Nideffer, R. M. (1976). Test of Attentional and Interpersonal Style. *Journal of Personality and Social Psychology, 34,* 394–404.

Nideffer, R. M. (1981). *The ethics and practice of applied sport psychology.* Ithaca, NY: Mouvement.

Nideffer, R. M. (1987). Issues on the use of psychological tests in applied settings. *The Sport Psychologist, 1,* 18–28.

Nideffer, R. M. (1990). Use of Test of Attentional and Interpersonal Style (TAIS) in sport. *The Sport Psychologist, 2,* 285–300.

Orlick, T. (1990). *In pursuit of excellence* (2nd ed.). Champaign, IL: Human Kinetics.

Ostrow, A. C. (1990). *Directory of psychological tests in sport and exercise sciences.* Morgantown, WV: Fitness Information Technology.

Pargman, D. (Ed.). (1993). *Psychological bases of sport injury.* Morgantown, WV: Fitness Information Technology.

Patrick, K., Sallis, J. F., Long, B., Calfas, K. J., Wooten, W., Heath, G., & Pratt, M. (1994). A new tool for encouraging activity: Project PACE. *The Physician and Sports medicine, 22*(11), pp. 45–46, 48–52.

Ravizza, K. (1988). Gaining entry with athletic personnel for season-long consulting. *The Sport Psychologist, 2,* 243–254.

Rushall, B., & Fox, D. (1980). *Scale for Sporting Environments.* Lakehead University, Thunder Bay, Ontario.

Sandweiss, J. H., & Wolf, S. L. (1985). *Biofeedback and sport science.* New York: Plenum Press.

Selye, H. (1956). *The stress of life.* New York: McGraw-Hill.

Singer, R. N. (1992). What in the world is happening in sport psychology? *Journal of Applied Sport Psychology, 4,* 63–76.

Smith, A. M., Scott, S. G., & Wiese, D. M. (1990). The psychological effects of sports injuries: Coping. *Sports Medicine, 9,* 352–369.

Spielberger, C. D., Gorsuch, R. L., & Luschene, R. L. (1970). *Manual for the State-Trait Anxiety Inventory.* Palo Alto, CA: Consulting Psychologists Press.

Spirduso, W. W. (1995). *Physical dimensions of aging.* Champaign, IL: Human Kinetics.

Straub, W. F. (Ed.). (1978). *Sport psychology: An analysis of athlete behavior.* Ithaca, NY: Mouvement.

Thompson, R. A., & Sherman, R. T. (1993). *Helping athletes with eating disorders.* Champaign, IL: Human Kinetics.

Tricker, R., & Cook, D. (1990). *Athletes at risk: Drugs in sport.* Dubuque, IA: William C. Brown.

Tutko, T. A., Lyon, L. & Ogilvie, B. C. (1969). *Athletic Motivation Inventory.* San Jose, CA: Institute for the Study of Athletic Motivation.

Vallerand, R. J. (1983). Attention and decision making: A test of the predictive validity of the Test of Attentional and Interpersonal Style (TAIS) in a sport setting. *Journal of Sport Psychology, 3,* 149–165.

Van Camp, S. P. & Boyer, J. L. (1989). Exercise guidelines for the elderly. *The Physician and Sports medicine, 17*(5), 83–86, 88.

Wadler, G. I., & Hainline, B. (1989). *Drugs and the athlete.* Philadelphia: Davis.

Williamson, D. A. (1990). *Assessment in eating disorders: Obesity, anorexia, and bulimia nervosa.* New York: Pergamon.

Williamson, D. A., Kelley, M. L., Davis, C. J., Ruggiero, L., & Blouin, D. C. (1985) Psychopathology of eating disorders: A controlled comparison of bulimic, obese, and normal subjects. *Journal of Consulting and Clinical Psychology, 53,* 161–166.

Winstead, B. A., & Cash, T. F. (1984, March). *Reliability and validity of the body-self relation questionnaire: A new measure of body image.* Paper presented at the annual meeting of the Southeastern Psychological Association, New Orleans, LA.

Wise, H. H., Jackson, D. W., & Rocchio, P. (1979). Preoperative psychological testing as a predictor of success in injury: A preliminary report. *The American Journal of Sportsmedicine, 7,* 287–292.

Zuckerman, M., Kolin, E. A., Price, L., & Zoob, I. (1964). Development of a sensation seeking scale. *Journal of Counseling and Psychology, 28,* 477–482.

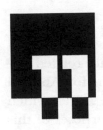

Psychopathology in Sport and Exercise

Britton W. Brewer and Trent A. Petrie

A t first glance, it may seem unusual to discuss psychopathology in association with sport and exercise. After all, there is evidence that "success in sport is inversely correlated with psychopathology" (Morgan, 1985, p. 71) and exercise has been used therapeutically for depression and other disorders (for a review, see Chapter 7, this volume). Nevertheless, because sport and exercise participants, as human beings, may be susceptible to psychopathology, examination of psychopathology in the context of sport and exercise is warranted (Heyman, 1986). Indeed, factors associated with sport and exercise may even foster certain types of psychopathology (Andersen, Denson, Brewer, & Van Raalte, 1994; Beisser, 1977; Heyman, 1986; House, 1989; Ogilvie & Tutko, 1971; Pinkerton, Hinz, & Barrow, 1989). For some disorders (e.g., developmental coordination disorder, bulimia nervosa), pathological symptoms may include sport and exercise behaviors.

Case studies and anecdotal reports have documented the occurrence of a wide variety of mental disorders in sport and exercise participants (Beisser, 1967; Ogilvie & Tutko, 1966). Examples of disorders experienced by top-level athletes include Tourette syndrome (Flatow, 1992; Page, 1990); panic disorder (Hales, 1993); obsessive compulsive disorder ("Malarchuk discloses," 1992); and bipolar disorder ("Yancey dead," 1994). In a national sample of 916 college football players (Brewer & Petrie, 1995), 10.5% (n = 96) were found to be depressed on the basis of their scores on the Center for Epidemiological Studies Depression scale (CES-D; Radloff, 1977). In large-scale surveys of clinical and counseling psychologists (Petrie & Diehl, 1995; Petrie, Diehl,

& Watkins, 1995), the primary areas of psychopathology addressed in individual therapy with athlete clients were reported to be anxiety and stress, depressive disorders, eating disorders, and substance-related disorders. Consistent with Association for the Advancement for Applied Sport Psychology (AAASP) certification criteria (AAASP, 1991), which require knowledge of basic psychopathology, the main purposes of this chapter are to highlight areas of psychopathology particularly relevant to sport and exercise, to review empirical research on the epidemiology of psychopathology in sport and exercise populations, and to provide recommendations for diagnosis and treatment of psychopathology in the context of sport and exercise.

Psychopathology Relevant to Sport and Exercise

Clearly, there is a wide range of disorders that may be experienced by sport and exercise participants. Nevertheless, some mental disorders are especially pertinent to sport and exercise contexts. Eating disorders, substance-related disorders, psychological factors affecting physical condition (i.e., psychosocial antecedents of athletic injury), and adjustment reactions (e.g., to athletic injury) are the forms of psychopathology that have been studied most extensively in association with sport and exercise. There are other disorders and subclinical syndromes (i.e., conditions in which impairment of behavioral, cognitive, or affective functioning is evident, but insufficient to satisfy diagnostic criteria) that also may be associated with sport and exercise participation, but they have been investigated less thoroughly. In this section, information regarding epidemiology, relevance to sport and exercise, and treatment is presented for each of the diagnostic categories identified as particularly relevant to sport and exercise.

Eating Disorders

For girls in late adolescence and women in early adulthood, approximately 0.5 to 1.0% and 1.0 to 3.0% meet diagnostic criteria for anorexia nervosa and bulimia nervosa, respectively; men and boys generally have a substantially lower rate (American Psychiatric Association [APA], 1994). For athletes, however, prevalence rates of eating disorders have varied considerably by study. Based on DSM–III–R criteria (APA, 1987), 1.6% and 4.2% of male and female intercollegiate athletes, respectively, could be classified with anorexia nervosa (Burckes-Miller & Black, 1988), and 1.3% of elite female Norwegian athletes were given a similar diagnosis (Sundgot-Borgen, 1994). Rucinski (1989) reported that 43% of a sample of female adolescent skaters scored in the anorexic range (> 30) on the Eating Attitudes Test (EAT; Garner & Garfinkel, 1979). For bulimia nervosa, frequencies have ranged from 4.1% for female collegiate gymnasts (Petrie & Stoever, 1993) to 8% for elite female Norwegian athletes (Sundgot-Borgen, 1994) to 39.2% for a cross-section of female college athletes (Burckes-Miller & Black, 1988). In considering these results, it is important to note that existing prevalence research has been limited by the use of small, circumscribed samples, the inconsistent measurement of eating disorders, and an absence of age-matched controls (Brownell & Rodin, 1992). Thus, these data provide only an emerging picture of the prevalence of eating disorders in athletes.

Although prevalence rates have been variable, researchers (e.g., Black & Burckes-Miller, 1988; Petrie & Stoever, 1993; Rosen & Hough, 1988; Sundgot-Borgen, 1994; Taub & Benson, 1992) consistently have shown that female athletes engage in disordered eating and weight-control behaviors, such as excessive exercise, rigorous dieting, binge eating, and vomiting. Considering these nondiagnosable behaviors is important for two reasons. First, they have been identified as risk factors—particularly excessive exercise and dieting—in the development of diagnosable disorders (Epling & Pierce, 1988; Polivy & Herman, 1985). Second, they have been independently related to psychological disturbances, such as body dissatisfaction (Petrie, 1993); neuroticism (Davis, 1992; Davis & Cowles, 1989); and lower self-esteem (Mintz & Betz, 1988). Although the exact number of athletes suffering from diagnosable eating disorders is not clear, athletes do exhibit other behavioral disturbances that suggest disordered eating problems are a major concern.

In addition to family, biological, personality, and genetic factors, the sport (i.e., sociocultural) environment has been strongly implicated in the etiology of eating disorder attitudes and behaviors (Burckes-Miller & Black, 1991; Striegel-Moore, Silberstein, & Rodin, 1986). Swoap and Murphy (1995) suggested that sport-specific weight restrictions (e.g., wrestling), pressure from coaches to lose weight or pursue an unrealistic body size and shape, and participation in sports where physical attractiveness is judged (e.g., gymnastics) are some of the factors that encourage athletes to develop an unhealthy focus on weight. In fact, athletes themselves have reported similar reasons for becoming preoccupied with weight and dieting, including pressure from coach, weight loss required for performance excellence, and improving physical appearance (Guthrie, 1991; Sundgot-Borgen, 1994). Wilson and Eldredge (1992) suggested that these psychosocial pressures lead to dietary restraint in athletes, which in turn interacts with psychopathological and pathophysiological factors to foster the development of disordered eating behaviors.

Because eating disorders are multidetermined, prevention and treatment should be too. Swoap and Murphy (1995) suggested that any eating-disorder sport-education program should focus on (a) fitness ideals (as opposed to body-weight ideals); (b) nutritional information provided by a nutritionist with sport performance knowledge; and (c) improvements in athletic personnel's (e.g., coaches) sensitivities to issues of weight control and dieting. Sesan (1989) described a three-level intervention program that focused on (a) education of athletic personnel about eating disorders and the relationship between the demands of sport participation and disordered eating, (b) early assessment and identification of at-risk athletes, and (c) educational outreach to sport teams where high numbers of athletes may be at risk. The scope of this chapter does not allow for a more detailed discussion of individual treatment issues, thus we strongly encourage readers to consider existing sources, such as Thompson (1987), Thompson and Sherman (1993), Ryan (1992), Garner and Garfinkel (1985) and the National Collegiate Athletic Association (1989), before undertaking such work.

Substance-Related Disorders

Although sport and exercise may connote images of clean living, health, and well-being, drug use by athletes is a serious concern. The highly publicized substance-related problems of well-known athletes, such as tennis player Jennifer Capriati, golfer John Daly, baseball player Steve Howe, and sprinter Ben Johnson, provide vivid examples of the potential consequences of drug use. The issue of substance use is more complicated for sport and exercise participants than for other individuals because athletes may use drugs for both "recreational" and performance-enhancement purposes (Anshel, 1993a, 1993b). In addition to the legal and health (physical and mental) ramifications of drug use experienced by the general population, competitive athletes may have their eligiblity to participate in sport restricted because many substances have been banned by sport governing bodies (Chappel, 1987).

Research has indicated that the prevalence of recreational drug use for athletes, at least at the high school and college levels, is roughly the same as that for nonathletes (Damm, 1991; Evans, Weinberg, & Jackson, 1992), although athletes may curb their use of recreational drugs during the competitive season (Selby, Weinstein, & Bird, 1990). Alcohol and marijuana are the primary substances used recreationally by athletes (Selby et al., 1990; Toohey, 1978; Toohey & Corder, 1981). In terms of performance-enhancement drugs, conservative prevalence estimates of 1.9% to 6.6% have been obtained for anabolic steroid use by high school students (Buckley et al., 1989; Cahill, Gaa, Griffith, & Tuttle, 1994; Windsor & Dumitru, 1989). It is likely that the use of banned substances by athletes is underreported in scientific research because of the penalties associated with the use of such substances. In addition to anabolic steroids, which are used to increase muscular size and strength, athletes may use other banned substances to reduce pain (e.g., morphine), to increase energy and arousal (e.g., amphetamines), to promote relaxation or reduce arousal (e.g., beta-blockers), or to control weight (e.g., diuretics; Anshel, 1993a).

In summarizing the empirical and theoretical literature, Anshel (1993a, 1993b) identified physical, psychological, and social causes of recreational and performance enhancement drug use by athletes. Physical causes include performance enhancement (e.g., heightened alertness, relaxation) and coping with pain and injury. Psychological causes include reduction of (or distraction from) unpleasant emotions (e.g., anxiety), boredom (e.g., during the off season), and personal problems. Social causes include peer pressure and experimentation. These reasons parallel explanations for drug use by members of the general population but take into account unique aspects of the sport environment.

Strategies for preventing drug use in sport have focused on deterrence (e.g., drug testing), education, coping skills training, and peer support (Anshel, 1993a, 1993b). Existing substance abuse prevention programs for athletes suffer from a number of limitations, including a reliance on one-time lectures and a lack of follow-up (Petitpas & Van Raalte, 1992). Treatment for athletes with an identified substance-related disorder is likely to involve outpatient or inpatient modalities, depending on the severity of the problem (Carr & Murphy, 1995; Damm, 1991). Although it is clear that scare tactics alone are not effective (Goldberg, Bents, Bosworth, Trevisan, & Elliot, 1991), intervention evaluation studies conducted with athletes are scarce and there is not currently an empirical basis for recommending the use of one particular type of intervention over another (Anshel, 1993a, 1993b).

Psychological Factors Affecting Medical Condition

Approximately 3 to 5 million athletic injuries occur each year in the United States (Kraus & Conroy, 1984). Because psychosocial factors such as coping resources, life stress, and social support may influence the occurrence of athletic injury (Andersen & Williams, 1988), it can be argued that the psychosocial antecedents of athletic injury constitute *psychological factors affecting medical condition* (APA, 1994, p. 675).

Research investigating the relationship of psychological variables to athletic injury has been conducted primarily with high school and college football players (Blackwell & McCullagh, 1990; Bramwell, Masuda, Wagner & Holmes, 1975; Coddington & Troxell, 1980; Cryan & Alles, 1983; Petrie, 1993a, 1993c; Thompson & Morris, 1994), although other sports, such as college volleyball (Williams, Tonymon, & Wadsworth, 1986); college gymnastics (Petrie, 1992); high school gymnastics, basketball, and wrestling (Smith, Smoll & Ptacek, 1990); and college baseball, softball, track, and tennis (Hardy & Riehl, 1988) have been considered. In certain studies (e.g., Blackwell & McCullagh, 1990; Coddington & Troxell, 1980; Cryan & Alles, 1983; Petrie, 1992), athletic injury was positively related to higher levels of life stress. In others, however, no direct relationship has been found between life stress and subsequent injury (e.g., Smith, Smoll & Ptacek, 1990; Williams, Tonymon, & Wadsworth, 1986).

In addressing inconsistent findings in the athletic injury literature, Andersen and Williams (1988) proposed a theoretical model describing the relationship between psychological variables and athletic injury. They suggested that athletic injuries were multiply determined and that researchers needed to consider the direct and moderating effects of other classes of variables, such as coping resources and personality, in addition to life stress. Subsequent research has supported their theoretical model, demonstrating that coping skills and social support (Smith, Smoll, & Ptacek, 1990); sensation seeking (Smith, Ptacek, & Smoll, 1992); social support (Petrie, 1992, 1993c); competitive trait anxiety (Petrie, 1993a); and playing status (i.e., starter vs. nonstarter; Petrie, 1993a, 1993c) moderated the life stress–injury relationship. Support for the direct effects of personality and coping variables on injury has been found for coping resources, competitive trait anxiety, and social support

(Blackwell & McCullagh, 1990; Hanson, McCullagh, & Tonymon, 1992). These results suggest that several psychological variables are related to athletic injury, either directly or indirectly through their moderation of life stress effects.

Andersen and Williams (1988) addressed the issue of intervention in their theoretical model, suggesting that various cognitive and behavioral approaches, such as cognitive restructuring, thought stopping, and relaxation, might be useful in addressing the potential psychological deficits that increase an athlete's risk of injury. In addition, strategies such as assisting athletes in increasing their coping skills or in becoming more satisfied with their support networks represent other potentially effective interventions. Regardless of the approach taken, it is essential that the intervention be specific to meet the needs of that individual. Unfortunately, little controlled research has been conducted in this area, so recommendations are based primarily on theory and are in need of empirical validation.

Adjustment Reactions

During the course of their involvement in sport and exercise, participants may experience a number of personally challenging transitions to which they must adjust (Pearson & Petitpas, 1990). For example, competitive athletes face the prospects of *deselection* (i.e., being cut from the team) and sport-career termination, and both competitive athletes and exercisers may become injured. Psychological adjustment to the latter transition—injury—is a topic of growing interest among researchers, who have examined the prevalence and correlates of postinjury emotional disturbance.

Research has indicated that an estimated 5% to 13% of athletes report clinically meaningful levels of psychological distress, at least in the short term (i.e., 1 to 2 months), following injury (Brewer, Linder, & Phelps, 1995; Brewer, Petitpas, Van Raalte, Sklar, & Ditmar, 1995; Leddy, Lambert, & Ogles, 1994; Smith, Scott, O'Fallon, & Young, 1990). Early theoretical formulations of the process of adjustment to athletic injury, which drew upon stage models of adjustment to loss (e.g., Kubler-Ross, 1969), considered postinjury emotional difficulties an inevitability. Extant research findings, however, support a conceptualization in which personal and situational variables interact to influence cognitive, emotional, and behavioral responses to injury (Brewer, 1994). Thus, characteristics of the person (e.g., age, personality, psychological investment in sport) and the situation (e.g., injury severity, injury duration, life stress) affect how the individual appraises the injury, reacts emotionally, and responds behaviorally. Managing affective responses to injury may be critical to the physical rehabilitation of athletic injuries, as postinjury emotional disturbance has been associated with poor adherence to sport injury rehabilitation regimens (Daly, Brewer, Van Raalte, Petitpas, & Sklar, 1995).

A variety of psychological treatments have been advocated for injured athletes, ranging from relaxation and imagery to counseling and psychotherapy (for a review, see Heil, 1993; Petitpas & Danish, 1995). Regardless of the particular intervention selected, which, of course, depends on the nature of the client's concerns and resources, Petitpas and Danish (1995) emphasized the importance of building rapport, educating injured athletes about their injury, helping injured athletes to develop coping skills, providing injured athletes with opportunities to practice their newly acquired coping skills, and evaluating the effectiveness of the intervention. Although studies investigating the impact of psychological interventions on outcomes of interest (e.g., emotional adjustment, physical rehabilitation) have not been conducted, there is evidence that psychological interventions such as counseling, goal setting, and imagery are credible with injured athletes and are well-received as long as they are integrated into the physical rehabilitation program and not perceived as "extra" (Brewer, Jeffers, Petitpas, & Van Raalte, 1994).

Various Disorders and Subclinical Syndromes

In addition to eating disorders, substance-related disorders, psychological factors affecting physical condition, and adjustment reactions, there are a number of other disorders and subclinical syndromes that have been documented in their association with sport and exercise participation. Because limited empirical information is available on each of these conditions, they will be discussed only briefly.

Dose–Response Reactions

Sport and exercise participants engage in physical activity presumably to prepare for competition or to enhance their fitness and well-being. Sometimes, however, the amount or dose of physical training can be excessive and counterproductive. Competitive athletes who engage in high-volume training regimens are at risk for developing *staleness*, a condition characterized by diminished performance and a variety of symptoms, including disturbances in mood, sleep, and appetite (for a review, see Raglin, 1993). Because the symptoms of staleness may mimic those of depressive disorders and chronic fatigue syndrome, careful evaluation is needed to rule out alternative causes of the symptoms (Puffer & McShane, 1991). At present, rest is the sole accepted treatment for staleness, although adjunctive psychological and medical care may also be appropriate (Raglin, 1993).

Although many individuals struggle to establish a regular exercise habit, some exercisers and recreational athletes have the opposite problem in that they become "dependent" on their involvement in physical activity and persist in their participation past the point at which physical and mental health benefits are gained. Exercise dependence, which has been labeled *negative addiction* (Morgan, 1979) and *obligatory exercise* (Yates, 1991), has been studied most extensively in association with running (for a review, see Pierce, 1994). Characteristics of exercise dependence include prioritizing exercise over other important activities and relationships, engaging in exercise despite the presence of exercise-related physical health problems (e.g., injury, pain), and experiencing withdrawal symptoms (e.g., mood disturbance) when restricted from participation in physical activity (Pierce, 1994). Comorbidity with eating disorders is a strong possibility among individuals with exercise dependence (de Coverley Veale, 1987). Although there is little information available on treatment of exercise dependence, Morrow (1988) developed a cognitive–behavioral intervention for exercise dependence in which clients are reinforced for gradually relinquishing exercise time to other activities after being assessed and trained in coping skills.

Anxiety Reactions

Anxiety is a central aspect of sport participation (Hackfort & Spielberger, 1989), with some athletes experiencing precompetitive anxiety to an extent that it interferes with performance (for a review, see Chapter 4, this volume). For the most part, the anxiety associated with sport involvement, even when it has an adverse effect on performance, is subclinical and can be addressed through performance-enhancement interventions. In rare cases, however, the level of anxiety experienced is more severe and warrants clinical attention (see Farkas, 1989; Friedberg, 1987). Silva (1994) identified a sport-specific condition in which anxiety is "isolated on an *element* of a total performance" (p. 104). As examples of this condition, termed *sport performance phobia*, Silva cited the behavior of a tennis player who was afraid to come to the net and a baseball catcher who developed an inability to throw the ball back to the pitcher despite being able to throw the ball to second base. Phobias and other extreme anxiety reactions should be addressed by sport and exercise psychology practitioners with clinical training.

Personality Disorders

A number of forces in competitive sport may contribute to the development and maintenance of personality disorders in athletes. For example, the coddling and adulation received by gifted athletes may help to foster narcissistic personality disorder (Andersen et al., 1994; House, 1989). Similarly, reinforcement of qualities such as toughness and aggressiveness in the sport environment may increase the likelihood of problem behavior among athletes with antisocial personality disorder (Andersen et al., 1994). Another factor that may exacerbate or contribute to the development of personality disorders in athletes is the dysfunctional, performance-contingent social support that athletes receive in many circumstances (House, 1989). Although there have been no empirical investigations on the prevalence and treatment of personality disorders in athletic populations, anecdotal evidence suggests that athletes with personality disorders may not respond well to performance-enhancement interventions and may require clinical attention (Andersen et al., 1994).

Recommendations for Diagnosis and Treatment

For sport and exercise participants with diagnosable psychopathology, appropriate treatment can improve their quality of life and enhance their sport or exercise involvement (e.g., Pelham et al., 1990). In the absence of empirical data suggesting otherwise, diagnosis and treatment of psychopathology in sport and exercise participants should be the same as with nonparticipants. Circumstances specific to sport and exercise, however, should be taken into consideration. Accordingly, the following recommendations for diagnosis and treatment of psychopathology in the context of sport and exercise are offered:

1. Practitioners should recognize that some of athletes' attitudes and behaviors that may appear to be pathological actually have adaptive value in sport and may be considered "normal" in the athletic subculture. For example, Folkins and Wieselberg-Bell (1981) found that finishers scored significantly higher on the

Psychopathic Deviate (Pd) scale of the Minnesota Multiphasic Personality Inventory (MMPI; Hathaway & McKinley, 1948) than nonfinishers in a 100 mile endurance run. The authors concluded that the detachment and lack of social conformity characteristic of high Pd scorers might assist endurance runners in training, which can be a solitary activity. Similarly, bodybuilders using anabolic steroids may be perceived positively by their fellow bodybuilders but not by the general public (Van Raalte, Cusimano, Brewer, & Matheson, 1993).

2. Practitioners should be sensitive to forces outside of the individual (e.g., coaches, competitive demands) that may be particularly influential in producing apparently pathological behavior. For example, the constant scrutiny faced by athletes both on and off the field may produce feelings of paranoia and anxiety (Ferrante & Etzel, 1991; House, 1989). Furthermore, characteristics such as aggressiveness and single-minded devotion to sport may be reinforced by coaches and teammates (Heyman, 1986). Thus, it is important to consider both the athlete and the athletic environment when assessing the behavior of sport and exercise participants (Miller, Vaughn, & Miller, 1990). Both personal and situational factors should be assessed thoroughly before concluding that a problem resides within the individual.

3. Practitioners should be aware that athletes in particular may be reluctant to seek treatment of a psychological nature. Research has shown that college student-athletes underutilize university mental health services relative to college student-nonathletes (Bergandi & Wittig, 1984; Carmen, Zerman, & Blaine, 1968; Pierce, 1969; Segal, Weiss, & Stokol, 1965). Athletes may be hesitant to become involved in psychotherapy because to do so could be construed as a sign of of personal "weakness," conflict with a desire to maintain autonomy, or cause them to be evaluated negatively by teammates, coaches, and others (Linder, Brewer, Van Raalte, & DeLange, 1991; Linder, Pillow, & Reno, 1989; Pierce, 1969; Pinkerton et al., 1989). Although athletes may be receptive to working with a sport psychologist for performance enhancement (Van Raalte, Brewer, Brewer, & Linder, 1992) and have expectations about counseling similar to those of nonathletes (Miller & Moore, 1993), the idea of consulting a mental health practitioner for psychotherapy may be met with resistance. Because entering treatment for psychopathology may

have negative ramifications for athletes' sport participation, athletes may be especially concerned about confidentiality. Practitioners should be attuned to this possibility and should make an effort to alleviate athlete-clients' concerns.

4. Practitioners should recognize that although sport may seem to be "just a game," many athletes are heavily invested in sport as a source of self-identity and self-worth (Brewer, Van Raalte, & Linder, 1993). Strong self-identification with sport involvement may benefit athletes in terms of developing a sense of self and enhancing motivation for training and competition, but may leave athletes vulnerable to psychological distress when they experience transitions such as deselection, injury, and sport-career termination (Brewer, 1993; Pearson & Petitpas, 1990). In extreme cases, threats to athletic self-identity may precipitate suicide (Petitpas & Danish, 1995; Smith & Milliner, 1994). Accordingly, the high degree of self-investment in sport participation possessed by some athletes should be acknowledged by practitioners and not dismissed as preoccupation with a frivolous activity.

5. Practitioners should be aware that although many athletic organizations may not ordinarily be receptive to psychological interventions, psychologists may be sought out in crisis situations such as a player death or a suicide attempt or threat (Rubin, 1991). In such situations, sport psychologists with crisis-intervention skills can provide counseling and consultation to help athletes, coaches, and administrators deal with the immediate and long-term consequences of the crisis (Heil, 1993).

6. In keeping with ethical guidelines, practitioners should provide referrals for their sport and exercise participant-clients who have presenting problems that are outside their realm of competence. Referral is clearly needed when the client's problem is centered on a technical aspect of sport performance or when the client requests a performance-enhancement intervention and the practitioner lacks sport- or exercise-specific knowledge. Referral also may be necessary when the client presents with psychopathology for which the clinically-oriented practitioner has not received training or where supervision or consultation is not available. For a review of referral processes in sport and exercise psychology, see Chapter 12, this volume).

Summary and Conclusions

In this chapter, we reviewed the major categories of psychopathology that have been identified and studied with sport and exercise participants. In addition, we provided recommendations for treatment and prevention as warranted by current research. Several points become clear from this review. First, athletes do experience psychopathology, such as eating disorders and substance abuse, at rates equal to and sometimes greater than the general population. Second, psychopathology specific to or exacerbated by sport or exercise involvement also exists. Third, research examining psychopathology in sport and exercise participants has been lacking, thus comments concerning this area still are tentative. Epidemiological, longitudinal, and well-controlled studies need to be conducted to expand the knowledge base. Finally, when treating psychopathology, it is essential that circumstances specific to sport and exercise be taken into consideration.

References

American Psychiatric Association. (1987). *Diagnostic and statistical manual of mental disorders* (3rd ed., rev.). Washington, DC: Author.

American Psychiatric Association. (1994). *Diagnostic and statistical manual of mental disorders* (4th ed.). Washington, DC: Author.

Andersen, M. B., Denson, E. L., Brewer, B. W., & Van Raalte, J. L. (1994). Disorders of personality and mood in athletes: Recognition and referral. *Journal of Applied Sport Psychology, 6*, 168–184.

Andersen, M. B., & Williams, J. M. (1988). A model of stress and athletic injury: Prediction and prevention. *Journal of Sport & Exercise Psychology, 10*, 294–306.

Anshel, M. H. (1993a). Psychology of drug use in sport. In R. N. Singer, M. Murphey, & L. K. Tennant (Eds.), *Handbook of research in sport psychology* (pp. 851–876). New York: Macmillan.

Anshel, M. H. (1993b). Drug abuse in sport: Causes and cures. In J. M. Williams (Ed.), *Applied sport psychology: Personal growth to peak performance* (2nd ed.) (pp. 310–327). Mountain View, CA: Mayfield.

Association for the Advancement of Applied Sport Psychology. (1991). Questions regarding certification. *Association for the Advancement of Applied Sport Psychology Newsletter, 6*(3), 3–4.

Beisser, A. R. (1977). *The madness in sports* (2nd ed.). Bowie, MD: Charles Press.

Bergandi, T., & Wittig, A. (1984). Availability of and attitudes toward counseling services for the collegiate athlete. *Journal of College Student Personnel, 25*, 557–558.

Black, D., & Burckes-Miller, M. (1988). Male and female college athletes: Use of anorexia nervosa and bulimia nervosa weight loss methods. *Research Quarterly for Exercise and Sport, 59*, 252–256.

Blackwell, B., & McCullagh, P. (1990). The relationship of athletic injury to life stress, competitive anxiety, and coping resources. *Athletic Training, 25*, 23–27.

Bramwell, S. T., Masuda, M., Wagner, N. N., & Holmes, T. H. (1975). Psychosocial factors in athletic injuries: Development and application of the Social and Athletic Readjustment Rating Scale (SARRS). *Journal of Human Stress, 1,* 6–20.

Brewer, B. W. (1993). Self-identity and specific vulnerability to depressed mood. *Journal of Personality, 61,* 343–364.

Brewer, B. W. (1994). Review and critique of models of psychological adjustment to athletic injury. *Journal of Applied Sport Psychology, 6,* 87–100.

Brewer, B. W., Jeffers, K. E., Petitpas, A. J., & Van Raalte, J. L. (1994). Perceptions of psychological interventions in the context of sport injury rehabilitation. *The Sport Psychologist, 8,* 176–188.

Brewer, B. W., Linder, D. E., & Phelps, C. M. (1995). Situational correlates of emotional adjustment to athletic injury. *Clinical Journal of Sport Medicine, 5,* 241–245.

Brewer, B. W., Petitpas, A. J., Van Raalte, J. L., Sklar, J. H., & Ditmar, T. D. (1995). Prevalence of psychological distress among patients at a physical therapy clinic specializing in sports medicine. *Sports Medicine, Training and Rehabilitation, 6,* 139–145.

Brewer, B. W., & Petrie, T. A. (1995, Spring). A comparison of injured and uninjured football players on selected psychosocial variables. *Academic Athletic Journal,* pp. 11–18.

Brewer, B. W., Van Raalte, J. L., & Linder, D. E. (1993). Athletic identity: Hercules' muscles or Achilles heel? *International Journal of Sport Psychology, 24,* 237–254.

Brownell, K. D., & Rodin, J. (1992). Prevalence of eating disorders in athletes. In K. D. Brownell, J. Rodin, & J. H. Wilmore (Eds.), *Eating, body weight, and performance in athletes* (pp. 128–145). Malvern, PA: Lea & Febiger.

Buckley, W. E., Yesalis, C. E., Friedl, K. E., Anderson, W. A., Streit, A. L., & Wright, J. E. (1988). Estimated prevalence of anabolic steroid use among high school seniors. *JAMA: Journal of the American Medical Association, 260,* 3441–3445.

Burckes-Miller, M., & Black, D. (1988). Male and female college athletes: Prevalence of anorexia nervosa and bulimia nervosa. *Athletic Training, 23,* 137–140.

Burckes-Miller, M., & Black, D. (1991). College athletes and eating disorders: A theoretical context. In D. Black (Ed.), *Eating disorders among athletes: Theory, issues and research* (pp. 11–26). Reston, VA: American Alliance for Health, Physical Education, Recreation & Dance.

Cahill, B. R., Gaa, G. L., Griffith, E. H., & Tuttle, L. D. (1994). Prevalence of anabolic steroid use among Illinois high school students. *Journal of Athletic Training, 29,* 216–218, 221–222.

Carmen, L., Zerman, J., & Blaine, G. (1968). Use of Harvard psychiatric service by athletes and nonathletes. *Mental Hygiene, 52,* 134–137.

Carr, C. M., & Murphy, S. M. (1995). Alcohol and drugs in sport. In S. M. Murphy (Ed.), *Sport psychology interventions* (pp. 283–306). Champaign, IL: Human Kinetics.

Chappel, J. N. (1987). Drug use and abuse in the athlete. In J. R. May & M. J. Asken (Eds.), *Sport psychology: The psychological health of the athlete* (pp. 187–212). New York: PMA.

Coddington, R. D., & Troxell, J. R. (1980). The effect of emotional factors on football injury rates—A pilot study. *Journal of Human Stress, 6,* 3–5.

Cryan, P. D., & Alles, W. F. (1983). The relationship between stress and college football injuries. *Journal of Sports Medicine and Physical Fitness, 23,* 52–58.

Daly, J. M., Brewer, B. W., Van Raalte, J. L., Petitpas, A. J., & Sklar, J. H. (1995). Cognitive appraisal, emotional adjustment, and adherence to sport injury rehabilitation. *Journal of Sport Rehabilitation, 4,* 23–30.

Damm, J. (1991). Drugs and the college student-athlete. In E. F. Etzel, A. P. Ferrante,

& J. W. Pinkney (Eds.), *Counseling college student athletes: Issues and interventions* (pp. 151–174). Morgantown, WV: Fitness Information Technology.

Davis, C. (1992). Body image, dieting behaviors and personality factors: A study of high performance female athletes. *International Journal of Sport Psychology, 23,* 179–192.

Davis, C., & Cowles, M. (1989). A comparison of weight and diet concerns and personality factors among athletes and non-athletes. *Journal of Psychosomatic Research, 33,* 527–536.

de Coverley Veale, D. M. W. (1987). Exercise dependence. *British Journal of Addiction, 82,* 735–740.

Epling, W. F., & Pierce, W. D. (1988). Activity-based anorexia: A biobehavioral perspective. *International Journal of Eating Disorders, 7,* 475–485.

Evans, M., Weinberg, R., & Jackson, A. (1992). Psychological factors related to drug use in college athletes. *The Sport Psychologist, 6,* 24–41.

Farkas, G. (1989). Exposure and response prevention in the treatment of an okeanophobic triathlete. *The Sport Psychologist, 3,* 189–195.

Ferrante, A. P., & Etzel, E. (1991). Counseling college student-athletes: The problem, the need. In E. F. Etzel, A. P. Ferrante, & J. W. Pinkney (Eds.), *Counseling college student athletes: Issues and interventions* (pp. 1–17). Morgantown, WV: Fitness Information Technology.

Flatow, S. (1992, August 23). 'Why is this happening?' *Parade Magazine,* pp. 18–19.

Folkins, C. H., & Wieselberg-Bell, N. (1991). A personality profile of ultramarathon runners: A little deviance may go a long way. *Journal of Sport Behavior, 4,* 119–127.

Friedberg, F. (1987). Coping skills treatment of situational vomiting: A case study. *Journal of Cognitive Psychotherapy: An International Quarterly, 1,* 183–188.

Garner, D., & Garfinkel, P. (1979). The eating attitudes test: An index of the symptoms of anorexia nervosa. *Psychological Medicine, 9,* 273–279

Garner, D., & Garfinkel, P. (Eds.). (1985). *Handbook of psychotherapy for anorexia nervosa and bulimia.* New York: Guilford.

Goldberg, L., Bents, R., Bosworth, E., Trevisan, L., & Elliot, D. L. (1991). Anabolic steroid education and adolescents: Do scare tactics work? *Pediatrics, 87,* 283–286.

Guthrie, S. R. (1991). Prevalence of eating disorders among intercollegiate athletes: Contributing factors and preventative measures. In D. Black (Ed.), *Eating disorders among athletes: Theory, issues and research* (pp. 43–66). Reston, VA: American Alliance for Health, Physical Education, Recreation & Dance.

Hackfort, D., & Spielberger, C. D. (Eds.). (1989). *Anxiety in sports: An international perspective.* New York: Hemispere.

Hales, D. (1993, December 19). When panic strikes. *Parade Magazine,* pp. 12–13.

Hanson, S. J., McCullagh, P., & Tonymon, P. (1992). The relationship of personality characteristics, life stress, and coping resources to athletic injury. *Journal of Sport and Exercise Psychology, 14,* 262–272.

Hardy, C. J., & Riehl, R. E. (1988). An examination of the life stress–injury relationship among noncontact sport participants. *Behavioral Medicine, 14,* 113–118.

Hathaway, S., & McKinley, C. (1948). *The Minnesota Multiphasic Personality Inventory.* New York: Psychological Corporation.

Heil, J. (1993). *Psychology of sport injury.* Champaign, IL: Human Kinetics.

Heyman, S. R. (1986). Psychological problem patterns found with athletes. *The Clinical Psychologist, 39,* 68–71.

House, T. (1989). *The jock's itch: The fast-track private world of the professional ballplayer.* Chicago: Contemporary Books.

Kraus, J. F., & Conroy, C. (1984). Mortality and morbidity from injuries in sports and recreation. *Annual Review of Public Health, 5,* 163–192.

Kubler-Ross, E. (1969). *On death and dying.* New York: Macmillan.

Leddy, M. H., Lambert, M. J., & Ogles, B. M. (1994). Psychological consequences of athletic injury among high level competitors. *Research Quarterly for Exercise and Sport, 65,* 347–354.

Linder, D. E., Brewer, B. W., Van Raalte, J. L., & DeLange, N. (1991). A negative halo for athletes who consult sport psychologists: Replication and extension. *Journal of Sport & Exercise Psychology, 13,* 133–148.

Linder, D. E., Pillow, D. R., & Reno, R. R. (1989). Shrinking jocks. Derogation of athletes who consult a sport psychologist. *Journal of Sport & Exercise Psychology, 11,* 270–280.

Malarchuk discloses an anxiety disorder. (1992, March 12). *The Boston Globe,* p. 68.

Miller, M. J., & Moore, K. K. (1993). Athletes' and nonathletes' expectations about counseling. *Journal of College Student Development, 34,* 267–269.

Miller, T. W., Vaughn, M. P., & Miller, J. M. (1990). Clinical issues and treatment strategies in stress-oriented athletes. *Sports Medicine, 9,* 370–379.

Mintz, L. B., & Betz, N. E. (1988). Prevalence and correlates of eating disordered behaviors among undergraduate women. *Journal of Counseling Psychology, 35,* 463–471.

Morgan, W. P. (1979). Negative addiction in runners. *The Physician and Sportsmedicine, 7*(2), 57–70.

Morgan, W. P. (1985). Selected psychological factors limiting performance: A mental health model. In D. H. Clarke & H. M. Eckert (Eds.), *Limits of human performance* (pp. 70–80). Champaign, IL: Human Kinetics.

Morrow, J. (1988, October). *A cognitive–behavioral interaction for reducing exercise addiction.* Paper presented at the annual meeting of the Association for the Advancement of Applied Sport Psychology, Nashua, New Hampshire.

National Collegiate Athletic Association. (1989). *Nutrition and eating disorder in collegiate athletics* [Video]. Kansas City, MO: Author.

Ogilvie, B. C., & Tutko, T. A. (1966). *Problem athletes and how to handle them.* London: Pelham.

Ogilvie, B. C., & Tutko, T. A. (1971). Sport: If you want to build character, try something else. *Psychology Today, 5*(10), 61–63.

Page, P. (1990). Tourette syndrome in athletics: A case study and review. *Athletic Training, 25,* 254–259.

Pearson, R. E., & Petitpas, A. J. (1990). Transitions of athletes: Pitfalls and prevention. *Journal of Counseling and Development, 69,* 7–10.

Pelham, W. E., Jr., McBurnett, K., Harper, G. W., Milch, R., Murphy, D. A., Clinton, J., & Thiele, C. (1990). Methylphenidate and baseball playing in ADHD children: Who's on first? *Journal of Consulting and Clinical Psychology, 58,* 130–133.

Petitpas, A., & Danish, S. J. (1995). Caring for injured athletes. In S. M. Murphy (Ed.), *Sport psychology interventions* (pp. 255–281). Champaign, IL: Human Kinetics.

Petitpas, A. J., & Van Raalte, J. L. (1992, Spring). Planning alcohol education programs for intercollegiate student-athletes. *The Academic Athletic Journal,* pp. 12–25.

Petrie, T. A. (1992). Psychosocial antecedents of athletic injury: The effects of life stress and social support on women collegiate gymnasts. *Behavioral Medicine, 18,* 127–138.

Petrie, T. A. (1993a). Coping skills, competitive trait anxiety, and playing status: Moderating effects on the life stress-injury relationship. *Journal of Sport and Exercise Psychology, 15,* 261–274.

Petrie, T. A. (1993b). Disordered eating in female collegiate gymnasts: Prevalence and personality/attitudinal correlates. *Journal of Sport & Exercise Psychology, 15,* 424–436.

Petrie, T. A. (1993c). The moderating effects of social support and playing status on the life stress-injury relationship. *Journal of Applied Sport Psychology, 5,* 1–16.

Petrie, T. A., & Diehl, N. S. (1995). Sport psychology in the profession of psychology. *Professional Psychology: Research and Practice, 26,* 288–291.

Petrie, T. A., Diehl, N. S., & Watkins, C. E., Jr. (1995). Sport psychology: An emerging domain in the counseling psychology profession? *The Counseling Psychologist, 23,* 535–545.

Petrie, T., & Stoever, S. (1993). The incidence of bulimia nervosa and pathogenic weight control behaviors in female collegiate gymnasts. *Research Quarterly for Exercise and Sport, 64,* 238–241.

Pierce, E. F. (1994). Exercise dependence syndrome in runners. *Sports Medicine, 18,* 149–156.

Pierce, R. (1969). Athletes in psychiatry: How many, how come? *Journal of the American College Health Association, 17,* 244–249.

Pinkerton, R., Hinz, L., & Barrow, J. (1989). The college student athlete: Psychological consideration and interventions. *Journal of American College Health, 37,* 218–226.

Polivy, J., & Herman, C. P. (1985). Dieting and binging: A causal analysis. *American Psychologist, 40,* 193–201.

Puffer, J. C., & McShane, J. M. (1991). Depression and chronic fatigue in the college student-athlete. *Primary Care, 18,* 297–308.

Radloff, L. (1977). The CES-D scale: A self-report depression scale for research in the general population. *Applied Psychosocial Measurement, 1,* 385–401.

Raglin, J. S. (1993). Overtraining and staleness: Psychometric monitoring of endurance athletes. In R. N. Singer, M. Murphey, & L. K. Tennant (Eds.), *Handbook of research in sport psychology* (pp. 840–850). New York: Macmillan.

Rosen, L., & Hough, D. (1988). Pathogenic weight-control behaviors of female college gymnasts. *The Physician and Sportsmedicine, 16,* 141–144.

Rubin, P. (1991, July 10–16). Bobby had a gun: And ASU's most promising wrestler turned it on himself. *New Times,* pp. 23, 28, 32, 35, 37, 38.

Rucinski, A. (1989). Relationship of body image and dietary intake of competitive ice skaters. *Journal of the American Dietetics Association, 89,* 98–103.

Ryan, R. (1992). Management of eating problems in athletic settings. In K. D. Brownell, J. Rodin, & J. H. Wilmore (Eds.), *Eating, body weight, and performance in athletes* (pp. 344–362). Malvern, PA: Lea & Febiger.

Segal, B. E., Weiss, R. J., & Stokol, R. (1965). Emotional adjustment, social organization, and psychiatric treatment rates. *American Sociological Review, 30,* 548–556.

Seime, R., & Damer, D. (1991). Identification and treatment of the athlete with an eating disorder. In E. F. Etzel, A. P. Ferrante, & J. W. Pinkney (Eds.), *Counseling college student athletes: Issues and interventions* (pp. 175–198). Morgantown, WV: Fitness Information Technology.

Selby, R., Weinstein, H. M., & Bird, T. S. (1990). The health of university athletes: Attitudes, behaviors, and stressors. *Journal of American College Health, 39,* 11–18.

Sesan, R. (1989). Eating disorders and female athletes: A three-level intervention program. *Journal of College Student Development, 30,* 568–570.

Silva, J. M., III. (1994). Sport performance phobias. *International Journal of Sport Psychology, 25,* 100–118.

Smith, A. M., & Milliner, E. K. (1994). Injured athletes and the risk of suicide. *Journal of Athletic Training, 29,* 337–341.

Smith, A. M., Scott, S. G., O'Fallon, W. M., & Young, M. L. (1990). The emotional responses of athletes to injury. *Mayo Clinic Proceedings, 65,* 38–50.

Smith, R. E., Ptacek, J. T., & Smoll, F. L. (1992). Sensation seeking, stress, and adolescent injuries: A test of stress-buffering, risk-taking, and coping skills hypotheses. *Journal of Personality and Social Psychology, 62,* 1016–1024.

Smith, R. E., Smoll, F. L., & Ptacek, J. T. (1990). Conjunctive moderator variables in vulnerability and resiliency research: Life stress, social support, and coping skills and adolescent sport injuries. *Journal of Personality and Social Psychology, 58,* 360–369.

Striegel-Moore, R., Silberstein, L., & Rodin, J. (1986). Toward an understanding of risk factors for bulimia. *American Psychologist, 41,* 246–263.

Sundgot-Borgen, J. (1994). Risk and trigger factors for the development of eating disorders in female elite athletes. *Medicine and Science in Sports and Exercise, 26,* 414–419.

Swoap, R. A., & Murphy, S. M. (1995). Eating disorders and weight management in athletes. In S. M. Murphy (Ed.), *Sport psychology interventions* (pp. 307–329). Champaign, IL: Human Kinetics.

Taub, D., & Benson, R. (1992). Weight concerns, weight control techniques, and eating disorders among adolescent competitive swimmers: The effect of gender. *Sociology of Sport Journal, 9,* 76–86.

Thompson, N. J., & Morris, R. D. (1994). Predicting injury risk in adolescent football players: The importance of psychological variables. *Journal of Pediatric Psychology, 19,* 415–429.

Thompson, R. A. (1987). Management of the athlete with an eating disorder: Implications for the sport management team. *The Sport Psychologist, 1,* 114–126.

Thompson, R. A., & Sherman, R. (1993). *Helping athletes with eating disorders.* Champaign, IL: Human Kinetics.

Toohey, J. (1978). Non-medical drug use among intercollegiate athletes at five American universities. *Bulletin on Narcotics, 30*(3), 61–65.

Toohey, J., & Corder, B. (1981). Intercollegiate sports participation and non-medical drug use. *Bulletin on Narcotics, 33*(3), 23–27.

Van Raalte, J. L., Brewer, B. W., Brewer, D. D., & Linder, D. E. (1992). NCAA Division II college football players' perceptions of an athlete who consults a sport psychologist. *Journal of Sport & Exercise Psychology, 14,* 273–282.

Van Raalte, J. L., Cusimano, K. A., Brewer, B. W., & Matheson, H. (1993). Perceptions of anabolic steroid users. *Journal of Applied Social Psychology, 23,* 1214–1225.

Williams, J. M., Tonymon, P., & Wadsworth, W. A. (1986). Relationship of life stress to injury in intercollegiate volleyball. *Journal of Human Stress, 12,* 38–43.

Wilson, G. T., & Eldredge, K. L. (1992). Pathology and development of eating disorders: Implications for athletes. In K. D. Brownell, J. Rodin, & J. H. Wilmore (Eds.), *Eating, body weight, and performance in athletes* (pp. 115–127). Malvern, PA: Lea & Febiger.

Windsor, R. E., & Dumitru, D. (1989). Prevalence of anabolic steriod use by male and female adolescents. *Medicine and Science in Sports and Exercise, 21,* 494–497.

Yancey dead at 56. (1994, August 27). *The Union-News,* pp. 23–24.

Yates, A. (1991). *Compulsive exercise and the eating disorders: Toward an integrated theory of activity.* New York: Brunner Mazel.

12 Referral Processes in Sport Psychology

Judy L. Van Raalte and Mark B. Andersen

Case #1

Malika began working with a sport psychologist because she lacked confidence during competitions and often was worried. As the consultation progressed, Malika learned ways to control her anxiety and bolster her confidence in her sport. She told her sport psychologist that she was able to manage her emotions in her sport but was now feeling worried because she was losing a lot of money betting on professional sports. Gambling had been a problem in high school and it was getting out of control again.

Case #2

Although Al sometimes seemed "different," he was an integral member of his team throughout the year. He wanted to improve in his sport and gladly put in extra hours training and working with a sport psychologist. At the team fund raiser, Al started acting strange again. He was rude to some of the people who were contributing to the team. The next week Al was found wandering around barefoot in a nearby town. He was disheveled and seemed to be disoriented.

Case #3

Chris was a team leader who took advantage of an opportunity to meet with a sport psychologist to discuss various issues. Chris told the sport psychologist that chronic knee pain kept her from performing in a relaxed manner. Chris asked the sport psychologist for performance enhancement suggestions that would allow her to compete and block out the pain.

Athletes begin working with sport psychologists for a variety of reasons. As described in the case examples above, consultation often begins with a focus on performance enhancement. Athletes may contact a sport psychology consultant or be referred to one for other problems as well (e.g., coach/teammate conflicts, career issues, injury). Over the course of consultation, the sport psychologist may come to believe that issues other than performance enhancement (e.g., gambling, psychopathology, physical injury) are of central concern to the athlete. When these issues are outside the sport psychologist's areas of expertise, or when the sport psychologist feels frustrated and is not making progress with a client, a referral may be in order (Bobele & Conran, 1988).

Referral is a delicate and potentially risky process. The structure of the referral can set the stage for the quality and efficacy of the therapeutic relationship that follows (Bobele & Conran, 1988). When working with athletes, referrals are complicated by the stigma associated with mental problems and the derogation of those who seek help from mental health practitioners. Research has indicated that male college students and older male sports fans derogate an athlete who consults a sport psychologist or a psychiatrist relative to an athlete who attempts to resolve the same problem by working with his coach (Linder, Brewer, Van Raalte, & DeLange, 1991). Although college athletes do not derogate a fellow athlete who consults a sport psychologist, they do have a negative regard for an athlete who consults a psychiatrist (Van Raalte, Brewer, Brewer, & Linder, 1992). Thus, fear of derogation may leave athletes hesitant to accept referrals to mental health professionals.

The purpose of this chapter is to address some of the complexities of the referral process in sport psychology. First, we will describe some of the typical problems requiring referral in sport psychology settings. Second, we will describe referral networks, and third, we will provide some *do's* and *don'ts* for the referral of athletes.

Typical Problems Requiring Referral

Athletes, in general, probably exhibit a smaller range and frequency of severe mental disorders than are found in the population at large. Severe pathology among athletes may be more rare because of a natural selection process. For example, maintaining an athlete's schedule and regimen is generally more than a severely depressed person or a person with borderline personality can handle for any significant length of time. The good mental health of athletes (Morgan, 1985) may also be due in part to their involvement in regular exercise. Various forms of physical activity have been found to be effective in treating depression and other psychological disorders (e.g., Martinsen, 1990; Sachs & Buffone, 1984). Nevertheless, problems requiring referral do occur in the athletic population (Andersen, Denson, Brewer, & Van Raalte, 1994). Depending on the specific knowledge and competencies of the sport psychologist, a variety of psychological problems may be detected that require referral. Some of the more common physical concerns, interpersonal and intrapersonal issues, and psychopathology that a sport psychologist might encounter, and make referrals for, are detailed below.

Physical Issues

Sport psychologists should make every effort to gain knowledge of the technical and physical aspects of sport and exercise activities. Such knowledge helps sport psychologists recognize when a problem is more physical than psychological and make appropriate referrals to coaches and sports medicine personnel. Knowledge of the technical aspects of the sport helps the sport psychologist better judge when an athlete's problems need the attention of the coach more than that of the sport psychologist. A case example illustrates this point. A beginning 110 meter hurdler was seeing one of the authors and starting work on imaging her event. On checking with the athlete about the quality, viewpoint, and pace of the hurdling images, the practitioner learned that the athlete was "watching" each hurdle as her leg went over it. The practitioner was fairly sure the hurdler's eyes should have been focused farther down the track and not on the hurdle that was being passed. Because this visual focus question was a coaching point outside of the sport psychologist's area of competence, it was suggested that the athlete discuss ideal focus techniques with her coach. This discussion resulted in improved hurdling for the athlete, enhanced the athlete's relationship with her coach, and gave the coach a favorable impression of the sport psychologist. Sport psychologists who interfere in the technical area of athletes' sport performances and cross the line into coaching may not last in the field.

Sport psychologists working in competitive sport may encounter athletes who are encouraged to "play through the pain." In some cases, athletes may be sent to a sport psychologist because they are not "tough" enough. That is, the coach may believe that athletes are "wimping out" or that psychological factors are causing recurrent injuries. Before working with an athlete on specific techniques such as concentration or pain management, as described in the case of Chris at the beginning of the chapter, the sport psychologist should refer the athlete to a sports medicine provider to make sure that additional athletic involvement will not cause physical damage. This referral can pose problems. The coach should be informed of any referral to sports medicine personnel. If this is not done, the coach may feel that an "end around" has been pulled. On the other hand, the sport psychologist cannot ethically reveal that a referral has been made without the express consent of the athlete. Referral for a thorough check-out framed as "just covering all the bases" may prove effective in putting both the athlete and coach at ease.

As relationships between sport psychologists and athletes develop, athletes may begin to feel comfortable voicing dissatisfaction with training schedules and techniques. Athletes may discuss technical problems with their training that they believe are contributing to poor performances. Naturally, athletes should talk to their coaches about technical issues, but some athletes are uncomfortable around their coaches and are rather fearful of coach reactions. Sport psychologists can help athletes develop strategies to facilitate dialogue. Although encouraging athletes to talk to their coaches is not a referral in the strict sense, it is getting athletes to the appropriate resource (cf. chapter 13, this volume).

Personal and Interpersonal Issues

Helping athletes cope with interpersonal issues may be within sport psychologists' realm of expertise, depending on their training. For those trained in exercise science or research psychology, or for those hired to work in performance enhancement only, the structure of the consultation setting necessitates referral for interpersonal concerns. For example, if sport psychologists are hired primarily to provide performance-enhancement services, they may decide to refer athletes to other sources for longer term consultation on interpersonal issues such as aggression and sexual issues.

Aggression is an accepted part of the athletic culture (Heyman, 1993). In some cases, however, athletes' aggression may become problematic. Difficulties can arise when athletes are so aggressive that they are unable to compete within the rules or are extremely aggressive off the field. For athletes who have been using alcohol, steroids, or other illegal drugs, the situation becomes even more complicated. A sport psychologist may have success helping athletes manage their aggression if the athletes have a history of reasonable anger and aggression control. Athletes with more problematic histories may require more extensive treatment, and may be good candidates for referral (Heyman, 1993).

The sexual activities of athletes are often considered newsworthy, although little research has been conducted on the actual sexual behavior of athletes (Heyman, 1993). Like the rest of the population, athletes confront a number of issues concerning relationships, sexuality, and gender role. Sport psychologists working primarily in the performance enhancement area still may come across sexuality issues with their athlete-clients. It is common for an athlete after a month or two of building up trust with the sport psychologist to then reveal some very personal information. In some cases, sexuality issues may be part of that information. For instance, in most cases, being a gay, lesbian, or bisexual athlete is not the problem; many of the problems these athletes face have to do with the homophobia in sport and society. Sport psychologists not familiar or comfortable with sexual-orientation and sexual-identity issues need to refer.

Psychopathology

As was highlighted in the case of Al, sport psychologists must be familiar with the symptoms associated with psychopathology so that they can appropriately treat or refer athletes (Andersen et al., 1994). The chapter on psychopathology (chapter 11) provides a discussion of some of the more common disorders that sport psychologists may encounter (e.g., adjustment reactions, anxiety disorders, eating disorders, personality disorders). Athletes who have problems with gambling, like Malika, described in case one, may also be appropriate candidates for referral.

Referral Networks

Having gathered information about the typical problems that may require referral, it is then incumbent on the sport psychologist to develop an appropriate referral network. A *sport psychology referral network* is a group of people with expertise in a variety of areas to whom athletes can be referred. Ideally, the professionals in the referral network have knowledge of sports and experience working with athletes. At the least, they should be interested in learning about sport and exercise and open to working with an athletic population.

Establishing a referral network takes time and motivation. First, appropriate professionals in the local area should be identified (Heyman, 1993). These might include coaches, exercise physiologists, sports medicine experts, physical therapists, athletic trainers, psychologists, psychiatrists, and social workers. Selecting both male and female professionals of various theoretical orientations and professional backgrounds can be useful. Second, an effort should be made to develop a relationship with these professionals. The referral process is often smoother and more comfortable if sport psychologists know the professionals to whom they are referring their athlete clients and if they have asked the referral sources how they would like athletes to be referred (Bobele & Conran, 1988). Athletes seem to find this "team approach," in which various sport professionals work together, to be appealing (Andersen, 1992). Third, the referral network should be evaluated and modified on an ongoing basis to provide the best service for athletes. Having a broad group of practitioners available allows the sport psychologist to have some flexibility in this process.

When developing a referral network, sport psychologists should keep in mind some of the specific concerns that athletes may have. Athletes generally have limited time due to the demands of training and work or school. Many athletes have limited funds. Thus, it is useful to select local practitioners, at least some of whom provide services on a sliding scale basis. For student-athletes attending colleges or universities, there are usually "free" on-campus services available. Developing a relationship with these providers increases the likelihood that athletes will follow through on referrals made.

The Referral Process

There is no one way to make the perfect referral. Nevertheless, there are several tips about the referral process that may be useful for sport psychology practitioners (see Exhibit 1).

Do prepare athletes for the referral. This preparation should begin at the first meeting with the athlete. Athletes should be informed that during the course of their work with the sport psychologist, referral to other practitioners is possible. Because a lot of information is covered in

---

Exhibit 1

Tips for Making Good Referrals

1. Prepare athletes for the possibility of referral.
2. Explain why you are making the referral (Bobele & Conran, 1988).
3. Describe to athletes what is generally involved in working with a mental health (or other) practitioner (Heil, 1993).
4. Be sensitive to athlete concerns in the referral process.
5. Get written consent from athletes to share information with the referral source if necessary.
6. Give athletes the necessary information to schedule an appointment or at the time that the referral is made, or schedule an appointment for the athlete at that time.
7. If athletes decide not to follow through, discuss alternate strategies. Do not hesitate to reintroduce the idea of referral (Heil, 1993).

---

the initial session, many psychologists (Strein & Hershenson, 1991) and sport psychologists have developed written handouts reiterating important details about the consultation process for athletes to read and take with them.

If it becomes evident that the athlete should be referred, *do* explain to the athlete why the referral is being made (Bobele & Conran, 1988; Heil, 1993). Athletes may be more receptive to the referral if it is explained in terms of their sport using performance-enhancement language rather than in terms of pathology. If appropriate referral networks have been cultivated, it also is possible for sport psychologists to match athletes with compatible, competent practitioners.

Do describe to athletes what is generally involved in working with the practitioner to whom they are being referred (Heil, 1993). This is particularly important for athletes who are being referred to mental health practitioners. Although athletes do not seem to differ from non-athletes in their expectations about counseling (Miller & Moore, 1993), there clearly are misconceptions about mental health treatments that exist. It is acceptable to tell athletes about various forms of payment available (e.g., insurance, sliding scale, pro bono), but the practitioner to whom an athlete is being referred should set the specific fee (Bobele & Conran, 1988).

Do be sensitive to the concerns and fears of the athlete during the referral process. Athletes may be afraid that if they pursue the referral, the practitioner may take away what made them "great" performers

---

Exhibit 2

Referral Don'ts

1. Don't oversimplify the situation (Bobele & Conran, 1988).
2. *Don't* disguise the expertise and/or function of the practitioner to whom the athlete is being referred (Bobele & Conran, 1988).
3. *Don't* use referral follow-through as a condition for a favorable report to the coach or a prerequisite to avoid negative consequences (Bobele & Conran, 1988).
4. *Don't* violate athlete confidentiality.
5. *Don't* undermine the treatment of the referral source.

(Heyman, 1993). Focusing on athletes' return to competition if athletes want to return is also important (Bobele & Conran, 1988).

If needed, *do* get written consent to share information about the athlete with the practitioner to whom the referral is being made (Strein & Hershenson, 1991). Information is appropriately shared on a "need-to-know" basis (Strein & Hershenson, 1991). Athletes who are aware of exactly what information will be provided may be more comfortable with the referral.

Do facilitate follow-through on the referral. Refer "in" as much as possible. That is, bring the referred practitioner in to work together with the athlete and the sport psychologist (Andersen, 1992). This team approach has the advantage of being convenient for the athlete and alleviating some athlete fears that if they pursue the referral they will be abandoned by their sport psychologist. When referring in is not feasible, give athletes the information needed for them to schedule an appointment with the practitioner. Some athletes may prefer to have the sport psychologist help them schedule the first appointment when the referral is made.

Do assess the effectiveness of the referral process. Sport psychologists may want to schedule follow-up meetings to see how the referral worked. If the athlete decides not to follow through on the referral, the sport psychologist should then discuss alternate strategies for dealing with the problem (Heil, 1993). Sport psychologists should not hesitate to reintroduce the idea of referral at a later date (Heil, 1993).

There are several *don'ts* for the referral process. Although this list is not exhaustive, avoiding these pitfalls may help referrals go more smoothly (see Exhibit 2).

During the referral process, *don't* oversimplify the situation and tell the athlete that the problem will easily be fixed if the athlete pursues the referral (Bobele & Conran, 1988). Although it is important to sound positive and confident about the skills of the referred practitioner, creating false expectations will make it more difficult for the practitioner to work effectively.

Don't disguise the expertise or function of the practitioner (Bobele & Conran, 1988). Particularly if the athlete is hesitant to pursue the referral, it may be tempting to omit some of the details of the practitioner's expertise. Failure to reveal relevant information, however, violates trust and can make it difficult for the practitioner to work effectively with the athlete.

Don't use referral follow-through as a condition for a favorable report to the coach or a prerequisite to avoid negative consequences (Bobele & Conran, 1988). Coaches may want to support the referral by punishing athletes who do not comply, but placing these additional conditions on the referral process can make it impossible for the practitioner to work effectively with the athlete.

Some athletes are referred to sport psychologists by significant others (e.g., coach, parent, dean) with an interest in the outcome of the athletes' consultation. When making new referrals for these athletes, *don't* violate confidentiality by informing these others of the referral process unless this has been agreed to by the athlete in writing. It may be useful to teach these significant others about sport psychologists' responsibility to protect athletes' confidentiality when the initial referral is accepted (Heyman, 1993). Information about confidentiality vis à vis these other interested parties should also be provided to athletes (McGrath, 1990).

Don't undermine the treatment of the practitioner to whom the athlete was referred. When a referral has been made for a specific problem, the sport psychologist should make an effort to focus on other issues to minimize the risk of athletes' confusion (American Psychological Association, 1992). If the athlete requires medical treatment, the sport psychologist can work as part of the sports medicine team, helping the athlete with psychological issues (Heil, 1993).

Conclusion

Referral comes in many varieties. For referrals that primarily have to do with the athlete's body (e.g., massage, sports medicine, nutrition), it is wise for athletes to keep the coach informed. For referrals of a more psychological or psychiatric nature (e.g., anxiety, depression, eating disorders), the specifics of the problem may dictate what the athlete chooses to reveal to the coach.

Some referrals, such as sending an athlete to a sport nutritionist to learn how to eat correctly during heavy training, are relatively easy. Referring an athlete to a psychiatrist because it appears medication could be of some benefit requires a delicate touch. We hope this chapter has helped clarify some of the varieties of referral that may be made for athletes.

References

American Psychological Association. (1992). Ethical principles of psychologists and code of conduct. *American Psychologist, 47,* 1597–1611.

Andersen, M. B. (1992). Sport psychology and procrustean categories: An appeal for synthesis and expansion of service. *Association for the Advancement of Applied Sport Psychology Newsletter, 7*(3), 8–9.

Andersen, M. B., Denson, E. L., Brewer, B. W., & Van Raalte, J. L. (1994). Disorders of personality and mood in athletes: Recognition and referral. *Journal of Applied Sport Psychology, 6,* 168–184.

Bobele, M., & Conran, T. J. (1988). Referrals for family therapy: Pitfalls and guidelines. *Elementary School Guidance, 22,* 192–198.

Heil, J. (1993). *Psychology of sport injury.* Champaign, IL: Human Kinetics.

Heyman, S. R. (1993). When to refer athletes for counseling of psychotherapy. In J. Williams (Ed.) *Applied sport psychology: Personal growth to peak performance* (2nd ed., pp. 299–308). Palo Alto, CA: Mayfield.

Linder, D. E., Brewer, B. W., Van Raalte, J. L., & DeLange, N. (1991). A negative halo for athletes who consult sport psychologists: Replication and extension. *Journal of Sport & Exercise Psychology, 13,* 133–148.

Martinsen, E. (1990). Benefits of exercise for the treatment of depression. *Sports Medicine, 9,* 380–389.

McGrath, R. J. (1990). Assessment of sexual aggressors. *Journal of Interpersonal Violence, 5,* 507–519.

Miller, M. J., & Moore, K. K. (1993). Athletes' and nonathletes' expectations about counseling. *Journal of College Student Development, 34,* 267–270.

Morgan, W. P. (1985). Selected psychological factors limiting performance: A mental health model. In D. J. Clark & H. M. Eckert (Eds.), *Limits of human performance* (pp. 70–80). Champaign, IL: Human Kinetics.

Rotella, R. J. (1992). Sport psychology: Staying focused on a common and shared mission for a bright future. *Association for the Advancement of Applied Sport Psychology Newsletter, 7*(3), 8–9.

Sachs, M. L., & Buffone, G. W. (Eds.). (1984). *Running as therapy: An integrated approach.* Lincoln, NE: University of Nebraska Press.

Strein, W., & Hershenson, D. B. (1991). Confidentiality in nondyadic counseling situations. *Journal of Counseling & Development, 69,* 312–316.

Van Raalte, J. L., Brewer, B. W., Brewer, D. D., & Linder, D. E. (1992). NCAA Division II college football players' perceptions of an athlete who consults a sport psychologist. *Journal of Sport & Exercise Psychology, 14,* 273–282.

Part Four

Working With Specific Populations

13 Psychosocial Interventions in Youth Sport

Ronald E. Smith and Frank L. Smoll

Athletic competition for children is a firmly established part of our society. Today in the United States, half of all youngsters between the ages of 8 and 18 participate in community-sponsored programs (e.g., Little League Baseball, Boys and Girls Clubs), where they are coached by approximately 2.5 million adult volunteers (Ewing & Seefeldt, 1995). Millions more participate in interscholastic programs. Sport scientists as well as popular writers have noted that the sport environment provides socialization opportunities and places adaptive demands on participants that parallel those of other important life settings (Martens, 1978; Michener, 1976; Smoll & Smith, 1995b). For this reason, organized athletic experiences are regarded as potentially important in child and adolescent development.

Although youth sports are firmly entrenched in our social and cultural milieu, concerns about their desirability have been expressed for some time. Those who favor youth sports emphasize that there are many aspects of the experience that contribute to personal development. Proponents generally view youth sports as miniature life situations through which participants can learn to cope with several of the important realities of life. Within sport, youngsters can compete and cooperate with others, they can learn risk taking and self-control, and they can deal with success and failure. Important attitudes are formed about achievement, authority, and persistence in the face of adversity. In addition, advocates point out, lifelong patterns of physical activity that promote health and fitness can be initiated through involvement in youth sports. Critics counter with claims that excessive physical and psychological demands are placed on young people and that programs exist primarily for the self-serving needs of coaches and parents. They suggest that children and youth would benefit far more if adults simply left them alone to participate in their own games and activities (Smith & Smoll, 1996).

A realistic appraisal of youth sports indicates that participation does not automatically result in beneficial or detrimental effects. We believe that the sport environment affords a strong potential for achieving desirable objectives. The question is not whether youth sports should continue to exist; they are here to stay, and if anything, they will continue to grow in spite of the criticisms that are sometimes leveled at them. The important issue is how the programs can be effectively structured and conducted in ways that ensure attainment of positive outcomes.

Research on Youth Sports

Sport consultants who choose to work in the arena of youth sports should be aware of the complex physical, psychological, and sociological phenomena that affect the developing child. Since the mid-1970s, the scientific community has increasingly studied the impact of the complex social network comprising coaches, parents, and peers. The accumulation of empirical evidence has resulted in a body of knowledge that spans several disciplinary areas, including psychology, sociology, and the sport sciences (see Smoll & Smith, 1995a, for an interdisciplinary review of youth sport research).

Personality Development and Sport Participation

Research on the psychological consequences of sport participation for personality development has centered on several variables of interest, most notably, self-concept and performance anxiety.

Sport experiences can have an important role in the development of the self-concept and can affect the child's self-esteem as well (Horn & Hasbrook, 1987; Smoll, Smith, Barnett, & Everett, 1993). Scanlan (1995) noted that youth sport participation occurs during a period when children have limited information about their competencies. They derive such information from both social and nonsocial sources, and this input helps form their self-concept and their evaluative responses to it (i.e., their self-esteem).

Three separate social evaluation processes, namely, comparative appraisal, reflected appraisal, and direct feedback, provide important information that is incorporated into the developing self-concept (Harter, 1978; Masters, 1972). Thus, children compare their abilities with those of their peers; they make inferences about themselves on the basis of meanings they infer from the reactions of others; and they receive direct feedback from "experts," such as parents, teachers, and coaches. Moreover, physical skills are highly valued throughout childhood, particularly by boys, and they are important determinants of peer acceptance (Chase & Dummer, 1992). Sports provide many opportunities for social comparison, and athletes receive a good deal of direct and indirect feedback from peers, parents, and coaches. The reactions of a high-status adult like a coach can make a strong impression on a child. The information received by the child in the course of sport participation can therefore contribute to either a positive or a negative self-concept, with resulting high or low self-esteem. Given this fact, the prospect of intervening in the sport system in such a way as to facilitate positive self-concept development is an exciting one.

Performance anxiety has also received a good deal of empirical attention. This form of anxiety involves high levels of somatic arousal, worry about the consequences of performing poorly, and concentration disruption caused mainly by cognitive interference (Smith, Smoll, & Schutz, 1990). In many ways, performance anxiety is the athlete's worst enemy, because fear of failure has been shown to interfere with performance, decrease enjoyment of sport participation, and promote avoidance of or withdrawal from sport participation (Smith and Smoll 1990b). In one study, more than half of a sample of 8- and 9-year-old sport nonparticipants indicated that they would like to compete but were fearful of performing poorly or failing to make a team (Orlick & Botterill, 1975). Brustad (1995) reviewed a number of studies that indicate that parents and coaches can be potent sources of anxiety for child athletes, particularly when the perceived demands and expectations of these significant adults severely tax the self-perceived abilities of the athlete. Concerns about negative evaluations from parents and coaches (as well as peers) are the primary source of worry (Brustad, 1988). Such worries are undoubtedly augmented by the fact that failure in sport occurs in a public context for all to see. Predictably, antecedents of performance anxiety include a history of being punished and criticized for achievement failures (Smith & Smoll, 1990b). Because of the negative effects of performance anxiety on both performance and enjoyment in sport, attempts to minimize its development within youth sports should be a high priority goal.

Coaches, Parents, and Athletes

The coach–parent–athlete triad has been referred to as the "athletic triangle" (Smith, Smoll, & Smith, 1989). The members of this social system interact with one another in complex ways, and the nature of those interactions can have significant consequences for the psychological development of the child. The coach–athlete relationship influences the child during important developmental periods, and the nature of the interpersonal transactions between coach and athlete have been shown to affect such variables as enjoyment of the activity, attraction toward coach and teammates, self-esteem, performance anxiety, team cohesion, and sport attrition (Fisher, Mancini, Hirsch, Proulx, & Staurowsky, 1982; Smith & Smoll, 1995; Westre & Weiss, 1991).

Parental influences on children's socialization into sport and on psychosocial consequences once involved have also been documented (Brustad, 1995; Greendorfer, Lewko & Rosengren, 1995). Although there is a paucity of research on observed parental behaviors and their consequences, the negative impact parents can have on child athletes is all too obvious. Parental misbehavior at competitive events has become such a problem that in some programs, parents are barred from attending games. Other programs have resorted to holding games during the morning or afternoon so that parents cannot easily attend. If the quality of supervision is a critical issue in youth sports, so also is the manner in which some misguided parents can undermine the laudable goals of youth sport programs and thereby detract from the benefits that athletic experiences should provide for children. Assisting parents in ensuring that sports will be a positive influence on their relationship with their child is a worthy target for sport psychology intervention.

The young athlete is a third point of intervention in the athletic triangle. Psychology has developed an impressive and effective arsenal of techniques to enhance human performance and well-being. The fact that children engage in youth sports during a formative period of their lives provides a window of opportunity for sport psychology interventions designed to foster the personal development of the athlete and to facilitate the development of life skills that generalize from sports to other areas of life.

In the sections to follow, we provide practical guidelines for the practitioner who wishes to work in the area of youth sports. It will become readily apparent that there already exist some promising and empirically validated intervention strategies but also that there is great opportunity for innovative approaches to enhancing the youth sport environment.

Coach-Based Interventions

Most athletes have their first sport experiences in programs staffed by volunteer coaches. Although many of these coaches are fairly well versed in the technical aspects of the sport, they rarely have had any formal training in creating a healthy psychological environment for youngsters. Moreover, through the mass media, these coaches are frequently exposed to college or professional coaches who model aggressive behaviors and a "winning is everything" philosophy that is highly inappropriate in a recreational and skill-development context. Because the vast majority of youth coaches have desirable motives for coaching (Martens & Gould, 1979; Smith, Smoll, & Curtis, 1978), one can assume that their limitations result primarily from a lack of information on how to create a supportive interpersonal climate. Several educational programs have been developed, therefore, for the purpose of positively affecting coaching practices and thereby increasing the likelihood that youngsters will have positive sport experiences.

Four training programs currently available in the United States include curricular components designed to influence the manner in which volunteer coaches interact with young athletes. The American Coaching Effectiveness Program (Martens, 1987), Coach Effectiveness Training (Smoll & Smith, 1993), the National Youth Sport Coaches Association program (Brown & Butterfield, 1992), and the Program for Athletic Coaches' Education (Seefeldt & Brown, 1992) have been administered to many thousands of youth coaches. The national coaching associations of Australia and Canada have also developed formal programs that provide training in sport psychology as well as other areas, such as sport pedagogy (teaching sport skills and strategies), sport physiology (conditioning, weight training, and nutrition), and sports medicine (injury prevention, care, and rehabilitation).

Unfortunately, only one of the programs mentioned, Coach Effectiveness Training (CET), has been subjected to systematic evaluation to determine its influence on coaches' behaviors and the effects of such behaviors on youngsters' psychosocial development (Brown & Butterfield, 1992). In this chapter, we present CET as an illustration of an empirical approach to the development and evaluation of intervention strategies in the youth sport setting. Specifically, overviews of (a) the development of CET, (b) the content of CET and procedures for its implementation, and (c) empirical studies that have assessed the efficacy of CET are provided.

Development of a Coach Training Program

A crucial first step in developing a training program is to determine what is to be presented. In this regard, our work was guided by a fundamental assumption that a training program should be based on scientific evidence rather than on intuition or what we "know" on the basis of informal observation. An empirical foundation for coaching guidelines not only enhances the validity and potential value of the program, but also increases its credibility in the eyes of consumers. Following is a description of our approach to generating an empirical database for CET.

Theoretical Model and Research Paradigm

In the early 1970s, recognition of the potential impact of youth coaches on athletes' psychological welfare prompted several questions that we felt were worth pursuing scientifically. For example, what do coaches do, and how frequently do they engage in such behaviors as encouragement, punishment, instruction, and organization? What are the psychological dimensions that underlie such behaviors? Finally, how are observable coaching behaviors related to children's reactions to their organized athletic experiences? Answers to such questions not only are a first step in describing the behavioral ecology of one aspect of the youth sport setting, but also provide an empirical basis for the development of psychologically oriented intervention programs.

To begin to answer such questions, we carried out a systematic program of research over a period of several years. The project was guided by a mediational model of coach–athlete interactions, the basic elements of which are represented as follows:

Coach Behaviors → Athlete Perception and Recall → Athlete's Evaluative Reactions.

This model stipulates that the ultimate effects of coaching behaviors are mediated by the meaning that athletes attribute to them. In other words, what athletes remember about their coach's behaviors and how they interpret these actions affects the way that athletes evaluate their sport experiences. Furthermore, a complex of cognitive and affective processes are involved at this mediational level. The athletes' perceptions and reactions are likely to be affected not only by the coach's behaviors, but also by other factors, such as the athlete's age, what he or she expects of coaches (normative beliefs and expectations), and certain personality variables such as self-esteem and anxiety. In recognition of this, the basic three-element model has been expanded to reflect these factors (Smoll & Smith, 1989). The expanded model specifies a number of situational factors as well as coach and athlete characteristics that could influence coach behaviors and the perceptions and reactions of athletes to them. Using this model as a starting point, we have sought to determine how observed coaching behaviors, athletes' perception and recall of the coach's behaviors, and athlete attitudes are related to one another. We have also explored the manner in which athlete and coach characteristics might serve to affect these relations.

Measurement of Coaching Behaviors

To measure leadership behaviors, we developed the Coaching Behavior Assessment System (CBAS), which permits the direct observation and coding of coaches' actions during practices and games (Smith, Smoll, & Hunt, 1977). The CBAS contains 12 categories divided into two major classes of behaviors. *Reactive* (elicited) *behaviors* are responses to immediately preceding athlete or team behaviors, whereas *spontaneous* (emitted) *behaviors* are initiated by the coach and are not a response to a discernible preceding event. Reactive behaviors are responses to either desirable performance or effort (reinforcement, nonreinforcement), mistakes and errors (mistake-contingent encouragement, mistake-contingent technical instruction, punishment, punitive technical instruction, ignoring mistakes), or misbehaviors on the part of athletes (keeping control). The spontaneous class includes general technical instruction, general encouragement, organization, and general communication. The system thus involves basic interactions between the situation and the coach's behavior. Use of the CBAS in observing and coding coaching behaviors in a variety of sports indicates that the scoring system is sufficiently comprehensive to incorporate the vast majority of coaching leader behaviors, that high interrater reliability can be obtained, and that individual differences in behavioral patterns can be discerned (Chaumeton & Duda, 1988; Cruz et al., 1987; Horn, 1984,

1985; Rejeski, Darracott, & Hutslar, 1979; Smith, Zan, Smoll, & Coppel, 1983; Wandzilak, Ansorge, & Potter, 1988).

Coaching Behaviors and Children's Evaluative Reactions

Following development of the CBAS, a field study was conducted to establish relations between coaching behaviors and several athlete variables specified in the conceptual model (Smith et al., 1978). Observed behaviors of 51 baseball coaches during 202 complete games were coded, and 542 children who played for the coaches were interviewed and administered questionnaires after the season ended.

At the level of overt behavior, three independent behavioral dimensions were identified through factor analysis: Supportiveness (composed of reinforcement and mistake-contingent encouragement), Instructiveness (general technical instruction and mistake-contingent technical instruction vs. general communication and general encouragement), and punitiveness (punishment and punitive technical instruction vs. organizational behaviors). Relations between coaches' scores on these behavioral dimensions and player measures indicated that players responded most favorably to coaches who engaged in higher percentages of supportive and instructional behaviors. Players on teams whose coaches created a supportive environment also liked their teammates more. A somewhat surprising finding was that the team's won–lost record was essentially unrelated to how well the players liked the coach and how much they wanted to play for the coach in the future. On the other hand, players on winning teams felt that their parents liked the coach more and that the coach liked them more than did players on losing teams. Apparently, winning made little difference to the children, but they knew that it was important to the adults. It is worth noting, however, that winning assumed greater importance beyond age 12, although it continued to be a less important attitudinal determinant than coach behaviors.

Another important issue concerns the degree of accuracy with which coaches perceive their own behaviors. Correlations between CBAS-observed behaviors and coaches' ratings of how frequently they performed the behaviors were generally low and nonsignificant. The only significant correlation occurred for punishment. Children's ratings on the same perceived behavior scales correlated much more highly with CBAS measures than did the coaches'! It thus appears that coaches have limited awareness of how frequently they engage in particular forms of behavior and that athletes are more accurate perceivers of actual coach behaviors.

Finally, analysis of the children's attraction responses toward the coaches revealed a significant interaction between coach supportiveness (the tendency to reinforce desirable performance and effort and to respond to mistakes with encouragement) and athletes' level of self-esteem (Smith & Smoll, 1990a). Specifically, the children with low self-esteem were especially responsive to variations in supportiveness in a manner consistent with a self-enhancement model of self-esteem (Shrauger, 1975; Swann, 1990; Tesser, 1988). This finding is consistent with the results of other studies that, collectively, suggest that self-enhancement motivation causes people who are low in self-esteem to be especially responsive to variations in supportiveness because of their greater need for positive feedback from others (Brown, Collins, & Schmidt, 1988; Dittes, 1959; Tesser & Campbell, 1983).

Program Evaluation: Assessing the Efficacy of CET

Sweeping conclusions are often drawn about the efficacy of intervention programs in the absence of acceptable scientific evidence. We therefore felt it was important not only to develop an empirical foundation for CET, but also to measure its effects on coaches and the youngsters who play for them.

We have focused on five important outcome questions in our program-evaluation studies. First, does the CET program affect the behaviors of the trained coaches in a manner consistent with the behavioral guidelines? Second, the program is designed to help coaches create an environment that would be expected to increase children's positive reactions to coach, teammates, and their sport experience; how does the program affect children's reactions to their athletic experience? Third, does exposure to a positive interpersonal environment created by trained coaches result in an increase in general self-esteem, particularly among children with low self-esteem? Fourth, does CET training help reduce performance anxiety among young athletes? Finally, do positive changes in the first four outcomes increase the likelihood that the young athletes will choose to return to the sport program?

Positive outcomes regarding all five of these questions have been established in a series of outcome studies in which experimental groups of youth baseball coaches exposed to the CET program were compared with untreated, control groups of coaches. Coaches exposed to CET differed in both observed behaviors and athlete-perceived behaviors in a manner consistent with the behavioral guidelines. Experimental-group coaches were more reinforcing, were more encouraging, gave more technical instruction, and were less punitive and controlling than control-group coaches. In turn, the athletes who played for the trained coaches indicated that they enjoyed their experience more and liked their coach and teammates more. They also demonstrated significant increases in general self-esteem and significant decreases in performance anxiety over the course of the season (Smith, Smoll, & Barnett, Barnett; Smith, Smoll, & Curtis, 1979; Smoll et al., 1993).

Finally, a recent study of attrition showed a dropout rate of 26% among children who played for control-group coaches, a figure that is consistent with previous reports of attrition in youth sport programs (Gould, 1987). In contrast, only 5% of the children who played for CET-trained coaches failed to return to the program the next season (Barnett, Smoll, & Smith, 1992). These positive psychosocial outcomes are all the more noteworthy in light of the fact that experimental and control groups did not differ in average won–lost percentages in any of the studies.

Guidelines for Conducting a CET Clinic

CET Principles

A set of five core principles underlies the behavioral coaching guidelines communicated in the CET program (Smith & Smoll, in press). A most important first principle is that "winning" is defined not in terms of won–lost records, but in terms of giving maximum effort and making improvement. The explicit and primary focus is on having fun, deriving satisfaction from being on the team, learning sport skills, and developing increased self-esteem. This philosophy is designed to maximize young athletes' enjoyment of sport and their chances of deriving the benefits of participation, partly as a result of combating competitive anxiety (Smoll & Smith, 1996). The focus on controllable effort rather than uncontrollable outcome also promotes separation of the athlete's feelings of self-worth from the game outcome, which serves to help overcome fear of failure.

Our second principle emphasizes a "positive approach" to coaching. In such an approach, coach–athlete interactions are characterized by the liberal use of positive reinforcement, encouragement, and sound technical instruction to help create high levels of interpersonal attraction between coaches and athletes. Punitive behaviors are strongly discouraged, because they have been shown to create a negative team climate and to promote fear of failure. We emphasize that positive reinforcement should not be restricted to the learning and performance of sport skills. Rather, it should also be liberally applied to the strengthening of desirable psychosocial behaviors (e.g., teamwork, leadership, sportsmanship). Coaches are urged to reinforce effort as much as they do results. This guideline has direct relevance to developing a healthy philosophy of winning and a reduction in performance anxiety.

CET includes several "positive-approach" guidelines pertaining to the appropriate use of technical instruction. For example, when giving instruction, we encourage coaches to emphasize the good things that will happen if athletes execute correctly rather than focusing on the negative things that will occur if they do not. This approach motivates athletes to make desirable things happen (i.e., develop a positive achievement orientation) rather than building fear of making mistakes.

The third coaching principle is to establish norms that emphasize athletes' mutual obligations to help and support one another. Such norms increase social support and attraction among teammates and thereby enhance cohesion and commitment to the team. Such norms are most likely to develop when coaches (a) model supportive behaviors and (b) reinforce athlete behaviors that promote team unity. We also instruct coaches in how to develop a "we're in this together" group norm. This norm can play an important role in building team cohesion among teammates, particularly if the coach frequently reinforces relevant bench behaviors of attention and mutual supportiveness.

A fourth principle is that compliance with team roles and responsibilities is most effectively achieved by involving athletes in decisions regarding team rules and reinforcing compliance with them rather than by using punitive measures to punish noncompliance. We believe that coaches should recognize that youngsters want clearly defined limits and structure.

The positive approach also applies to promoting compliance with team rules. One of the most effective ways of eliminating negative behaviors (and avoiding the negative side effects of punishment) is to strengthen positive behaviors that are incompatible with the negative ones. Thus, coaches are encouraged not to take rule compliance for granted, but to acknowledge instances of compliance with the rules. By using positive reinforcement to strengthen desirable behaviors, coaches can often avoid having to deal with misbehaviors on the part of athletes.

Finally, CET coaches are urged to obtain behavioral feedback and to engage in self-monitoring to increase awareness of their own behaviors and to encourage compliance with the positive-approach guidelines.

CET Procedures

In a CET workshop, which lasts approximately 2.5 hours, behavioral guidelines are presented both verbally and in written materials (a printed outline and a 12-page pamphlet) given to the coaches. The pamphlet supplements the guidelines with concrete suggestions for communicating effectively with young athletes, gaining their respect, and relating effectively to their parents. The importance of sensitivity and being responsive to individual differences among athletes is also stressed. The written materials serve to (a) help keep the workshop organized, (b) facilitate coaches' understanding of the information, (c) eliminate the need for coaches to take notes, and (d) give coaches a tangible resource to refer to in the future. Also, audio–visual aids, such as content slides and cartoons illustrating important points, are used to facilitate comprehension and retention as well as to add to the organizational quality of the session.

Not only do we believe in the importance of establishing an empirical foundation for training guidelines, but also we feel that the ability to present supportive data increases the credibility of the guidelines for the coaches. A CET workshop therefore includes a description of the development and testing of the program. Using lay terms and avoiding scientific jargon, we describe the 12 coaching behaviors that we studied as well as the manner in which they were related to athletes' reactions to their sport experience (see Smith & Smoll, 1991, for a summary of this work). This information sets the stage for the presentation of coaching guidelines.

In introducing coaching guidelines, we emphasize that they should not be viewed as a "magic formula," and that mere knowledge of the principles is not sufficient. We stress that the challenge is not so much in learning the principles; they are relatively simple. Rather, the challenge is for the coach to integrate the guidelines into his or her own coaching style.

The most basic objectives of CET are to communicate coaching principles in a manner that is easily comprehended and to maximize the likelihood that coaches will adopt the information. As part of our approach to creating a positive learning environment, we encourage coaches to share their own experiences and associated practical knowledge with the group. CET workshops are thus conducted with an interactive format in which coaches are treated as an integral part of the session rather than a mere audience. The open atmosphere for exchange promotes active rather than passive learning, and the dialogue serves to enhance the participants' interest and involvement in the learning process.

The didactic instruction described contains many verbal modeling cues that essentially tell coaches what to do. To supplement the didactic verbal and written materials, coaching guidelines are transmitted through behavioral modeling cues (i.e., demonstrations showing coaches how to behave in desirable ways). In CET, such cues are presented by a live model (the trainer) and by symbolic models (coach cartoons). In addition, modeling is frequently used in conjunction with later role-playing of positive behaviors. Coaches are kept actively involved in the training process through presentation of critical situations and asking them to role-play appropriate ways of responding. This form of behavioral rehearsal has great promise in enhancing acquisition of desired behaviors, in providing the opportunity to practice the behaviors, and in establishing an increased level of participant involvement during the workshops.

One of the striking findings from our initial research was that coaches had very limited awareness of how often they behaved in various ways (Smith et al., 1978). Thus, an important component of a training program should be an attempt to increase coaches' awareness of what they are doing as well as their motivation to comply with behavioral guidelines. In CET, coaches are taught the use of two proven behavioral-change techniques, namely, behavioral feedback (Edelstein & Eisler, 1976; McFall & Twentyman, 1973) and self-monitoring (Kanfer & Gaelick-Buys, 1991; Kazdin, 1974; McFall, 1977). To obtain feedback, coaches are encouraged to work with their assistants as a team and share descriptions of each other's behaviors. They can discuss alternate ways of dealing with difficult situations and athletes and prepare themselves for dealing with similar situations in the future. Other potential feedback procedures include coaches' soliciting input from athletes and provision of feedback by a league committee.

Self-monitoring (observing and recording one's own behavior) is another behavioral-change technique that has the potential for increasing coaches' awareness of their own behavioral patterns and encouraging their compliance with the guidelines. This method of self-regulation has proved to be an effective behavioral-change procedure in a variety of intervention contexts (see Kanfer & Gaelick-Buys, 1991; Kazdin, 1974; McFall, 1977). Because it is impractical to have coaches monitor and record their own behavior during practices or games, CET coaches are given a brief self-monitoring form that they are encouraged to complete immediately after practices and games (see Smoll & Smith, 1993, pp. 53–54). On the form, they indicate approximately what percentage of the time they engaged in the recommended behaviors in relevant situations. For example, coaches are asked, "Approximately what percentage of the times they occurred did you respond to mistakes/errors with encouragement?" Self-monitoring is restricted to desired behaviors in light of evidence that tracking of undesired behaviors can be detrimental to effective self-regulation (Cavior & Marabotto, 1976; Gottman & McFall, 1972; Kirschenbaum & Karoly, 1977). Coaches are encouraged to engage in self-monitoring on a regular basis to achieve optimal results.

Parent-Based Interventions

Anecdotes abound concerning parental influences that can potentially undermine the best-intentioned youth sport program. Consider the following example, provided by a youth baseball coach:

> One night last season my team lost a close game. I sat the whole team down on the bench and congratulated them for trying, for acting like gentlemen. I said I couldn't have been more proud of them if they had won. Most of all, I said, it is as important to be a good loser as a gracious winner. As I talked, I could see their spirits lifting. I felt they had learned more than just how to play baseball that night. But as I mingled with the parents in the stands afterward, I was shocked to hear what they were saying to the boys. The invariable theme was, "Well, what happened to *you* tonight?" One father pulled out a note pad and went over his son's mistakes play by play. Another father dressed down his son for striking out twice. In five minutes, the parents had undermined every principle I had set forth. (McNeil, 1961, p. 142)

The importance of parents in the youth sport experience cannot be overemphasized. Research has shown that parents play an important role in the socialization of children into sports and influence the psychosocial outcomes of sport experiences, including self-concept development and enjoyment of the activity (Brustad, 1995; Greendorfer,

Lewko, & Rosengren, 1995). Thus, a potentially influential focus of intervention is the parent.

Several books have been written for the youth sport parent (e.g., Hanlon, 1994; McInally, 1987; Rosen, 1967; Rotella & Bunker, 1987; Smith et al., 1989). Workshops for parents similar to those developed for coaches can be another vehicle for reaching parents and influencing the ways in which they interact with their child athlete.

Elsewhere, we have advanced a set of guidelines for parents that parallel those emphasized in Coach Effectiveness Training (Smith et al., 1989), and we have also provided coaches with guidelines for conducting a workshop with the parents of the athletes they are coaching (Smoll, 1993). However, in contrast to the empirical base for CET, no outcome data are currently available for assessing the efficacy of the parent program we have developed. Nonetheless, we now delineate some of the issues that a sport psychologist might choose to cover in a workshop for parents.

Developmental Versus Professional Models of Sport

A fundamental issue is the distinction between youth and professional models of sport. Youth sports are intended to provide an educational medium for the development of desirable physical and psychosocial characteristics. The sport environment is viewed as a microcosm of society in which children can learn to cope with realities they will face in later life. Thus, athletics provides a developmental setting within which an *educational* process can occur. On the other hand, professional sports are an explicitly commercial enterprise. Their goals, simply stated, are to entertain and, ultimately, to make money. Financial success is of primary importance and depends heavily on a *product orientation,* namely, winning. Is this wrong? Certainly not. The professional sports world is a part of the entertainment industry, and as such, it is enormously valued in our society.

What, then, is the problem? Most of the negative consequences of youth sports occur when adults erroneously impose a professional model on what should be a recreational and educational experience for children. When excessive emphasis is placed on winning, it is easy to lose sight of the needs and interests of the young athlete.

Objectives of Youth Sports

As noted previously, there are many possible benefits of participating in youth sports. Some of them are physical, such as attaining sport skills and increasing health and fitness. Others are psychological, such as developing leadership skills, self-discipline, respect for authority, competitiveness, cooperativeness, sportsmanship, and self-confidence. Youth sports are also an important social activity in which children can make new friends and acquaintances and become part of an ever-expanding social network. Furthermore, the involvement of parents in the athletic enterprise can serve to bring families closer together and strengthen family unity. Finally, of course, youth sports are (or should be) just plain *fun*.

The basic right of the child athlete to have fun in participating should not be neglected. One of the quickest ways to reduce fun is for adults to begin treating children as if they were professional athletes. Coaches and parents alike need to keep in mind that young athletes are not miniature adults. They are children, and they have the right to play as children. Youth sports are first and foremost a play activity, and children deserve to enjoy sports in their own way. In essence, it is important that programs remain child-centered and do not become adult-dominated.

What about *winning*? The common notion in sports equates success with victory. However, with a "winning is everything" philosophy, young athletes may lose opportunities to develop their skills, to enjoy participation, and to grow socially and emotionally. Well-informed parents realize that success is not equivalent to winning games, and failure is not the same as losing. Rather, the most important kind of success comes from striving to win and giving maximum effort. The only thing athletes can control is the amount of effort they give. They have incomplete control over the outcome that is achieved. Athletes should be taught that they are never "losers" if they give maximum effort in striving for excellence. This philosophy of success is relevant to parents as well as coaches. In fact, it may be more important for parents to understand its meaning. They can apply it to many areas of their child's life in addition to athletics.

What are some criteria for determining when the desire for winning is out of perspective? Martens (1978) suggested that winning is out of perspective (a) when a display of comradeship with an opponent is considered a sign of weakness or laughter is judged to be a lack of competitiveness; (b) when a coach instructs athletes in strategies designed to take unfair advantage of an opponent; (c) when youngsters are given drugs, coaxed to cheat, or intimidated to excel; or (d) when winning the game becomes more important than winning friends, respect, self-confidence, skill, health, and self-worth. When winning is kept in perspective, the child comes first and winning is second (Martens & Seefeldt, 1979). In this case, rather than focusing on a won–lost record, the most important sport product is the quality of the experience provided for young athletes.

What about the objectives that young athletes seek to achieve? A survey of more than 100,000 youth sport participants in the state of Michigan indicated that young athletes most often participated in organized sports for the following reasons: (a) to have fun, (b) to improve their skills and learn new skills, (c) to be with their friends or make new friends, and (d) to succeed or win (Universities Study Committee, 1978). These goals should be communicated to parents, and parents should be cautioned that none of these outcomes is achieved automatically through participation in sports. Coaches, parents, and sport administrators should be part of a team trying to accomplish common goals. By working together to reduce chances of misunderstanding and problems, these adults can help children to attain their objectives. In this regard, parents should be encouraged to view their involvement in youth sports as an integral part of their childrearing responsibilities.

Parent Roles and Responsibilities

When a child enters a sport program, parents automatically take on some obligations. Some parents do not realize this at first and are surprised to find what is expected of them. Others never realize their responsibilities and miss opportunities to help their children grow through sports, or they may do things that interfere with their children's development.

To begin, parents must realize that children have a right to choose not to participate (Martens & Seefeldt, 1979). Although parents might choose to encourage participation, children should not be pressured, intimidated, or bribed into playing. In fulfilling their responsibility, parents should counsel their children, giving consideration to the sport selected and the level of competition at which the children want to play. And of course, parents should respect their children's decisions.

Parents can enjoy their children's participation more if they acquire an understanding and appreciation of the sport. This includes knowledge of basic rules, skills, and strategies. Coaches can serve as valuable resources by answering parents' questions and by referring parents to a community or school library or a bookstore for educational materials. In addition, coaches should devote part of an early season practice to a lecture–demonstration of the fundamentals of the sport, and parents who have little background in the sport should be encouraged to attend this session.

The Reversed-Dependency Trap

Parents often assume an extremely active role in youth sports, and in some instances, their influence becomes an important source of children's stress (Passer, 1984; Scanlan, 1986; Smith, 1986; Smoll & Smith, 1995b). One factor in parent-induced stress is what we refer to as the *reversed-dependency phenomenon*. All parents identify with their children to some extent and thus want them to do well. Unfortunately, in some cases, the degree of identification becomes excessive. The child becomes an extension of the parents. When this happens, parents begin to define their own self-worth in terms of how successful their son or daughter is. The father who is a ''frustrated jock'' may seek to experience through his child the success he never knew as an athlete. The parent who was a star may be resentful and rejecting if the child does not attain similar achievements. Some parents thus become ''winners'' or ''losers'' through their children, and the pressure placed on the children to excel can be extreme. A child *must* succeed or the parent's self-image is threatened. Much more is at stake than a mere game, and the child of such a parent carries a heavy burden. When parental love and approval are dependent on adequacy of performance, sports are bound to be stressful (see Smith, Smoll, & Smith, 1989; Smoll, 1990).

Youth sport consultants may be able to counteract this tendency by explaining the identification process to parents. They can tell parents that if they place excessive pressure on children, they can decrease the potential of sports for enjoyment and personal growth. A key to reducing parent-produced stress is to impress on parents that youth sport programs are for young athletes and that children and youth are *not* adults. Parents must acknowledge the right of each child to develop athletic potential in an atmosphere that emphasizes participation, personal growth, and fun.

Commitments and Affirmations

To contribute to the success of a sport program, parents must be willing and able to commit themselves in many different ways. Al Rosen (1967), a former Major League Baseball player, developed some questions that can serve as thought-provoking reminders of the scope of parent responsibilities, questions to which parents must honestly answer *yes*.

1. *Can the parents give up their child?* This requires putting the child in the coach's charge and trusting him or her to guide the sport experience. It involves accepting the coach's authority and the fact that he or she may gain some of the child's admiration and affection that the child once directed solely at the parent. This responsibility does not mean that parents cannot have input, but they need to accept that the coach is the ultimate decision maker. If parents are going to undermine the coach's leadership, it is best that their child not join the program.

2. *Can the parents admit their shortcomings?* Parents must be convinced that the proper response to a mistake or not knowing something is an honest disclosure. For example, if their child asks a question about sports and they do not know the answer, they should not be afraid to admit it. An honest response is better than a wrong answer. Coaches and parents alike should show children that they realistically accept their own limitations. Surely, nobody is perfect, but sometimes children do not learn this because adults fail to teach them.

3. *Can the parents accept their child's triumphs?* Every child athlete experiences "the thrill of victory and the agony of defeat" as part of the competition process. Accepting a child's triumphs sounds easy, but it is not always so. Some parents do not realize it, but fathers in particular may be competitive with their sons. For example, if a boy does well in a contest, his father may point out minor mistakes, describe how others did even better, or bring up something more impressive from memories of his own sport achievements.

4. *Can the parents accept their child's disappointments?* In addition to accepting athletic accomplishments, parents are called on to support their children when they are disappointed and hurt. This may mean watching their child lose a contest while others triumph or not being embarrassed, ashamed, or angry when their 10-year-old cries after losing. When an apparent disappointment occurs, parents should be able to help their children see the positive side of the situation.

5. *Can the parents give their child some time?* Some parents are very busy, although they may be interested and want to encourage their children. To avoid disappointment and potential conflicts,

the best advice to give parents is to tell them to deal honestly with their time-commitment issue and not promise more time than they can deliver. Parents should ask their children about their sport experiences and make every effort to watch some of their contests.

6. *Can the parents let their child make his or her own decisions?* This is an essential part of growing up and a real challenge for parents. Parents should be encouraged to offer suggestions and guidance about sports, but ultimately, within reasonable limits, they should let the child go his or her own way. All parents have ambitions for their child, but they must accept the fact that they cannot dominate the child's life. Sports can offer an introduction to the major process of letting go.

7. *Can the parents show their child self-control?* Parents should be reminded that they are important role models for their children's behavior. It is not surprising that parents who lose control of themselves often have children who are prone to emotional outbursts and poor self-discipline. Coaches can hardly be expected to teach sportsmanship and self-control to youngsters whose parents lack these qualities.

Conduct at Sport Events

The most noticeable parent problem is misbehavior at games. As part of their responsibilities, parents should watch their children compete in sports, but their behavior must meet acceptable standards. In this regard, Martens and Seefeldt (1979) recommended the following rules:

1. Parents should remain seated in the spectator area during the contest.
2. Parents should not yell instructions or criticisms to the children.
3. Parents should make no derogatory comments to players, parents of the opposing team, officials, or league administrators.
4. Parents should not interfere with their children's coach. They must be willing to relinquish the responsibility for their child to the coach for the duration of the contest.

Good sportsmanship among spectators is a goal worth working for. Parents have the obligation not only to control their own behavior, but also to remind others of the responsibility, if necessary. When parents misbehave, it is the duty of other parents and league administrators to step in and correct the situation. The rule of thumb for all spectators is that nothing in their actions should interfere with any child's enjoyment of the sport.

Athlete-Based Interventions

The third point in the athletic triangle is the young athlete. Recently, intervention programs directed at the athlete have begun to appear. Some of these interventions involve the application of psychological principles to enhance sport performance. Others are directed at psychosocial outcomes.

Performance-Enhancement Interventions

Notable among the performance-enhancement interventions is "behavioral coaching" (Martin & Hyrcaiko, 1983), which involves teaching coaches to adopt operant techniques, such as analysis and behavioral assessment of skill components, videotaped feedback, response-contingent reinforcement of response execution, shaping procedures, self-monitoring and behavioral graphing of the skill-acquisition process, and modeling procedures. More than a dozen studies have shown that operant techniques can be highly effective in facilitating skill acquisition and enhancing performance for a variety of sports and age levels (see Lee, 1993; Martin, 1992; and Smith, Smoll, & Christensen, 1996, for reviews). Sport consultants who are conversant with the application of operant principles will find an eager audience of coaches who wish to be trained in these powerful performance-enhancement techniques.

Imagery-based performance-enhancement techniques have also been applied to child-athlete populations. For example, a study by Zhang, Ma, Orlick, and Zitzelberger (1992) tested the efficacy of a mental-imagery program designed to increase the performance of promising Chinese table tennis players between the ages of 7 and 10. The children were divided into three groups. Subjects in the first condition received a comprehensive 22-week mental-training program that included relaxation, video observation, and mental-imagery sessions. A second treatment group received only the video–observation component of the training. The third group was a no-treatment control condition. Results indicated that compared with the other two groups, the children who received the full mental-training package significantly improved both the accuracy and the technical quality of their table tennis fore-hand attack.

Sportsmanship and Moral Development

Although it is frequently asserted that sport builds sportsmanship and character, research on moral reasoning and behavior suggests a less optimistic view. For example, recent research indicates that the sanctioning of aggressive and competitive behavior in sport may have negative consequences on moral development (Bredemeier & Shields, 1987, 1995). Using measurement tools derived from Haan's (1978) structural–developmental model of morality, researchers have found that child and adolescent athletes exhibit lower levels of moral reasoning than nonathletes and show greater acceptance of aggression in sport as legitimate (Bredemeier & Shields, 1984). Whether sport participation contributes to lower levels of moral reasoning or children who are lower in moral development are more likely to be drawn to sport is a question as yet unanswered. Nevertheless, these findings are provocative in pointing to sport as a potentially important arena for moral development.

Paralleling the results of the leadership–coaching research described previously, there are indications that psychological intervention may have salutary effects on moral development. Several studies have shown that explicit attention to moral training in sport and physical activity settings can promote significant advances in the moral reasoning maturity of children (Bredemeier, Weiss, Shields, & Shewchuk, 1986; Romance, Weiss, & Bockoven, 1986). In one study (Bredemeier et al., 1986), children participating in a summer sports camp were exposed to one of two 6-week moral education programs derived from different theoretical approaches to moral development. In the first, which was based on a social learning model emphasizing the learning of moral principles through modeling and vicarious and direct reinforcement, adult leaders described to the children how they themselves thought about and responded to moral issues involving themes of fairness, sharing, verbal and physical aggression, and distributive and retributive justice. They also acknowledged and reinforced instances of verbal and nonverbal moral behavior performed by the children. In the other moral education condition, which was based on structural–developmental theory, the instructors used dialogue aimed at resolving interpersonal disruptions and conflicts among the children as a vehicle for promoting moral growth. Children in a control condition participated in the normal camp program.

In a pre–post design, moral reasoning maturity was assessed by means of the Piagetian Intentionality Task and a measure of children's understanding of fairness, or distributive justice. On both measures, both the social learning and the structural–developmental conditions yielded significant positive changes in moral reasoning, but the two conditions did not differ from one another. Children in the control group exhibited no significant changes in their moral reasoning.

Many important issues concerning moral education in sport remain to be studied. One important question involves the effects of interventions not only on moral reasoning, but also on behavior. Another involves the extent to which moral principles learned in sport generalize to other life settings. Sport would appear to be a two-edged sword as far as moral development is concerned, and it is important to identify the factors that promote positive and negative outcomes. The very act of "sportsmanship" implies the exercise of moral decision making, and sport is a setting in which children can be guided in dealing with moral dilemmas.

Life Skills Interventions

A third recent emphasis has been on training children in skills that not only enhance their sport performance, but also extend as "life skills" to other areas of the child's life, such as academics and social interactions. For example, Orlick and McCaffrey (1991) described a psychological skills program for elementary school children that includes training in relaxation, imagery, focusing, and refocusing. Another promising program featuring goal-setting procedures has been developed by Danish and his collaborators (Danish et al., 1992). In both programs, the skills training is adapted to the child's level. For example, relaxation training includes comparing tense muscles to uncooked spaghetti and relaxed muscles to limp, cooked spaghetti (Orlick & McCaffrey, 1991). Likewise, goal-setting training is embellished with exciting imagery and games (Danish et al., 1992).

Although controlled outcome studies are needed, this approach may hold considerable promise for promoting the development of important psychological skills. Such training could easily be applied to child athletes as well, with the inclusion of generalization training to facilitate transfer of the skills to other life areas. Such training might be particularly useful in working with high-risk inner-city youth, who are typically resistant to life skill programs implemented within the school setting. Such youngsters might be more enthusiastic about a program designed and conducted within the realm of sport.

Conclusions

Sport psychology interventions are a promising development that can enhance the well-being and psychosocial development of children and youth. This area constitutes an exciting arena for both psychological research and intervention. The researcher can discover the principles that govern the youth sport social system and that make a difference in the well-being of its members. Similarly, the practitioner is in a position to apply the principles and procedures of sport psychology in a manner that can better the lives of many young athletes, their coaches, and their parents.

We presented CET as an example of a scientifically developed program. The 3-hour CET program has proved to be a brief and effective program that alters coaching behaviors in a desirable fashion and thereby has positive psychosocial effects on the children who play for trained coaches. All five classes of outcome variables—coaching behaviors, children's attitudes, self-esteem, performance anxiety, and attrition—have been significantly influenced by the training program. Nonetheless, a number of important research questions remain. For example, dismantling studies are needed to assess the relative contributions of the various components of the training program, which include didactic instruction, modeling and role-playing of desired behaviors, training in self-monitoring of coaching behaviors, and behavioral feedback. Such research could help to establish the necessary and sufficient components of an effective program and could facilitate the development of improved training programs.

Likewise, little is known about the efficacy of parent interventions. Do the parent guidelines described in this chapter influence parents in desirable ways? Do they have salutary consequences on nonsport-related areas of the parent–child relationship? If the interventions are efficacious, does it matter whether the guidelines are presented by a coach or by a sport consultant? These are empirical issues that have not yet been addressed. Clearly, more data are needed on the effects of both coach- and parent-directed interventions.

A promising recent development is the application of psychological skills training programs to young athletes (e.g., Orlick & McCaffrey,

1991; Zhang et al., 1992). Preliminary results suggest that training in such skills as relaxation, mental rehearsal, and goal setting can be of value to children. These skills can be readily taught in a sport setting, and appropriate generalization training should permit transfer to other life areas as well. Psychological skills training in sport contexts may be especially valuable for high-risk children who do not respond positively to life skills training carried out in academic settings.

Children's sports is an area that invites the attention of both researchers and practitioners. Many important empirical questions remain to be addressed, and the skillful application of psychological principles and intervention procedures can have a salutary impact on sport participants during a period of development when important foundations for later life are being established.

References

Barnett, N. P., Smoll, F. L., & Smith, R. E. (1992). Effects of enhancing coach–athlete relationships on youth sport attrition. *The Sport Psychologist, 6*, 111–127.

Bredemeier, B. J., & Shields, D. (1984). The utility of moral stage analysis in the understanding of athletic aggression. *Sociology of Sport Journal, 1*, 138–149.

Bredemeier, B. J., & Shields, D. (1987). Moral growth through physical activity: A structural/developmental approach. In D. Gould & M. R. Weiss (Eds.), *Advances in pediatric sport sciences: Vol. 2. Behavioral issues* (pp. 143–165). Champaign, IL: Human Kinetics.

Bredemeier, B. J. L., & Shields, D. L. L. (1995). Moral development in children's sport. In F. L. Smoll & R. E. Smith (Eds.), *Children and youth in sport: A biopsychosocial perspective* (pp. 381–402). Dubuque, IA: Brown & Benchmark.

Bredemeier, B. J., Weiss, M. R., Shields, D., & Shewchuk, R. M. (1986). Promoting moral growth in a summer sport camp: The implementation of theoretically grounded instructional strategies. *Journal of Moral Education, 15*, 212–220.

Brown, B. R., & Butterfield, S. A. (1992). Coaches: A missing link in the health care system. *American Journal of Diseases in Childhood, 146*, 211–217.

Brown, J. D., Collins, R. L., & Schmidt, G. W. (1988). Self-esteem and direct versus indirect forms of self-reinforcement. *Journal of Personality and Social Psychology, 55*, 445–453.

Brustad, R. J. (1988). Affective outcomes in competitive youth sport: The influence of intrapersonal and socialization factors. *Journal of Sport & Exercise Psychology, 10*, 307–321.

Brustad, R. J. (1995). Parental and peer influence on children's psychological development through sport. In F. L. Smoll & R. E. Smith (Eds.), *Children and youth in sport: A biopsychosocial perspective* (pp. 112–124). Dubuque, IA: Brown & Benchmark.

Cavior, N., & Marabotto, C. M. (1976). Monitoring verbal behaviors in a dyadic interaction. *Journal of Consulting and Clinical Psychology, 44*, 68–76.

Chase, M. A., & Dummer, G. M. (1992). The role of sports as a social status determinant for children. *Research Quarterly for Exercise and Sport, 63*, 418–424.

Chaumeton, N. R., & Duda, J. L. (1988). Is it how you play the game or whether you win or lose? The effect of competitive level and situation on coaching behaviors. *Journal of Sport Behavior, 11,* 157–173.

Cruz, J., Bou, A., Fernandez, J. M., Martin, M., Monras, J., Monfort, N., & Ruiz, A. (1987). Avaluacio conductual de les interaccions entre entrenadors i jugadors de basquet escolar. *Apunts Medicina de L'esport, 24,* 89–98.

Danish, S. J., Mash, J. M., Howard, C. W., Curl, S. J., Meyer, A. L., Owens, S., & Kendall, K. (1992). *Going for the goal: Leader manual* (5th ed.). Richmond, VA: Virginia Commonwealth University

Dittes, J. E. (1959). Attractiveness of group as a function of self-esteem and acceptance by group. *Journal of Abnormal and Social Psychology, 59,* 77–82.

Edelstein, B. A., & Eisler, R. M. (1976). Effects of modeling and modeling with instructions and feedback on the behavioral components of social skills. *Behavior Therapy, 7,* 382–389.

Ewing, M. E., & Seefeldt, V. (1995). Patterns of participation and attrition in American agency-sponsored youth sports. In F. L. Smoll & R. E. Smith (Eds.), *Children and youth in sport: A biopsychosocial perspective* (pp. 31–46). Dubuque, IA: Brown & Benchmark.

Fisher, A. C., Mancini, V. H., Hirsch, R. L., Proulx, T. J., & Staurowsky, E. J. (1982). Coach–athlete interactions and team climate. *Journal of Sport Psychology, 4,* 388–404.

Gottman, J. M., & McFall, R. M. (1972). Self-monitoring effects in a program for potential high school dropouts: A time series analysis. *Journal of Consulting and Clinical Psychology, 39,* 273–281.

Gould, D. (1987). Understanding attrition in children's sport. In D. Gould & M. R. Weiss (Eds.), *Advances in pediatric sport sciences* (pp. 61–85). Champaign, IL: Human Kinetics.

Greendorfer, S. L., Lewko, J. H., & Rosengren, K. S. (1995). Family and gender-based influences in sport socialization of children and adolescents. In F. L. Smoll & R. E. Smith (Eds.), *Children and youth in sport: A biopsychosocial perspective* (pp. 89–111). Dubuque, IA: Brown & Benchmark.

Haan, N. (1978). Two moralities in action contexts: Relationship to thought, ego regulation, and development. *Journal of Personality and Social Psychology, 36,* 286–305.

Hanlon, T. (1994). *Sport Parent.* Champaign, IL: Human Kinetics.

Harter, S. (1978). Effectance motivation reconsidered. *Human Development, 21,* 34–64.

Horn, T. S. (1984). Expectancy effects in the interscholastic athletic setting: Methodological considerations. *Journal of Sport Psychology, 6,* 60–76.

Horn, T. S. (1985). Coaches' feedback and changes in children's perceptions of their physical competence. *Journal of Educational Psychology, 77,* 174–186.

Horn, T., & Hasbrook, C. (1987). Psychological characteristics and the criteria children use for self-evaluation. *Journal of Sport Psychology, 9,* 208–221.

Kanfer, F. H., & Gaelick–Buys, L. (1991). Self-management methods. In F. H. Kanfer & A. P. Goldstein (Eds.), *Helping people change: A textbook of methods* (4th ed., pp. 305–360). New York: Pergamon Press.

Kazdin, A. E. (1974). Self-monitoring and behavior change. In M. J. Mahoney & C. E. Thoresen (Eds.), *Self-control: Power to the person* (pp. 218–246). Monterey, CA: Brooks/Cole.

Kirschenbaum, D. S., & Karoly, P. (1977). When self-regulation fails: Tests of some preliminary hypotheses. *Journal of Consulting and Clinical Psychology, 45,* 1116–1125.

Lee, C. (1993). Operant strategies in sport and exercise. *International Journal of Sport Psychology, 24,* 306–325.

Martens, R. (1978). *Joy and sadness in children's sports.* Champaign, IL: Human Kinetics.

Martens, R. (1987). *American coaching effectiveness program: Level 1 instructor guide* (2nd ed.). Champaign, IL: Human Kinetics.

Martens, R., & Gould, D. (1979). Why do adults volunteer to coach children's sports? In G. C. Roberts & K. M. Newell (Eds.), *Psychology of motor behavior and sport— 1978* (pp. 79–89). Champaign, IL: Human Kinetics.

Martens, R., & Seefeldt, V. (1979). *Guidelines for children's sports.* Reston, VA: American Alliance for Health, Physical Education, Recreation, and Dance.

Martin, G. L. (1992). Applied behavior analysis in sport and physical education. In R. P. West & J. Hammerlynck (Eds.), *Designs for excellence in education: The legacy of B. F. Skinner* (pp. 223–257). Longmont, CO: Sopris West.

Martin, G. L., & Hyrcaiko, D. (Eds.). (1983). *Behavior modification and coaching: Principles, procedures, and research.* Springfield, IL: Charles C Thomas.

Masters, J. C. (1972). Social comparison in young children. In W. W. Hartup (Ed.), *The young child* (pp. 320–339). Washington, DC: National Association for Education of Young Children.

McFall, R. M. (1977). Parameters of self-monitoring. In R. B. Stuart (Ed.), *Behavioral self-management: Strategies, techniques and outcomes* (pp. 196–214). New York: Brunner/Mazel.

McFall, R. M., & Twentyman, C. T. (1973). Four experiments on the relative contributions of rehearsal, modeling, and coaching to assertion training. *Journal of Abnormal Psychology, 81,* 199–218.

McInally, P. (1987). *Moms & dads, kids & sports.* New York: Macmillan.

McNeil, D. R. (1961, June). Little leagues aren't big leagues. *Reader's Digest,* p. 142.

Michener, J. A. (1976). *Sports in America.* New York: Random House.

Orlick, T., & Botterill, C. (1975). *Every kid can win.* Chicago: Nelson-Hall.

Orlick, T., & McCaffrey, N. (1991). Mental training with children for sport and life. *The Sport Psychologist, 5,* 322–334.

Passer, M. W. (1984). Competitive trait anxiety in children and adolescents: Mediating cognitions, developmental antecedents and consequences. In J. M. Silva & R. S. Weinberg (Eds.), *Psychological foundations of sport and exercise* (pp. 130–144). Champaign, IL: Human Kinetics.

Rejeski, W., Darracott, C., & Hutslar, S. (1979). Pygmalion in youth sport: A field study. *Journal of Sport Psychology, 1,* 311–319.

Romance, T. J., Weiss, M. R., & Bockoven, R. (1986). A program to promote moral development through elementary school physical education. *Journal of Teaching in Physical Education, 5,* 126–136.

Rosen, A. (1967). *Baseball and your boy.* New York: Funk & Wagnalls.

Rotella, R. J., & Bunker, L. K. (1987). *Parenting your superstar.* Champaign, IL: Human Kinetics

Scanlan, T. K. (1986). Competitive stress in children. In M. R. Weiss & D. Gould (Eds.), *Sport for children and youths* (pp. 113–118). Champaign, IL: Human Kinetics.

Scanlan, T. K. (1995). Social evaluation and the competition process: A developmental perspective. In F. L. Smoll & R. E. Smith (Eds.), *Children and youth in sport: A biopsychosocial perspective* (pp. 298–308). Dubuque, IA: Brown & Benchmark.

Seefeldt, V., & Brown, E. W. (Eds.). (1992). *Program for athletic coaches' education.* Dubuque, IA: Brown & Benchmark.

Shrauger, J. S. (1975). Responses to evaluation as a function of initial self-perceptions. *Psychological Bulletin, 82,* 581–596.

Smith, R. E. (1986). A component analysis of athletic stress. In M. Weiss & D. Gould (Eds.), *Sport psychology for children and youths* (pp. 107–112). Champaign, IL: Human Kinetics.

Smith, R. E., & Smoll, F. L. (1990a). Self-esteem and children's reactions to youth sport coaching behaviors: A field study of self-enhancement processes. *Developmental Psychology, 26,* 987–993.

Smith, R. E., & Smoll, F. L. (1990b). Sport performance anxiety. In H. Leitenberg (Ed.), *Handbook of social and evaluation anxiety* (pp. 417–454). New York: Plenum Press.

Smith, R. E., & Smoll, F. L. (1991). Behavioral research and intervention in youth sports. *Behavior Therapy, 22,* 329–344.

Smith, R. E., & Smoll, F. L. (1995). The coach as a focus of research and intervention in youth sports. In F. L. Smoll & R. E. Smith (Eds.), *Children and youth in sport: A biopsychosocial perspective* (pp. 125–141). Dubuque, IA: Brown & Benchmark.

Smith, R. E., & Smoll, F. L. (1996). Way to go, coach: A scientifically-proven approach to coaching effectiveness. Portola Valley, CA: Warde.

Smith, R. E., & Smoll, F. L. (in press). Coach-mediated team building in youth sports. *Journal of Applied Sport Psychology.*

Smith, R. E., Smoll, F. L., & Barnett, N. (1995). Reduction of children's sport performance anxiety through social support and stress-reduction training for coaches. *Journal of Applied Developmental Psychology, 16,* 125–142.

Smith, R. E., Smoll, F. L., & Christensen, D. S. (1996). Behavioral assessment and interventions in youth sports: A review. *Behavior Modification, 20,* 3–44.

Smith, R. E., Smoll, F. L., & Curtis, B. (1978). Coaching behaviors in Little League Baseball. In F. L. Smoll & R. E. Smith (Eds.), *Psychological perspectives in youth sports* (pp. 173–201). Washington, DC: Hemisphere.

Smith, R. E., Smoll, F. L., & Curtis, B. (1979). Coach Effectiveness Training: A cognitive–behavioral approach to enhancing relationship skills in youth sport coaches. *Journal of Sport Psychology, 1,* 59–75.

Smith, R. E., Smoll, F. L., & Hunt, E. B. (1977). A system for the behavioral assessment of athletic coaches. *Research Quarterly, 48,* 401–407.

Smith, R. E., Smoll, F. L., & Schutz, R. W. (1990). Measurement and correlates of sport-specific cognitive and somatic trait anxiety: The Sport Anxiety Scale. *Anxiety Research, 2,* 263–280.

Smith, R. E., Smoll, F. L., & Smith, N. J. (1989). *Parents' complete guide to youth sports.* Reston, VA: American Alliance for Health, Physical Education, Recreation, and Dance.

Smith, R. E., Zane, N. W. S., Smoll, F. L., & Coppel, D. B. (1983). Behavioral assessment in youth sports: Coaching behaviors and children's attitudes. *Medicine and Science in Sports and Exercise, 15,* 208–214.

Smoll, F. L. (1990). Psychology of the young athlete: Stress-related maladies and remedial approaches. *Pediatric Clinics of North America, 37,* 1021–1046.

Smoll, F. L. (1993). Enhancing coach–parent relationships in youth sports. In J. M. Williams (Ed.), *Applied sport psychology: Personal growth to peak performance* (2nd ed., pp. 58–67). Mountain View, CA: Mayfield.

Smoll, F. L., & Smith, R. E. (1989). Leadership behaviors in sport: A theoretical model and research paradigm. *Journal of Applied Social Psychology, 19,* 1522–1551.

Smoll, F. L., & Smith, R. E. (1993). Educating youth sport coaches: An applied sport psychology perspective. In J. M. Williams (Ed.), *Applied sport psychology: Personal growth to peak performance* (2nd ed., pp. 36–57). Mountain View, CA: Mayfield.

Smoll, F. L., & Smith, R. E. (Eds.) (1995a). *Children and youth in sport: A biopsychosocial perspective.* Dubuque, IA: Brown & Benchmark.

Smoll, F. L., & Smith, R. E. (1995b). Competitive anxiety: Sources, consequences, and intervention strategies. In F. L. Smoll & R. E. Smith (Eds.), *Children and youth in sport: A biopsychosocial perspective* (pp. 359–380). Dubuque, IA: Brown & Benchmark.

Smoll, F. L., Smith, R. E., Barnett, N. P., & Everett, J. J. (1993). Enhancement of children's self-esteem through social support training for youth sport coaches. *Journal of Applied Psychology, 78,* 602–610.

Swann, W. B., Jr. (1990). To be known or to be adored? The interplay of self-enhancement and self-verification. In R. M. Sorrentino & E. T. Higgins (Eds.), *Handbook of motivation and cognition: Foundations of social behavior* (Vol. 2, pp. 69–92). Orlando, FL: Academic Press.

Tesser, A. (1988). Toward a self-evaluative maintenance model of social behavior. In L. Berkowitz (Ed.), *Advances in experimental social psychology* (Vol. 21, pp. 69–92). San Diego, CA: Academic Press.

Tesser, A., & Campbell, J. (1983). Self-definition and self-evaluation maintenance. In J. Suls & A. G. Greenwald (Eds.), *Psychological perspectives on the self* (Vol. 2, pp. 1–31). Hillsdale, NJ: Erlbaum.

Universities Study Committee. (1978). *Joint legislative study on youth programs: Phase III. Agency sponsored sports.* East Lansing, MI: Michigan Institute for the Study of Youth Sports.

Wandzilak, T., Ansorge, C. J., & Potter, G. (1988). Comparison between selected practice and game behaviors of youth soccer coaches. *Journal of Sport Behavior, 11,* 78–88.

Westre, K., & Weiss, M. (1991). The relationship between perceived coaching behaviors and group cohesion in high school football teams. *The Sport Psychologist, 5,* 41–54.

Zhang, L., Ma, Q., Orlick, T., &, Zitzelberger, L. (1992). The effect of mental-imagery training on performance enhancement with 7–10-year-old children. *The Sport Psychologist, 6,* 230–241.

14 Working With College Student-Athletes

Mark B. Andersen

For many student-athletes, starting college brings about substantial psychosocial change and adjustment (Gould & Finch, 1991). The demands placed on student-athletes (e.g., academic pressures, sport performance, training, travel) usually exceed the demands experienced by nonathlete students. Student-athletes face a variety of developmental issues and have a number of special pressures, including maintaining academic eligibility and staying in compliance with the myriad regulations of the National Collegiate Athletic Association (NCAA; Renfro, 1993). The purpose of this chapter is to describe student-athletes in general, to discuss some of the important developmental issues that affect them, to identify special pressures that college student-athletes are under, and to provide some practical information about the NCAA and intercollegiate athletics for practitioners interested in working with this population.

Varieties of Student-Athletes

Student-athletes, like everyone else, come in a variety of shapes, sizes, talents, and commitments. Some demographic variables of student-athletes (e.g., gender, division status, scholarship) may have a large effect on some of the problems and issues they confront.

NCAA Divisions I, II, and III

NCAA Division I athletic programs are usually the largest and best funded. Many of the student-athletes receive full or partial scholarships.

NCAA Division I programs also have high regional, and often high national, visibility. Athletes in these programs face a great deal of public scrutiny. These are usually high-power programs, and some of the issues student-athletes may bring to the sport psychologist include worries over maintaining scholarships, pressure from coaches, and exposure in the media. NCAA Division I schools are often "pressure cookers" for athletes, especially in the revenue sports of football, basketball, and baseball. Many schools also specialize in one or two nonrevenue sports (e.g., swimming at Stanford and the University of Texas), and pressures on athletes in those sports can be substantial.

NCAA Division II student-athletes may not experience the national exposure and pressure of NCAA Division I athletes, but the local and statewide attention may be considerable. NCAA Division II schools offer scholarships to student-athletes but on a more limited basis than NCAA Division I schools.

NCAA Division III schools offer no athletic scholarships and usually do not receive the attention and pressures of NCAA Division I and II programs. The media attention at the local level, however, may be extensive. Although sport psychologists do not encounter anxieties about athletic scholarships, the NCAA Division III athlete may feel substantial pressures from the team, coach, and press.

A distinction in intercollegiate athletics that is probably more important than the NCAA Division I, II, and III designations is the difference between revenue and nonrevenue sports. The revenue sports are usually football and men's basketball, with baseball a distant third. There are a few exceptions, but it is usually these programs that get the most attention, acknowledgement, and money. Athletes and coaches in nonrevenue sports may feel resentment toward those in football and basketball for their "hogging" of attention and money. Poor relationships between revenue and nonrevenue sports are not helped when coaches in revenue sports remind those affiliated with other sports that it is the football and basketball programs that support the rest of the sports. This is a commonly held belief, even by coaches and athletes, but in a vast majority of cases, football and basketball programs operate in the red and are themselves a drain on university resources (Sperber, 1990).

Another distinction in intercollegiate athletics is between men's and women's sports. Even though Title IX is over 20 years old, women athletes and women's programs, with some exceptions, are still second-class entities. Title IX helped increase the number of collegiate teams for women in the United States, but it also brought with it a large number of men to coach those new teams. Communication problems between coaches and athletes occur in all types of coaching situations, but the potential for difficulties between female athletes and male coaches may be greater than in same-sex coaching relationships.

Junior College

Junior-college athletes are another group that sport psychologists may serve. Often, high school athletes with academic difficulties, financial concerns, or athletic deficiencies (e.g., size, strength, speed) go to a junior college, play their sport, hone their skills, and shore up their academic record. Some of these athletes, after 2 years, apply to NCAA Division I, II, or III institutions. The transfer to a 4-year school may not be an easy one. The problems of the transferring junior-college student bring up the issues of transitions in student-athletes' lives, and these concerns are covered, along with other developmental landmarks, in the following section.

Developmental Issues

Intercollegiate athletes usually range in age from 17 to 23. In Eriksonian terms, the developmental tasks they face concern identity and establishing intimate relationships (Erikson, 1968). Many student-athletes identify more with the "athlete" part than with the "student" part. Over-identification with the role of athlete may predispose a student-athlete to difficulties in several stages of a college career.

Transition

The first potential difficult period is the transition into college. High school student-athletes may have some of their first experiences in the realm of ethics and sport (e.g., inducements, promises, cash; see Davenport, 1985; Lapchick, 1989a). Also, many athletes go from being a star player on their high school team to being just another member of the team in college. An athlete's identity may take a blow when the high school thinking was "I am a great ballplayer," and the college reality is that "there's a bunch of players way better than I am here." Learning such lessons may be even more difficult for athletes who have moved away from home for the first time and are in a new environment (Pearson & Petitpas, 1990).

Sometimes the move to college is also a cultural transition. For example, a Northeast urban student may have some adjustment problems if he or she accepts a scholarship at a rural university in the Southwest. The move to college can make some athletes feel like strangers in a strange land. Again, self-concept and identity may suffer in a foreign environment.

The overidentification with the athlete role may lead to maladaptive thinking and behavior. Many athletes in revenue sports come to college with the plan of going on to a career in professional sport (Scales, 1991). The painful fact is that very few athletes even get a tryout with a professional team and that professional careers are extremely short. This thinking about and planning for professional careers can lead to neglect of other career options and working in class only to maintain eligibility. For students who end their college careers with little career planning, poor academic records, and no professional opportunities, the transition out of sport can be traumatic. For athletes who sustain career-ending injuries, the sudden loss of dreams and identity can leave them susceptible to severe adjustment problems and possibly depression (Brewer, 1993; Kleiber & Brock, 1992).

Sport psychologists working with collegiate athletes might want to assess identification with the athlete role, especially in junior and senior class athletes, because for many, their careers will soon come to an end. Ideally, career planning should start for collegiate athletes at the freshman level and continue throughout their college days. Career counseling is available at most universities, but usually such services do not have a delivery agreement in place for intercollegiate athletics (see Coleman & Barker, 1991; Petitpas, Danish, McKelvain, & Murphy, 1992; and Wittmer, Bostic, Phillips, & Waters, 1981, for discussions of career counseling for student-athletes). Many academic athletic advisors, however, do a good job of guiding athletes in their exploration of alternate career tracks. "Exploration" is a critical task of late adolescence and early adulthood, and college provides many avenues (and pressures) for exploration and experimentation.

Substance Use and Abuse

For many, college is a continuation of the exploration and experimentation that began in high school (or even earlier). College may offer a greater variety of experiences and relationships, however, along with greater freedom to pursue those experiences. Student-athletes probably differ little from students in general in the area of substance use and abuse. In a recent chapter on drugs and sport, Damm (1991) reported that past research has shown that drug and alcohol use among student-athletes reflects the patterns of use among students in general (cf. Tricker, Cook, & McGuire, 1989). The difference is that student-athletes have to take drug tests occasionally, a process that is, at best, embarrassing and, at worst, dehumanizing. Many universities, in compliance with NCAA directives, have initiated drug education and substance-abuse prevention programs. Unfortunately, many of these programs are one-time affairs with a primary prevention approach (Tricker & Cook, 1989) and probably have little effect on student patterns of drug and alcohol use. For college populations, secondary and tertiary prevention and care programs seem more appropriate because attitudes and experiences with drugs and alcohol usually have their roots in high school and middle school (Damm, 1991; Marcello, Danish, & Stolberg, 1989).

Sport psychologists who wish to offer services in the area of substance abuse education and prevention aimed at college populations might wish to consult the work of Petitpas and Van Raalte (1992) for some guidelines on designing programs better suited to the needs of university student-athletes. They suggested a six-component program that involves (a) education on substance abuse and substance-abuse recognition held in small-group discussion formats, (b) enhancement of life skills to help student-athletes manage stress better and increase coping resources, (c) support groups for alcohol and drug issues as well as other problems facing student-athletes such as the transitions into and out of college sports, (d) counseling services for student-athletes with substance-abuse problems, (e) follow-up on student-athletes who have participated in the program to determine whether new behaviors regarding drugs and alcohol have been maintained, and (f) program evaluation and revision. Offering such a comprehensive program may meet with resistance because of the usual problems in intercollegiate athletics of insufficient time and money, but it is a good outline to start with, and it is more likely to meet with success than the few hours of drug education required by the NCAA.

One last word on student-athletes using drugs and alcohol: Student-athletes do differ from the general student population when it comes to the legal (and media) ramifications of drug and alcohol use. A college student caught smoking marijuana or drunk and acting disorderly in most universities garners a mention on the back page of the local paper's police report. If the infraction does not occur on university property, it probably does not come to the attention of university officials. An intercollegiate athlete arrested for drug possession or public drunkenness, no matter where it occurs, will make at least the sports page and, depending on the athlete's status, possibly the front page of the newspaper. When it comes to legal and "moral" behavior, many student-athletes live under extremely close scrutiny. The use of alcohol is part of many student-athletes' experiences in college, as is the exploration of sexuality and intimate behavior.

Sexuality

College is a time for developing relationships, sexual and otherwise. There is a vast literature on the sexuality and sexual behavior of college-age populations. In general, there is little reason to suspect that the issues of sexuality and sexual behavior among college student-athletes differ significantly from those of the college population as a whole. In a few areas, such as living up to stereotypes of sexual athleticism and hypervirility and dealing with expectations about sexual orientation (e.g., females in "masculine" sports, males in "expressive" sports), student-athletes may have special concerns. The reader should consult chapter 16, this volume, for a review of sexual orientation issues in sport.

There is little specific literature on college athletes and sexual behavior. Some recent studies have revealed, however, that compared to student nonathletes, student-athletes reported having significantly more sexual partners in the course of a year (Butki, Heyman, & Andersen, 1994; Heyman, Varra, & Keahey, 1993). Both athletes and nonathletes also reported low frequencies of condom use. More partners and low condom use suggest that many athletes, and college students in general, are involved in risky sexual behavior. Offering psychoeducational programs on responsible sexual behavior might be another way sport psychologists can assist athletic departments to improve care for their athletes.

Special Pressures on Student-Athletes

The life of a student-athlete when school is in session is often a seemingly never-ending story of getting caught up. It is the rare student-athlete who is well ahead in his or her studies. A certain standard of academic performance is necessary to maintain eligibility. The pressures and demands of academic and athletic performance combined often leave little time for student-athletes to engage in common student activities such as play and socializing. The following sections discuss some of the special pressures on student-athletes.

Academic Performance

By their junior year, student-athletes must have earned at least a 2.0 overall grade point average and have passed at least 24 semester units per year to maintain eligibility (see the latest NCAA regulations for a complete discussion of academic eligibility rules; NCAA rules are constantly changing). At some universities, the student-athletes who do not have the required grade point average must attend study hall, see tutors, or both. A student-athlete's day might look something like this: classes 9:00 to 1:00, lunch 1:30, practice 2:30 to 5:30, dinner 6:00, study hall 7:00 to 10:00, and maybe more studying at home, later. Time for scheduling extra activities (including sport psychology consultation) is limited.

Time Management

Organizing student-athletes' time is often not a problem. Much of their time is already scheduled. Pinkney (1991) made the wise suggestion that some common time-management techniques are not appropriate for many student-athletes. For example, student-athletes should not be asked to find more time in the day or to set aside more time to get things done. They do not have "extra" time. In a true sense, they already have great time-management skills. They get to practice on time; they use their time effectively in the pool or in the weight room. Time management for student-athletes needs to focus not on finding more time but on using the time they have more effectively and efficiently.

The area of time management for student-athlete study time is probably a good place to start teaching student-athletes how to use their time more efficiently. Pinkney (1991) suggested a variety of techniques such as use of flash cards, short bouts of studying during the day between classes, and transferring time-management skills learned in sport to the academic realm such as reframing the academic environment into a long series of competitions (e.g., tests, papers). The transfer of training from the playing field can also play a role in common study and performance problems such as test anxiety.

Test Anxiety

A sport psychologist working with athletes on performance issues is likely to introduce the techniques of relaxation and imagery. Thus, when it comes to dealing with test anxiety, the student-athlete already has the basic tools for systematic desensitization. Coupling imagery and relaxation with more efficient study skills may help raise the comfort level of the student in the classroom.

One major problem student-athletes face involves missing classes owing to travel and competitions. This remains a thorny problem. Many university professors are more than willing to let student-athletes take tests at different times, especially if the student-athletes notify them in advance. Some professors are rigidly attached to their own schedules, however, which leaves student-athletes in "damned if you do, damned if you don't" situations. A sport psychologist speaking to a stubborn professor on behalf of a student-athlete needs to use great tact and advanced negotiating skills to avoid alienating the professor and making the matter worse.

Academic performance is the student-athlete's responsibility, and making up missed class time is part of being a student-athlete. The sport psychologist, however, can help the student-athlete by occasionally checking on how things are going and suggesting various strategies for making up for time missed (e.g., arranging for another student to record the lecture, getting lecture notes from others). The sport psychologist must remember that academic progress and eligibility fall in the realm of responsibility of the academic athletic advisors and the NCAA eligibility coordinator. Making sure all persons involved in the academic progress of student-athletes know what the others are doing helps reduce the potential for conflicting suggestions.

Athletic Injury

Connecting with student-athletes through the sports medicine unit may be one of the best routes to take for a sport psychologist wishing to work with student-athletes. Establishing good rapport with sports medicine personnel and working in the training room can help the sport psychologist ease into helping student-athletes with the often difficult physical and psychological demands of the rehabilitation process. Sport psychologists, unfamiliar with general rehabilitation psychology, may wish to do some reading in this field to gain knowledge about helping athletes with rehabilitation (e.g., Wiese & Weiss, 1987) and working with sports medicine organizations (e.g., Andersen & Brewer, in press).

Dealing With the Media

Student-athletes, especially those in highly visible sports, may encounter the media for the first time. Many NCAA Division I schools require some of their athletes to attend seminars on how to interact with the press. The sport psychologist may be able to offer services and viewpoints that help the athlete keep the media attention in perspective (e.g., how to keep cool in interview situations, how to keep one's head from getting "too big" from all the attention). The suggestions offered by Baillie and Ogilvie about elite athletes dealing with the media are relevant to collegiate athletes (see chapter 15, this volume).

Olympic years, World Series, and Grand Slam tennis tournaments often provide opportunities for the press to bring up sport psychology and sport psychologists. The result is good news and bad news. The good news is that sport psychology gets some air time, which may help increase the acceptance of sport psychology among the sporting community and the general public. The bad news is that the media portrayals of sport psychology and sport psychologists are often slanted or misrepresentative of how most sport psychologists operate. A major error by the media (and by some athletes) is to attribute athletes' success to their interactions with sport psychologists. This can lead to resentment on the part of athletes who should be recognized for their performances. Excessive media attention also challenges sport psychologists' attempts to maintain appropriate confidentiality. It is recommended that sport psychologists remain in the background as much as possible and inform athletes that that is where they want to remain.

The Practitioner and the NCAA

Knowing the Rules

The NCAA has a byzantine set of ever-changing rules and regulations concerning what one can and cannot do for athletes. The sport psychologist needs to become familiar with these rules to avoid putting the athlete or the team in jeopardy of NCAA violations (Renfro, 1993).[1] Depending on the NCAA rule infraction, the consequences can range

---

1. The practitioner who begins sport psychology or counseling work with intercollegiate athletes should obtain a current copy of the NCAA regulations, available from the NCAA, 6201 College Boulevard, Overland Park, KS 66211-2442, tel.: 913-339-1906.

from a warning to the loss of the student's eligibility to the whole team being placed on probation (or worse).

Current NCAA regulations have been interpreted as stating that psychological consultation should occur only in a group (classroomlike) setting or the sport psychologist's office. The minute sport psychologists go out on the playing field to work with athletes (e.g., helping athletes with on-site self-talk strategies), they are considered extra coaches. If the team has the maximum number of coaches allowed by the NCAA, the sport psychologist has just placed the team in violation. If the team has fewer coaches than the maximum allowed, on-site interventions might not pose a problem. There are no NCAA regulations about a sport psychologist simply attending and observing practice.

Regarding the services the sport psychologist offers, a wise tack would involve a "whole-person" approach (Chartrand & Lent, 1987; Greenspan & Andersen, 1995; Petitpas & Champagne, 1988). If a coach or administrator employs a sport psychologist for the sole purpose of making more points or winning more games, the NCAA is likely to take a dim view of the practice and consider it a type of exploitation.

Sport psychologists may hold group psychoeducational sessions with the whole team, but the coach needs to include that time in the weekly allotment of hours for practice and team meetings (i.e., 20 hours). If sport psychologists work for the intercollegiate athletics department or the university, they may not buy anything for the athlete, not even a hamburger, nor may they phone prospective players unless the contact is counted as an official call. This last prohibition speaks to the area of recruitment. Although a sport psychologist may be involved with the recruitment process, it is advised that the role be limited. The NCAA rules for recruiting are quite strict. The level of recruitment involvement that seems best and safest would be for the sport psychologist to meet with interested prospective student-athletes when they make their campus visit. Deeper involvement than that and forays into the selection of recruits should be avoided.

If a student-athlete develops a working relationship with a sport psychologist, those one-on-one meetings do not count as part of the NCAA's 20 hours of "athletically related activities." So there is no limit to performance counseling, or any counseling for that matter, as long as the student-athlete initiates the counseling session. As stated earlier, sport psychologists need to be familiar with the current NCAA regulations and should get to know the institution's NCAA compliance coordinator, who can help clear up any doubts or misunderstandings the sport psychologist may have about service delivery and NCAA regulations.

Other University Contacts

At a medium-size or large university, student-athletes may have access to a variety of sources that provide psychological and other one-on-one services. At smaller colleges, the range of such services may be limited. Many departments and campus organizations may supply services (of a psychological, academic, or counseling nature) to athletes *if* the athlete is the one who initiates contact. University personnel who work with student-athletes may include academic athletic advisors, tutors, counseling-center staff, academic department staff (e.g., exercise-science professors), and university job-placement staff. Some of the most common sources of services for athletes are discussed in more detail subsequently in this section.

Large universities usually have a fair number of staff persons at the university counseling center. In some cases, one or two of the staff members may have made contact with the athletics department or have some history of working with athletes. Another source of services in many large universities is the psychology department (or the counseling department) clinic. The schematic diagram in Figure 1 represents a generic picture of a large university and the potential agencies and university groups that may provide services to student-athletes. Although not all universities have such complex hierarchical lines of reporting, accountability, and service delivery, one can see that entering into a consulting relationship with student-athletes or teams can involve a multitude of agencies, organizations, and subgroups.

For those who have little or no contact with intercollegiate athletics (e.g., private practitioners, academics) and wish to establish a relationship with athletes and coaches, there are several paths to take. The first path leads to the academic athletic counselors. These individuals counsel athletes on academic matters, eligibility, registration, and so forth. They are intimately familiar with the factors that influence academic success for student-athletes (see Hurley & Cunningham, 1984; Lang, Dunham, & Alpert, 1988; Lapchick, 1989a). Many academic athletic counselors also get to hear about athletes' concerns about sport performance and life in general. These people are often overworked, and many would welcome good referral sources for athletes who want to work on performance enhancement or other personal issues. Forming

Figure 1

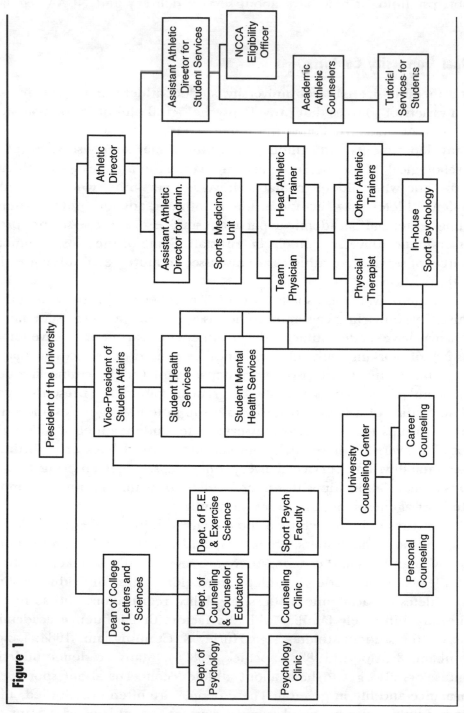

Schematic of a large university's potential service-delivery resources for student-athletes.

a liaison with academic athletic counselors is probably one of the smarter moves a university counseling-center psychologist (or any other practitioner) could make.

A second path for developing a relationship with intercollegiate athletics involves connections with the sports medicine unit. A recent survey found that athletic trainers would like to see more training in psychology and more psychological services in sports medicine settings (Wiese, Weiss, & Yukelson, 1991). It appears that many athletic trainers welcome contact with sport psychologists, especially those with experience and knowledge of psychological processes in injury rehabilitation. One caveat needs mentioning: Sports medicine units in intercollegiate athletics departments often have convoluted structures (Andersen & Brewer, 1995), and thorough familiarity with the structure and reporting lines of such organizations may help avoid faux pas when offering services.

At a few universities in the United States, the intercollegiate athletics department has hired a full-time sport psychologist to work with student-athletes (e.g., University of Arizona, Washington State University). More commonly, athletics departments send a troubled athlete to an outside psychologist or psychiatrist for treatment of a problem (e.g., substance abuse, gambling) or in response to a court order stemming from unlawful behavior. Rarely do athletics departments send an athlete outside the university for something such as mental skills training for performance enhancement.

One last pathway to working with intercollegiate athletes is to offer services pro bono. The disadvantage of this practice follows the simple maxim, "If you give it to them for free, they won't pay for it." Many intercollegiate athletics departments are essentially businesses, and sport psychology is an expense of low priority. Thus, sport psychologists who provide services for free might receive a warm welcome, but they may experience a "cold shoulder" when they later begin to talk about fees. If one plans to offer services pro bono, going through sports medicine and student services administrators may be the best plan.

Working in Intercollegiate Athletics

Intercollegiate athletic departments can assume complex organizational structures, especially at large universities. Unless a sport psychologist was a college athlete, an intercollegiate athletics department can be somewhat bewildering. To increase understanding of athletics departments, the sport psychologist should keep in mind that intercollegiate athletics is in the entertainment business with an entertainment product to sell (often a football or basketball team). Different pressures come to bear on administrators, coaches, and athletes from what happens "across the street" at the university, where teaching and research receive the most attention.

Large universities may have a chief athletic director and several associate and assistant athletic directors to cover areas such as marketing, sports information, contest management, student support services, and so forth. The athletic administrators that a sport psychologist should make connections with usually are the ones responsible for sports medicine units and student services. The sport psychologist may enter at any level of the complex intercollegiate athletic structure. Whenever sport psychologists enter the system, the assistant athletic director or other administrator responsible for the "area of service" (e.g., sports medicine) in which the sport psychologist is working needs to be advised that the sport psychologist is on board. Entering into the system without checking in with the "top brass" may set off the organizational "immune system" and get the sport psychologist hastily removed.

Confidentiality

An administrator, a coach, or a team member may seek out services. This presents a challenge to the sport psychologist, who must remain clear on who the client is. Who receives service and who pays for it in college athletics are usually not the same person. If administrators allocate money for services for an athlete, they may want information about what that money is buying and how the services are going. Administrators, coaches, and athletes may not know the subtleties of confidentiality, protection, and privilege. The sport psychologist should plan on providing preemptive education about psychologists' ethical codes.

Boundaries

Sport psychologists often have boundaries that differ from those observed in more traditional clinical or counseling psychology. Sport psychologists may attend practices and competitions and even travel to out-of-town games and meets. This rather "familiar" behavior may pose some problems. Sport psychologists might want to clarify their boundaries to themselves and their clients. There are some sport psychologists who travel with the team, eat with the team, and even work out with the team. The rationale behind this behavior involves getting the sport psychologist to be accepted as one of the team or coaching staff. Although the intentions seem honorable, the results of such familiar behavior pose some problems (Ellickson & Brown, 1990).

Sport psychologists with wide boundaries enter into multiple roles, becoming psychologist, coach, dinner companion, and teammate. Multiple roles may lead to confusion for both the client and the sport psychologist. An example from my own case book illustrates this point. I worked for 2 years rather closely with a university women's gymnastics team. We held team meetings to discuss performance, academic pressures, time management, stress management, and interpersonal issues. I also met individually with some of the team members. These individual meetings usually involved sensitive material that the gymnasts did not want to bring up in the team sessions. My contact with team members outside the group and individual sessions was limited to occasional observation of practices and competitions. During these observations, I never engaged in any on-site interventions and kept well in the background. At the end of the second year, the coaches invited me to the annual awards dinner. I accepted the invitation. I was seated right across from a gymnast I had seen on a one-to-one basis, who had discussed with me some painful experiences from her childhood. I was uncomfortable and could see that she seemed a bit out of sorts. She confirmed this by leaning across the table and saying in a confused and somewhat disconcerted manner, "It is so weird to have you sitting here." And she was exactly right. Having dinner together (even at a team function) was not part of the relationship we had developed. It was an uncomfortable but valuable lesson about boundaries and dual roles.

Travel with the team can provide rich information about team dynamics and performance at different venues. It has pitfalls, however, and can lead to role confusion. Recommendations for team travel might include separate travel for the sport psychologist. One would not want to be seated next to a client for a 5-hour plane flight. Because rooming with coaches or athletes sets up more boundary issues, lodging arrangements should allow the sport psychologist some distance. Such an arrangement also allows athletes to talk with the sport psychologist in private without interruptions.

Large NCAA Division I universities may send sport psychologists or, more often, academic athletic counselors to away games and meets.

Sport psychologists, especially those outside the intercollegiate athletics department, usually have to supply their own transportation and lodging if they wish to observe the team at an away event. Although NCAA Division I universities are the ones most likely to have funds to pay for a sport psychologist's travel and services, institutions at other NCAA divisional levels may also request psychological services at away competitions.

Conclusion

This chapter does not cover all of the potential services sport psychologists could offer to collegiate athletes or touch on even the majority of college athletes' concerns. The problems of athletes in college are similar to those of athletes in general. For example, in many sports, weight control and appearance are major issues (e.g., diving, gymnastics), and disorders in eating may arise (Black & Burckes-Miller, 1988; Borgen & Corbin, 1987; Parker, Lambert, & Burlington, 1994; Petrie, 1993; Rosen & Hough, 1988). Issues of prejudice and discrimination confront minority athletes throughout their careers and afterward (Anshel, 1990; Anshel & Sailes, 1990; Cashmore, 1982; Lee & Rotella, 1991; Scales, 1991). These topics and more are covered in chapter 16, this volume.

References

Andersen, M. B., & Brewer, B. W. (1995). Organizational and psychological consultation in collegiate sports medicine groups. *Journal of American College Health, 44,* 63–69.

Anshel, M. M. (1990). Perceptions of black intercollegiate football players: Implications for the sport psychology consultant. *The Sport Psychologist, 4,* 235–248.

Anshel, M. M., & Sailes, G. (1990). Discrepant attitudes of intercollegiate team athletes as a function of race. *Journal of Sport Behavior, 13,* 68–77.

Black, D. R., & Burckes-Miller, M. E. (1988). Male and female college athletes: Use of anorexia nervosa and bulimia nervosa weight loss methods. *Research Quarterly for Exercise and Sport, 59,* 252–256.

Borgen, J. S., & Corbin, C. B. (1987). Eating disorders among female athletes. *The Physician and Sportsmedicine, 15*(2), 89–95.

Brewer, B. W. (1993). Self-identity and specific vulnerability to depressed mood. *Journal of Personality, 61,* 343–364.

Butki, B. D., Heyman, S. R., & Andersen, M. B. (1994, October). *Athletes' knowledge and sexual behaviors related to acquired immunodeficiency syndrome.* Paper presented at the annual meeting of the Association for the Advancement of Applied Sport Psychology, Incline Village, NV.

Cashmore, E. (1982). *Black sportsmen*. London: Routledge & Kegan Paul.

Chartrand, J. M., & Lent, R. W. (1987). Sports counseling: Enhancing the development of the student-athlete. *Journal of Counseling and Development, 66,* 164–167.

Coleman, V. D., & Barker, S. A. (1991, Spring). A model of career development for student-athletes. *Academic Athletic Journal*, pp. 33–40.

Damm, J. (1991). Drugs and the college student athlete. In E. F. Etzel, A. P. Ferrante, & J. W. Pinkney (Eds.), *Counseling college student athletes: Issues and interventions* (pp. 151–176). Morgantown, WV: Fitness Information Technology.

Davenport, J. (1985). From crew to commercialism: The paradox of sport in higher education. In D. Chu, J. O. Segrave, & B. J. Becker (Eds.), *Sport and higher education* (pp. 5–16). Champaign, IL: Human Kinetics.

Ellickson, K. A., & Brown, D. R. (1990). Ethical considerations in dual relationships: The sport psychologist–coach. *Journal of Applied Sport Psychology, 2,* 186–190.

Erikson, E. H. (1968). *Identity: Youth and crisis*. New York: Norton.

Gould, D., & Finch, L. (1991). Understanding and intervening with the student-athlete-to-be. In E. F. Etzel, A. P. Ferrante, & J. W. Pinkney (Eds.), *Counseling college student athletes: Issues and interventions* (pp. 51–69). Morgantown, WV: Fitness Information Technology.

Greenspan, M., & Andersen, M. B. (1995). Providing psychological services to student athletes: A developmental psychology approach. In S. M. Murphy (Ed.), *Sport psychology interventions* (pp. 177–191). Champaign, IL: Human Kinetics.

Heyman, S. R., Varra, E. M., & Keahey, J. (1993, August). Comparison of high school varsity athletes and non-varsity students on measures of homophobia, sexuality activity, and knowledge about AIDS. In S. R. Heyman (Chair), *Homophobia in sport: Confronting the fear.* Symposium conducted at the annual meeting of the American Psychological Association, Toronto, Ontario, Canada.

Hurley, R. B., & Cunningham, R. L. (1984). Providing academic and psychological services for the college athlete. In A. Shriberg & F. R. Brodzinski (Eds.), *Rethinking services for college athletes* (pp. 51–58). San Francisco: Jossey-Bass.

Kleiber, D. A., & Brock, S. C. (1992). The effect of career-ending injuries on the subsequent well-being of elite college athletes. *Sociology of Sport Journal, 9,* 70–75.

Lang, G., Dunham, R., & Alpert, G. (1988). Factors related to the academic success and failure of college football players: A case of mental dropout. *Youth and Society, 20,* 209–222.

Lapchick, R. E. (1989a). The high school student-athlete: Root of the ethical issues in college sport. In R. E. Lapchick & J. B. Slaughter (Eds.), *The rules of the game.* New York: Macmillan.

Lapchick, R. E. (1989b). *Pass to play: Student athletes and academics*. Washington, DC: National Education Association.

Lee, C. C., & Rotella, R. J. (1991). Special concerns and considerations for sport psychology consulting with black athletes. *The Sport Psychologist, 5,* 365–369.

Marcello, R. J., Danish, S. J., & Stolberg, A. L. (1989). An evaluation of strategies developed to prevent substance abuse among student-athletes. *The Sport Psychologist, 3,* 196–211.

National Collegiate Athletic Association (1995). *1995–1996 NCAA Manual.* Overland Park, KS: Author.

Parker, R. M., Lambert, M. J., & Burlington, G. M. (1994). Pathological features of female runners presenting with pathological weight control behaviors. *Journal of Sport & Exercise Psychology, 16,* 119–134.

Pearson, R. E., & Petitpas, A. J. (1990). Transitions of athletes: Developmental and preventive perspectives. *Journal of Counseling and Development, 69,* 7–10.

Petitpas, A. J., & Champagne, D. (1988). Developmental programming for intercollegiate athletes. *Journal of College Student Development, 29,* 454–460.

Petitpas, A. J., Danish, S., McKelvain, R., & Murphy, S. (1992). A career assistance program for elite athletes. *Journal of Counseling and Development, 71,* 383–386.

Petitpas, A. J., & Van Raalte, J. L. (1992, Spring). Planning alcohol education programs for intercollegiate student-athletes. *Academic Athletic Journal,* pp. 12–25.

Petrie, T. A. (1993). Disordered eating in female collegiate gymnasts: Prevalence and personality/attitudinal correlates. *Journal of Sport & Exercise Psychology, 15,* 424–436.

Pinkney, J. W. (1991). Student-athletes and time management for studying. In E. F. Etzel, A. P. Ferrante, & J. W. Pinkney (Eds.), *Counseling college student athletes: Issues and interventions* (pp. 121–134). Morgantown, WV: Fitness Information Technology.

Renfro, W. I. (Ed.). (1993). *1993–1994 NCAA guide for the college-bound student-athlete.* Overland Park, KS: The National Collegiate Athletic Association.

Rosen, L., & Hough, D. (1988). Pathogenic weight control behaviors of female college gymnasts. *The Physician and Sportsmedicine, 16*(9), 141–144.

Scales, J. (1991). African-American student-athletes: An example of minority exploitation in collegiate athletics. In E. F. Etzel, A. P. Ferrante, & J. W. Pinkney (Eds.), *Counseling college student-athletes: Issues and interventions* (pp. 71–99). Morgantown, WV: Fitness Information Technology.

Sperber, M. (1990). *College sports, Inc.: The athletic department vs. the university.* New York: Holt.

Tricker, R., & Cook, D. L. (1989). The current status of drug intervention and prevention in college athletic programs. *Journal of Alcohol and Drug Education, 34*(2), 38–45.

Tricker, R., Cook, D. L., & McGuire, R. (1989). Issues related to drug use in college athletics: Athletes at risk. *The Sport Psychologist, 3,* 155–165.

Wiese, D. M., & Weiss, M. R. (1987). Psychological rehabilitation and physical injury: Implications for the sportsmedicine team. *The Sport Psychologist, 1,* 318–330.

Wiese, D. M., Weiss, M. R., & Yukelson, D. P. (1991). Sport psychology in the training room: A survey of athletic trainers. *The Sport Psychologist, 5,* 15–24.

Wittmer, J., Bostic, D., Phillips, T., & Waters, W. (1981). The personal, academic, and career problems of college student athletes: Some possible questions. *Personnel and Guidance Journal, 60,* 52–55.

15 Working With Elite Athletes

Patrick H. F. Baillie and Bruce C. Ogilvie

If applied sport psychology has an area of glamour, it likely rests in the realm of providing services to elite athletes. We define *elite athletes* as those whose pursuit of excellence in sport has led to their participation and success in competition at the Olympic or professional level. Unfortunately, there is a tendency among some practitioners to promote themselves on the basis of the number of medals or championship teams with which they have been associated. More appropriately, working with elite athletes should be seen as an opportunity to work with talented and dedicated clients, athletes who have reached the pinnacle of their sport.

Work with elite athletes brings into play special challenges for the sport psychologist. It is more than an extension of services offered to amateur sports clubs and other competitors. Travel schedules can disrupt the regularity of involvement. The media may look to the sport psychologist for that extra insight or news tip. Administrative structures may become increasingly burdensome. Substance-abuse issues may be prevalent and may put the sport psychologist in an ethical or even legal dilemma. At times, when consultation fails to lead to effective changes in service delivery, one side or the other may choose to terminate the consultation process abruptly.

This chapter aims to address some of these unique issues, including gaining entry and acceptance with Olympic and professional athletes, recognizing differences between work with teams and work with indi-

We thank Ken Ravizza and Hap Davis, who provided commentary and suggestions on earlier drafts of this chapter.

viduals, coping with the distractions and obligations that face the athlete and the sport psychologist at this level of competition, and evaluating the ongoing effectiveness of the consultation for both the client and the practitioner. Although there is no doubt that there are special pleasures that may come from working with elite athletes, there are also specific perils that a prepared consultant must be aware of.

The Starting Point: Gaining Entry With Elite Athletes

The value of first impressions has seldom been denied, and the image that sport psychologists present at their first meeting with elite athletes often characterizes the nature and duration of the professional relationship. Honesty, genuineness, and the ability to earn athletes' trust are frequently mentioned as essential elements on which practitioners build their reputation.

Strategies for Access and Acceptance by Professional and Olympic Athletes

It is essential for sport psychology consultants to use a variety of methods to gain access to and acceptance by professional and Olympic athletes (Exhibit 1). Many athletes and coaches realize the importance of sport psychology, but their enthusiasm for working with a mental-training consultant may be restrained. Coaches, for example, may feel that sport psychology techniques such as goal setting, focus control, and avoidance of burnout are basic skills that fall under the coach's purview. Athletes, on the other hand, may believe that consultation with a sport psychologist is an admission of weakness. Other significant barriers to the involvement of a sport psychologist are negative connotations associated with the image of a "shrink," lack of sport-specific knowledge by the practitioner, and inadequate experience in the elite sport environment (Ravizza, 1988). Ravizza recommended using terms such as *mental training* or *mental toughness* instead of sport psychology, because athletes are likely to be more comfortable with these alternatives. For athletes referred to a sport psychologist, feelings of paranoia are not uncommon (Ogilvie, 1979). Supervised experience with amateur sports clubs or college teams provides the practitioner with exposure to the sport and to introductory administrative issues. As the summer and fall of 1994 showed, with cuts to Olympic program funding and strikes or lockouts

Exhibit 1

Strategies for Access to and Acceptance by Professional and Olympic Athletes

1. Gain experience working with athletes in a variety of settings including schools and universities, local sports clubs, development teams, and other amateur organizations.
2. Develop name-recognition by volunteering with sports teams, presenting at coaching clinics, working with individual athletes, making cold calls to sports organizations and following up with written materials, and giving public presentations or lectures to other interested audiences.
3. Accurately assess the needs of the athletes, rather than imposing a predetermined program developed elsewhere. Assessment includes identification of the athletes' strengths, requirements, experiences with applied sport psychology, and interests in performance enhancement and mental training.
4. Be sensitive to the needs of the athletes, including scheduling, flexibly providing support for the athletes, and providing clear strategies with a positive focus.
5. Use language that is appropriate to the sport setting, emphasizing plain language, direct communication, and simple ideas instead of psychological jargon. Knowledge and use of terms related to player positions, game rules, and sport strategies assist in the early development of rapport.

in two professional sports, elite athletics is business-driven; sport psychologists often need to prove immediately to be worth their fees. On-the-job training is rare.

Sport psychology positions working with elite athletes are rare and are almost never advertised. In North America, there are perhaps 25 practitioners working with professional sports teams and an approximately equal number involved with Olympic athletes. For a handful of skilled practitioners, years of experience and a track record of proficiency may lead to unsolicited offers of employment. For others, presentations to coaching conferences, publications in popular magazines or books, and involvement with development teams serve to provide name-recognition when approaching teams or national governing bodies (NGB), the organizations that allocate funding and determine policy for Olympic sports. In short, experience helps, but "cold calls" and other sales techniques are required before novice practitioners are able to get their foot in the door. Experience with a single team member, collegiality with an administrator, and a willingness to start with volunteer services have proved to be useful approaches.

Despite obvious differences in the financial benefits of sports involvement, Olympic and professional athletes are joined in their opinions about the importance of being able to challenge themselves to excellence through sport and about the excitement of competition (Baillie, 1992). Understanding athletes' motivations and commitment is an important step in earning their respect and trust. As a result, Ravizza (1988), Orlick (1989), and some of the contributors to a special edition of *The Sport Psychologist* (i.e., Botterill, 1990; Ravizza, 1990) recommended that the consultation process begin with a detailed assessment of the athlete's or team's needs, rather than the imposition of a packaged program. Orlick (1989) stated, "I never begin an individual consultation session with a preconceived notion of what a particular high performance athlete might want or need. Each one has different needs, and these needs differ at various times in his or her career" (pp. 358–359). Orlick described beginning the assessment by discussing the athlete's goals, experiences with mental preparation, and identification of mental tasks that require focused work. Ravizza (1988) added that the practitioner must also determine how to integrate mental skills training into the coach's schedule to minimize disruption. Coaches are likely to be more comfortable with a consultant who provides assurances that sport psychology interventions are intended to complement the coach's role and not to impinge on typical coaching domains such as skill acquisition, game strategy, and roster decisions.

Athletes also may need sport psychologists to be sensitive to scheduling issues. Given the pressures and commitments of elite-level athletic competition, several authors (e.g., Botterill, 1990; Halliwell, 1990) have suggested that time with family is important for the athlete and that sport psychology interventions offered on road trips, when "downtime" is more common, may be better received. Other dimensions of access reflect the practitioner's own values, such as being in the locker room before games, on the field during practices, or in a conveniently located arena office. Preferences vary. "I have found that I can be most effective by keeping a low profile and being available on planes, buses, or in my hotel room. An open-door policy based upon a genuine interest in each player has proven to be the most effective approach for me" (Ogilvie, 1979, p. 51).

Personality may also play a central role in determining the goodness of fit between an athlete or team and a practitioner. Orlick and Partington (1987) surveyed 75 Canadian Olympic athletes and found that sport psychology consultants were given positive evaluations when they were accessible, practical, flexible, seen to have something concrete

to offer, and willing to provide athlete-specific input. Negative evaluations were given to consultants who lacked sensitivity, failed to provide
sufficient feedback, or had poor application of psychology to sport, and
to those whose interpersonal styles were described, among other adjec-
tives, as *wimpy* or *domineering*. Orlick and Partington (1987) concluded,
"As a result of this study, ... we have become acutely aware of the
importance of having people with the right kind of personal qualities
enter the field" (pp. 16–17). Gould, Murphy, Tammen, and May (1991)
found that effectiveness of the consultant was highly correlated with his
or her fitting in with the team, drawing on the athletes' strengths, being
trustworthy, having a positive focus, and providing clear strategies.

Effectiveness may also be improved if consultants modify their use
of language. For those practicing from a clinical perspective, diagnostic
labels and psychological terms offer efficient professional communication but are likely to carry negative connotations among athletes and
administrators. Even nonclinical terms such as *sensitive*, *loner*, and *having
an edge* have different meanings in the sport context. Evaluative language, particularly when used by the practitioner, may interfere with
the development of a trusting relationship between the sport psychologist and the athlete. Experience with professional and Olympic sports
quickly focuses the consultant's vocabulary on words and phrases that
provide specific direction and clarity for the athlete. Through this sort
of adjustment, consultants begin to develop rapport with their clients,
which is likely to enhance trust and commitment.

Negotiating and Detailing the Terms of Consultation

Multiple models of service delivery exist within applied sport psychology. These models are at times related to the practitioner's self-
perceived competencies and, at other times, a reflection of coaching
philosophies and team needs. Murphy (1988), for example, compared
medical, consultation, and educational models in applied sport psychology and recommended a consultation-type model drawn from a
base in industrial–organizational psychology. Neff (1990) described a
wide-ranging employee assistance program with a professional sports
organization, including personal counseling and testing. Ravizza (1990)
presented an educational model that consists of information, practice,
and support for the athlete, similar to that of Rotella (1990), who argued for a role in performance enhancement only, avoiding counseling
areas and any part in player selection. Dorfman (1990) offered a com-

Exhibit 2

Recommendations for the Content of Contracts for Sport Psychology Services With Elite Athletes

1. Financial terms
   a. Determine an appropriate level of compensation for services rendered.
   b. Attempt to avoid contracts that are based on barter, particularly with individual athletes.
   c. Specify the time period during which the contract is in effect.
   d. Identify escape clauses through which either side may prematurely terminate services, with associated periods of notification.
2. Orientation
   a. Present orientation workshops for the entire coaching staff.
   b. Schedule individual meetings with each athlete.
3. Professional issues
   a. Detail professional boundaries.
   b. Describe specific competencies.
   c. Explain referral process.

bined clinical–educational approach with personal and family counseling and referrals for drug rehabilitation, financial advice, and academic assistance.

The issue of philosophy of service delivery must be clarified before a contract between practitioner and client can be formalized. Recommendations regarding the content of the contract are presented in Exhibit 2. Essential elements include financial terms, clarification of access, clarification of role, and details of the referral process. Specific services to be provided vary, as does the amount of time to be provided by the practitioner, the term of the contract, and the level of compensation. Contracts that are based on a barter system are not uncommon, for example, providing season tickets to the consultant, but barter should be avoided when it is clinically contraindicated or exploitative. The sport psychologist is well advised to review the relevant literature on the impact of remuneration on therapeutic outcome (e.g., Cerney, 1990; Yoken & Berman, 1987) before agreeing on this type of payment. In short, the value that the team or athlete writes into the practitioner's contract is an early reflection of the importance or relevance that the client is giving to mental training and a comment on what sport psychology services are worth.

We have found that proper orientation to sport psychology programs is essential for consultation work with teams. Meetings with the coaching staff, team members, and team trainer and physician each may serve to introduce the services of a sport psychologist.

The primary goal of the meeting with the coaches is to have them see the sport psychologist as a contributor to their personal goals, while at the same time respecting the individual needs of the players. With team members, the focus shifts to describing sport psychology strategies and interventions, detailing the nature of privileged communication, and explaining that all psychological insights, be they from testing, interviews, or coaches, are designed to enhance the athlete's performance. In some cases, the sport psychologist may choose to offer appropriate readings, to give practical examples of interventions, and to inform players that sports psychologists contribute most when athletes seek their services on the basis of their particular concerns. The central theme is that the services will be tailored to the needs of the individual athlete.

Finally, the initial meeting with the team physician and trainer serves to establish open communication that will assist in integration of later programs for injury recovery, substance abuse, eating disorders, and other elements of physical conditioning that the sport psychologist feels competent to address. An ongoing collaborative effort is needed to address each of these topics effectively.

The orientation process can be facilitated by clear delineation of the specific role of the sport psychologist. Professional boundaries related to test materials, the voluntary nature of athlete involvement, and the referral process should be stipulated at the outset. The sport psychologist should clarify with the contract holder the nature of feedback regarding the team and its performance. The sport psychologist should assure the contract holder that all services will be delivered within the ethical framework of the field. When the sport psychologist has authority for referrals to outside services, such as substance-abuse programs, the contract should also identify at least one individual with whom the sport psychologist shares a privileged relationship should subsequent referrals require that level of professional protection.

The contract is also the place to begin to clarify issues concerning competencies of the sport psychologist. In their study of 19 sport psychology consultants, Partington and Orlick (1991) found a common core of services. "The eight most frequently mentioned services in descending order included focus and refocus control, activation and anxiety control, competition planning, monitoring and evaluation, imagery, pre-competition planning, goal-setting, and interpersonal com-

Exhibit 3

Sample Contract for the Provision of Sport Psychology Services

1. This agreement is between [the sport psychologist(s)] and [the client(s)] for the provision of sport psychology services by [the sport psychologist(s)] with [the client(s)].

2. The agreement covers the period between [the present date or the first day of the season] and [one year less a day from the present date or the last possible day of competition]. Either party of the agreement may terminate services at any time while the agreement is in effect, on provision of written notice [one month] prior to the termination.

3. Areas in which [the sport psychologist] is competent to provide service include: (add or delete as applicable) goal setting, stress management, substance-abuse counseling, focus control, psychometric assessment, marital or couples counseling, imagery, pre-competition and competition planning, crisis management, interpersonal communication, self-talk strategies, and regulation of arousal. [Data collection for research by the sport psychologist, assessments of draft prospects, and] other services will be negotiated separately.

4. Required services outside of these areas of competence will be accessed through referrals at the discretion of [the sport psychologist], wherever possible in consultation with [the client]. Costs associated with additional treatment resources will be paid by [the client]. Such services may include residential substance-abuse treatment, family or marital counseling, or career transition programs.

5. Fees for the provision of sport psychology services by [the sport psychologist] will be in the amount of $[ ], to be paid in [ ] equal installments, on [date(s)] by [the client].*

6. The nature and content of all services provided by [the sport psychologist] to an individual athlete are privileged and will not be disclosed by [the sport psychologist] to anyone without the written consent of the athlete. The nature and content of services provided to the team as a whole are also privileged and will not be disclosed outside of the team by [the sport psychologist] without the written consent of [the head coach].

7. (When working with a team or NGB:) [The sport psychologist] will consult [every 2 weeks] with [the head coach] in order to discuss issues of team cohesion, communication, and mental focus, and other topics as determined by mutual concern.

8. At the beginning of the term of this agreement, or at a time agreed on by the parties, [the sport psychologist] will hold an introductory meeting with [the athlete(s)] in order to outline expectations for the provision of sport psychology services and to answer questions from [the athlete(s)]. This meeting will be held at [the client's training facility] and will outline the

continued

Exhibit 3, continued

training and background of [the sport psychologist], services to be offered, relevant readings, ethical standards, and scheduling. Meetings with each individual athlete will be arranged at times of mutual convenience.

9. At the beginning of the term of this agreement, or at a time agreed on by the parties, [the sport psychologist] will meet separately with the coaching staff, the medical staff, and any other team personnel as may be appropriate in order to outline the training and background of [the sport psychologist], services to be offered, procedures for interdisciplinary consultation, relevant readings, ethical standards, and scheduling, and to answer questions from each of these groups.

10. Any modifications to this agreement must be made by mutual consent of the parties.

Dated ___[date]___ at ___[city]___ ,

Signed [the sport psychologist] ___[name of the sport psychologist —printed]___

___[the athlete or head coach]___ ___[name of the signatory/client —printed]___

*Fees may cover all or part of the services to be provided. When the fees cover preseason training and regular contact during the season but not crisis-management issues or other circumstances such as attendance at nonlocal competitions, additional fees should be specified in the contract. An informal survey by the authors suggests that, at the present time, fees for a season of service to a professional team range from barter for a pair of season tickets to over $50,000.

munication'' (p. 186). Crisis management is another element that is frequently cited. Gould et al. (1991) found that coaches and athletes were most interested in imagery and visualization techniques, concentration and attention training, stress management, relaxation, self-talk strategies, and regulation of arousal. Career transition planning, eating disorders, substance-abuse concerns, and personal development were rated as less important.

Inevitably, occasions arise when consultants are asked, with next to no warning, to aid in the resolution of critical problems of an extremely complex nature. It is imperative that consultants define their roles. Although it may be ideal to refer or to leave the situation and take the time to discuss options with colleagues, the reality is that circumstances often conspire to limit flexibility. For example, when a star athlete is traded or hurt, a press release may precede any discussion with other team members. Does one hold a team meeting or hope to chat with each athlete before the day is through? The sport psychologist might even be asked to break the news of a trade to the athlete, a decision that will affect future relationships with other team members, who may believe that he was part of the trade decision. This type of request is more likely to arise in situations when the practitioner has either opted for comprehensive counseling services or failed to specify the exact nature of the mental training program.

Many potential problems can be avoided through the development and use of an appropriate contract such as that presented in Exhibit 3. At every opportunity, sport psychology consultants should clarify that their work should be evaluated on the basis of improved use of mental skills strategies by the athlete, or other parameters, but not on the basis of winning or losing by the athlete or team. Although the ethical and moral stance of sport psychologists may involve separating their services from the goal of producing winners, they will find that managers, coaches, and parents continue to evaluate them and sport psychology in terms of how they contribute to this end. When financial pressures increase for the athlete or team as a result of losing competitions and losing fans or sponsors, sport psychologists are likely to learn quickly their true significance to the organization.

With an employee assistance program as the model of service, the sport psychology consultant needs to clarify the procedures for referral and payment of costs associated with outside services, for example, substance-abuse programs, family counseling, and financial-management professionals. Because confidentiality issues can limit the ability of practitioners to make referrals (e.g., the sport psychologist may be put in a position of having to disclose personal information about an athlete before the team, or the NGB may authorize funds for other treatment), consultants may have to make independent decisions to spend a significant amount of a team's or an NGB's money or to impact on training and travel schedules should the needs of the athlete include comprehensive treatment alternatives.

Individual Versus Team Clients

The single most important ethical issue to face a sport psychologist working with elite athletes is clarification of exactly who the client is. Is the practitioner's primary allegiance to the athlete, coach, general manager, or NGB? The nature of this element of the relationship must be clarified during initial negotiations, but it also requires careful monitoring throughout the term of the contract.

Respecting Boundaries With Administrators, Coaches, and Athletes

Although many authors have commented on their preference for work with individual athletes rather than with a team as a group (e.g., Dorfman, 1990; Ravizza, 1990), clarification of primary allegiance and ethical issues has been less widely discussed. When it has been discussed, the results have often been fractious. On the one hand, many practitioners are licensed or chartered psychologists and function within the professional framework provided by the standards of the American Psychological Association (APA). On the other hand, individuals with a sport science background, who clearly may have much to offer a prospective client, may have a different perspective on interventions and ethics. As one example, APA ethics prohibit the therapist from involvement in a second, nontherapeutic role with the client (e.g., providing treatment services while instructing the student in a required university course), but such dual relationships as coach and sport psychologist depend on the personal ethics of practitioners who are not covered under the aegis of the APA. In such a circumstance, boundary issues between the service provider and the athlete become even more salient.

Working with individual athletes may result in a reduction of the number of extraneous factors than can disrupt the therapist–athlete relationship. When golf or tennis professionals seek service, responsibility is usually restricted to the clients and their agents. There are notable occasions when sponsors or parents, by the nature of their relationship to the athlete, have influenced the implementation of mental skills training programs. Ideally, the practitioner–athlete relationship is based totally on collaborative efforts. When service is extended to an entire team or NGB, functioning within established ethical guidelines becomes a continuous challenge.

In working with teams, the approval of the coach is necessary before the sport psychologist can develop rapport with the team and implement any sort of program. As a result, some practitioners view an allegiance to the coach as being a prerequisite to working with sports teams (Ogilvie, 1979; Ravizza, 1990). Others find this relationship troubling or at least limiting in perspective: "If a sport psychology consultant failed to deal with problems identified by athletes, and only dealt with those viewed as real by the coach, he or she would turn away from everything we have learned about high quality consulting from athletes and coaches" (Partington & Orlick, 1987a, p. 101). In any event, the nature of the relationship must be clear for all participants. A coach may feel that the sport psychology consultant is sharing traditional coaching territory, such as enhancing team motivation or helping the athlete to focus, and therefore expect the practitioner's allegiance. The athlete, by contrast, is a high-functioning individual for whom the acknowledgement of a need for psychological help is such a violation of self-concept that any suggestion of collusion between the coach and the consultant may obstruct the athlete's openness. The balance between allegiance and ethics becomes all the more precarious.

In working with teams, the sport psychology consultant may find varying levels of acceptance among the athletes. Issues such as race, history with other consultants, overall trust, and personal motivation influence the comfort of athletes in seeking mental skills training. Ravizza (1988) suggested that three groups may arise: "In general, I find that about one third of the athletes on a team are very receptive to the program in the beginning, one third will seek it out when they are struggling, and one third are not receptive" (p. 249). Put simply, not all members of a team feel comfortable in accessing sport psychology services. Practitioners must identify whether they need to address this reluctance or allow for a more gradual building of acceptance by the team. Goodness of fit applies to the whole team and the sport psychologist, not necessarily each team member.

Maintaining Confidentiality

One of the most potentially lethal issues facing the sport psychology consultant concerns information gained through work with an individual athlete about which the coach or administrator seeks disclosure. The most acute focus of this issue occurs when the sport psychologist becomes involved in personnel decisions. If assessment of potential draft choices is one of the services being provided, team members may question the allegiance of the practitioner, perhaps fearing that confidential information will be passed along to management. Whenever possible, the practitioner should revert to an educational role and explain the nature of privileged communication to the athletes and their coach. Primary emphasis on the relationship with the coach does not imply a flow of confidential material or the coach's expectation of such communication if the coach understands that privilege is necessary for consultants to maximize their effectiveness.

Additional questions of allegiance arise when sport psychologists begin, as they must, to interact with administrators. Throughout the hierarchy of the team or NGB, there are individuals with private agendas. These agendas reflect the various administrative roles played by each member within the organization. Professional survival often depends on one's skill in identifying each agenda and deciding on an appropriate course of behavior. Consultants are ultimately involved with athletes in whom the team or NGB has made great financial investments. Protection of the capital investment is a primary concern. If a sport psychologist works with an athlete on sensitive issues such as substance abuse, the situation can become quite difficult. One of the authors worked in a professional sport that had a substance-abuse policy that provided for fines "of any team official knowing of a player's drug use and not reporting such use." To respect confidentiality, the contract stated that the team would pay any fines levied against the consultant.

Factors That May Impair Athletes' Performance

Competition at the Olympic or professional level may offer athletes the ultimate showcase for their talents. It is also likely to bring into play new time demands, new sources of competitive stress, and other challenges such as dealing with the media, life on the road, and heightened pressure, either self-imposed or external, for consistent excellence. For the sport psychology consultant, these issues must be addressed in order to assist athletes in maintaining focus during training and competitions. However, the disturbances also interfere with athletes' time and may, therefore, impinge on access and the availability of suitable consultation sessions.

Coping With Travel, Outside Employment, and Other Distractions

Most professional sports teams spend half of their season on the road. For golfers, bowlers, and tennis players, among others, the entire season may be spent traveling. Unless they are well sponsored, Olympic athletes may need to balance training and competition with the demands of earning a living outside of sport. These and other factors not only conspire against the best performances of the athletes, but also affect the delivery of sport psychology services.

Michelle Mullen, a professional bowler interviewed by Gould and Finch (1990), described life on tour as being extremely stressful as a result of struggling to make a living and to maintain a healthy perspective on the role of sport:

> You must be able to keep your bowling in the right regard and not let it become your total life. Sometimes the tour can become so all consuming, and in many ways it has to be. However, you must remember that it's just part of your life and not necessarily the total essence of it. (Gould & Finch, 1990, p. 422)

Discussing possible research areas for sport psychology, Mullen noted the following:

> Interesting things to study have to do with lifestyle and getting an understanding for the stressful lifestyle. It's different in every sport for different reasons. Finances have a lot to do with it, depending on what you're competing for. Understanding what kind of roller coaster it is as a professional athlete, especially the uncertainty. . . . dealing with different issues like that, the stress levels are underestimated by far. (Gould & Finch, 1990, p. 426)

Gould and Finch also commented that "the ability to compete effectively on television while audiences of millions may watch is a stress source that may be more prevalent in the professional rather than the amateur ranks" (p. 427). Attention to these sorts of stresses is necessary to optimize performance.

Botterill (1990) described the importance of spouses, families, and friends in the life of the professional athlete; when serving as sport psychology consultant, he offers his services to these people. Botterill has also noted the difficulty of scheduling interventions: "Road trips often contain unique challenges to work through and players can be more receptive to spending additional time on things on the road. Professional players spend so much time away from home they are often well advised to maximize time with their families when at home" (p. 366). A broader analysis of the scheduling of interventions suggests that team meetings or coach referrals after a home practice are likely to be met with annoyance and disinterest by team members. Athletes, as noted earlier, like a consultant to be available, but flexible. When a program is truly supported by the coaching staff, mental-training exercises may replace some or all of the allotted practice time. Other times for less intrusive interventions include travel times (e.g., at airports or bus stations, en route, and at hotels) and during meals. Sport psychologists should discuss the issue of scheduling during the introductory stage of the consultation. Sensitivity to scheduling, to avoid adding to the demands on the athlete, is likely to be favorably received.

Dealing With the Media

Just as professional sport is a business, so is the media's function in covering it. For this reason, the athlete and the sport psychologist both must learn about handling inquiries from reporters. Exposure on television or in print may improve the marketability of both athlete and consultant, but an ongoing relationship with the media also increases the risk of making a potentially damaging off-the-cuff comment (never "off the record"—reporters are always researching, even if not actually quoting). The simple fact that an athlete is seeing the "shrink" may become a story.

In most elite sport organizations, there are public relations staff who provide excellent counsel regarding media contacts. Reporters gain access to the athletes at limited times only, although they may freely editorialize about issues that, when read or seen by athletes, can interfere with their training and competitive focus. Among the worst mistakes that an athlete might make is to suggest dissension among team members or to insult an opponent, thereby offering a grudge motivation. Complete avoidance of the media has worked only for the rare athlete and is likely to hamper the athlete in developing community involvement and the potential revenues from endorsements. Careful management of media interactions, therefore, becomes an asset.

The same concerns may be raised for the sport psychology consultant. Directing media to the press officer is often the safest way to avoid an errant comment. When the practitioner becomes the focus of a story, extreme caution must be exercised by the team and the consultant. Although the original story may be a favorable account of the sport psychologist's activities, competing media sources are likely to reframe the idea to boost their own sales. Taking a broad educational role, for example, describing the purpose and techniques of applied sport psychology in performance enhancement, is perhaps the best way to limit media interactions. Discussing team dynamics, coaching styles, and athlete preparedness with the press may lead to a quick end to the consultant relationship with the sports organization.

End-of-Season

After each involvement with elite athletes, it is important that practitioners undertake an evaluation of the consultation process, including self-assessment and the eliciting of feedback from athletes, coaches, and administrators. Such a procedure is likely to provide valuable insights that can prepare consultants for future opportunities or for marketing themselves in another setting. The Consultant Evaluation Form developed by Partington and Orlick (1987b) may be a useful tool for this process.

Assessing the Effectiveness of the Consultation

In a study of consultants, administrators, coaches, and athletes, Gould et al. (1991) used the Consultant Evaluation Form to assess the characteristics of effective services provided to 25 NGBs. A similar process was employed by Orlick and Partington (1987). Both studies provide a practical basis for comparing the results of athlete, coach, and self-evaluation. Ultimately, the goodness of fit with the organization and the use of the sport psychology consultant by the athlete are the measures of overall effect. Shortcomings, however, may be the result of elements that are beyond the control of the practitioner. Athletes, for example, may fear their coach and, hence, fear the sport psychologist whose allegiance has been demanded by the coach. Beginning a consultation in a crisis-management mode is also likely to influence its usefulness. The length of the relationship with an athlete or team may affect effectiveness. "Establishing initial rapport with coaches takes time. Yet the pressure on coaches of elite teams is for quick results," writes Ravizza (1988, p. 247). Orlick (1989) confirmed the benefit of time: "In my best or most effective consulting situations I have enough time to make a difference, which means multiple contacts at the individual level. . . . Usually it takes about 3 years of ongoing work before things really come together mentally for highly committed athletes" (p. 363).

The evaluation process should include an assessment of the contracting body as well, to determine what changes might enhance the implementation of consulting services in the future. For example, the following questions may need to be answered: Were adequate facilities made available to the consultant? What support did the coach provide for learning and practice of mental skills strategies? Could the issues of confidentiality and privilege have been better introduced or explained? Was enough time made available for consultations? Were team meetings (if any) appropriately scheduled and attended? This type of evaluation is also useful *during* the consultation process.

Contending With the End of a Relationship

Athletes retire or are traded; coaches resign or are fired; teams shift priorities or look for scapegoats in seasons of underachievement. For these and other reasons, the job of sport psychology consultant may come to an abrupt end. On occasion, it is consultants who make the decision to fire themselves.

Whether the practitioner's relationship continues with a team or NGB after significant personnel changes depends on the consultant's ability to market services to the new power brokers. When possible and appropriate, an introduction to a new coach is best made by the general manager or other team official, privately, with discussion about the effectiveness of the previous consultation. Sometimes the departure of a coach or general manager spells the beginning of a major housecleaning that is likely to include the sport psychologist. "The sign that you should take your Rorschach cards and run will be when you go to the box office for your free tickets to the game and find that the attendant has forgotten your name" (Ogilvie, 1979, p. 55).

Marketing One's Services

The end of a consulting relationship also offers an appropriate opportunity for self-evaluation. Before marketing in search of a new contract, it may be helpful to reflect on success (or failure) in achieving the objectives of the previous consultation. Even if won–lost ratios and excellence in competition have not changed, subtler variables may be analyzed. These variables include the athletes' knowledge of sport psychology strategies, effective use of the techniques, rapport between the athlete or athletes and the sport psychologist, use of the sport psychologist's services, team cohesion, and athletic skill development, among others. The period between contracts is also a good time to consider necessary changes in service delivery, such as accessibility and availability of the consultant, communication with coaches, team versus individual sessions, and the model of consultation.

Obtaining letters of introduction or reference may be a suitable way to mark the end of a positive consultation process while laying the foundation for the next contract. Testimonials, although now acceptable under APA ethical standards (APA, 1992), draw a range of responses from practitioners. Loehr (1990), for example, described negotiating endorsements by athlete–clients in lieu of financial remuneration. Because of the issues of confidentiality and barter raised by this approach, it is widely discouraged. Use of written evaluations by coaches and NGBs, rather than from athletes, may be a more acceptable method for presenting documentation of previous experiences and accomplishments to potential clients. Cold calls, submissions of proposals, and all the other procedures used previously are needed in the search for another position.

The end of a consultation may begin a trying time for the sport psychologist. There may be financial implications and feelings of loss. Finding the next job can be just as difficult as finding the first. Even a positive reputation as a sport psychologist will not easily create a new elite- or professional-level position. As a result, the process of marketing, gaining access, and establishing the trust and respect of athletes and coaches begins again.

Conclusion

This chapter provided a perspective on the role of the sport psychologist working with Olympic and professional athletes. Although this level of competition offers athletes the pinnacle of sport excellence, it also introduces new challenges for the provision of mental training or broader psychological interventions. Practitioners intending to work at this level must first gain experience in other sport settings, to clarify for themselves issues such as the model of service delivery, negotiation of contracts, guarantees regarding confidentiality, and the scope of skills and programs they are competent to offer.

The difficulties of gaining access, earning the trust of athletes and coaches, providing effective service, and evaluating the usefulness of the consultation may make the provision of sport psychology services to elite athletes a demanding and, at times, perilous process. As Ravizza (1990) wrote, "in every situation there is an ideal way to do your job, and then there is reality" (p. 331). In their profiles of 10 leading sport psychologists, Straub and Hinman (1992) cited the opinion of Tara Scanlan, 1995 president of the Association for the Advancement of Applied Sport Psychology, that "sport psychology is not for the faint hearted. She advises prospective sport psychologists to seriously assess the strength of their 'pioneering spirit.' Sport psychologists, Scanlan continues, often have to travel uncharted routes, and they should make sure they can handle the challenges" (p. 307).

We invite the interested reader to study additional perspectives on consultation with elite athletes, such as those offered in the journal *The Sport Psychologist*. We recommend supervised experience in beginning all levels of involvement, and we encourage the development and maintenance of a network of colleagues and mentors. Finally, we promote the attendance and contributions of consultants working in elite sport at conferences and other forums that allow for the exchange of ideas or concerns and work toward the improvement of techniques for sport psychology with Olympic and professional athletes and teams.

References

American Psychological Association. (1992). Ethical principles of psychologists and code of conduct. *American Psychologist, 47,* 1597–1611.

Baillie, P. H. F. (1992, October). *Career transition in elite and professional athletes: A study of individuals in their preparation for and adjustment to retirement from competitive sports.* Colloquium presented at the annual meeting of the Association for the Advancement of Applied Sport Psychology, Colorado Springs, CO.

Botterill, C. (1990). Sport psychology and professional hockey. *The Sport Psychologist, 4,* 358–368.

Cerney, M. S. (1990). Reduced fee or free psychotherapy: Uncovering the hidden issues. *Psychotherapy Patient, 7,* 53–65.

Dorfman, H. A. (1990). Reflections on providing personal and performance enhancement consulting services in professional baseball. *The Sport Psychologist, 4,* 341–346.

Gould, D., & Finch, L. (1990). Sport psychology and the professional bowler: The case of Michelle Mullen. *The Sport Psychologist, 4,* 418–430.

Gould, D., Murphy, S., Tammen, V., & May, J. (1991). An evaluation of U.S. Olympic sport psychology consultant effectiveness. *The Sport Psychologist, 5,* 111–127.

Halliwell, W. (1990). Providing sport psychology consulting services in professional hockey. *The Sport Psychologist, 4,* 369–377.

Loehr, J. (1990). Providing sport psychology consulting services to professional tennis players. *The Sport Psychologist, 4,* 400–408.

Murphy, S. M. (1988). The on-site provision of sport psychology services at the 1987 U.S. Olympic Festival. *The Sport Psychologist, 2,* 337–350.

Neff, F. (1990). Delivering sport psychology services to a professional sport organization. *The Sport Psychologist, 4,* 378–385.

Ogilvie, B. (1979). The sport psychologist and his professional credibility. In P. Klavora & J. V. Daniel (Eds.), *Coach, athlete and the sport psychologist* (pp. 44–55). Champaign, IL: Human Kinetics.

Orlick, T. (1989). Reflections on sportpsych consulting with individual and team sport athletes at Summer and Winter Olympic Games. *The Sport Psychologist, 3,* 358–365.

Orlick, T., & Partington, J. (1987). The sport psychology consultant: Analysis of critical components as viewed by Canadian Olympic athletes. *The Sport Psychologist, 1,* 4–17.

Partington, J., & Orlick, T. (1987a). The sport psychology consultant: Olympic coaches' views. *The Sport Psychologist, 1,* 95–102.

Partington, J., & Orlick, T. (1987b). The Sport Psychology Consultant Evaluation Form. *The Sport Psychologist, 1,* 309–317.

Partington, J., & Orlick, T. (1991). An analysis of Olympic sport psychology consultants' best-ever consulting experiences. *The Sport Psychologist, 5,* 183–193.

Ravizza, K. (1988). Gaining entry with athletic personnel for season-long consulting. *The Sport Psychologist, 2,* 243–251.

Ravizza, K. (1990). Sportpsych consultation issues in professional baseball. *The Sport Psychologist, 4,* 330–340.

Rotella, R. J. (1990). Providing sport psychology consulting services to professional athletes. *The Sport Psychologist, 1,* 100–117.

Straub, W. F., & Hinman, D. A. (1992). Profiles and professional perspectives of 10 leading sport psychologists. *The Sport Psychologist, 6,* 297–312.

Yoken, C., & Berman, J. S. (1987). Third-party payment and the outcome of psychotherapy. *Journal of Consulting and Clinical Psychology, 55,* 571–576.

16

Diversity in Sport

Karen D. Cogan and Trent A. Petrie

U nderstanding and appreciating individual differences that are based on gender, race–ethnicity, sexual orientation, and physical disabilities has long been a central tenet in counseling psychology and related mental health fields (e.g., Sue et al., 1982). Recently, these differences have become a subject of focus in sport psychology. Sport experiences differ for some subgroups of athletes, suggesting the necessity of addressing diversity issues in sport as well (Chartrand & Lent, 1987). The importance of recognizing the potential influences of individual differences also is seen in recent revisions of professional organizations' ethical principles. The American Psychological Association's (APA, 1992) ethical principles, Section 1.08 on human differences, states that "psychologists obtain the training, experience, consultation or supervision necessary to ensure the competence of their services" (p. 1601). In a recent adaptation of these principles, the Association for the Advancement of Applied Sport Psychology (AAASP) included awareness of individual differences in Principle D, Respect for People's Rights and Dignity (AAASP, 1994). Thus, sport psychology consultants have an ethical and practical responsibility to be knowledgeable about individual differences in general and those specific to the sport environment.

In this chapter, we focus on four sources of individual differences —gender, race–ethnicity, sexual orientation, and physical disabilities— and present information on both general and specific issues of athletes who are women, racial or ethnic minority group members; gay, lesbian, or bisexual; or the physically disabled. The purposes of this chapter are to provide (a) an overview of four groups, including a description of the population and current empirical research specific to the athletic environment, and (b) practical suggestions on how one might recognize issues and work more effectively with athletes from each group.

Gender

The Population

Since the early 1970s, women's and girls' participation in sport has increased dramatically owing to new opportunities, legislative changes demanding equal treatment, and greater publicity for female athletes (Coakley, 1990). Historically, however, sport psychology research has focused on male athletes' sport experiences, limiting the generalizability of findings to female athletes. Current research and scholarship are beginning to address gender issues (Duda, 1991; Gill, 1994; Krane, 1994) and to focus on how women's sport experiences differ from men's. Because there is a general lack of information about female athletes, we focus primarily on women's sport experiences.

Empirical Findings

In examining men's and women's sport experiences, it is helpful to consider the influence of societal factors. A primary factor, socialization, is defined as "the process whereby individuals learn the skills, values, norms, and behaviors enabling them to function competently in many different social roles within their group or culture" (Weiss & Glenn, 1992, p. 140). Historically, as well as currently, society communicates through many media (e.g., school, family, television) the gender roles children are expected to adopt. Boys usually are taught to be competitive, active, and independent, characteristics that are congruent with the general sport environment (Oglesby, 1983). Girls, however, are expected to be nurturing, kind, cooperative, and even passive (Ortner, 1974). Although females may view the general sport environment as inconsistent with their gender identity, certain sports, such as gymnastics and figure skating, may fit this female gender profile better than others (Csizma, Wittig, & Schurr, 1988).

During childhood, the groundwork is laid for future athletes to determine how they will participate in sport. In their model of activity choice, Eccles et al. (1983) proposed that gender-role stereotypes as well as beliefs and behaviors of significant socializers mediate expectancies and activity choices. The gender-role stereotypes held by significant individuals in children's lives can easily influence their development of self-concept, perceived value of various activities, and performance expectations. Likewise, the beliefs and behaviors of important figures in a child's world can influence the child's self-perception. Research on this model using kindergartners through seventh graders indicates that girls express more negative assessments of their general athletic ability than boys. These gender differences at such young ages appear to be more of a consequence of gender-role socialization than of natural aptitudinal differences (Eccles & Herold, 1991).

In adolescence, girls often learn that general achievement and femininity are incompatible and believe they need to make a choice between the two (Hyde, 1992). A girl may find her interests evolving from sport and competition to dating and developing interpersonal relationships. After all, girls are taught to be cooperative and to focus on social relationships, not sport. Such a pervasive and limiting message may discourage some talented young athletes from persisting in sport (Allison, 1991).

During the traditional college years (ages 18–22), male and female students shift from dependence on family to separation and individuation. Moving into the collegiate environment can be a stressful time as students cope with increasing independence and financial responsibility, exposure to drugs and alcohol, identity development, and romantic and peer relationships. W. D. Parham (1993) argued that student-athletes face additional challenges that make the resolution of these "normal" developmental tasks even more difficult, including balancing academics and athletics, isolation from mainstream campus activities, managing athletic successes and failures, maintaining high levels of physical health, and ending an athletic career. In addressing gender-specific stressors, Parham noted that female athletes might be more likely to struggle with eating disorders or weight management, the ramifications of participating in low-budget sports, and the societal biases concerning women's participation in sport. (See Cogan and Petrie, in press, for a more thorough review of the effects of clinical issues such as eating disorders and sexual abuse on women's sport experiences and performances.)

Past research on women in sport has examined role conflict, which refers to the conflict between a woman's femininity (submissiveness, grace, beauty) and attributes needed to succeed in her sport (strength, achievement, aggressiveness). Initially, role conflict was thought to hinder women in sport (Duquin, 1978; Felshin, 1974; Harris, 1979), but more recent research indicates that the majority of women athletes experience little or no conflict (Anthrop & Allison, 1983; Desertrain & Weiss, 1988; Sage & Loudermilk, 1979) and perhaps even less conflict than women in the general population (Allison, 1991). Allison suggested that by focusing on this topic, sport psychologists are missing the "real" issue, which is the societal belief that women are supposed to experience such conflict. Female athletes, for the most part, seem comfortable with their roles; thus, changes need to occur in society's attitudes toward women's participation in sport and not in the athletes themselves.

Another societal issue concerns negative stereotypes of female sport participants. Females who participate in sports such as basketball (Pedersen & Kono, 1990; Snyder & Spreitzer, 1983), softball, and track and field (Snyder & Spreitzer, 1983) often are stigmatized, viewed as unfeminine, and questioned about their sexual orientation (Snyder & Spreitzer, 1983). Some sports, however, such as gymnastics and tennis (Pedersen & Kono, 1990; Snyder & Spreitzer, 1983) and swimming (Snyder & Spreitzer, 1983), are considered more "acceptable" or "appropriate" for women. Women who participate in such gender-appropriate sports are chosen more often as a dating partner by men and as a best friend by women than those who participate in less gender-appropriate sports (Kane, 1988). Society's biases add an extra burden for women who participate in some sports.

Women also have different athletic-related career opportunities than men. Although athletic budget disparities still exist, women currently have more opportunities than ever to participate at the collegiate level (Coakley, 1990). However, women still have limited possibilities for professional sport or coaching careers (e.g., Acosta & Carpenter, 1992) and continue to experience this aspect of sport involvement differently from men. Thus, women may harbor fewer unrealistic expectations about making a career out of sport and place more emphasis on obtaining an education (Meyer, 1990).

Intervention Strategies

Working With Women Athletes

Guidelines for working competently with women have been suggested for psychologists (American Psychological Association, 1975; Fitzgerald

& Nutt, 1986). These guidelines are useful for any professional who works with women in a psychology-related manner and can be adapted for working with female athletes. First, sport psychology consultants must have some knowledge of how men's and women's lives and sport experiences are different because of gender. Second, sport psychology consultants must be sensitive to circumstances in which a woman would work best with a female or male counselor and make referrals as needed. With some issues, such as sexual abuse or eating disorders, a woman athlete may feel more comfortable working with a woman consultant. On the other hand, some women athletes may relate better to or be more comfortable consulting with a man. The sport psychology consultant must respect an athlete's wishes and assist her in determining who might best meet her individual needs. Regardless of their gender, all sport psychology consultants should become aware of the unique factors in women's athletic experiences and, when needed to work effectively and ethically, should seek supervision or consultation with colleagues knowledgeable in this area. (See Gill, 1994, for an overview of feminist approaches to educational sport psychology consultation.)

Female Sport Psychology Consultants Working With Male Athletes

Most sport psychology consultants working with U.S. Men's Olympic Teams are male (Gould, Tammen, Murphy, & May, 1989). (Because same-gender combinations seem to be accepted, we do not focus here on men working with male athletes or women working with female athletes.) Female sport psychology consultants working with male athletes, however, may face a variety of stereotypes owing to their gender. Athletes or coaches may question female consultants' competence, acceptability, and trustworthiness, citing the impression that women like to "gossip" and will not honor confidentiality, the possibility of attraction and transference, the view that women will be manipulative to get athletes to comply, and the perception that women are less knowledgeable about sport than men (Yambor & Connelly, 1991). Because sport remains primarily a male domain (Coakley, 1990), it is important for female consultants to recognize that these misperceptions exist and can interfere with their work with athletes and sport teams. It is useful to address the issues proactively at the beginning of consultation, exploring any concerns the male athlete or coach has about a female consultant's potential effectiveness.

Race–Ethnicity: Athletes of Color

The Population

As W. D. Parham (1993) noted, the term *athletes of color* (at least at the collegiate level) usually refers to African American athletes. Concerning other racial or ethnic groups, researchers have commented on the lack of attention given to male athletes who are Native American or Hispanic or to female athletes representing any racial or ethnic group (Coakley, 1990). Information on Asian American athletes is virtually nonexistent. In general, athletes of color are overlooked in the current sport psychology literature.

Some information exists in the sport sociology literature and in popular magazines, however, such as *Ebony* and *Hispanic*, which have focused on the sport accomplishments of people of color. For instance, compared to other American institutions, sport has been more open to African Americans (Curry & Jiobu, 1984), men in particular. In some professional sports, African Americans are overrepresented, composing 75%, 60%, and 18% of basketball, football, and baseball players, respectively ("Blacks in Sports," 1992). In sports such as swimming, fencing, gymnastics, skiing, skating, and cycling, however, African Americans are underinvolved (Coakley, 1990; Curry & Jiobu, 1984). In Olympic competition, African American athletes won 76 individual medals in Barcelona in 1992, half of which were gold ("Barcelona Gold," 1992). Hispanic athletes are largely recognized in baseball, where 14% of the players and 17% of the leading salary earners are Hispanic ("The Best," 1993). Concerning minority athletes' early involvement in sport, a recent study of male and female high school athletes reported that 12.6% and 13.1% identified themselves as African American and Hispanic, respectively (Melnick, Sabo, & Vanfossen, 1992).

Empirical Findings

Very little empirical research exists concerning athletes of color, and the available articles focus primarily on African American males. In this review of the available literature, therefore, the lack of focus on some groups in no way reflects an intention to ignore these athletes.

Historically, African American athletes have faced discrimination on the playing field as well as in other areas of life. At the collegiate level, for example, Wiggins (1991) documented the racial turmoil in athletics that existed on college campuses between 1968 and 1972. At the professional level, it was not until the mid-1940s that African Americans were allowed to play in the National Football League and Major League Baseball ("Before Jackie," 1992; Rader, 1983). When these players finally were included, they clearly contributed to the development of the sport ("Before Jackie," 1992).

Theories have been proposed to explain the differential representation of African Americans in certain sports. Genetic explanations have not been supported by the research and have been considered racist (e.g., Davis, 1990). Thus, the focus has shifted to sociological–cultural explanations. Poor African American children may have more opportunities to participate in sports such as basketball and track and field because of the low cost of equipment (Coakley, 1990). In addition, sport is more salient in African American as opposed to Caucasian communities and is considered an important activity, especially for boys (Spreitzer & Snyder, 1990). With many African American role models being athletes, athletic fame is viewed, often unrealistically, as a way out of poverty for young boys (Curry & Jiobu, 1984).

At the collegiate level, African American athletes do not escape the discrimination and racism they have faced for all of their lives (W. D. Parham, 1993). They continue to deal with professors and peers who have little understanding of their culture (W. D. Parham, 1993) and may face assumptions that they are in college only because of affirmative action (Scales, 1991) or an athletic scholarship. Such experiences can leave an athlete feeling confused, angry, hurt, or bitter and contribute to a challenging athletic experience that a White athlete may not face (W. D. Parham, 1993).

To increase understanding of minority athletes' perceptions of their sport experiences, Anshel (1990) interviewed African American collegiate football players. Findings indicated that these players (a) preferred a more subdued and individualized pregame mental-preparation strategy as opposed to a pregame talk and coach instructions, (b) felt personal accomplishments were more important than a winning team, (c) felt coaches might lack objectivity in assessing their competence, (d) felt Anglo coaches did not understand their culture, (e) experienced racism and unfairness, (f) did not respond well to harsh criticism from coaches, and (g) wanted the coaches to earn their respect. Further exploring minority athletes' perceptions, Anshel and Sailes (1990) examined potential differences between African American and White football players' attitudes. When compared to White athletes, African American athletes were less trusting of White coaches, perceived coaches as too authoritarian, preferred independent pregame preparation, and were more upset if the team won but they did not experience personal success. In terms of similarities, all the athletes admired coaches and got along well with teammates. Anshel (1990) noted that although his research dealt primarily with general racial differences, variability exists within groups, and individualized approaches were warranted with athletes.

Recognizing the absence of studies on minority females, Howard-Hamilton (1993) examined issues African American female athletes face. Athletic participation is encouraged primarily by the family when girls enter sport, and athletic achievements are considered important. Through sport involvement, the female African American athlete can stand out on her own without compromising her femininity. When she attends a predominantly Caucasian college, however, she may experience tremendous psychological, and cultural barriers. Specific issues she may face in this environment include self-worth that is closely tied to athletic ability; lack of fame, fortune, and sport-related job opportunities after college; and failure to prepare for a nonsport career.

Trusdell (1991) offered several explanations for the low involvement of Hispanic athletes in high-profile college sports such as football and basketball. One reason is cultural; baseball and soccer are sports to which many Hispanic emigrants were exposed as children. The effects of this cultural influence can be seen in the percentage of Hispanic professional baseball players. Another reason is size; Hispanic people tend to be smaller in size, and for basketball and football, size is a benefit. As Hispanics are exposed to and find opportunities in other sports, representation is likely to increase.

Intervention Strategies

All too often, people of color are placed into categories, and their experiences are described solely on the basis of their race or ethnicity. We cannot assume, however, that every person of color experiences his or her race or ethnicity in the same manner nor that race–ethnicity is the person's defining feature. In fact, tremendous variation exists within racial and ethnic groups, some of which may be due to acculturation (Atkinson, Morten, & Sue, 1993) or racial identity development (e.g., Helms, 1984; T. A. Parham, 1989). Race–ethnicity is but one of several factors to consider when attempting to understand an individual's worldview (Speight, Myers, Cox, & Highlen, 1991).

Similarly, athletes are exposed to a broad range of experiences—athletic, personal, and cultural—that help to define them as individuals. Thus, a discussion of how a particular racial or ethnic group experiences sport would not fit all athletes in that group. Even so, suggestions on how consultants might work effectively with athletes of color, specifically African Americans, have been offered (Howard-Hamilton, 1993; Lee & Rotella, 1991). We do not review these comments here but suggest the reader pursue these resources as needed. Instead, we encourage sport psychology consultants to heed Sue and Sue's (1990) caution about stereotypes and generalizations:

> Generalizations are necessary for us to use; without them, we would become inefficient creatures. However, they are guidelines for our behaviors, to be tentatively applied in new situations, and they should be open to change and challenge. (p. 47)

It is essential for the consultant to view athletes of color as individuals, for whom culture is one important defining feature, and to tailor interventions to fit the athletes' needs as opposed to applying a package designed for a certain racial–ethnic group. A sport psychology consultant might begin by reviewing the resources provided, taking a multicultural counseling course, or receiving supervision from or arranging consultation with a colleague experienced in this area.

Sexual Orientation: Gay, Lesbian, and Bisexual Athletes

The Population

Recent research suggests that the prevalence of homosexuality in the general population of the United States ranges from 4% to 17% (Gonsiorek & Weinrich, 1991), but opinions differ regarding percentages of homosexual athletes (Rotella & Murray, 1991). Heyman (1986) and Griffin (1994) suggested that there is a higher percentage of lesbians in women's sports than in the general population, which may constitute a support system for lesbians. Regardless of the exact numbers, gay, lesbian, and bisexual athletes exist, and their sport experiences may differ from those of heterosexual athletes. For example, lesbian athletes often face double societal barriers: being female and being homosexual.

Although we combine gay, lesbian, and bisexual (GLB) athletes into one group in our discussion, we recognize that many differences exist among these three groups of athletes. The issues we raise are general, and a sport psychology consultant should heed the caution offered in the section on athletes of color. Within- and between-group differences exist, and athletes should be assessed individually to determine their specific needs and the most viable interventions.

Empirical Findings

The experiences of GLB athletes have long been ignored. Although selected articles, conference presentations, and book chapters have focused on GLB athletes and homophobia in sport (Cogan & Petrie, 1993, in press; Griffin, 1994; Heyman, 1986; Johnston, 1994; Krane & Vealey, 1994; Lenskyj, 1991; Rotella & Murray, 1991), relatively little of the sport psychology literature addresses these athletes' experiences. No specific information on bisexual athletes could be found.

Because of general societal biases against and stigmatization associated with homosexuality, a GLB athlete is likely to face the same issues that a GLB nonathlete would encounter (Cogan & Petrie, in press). Such issues include but are not limited to (a) the need to hide sexual orientation or censor comments or actions for fear of giving oneself away; (b) difficulty trusting others; (c) feelings of shame and lack of pride; (d) overt and subtle pressure from society, self, family, or friends to change sexual orientation; (e) reconciliation of religious beliefs that may not condone a GLB lifestyle; (f) destructive coping strategies such as use of drugs or alcohol to escape the isolation and self-hatred (Griffin, 1994) or use of food (either restricting or bingeing); and (g) the bias that heterosexual relationships are better and preferred. Concomitant feelings may include depression, anger, isolation, anxiety, and confusion, all of which can undermine athletic performance.

GLB athletes might experience some additional, unique stressors related to their sexuality in the athletic environment. First, they may experience fears about being forced out of the closet ("outed") and going public. Rotella and Murray (1991) noted that some athletes may avoid success and notoriety to avoid being outed by the media. Athletes who choose to be out and are proud of it still may face negative consequences such as disapproval, rejection, harassment and discrimination (Lenskyj, 1991). Athletes also may be "encouraged" directly or indirectly to leave the team or be less visible. A second issue is the lack of role models and support from family and society. GLB athletes may feel isolated, alienated, and lonely unless they have found a support system in their sport or social network. Because going public is so risky, few

GLB athlete role models may exist to provide support, knowledge, and options. A third issue is the potential for team divisions and conflicts surrounding sexual orientation. When a team is composed of both GLB and non-GLB athletes, team conflicts and divisions may occur, especially in an environment where homophobia and related biases exist. Given their potential divisiveness, such conflicts may negatively affect team cohesion and performance.

Intervention Strategies

Sexual Orientation Is Not Always An Issue

Like any athletes who seek counseling, GLB athletes may have issues that are not linked with sexual orientation. It is important to be open to discussing sexual orientation, but it also is important to realize that a GLB athlete may want only cognitive–behavioral strategies for enhancing performance.

Self-Awareness

Sport psychology consultants who work with GLB athletes must be comfortable with their own as well as others' same-gender attractions and aware of their own homophobia. If a sport psychology consultant is struggling with the acceptability of these feelings, a referral is in order.

When Sexual Orientation Is An Issue

If sexual orientation is a central concern, the primary objective is to help athletes accept and appreciate themselves and resolve identity conflicts in a homophobic world. This goal may involve helping them to embrace their sexuality and deprogram from the negative stereotypes, homophobic messages, and second-best images that society has communicated (Clark, 1987). As Garnets, Hancock, Cochran, Goodchilds, and Peplau (1991) noted, "a therapist does not attempt to change the sexual orientation of the client without *strong* (italics added) evidence that this is the appropriate course of action and that change is desired by the client" (p. 969). Clark has argued, however, that clients who seek such a change really are asking for acceptance.

Social Support

One should encourage the development of a support system (Clark, 1987). The GLB athlete may feel alone and isolated; contact with other GLB athletes or nonathletes is a vital step. Sport psychology consultants need to become informed about resources for GLB individuals to be able to facilitate such connections. Knowledge of GLB role models (e.g., Martina Navratilova) and sport opportunities for GLB athletes (e.g., the Gay Games) can prove useful.

Handling Team Conflicts

Because of homophobic team environments, GLB athletes may feel acutely different from and uncomfortable with their teammates. Thus, they may seek counseling concerning how to cope. If they want to confront homophobic teammates, consultants may assist them by role-playing different approaches and discussing possible reactions of team-mates and coaches. If athletes are uncomfortable confronting others, consultants may assist them by providing the opportunity to discuss their feelings about the environment and helping them find alternative en-vironments.

Coming Out

Disclosure should be the athlete's decision; it is not a requirement. If GLB athletes choose to come out, they need to do so at their own pace with much support and encouragement. Pressuring athletes to move too quickly through the coming-out process may be damaging to their self-esteem and coping abilities.

Formation of a GLB Identity

Much has been written about the developmental stages associated with the formation of homosexual identities (e.g., Cass, 1979; Troiden, 1989), and consultants may want to avail themselves of this literature to improve their understanding of some of the individual differences that exist among GLB athletes.

Athletes With Disabilities

The Population

A number of organized sport programs exist in the United States for persons with disabilities; however, many persons with disabilities are not aware of such programs (Asken, 1989). Although possibilities exist for sport psychology consultants to assist athletes with disabilities with mental-training strategies, few sport psychology consultants have be-come involved (Asken, 1989). Such a lack of involvement is not sur-prising given the dearth of sport psychology literature focusing on athletes with disabilities. With over 3,000 athletes participating in disabled sport in the United States (Henschen, Horvat, & Roswal, 1992), it is hardly an area for sport psychology consultants to ignore.

Many disabilities, including blindness, deafness, cerebral palsy, spinal cord injuries, amputations, and mental retardation or delay, do not prevent athletes from engaging in competitive sport (Asken, 1989). Asken cited a variety of competitive opportunities that exist for athletes with disabilities, with most sports being available. Recreational opportunities such as downhill skiing for blind athletes also are available, although clearly some alterations (e.g., a sighted guide) may be required. Physical activity is no longer merely a rehabilitative process.

Although persons with disabilities can partake in physical activity on a variety of levels, the information in this section focuses on competitive athletes with disabilities, because they are the ones most likely to seek sport psychology consultation. Since 1986, the U.S. Olympic Festival has offered opportunities for athletes with disabilities to compete (Paciorek, Jones, & Tetreault, 1991), as have the Olympics for the Physically Disabled, the Special Olympics, and the ParaOlympics. In addition, the United States Olympic Committee has made a commitment to athletes with disabilities by forming the Committee on Sport for the Disabled (COSD; Asken & Goodling, 1986).

Empirical Findings

Literature on athletes with disabilities has been lacking, with empirical information virtually nonexistent through the 1980s (Asken, 1989). During the 1990s, more research on athletes with disabilities has been conducted, although few studies exist that assist athletic personnel in understanding these athletes' experiences.

Much existing research has examined mood states of athletes with disabilities, often making comparisons with able-bodied athletes (e.g., Henschen, Horvat, & French, 1984; Horvat, Roswal, & Henschen, 1991). Mood states typically have been measured with the Profile of Mood States (POMS). "Healthier" competitors have been defined as those who display high vigor and low tension, depression, anger, fatigue, and confusion. This combination creates an "iceberg profile" and results in low overall mood disturbance scores (Henschen, Horvat, & Roswal, 1992).

Although some studies used "visual comparisons" rather than statistical methods to determine comparisons (e.g., Henschen et al., 1984), general findings indicate that male wheelchair-bound athletes exhibit similar mood states (high psychological health) to able-bodied athletes (Henschen et al., 1992; Horvat, French, & Henschen, 1986; Horvat, Roswal, Jacobs, & Gaunt, 1989). Horvat et al. (1991) extended these findings to disabled track and field athletes, swimmers, weightlifters, and table tennis players. In one study, Horvat et al. (1989) found no gender differences among wheelchair-bound athletes; however, Horvat et al. (1986) found that women had significantly higher mood disturbance scores (lower psychological health) than men, even though the women still exhibited an iceberg profile. Research on commitment has indicated that wheelchair marathon athletes have at least the same level of commitment to their sport as highly motivated able-bodied exercisers (Fung, 1992).

Research on other types of disabilities is even more sparse. Clark and Sachs (1991) measured the psychological skills of deaf athletes and noted that these athletes were more similar to than different from hearing athletes. Travis and Sachs (1991) discussed mentally retarded athletes and presented a case study to illustrate some appropriate intervention strategies for this population.

Intervention Strategies

Sport psychology techniques are underused with athletes with disabilities, and few if any sport psychology programs have been made available to this group of athletes (Asken, 1989, 1991). Thus, many opportunities exist for sport psychology consultants to work with athletes with disabilities.

One goal of competitive sport for persons with disabilities is to minimize the differences from sport with able-bodied persons as much as possible and maintain the same structure whenever feasible (Asken, 1991). Athletes with disabilities have some unique needs, however, and sport psychology consultants must have special knowledge in the following areas (Asken, 1991):

1. The psychology of physical disability and the physical and psychological trauma these athletes may have experienced.
2. The physiological and medical considerations unique to this population that can influence future injury and performance.
3. The complexities in motivation to compete, which range from the usual desires for challenge and fitness to denial of the physical disability.

4. Unique performance problems such as anxiety owing to a limitation caused by the disability.
5. The varied organizational structures of sports for persons with disabilities.
6. The social environment, which includes physical and social barriers.

According to Asken (1989), athletes with disabilities can use arousal control, concentration, goal setting, self talk, negative thought stopping, interpersonal–assertiveness skills training, and confidence enhancement similarly to able-bodied athletes. Some of these standard interventions may need to be adapted, however, depending on the disability. For instance, with a paralyzed athlete, progressive muscle relaxation presents a special concern because the athlete has no feeling in some areas. Research is needed to determine appropriate applications. With a blind athlete, standard mental imagery may not be a viable option and may need to be altered to fit the athlete's needs. Communication training may need to be adapted so that hearing-impaired athletes can participate.

Conclusion

In this chapter, we reviewed the influences of individual differences related to gender, race–ethnicity, sexual orientation, and physical disability on sport experiences and offered suggestions for working effectively with athletes from each group. Although becoming familiar with issues and characteristics specific to these four groups is important, it is essential that generalities not become the sole criterion for guiding assessment and intervention. Instead, we encouraged sport psychology consultants to approach athletes from these groups as individuals, recognizing that culture or group membership is but one important factor that defines each person.

References

Acosta, R. V., & Carpenter, L. J. (1992). As the years go by: Coaching opportunities in the 1990s. *Journal of Physical Education, Recreation, and Dance, 63,* 36–41.

Allison, M. T. (1991). Role conflict and the female athlete: Preoccupation with little grounding. *Journal of Applied Sport Psychology, 3,* 49–60.

American Psychological Association. (1975). Report on the task force on sex bias and sex-role stereotyping in psychotherapeutic practice. *American Psychologist, 30,* 1169–1175.

American Psychological Association. (1992). Ethical principles of psychologists and code of conduct. *American Psychologist, 47,* 1597–1611.

Anshel, M. H. (1990). Perceptions of Black intercollegiate football players: Implications for the sport psychology consultant. *The Sport Psychologist, 4,* 235–248.

Anshel, M. H., & Sailes, G. (1990). Discrepant attitudes of intercollegiate team athletes as a function of race. *Journal of Sport Behavior, 13,* 68–77

Anthrop, J., & Allison, M. T. (1983). Role conflict and the high school female athlete. *Research Quarterly for Exercise and Sport, 54,* 104–111

Asken, M. J. (1989). Sport psychology and the physically disabled athletes: Interview with Michael D. Goodling, OTR/L. *The Sport Psychologist, 3,* 166–176.

Asken, M. J. (1991). The challenge of the physically challenged: Delivering sport psychology services to physically disabled athletes. *The Sport Psychologist, 5,* 370–381.

Asken, M. J., & Goodling, M. D. (1986). Sport psychology: I. An introduction and overview. *Sports 'n Spokes, 12,* 12–15.

Association for the Advancement of Applied Sport Psychology. (1994). *Ethical principles of the Association for the Advancement of Applied Sport Psychology.* [Brochure]. Boise, ID: Author.

Atkinson, D. R., Morten, G., & Sue, D. W. (1993). *Counseling American minorities: A cross-cultural perspective.* Dubuque, IA: Brown & Benchmark.

Barcelona gold: African-American athletes win medals and acclaim during the XXV Olympiad. (1992, October). *Ebony,* pp. 30–32.

Before Jackie. (1992, August). *Ebony,* pp. 34–36.

The best in their field. (1993, July). *Hispanic Business,* pp. 52–56.

Blacks in sports. (1992, August). *Ebony,* p. 26.

Cass, V. C. (1979). Homosexual identity formation: A theoretical model. *Journal of Homosexuality, 4,* 219–235.

Chartrand, J. M., & Lent, R. W. (1987). Sport counseling: Enhancing the development of the student-athlete. *Journal of Counseling and Development, 66,* 164–166.

Clark, D. (1987). *The new loving someone gay.* Berkeley, CA: Celestial Arts.

Clark, R. A., & Sachs, M. L. (1991). Challenges and opportunities in psychological skills training in deaf athletes. *The Sport Psychologist, 5,* 392–398.

Coakley, J. J. (1990). *Sport in society: Issues and controversies.* St. Louis: Times Mirror/ Mosby.

Cogan, K. D., & Petrie, T. A. (1993, October). *Counseling women athletes: Issues and strategies.* Paper presented at the annual meeting of the Association for the Advancement of Applied Sport Psychology. Montreal, Quebec, Canada.

Cogan, K. D., & Petrie, T. A. (in press). Counseling women college student-athletes. In E. Etzel, A. Ferrante, & J. Pinkney (Eds.), *Counseling college student-athletes* (2nd ed.). Morgantown, WV: Fitness Information Technology.

Csizma, K. A., Wittig, A. F., & Schurr, K. T. (1988). Sport stereotypes and gender. *Journal of Sport & Exercise Psychology, 10,* 62–74.

Curry, T. J., & Jiobu, R. M. (1984). *Sports: A social perspective.* Englewood Cliffs, NJ: Prentice-Hall.

Davis, L. (1990). The articulation of difference: White preoccupation with the question of racially linked genetic differences among athletes. *Sociology of Sport Journal, 7,* 179–187.

Desertrain, G. S., & Weiss, M. R. (1988). Being female and athletic: A cause for conflict? *Sex Roles, 18,* 567–582.

Duda, J. L. (1991). Perspectives on gender roles in physical activity. *Journal of Applied Sport Psychology, 3,* 1–6.

Duquin, M. (1978). The androgynous advantage. In C. Oglesby (Ed.), *Women in sport: From myth to reality* (pp. 89–106). Philadelphia: Lea & Febiger.

Eccles (Parsons), J., Adler, T. F., Futterman, R., Goff, S. B., Kaczala, C. M., Meece, J. L., & Midgley, C. (1983). Expectations, values and academic behaviors. In J. T. Spence (Ed.), *Achievement and achievement motives: Psychological and sociological approaches* (pp. 75–146). New York: Freeman.

Eccles, J. S., & Herold, R. D. (1991). Gender differences in sport involvement: Applying the Eccles' expectancy-value model. *Journal of Applied Sport Psychology, 3,* 7–35.

Felshin, J. (1974). The dialectics of women and sport. In E. Gerber, J. Felshin, P. Berlin, & W. Wyrick (Eds.), *The American woman in sport* (pp. 179–210). Reading, MA: Addison-Wesley.

Fitzgerald, L. F., & Nutt, R. (1986). The Division 17 principles concerning the counseling/psychotherapy of women: Rationale and implementation. *The Counseling Psychologist, 14,* 180–216.

Fung, L. (1992). Commitment to training among wheelchair marathon athletes. *International Journal of Sport Psychology, 21,* 138–146.

Garnets, L., Hancock, K. A., Cochran, S. D., Goodchilds, J., & Peplau, L. A. (1991). Issues in psychotherapy with lesbians and gay men: A survey of psychologists. *American Psychologist, 46,* 964–972.

Gill, D. L. (1994). A feminist perspective on sport psychology practice. *The Sport Psychologist, 8,* 411–426.

Gonsiorek, J. C., & Weinrich, J. D. (1991). The definition and scope of sexual orientation. In J. C. Gonsiorek & J. D. Weinrich (Eds.), *Homosexuality: Research implications for public policy* (pp. 1–12). Newbury Park, CA: Sage.

Gould, D., Tammen, V., Murphy, S., & May, J. (1989). An examination of U.S. Olympic sport psychology consultants and the services they provide. *The Sport Psychologist, 3,* 300–312.

Griffin, P. (1994). Homophobia in sport: Addressing the needs of lesbian and gay high school athletes. *The High School Journal, 77,* 80–87.

Harris, D. (1979). Female sport today: Psychological considerations. *International Journal of Sport Psychology, 10,* 168–172.

Helms, J. E. (1984). Toward a theoretical explanation of the effects of race on counseling: A black and white model. *The Counseling Psychologist, 12,* 153–164.

Henschen, K., Horvat, M., & French, R. (1984). A visual comparison of psychological profiles between able-bodied and wheelchair athletes. *Adapted Physical Activity Quarterly, 1,* 118–124.

Henschen, K., Horvat, M., & Roswal, G. (1992). Psychological profiles of the United States wheelchair basketball team. *International Journal of Sport Psychology, 23,* 128–137.

Heyman, S. R. (1986). Psychological problem patterns found with athletes. *The Clinical Psychologist, 39,* 68–71.

Horvat, M., French, R., & Henschen, K. (1986). A comparison of the psychological characteristics of male and female able-bodied and wheelchair athletes. *Paraplegia, 24,* 115–122.

Horvat, M., Roswal, G., & Henschen, K. (1991). In the field: Psychological profiles of disabled male athletes before and after competition. *Clinical Kinesiology, 45,* 14–18.

Horvat, M., Roswal, G., Jacobs, D., & Gaunt, S. (1989). Selected psychological comparisons of able-bodied and disabled athletes. *The Physical Educator, 45,* 202–208.

Howard-Hamilton, M. (1993). African-American female athletes: Issues and implications for educators. *NASPA Journal, 30,* 153–159.

Hyde, J. S. (1992). *Half the human experience: The psychology of women* (2nd ed.). Lexington, MA: Heath.

Johnston, F. (1994, October). *Breaking the silence: Gays and lesbians in sport.* Paper presented at the annual meeting of the Association for the Advancement of Applied Sport Psychology, Lake Tahoe, NV.

Kane, M. J. (1988). The female athletic role as a status determinant within the social systems of high school adolescents. *Adolescence, 23,* 253–264.

Krane, V. (1994). A feminist perspective on contemporary sport psychology practice. *The Sport Psychologist, 8,* 393–410.

Krane, V., & Vealey, R. (1994, October). *Transforming the silence on lesbianism in sport.* Paper presented at the annual meeting of the Association for the Advancement of Applied Sport Psychology, Lake Tahoe, NV.

Lee, C. C., & Rotella, R. J. (1991). Special concerns and considerations for sport psychology consulting with black student athletes. *The Sport Psychologist, 5,* 365–369.

Lenskyj, H. (1991). Combating homophobia in sport and physical education. *Sociology of Sport Journal, 8,* 61–69.

Melnick, M. J., Sabo, D. F., & Vanfossen, B. (1992). Educational effects of interscholastic athlete participation on African-American and Hispanic youths. *Adolescence, 27,* 295–308.

Meyer, B. (1990). From idealism to actualization: The academic performance of female collegiate athletes. *Sociology of Sport Journal, 7,* 44–57.

Oglesby, C. A. (1983). Interactions between gender identity and sport. In J. M. Silva & R. S. Weinberg (Eds.), *Psychological foundations of sport* (pp. 387–399). Champaign, IL: Human Kinetics.

Ortner, S. (1974). Is female to male as nature is to culture? In M. Rosaldo & L. Lamphere (Eds.), *Woman, culture and society* (pp. 67–87). Stanford, CA: Stanford University Press.

Paciorek, M. J., Jones, J., & Tetreault, P. (1991). Disabled athlete participation at the 1990 U.S. Olympic Festival. *Palaestra, 7,* 18–25.

Parham, T. A. (1989). Cycles of psychological nigrescence. *The Counseling Psychologist, 17,* 187–226.

Parham, W. D. (1993). The intercollegiate athlete: A 1990s profile. *The Counseling Psychologist, 21,* 411–429.

Pedersen, D. M., & Kono, D. M. (1990). Perceived effects on femininity of the participation of women in sport. *Perceptual and Motor Skills, 71,* 783–792.

Rader, B. G. (1983). *American sports: From the age of folk games to the age of spectators.* Englewood Cliffs, NJ: Prentice-Hall.

Rotella, R., & Murray, M. (1991). Homophobia, the world of sport, and sport psychology consulting. *The Sport Psychologist, 5,* 355–364.

Sage, G. H., & Loudermilk, S. (1979). The female athlete and role conflict. *Research Quarterly, 50,* 88–96.

Scales, J. (1991). African-American student athletes: An example of minority exploitations in collegiate athletics. In E. Etzel, A. P. Ferrante, & J. Pinkney (Eds.), *Counseling college student-athletes: Issues and interventions.* Morgantown, WV: Fitness Information Technology.

Snyder, E. E., & Spreitzer, E. (1983). Change and variation in the social acceptance of female participation in sports. *Journal of Sport Behavior, 6,* 3–8.

Speight, S. L., Myers, L. J., Cox, C. I., & Highlen, P. S. (1991). A redefinition of multicultural counseling. *Journal of Counseling and Development, 70,* 29–36.

Spreitzer, E., & Snyder, E. E. (1990). Sports within the Black subculture: A matter of social class or a distinctive subculture? *Journal of Sport and Social Issues, 14,* 48–58.

Sue, D., Bernier, J., Durran, A., Feinberg, L., Pederson, P., Smith, E., & Vasquez-Nuttal, E. (1982). Position paper: Cross-cultural counseling competencies. *The Counseling Psychologist, 10,* 45–52.

Sue, D. W., & Sue, D. (1990). *Counseling the culturally different: Theory and practice.* New York: Wiley.

Travis, C. A., & Sachs, M. L. (1991). Applied sport psychology and persons with mental retardation. *The Sport Psychologist, 5,* 382–391.

Troiden, R. R. (1989). The formation of homosexual identities. *Journal of Homosexuality, 17,* 41–73.

Trusdell, B. (1991, January/February). Getting in the game. *Hispanic,* pp. 24–26.

Weiss, M. R., & Glenn, S. D. (1992). Psychological development and female sport participation: An interactional perspective. *Quest, 44,* 138–157.

Wiggins, D. K. (1991). Prized performers but frequently overlooked students: The involvement of Black athletes in intercollegiate sports on predominantly white university campuses, 1890–1972. *Research Quarterly for Exercise and Sport, 62,* 164–177.

Yambor, J., & Connelly, D. (1991). Issues confronting female sport psychology consultants working with male student athletes. *The Sport Psychologist, 5,* 304–312.

Part Five

Professional Issues

Education and Training in Sport and Exercise Psychology

Penny McCullagh and John M. Noble

In recent years, the term *sport psychologist* has been used with increasing frequency in sport as well as academic settings. Combining the domain areas of sport and psychology is intuitively appealing, and the methods for defining and becoming a sport psychologist are varied. These concerns are not necessarily new. In 1925, Coleman Griffith stated that "although a great many men have hitherto used the words 'psychology' and 'athletics' in the same sentence, no one has, until the present, undertaken a thorough survey of all that might be done in the field" (p. 193). Griffith (1925) then went on to suggest that there were three ways psychologists could contribute to the area of athletics. One way was to demonstrate to young coaches the psychological principles practiced by experienced coaches. The second was to apply principles discovered in the laboratory to athletics. The third was for psychologists to bring a scientific approach to the area of coaching. Thus, the interdisciplinary nature of psychology and physical activity has a well-established history, although the development of the field has only recently begun. The purpose of this chapter is to highlight the educational and career paths available to the aspiring sport and exercise psychologist.

People frequently ask for a definition of a sport psychologist. The term *sport psychologist* itself is problematic. Because the term *psychologist* is restricted by laws in each state in the United States and typically refers only to individuals schooled in mainstream psychology, individuals with training emphasis in sport and exercise should not technically be called a psychologist. For simplification, we use the term *sport psychologist* in a broad sense to refer to individuals working from either a research or an applied perspective in the area of human movement. It should be emphasized that the practice can extend well beyond the sport environment and include exercise, rehabilitation, or basic movement settings (Rejeski & Brawley, 1988). For this reason, the term *sport psychologist* may not be the most appropriate.

Sport psychologists typically receive their degrees from either a psychology department or a kinesiology–physical education department. Recommending direction toward one department or another is difficult. The choice depends on a variety of issues, most notably specific career goals and interests. The purpose of this chapter is to identify potential educational paths and the careers they lead toward. Because much of the early course work in sport psychology was offered in kinesiology-related departments (e.g., physical education, sport science, movement science), we focus first on typical training within this discipline.

Psychological Kinesiology

Although many believe that the field of sport psychology has emerged only in the last decade, this view is refuted by the previous quotation of Griffith (1925). Furthermore, as early as the 1960s, sport psychology classes were being offered in numerous physical education programs across the country. An examination of early textbooks in the field reflects the academic content of sport psychology in the 1960s and 1970s (e.g., Cratty, 1968; Lawther, 1972; Martens, 1975; Morgan, 1970; Singer, 1975). Many of these early classes had as a primary goal to facilitate the application of psychological principles to teaching and coaching. As physical education departments moved from a strong pedagogical (teacher preparation) focus to a research-oriented focus, the role of sport psychology within these departments also evidenced a change. During this period, many departments of physical education selected other names such as exercise science, movement science, sport science, and kinesiology to reflect this research emphasis. For the purposes of this chapter, the term *kinesiology* refers to the broad realm of movement-oriented science departments.

The early emphasis of sport psychology within kinesiology departments is reflected in the establishment of academic societies and scholarly conferences devoted to sport psychology, which were developed from within this discipline. The International Society of Sport Psychology (ISSP) first met in Rome in 1965, and the North American Society for the Psychology of Sport and Physical Activity (NASPSPA) was organized in 1967. The *International Journal of Sport Psychology* was established in 1970 and the *Journal of Sport Psychology* in 1979. These organizations and journals initially were devoted to the development of a knowledge base of information concerning sport psychology and the dissemination of that information, and they continue to serve that purpose today.

Undergraduate Training

Before they begin specific training in sport psychology, students at the undergraduate level should receive a broad-based education in movement-related fields. Basic courses at the undergraduate level include exercise physiology, biomechanics, motor learning and control, sport sociology, and sport and exercise psychology. Depending on the academic focus of the department, many programs offer specialized tracks that prepare students for professional careers. For example, programs may prepare students for athletic training, fitness management, coaching, teaching physical education, sport administration, and so on. Other programs are not professionally based and provide a liberal arts degree that may lead to graduate training in medically related fields (e.g., physical therapy, physician assistant programs, occupational therapy, nursing, or medicine) or in research within the field of kinesiology. Regardless of the focus of the program, most departments offer an undergraduate course in sport psychology that may be titled Psychology of Physical Activity, Sport and Exercise Psychology, or Psychological Basis of Human Movement.

Questions frequently arise about the rationale for taking movement-related courses that cover information beyond the psychology of sport and exercise. This may be best explained by briefly describing each of these areas and their importance to the sport psychologist. *Exercise physiology* is the study of body function during exercise. Exercise physiology attempts to answer such questions as, "What are the limits of physical performance? Is it possible to run the 100-meter dash in 9 seconds? Can the routines of Olympic gymnasts become more complex and better executed than they are now?" (Brooks & Fahey, 1985, p. 1).

Although these questions highlight the importance of exercise physiology, their answers provide essential background information for the aspiring sport and exercise psychologist. Because exercise physiology is dependent on other disciplines such as anatomy, physiology, and biochemistry, many universities require course work in these basic disciplines as a prerequisite to an exercise physiology course. Although the topics covered in the courses vary, several issues are especially relevant for individuals interested in sport and exercise psychology. For example, to consult with an athlete who is striving to reach optimal performance, understanding the basic mechanisms of physical training is essential. If an athlete has reached an apparent "plateau" in performance, the knowledgeable sport psychologist can discern whether physical overtraining or some psychological phenomenon is the issue of concern. Thus, issues revolving around body composition, nutrition, training in different altitudes or other environmental conditions, fatigue, sex differences, and special populations are essential to exercise physiologists as well as sport psychologists.

"The internal and external sources acting on a human body and the effects produced by these forces" are known as *biomechanics* (Hay, 1985, p. xv). A primary emphasis in biomechanics is on human structure or anatomy and how the body functions mechanically. Topics covered include linear motion, projectile motion, angular motion, flotation, and center of gravity. Determining what is mechanically unsound about a particular movement pattern is primarily the domain of coaches and biomechanists. However, for communication purposes, it is essential for the sport and exercise psychologist to understand these topics.

> For many, there are few things as exciting as a close race, match, or game where the competitors demonstrate nearly incredible levels of skill to achieve victory. And, for many, there are few things as satisfying as having been committed to a long-term program of training and skill learning, and then experiencing the thrill of achieving the goal in an important performance. (Schmidt, 1991, p. vii)

An examination of the processes underlying the principles of skilled learning and performance in teaching, coaching, and rehabilitation settings is the focus of many undergraduate courses in *motor learning and control.* Information processing and attention, the role of feedback in motor skill learning, strategies for designing effective practice sessions, and the assessment of motor memory are central issues to this field.

In contrast to exercise physiology, biomechanics, and motor learning and control, *sport sociology* focuses at a macroscopic level on categories or groups of people. Sport sociologists examine the connection between sports and other spheres of social life including family, education, social class, ethnicity, disability, economy, and religion (Coakley, 1994). Other topics of interest include socialization factors, drug use, aggression, and media or political issues. Knowledge about these topics might prove invaluable for a practicing sport and exercise psychologist.

Typical *sport and exercise psychology* classes within kinesiology departments focus on the research and application of psychological principles in movement, sport, and exercise settings. Specifically, these courses focus on antecedent variables that may predispose an individual to engage in physical activity or on the consequences of participation in physical activity for a host of psychological characteristics. Basic topics covered may include anxiety and arousal effects on physical activity, attention, motivation, gender differences, aggression, group dynamics, modeling, socialization, and exercise adherence. Application of mental imagery, goal setting, and relaxation skills to physical activity settings are also likely to be included.

Although the aforementioned courses cover the basics, numerous other classes add to a movement-based education. Courses in sports medicine that focus on injury prevention and rehabilitation, sport nutrition, and the teaching of sport skills all may be useful to the sport psychologist. The primary purpose of these classes is not to establish competencies in these areas, but rather to ensure basic knowledge to enhance communication with clients and coaches.

Graduate Training

At the graduate level, training in sport and exercise psychology becomes more specialized. Typically, students complete a master's degree before being selected for a PhD program. To gain admission to a master's program, students generally must provide evidence that they have completed prerequisites in the previously mentioned kinesiology-based courses. If students come from another discipline such as psychology, they may need to complete these courses as part of their graduate training. The course offerings in graduate programs and the focus of programs are diverse. Programs tend to take either a basic research approach to the topic of sport and exercise psychology, an applied approach in which emphasis is on interventions to enhance performance, or some combination of research and application. Interested students should carefully weigh the pros and cons of each approach to determine how each will enhance their goals. Individuals are advised to examine carefully the *Directory of Graduate Programs in Applied Sport Psychology* (Sachs, Burke, & Butcher, 1995) as well as *The World Sport Psychology Sourcebook* (Salmela, 1992) for more information on specific programs. The *Graduate Training and Career Possibilities in Exercise and Sport Psychology* brochure (APA, 1994) is also a useful source of information.

A typical graduate program (master's or PhD) in psychological kinesiology includes courses in research methods and statistics, motor behavior (motor development, motor learning and control), and other advanced kinesiology subjects (biomechanics, exercise physiology, sport sociology), as well as supportive courses outside the discipline in sociology, psychology, educational psychology, or perhaps anthropology. At the graduate level, students often enroll in two or more sport psychology courses that focus on topics such as applied issues in sport psychology, youth sport, social psychological aspects of physical activity, psychophysiological approaches, or exercise motivation. Depending on the focus of the program, students can engage in internships working in sport or exercise settings under the supervision of an advisor.

Because the field of sport and exercise psychology is intimately tied to the disciplines of both kinesiology and psychology, it is wise to heed the advice of Coleman Griffith, given 70 years ago, and recognize that "the athlete who goes into a contest is a mind–body organism and not merely a physiological machine" (1925, p. 193). Of course, this statement could be applicable to involvement in exercise as well as sports. Therefore, we suggest that those working in the area have knowledge about the movement domain as well as psychology.

One of the basic purposes of most graduate programs in kinesiology departments is to conduct research. At the PhD level, students may become involved with various aspects of their advisor's research program before moving on to more independent research experiences. Training students to conduct presentable and publishable research in an ethical fashion are important concerns within a graduate program. The advisor's primary role is to mentor students for a future career. A recent survey of 175 sport psychology graduate students indicated that students were quite pleased with the current level of training in research and writing for publications and presentations (Butki & Andersen, 1994). In terms of ethics, however, students expressed concern about their training. A perusal of the following papers may help fill this apparent void. The topic of ethical considerations across a wide variety of academic settings including human and animal research, teaching, and advising was addressed by The Academy of Kinesiology and Physical Education, and an entire issue of *Quest* was devoted to these topics. Articles by both Berger (1993) and Roberts (1993) in that issue highlighted ethical considerations in the advisor–advisee relationship, and a recent paper by Andersen (1994) on supervision in sport psychology reinforced the importance of examining supervision practices within the field.

Training in the applied aspects, or provision of services, varies widely depending on the program. Typical service provision includes presenting techniques such as goal setting, imagery, relaxation, and coping with stress to groups and individuals. Some sport and exercise psychology supervisors have developed opportunities for their graduate students to work in applied settings at local high schools, on campus, or at other universities (Van Raalte et al., 1994). Some graduate programs offer no opportunities for students to engage in applied practices, and if the students in these programs decide to offer services, they probably do so without any supervision. We believe that allowing students to practice without adequate supervision is not acceptable. Identifying suitable sport and exercise psychology supervisors may be difficult considering that recent reviews of supervision in sport psychology indicate that a majority of supervisors (56%) have never been supervised in their own work (Andersen, Van Raalte, & Brewer, 1994). Suggestions for improved supervision in the field include requiring faculty to audit graduate courses on supervision or continuing education courses and requiring more empirical examinations (Andersen et al., 1994).

Employment Opportunities

The primary employment opportunity for individuals trained in psychological kinesiology at the PhD level is an academic position. These academic positions may or may not involve opportunities to work with individuals in performance-enhancement settings. The primary responsibilities of academicians are research, teaching, and service, and the relative importance of these responsibilities varies from institution to institution. For example, although some departments may view delivery of sport and exercise psychology services as a viable function that contributes to tenure and promotion, other universities place heavy emphasis on data-based research published in refereed journals. Most academic positions require teaching in sport and exercise psychology, and many also include teaching in other, related fields (e.g., statistics, motor learning).

Examination of the characteristics of individuals publishing in sport and exercise psychology journals indicates a shift over the last decade. In the first 6 years of the existence of the *Journal of Sport & Exercise Psychology* (renamed from the *Journal of Sport Psychology*) (1979–1985), 65% of the contributing authors were from kinesiology–physical education departments and 21% were from psychology programs (Landers, Boutcher, & Wang, 1986). During the period from 1985 to 1990, only 54% of the papers came from kinesiology–physical education departments, 29% from psychology departments, and 18% from other areas (sociology, medicine, business, counseling) (Gill, 1992). These trends may be indicative of the growing interest in sport psychology in mainstream psychology. Most of the academic jobs with an emphasis in sport psychology, however, are in kinesiology departments rather than psychology departments.

Academic applied sport psychologists can do applied work with the athletic teams on campus, provide information to youth sport leagues, and work with individual athletes. Consultation with sports medicine and physical therapy clinics is also a potential means of providing applied services. Because individuals trained in psychological kinesiology are not qualified to deal with clinical issues (e.g., eating disorders, depression), their primary role is one of education or performance enhancement.

Another opportunity for people trained in kinesiology is to conduct research in medical laboratories or as part of a medical team. Basic research issues as well as application of services related to exercise participation or rehabilitation might be a prime focus for such individuals. Psychological aspects of rehabilitation from injury, adherence to exercise during the cardiac rehabilitation process, or effective stress-management techniques are all possible research and application topics.

Although the preceding career opportunities are probably the most prevalent ones for individuals trained in kinesiology, alternative possibilities exist that depend on the specific training and talents of the individual. These alternatives include jobs in coaching, corporate fitness, or other allied health fields.

Psychology

Undergraduate Training

Most psychology departments are housed in a College of Arts and Sciences and provide students with a liberal arts undergraduate degree. A psychology degree provides a broad understanding of the content, concepts and research methods of contemporary psychology. *Psychology*, recognized as a fairly young science, has been defined in numerous ways; one recent definition is "the scientific study of behavior and mental processes" (Atkinson, Atkinson, Smith, & Hilgard, 1987, p. 13). Psychologists can serve a variety of functions, and an array of course work and specialty areas is necessary to encompass the field adequately.

Students at the undergraduate level select courses from a variety of options spanning a wide range of subdisciplines. Courses in *biological psychology* examine the relationship between biological processes and behavior. The influence of specific hormones on behavior and the study of drugs and behavior are topics of relevance for biological psychologists. *Cognitive psychology* is concerned with topics related to attention, perception, memory, learning, and decision making. Determining how experts acquire high levels of skill is a basic research question of a cognitive scientist (e.g., Ericsson & Charness, 1994). *Educational psychology* is closely linked to cognitive psychology but emphasizes cognitive aspects involved in learning and teaching. *Industrial and organizational psychology* is primarily concerned with management or leadership structures in groups as well as developing selection criteria for successful job performance. *Social psychology* examines interpersonal processes and how interactions among individuals influence attitudes and behaviors. Cultural and gender differences, self-perceptions, and social learning are all relevant topics to the social psychologist. *Developmental psychology* addresses physical, cognitive, and social development across the life span.

Typically, undergraduate students take course work across this entire spectrum of psychology. Of course, the emphasis and course offerings vary depending on the expertise of faculty members at the college or university. The emphasis in psychology departments typically does not include human movement issues, particularly sport and exercise. However, a recent survey of psychology department chairpersons revealed that only 15% of 102 respondents offered an undergraduate course in sport psychology (LeUnes & Hayward, 1990). The majority of such courses are offered in kinesiology departments. Recently, psychologists have begun to examine exercise-related issues from a health psychology perspective (a field with great relevance to sport psychology). Interested readers should peruse issues of *Health Psychology*, a journal published by the American Psychological Association to address many of these issues.

Graduate Training and Employment Opportunities

Graduate students in psychology departments focus on any one of the previously mentioned specialization areas. This graduate training prepares students for an academic career, a research career in a clinical institute, or perhaps a career in business (especially for industrial–organizational psychologists). Consultation with athletes may occur, but this feature is typically a minimal part of employment or lies entirely outside regular employment. As previously noted, most psychology departments do not offer course work in sport psychology, so that training in sport psychology must be obtained elsewhere.

Graduate students interested in applied sport psychology may choose to earn a PhD or PsyD degree in clinical or counseling psychology. The PsyD is a relatively new degree, designed for people who want to engage in applied practice with less emphasis on research. It should be noted that entrance to clinical and counseling psychology programs is extremely competitive. Many programs have as many as 500 applicants for only five or six positions. *Clinical psychology* is the "application of psychological principles to the diagnosis and treatment of emotional and behavioral problems" (Atkinson et al., 1987, p. 15). Clinical psychologists typically work with people with mental illness, personality disorders, criminal behavior, drug addiction, eating disorders, or other behavior problems. Clinical psychologists work in mental hospitals, juvenile courts, mental health clinics, prisons, medical schools, or private practice. *Counseling psychologists* work with similar populations but usually deal with less serious problems and help individuals deal with social adjustments or vocational issues. Although some psychology faculty members may have interest in sport and exercise psychology (LeUnes & Hayward, 1990), it is clearly not the main focus of most programs. Students who want to pursue a counseling or clinical degree and apply some of their knowledge to athletes should carefully discuss these options with faculty advisors before choosing a program. Once a program is selected, students must obtain sufficient knowledge in the kinesiological sciences to facilitate this application. To obtain further information about graduate training in psychology, one may consult *The Complete Guide to Graduate School Admission: Psychology and Related Fields* (Keith-Spiegel, 1991).

Supervised practicums in psychology begin as early as the first year and typically culminate with a year-long supervised internship. The American Psychological Association accredits programs and publishes a yearly list in the December issue of the *American Psychologist.* Combining a degree in psychology with course work in exercise and sport psychology prepares individuals to work with both athlete and nonathlete populations. Because few individuals earn a living consulting only with athletes, this career option provides a viable opportunity to earn the major portion of income from other sources (e.g., consulting with businesses or medical clinics). The United States Olympic Committee and some universities have hired sport psychologists to work with their athletes on a full-time basis, but these positions are limited.

There are some employment possibilities for individuals who complete their graduate training before obtaining the PhD. For example, a master's degree in clinical or counseling psychology (with course work in kinesiology) or a master's degree in kinesiology (with course work in psychology) prepares a person to work in academic advising, health promotion, or coaching. People with master's degrees may *not* be labeled as psychologists nor will they have the necessary credentials to obtain the status of "certified consultant" by the Association for the Advancement of Applied Sport Psychology (AAASP). See chapter 18, this volume.

Integration

For a person to be well equipped to deal with sport and exercise psychology issues, it is imperative to have training in both psychology and kinesiology. Depending on the specific career path chosen, the emphasis of these disciplines varies. Persons interested in applying interventions, whether they come from a psychological or kinesiological background, need to understand the research process to evaluate the effectiveness of their interventions. For example, an individual wanting to help an athlete cope with stress needs sufficient psychological knowledge about coping behaviors and sources of stress as well as knowledge about the particular sport they are dealing with. Likewise, researchers

Figure 1

ACADEMIC BACKGROUND

Primary Interest Area	Kinesiology or Nonclinical Psychology		Clinical or Counseling Psychology	
	Potential Areas of Employment	Typical Issues	Potential Areas of Employment	Typical Issues
Research	1. Academic 2. Medical setting 3. Part-time consultation w/athletic teams, youth sport, etc.	1. Testing models/theories 2. Developing inventories 3. Scientific method of data collection 4. Data analysis 5. Publication of results 6. Undergraduate and graduate teaching 7. Training doctoral students	1. Academic 2. Clinical institution	1. Testing models/theories 2. Developing inventories 3. Scientific method of data collection 4. Data analysis 5. Publication of results 6. Undergraduate and graduate teaching 7. Testing of hypothesized interventions 8. Training of doctoral students to become clinicians

Practice	1. Part-time academic
	2. Allied health field
	3. Coaching clinics
		1. Group work with players on a team
		2. Work with coaches
		3. Issues related to performance enhancement
		  - anxiety reduction
		  - goal setting
		  - attentional focus
		  - preperformance plans
			1. Academic (part- or full-time)
			2. Private practice
			3. Hospital
			4. Clinic
			5. Law enforcement
				1. Underlying personality constructs accounting for performance deficits
				2. Individualized, personalized, consulting/counseling; sport or nonsport related:
				  - family problems
				  - marital problems
				  - eating disorders
				  - stress issues

Employment areas and typical issues addressed by sport psychologists with various academic backgrounds.

need to understand and help impart the practical applications of the knowledge they generate. Although it is not necessary to obtain a degree in both psychology and kinesiology, it is imperative to receive adequate training in both areas to fulfill the likely requirements of future employment in sport and exercise psychology. For more information on this issue, see Taylor (1991).

Figure 1 provides a taxonomy for the education and roles of individuals trained in psychology and kinesiology with interests in research or practice. Sage advice would be to determine carefully where one wants to work in this classification and follow the appropriate educational route to achieve that goal. Although these appear to be four mutually exclusive categories, anyone operating within the field of sport and exercise psychology should have knowledge of the other quadrants. It should also be noted that the same general issue might be examined from the perspective of someone working within any of the quadrants. For example, the psychological factors associated with sport and exercise injury is currently a popular topic that may fall within any one of these categories.

A number of significant issues are currently of concern in the field of sport and exercise psychology. These issues are discussed elsewhere in this volume. Some of these issues have been discussed and debated for a number of years and others have only recently surfaced. These professional issues include accreditation of sport psychology programs, certification as a sport psychologist, the realm of sport psychology, ethical principles involved in the practice of applied sport psychology, and defining of the field. Many of these issues became prevalent in the late 1970s and 1980s with the publication of new journals devoted to the psychology of sport and physical activity (see, for example, Danish & Hale, 1981, 1982; Dishman, 1983; Harrison & Feltz, 1979; Heyman, 1982; and Nideffer, DuFresne, Nesvig, & Selder, 1980). Others are newer concerns and are debated in journals and newsletters and at annual conventions.

Professional Organizations and Journals in Sport Psychology

Since the birth of the ISSP in 1965, a number of professional organizations have been formed to represent sport psychologists as well as the profession as a whole. LeUnes and Nation (1989) listed 11 professional organizations involved in sport psychology, although some of these

Exhibit 1

Professional Organizations Dealing Entirely or Partially with Sport and Exercise Psychology

American Alliance for Health, Physical Education, Recreation and Dance (AAHPERD, Sport Psychology Academy)
This large organization has one small section devoted to sport psychology. AAHPERD, 1900 Association Drive, Reston, VA 22091.

American College of Sports Medicine (ACSM)
This large society focuses on numerous subdisciplines including exercise physiology, biomechanics, sport psychology, fitness, wellness, and other areas. ACSM, 401 West Michigan Street, Indianapolis, IN 46202-3233.

American Psychological Association (APA)
This is a large organization of which two sections have particular relevance for exercise and sport psychology: Division 47 (exercise and sport psychology) and Division 38 (health psychology). APA, 750 First Street, NE, Washington, DC 20002-4242.

Association for the Advancement of Applied Sport Psychology (AAASP)*
This society is devoted entirely to sport psychology with three distinct interest areas: health psychology, social psychology, and performance enhancement.

Canadian Society for Psychomotor Learning and Sport Psychology (CSPLSP)*
This organization is the Canadian counterpart of NASPSPA and focuses on motor learning and control, motor development, and sport psychology.

International Society for Sport Psychology (ISSP)*
This international society focuses on motor learning and control, motor development, and sport psychology.

North American Society for the Psychology of Sport and Physical Activity (NASPSPA)*
This organization focuses on motor learning and control, sport psychology, and motor development.

*These organizations do not have permanent addresses because individuals in charge of memberships rotate every 2–4 years. Individuals should check the *Encyclopedia of Associations*, published on an annual basis by Gale Research Inc., Washington, DC.

maintain only cursory interest in sport psychology. The NASPSPA, an influential national organization that originated in 1965 with 10 charter members, primarily focuses on research in sport psychology, motor learning and control, and motor development. The Canadian counterpart to NASPSPA, the Canadian Society for Psychomotor Learning and Sport Psychology (CSPLSP), was started in 1969 as a means of representing the Canadian interests in the field. As a response to a growing

---

Exhibit 2

Journals Dealing Primarily With Sport and Exercise Psychology Issues

International Journal of Sport Psychology
Official publication of the International Society of Sport Psychology (ISSP). Publisher: Pozzi, Rome, Italy. Began in 1970.

Journal of Applied Sport Psychology
Official publication of the Association for the Advancement of Applied Sport Psychology (AAASP). Publisher: Allen Press, Inc., Lawrence, KS. Began in 1989.

Journal of Sport & Exercise Psychology
Official publication of the North American Society for the Psychology of Sport and Physical Activity (NASPSPA). Publisher: Human Kinetics, Champaign, IL. Began in 1979.

Journal of Sport Behavior
Publisher: United States Sports Academy, Mobile, AL. Began in 1978.

The Sport Psychologist
Official publication of the International Society of Sport Psychology (ISSP). Publisher: Human Kinetics, Champaign, IL. Began in 1987.

---

concern with professional issues and the delivery of services in sport psychology, the AAASP was started in 1985. The AAASP is composed of three major sections: social psychology, health psychology, and intervention–performance enhancement. The American Psychological Association (APA), with over 81,000 members, recently established a 47th division, the Division of Exercise and Sport Psychology. The American College of Sports Medicine also has an active membership of individuals interested in sport and exercise psychology. The American Alliance for Health, Physical Education, Recreation, and Dance (AAHPERD) has 2,000 members who select sport psychology as a primary interest area. With the exception of the ISSP, which convenes for international meetings on a quadrennial basis, each of these organizations meets for an annual conference. For a listing of organizations that deal with sport and exercise psychology, please refer to Exhibit 1.

There are a number of professional journals that are devoted specifically to the research, practice, or other professional issues of sport psychology. Journal names, publishers, and subscription information are provided in Exhibit 2. Many university libraries carry these journals. Besides these specific sport psychology journals, a number of sport,

---

Exhibit 3

Journals Dealing Frequently with Sport and Exercise Psychology Issues

Medicine and Science in Sports and Exercise
Official journal of the American College of Sports Medicine (ACSM). Publisher: American College of Sports Medicine, Madison, WI. Began in 1969.

Pediatric Exercise Science
Official journal of the North American Society of Pediatric Exercise Science. Publisher: Human Kinetics, Champaign, IL. Began in 1989.

Research Quarterly for Exercise & Sport
Official publication of the Research Consortium of the American Alliance for Health, Physical Education Recreation, and Dance (AAHPERD). Publisher: AAHPERD, Washington, DC. Began in 1930.

---

exercise-science, and general psychology journals publish in the area of sport psychology. A selected list of these journals is provided (see Exhibits 3 and 4), but it should be emphasized that this list does not contain all the journals that publish articles of interest. Reflecting the eclectic nature of the field, some of these journals emphasize research and some emphasize practice. We recommend that interested individuals obtain copies of these journals from a library before subscribing.

Exhibit 4

Psychology Journals That May Include Topics Related to Sport and Exercise Psychology

*Health Psychology**
*Journal of Applied Psychology**
*Journal of Consulting and Clinical Psychology**
*Journal of Counseling Psychology**
*Journal of Personality and Social Psychology**
Perceptual and Motor Skills. Publisher: Perceptual & Motor Skills, Missoula, MT
*Psychology and Aging**
The Gerontologist. Publisher: The Gerontological Society of America, Washington, DC

---

*Published by the American Psychological Association, Washington, DC.

Conclusion

There are numerous options for pursuing educational goals related to the field of sport and exercise psychology. Before embarking on a career, individuals are advised to talk to both students and professionals in the field, read published materials that outline career options, and investigate or perhaps even join some professional societies. Before applying to graduate school, it is important to spend time carefully examining the requirements of the program and discussing career goals with faculty advisors in the area. Interdisciplinary work divided between a psychology and a kinesiology program is ideal but not readily available at all institutions. Continued development in the field can be achieved by joining professional organizations and keeping abreast of research in appropriate journals.

References

American Psychological Association. (1994). *Graduate training and career possibilities in exercise and sport psychology.* [Brochure]. Washington, DC: Author.

Andersen, M. B. (1994). Ethical considerations in the supervision of applied sport psychology graduate students. *Journal of Applied Sport Psychology, 6,* 152–167.

Andersen, M. B., Van Raalte, J. L., & Brewer, B. W. (1994). Assessing the skills of sport psychology supervisors. *The Sport Psychologist, 8,* 238–247.

Atkinson, R. L., Atkinson, R. C., Smith, E. E., & Hilgard, E. R. (1987). *Introduction to psychology* (9th ed.). New York: Harcourt Brace Jovanovich.

Berger, B. G. (1993). Ethical issues in clinical settings: A reaction to ethics in teaching, advising, and clinical services. *Quest, 45,* 106–119.

Brooks, G. A., & Fahey, T. D. (1985). *Exercise physiology: Human bioenergetics and its applications.* New York: Macmillan.

Butki, B. D., & Andersen, M. B. (1994). Mentoring in sport psychology: Students' perceptions of training in publications and presentation guidelines. *The Sport Psychologist, 8,* 143–148.

Coakley, J. J. (1994). *Sport in society: Issues and controversies* (5th ed.). St. Louis: Mosby.

Cratty, B. J. (1968). *Psychology and physical activity.* Englewood Cliffs, NJ: Prentice-Hall.

Danish, S. J., & Hale, B. D. (1981). Toward an understanding of the practice of sport psychology. *Journal of Sport Psychology, 3,* 90–99.

Danish, S. J., & Hale, B. D. (1982). Further considerations on the practice of sport psychology. *Journal of Sport Psychology, 4,* 10–12.

Dishman, R. K. (1983). Identity crises in North American sport psychology: Academics in professional issues. *Journal of Sport Psychology, 5,* 123–134.

Ericsson, K. A., & Charness, N. (1994). Expert performance: Its structure and acquisition. *American Psychologist, 49,* 725–747.

Gill, D. L. (1992). Status of the Journal of Sport & Exercise Psychology, 1985–1990. *Journal of Sport & Exercise Psychology, 14,* 1–12.

Griffith, C. R. (1925). Psychology and its relation to athletic competition. *American Physical Education Review, 30,* 193–199.

Harrison, R. P., & Feltz, D. L. (1979). The professionalization of sport psychology: Legal considerations. *Journal of Sport Psychology, 1,* 182–190.

Hay, J. G. (1985). *The biomechanics of sports techniques* (3rd ed.). Englewood Cliffs, NJ: Prentice-Hall.

Heyman, S. R. (1982). A reaction to Danish and Hale: A minority report. *Journal of Sport Psychology, 4,* 7–9.

Keith-Spiegel, P. (1991). *The complete guide to graduate school admission: Psychology and related fields.* Hillsdale, NJ: Erlbaum.

Landers, D. M., Boutcher, S. H., & Wang, M. Q. (1986). The history and status of the *Journal of Sport Psychology:* 1979–1985. *Journal of Sport Psychology, 8,* 149–163.

Lawther, J. D. (1972). Sport psychology. Englewood Cliffs, NJ: Prentice-Hall.

LeUnes, A. D., & Hayward, S. A. (1990). Sport psychology as viewed by chairpersons of APA–approved clinical psychology programs. *The Sport Psychologist, 4,* 18–24.

LeUnes, A. D., & Nation, J. R. (1989). *Sport psychology.* Chicago: Nelson-Hall.

Martens, R. (1975). *Social psychology and physical activity.* New York: Harper & Row.

Morgan, W. P. (Ed.). (1970). Contemporary readings in sport psychology. Springfield, IL: Charles C Thomas.

Nideffer, R. M., DuFresne, P., Nesvig, D., & Selder, D. (1980). The future of applied sport psychology. *Journal of Sport Psychology, 2,* 170–174.

Rejeski, W. R., & Brawley, L. R. (1988). Defining the boundaries of sport psychology. *The Sport Psychologist, 2,* 231–242.

Roberts, G. C. (1993). Ethics in professional advising and academic counseling of graduate students. *Quest, 45,* 78–87.

Sachs, M. L., Burke, K. L., & Butcher, L. A. (1995). *Directory of graduate programs in applied sport psychology* (4th ed.). Morgantown, WV: FIT.

Salmela, J. H. (1992). *The world sport psychology sourcebook.* Champaign, IL: Human Kinetics.

Schmidt, R. A. (1991). *Motor learning and performance: From principles to practice.* Champaign, IL: Human Kinetics.

Singer, R. N. (1975). *Myths and truths in sport psychology.* New York: Harper & Row.

Taylor, J. (1991). Career direction, development, and opportunities in applied sport psychology. *The Sport Psychologist, 5,* 266–280.

Van Raalte, J. L., Dale, G. A., Wrisberg, C. A., Janssen, J. J., Wiechman, S. A., Leffingwell, T. R., Ryder, S. P., Harmison, R. J., & Williams, J. M. (1994, October). *Applied sport psychology internships with university athletes: Programs and possibilities.* Paper presented at the annual meeting of the Association for the Advancement of Applied Sport Psychology, Lake Tahoe, NV.

Certification in Sport and Exercise Psychology

18

Leonard Zaichkowsky and Frank Perna

Sport and exercise psychology is a multidisciplinary profession. Scientists, educators, and practitioners of sport and exercise psychology share a common interest, but these professionals have received their primary training from an array of general fields spanning psychology, sport science, and medicine that include subspecialties such as clinical and counseling psychology, exercise physiology, and biomechanics to name a few. Currently, a leading sport and exercise psychology organization, the Association for the Advancement of Applied Sport Psychology (AAASP), lists roughly equal distributions of members trained in psychology specialties and in one of the sport sciences.

Similar to other applied disciplines in an early stage of development, sport and exercise psychology faced the task of generating a mutually accepted mode of professional training, code of practice, and espoused core knowledge base. Perhaps no other area in an applied profession generates as much attention and controversy as codifying standards for professional preparation and practice, because the practice of a profession serves as the primary interface of the field to the general public and encompasses both legal and professional issues. One may refer to articles on the credentialing of counselors (Brooks & Gerstein, 1990) and professional psychologists (Cummings, 1990; Fretz & Mills, 1980). Fairly or unfairly, the general public views the educational background of professionals who practice as the model for the field. The field of sport and exercise psychology offers no exception. Similar to other applied professions at a beginning stage of development, issues surrounding the provision of sport and exercise psychology services have generated considerable debate concerning whether services should be provided (Kirschenbaum, 1994; Morgan, 1988), how individuals should be trained, and who should provide services (Anshel, 1992, 1993; Danish & Hale, 1981; Dishman, 1983; Gardner, 1991; Harrison & Feltz, 1979; Heyman, 1993; May, 1993; Monahan, 1987; Silva; 1989; Zaichkowsky, 1993; Zaichkowsky & Perna, 1992).

Certification is a function of a professional organization that attempts to codify a common standard of preparation and practice. At a beginning stage, these standards must serve the dual purpose of recognizing the experience of members currently in the field as well as setting guidelines for newer members. A leading sport and exercise psychology organization in the United States, AAASP initially implemented and continues to revise a certification process for sport and exercise psychology consultants. The purposes of this chapter are (a) to define terminology associated with certification, which in our opinion has been at the root of much controversy; (b) to provide a brief history of certification internationally; (c) to provide a rationale for the existence of the certification process; (d) to present AAASP certification criteria; and (e) to outline and respond to criticisms that have been levied against certification and the associated criteria in sport and exercise psychology.

Defining Certification and Related Terms

It is clear that a large number of current and aspiring professionals are unclear about the terminology associated with the credentialing process in general and in sport and exercise psychology in particular. For instance, confusion exists regarding statutory versus nonstatutory designations and regarding certification versus licensure. This section defines the many terms that are related to the credentialing process.

Credentialing

This broad, generic term is commonly defined as a process of giving a title or claim of competence. Credentialing includes *statutory* designations, which are protected by law and enacted by a legislative body, as well as *nonstatutory* designations, such as recognition by organizations and registries, which are not protected by law. In the mental health field, credentialing takes five basic forms: association membership, accreditation of educational and training programs, certification by a non-governmental agency, government licensure, and registration on an official roster (Anchor, 1988).

Certification

Although this is generally a nonstatutory designation granted by an organization rather than a legislative body, some states use the label *certification* in reference to statutory designations (e.g., certified teacher, certified psychologist). Certification is usually a transitional designation that may serve as a preliminary step toward statutory standards for a profession (Smith, 1986). The National Coaching Certification Program in Canada and AAASP certification are examples of nonstatutory certification, whereas public school certification and mental health counselor certification are examples of statutory certification.

Registry

A listing in a registry is generally a nonstatutory designation indicating "that an individual has been publicly identified as meeting qualifications as specified by the organization and is eligible for formal listing" (Smith, 1986, p. 13). The National Register of Health Service Providers in Psychology and the Canadian Mental Training Registry are examples of registries.

Licensure

Licensure is a statutory process and is the most restrictive of all the terms discussed. The statutory designation of licensure indicates a state or provincial process that is designed to regulate professional conduct within a particular field. At times, a state may adopt a professional organization's admission standards or code of ethics, and it may even relegate the monitoring of the field to a professional board of the organization. However, the state legislature retains legal authority and determines the professional organization's involvement. Licensure as a psychologist is an example of a statutory process that protects the use of the title (i.e., psychologist) and scope of practice (e.g., psychological test interpretation).

Psychologist

The title "psychologist" is restricted in many states and provinces in the United States and Canada to those who are licensed or certified to offer services to the public. These individuals generally have a doctoral degree in counseling or clinical psychology. Exceptions to this restricted use of the title include individuals who teach and conduct research in psychology and individuals from selected states and provinces that recognize master's-level psychologists.

Counselor

This is a term that appears to apply to, literally, a "cast of thousands." Any person who is helping another is in fact offering counseling services. For instance, there are academic counselors, drug and alcohol counselors, career counselors, marriage counselors, and so forth. In many cases, little or no training is provided for these "lay" counselors; however, in other cases, counselors undergo rigorous training, making them eligible for a statutory designation such as "licensed mental health counselor."

Accredited or Approved Program

These terms generally refer to an educational, training, or service program that has met standards that may or may not be related to certification or licensure. Accreditation is usually the result of a review of relevant documentation and a site visit by a team of reviewers from the accreditation agency. The American Psychological Association (APA) has an accreditation program that approves training programs in counseling, school, and clinical psychology. It should be emphasized, however, that by participating in an APA-approved program, one does not automatically become licensed to practice psychology. This point is particularly confusing to aspiring young professionals who may be unaware that licensing is a state function and not a function of APA.

A Brief History of Sport Psychology Certification

The question of who is qualified to be a "sport psychologist" has been an issue ever since sport psychology expanded from being primarily a topic for research and teaching in universities to providing "professional services" to athletes and coaches. A number of position papers were written on the topic beginning in the late 1970s (e.g., Harrison & Feltz, 1979) and continuing to the present (Anshel, 1992; Danish & Hale, 1981; Dishman, 1983; Nideffer, Feltz, & Salmela, 1982; Zaichkowsky & Perna, 1992).

The United States Olympic Committee (USOC) initiated the first systematic attempt in North America to credential sport and exercise psychologists. In the early 1980s, the USOC chose to improve the provision of sport science services to athletes. The USOC Sports Medicine Council was comfortable with identifying qualified biomechanists and exercise physiologists but thought that the standards for quality control in sport psychology were "elusive." In August of 1982, the USOC brought together 12 individuals with established expertise and experience with the differing orientations of sport psychology to develop an approach to standards and identify organizational and referral processes and relationships.

Guidelines proposed by this committee were subsequently published (U.S. Olympic Committee, 1983). The main recommendation made by this committee was that a sport psychology registry be established that would include the names of qualified workers in three separate categories of sport psychology. These categories included (a) clinical–counseling sport psychologists, (b) educational sport psychologists, and (c) research sport psychologists. The committee provided criteria for the three categories (USOC, 1983) and invited sport psychologists to apply for membership in the registry. From 1983 to 1995, a total of 67 sport psychologists were listed on the USOC Registry. Recently the USOC and AAASP announced the formation of a certification partnership (McCann & Scanlan, 1995). All AAASP certified consultants who are also members of APA will meet criteria for acceptance on the registry.

In 1989, after several years of committee deliberations, the AAASP approved a certification program. The first certificates were awarded in 1991 under criteria established for "grandparenting." The time frame for grandparenting is currently over, and "regular" application is ongoing. A total of 89 AAASP members have been certified through 1994.

Several issues faced the AAASP Executive Board, Certification Committee, and fellows. Most notable were matters pertaining to *role definition* (i.e., what can sport and exercise psychologists do?) and *title* (i.e., what is the most appropriate legally acceptable title for members working in sport and exercise psychology?). Numerous experts in law and

Exhibit 1

Criteria for AAASP Certification

1. Completion of a doctoral degree from an institution of higher education accredited by one of the regional accrediting bodies recognized by the Council of Postsecondary Accreditation; in Canada, an institution of higher education must be recognized as a member in good standing of the Association of Universities and Colleges of Canada. Programs leading to a doctoral degree must include the equivalent of three full-time academic years of graduate study, 2 years of which are at the institution from which the doctoral degree is granted, and 1 year of which is in full-time residence at the institution from which the doctoral degree is granted.

2. Knowledge of scientific and professional ethics and standards. This requirement can be met by taking one course on these topics or by taking several courses in which these topics compose parts of the courses or by taking part in other comparable experiences.

3. Knowledge of the sport psychology subdisciplines of intervention–performance enhancement, health–exercise psychology, and social psychology as evidenced by three courses or two courses and one independent study in sport psychology (two of these courses must be taken at the graduate level).

4. Knowledge of the biomechanical and physiological bases of sport (e.g., kinesiology, biomechanics, exercise physiology).

5. Knowledge of the historical, philosophical, social, or motor behavior bases of sport (e.g., motor learning–control, motor development, issues in sport–physical education, sociology of sport, history and philosophy of sport–physical education).

6. Knowledge of psychopathology and its assessment (e.g., abnormal psychology, psychopathology).

7. Training designed to foster basic skills in counseling; (e.g., course work on basic intervention techniques in counseling; supervised practicums in counseling, clinical, or industrial–organizational psychology).*

8. Supervised experience with a qualified person (i.e., one who has an appropriate background in applied sport psychology), during which the individual receives training in the use of sport psychology principles and techniques (e.g., supervised practicums in applied sport psychology in which the recipients of the assessments and interventions are participants in physical activity, exercise, or sport).*

9. Knowledge of skills and techniques within sport or exercise (e.g., supervised practicums in applied sport psychology in which the recipients of the assessments and interventions are participants in physical activity, exercise, or sport).

10. Knowledge and skills in research design, statistics, and psychological assessment.*

continued

Exhibit 1, continued

At least two of the following four criteria must be met through educational experiences that focus on general psychological principles (rather than sport-specific ones):

11. Knowledge of the biological bases of behavior (e.g., biomechanics–kinesiology, comparative psychology, exercise physiology, neuropsychology, physiological psychology, psychopharmacology, sensation).
12. Knowledge of the cognitive–affective bases of behavior (e.g., cognition, emotion, learning, memory, motivation, motor development, motor learning–control, perception, thinking).
13. Knowledge of the social bases of behavior (e.g., cultural, ethnic, and group processes; gender roles in sport; organizational and systems theory; social psychology; sociology of sport).
14. Knowledge of individual behavior (e.g., developmental psychology, exercise behavior, health psychology, individual differences, personality theory).

---

*Graduate level only.

psychology were consulted regarding the issue of title. After extensive deliberation, it was concluded that if the AAASP certified individuals as "sport psychologists," the association might be in violation of state and provincial laws. Because of this legal issue, AAASP fellows voted to use the title "Certified Consultant, AAASP" rather than a title supported by many members, "certified sport psychologist." The criteria for AAASP certification are presented in Exhibit 1.

International Developments

Canada

In 1987, under the leadership of Dr. Murray Smith, Canada instituted The Canadian Registry for Sport Behavioral Professionals. This national registry was a part of the Canadian Association of Sport Sciences (CASS) and was designed to provide a list of names of persons who were qualified to provide professional services to the sport community, including athletes, coaches, parents, teams, administrators, agencies, and sport governing bodies. The registry was similar to the USOC registry in that it listed qualified professionals in three categories: (a) licensed psychologists, (b) sport educators–counselors, and (c) sport researchers. For a variety of reasons, this version of the Canadian Registry ceased to function and was replaced by the Canadian Mental Training Registry (CMTR) in 1994.

The CMTR, which had 29 registrants as of July 1994, states as its purposes: (a) to identify people in Canada who may be able to assist athletes and coaches with mental training and performance enhancement and (b) to promote the continued development of effective mental-training services for athletes and coaches in Canada. The Registry Review Committee is a subcommittee of the High Performance Sport Committee (HPSC) of the Canadian Society for Exercise Physiology. The HPSC has identified the following areas of preparation and experience as important for "effective mental training in an applied sport setting" (CASS, 1994, p. 2):

1. Academic training that generates an appropriate knowledge base with respect to (a) mental links to excellence, (b) applied mental-training consulting, and (c) allied sport sciences.
2. Demonstrated personal experience in sport as a participant, athlete, performer, or teacher–coach.
3. Completion of a supervised internship in mental, training or demonstrated experience in mental-training consulting.
4. Favorable client evaluations.

The CMTR review committee specifies that registrants normally have acquired a master's or doctoral degree with specialization in sport psychology or mental training and have completed a supervised internship or consulting experience with athletes and coaches. In their publication, the CMTR is careful to state "what registrants do not do":

> Mental training consultants do not conduct psychometric testing for the purpose of diagnosing or treating psychiatric disorders; nor do they provide psychotherapy, prescribe drugs, deal with deep-seated personality disorders or mental illness. The treatment of patients with mental disorders clearly falls outside the scope of ongoing mental training consulting work with athletes or others pursuing excellence. This is a distinctly different role from the mental strengthening role that mental training consultants engage in with athletes and coaches. (CASS, 1994, p. 4)

Australia

Like their colleagues in North America, Australians have struggled with the question of who can be a sport psychologist. Jeffrey Bond was appointed to be the first "applied" sport psychologist at the Australian Institute of Sport in 1982. Since that time, educational programs as well as opportunities in the field of sport and exercise psychology have grown at a rapid rate. After many years of debate regarding credentialing of sport psychologists, the Australians have determined that to be called a "sport psychologist" one needs to be a full member the Australian Psychological Society (APS) and accepted as a member of the Board of Sport Psychologists. The board has been sanctioned by and held directly accountable to the APS. As such, sport and exercise psychology is closely linked to the profession of psychology (Chairperson's Report, 1993).

In Australia, psychologists do not have to have a doctoral degree in order to call themselves "psychologists." Today, in Australia, individuals can provide psychological services to the public if they are full members of APS. The criteria for full membership, in the absence of a psychology degree from a certified APS university program, include a record of research publications, letters of endorsement from current APS members, and successful completion of a supervised field experience. Recent changes within the APS require future psychologists to have 6 years of university training plus 2 years of supervised clinical experience. Several universities have recently instituted master of psychology in sport psychology programs to provide the type of interdisciplinary training that is needed for preparing professionals with a specialization in sport and exercise psychology.

Great Britain

The British Association of Sport and Exercise Sciences (BASES) has recently approved accreditation criteria for sport and exercise scientists—psychology section. Their purpose was to "set, maintain and enhance the professional and ethical standards of its members who are actively involved in the sport and exercise sciences" (BASES, 1994). Accreditation was made available in two categories: (a) research accreditation and (b) support accreditation. To be accredited as a researcher, one has to make presentations and publish articles on sport and exercise psychology. For support accreditation, a candidate must submit a portfolio that demonstrates involvement in the scientific study of sport and exercise and an ability to transpose relevant scientific knowledge into effective work in the field with clients. The accreditation process also requires supervised experience for accreditation as a "sport and exercise psychologist."

The Benefits of Certification

In every instance in which certification has been instituted, the sponsoring organization has written about the benefits of certification. The following statement issued by the AAASP captures much of what other organizations have said:

> Because the Association for the Advancement of Applied Sport Psychology (AAASP) and its membership are committed to the promotion of applied sport psychology, its members strive to maintain high standards of professional conduct while rendering consulting service, conducting research, and training others. AAASP has made a commitment to promoting excellence in sport psychology by instituting a certification program. (Questions Regarding Certification, 1991)

This declaration was followed by a statement of the benefits to a certification program, which are described in the following sections:

Accountability and Professionalism

The primary objective of the certification program is to provide a standard by which sport administrators, coaches, psychologists, other health care professionals, the media, and the public may accept as reliable evidence that an individual has attained specified professional competency. In this way, the AAASP is assuming accountability for high standards of performance in sport and exercise psychology. Certification also attests to the professionalism of the individual, thereby serving to protect the public interest.

Recognition

Certification means that each individual certified as a consultant is listed in a registry of accredited specialists and is recognized for having fulfilled prescribed standards of performance and conduct. This registry is made available to all amateur and professional sport organizations as well as other professional groups. In this way, certification serves to provide a vehicle for identifying qualified practitioners.

Credibility

The certification process affords credibility because certification procedures for identifying qualified professionals are rigorous and based on peer review. The public can be assured that sport and exercise psychology is maintaining high standards of performance because of the recertification procedures, which require upgrading of skills monitored by AAASP.

By specifying what is considered to be appropriate preparation of professionals, the AAASP certification process provides colleges and universities with guidelines regarding programs, courses, and practicum experiences in the field of sport and exercise psychology.

Public Awareness

Certification serves to raise awareness and understanding of sport and exercise psychology for all members of the sport community as well as the public at large.

Another benefit to certification not listed in the AAASP document but stated by Smith (1986, 1987) in the Canadian registry document is that of "proactive self-determination." There is clearly an advantage to having the sport and exercise psychology profession proactively define education–training, roles, ethical standards, and so forth, rather than having external professional organizations define conditions in possibly unacceptable ways.

Criticisms of AAASP Certification

Considering that sport and exercise psychology is a new field and the AAASP is a new professional organization, it is not surprising that the organization's attempt to codify guidelines for professional practice has been met with mixed reactions. It is our position that division in opinion is not only understandable but desirable. In this section, we present a rationale for AAASP certification as well as address the major criticisms that have been levied against it. The reader is referred to Anshel (1992, 1993) and Zaichkowsky and Perna (1992) for a full discussion of these issues.

Briefly, Anshel (1992, 1993) suggested that vague language permeates the certification guidelines. He also asserted that the process and criteria associated with AAASP certification are flawed in three ways: (a) Certification is overexclusionary; (b) the criteria are discriminatory toward individuals trained in the sport sciences; and, perhaps most important, (c) certification in sport and exercise psychology has greater potential for harm than for good.

Generic and Specific Language

As indicated in the previous sections outlining AAASP certification, many specific behaviors are clearly identified, although some guidelines describe the practice of sport and exercise psychology in generic terms. Guidelines specifically address required preparatory course work, educational degrees, and field experiences as well as identify professional behaviors that are outside the scope of practice for AAASP-certified consultants. Although it is true that some guidelines are left to interpretation, this is the case for most professional codes of conduct. Broad language is necessary because guidelines attempt to convey heuristics to govern practice rather than concretely specify a wide array of behavior constituting either wrongful or desirable practice. This feature enables a document to have longevity and sensitivity to the organization membership's views, which may change as a function of new information such as legal statutes and public feedback. The Constitution of the United States is based on the same principle, providing constituents with both the specific letter of the law and an opportunity for an interpretative review of the spirit of the law. Similarly, AAASP certification guidelines allow professional peers to determine whether adherence to the spirit of the guidelines was followed and whether a particular guideline is presently appropriate.

Overexclusion

It has been stated that AAASP certification "fails to recognize the expertise of individuals who meet many, but not all, of the criteria for certification" (Anshel, 1993, p. 345). Anshel presented the scenario of an emigré to the United States who is recognized by his or her country as a sport psychologist and the case of a licensed, but not AAASP-certified, U.S. psychologist who wants to provide clinical services to athletes with eating disorders as examples of competent individuals who would be excluded from AAASP certification or precluded from providing clinical services.

Because the AAASP certification process is at an early stage, certification guidelines state that current professionals desiring certification are not expected to meet all of the stated educational criteria, particularly if they can document applied experience or expertise by training, research, or continuing education. A 5-year grandparent clause was instituted specifically to recognize such individuals and to serve as an appeals process providing a forum for professionals to state their case. No statement in AAASP certification guidelines should be construed to preclude professionals from practicing within a protected scope of practice in their recognized areas of expertise.

Returning to the first scenario, a foreign sport psychologist would be eligible for AAASP certification by virtue of experience and recognized expertise. Additionally, AAASP certification does not require U.S. citizenship. However, the burden of proof of eligibility lies with the individuals seeking certification regardless of their country of origin.

In the case of the psychologist, AAASP certification guidelines do not govern the practice of professionals other than certified consultants. Additionally, although statutes may vary from state to state, the use of psychological methods and testing to diagnose and treat psychological disorders, disorders of habit or conduct, and psychological issues accompanying physical illness, injury, or disability are but a few of the functions protected by law. Therefore, psychologists cannot be prevented from providing services that are within their legal scope of practice and area of expertise even if their clients are athletes. It is important to note, however, that licensure as a psychologist is not sufficient to qualify for AAASP-certified consultant status.

Discrimination Against the Sport Sciences

A major criticism that has been levied against AAASP certification suggests that representation of the certification committee was biased and that the guidelines favor individuals with psychology over sport science backgrounds. However, there are no data to support this view. AAASP Certification Committee minutes document that representative experts from the fields of psychology and sport science, the legal and medical disciplines, and the AAASP membership contributed input at the inception of proposed guidelines and in ensuing years. Additionally, a recent empirical analysis comparing the educational backgrounds of applicants accepted or rejected for AAASP-certified consultant status revealed that significantly more sport-science-trained than psychology-trained individuals achieved certification (Zaichkowsky & Perna, 1992).

Potential for Harm

It has been suggested that credentialing an individual as a certified consultant may diminish rather than promote quality service. This criticism is based largely on the premise that certification may create the illusion of sanctioning fraudulent practice (Anshel, 1992; Zaichkowsky & Perna, 1992). Fraudulent practices in sport and exercise psychology primarily include practitioners who misrepresent the efficacy of sport and exercise psychology interventions and those who engage in practice without proper training. Although it is true that certified consultants who make fraudulent claims, misapply techniques, and generally practice outside of their area of expertise would likely damage the field of sport and exercise psychology, there is no evidence to suggest that certification would promote this occurrence. More arguments can be made supporting the opposite view: that certification would likely minimize unethical practice.

First, an ample knowledge base exists supporting the efficacy of many of the interventions used in the provision of sport and exercise psychology services (Druckman & Bjork, 1991; Greenspan & Feltz, 1989; Kendall, Hrycaiko, Martin, & Kendall, 1990; Meyers, 1994; Meyers, Schleser, & Okwumabua, 1982; Zaichkowsky & Fuchs, 1988). The course work and supervised practicums required for certification are intended to document that applicants for certification not only are exposed to these techniques, but also demonstrate proficient skill and judgment in their application. Present AAASP-certified consultants, similar to other applied professionals, are encouraged to apprise themselves regularly of new developments through journals, conferences, workshops, and consultation. To maintain certified status, consultants are also required to complete continuing education credits to keep abreast of new information and applications within the field.

It is true that certification, similar to all credentialing processes, can only minimally define competent practice. Whether or not consultants seek to adjust their practice as new evidence accumulates or engage in consultation and referral when appropriate is not an issue plaguing certification, but rather an issue of professional integrity. However, we contend that certification standards serve to promote competent practice by providing a structure and training guidelines for students and professionals seeking to expand their practice.

A related criticism that often arises concerns the belief that licensed mental health practitioners without requisite experience in the practice of sport and exercise psychology—specifically, psychologists—would be eligible for AAASP-certified consultant status. This is simply not the case. Nor is it appropriate to assume that a psychologist without demonstrated expertise may opt to advertise and practice as a "sport and exercise psychologist" without the potential for censure. Although state statutes typically protect the title "psychologist" and variations thereof, state regulatory boards prohibit psychologists and other mental health professionals from practicing and advertising in areas outside of their expertise. Professionals may be reported to their respective certifying or licensing boards for practicing outside of their area of expertise. Therefore, although AAASP has no legal jurisdiction over professionals who practice unethically, publicly stated AAASP certification criteria put individuals and sport and exercise psychology organizations in a better position to curtail practice that is detrimental to the field of sport psychology.

It is our view that certification, as designed by the AAASP, provides the public with standard criteria that certified consultants have met and a means by which certified and noncertified professionals can be compared. With time, professional sport and exercise psychology organizations and the public will decide whether distinction by AAASP certification is important. In the interim, the public is protected, to the extent possible, from fraud. However, as is the case with credentialing in other professional fields, certification does not, and never was intended to, guarantee expertise or personal integrity. All professional organizations contain isolated individuals who have engaged in unethical and at times criminal conduct. To allege that certification potentially promotes inappropriate behavior detrimental to the field is unsubstantiated. On the contrary, to dispense with certification and let "the market" determine quality, as has been suggested (Anshel, 1992), would likely be a professional disaster.

Conclusion

Because a great deal of confusion exists regarding what certification is, who engages in certification, and why there is certification, this chapter defines nomenclature associated with certification, emphasizes legal issues concerned with the title "psychologist," and presents arguments for and against the process. Important papers associated with certification are referenced. We also provide a brief history of certification of sport and exercise psychologists in the United States, Canada, Australia, and Great Britain. Emphasis is placed on the certification process used by AAASP.

References

Anchor, K. N. (1988). Professional regulation in the U.S.: Task force on issues and problems in current credentialing practices. *Medical Psychotherapy: An International Journal, 1,* 173–180.

Anshel, M. H. (1992). The case against the certification of sport psychologists: In search of the phantom expert. *The Sport Psychologist, 6,* 265–286.

Anshel, M. H. (1993). Against the certification of sport psychology consultants: A response to Zaichkowsky and Perna. *The Sport Psychologist, 7,* 344–353.

British Association of Sport and Exercise Sciences. (1994). *Accreditation criteria for sport and exercise scientists—psychology section.* Unpublished manuscript.

Brooks, D. K., & Gerstein, L. H. (1990). Counselor credentialing and interprofessional collaboration. *Journal of Counseling & Development, 68,* 476–490.

Canadian Association of Sport Sciences. (1994). *Canadian Mental Training Registry CMTR: Information for prospective users.* [Brochure]. Gloucester, Ontario, Canada: Author.

Chairperson's report. (1993). *Australian Sport Psychology Association Bulletin, 2,* 4–6.

Cummings, N. A. (1990). The credentialing of professional psychologists and its implication for the other mental health disciplines. *Journal of Counseling and Development, 68,* 485–490.

Danish, S. J., & Hale, B. D. (1981). Toward an understanding of the practice of sport psychology. *Journal of Sport Psychology, 3,* 90–99.

Dishman, R. K. (1983). Identity crisis in North American sport psychology. *Journal of Sport Psychology, 5,* 123–134.

Druckman, D., & Bjork, R. A. (1991). *In the mind's eye: Enhancing human performance.* Washington, DC: National Academy Press.

Fretz, B. R., & Mills, D. H. (1980). *Licensing and certification of psychologists and counselors: A guide to current policies, procedures and legislation.* San Francisco: Jossey-Bass.

Gardner, F. L., (1991). Professionalization of sport psychology: A reply to Silva. *The Sport Psychologist, 5,* 55–60.

Greenspan, M. J., & Feltz, D. L. (1979). Psychological interventions with athletes in competitive situations: A review. *The Sport Psychologist, 3,* 219–236.

Harrison, R. P., & Feltz, D. L. (1979). The professionalization of sport psychology: Legal considerations. *Journal of Sport Psychology, 1,* 182–190.

Heyman, S. (1993, August). *The need to go slowly: Educational and ethical issues in proposed sport psychology certification.* Paper presented at the annual meeting of the American Psychological Association, Toronto, Ontario, Canada.

Iso-Ahola, S. E., & Hatfield, B. (1986). Evolution of the field. In S. E. Iso-Ahola & B. Hatfield (Eds.), *Psychology of sports: A social psychological approach* (pp. 15–28), Dubuque, IA: William C. Brown.

Kendall, G., Hrycaiko, D., Martin, G. L., & Kendall, T. (1990). The effects of imagery rehearsal, relaxation and self-talk package on basketball game performance. *Journal of Sport & Exercise Psychology, 12,* 157–166.

Kirschenbaum, D. S. (1994, August). *Helping athletes improve sport performance: Best guesses.* Division 47 Presidential Address at the annual meeting of the American Psychological Association, Los Angeles, CA.

May, J. (1993, August). *Issues concerning certification of sport psychologists.* Paper presented at the annual meeting of the American Psychological Association, Toronto, Ontario, Canada.

McCann, S. C., & Scanlan, T. (1995). A new USOC-AAASP partnership: Olympic world opens to interested certified consultants, AAASP. *AAASP Newsletter, 10*(3), 9.

Meyers, A. W. (1994, August). *Status of psychological interventions for athletic performance enhancement.* Paper presented at the annual meeting of the American Psychological Association, Los Angeles, CA.

Meyers, A. W., Schleser, R., & Okwumabua, T. M. (1982). A cognitive–behavioral intervention for improving basketball performance. *Research Quarterly for Exercise and Sport, 53,* 344–347.

Monahan, T. (1987). Sport psychology: A crisis identity? *The Physician and Sportsmedicine, 15,* 203–212.

Morgan, W. P. (1988). Sport psychology in its own context: A recommendation for the future. In J. S. Skinner, C. B. Corbin, D. M. Landers, P. E. Martin, & C. L. Wells (Eds.), *Future directions in exercise and sport science* (pp. 97–110). Champaign, IL: Human Kinetics.

Nideffer, R. M., Feltz, D., & Salmela, J. (1982). A rebuttal to Danish and Hale: A committee report. *Journal of Sport Psychology, 2,* 2–4.

Questions regarding certification. (1991, Winter). *AAASP Newsletter, 6,* 3–4.

Silva, J. M. (1989). Toward the professionalization of sport psychology. *The Sport Psychologist, 3,* 265–273.

Smith, M. F. R. (1986, October). *Background to the proposal for a Canadian registry for sport psychology.* Paper presented at the annual meeting of the Canadian Association of Sport Science. Ottawa, Ontario, Canada.

U.S. Olympic Committee establishes guidelines for sport psychology services. (1983). *Journal of Sport Psychology, 5,* 4–7.

Zaichkowsky, L. D. (1993, August). *Certification program of AAASP.* Paper presented at the annual meeting of the American Psychological Association, Toronto, Ontario, Canada.

Zaichkowsky, L. D., & Fuchs, C. Z. (1988). Biofeedback applications in exercise and athletic performance. In K. Pandolf (Ed.), *Exercise and sport science reviews* (pp. 381–421). New York: Macmillan.

Zaichkowsky, L. D., & Perna, F. M. (1992). Certification of consultants in sport psychology: A rebuttal to Anshel. *The Sport Psychologist, 6,* 287–296.

Incorporating Sport and Exercise Psychology Into Clinical Practice

Kate F. Hays and Robert J. Smith

The emerging field of sport and exercise psychology offers consid-erable potential and promise for individuals considering a career in psychology (APA, 1994). For established practitioners, the route to sport and exercise psychology may be somewhat different. How can sport and exercise psychology be used in clinical practice? What skills are needed? How is a sport and exercise psychology practice created? What are the potential pitfalls? This chapter is intended to address these questions.

Why Sport and Exercise Psychology?

The field of sport and exercise psychology holds considerable appeal for both the public and practitioners. Several factors contribute to its emergence as a field in which special skills and knowledge can be de-veloped. Our culture values both exercise (i.e., fitness) and sport (i.e., competition). Furthermore, changes in health care practice and fund-ing are presenting a challenge to practitioners to adapt and innovate. Market pressures for diversification, cost-effectiveness, and special-ization all can be met through the practice of sport and exercise psy-chology.

In surveys of the most important things in people's lives, good health ranks highest (Ribisl, 1984). At least attitudinally, if not in prac-

The material presented in this chapter is based in part on an article "Putting Sport Psychology Into (Your) Practice" by Kate F. Hays that appeared in *Professional Psychology: Research & Practice, 26,* 1995.

tice, people are developing a holistic perspective. They recognize that exercise and good health, and wellness contribute to an enhanced quality of life (Antonovsky, 1984; Berger, 1993). The past few years have seen psychology and mental health placed within the spectrum of health care (Yenney & APA Practice Directorate, 1994). Sport and exercise psychology, with its focus on the interaction of mind and body, fits naturally within this general framework.

Cost effectiveness is increasingly a driving force for practitioners (Austad & Hoyt, 1992). A recent Delphi poll suggested that therapies of the future will be brief, directive, present-centered, and problem-focused (Norcross, Alford, & DeMichele, 1992). These characteristics are descriptive of the practice of sport and exercise psychology (Hays, 1995a).

Specialization is important for both one's business and one's professional identity. Finding a niche is a constructive way to become "identifiable"—distinct from the competition. Furthermore, by focusing either on healthier populations or on the healthier aspects of people's lives, sport and exercise psychology may also prevent burnout or ameliorate the effects of practitioner vicarious traumatization (McCann & Pearlman, 1990).

The field of sport and exercise psychology has increasingly been of interest to psychologists and, in particular, practitioner psychologists. More than half the members of the Association for the Advancement of Applied Sport Psychology (AAASP) identify themselves as psychologists (AAASP, 1994). The majority of members of the Division of Exercise and Sport Psychology (Division 47), one of the newer divisions of the American Psychological Association (APA), describe themselves as mental health providers, and one third list themselves as employed full-time in independent practice (APA, 1993).

Sport and Exercise Psychology in Clinical Practice

There are three somewhat distinct ways in which the practitioner may engage in sport and exercise psychology: focusing on the body-to-mind aspect (i.e., the acknowledgement of the effect of exercise on mental health), focusing on the mind-to-body aspect (i.e., the use of mental techniques within sports), and practicing psychotherapy with athletes.

Body-to-Mind: Exercise and Mental Health

As noted in chapter 7, this volume, there is a positive connection between physical and mental functioning. Moderate exercise performed regularly (e.g., aerobic exercise performed three times a week for one-half hour at a time) has profound effects not only on the cardiovascular system but also on mood and sense of well-being (Berger, 1993; Kirkcaldy & Shephard, 1990; Morgan, 1985a). There is, as Morgan (1985a) described, an "affective beneficence" to exercise. Research suggests that exercise is associated with a reduction in depression and the amelioration of anxiety (e.g., Martinsen, 1990; Morgan & Goldston, 1987; Sime & Sanstead, 1987). Furthermore, exercise appears to result in improvements in self-esteem, mastery, body image, and socialization, all contributory to improvements in mental and emotional functioning (Berger, 1984; Boutcher, 1993; Sonstroem, 1984). Although only minimal research in this arena has been conducted among the severely mentally ill, exercise appears to have a salutary effect with this population as well (Auchus, 1993; Martinsen, 1990; Skrinar, Unger, Hutchinson, & Faigenbaum, 1992).

Exercise has multiple potential uses in the psychotherapy setting (Hays, 1993). Exercise may be prescribed as a form of therapy, encouraged as adjunctive to psychotherapy, or used as the setting in which the therapy is conducted. The therapist's engagement with the client in relation to exercise may include consultation, modeling, or participation. The client's own level of involvement in sport or exercise may range from that of a sedentary nonathlete to that of a competitive or professional athlete.

Mind-to-Body: Peak Performance Training

Psychological skills training (PST) programs are based on the assumption that aspects of thoughts and feelings can inhibit effectiveness and that use of mental skills can enhance optimal performance. Considerable research, especially with competitive athletes, suggests that educational psychological skills intervention improves competitive performance (see metaanalyses by Greenspan & Feltz, 1989; Meyers, Whelan, & Murphy, in press). PST programs typically include training in relaxation, imagery, goal setting, concentration, and cognitive self-management.

The cognitive–behavioral techniques used in PST are consonant with a specific, goal-focused, time-limited framework that can result in marked behavior change. These techniques are most effective when individually prescribed rather than packaged or presented en masse (Meyers, Whelan, & Murphy, in press). As with any other techniques, they must be understood and practiced correctly to have the greatest impact. For the clinician, PST can also function as a diagnostic tool: If the performance-enhancement intervention is rapidly effective, there may not be underlying pathology. To the extent that a person does not respond easily to PST, additional issues may need to be addressed (Hays, 1995a; May, 1986).

Psychotherapy With Athletes

In an early prospective study, Pierce (1969) found college athletes less likely than other students to seek psychotherapy. Athletes may tend to be mentally healthier than the general population; however, they may exhibit fairly severe psychopathology by the time they seek services (Morgan, 1985b).

Typical presenting problems include anxiety, depression, eating disorders, substance abuse, fears of success or failure, and relationship and motivational concerns, suggesting that there is substantial overlap between athletic and nonathletic clinical populations (Mahoney & Suinn, 1986). The athlete seeking psychotherapy may be more comfortable working with a therapist who is knowledgeable about sport and respectful of its role in the athlete's life (May, 1986). Psychotherapists should be sensitive to the client in context: respecting the client's identification as an athlete, taking seriously the client's engagement in competitive sport, and recognizing the legitimacy of time constraints created by competitive schedules.

In real life, the distinction between PST and counseling or psychotherapy may at times be arbitrary. In the only large-scale survey of its kind, Meyers et al. (in press) found that even though the initial focus of services at the U.S. Olympic Training Center concerned performance, 85% of all persons seen by the sport psychology staff involved personal counseling with athletes.

The Business of Clinical Sport and Exercise Psychology

Integrating sport and exercise psychology into clinical practice raises a number of issues that can be subsumed under three central questions:

(a) Where am I? (b) Where do I want to be? and (c) How do I get there? Careful consideration of these questions will facilitate the transition necessary to integrate sport and exercise consultation into a practice.

Where Am I? Current Interests and Skills

Interest Level

Hill (1960) proposed that people ask themselves what they are willing to give up to achieve their goals. Researchers in the area of self-regulation (Karoly & Kanfer, 1982; Kirschenbaum, 1992) agree that persistence underlies the success of any program of change. Strong motivation is vital when incorporating sport and exercise psychology into applied practice. The level of commitment one has to this field is strongly related to the quality of subsequent experiences.

There are potential intrinsic (e.g., intellectual stimulation, personal growth) and extrinsic (e.g., financial reward, visibility, special "perks") motives for entering a new field. When reviewing reasons for becoming a sport and exercise consultant, it is useful to recognize that relatively few professionals in this field report significant external incentives such as lucrative contracts with professional sports teams. Psychologist Fredrick Neff, for example, is the team sport psychology consultant for the Boston Bruins Hockey Club and even he must supplement his income with a general clinical practice (Neff, 1990; F. Neff, personal communication, July 16, 1992). Some evidence suggests that people pursuing goals for money or notoriety are less persistent than those with more personal investment (Kirschenbaum, 1992).

Relevant Skills

Sport and exercise psychologists have argued that consultants need to have knowledge in both psychological and sport sciences (e.g., Danish & Hale, 1981; Taylor, 1994). Among the most common psychological techniques used in sport psychology are arousal regulation (Orlick, 1986; Weinberg, 1984), mental imagery (Orlick, 1990; Suinn, 1980), goal setting (Locke & Latham, 1985; Weinberg, 1994), and attentional control (Nideffer, 1981; Orlick, 1990).

Psychologists with skills in organizational development, cognitive–behavioral techniques, and hypnosis already have a solid foundation on which to base work with athletes and coaches. Moreover, clinical assessment, teaching skills, and knowledge of how people behave in family and other group systems become crucial in the consultative process.

Beyond general psychological skills, sport and exercise psychologists must have specialized knowledge. Sport sciences—exercise physiology, biomechanics, and motor learning—provide consultants with important knowledge about physiological contributions to athletic performance. Formal training is also needed in the areas of nutrition and performance-enhancing drugs. Knowledge of sport-specific terminologies, rules, assessment and intervention techniques is also essential.

Sport and exercise psychologists with firsthand experience of specific sport or exercise skills are at an advantage when consulting. It is also possible to gain experience and learn more about a sport through reading, observation, and discussion with athletes, coaches, and others who are knowledgeable about that sport. Athletes generally are less concerned that a consultant has specific knowledge of their sport than that the consultant is open to learning the common terms used and willing to help them achieve their goals (Parham & Singer, 1994). Perhaps this reflects athletes' appreciation for the practical reality that even experienced sport and exercise psychologists cannot possibly have firsthand expertise in all sports.

Although sport experience is important, too much knowledge or investment in a specific sport could potentially interfere with a consultant's effectiveness. If a consultant played tennis in college, for example, advanced knowledge of the sport might make it harder to avoid giving advice on physical skills when working with tennis players. This situation can cause conflicts with coaches, who perceive the role of a sport psychologist to be strictly that of a mental skills consultant (May, 1986).

No matter how much knowledge sport psychology consultants have, they must be able to communicate their findings and recommendations in lay terms. Consultants should speak with athletes and coaches appropriately, using proper terminology (Eklund, 1993). Additionally, consultants who let go of clinical language and formality communicate better with their clients and are rewarded with better results (Van Raalte, in press).

These skill areas require a significant investment of time and resources. Aspiring sport and exercise psychology consultants can gain knowledge and experience by (a) reading some of the introductory texts on sport psychology (e.g., Horn, 1992; Orlick, 1990; Silva & Weinberg, 1984; Suinn, 1980; Williams, 1993); (b) pursuing continuing education offerings at conferences and seminars (e.g., APA regularly offers an all-day sport psychology workshop at its annual convention, and AAASP has recently designed preconference continuing education workshops); (c) obtaining a comprehensive list of graduate programs in sport psychology training (e.g., Sachs, Burke, & Salitsky, 1992); (d) attending practices and competitive events to learn more about specific sports; and (e) finding a mentor.

Where Do I Want to Be and How Do I Get There?

In *The Seven Habits of Highly Effective People*, Covey (1989) advised people pursuing a goal to "begin with the end in mind." With the goal in mind of incorporating sport and exercise psychology into clinical practice, what would an ideal sport and exercise psychology practice look like? Important areas to consider include the target market, services offered, financial goals, the optimal ratio of sport and exercise psychology to general clinical practice, and the development of professional supports.

Target Market

Taylor (1994) aptly noted that training and experience with specific presenting problems, intervention skills, and client populations guide the decision about whom to serve. Within the boundaries of one's competence, it is useful to identify both the *most* and the *least* desirable types of consultation.

The search for a target market can begin with a written description of an ideal client referral. Demographic variables include age group, gender, race–ethnicity, sports ability level, type of sport, referral source, and whether the client is a team, an individual athlete, a coach, a parent, an official, or an administrator (Taylor, 1994). The type of work settings preferred (e.g., professional sports, business, school, fitness or country clubs) also helps shape the target market and sources of referrals.

Developing referral sources is a challenging process. Suggestions for building a referral network include (a) identifying potential referral sources in the local area (e.g., gathering names of coaches, athletic trainers, doctors, physical therapists, fitness instructors, sport–exercise scientists, and sports agents); (b) brainstorming ways to educate these potential sources about services offered (e.g., through association newsletters, workshop flyers, introductory letters and follow-up phone calls, brochures, and topical newspaper or magazine articles); (c) attending awards dinners and networking functions; (d) inviting referral sources to breakfast or lunch; (e) offering free training workshops ("foot-in-the-door" approach); (f) carrying business cards and keeping extra supplies in the car or office in case someone offers to distribute them to prospective clients; and (g) keeping an alphabetical file with names of sports contacts.

Services

The services provided by sport and exercise psychologists vary greatly. They include psychotherapy, mental skills training, workshops for laypersons and professionals, and supervision to apprentice consultants. In a survey of sports medicine physicians, Brewer, Van Raalte, and Linder (1991) found that the five most common problems for which physicians referred athletes to sport psychologists were depression, stress–anxiety, substance abuse, family adjustment issues, and pain.

A critical task in practice development involves conducting a needs analysis of the target market. It makes no sense to offer a service if prospective clients fail to see a need for it. Important information can be gathered by hiring a marketing consultant or conducting surveys by oneself (i.e., asking numerous prospective clients or referral sources what they want). Athletes, coaches, doctors, athletic trainers, and sports agents can be asked questions such as, Would you ever seek or refer someone for consultation with a sport and exercise psychologist, and why? If so, how much would you (or others) be willing to pay for this service? What are the top five psychological factors affecting your (or your athletes') game, and ranked in order? Do you think sport and exercise psychologists can serve an important role in resolving some of these problems, and if so, how?

Additionally, it is useful to find out what services local sport and exercise psychologists provide and how they get paid. Generally, the likelihood of success as a consultant increases when one offers what competitors do not. If other sport and exercise psychology consultants work only with athletes and coaches, there may be a market for specializing in services to their families.

Finally, as in a general practice, there should be limitations in the services offered to clients. In addition to the ethical issue of practicing within one's areas of competence, there is also the potential for a lack of focus. Trying to be all things to all people usually results in being spread too thin, causing all one's work to suffer. Thus, it is wise to identify two or three areas of concentration and refer clients who need other services to colleagues who can better meet their needs.

When determining which services to offer sport and exercise psychology clients, one should consider (a) using a marketing consultant; (b) conducting a needs analysis of athletes and coaches to determine what to offer; (c) contacting other sport and exercise psychologists, athletes, coaches, and sports agents to explore how much they think these services are worth (i.e., how much the market will bear); (d) choosing specific sports to specialize in and concentrating efforts on these sports; and (e) developing a "boilerplate" contract outlining services, fees, and collections procedures (consult an attorney or see Yenney & APA, 1994).

Financial Goals

During a presentation to a summer basketball clinic, one of the authors asked the group what they thought a sport psychologist offers to athletes. A 12-year-old boy stood up confidently and said, "That's when you get paid a million dollars to have some athlete sit on your couch and talk about their problems." Although it was a naive and bald statement, it reflected a belief that sport and exercise psychology is a readily lucrative field. Some individuals do indeed make a good living as sport and exercise psychology consultants, but the vast majority supplement their income with general clinical work or academic positions.

Different segments of the sport and exercise psychology market offer varying levels of financial remuneration. To earn more, one might consider providing services to a specific population who can afford to pay higher fees. Professional athletes and coaches certainly provide one market. Among amateur enthusiasts, golfers, tennis players, figure skaters, rowers, marksmen, polo players, and equestrians tend to be more affluent; college athletes tend to have fewer resources to spend on mental training.

Although pro bono work does not add directly to the income stream, it does provide sport and exercise psychology services to athletes who might benefit from them. Besides being a good deed, offering free workshops and consultations to specific people or groups often leads to other, paying opportunities. Careful attention to the proportion of pro bono to paid services provided is an important aspect of realistic financial planning.

Phasing in the Practice

Typically, sport and exercise psychology work develops slowly enough that the desirable balance between consultations within athletics and other work can emerge. Nevertheless, it pays to consider how much time to invest in general practice maintenance (including marketing efforts) while concurrently pursuing sport psychology opportunities. In fact, we recommend continued attention to the "bread and butter" business, phasing in sport and exercise psychology marketing and networking gradually. This approach allows for a smoother transition.

Developing Professional Supports

Solo practitioners know all too well how isolated consultants can feel. Therefore, nurturing connections with professionals from sport and exercise psychology and other related fields is critical. A professional support network can be developed by (a) identifying colleagues who can provide supervision–consultation services; (b) creating informal networks or legal partnerships with other sport and exercise psychologists, sports medicine professionals, fitness professionals, or sports agents; (c) identifying professionals in other fields who can provide guidance in setting up a practice, such as attorneys, certified public accountants, marketing consultants, and public relations consultants; and (d) joining local or national sport and exercise psychology associations for continuing education, referrals, credentialing, and visibility. In particular, consider APA's Division of Exercise and Sport Psychology (Division 47) and the Association for the Advancement of Applied Sport Psychology.

Potential Pitfalls

Despite the promise presented by the inclusion of sport and exercise psychology in one's practice, a number of issues need to be addressed. Coping with becoming a novice again, suffering setbacks, scheduling, and managing diagnostic concerns and ethical issues are especially salient concerns. Other chapters in this book focus on some of these topics (e.g., chapters 17 and 20), yet for the practitioner psychologist, particular issues bear special emphasis and even reiteration.

A Novice Again

Expanding one's practice into an unfamiliar area involves the acquisition of new information and skills as well as their integration into existing knowledge and practice. The seasoned practitioner may experience discomfort in being placed in the position of learner once again. Yet acknowledging ignorance can assist in lowering the barriers so that learning can occur, whether through reading, course work, or supervised practice. An attitude of humility, openness, and curiosity makes this process more interesting and effective.

Rejection, Setbacks, and Ambiguity

In part because of its emergent status, sport and exercise psychology has not yet found a comfortable niche. Practitioners, whether new to the field or seasoned, are therefore likely to encounter a series of dead ends and opportunities that do not quite jell. In assessing rejections, it is important to differentiate between situations in which a sport and exercise psychologist is undertrained or inappropriate from instances in which others (e.g., coaches and athletic staff or sports medicine personnel) need education concerning the field's potential value to them. When starting commercial enterprises, it is considered preferable to be the second or subsequent person bringing a new product or service to an area. Because of the newness of this field, however, it may be necessary to create a market before fulfilling that market's need, depending on the target population and location.

Disruptions of Schedule

Working with amateur and professional athletes may require some flexibility and variation in scheduling, depending on the particular sport and the nature and length of the contact with the athlete. Some sports arc seasonal, and an athlete may not see the relevance of contact during the off-season. Some athletes may require intensive work before important events. Athletic teams may expect the sport and exercise psychologist to travel with them. The psychologist who has other clients needs to develop backup services to ensure sufficient and appropriate coverage when necessary. If sport and exercise psychology obligations occur at predictable times, it may be helpful to print up a schedule beforehand, so that other clients know these plans well in advance. As in taking vacations, it is important to pay attention to clients' subjective experience of absences.

Involvement in seasonal sports can create a "boom or bust" cycle. There are various ways to handle this problem. One is to become involved with athletes whose sports have different seasons; another is to adapt other aspects of the overall practice to these demands. Even in the face of high demand at the peak of a season, it is important to set aside regular time for marketing.

Psychopathology and Diagnosis

The clinical practitioner working in sport and exercise psychology often operates on the cusp of the wellness–illness continuum. Clients may not be seeking psychotherapy and may not have definable psychopathology. Although therapeutic, the services provided may not be psychotherapy. Furthermore, it has been suggested that pathologizing normative experiences may have demoralizing effects on clients (Danish, Petitpas, & Hale, 1993). The practitioner accustomed to diagnosis and third-party billing thus confronts both ethical and legal dilemmas in considering the source of payment for services, particularly with individuals. False diagnosis for the purpose of reimbursement is unethical; however, when the consultation involves more than PST, diagnostic criteria for reimbursement may be met. It is prudent to consider sources of reimbursement before embarking on a course. It is also important to review payment options with the contracting party.

Boundary Issues

Concerns about boundaries, present for all psychologists (see chapter 20, this volume), take on particular significance for the practitioner entering this field (Hays, 1995a; Sachs, 1993). As one's practice shifts toward consultation, it is important to note changes in the relationship between psychologist and client and how those differences are understood and monitored. The potential for increased engagement with the client away from the office setting increases the possibility for loss of traditional structures and a more casual relationship. Exercising with clients, observing them on the playing field (whether in practice or competition), traveling with a team, and working with high-profile clients all involve changes from the standard therapist–patient 50-minute hour. Sport and exercise psychologists need to monitor possible shifts in role relationships, levels of self-disclosure, and power and gender imbalances (Hays, 1995b). It is vital to have an ongoing way to review these questions, whether through reflection, supervision, or consultation.

Sport Psychology as a "Title"

With the professionalization of applied sport psychology has come considerable discussion about which clinicians can call themselves "sport psychologists." The title "psychologist" is restricted by states to persons so certified or licensed. Beyond this restriction, psychologists are additionally bound by ethics to practice within their level of competence (APA, 1992). Recently, Taylor commented that "licensed psychologists do not have de facto grounds to hold themselves out to the public as sport psychologists" (1994, p. 188). By virtue of specialized education, training, and experience in exercise and sport, it becomes appropriate for psychologists to claim this title. Without further clinical, counseling, or psychotherapy training, those with training only in sport science should not have an independent counseling or psychotherapy practice (for further discussion, see chapter 18, this volume).

Confidentiality

Confidentiality issues are reflected in many aspects of exercise and sport psychology. Psychologists are obligated not to disclose information concerning clients except as that privilege is waived by clients (APA, 1992). In contrast, coaches are routinely quoted in the press discussing their players. Does psychologists' commitment to confidentiality change when they work in the arena of sport and exercise psychology? The temptation of disclosure to the media becomes increasingly seductive, the more important or famous the client is. As in other contractual or consultative contexts, there is the common ethical dilemma of disclosure if hired by a team administrator to work with individuals who are members of the team. It is important to discuss and specify, possibly in writing, how this will be handled before the work starts.

Further confidentiality issues can arise as a function of the entrepreneurial nature of sport and exercise psychology and the high public visibility of some athletes. For example, there is a marketing dilemma in the use of client endorsements and the public identification of those clients. At present, no standard exists, and practitioners handle these issues in markedly different ways. There is a wide range of practice, from offering services in exchange for endorsements to insisting that athletes not indicate that they are working with a sport psychologist (Botterill, Rotella, Loehr, Ravizza, & Halliwell, 1993; D. S. Kirschenbaum, personal communication, October 14, 1993). We would err on the side of caution and respect for privacy; even if clients waive their rights to confidentiality, such decisions may reflect the power differential between the sport and exercise psychologist and the client rather than a freely accepted agreement. The sport and exercise psychologist should weigh carefully the implications and effects of any decision that does not fully protect the client's identity.

Conclusion

The opportunities to include sport and exercise psychology in clinical practice are rich and varied. The professional who is retooling combines the inquiry of the scientist with the attention to individual differences of the practitioner. Practice opportunities range from injury prevention and performance enhancement to psychotherapy and remediation.

The business of learning about and developing a new practice in sport and exercise psychology involves an assessment of both current practice and future goals. Various potential problem areas also require careful consideration.

It cannot be overemphasized that, for one's own protection as well as growth in regard to all of these issues, it is helpful to have informal or formal networks of colleagues with whom to consult. To the extent that one's education in this field has been ''on-the-job training,'' it is even more important to develop viable ways of addressing troublesome issues before they arise.

As one navigates from where one is to where one wants to be, these suggestions are designed to assist in reading the map, plotting the route, and attending to the road signs. One needs to be persistent, to expect mistakes, to learn from them, and to maintain a positive outlook. The satisfaction deriving from new vistas and deeper knowledge provides the reward.

References

American Psychological Association. (1992). Ethical principles of psychologists and code of conduct. *American Psychologist, 47,* 1597–1611.

American Psychological Association. (1993). *Profile of Division 47 members: 1993.* (Report prepared by American Psychological Association Office of Demographic, Employment, and Educational Research.) Washington, DC: Author.

American Psychological Association. (1994). *Graduate training and career possibilities in exercise and sport psychology* (2nd ed.). Washington, DC: Author.

Antonovsky, A. (1984). The sense of coherence as a determinant of health. In J. D.

Matarazzo, S. M. Weiss, J. A. Herd, N. E. Miller, & S. M. Weiss (Eds.), *Behavioral health* (pp. 114–129). New York: Wiley.

Association for the Advancement of Applied Sport Psychology. (1994). *AAASP Newsletter, 9*(3), 9.

Auchus, M. P. (1993). Therapeutic aspects of a weight lifting program with seriously psychiatrically disabled outpatients. *The Psychotherapy Bulletin, 28*, 30–31, 34–36.

Austad, C. S., & Hoyt, M. F. (1992). The managed care movement and the future of psychotherapy. *Psychotherapy, 29*, 109–118.

Berger, B. G. (1984). Running toward psychological well-being: Special considerations for the female client. In M. L. Sachs & G. W. Buffone (Eds.), *Running as therapy* (pp. 172–197). Lincoln, NE: University of Nebraska Press.

Berger, B. G. (1993). Exercise and the quality of life. In R. N. Singer, M. Murphey, & L. K. Tennant (Eds.), *Handbook of research on sport psychology* (pp. 729–760). New York: Macmillan.

Botterill, C., Rotella, R., Loehr, J., Ravizza, K., & Halliwell, W. (1993, October). *Issues and implications in professional sport consulting.* Symposium conducted at the annual meeting of the Association for the Advancement of Applied Sport Psychology, Montreal, Quebec, Canada.

Boutcher, S. (1993). Emotion and aerobic exercise. In R. N. Singer, M. Murphey, & L. K. Tennant (Eds.), *Handbook of research on sport psychology* (pp. 799–814). New York: Macmillan.

Brewer, B. W., Van Raalte, J. L., & Linder, D. E. (1991). Role of the sport psychologist in treating injured athletes: A survey of sports medicine providers. *Journal of Applied Sport Psychology, 3*, 183–190.

Covey, S. R. (1989). *The seven habits of highly effective people.* New York: Fireside/Simon & Schuster.

Danish, S. J., & Hale, B. D. (1981). Toward an understanding of the practice of sport psychology. *Journal of Sport Psychology, 3*, 90–99.

Danish, S. J., Petitpas, A. J., & Hale, B. D. (1993). Life development intervention for athletes: Life skills through sports. *The Counseling Psychologist, 21*, 352–385.

Eklund, R. (1993). Considerations for gaining entry to conduct sport psychology field research. *The Sport Psychologist, 7*, 232–243.

Greenspan, M. J., & Feltz, D. F. (1989). Psychological interventions with athletes in a competitive situation: A review. *The Sport Psychologist, 3*, 219–236.

Hays, K. F. (1993). The use of exercise in therapy. In L. Van de Creek, S. Knapp, & T. L. Jackson (Eds.), *Innovations in Clinical Practice: A Source Book, 12*, 155–168.

Hays, K. F. (1995a). Putting sport psychology into (your) practice. *Professional Psychology: Research & Practice, 26*, 33–40.

Hays, K. F. (1995b). Running therapy: Special characteristics and therapeutic issues of concern. *Psychotherapy, 31*, 725–734.

Hill, N. (1960). *Think and grow rich.* New York: Fawcett Crest.

Horn, T. (Ed.) (1992). *Advances in sport psychology.* Champaign, IL: Human Kinetics.

Karoly, P., & Kanfer, F. H. (1982). *Self-management and behavior change: From theory to practice.* New York: Pergamon Press.

Kirkcaldy, B. D., & Shephard, R. J. (1990). Therapeutic implications of exercise. *International Journal of Sport Psychology, 21*, 165–184.

Kirschenbaum, D. S. (1992). Elements of effective weight control programs: Implications for exercise and sport psychology. *Journal of Applied Sport Psychology, 4*, 77–93.

Locke, E. A., & Latham, G. P. (1985). The application of goal setting to sports. *Journal of Sport Psychology, 7*, 205–222.

Mahoney, M. J., & Suinn, R. M. (1986). History and overview of modern sport psychology. *The Clinical Psychologist, 39,* 64–68.

Martinsen, E. W. (1990). Benefits of exercise for the treatment of depression. *Sports Medicine, 9,* 380–389.

May, J. R. (1986). Sport psychology: Should psychologists become involved? *The Clinical Psychologist, 39,* 77–81.

McCann, I. L., & Pearlman, L. A. (1990). *Psychological trauma and the adult survivor: Theory, therapy and transformation.* New York: Brunner/Mazel.

Meyers, A. W., Whelan, J. P., & Murphy, S. M. (1996). Cognitive behavioral strategies in athletic performance enhancement. In M. Hersen & A. S. Belack (Eds.), *Handbook of behavior modification* (Vol. 30, pp. 137–164). New York: Plenum Press.

Morgan, W. P. (1985a). Affective beneficence of vigorous physical activity. *Medicine and Science in Sports and Exercise, 17,* 94–100.

Morgan, W. P. (1985b). Selected psychological factors limiting performance: A mental health model. In D. H. Clarke & H. M. Eckert (Eds.), *Limits of human performance* (pp. 70–80). Champaign, IL: Human Kinetics.

Morgan, W. P., & Goldston, S. E. (1987). *Exercise and mental health.* New York: Hemisphere.

Neff, F. (1990). Delivering sport psychology services to a professional sport organization. *The Sport Psychologist, 4,* 378–385.

Nideffer, R. M. (1981). *The ethics and practice of applied sport psychology.* Ithaca, NY: Mouvement.

Norcross, J. C., Alford, B. A., & DeMichele, J. T. (1992). The future of psychotherapy: Delphi data and concluding observations. *Psychotherapy, 29,* 150–158.

Orlick, T. (1986). *Psyching for sport: Mental training for athletes.* Champaign, IL: Human Kinetics.

Orlick, T. (1990). *In pursuit of excellence: How to win in sport and life through mental training.* Champaign, IL: Human Kinetics.

Parham, W. D., & Singer, R. N. (1994, August). *A discussion with elite coaches and athletes.* Discussion conducted at the annual meeting of the American Psychological Association, Los Angeles, CA.

Pierce, R. A. (1969). Athletes in psychotherapy: How many, how come? *Journal of the American College Health Association, 17,* 244–249.

Ribisl, P. M. (1984). Developing an exercise prescription for health. In J. D. Matarazzo, S. M. Weiss, J. A. Herd, N. E. Miller, & S. M. Weiss (Eds.), *Behavioral health* (pp. 448–466). New York: Wiley.

Sachs, M. L. (1993). Professional ethics in sport psychology. In R. N. Singer, M. Murphey, & L. K. Tennant (Eds.), *Handbook of research on sport psychology* (pp. 921–932). New York: Macmillan.

Sachs, M. L., Burke, K. L., & Salitsky, P. B. (1992). *Directory of graduate programs in applied sport psychology* (3rd ed.). Boise, ID: Association for the Advancement of Applied Sport Psychology.

Silva, J. M., & Weinberg, R. S. (Eds.). (1984). *Psychological foundations of sport.* Champaign, IL: Human Kinetics.

Sime, W. E., & Sanstead, M. (1987). Running therapy in the treatment of depression: Implications for prevention. In R. F. Munoz (Ed.), *Depression prevention* (pp. 125–138). New York: Hemisphere.

Skrinar, G. S., Unger, K. V., Hutchinson, D. S., & Faigenbaum, A. D. (1992). Effects of exercise training in young adults with psychiatric disabilities. *Canadian Journal of Rehabilitation, 5,* 151–157.

Sonstroem, R. (1984). Exercise and self-esteem. In R. Terjung (Ed.), *Exercise and sport sciences reviews* (pp. 123–154). New York: Macmillan.

Suinn, R. M. (Ed.). (1980). *Psychology in sports: Methods and applications.* Minneapolis: Burgess.

Taylor, J. (1994) Examining the boundaries of sport science and psychology trained practitioners in applied sport psychology: Title usage and area of competence. *Journal of Applied Sport Psychology, 6,* 185–195.

Van Raalte, J. L. (in press). The competitive athlete. *The Psychotherapy Patient.*

Weinberg, R. S. (1984). Mental preparation strategies. In J. M. Silva & R. S. Weinberg (Eds.), *Psychological foundations of sport* (pp. 145–156). Champaign, IL: Human Kinetics.

Weinberg, R. S. (1994). Goal setting and performance in sport and exercise settings: A synthesis and critique. *Medicine and Science in Sports and Exercise, 26,* 469–477.

Williams, J. M. (1993). *Applied sport psychology* (2nd ed.). Mountain View, CA: Mayfield.

Yenney, S. L., & American Psychological Association Practice Directorate. (1994). *Business strategies for a caring profession.* Washington, DC: American Psychological Association.

Ethics in Sport and Exercise Psychology

20

James P. Whelan, Andrew W. Meyers, and T. David Elkin

One might guess that a discussion about ethical issues in the area of sport and exercise psychology would be straightforward and simple. Professionals in sport and exercise psychology, although originating from various academic traditions, participate in the same range of activities and services as professionals in other areas of psychology (Cox, Qiu, & Liu, 1993; Singer, 1993). Some sport and exercise psychologists hold academic positions that enable them to teach, perform research, and mentor, whereas others focus on the application of scientific knowledge about human behavior (e.g., Smith, 1989), providing evaluations, interventions, educational training, and other types of consultation. There is a clear concern for the quality of services delivered and for the general well-being of individuals and groups with whom these professionals work (e.g., Taylor, 1994; Weinberg, 1989). Logically then, a discussion about ethical issues could focus on the American Psychological Association's (APA) code of ethics (APA, 1992) as applied to sport and exercise settings.

Historically, such discussions have been neither straightforward nor simple. One complication has been that the creation of unique ethics guidelines is seen as central to the professional autonomy of sport and exercise psychology. Zeigler (1987), for example, argued that a code of ethics designed specifically for sport and exercise psychology is a "vital aspect of the overall professionalization of the field" (p. 138). Adoption of the APA code of ethics would be inconsistent with the goal of public recognition of this profession. Successful professionalization, it follows, requires a profession-specific ethics code. A related complication has been that the application of the APA code of ethics often leads to conflicts among sport and exercise professionals, involving issues such as boundaries of practice, title usage, and academic identity of sport psychology (Brown, 1982; May, 1986; Nideffer, 1981; Rejeski & Brawley, 1988; Taylor, 1994). Many competent exercise and sport scientists who are the backbone of this relatively new profession were not trained in psychology departments. These scientists become understandably bothered by laws governing the provision of psychological services that restrict the application of their science (Silva, 1989).

Other complications to these ethics discussions have been related to the debate concerning whether sport and exercise psychology services are unique psychological services that require unique standards for ethical conduct (e.g., Petitpas, Brewer, Rivera, & Van Raalte, 1994; Sachs, 1993; Singer, 1993; Whelan, 1993; Willis & Cambell, 1992). Clearly, there are similarities and differences between sport and exercise psychology services and traditional psychological services. Sport and exercise psychology services may be delivered in the context of therapy or counseling (Whelan, Meyers, & Donovan, 1995); however, performance enhancement and psychological skill training and consultation are not necessarily therapy and not necessarily clinical (Singer, 1993). Application of the 1992 APA code of ethics to similar behaviors in different contexts can be confusing. In addition, the APA code of ethics fail to provide specific guidance for some applied sport and exercise psychology situations (e.g., Petitpas et al., 1994; Sachs, 1993; Singer, 1993; Willis & Cambell, 1992). The APA code of ethics seems to lack the specificity to be practical and interpretable to many who provide services in sport and exercise settings.

Although we would like to say that the discussion that follows will remove these complications and proceed with a straightforward and simple presentation about how to be an ethical sport and exercise psychologist, unfortunately, we cannot. We can put aside discussion of the role of an ethics code in the professionalization of sport psychology and the conflicts about professional organization and identity. These issues are important, but they are not really about ethics or ethical obligation. They need to be considered elsewhere. The complications related to the frustrations of not having specific ethical rules that anticipate unique and specific sport and exercise psychology situations or dilemmas, however, cannot be eradicated. Ambiguity, uncertainty, and uniqueness seem to be part of each complex ethical situation sport and exercise psychology professionals face (Windt, Appleby, Battin, Francis,

& Landesman, 1989). It would be impossible to have ethical standards or rules for every situation. Professionals, therefore, need to understand how to use the ethics code to guide the process of deciding between right and wrong actions (Windt et al., 1989). The foundation for this emphasis is the shared sense of values and responsibilities that is part of the role of the sport and exercise psychology professional, regardless of training background or type of credentials.

Our discussion begins with a declaration about the purpose of professional ethics and a brief history of the APA code of ethics. This history concludes with a summary of the criticisms of the most recent version of this code. Next, an exploration of two primary traditions in ethical theory of right and wrong is provided, with details about the major premises of these theories. The focus then turns to pragmatics of applying these ideas. Specifically, the applications of ethical reasoning to the issues and areas of practical concern to those working in exercise and sport settings are addressed. Using a recent survey of dilemmas and controversial behaviors found in these settings (Petitpas et al., 1994), we consider how professionals can approach problematic situations ethically in an a priori manner.

Professional Ethics

Purpose of Ethics Codes

Questions about ethical conduct permeate our culture. One need only pick up a newsmagazine or newspaper or spend a few evenings watching television to find aggressive inquiries into the ethics of politicians, lawyers, physicians, psychologists, and a variety of other professionals. Our society, with good reason, has become less trusting and more cynical about the judgments of its professionals and experts. In turn, this mistrust and cynicism has led to decreased tolerance for professional misbehavior and increased demands for ethical reform (Windt, 1989). It is expected that the professional can judge between right and wrong and should behave in accordance with what is right. Partly as a consequence of this cultural mistrust, the study of ethics and the development of written codes of ethics in the social sciences and helping professions has absorbed much energy and generated a great deal of debate in recent years (Ellickson & Brown, 1990; Johns, 1993; Windt et al., 1989). This activity in the realm of ethics reflects the concern felt by many

that ethics codes need to address the cultural concerns and fears artic-
ulated by society.

To address these concerns, a profession and its members must attend to both the privileges and the responsibilities of professional status
(Windt, 1989). Privileges derive from society's agreement to designate
a group of trained individuals as possessing specialized knowledge and
holding the power implicit in this knowledge. The profession's responsibilities result from society's expectation that the profession will regulate itself to "do no harm" and will govern itself to ensure the dignity
and welfare of individuals and the public. The profession also agrees to
ensure the quality of its interactions with society. To maintain this status,
professional organizations must develop and enforce guidelines that
regulate their members's professional conduct. Ethical principles, which
go above and beyond personal ethics, are one such set of self-regulatory
guidelines. These principles, written as an ethics code, guide professionals to act responsibly as they employ the privileges granted by society. A profession's inability to regulate itself violates the public's trust
and perpetuates cultural and societal cynicism toward the profession.

The APA Code of Ethics

Psychology as a field has a long and successful history of acting responsibly and proactively on issues of ethical conduct. The APA first adopted
a code of ethics in 1953, which was fairly early in the history of the
profession (APA, 1953). This first ethics code was developed by polling
members for specific vignettes that related to ethical situations. The
response was so great that the code was unwieldy by reason of its sheer
size (O'Donohue & Mangold, in press). The code has been revised
seven times in the ensuing years to meet the needs of the profession
and to fulfill obligations to society. The code thus has become a living
document; as psychology has changed, the code has changed with it
(Pope & Vetter, 1992).

The current code (APA, 1992) consists of six general principles:
competence, integrity, professional and scientific responsibility, respect
for people's rights and dignity, concern for others' welfare, and social
responsibility. Under each of these principles are specific standards, or
practical applications of the general principles. These standards are
generally thought of as rules of ethical behavior. The primary goal of
the code has always been to respect the dignity of the individual and to
guarantee the welfare of the consumer and the profession (Peyton,

1994). This foundational goal of the code can be conceptualized in general terms as "do no harm," and it serves to inform the six general principles. The general principles then become specific in the form of the standards, the discrete rules and regulations that result from the application of the general principles to real-life situations. The entire model can be conceptualized as a triangle: At the widest point on the bottom are the specific standards, or the individual rules that make the ethics code enforceable; these are seen as flowing logically from the general principles, which constitute the next tier. These general principles are derived from the top point, which is the foundational goal of the ethics code, respect for human beings.

The code has not been without criticism. The 1992 version is generally seen as a great improvement over previous renditions (Bersoff, 1994); however, the current code has been criticized for being too concerned with protecting the profession rather than the public (Bersoff, 1994), indifferent to the concerns of diverse groups (Peyton, 1994), equivocal about multiple relationships (Sonne, 1994), and in general, vague (Vasquez, 1994). These criticisms seem to occur because of two problems inherent to the nature of the ethics code itself: (a) It seeks to address a wide range of activities, and thus necessitates a cursory treatment of each, and (b) it fails to anticipate the unique and specific situations in which psychologists find themselves.

A study of the philosophy of ethics may help to clarify these concerns regarding specific ethics codes. Although a thorough understanding of the philosophy of ethics is not a prerequisite for further discussion of ethics and ethics codes, a brief treatment of the philosophy of ethics will aid the professional in understanding the foundations of ethics and in applying ethics in difficult situations.

Philosophy of Ethics in the History of Psychology

The philosophical study of ethics involves the inquiry into the principles and presuppositions that operate in moral judgments. It has been traditionally concerned with the study of what is good and bad, what is right and wrong, or the values that define a "good life." Ethical codes, therefore, are an attempt to put into practice this good life. Codes of ethics may exist for many different populations and diverse situations: Different cultures, religions, and professions may have quite different codes of ethics. The one common factor underlying different codes, however, is their definitional acceptance of ethical codes as "moral guides to self regulation" (O'Donohue & Mangold, in press). Thus, the function of ethics in general and ethical codes in particular is to define right and wrong behavior for a given population, especially as that population interacts with other populations.

It is apparent that the philosophy of ethics must be theory-driven. In other words, one cannot make a determination of what is right and wrong behavior on the basis of personal whims. If that were the case, then ethics and, by implication, codes of ethics would merely be the fickle voice of the majority. Codes of ethics cannot exist without some sort of theory behind them, informing them, grounding them, and providing for their application. This does not mean, however, that codes of ethics are therefore vastly different from ordinary morality. Indeed, professional codes of ethics do not have a "hierarchy of values" different from ordinary morality (O'Donohue et al., 1987, p. 394).

In the history of philosophy, many distinct sources for ethics and ethics codes exist. From the Judeo–Christian ethic to Aristotle to Nietzsche, philosophies of ethics have abounded. However, the works of the deontologists and the consequentialists have been described as particularly influential in the field of psychology and especially on the APA ethics code (Eyde & Quaintance, 1988; O'Donohue & Mangold, in press). The following sections present a brief description of these competing ethical philosophies.

Consequentialists

This school of philosophy argues that actions are ethical or not on the basis of what their consequences are. Behaviors are not determined in an a priori manner to be ethical or not. We can determine if an action is ethical only by making judgments after the behavior occurs. It is the end that is important, not the means by which one arrives at the end. To be ethical, an individual must follow specific rules that make an attempt to guarantee that the consequences of actions will be ethical. A representative of this school is John Stuart Mill, whose contribution to ethical philosophy is known as utilitarianism (Mill, 1861/1979). Although this principle has been stated in many ways, it can be summarized in the well-known statement, "the greatest good for the greatest number." Mill assumed that human beings do not solely desire lofty things such as virtue and duty, nor only desire base things, like wealth. What human beings desire is happiness, and when things like virtue and wealth make them happy, they seek them. The goal of morality, then, becomes one of maximizing happiness, and happiness is maximized when the greatest number of people have it.

In creating moral and ethical codes, the necessity of maximizing pleasure for the majority of human beings is paramount. The way to maximize this happiness is by ensuring that the rules that are developed for that purpose are followed. If it can be shown that a particular action produces the greatest good for the greatest number, then people should engage in that action. Ethics codes are rules that are based on past experiences.

Deontologists

In contrast to consequentialism, the deontological viewpoint holds that before any discussion of ethics and ethics codes can take place, a philosophical foundation must be established. The deontological view argues that ethics needs to be founded on firm and lasting principles that can be applied to many different situations. These principles are, in a sense, immutable; otherwise, ethics would exist merely by the will of the majority. The deontologists point out that the whole point of discussions about ethics is to center on the ideal. Ethics is concerned with what should be, not with what is; therefore, what needs to be established is the ideal, or what ought to be. The ideal is encapsulated in principles, which are not specific but can be applied to many different areas. For example, philosophers of this school would prefer to have general principles, such as "respect other people," than to have a litany of specific rules that apply this principle in many different areas. The problem becomes one of deciding which principles to emphasize.

A philosopher of the deontological school was Immanuel Kant. Kant argued that morality entails duty to one's conscience. He stated that rationality exists in every human and that reason is capable of generating the possibilities of future experiences. People can think ahead in time and judge whether an action will be ethical or not on the basis of past experiences. Morality, therefore, is a duty to the future possibilities of experience and is based on the general principle of respect for other human beings.

In *Grounding for the Metaphysics of Morals*, Kant (1785/1977) described the categorical imperative, which has several qualifications and conditions. It states that a moral action is one that obeys the dictates of universality and consistency. Stated differently, a moral action must be able to be applied to all human beings and must involve no contradictions. The categorical imperative is then used to test whether actions are moral or not. In other words, one could test a maxim (I will borrow money and never repay it) by thinking, if everyone were to do this, could they continue to do it forever? In this example, everyone could of course engage in this behavior, but everyone could not continue to engage in it forever; it would become a self-destructive action. Out of this example comes one of the underlying principles in discussions such as this one: respect for human beings. Actions that are destructive to human beings are not moral because they cannot be universalized. The work of Kant provides philosophical justification for the grounding of morals and a framework from which specific moral maxims can be generated for novel situations that have never been questioned before.

Integrating Philosophy and Ethics

These two philosophers and the views that they espouse have had a unique effect on the creation of the code of ethics of the APA. On the one hand, Kant would argue for the general principles; with his emphasis on duty to conscience and the use of reason to test all possible actions, his view of ethics points to the understanding and documentation of general principles, or general plans of action that would guide future tests of actions for ethicality. His philosophy allows no room for particular rules; it is a dynamic system that is constantly capable of evaluating every single possible action that can be thought of at any moment.

The philosophy of Mill, on the other hand, comes at the problem from quite a different direction. His philosophy points to the necessity of specific codes and standards that deal with specific situations. Only by dealing with the specific contingencies of the environment and behavior can the happiness and the good of the greatest number be ensured. Only by looking to past experiences can rules be generated that will cover future experiences. Mill would make no provisions for general principles that inform ethics in a global sense; rather, his framework demands the specific and works toward spelling out exactly what contributes to the greatest good for the greatest number. Thus, the work of the consequentialists can be seen as arguing for the creation of specific rules, or standards that govern behavior.

The APA ethics code (1992) operates according to both of these assumptions. The code is functionally a mixture of the different philosophical frameworks epitomized by Kant and Mill. From the deontologists, the code derives its six general principles, all of which operate as ethical maxims capable of being universalized and consistent without resorting to individual rules for specific cases. These principles are designed to be portable, in a sense; they transcend specific situations and therefore are capable of influencing a wide range of behaviors. Likewise, the code follows the consequentialists, with its standards. These are specific rules that are thought to flow out of the general principles and that apply to specific situations within the field of psychology. The problem with attempting to create an exhaustive list is that one cannot anticipate every problematic circumstance. Undoubtedly, the standards as they are currently written do not represent all of the possible rules that a psychologist would need to follow to behave ethically. However, the code claims to be "enforceable," and ethics codes can be enforceable only if specific rules are spelled out. The question of other rules that are also enforceable but have not yet been codified naturally arises. The code recognizes this dilemma and provides for the creation of additional rules: "The Ethical Standards are not exhaustive. The fact that a given conduct is not specifically addressed by the Ethics Code does not mean that it is necessarily ethical or unethical" (APA, 1992, p. 1598).

This dynamic model of ethics, in which standards often fail to fit perfectly and principles give guidance across context areas, may make some people uncomfortable. People seem naturally to desire specificity and ease of applicability, which a list of rules seemingly provides. However, codes of ethics are moving away from the conception of a mere list of rules and toward a dynamic model of ethics, one that treats ethics in a thematic sense by emphasizing the general principles. The Association for the Advancement of Applied Sport Psychology (AAASP) is considering adopting a model of this type. In the AAASP model, the general principles are listed and then provision is made for future clarification of these principles, as time goes by and as the field develops. This flexibility, is particularly appropriate for professionals who are working in a new field but attempting to develop and adhere to specific statements.

Ethical Philosophy Applied to Sport and Exercise Psychology

Sport and exercise psychologists frequently encounter ethically challenging situations. Consider the following situation: A man with a PhD in counseling with a background in exercise and sport sciences (let's call him Dr. Bob) accepted a split position funded by a university counseling center and the university's athletic department. His charge in this new position included sport psychology and personal counseling services to the university's sports teams and the individual student-athletes. While moving into his office, Dr. Bob received a call from the head coach for one of the women's sport teams. The coach reported that her team really needed a psychologist. She requested mental skills training for her team, assistance with a couple of "head cases," and information about the psychology of coaching, and feedback about her coaching. The coaching issue centered on more effective communication between herself and the team. The coach said that several players seemed to be insulted and discouraged by her feedback. Because the coach had worked with a sport psychologist as an athlete, she was very responsive to Dr. Bob's clarifications about confidentiality and his role with the coach and team. Dr. Bob was confident that he and the coach had a clear understanding of his role with her and her team.

Through the early fall, Dr. Bob's efforts appeared to pay off. The coach was initially receptive during the preseason consultation meetings about communication with her team. Unfortunately, the pressure of conference play precipitated a return to what, for the sake of simplicity, could be labeled an authoritarian and condescending style of coaching. The team benefited from the psychological skills training meetings and appeared to be mastering some basic psychological skills related to performance preparation. Several of the team members had confidentially contacted Dr. Bob with concerns about their relationship with the coach. He assured each of these women that their meetings were confidential and that this confidentiality was understood by the coach. An added bonus was that the coach had mentioned to the athletic director and other coaches that "sport psychology" was okay.

At the end of a successful season for this team, Dr. Bob's experience was drastically altered. One third of the squad—including many of the starters—requested to meet with Dr. Bob as a group. They each reported feeling abused by the coach, and with their parents' support they wanted to seek a release from the team. They wanted to know how to get this release. The women and their parents considered calling the university president to secure their release. Several described specific incidents in which the coach's behavior could be viewed as psychologically abusive. Dr. Bob had neither witnessed nor heard of these incidents before. Instantly, Dr. Bob found himself in an ethical dilemma.

He had a fiduciary relationship with both the coach and the team members. The seriousness of the conflict between these two parties meant that he was in position to fail the trust of one of these relationships. In fact, his fiduciary responsibilities were threatened by his simply listening to the team members and engaging them in a discussion of their options. A further complication was that this scenario could jeopardize his job and the degree to which the athletic department and the student-athletes had access to a sport psychologist. Although Dr. Bob had educated all parties involved about his ethical responsibilities, he was not ready for the specifics of this situation. However, Dr. Bob cannot be blamed. There are no specific rules concerning a situation like this one. A simple answer stating what is the right action to take does not exist for such circumstances.

Unpredictable and complicated situations such as this occur for professionals working in clinical psychology (Pope, Tabachnick, & Keith-Spiegel, 1987; Pope & Vasquez, 1991; Pope & Vetter, 1992), sport psychology (Petitpas et al., 1994; Sachs, 1993), and other public service areas (Bayles, 1981; Windt et al., 1989). These situations challenge the professional's knowledge of the meaning and the application of ethics codes. They call for psychologists to identify and clarify their personal values as well as their professional and institutional guidelines.

Responses to a sample of situation such as this one in sport psychology were recently elicited in a national survey of the beliefs and behaviors of psychologists and sport scientists interested in the application of psychology to exercise and sport settings (Petitpas et al., 1994). Petitpas and colleagues mailed questionnaires to 508 student and professional members of the Association for the Advancement of Applied Sport Psychology (AAASP). Respondents were provided with 47 ethical situations and asked to report their own behavior and their belief about the ethicality of the choices. This survey also requested a brief description of difficult ethical situations experienced by members. Of the 165 members who returned the survey, approximately half of the respondents identified themselves as psychologists, with most of the other half identifying themselves as exercise scientists. It is interesting that over 90% of the respondents reported that they engage in sport psychology services less than 17 hours per week and 70% less than 5 hours per week. Therefore, individuals in this sample, representing the two major traditions within sport psychology, were only minimally engaged in applied sport psychology services. The central findings of this survey replicated the work of Pope et al. (1987), with most of these professionals

---

Exhibit 1

Behaviors Identified as Difficult Judgments

1. Conflict with confidentiality:
   a. Reporting recruiting violations to appropriate officials.
   b. Reporting an athlete's gambling activity.
   c. Reporting an athlete who acknowledged committing rape in the past.
2. Conflict between personal values and professional ethics:
   a. Consulting with athletes in a sport that you find morally objectionable (e.g., boxing).
   b. Working with an athlete who uses steroids.
   c. Refusing to continue consulting with a client after you discover that he or she is involved in illegal activity.
3. Conflict with dual relationships:
   a. Socializing with clients (e.g., partying with the team).
   b. Allowing out-of-town clients to reside in your home while services are being provided.

---

reporting that they behaved in accordance with their beliefs about ethics. There were only minor differences between members identified as psychologists and those identified as sport and exercise scientists in terms of ethical beliefs and behaviors. The dilemmas that these professionals identified were not inconsistent with themes addressed in the APA code of ethics.

Of the 47 ethical situations, respondents found 8 to be difficult ethical judgments and 24 to be controversial behaviors. Difficult ethical judgments were defined as situations for which over 25% of the respondents indicated that they were unsure whether the behavior was ethical. Controversial behaviors were items for which the opinions of the respondents were significantly diverse. The 8 difficult ethical situations can be classified into three general categories (see Exhibit 1).

The behaviors that were rated as controversial can be classified into four general categories (see Exhibit 2). Using these classifications generated by controversial ethical situations, specific ethical dilemmas faced in sport and exercise settings become apparent.

First, *issues of confidentiality* are frequently encountered by professionals working in sport and exercise psychology, as in the following hypothetical example: A PhD psychologist is contracted by a major university to work with an athlete who reports "anxiety." Before beginning the consultation, the professional is instructed about National Collegiate Athletic Association (NCAA) rules and regulations that specifi-

---

Exhibit 2

Behaviors Identified as Controversial

1. Conflict with confidentiality:
   a. Reporting recruiting violations to appropriate officials.
   b. Reporting an athlete who uses cocaine.
   c. Reporting an athlete who uses steroids.
   d. Reporting abusive coaching practices.
   e. Reporting an athlete's gambling activity.
   f. Reporting an athlete who committed burglary.
   g. Reporting an athlete who acknowledged committing rape in the past.
2. Conflict between personal values and professional ethics:
   a. Working with an athlete whose sexual or religious practices you oppose.
   b. Consulting with athletes in a sport that you find morally objectionable (e.g., boxing).
   c. Working with an athlete who uses steroids.
   d. Refusing to continue consulting with a client after you discover that he or she is involved in illegal activity.
3. Conflict with dual relationships:
   a. Accepting goods or services in exchange for sport psychology consultation.
   b. Serving concurrently as coach and sport psychologist for a team.
   c. Serving concurrently as college instructor and psychologist for a student-athlete.
   d. Being sexually attracted to a client.
   e. Becoming sexually involved with a client *after* discontinuing a professional relationship.
   f. Entering into a business relationship with a client.
4. Conflict with self-presentation or advertising:
   a. Publicly claiming to be a sport psychologist.
   b. Advertising sport psychology services.
   c. Including athlete testimonials in advertising.
   d. Using institutional affiliation to recruit private clients.

---

cally state that the professional cannot attend practices or performance situations because that professional would be considered part of the coaching staff. Over the course of consultation, this issue becomes problematic for the professional, who knows that effective treatment for anxiety should involve on-site exposure to anxiety-eliciting stimuli by the athlete and behavior monitoring of the athlete by the professional. Also, after 1 month of consultation, the professional is approached by the coaching staff, who claim that the athlete has signed a consent waiver, and they want to know what has happened during the consultation process. This, too, is problematic, because the professional has discovered information relating to the anxiety of the athlete that might result in the athlete losing eligibility. What can the professional do? The ethics code is not particularly clear at this point. It must be remembered that the professional's primary responsibility is to the athlete and that behaving ethically involves being true to the foundational principle of doing no harm to the athlete. Therefore, the professional should not divulge information concerning the athlete without the athlete's permission. The professional should contact the athlete, discuss what is to be revealed, and proceed from there. This is an example in which issues of confidentiality become clouded; even though the professional is under contract by the university, however, the professional's primary fiduciary responsibility lies with the athlete.

Second, *conflicts between personal and professional ethics* frequently occur to those who work in sport and exercise psychology (Appleby, 1989). It is always recommended that ethical issues be clearly defined and clarified before one enters into a formal consultation (Dougherty, 1990). Although this advice is helpful, it is not always possible to follow. Often, issues arise during the consultation process that were not foreseeable from the outset and involve conflicts between personal and professional ethics. Returning to the earlier example, suppose that during the consultation process the professional discovers that one of the sources of anxiety that the athlete is experiencing is the athlete's frequent use of illegal drugs. The professional may be personally against the use of drugs but must take into account, first and foremost, the obligation to professional ethics. What should the professional do? The professional may feel that it would benefit the athlete in the long run to enter a drug rehabilitation program, but the athlete does not want to do this. Here, the professional's obligation involves acting in the athlete's best interest as far as sport and exercise performance is concerned, in line with the professional's original contract with the university. Again, the specific rules are not clear, but the professional is aided by an understanding of the philosophy of ethics and complying with general principles.

Dual-role conflicts in sport and exercise psychology are especially problematic. There are times when professionals may find that the relationship boundary between themselves and clients becomes clouded. In the preceding example, if the professional chooses to use on-site exposure by attending practices and games, the role of the professional changes slightly; the professional is now part of the coaching staff and hence may be viewed by the athlete as less objective. Likewise, the visual intimacy that a locker room affords can be problematic for the professional and may lead to feelings of decreased objectivity by both the professional and the athlete (Sachs, 1993). Dual-role relationships open the possibility of distorting the professional relationship, creating conflicts of interest, and undermining the fiduciary nature of the consultation process (Pope & Vasquez, 1991; Sonne, 1994). For the professional, the difficulty lies in avoiding dual-role relationships; however, there are no rules that clearly delineate all possible dual-role relationships. The professional must operate from general principles with a view toward clearly defining future dual-role relationships.

Finally, in regard to *self-presentation and advertising*, the APA code of ethics frequently finds itself at odds with the rules and regulations of the Federal Trade Commission (FTC) (Koocher, 1994). The basic rule applied by the ethics code is that advertising by a professional is wrong; however, the FTC has in the past investigated whether this prohibition is correct (Koocher, 1994). To return to the preceding example again, the athlete with whom the professional has worked is now, after a period of time, showing no signs of anxiety, is playing in top form, and credits the professional for the comeback. The athlete has an upcoming television interview and has told the professional that he plans to mention the professional's name on the air. What should the professional do? Although the professional has not actively sought out this endorsement from the athlete, it is not something that the professional can easily reject. It could mean many more referrals in the future for other athletic consultations. However, the professional knows that advertising is not encouraged in the ethics code. In this case, the professional again should remember the general principles, which state that the primary goal of consultation is to benefit the athlete, not the professional.

As one might imagine, a virtually endless number of difficult situations could easily be offered. The point is that professionals who are currently working in the field of sport and exercise psychology frequently find themselves in ethical dilemmas for which no clear rules are present to guide their behavior. Although rules and standards are needed that address these situations, these take time to generate, and until then the professional may feel at a loss for ethical guidance. In this situation, an understanding of the philosophy of ethics and the foundations of ethics codes can be helpful for the professional. The first step is always to consult the standards. If there are no specific standards to address a situation, the professional should attempt to use the general principles and, ultimately, the foundational principle in an effort to guide behavior. Over time, it is the hope that specific standards will be generated.

Conclusion

An ethics code is a helpful tool in guiding behavior. It is especially helpful for a profession that in part fulfills its societal contract by providing for the regulation of its members' behavior. But ethics codes change as the profession changes in its relation to society. Furthermore, as developing fields emerge, ethical situations are encountered that an existing ethics code may not adequately address. Although sport and exercise psychology is by definition a branch of psychology, the professionals who practice it often encounter ethical situations that are difficult and controversial. It is clear from the examination of difficult and controversial situations that behaving ethically does not involve simply following the rules of the ethics code. Understanding the philosophy of ethics guides the professional toward ethical behavior. The ultimate goal would naturally be the creation of standards that clearly delineate ethical behavior; however, the creation of standards is an ongoing, developmental process. The professional is aided, therefore, by an understanding of the foundational principle and the general principles of an ethics code until such time as specific standards are created that address the particular situations of concern to the professional.

References

American Psychological Association. (1992). Ethical principles of psychologists and code of conduct. *American Psychologist, 47,* 1597–1611.

Appleby, P. C. (1989). Personal, professional, and institutional obligations. In P. Y. Windt, P. C. Appleby, M. P. Battin, L. P. Francis, & B. M. Landesman (Eds.), *Ethical issues in the professions* (pp. 229–255). Englewood Cliffs, NJ: Prentice-Hall.

Bayles, M. D. (1981). *Professional ethics.* Belmont, CA: Wadsworth.

Brown, J. (1982). Are sport psychologists really psychologists? *Journal of Sport Psychology, 4,* 13–18.

Cox, R. H., Qiu, Y., & Liu, Z. (1993). Overview of sport psychology. In R. N. Singer, M. Murphey, & L. K. Tennant (Eds.), *Handbook of research on sport psychology* (pp. 3–31). New York: Macmillan.

Dougherty, A. M. (1990). *Consultation: Practice and perspectives.* Pacific Grove, CA: Brooks/Cole.

Ellickson, K. A., & Brown, D. R. (1990). Ethical considerations in dual relationships: The sport psychologist-coach. *Journal of Applied Sport Psychology, 2,* 186–190.

Kant, I. (1785/1977). Grounding for the metaphysics of morals. In S. M. Cahn (Ed.), *Classics of Western Philosophy* (pp. 925–976). Indianapolis, IN: Hackett.

May, J. (1986). Sport psychology: Should psychologists become involved? *The Clinical Psychologist, 39,* 77–81.

Mill, J. S. (1861/1979). Utilitarianism. In G. Sher (Ed.), *John Stuart Mill: Utilitarianism* (pp. 1–63). Indianapolis, IN: Hackett.

Nideffer, R. (1981). *The ethics and practice of applied sport psychology.* Ithaca, NY: Movement.

O'Donohue, W., & Mangold, R. (in press). A critical examination of the ethical principles of psychologists and code of conduct. *Psychology and philosophy: Interdisciplinary problems and responses.* New York: Allyn & Bacon.

Petitpas, A., Brewer, B., Rivera, P., & Van Raalte, J. (1994). Ethical beliefs and behaviors in applied sport psychology: The AAASP ethics survey. *Journal of Applied Sport Psychology, 6,* 135–151.

Pope, K. S., Tabachnick, B. G., & Keith-Spiegel, P. (1987). Ethics of practice: The beliefs and behaviors of psychologists as therapists. *American Psychologist, 42,* 993–1006.

Pope, K. S., & Vasquez, M. J. T. (1991). *Ethics in psychotherapy and counseling: A practical guide for psychologists.* San Francisco: Jossey-Bass.

Pope, K. S., & Vetter, V. A. (1992). Ethical dilemmas encountered by members of the American Psychological Association. *American Psychologist, 47,* 397–411.

Rejeski, W. J., & Brawley, L. (1988). Defining the boundaries of sport psychology. *The Sport Psychologist, 2,* 231–242.

Sachs, M. (1993). Professional ethics in sport psychology. In R. N. Singer, M. Murphey, & L. K. Tennant (Eds.), *Handbook of research on sport psychology* (pp. 921–932). New York: Macmillan.

Silva, J. (1989). Toward the professionalization of sport psychology. *The Sport Psychologist, 3,* 265–273.

Singer, R. N. (1993). Ethical issues in clinical services. *Quest, 45,* 88–145.

Smith, R. E. (1989). Applied sport psychology in an age of accountability. *Journal of Applied Sport Psychology, 1,* 166–180.

Taylor, J. (1994). Examining the boundaries of sport science and psychology trained practitioners in applied sport psychology: Title usage and area of competence. *Journal of Applied Sport Psychology, 6,* 185–195.

Weinberg, R. S. (1989). Applied sport psychology: Issues and challenges. *Journal of Applied Sport Psychology, 1,* 181–195.

Whelan, J. P. (1993, Summer). Considering ethics. *AAASP Newsletter, 8,* 24, 27.

Whelan, J. P., Meyers, A. W., & Donovan, C. (1995). Interventions with competitive recreational athletes. In S. Murphy (Ed.), *Sport psychology interventions* (pp. 71–116). Champaign, IL: Human Kinetics.

Willis, J., & Campbell, L. (1992). Counseling in the fitness profession. In J. Willis & L. Campbell (Eds.), *Exercise psychology* (pp. 147–171). Champaign, IL: Human Kinetics.

Windt, P. Y. (1989). Professions and professional ethics: The theoretical background. In P. Y. Windt, P. C. Appleby, M. P. Battin, L. P. Francis, & B. M. Landesman (Eds.), *Ethical issues in the professions* (pp. 1–24). Englewood Cliffs, NJ: Prentice-Hall.

Windt, P. Y., Appleby, P. C., Battin, M. P., Francis, L. P., & Landesman, B. M. (Eds.). (1989). *Ethical issues in the professions.* Englewood Cliffs, NJ: Prentice-Hall.

Zeigler, E. F. (1987). Rationale and suggested dimensions for a code of ethics for sport psychologists. *The Sport Psychologist, 1,* 138–150.

Part Six

Conclusion

Future of Sport and Exercise Psychology

Robert N. Singer

It has been said that "predicting is difficult—especially if it's about the future!" Even weather forecasters experience great challenges in determining the next day's weather, in spite of the availability of advanced technology. It is no easier to project developments and directions in a specialized field of study. With reservations, we attempt to make a brief excursion from the present to the future with regard to perspectives about sport and exercise psychology (SEP).

In 1994, APA President Frank Farley convened a group of highly recognized psychologists for a conference titled "The Assembly of the 21st Century." The general purpose was to brainstorm about the future of psychology (Meade, 1994). Three questions were framed by Farley:

- What common ground exists in psychology in the 1990s?
- Where should psychology be headed as the 21st century approaches?
- How can psychology help the world to be a better place?

Certainly the same questions are significant for the SEP field. Perhaps "wise people," identified leaders in SEP, should be brought together for this purpose (e.g., see Straub & Hinman, 1992). Lengthy and insightful dialogue could lead to more intelligent planning for the shaping of SEP as we approach the 21st century. At the very least, leaders in SEP could be surveyed, as done by Boneau (1992) with senior psychologists for psychology in general, to gain insights into currently and potentially significant developments in the field; included would be implications for the future concerning subject matter (or knowledge base) and application (or practice).

Although the scope of SEP is broad, commonalities appear in the interests and pursuits of academic scholars and professionals with more applied concerns, as I explain later. There are many productive and beneficial directions the field could take and is taking to enhance its identity and meaningfulness. It should be possible to determine how users of SEP knowledge and services are better off and how and why contributions "make a difference." The challenges are great and somewhat overwhelming but necessary to meet.

What will all this activity and interest lead to? What major issues will surface? What developments will occur? How will SEP fare in the future in terms of the respect it receives, the identity it creates, and the impact it makes? This chapter begins with a discussion of the uniqueness of SEP, and continues with a description of ways to bridge boundaries. Commentary on specializing within SEP and career possibilities is followed with a discussion of emerging opportunities for services, activities, and networking in the field. Finally, a discussion of research allows an exploration of the future of SEP with reference to present concerns.

A Unique Sport Science

Although SEP has its roots in both psychology and sport science, it is somewhat unique as a sport science. A commonality among the sport sciences includes the intent to contribute to the understanding and maximizing of human performance and achievement, for example, to help an athlete be the best that he or she can be. In addition, however, SEP can and should be concerned with the well-being of the athlete or exercise participant. This special contribution of the field needs to be emphasized more in the future.

This unique contribution is especially valued in the world of high-level sport, where the pressure to win is incredibly great. Any advantage over opponents, such as through potentially useful products or approaches to training and competition, is eagerly sought. Sport science and medical breakthroughs are becoming increasingly available for this purpose; however, SEP can represent more than this to athletes. Their personal development, responsibility, decision-making skills, rights, and happiness should also be addressed. Of the cadre of specialists enlisted to ensure the competitive edge of athletes and teams, the sport and exercise psychologist might be the only one who clearly assumes the designated role of a support person caring about more than the winning of an event. Sport and exercise psychologists help to place sport in perspective in the lives of athletes. It is hoped that this function increases in subsequent years.

The field is clearly more directly in tune with the welfare of people when considering exercise and health for the general population than when concerned with success for the elite athlete. Specialists with a focus on the lifestyles and well-being of individuals help them to become involved with and committed to meaningful physical activity programs throughout their lives.

Multidisciplinary Nature

The legitimate academic home of SEP may be claimed by both departments of psychology and departments of sport and exercise science. However, on the basis of current SEP courses offered (Petrie & Watkins, 1994), employment possibilities, and academic specializations within a department in this country, SEP is most likely to be associated with departments of exercise and sport science or departments with a similar title. (See, for example, the *Directory of Graduate Programs in Applied Sport Psychology*, written by Sachs, Burke, & Salitsky, 1992 for the Association for the Advancement of Applied Sport Psychology.) Furthermore, LeUnes and Hayward (1990) noted that clinical psychology program chairpersons feel that sport psychology is not a significant curricular component in major psychology departments. Course offerings in sport psychology in such departments are rare. Nevertheless, psychology and sport and exercise science departments are expected to collaborate increasingly in contributing to the academic preparation of sport and exercise psychologists.

Experiences in the study of psychology and of movement, especially as associated with sport and exercise, are important in preparing to be a sport and exercise psychologist. SEP is indeed multidisciplinary. Scientists and practitioners from different academic backgrounds can and should collaborate to further understanding and improve the services delivered. The bodies of knowledge and language associated with psychology as well as sport and exercise science need to be shared and understood.

The notion of sharing knowledge and interests, leading to expanding interpretations of the field, can also be identified with the terms "sport" and "exercise." Historically, the field was labeled *sport psychol-*

ogy. The focus was exclusively on athletic performance. In more recent years, health and well-being through regular participation in vigorous physical activity programs has become of increasing interest. Sport and exercise are related movement mediums, and certain themes of interest, such as motivation, self-efficacy, and attributional styles, concern the sport psychologist as well as the exercise psychologist. Even though each area will become increasingly specialized, professionals with a primary commitment to either one should remain as partners.

Specializing Within the Specialization

As the body of knowledge is developed in any specialization, the specialization itself typically becomes more diverse and fractionated. As well, themes and interests are explored more scientifically and advanced more acceptably. Perhaps SEP lacks a clear identity, a complaint Scott (1991) has made about the field of psychology in general. A clear identity is badly needed in the case of SEP. Considerations should be given to (a) an advanced body of knowledge, and (b) potential functions and roles of those trained in the area.

The Body of Knowledge

It has been proposed (Singer, in press) that the commonality of interest to exercise and sport psychologists is in *human achievement and welfare* in and through the *medium of movement.* Sport, exercise, recreation, and play are representative of this medium.

It should be realized that sport and exercise sport psychologists are becoming more specialized, and the trend will continue. Expertise is function-specific. Areas of specialization include the following:

1. *Youth sport* (developmental considerations, motivational factors, optimal learning periods, ideal experiences)
2. *Group dynamics* (morale, productivity, leadership)
3. *Learning and expertise* (learning processes, practice conditions and simulations, demands of events, expert systems)
4. *Counseling* (coping with problems and maladaptive behaviors, substance abuse, depression, injury, severe anxiety)
5. *Psychometrics* (sport-specific psychological test construction, diagnosis, selection, prediction of success)

6. *Performance enhancement* (mental preparation routines, intervention techniques, motivation, self-regulation approaches)
7. *Well-being* (wellness and quality of life, motivational factors, psychological benefits)

The body of knowledge has been increasing steadily in recent years owing to the scholarly efforts of exercise and sport psychologists (e.g., Singer, Murphey, & Tennant, 1993). The range and depth of the growing body of knowledge in SEP indicates the increased focus within the specialization.

Functions and Roles

The increasing functions and roles of sport and exercise psychologists suggest the need for greater specialization. The following updated list of potential roles and functions of sport and exercise psychologists is based on the work of Singer (1984):

1. Scientist: developing the body of knowledge.
2. Scholar–educator: developing and transmitting the body of knowledge and guiding the experiences of would-be sport and exercise psychologists.
3. Counselor: aiding athletes in dealing with maladaptive behaviors and personal adjustment problems.
4. Performance-enhancement consultant: helping athletes to improve performance potential through intervention and self-regulation techniques.
5. Psychodiagnostician: assessing the psychological attributes associated with achieving.
6. Spokesperson: promoting the welfare and the ethical treatment of athletes.
7. Health promotion specialist: contributing to the well-being of the average person in need of regular exercise involvement.

Some sport and exercise psychologists have assumed just one of these roles, at least in terms of primary focus, and some have been able to handle various roles well. Nevertheless, it must be realized by both specialists and clients that a sport and exercise psychologist cannot be all things to all people. Like mastering the body of knowledge and specializing in some aspect of it, excellence in pursuing a particular role is somewhat specialized as well.

Most students preparing to be sport and exercise psychologists would like to be performance enhancers, helping highly skilled athletes to be even more proficient. Unfortunately, athletes oftentimes view sport psychologists mainly as shrinks (Van Raalte, Brewer, Brewer, & Linder, 1992). College students also tend to classify sport psychologists as working with mental problems (Linder, Brewer, Van Raalte, & De-Lange, 1991). The connotations associated with the term *mental problem* may lead athletes to shy away from involvement with sport psychologists or to keep a consultation secret. Athletes do not want to be labeled as mental cases when, in reality, no deep-seated disorders exist. Of course privacy and confidentiality are imperative.

Another function is in health promotion. Understanding and contributing to healthy lifestyles to enhance one's quality of life is of great significance. The challenge is in determining ways to get more people involved in regular programs of physical activity. Physiological and physical benefits are obvious. Psychological benefits are not so apparent and easily measured, but a variety of them exist, as is indicated later in this chapter and reported increasingly in recent research.

Sport and exercise psychologists should understand their capabilities. The APA's *Ethical Principles for Psychologists and Code of Conduct* (1992) requires this of all psychologists. The acceptability and respectability of a profession is at stake, and the importance of realizing one's limitations of knowledge or practice is perhaps of greater importance than recognizing what one can do well.

Career Choices

Although career choices in SEP may be apparent, the paths to realize such choices are not well laid out. Nor are the career opportunities well established and recognized in society at present. These matters may change for the better in the near future. As the trend continues for more and better graduate students to be academically prepared to function effectively in occupations that range from university positions to service providers, greater credibility and acceptance of the field will be realized.

Despite these problems, survey data of recently graduated sport psychology doctorate holders have indicated that these professionals are satisfied with their careers (Waite & Pettit, 1993). They are involved in a variety of work activities, typically with some combination of teaching, research, consulting, administration, and coaching. Most of the respondents were employed in academic settings, and about half of them were consulting with and counseling athletes.

No university presently offers an undergraduate specialization in SEP. A number of them, however, have faculty who have developed SEP curricula at the master's and doctoral levels. However, there is grave concern in higher education about the overproduction of graduates in virtually every field with PhD's and postdoctorate degrees. Many graduates cannot locate positions in their specialization and are considered to be fortunate to get any kind of employment. Perhaps pressure will be put on graduate school faculties to think the dilemma through carefully and to reduce the size of their programs. If this happens, an undergraduate or master's degree might be more valued than it is presently. Exercise science specialists with undergraduate and master's degrees seem to find employment reasonably well. Physical therapists and athletic trainers locate excellent positions without doctorates.

Will reasonably comprehensive programs in the sport and exercise field be proposed at the undergraduate and master's levels, and will graduates from these programs be marketable? It will be interesting to see what happens with regard to these issues. Presently, most professional employment requires a doctorate from a psychology or exercise and sport sciences department, with an emphasis in SEP. In addition, to be a licensed psychologist in most states, one must hold a doctorate in an APA-approved doctoral program, as one criterion.

There has been a steady increase in the number of sport psychologists consulting with athletes and teams, although on an irregular basis. If they are effective with athletes and coaches, even on a part-time basis, the situation may change. But students should not be naive about their chances for employment in this capacity. Furthermore, when positions arise in athletic programs for sport psychologists, direct performance enhancement may be of low priority. For example, a university athletic department may hire a sport psychologist as a counselor–advisor to help student-athletes make responsible decisions about their lifestyles and education and remain academically eligible to compete. When a professional sports team searches for a sport psychologist, it may be concerned with substance-abuse education and other factors related to the private lives of athletes.

Performance enhancement—helping athletes through the use of intervention techniques, education, and self-regulation strategies—is at the beginning stage of understanding and application in sport programs in this country. Sport psychologists who know how to be effective businesspeople are making breakthroughs, creating a niche for themselves. Professional education, experience, and the ability to sell oneself are critical considerations. As sport continues to grow as an entertainment medium, with more and more at stake in winning and much media attention and money riding on the outcomes of events, sport psychologists are likely to be more involved in more clearly defined roles. If visibility of sport psychologists in the media grows and the reporting of their involvement is favorable, recreational athletes and exercise participants will become more interested in availing themselves of similar services.

Emerging Opportunities

The career paths of sport and exercise psychologists are varied, which can make the field seem confusing and unstable. This variety can also be interpreted as opportunity. There are many opportunities to do research, to provide services to various constituencies, and to be involved in interesting and challenging activities. There are also opportunities to be an educator.

Full-Time Occupations

Faculty
Increasing numbers of exercise and sport science departments are employing sport and exercise psychologists to teach and to undertake research. Especially valuable is the person who can attract research grants. The specialty area in which this is most likely to occur is exercise psychology, because Americans are preoccupied with their quality of life and with aging with minimal health problems.

University Athletic Department Counseling
Athletic directors are realizing the importance of providing advising and counseling services to athletes that go beyond course selection. The perspective is not typically for athletic performance enhancement, however. Rather, the functions include helping athletes in making lifestyle choices, motivating them to study and graduate, and enabling them to deal with personal problems.

Private Practice

A counseling and performance-enhancement practice for serious athletes is possible, but it should be incorporated into a larger practice that services nonathletes as well.

Corporations

Possibilities exist for exercise psychologists in larger corporations with exercise and recreational facilities and a commitment to encouraging employees to take advantage of them. These professionals can develop motivational conditions and individualized programs suited for different personality styles and psychological needs.

Part-Time Occupations

Consulting is the leading candidate for part-time involvement in SEP. It helps to have a stable position and income when attempting to consult with athletic teams or individual athletes, because the sport world has become accustomed to free or low-priced support services. Furthermore, although services may be reimbursed, one is not able to make a living from what right now amounts to less than part-time work. On the positive side, coaches and athletes are becoming more receptive to sport psychological services, and more and more psychologists and sport scientists are becoming involved in consulting activities. Consulting activities performed by exercise psychologists can be established with local health and fitness clubs. Although this has been done rarely, health and fitness clubs are a potential area for future involvement.

Consulting could also be offered to local recreational youth sport programs to provide guidance for their structure, format of instruction, and work with participants. Volunteer coaches may lack information about children: their readiness to learn, performance capabilities, ability to deal with competition, and response to motivational approaches. For those interested in occasional consulting or pro bono work, there are many other potential constituencies, such as people with handicaps, older people, and people with mental retardation, who are virtually unnoticed by sport and exercise psychologists, who primarily target highly skilled athletes. Perhaps the scope of involvement with these populations will increase in the future.

Professional Activities and Service

To keep abreast of the latest information and activities in SEP and to help shape the future, North American sport and exercise psychologists have the opportunity to be directly active in Division 47 (exercise and sport psychology) of the American Psychological Association, the North American Society for the Psychology of Sport and Physical Activity (NASPSPA), and the Association for the Advancement of Applied Sport Psychology (AAASP). They can also be involved with such international organizations as the International Society of Sport Psychology (ISSP).

By providing services to organizations and being an active member, a sense of belonging and fulfillment is experienced, along with feelings of contributing to the field. Personal growth occurs from interactions with others with similar interests.

International Networking

Each year seems to bring about more opportunities for sport and exercise psychologists from various parts of the world to collaborate, share ideas, and learn more about "happenings." Sports medicine and sport science conferences in general as well as sport psychology conferences specifically are being hosted more frequently by various countries, national societies, and international organizations. (Leading organizations that hold regular conferences were identified in the preceding section.)

Professional activities vary in different countries and locations in the world. Some countries have benefited from an economic and educational structure that has provided support and opportunities. Regardless of advantages and disadvantages, one point is clear: Sport and exercise psychology is emerging at a rapid rate all over the globe as a legitimate scholarly specialization capable of offering valuable services.

Recognition and Respectability

A potential rosy path in SEP is not without prickly weeds. The excitement surrounding the emergence of educational and intervention programs associated with sport and exercise, with considerable media exposure, has led to unfortunate consequences on occasion. Claims for efficacy and speed of techniques are sometimes unjustified. Some individuals with inadequate academic preparation in psychology and the sport sciences as well as limited experiences in sport settings are promising services that are not scientifically valid. Some try to start at the top—with professional or Olympic athletes—before they have had sufficient experiences with average athletes. Regular quality checks on what is happening in the name of SEP need to be made, and a structure for such a purpose should be established. SEP must proceed carefully if acceptance is to be steady and the outcomes fruitful. The dangers are clear when one tries to run before knowing how to walk. Progress is a slow and painful but exciting process. Competent sport and exercise psychologists should possess values and ethics, and continue to develop guidelines for the field. This is a major challenge in the immediate future. Athlete's skills take many years of dedicated training and practice to hone, and the same is the case for the services that can be provided to them and others, as well as the research themes that can be undertaken satisfactorily.

Research

As in many academic specializations, professionals may become primarily motivated to pursue an educational path, a research path, or a practice path. Many try to blend two or even all three of the paths. The usual *educational* role is that of university professor. For those committed to the *practice* of SEP, possible roles have been discussed earlier in the chapter. In this section, the focus is on research directions for the field.

Other attempts have been made to suggest future scholarly directions (e.g., Singer, 1986, 1994; Strean & Roberts, 1992). Such projections become more complex and hazardous if one tries to predict (a) topical themes, (b) type of focus (e.g., more applied vs. more basic), (c) methodological approaches (e.g., quantitative vs. qualitative), (d) multidisciplinary possibilities, and (e) appropriate models and theories. Geographical and cultural differences among countries result in differing interests and approaches, which also makes prediction difficult. Research trends in sport psychology, as expected, reflect trends in psychology in general.

The Significance of Science and a Body of Knowledge

A fundamental assumption is the need for the formulation and continual advancement of a scholarly body of knowledge in SEP. The 1970s and early 1980s witnessed the generation of lines of research, usually laboratory-centered, to establish the credibility and acceptability of SEP within university settings. Although some of the work has been sustained, many scholars have shifted gears. Applied, or application-oriented, research is in vogue. The goal is to work with more ecologically valid settings to have a more direct impact on the potential and practical concerns of the consumers of the information generated from this research (Singer, 1989).

The critical point is the need for SEP to be anchored in a legitimate body of knowledge. Both applied and basic (fundamental) research are necessary; they have different primary missions. What is important is that the research advance the body of knowledge and provide a suitable and defensible basis for services rendered. Those who practice SEP should be well versed in the values, methods, and outcomes of scientific research, as Howell (1992) suggested for psychology in general. A solid scientific base provides credibility for SEP in the minds of fellow scholars in other specializations as well as the general public. We share Howell's concern that more and more psychology students seem to want applied courses and careers. There is a growing scientific deficit. The body of knowledge associated with SEP must grow with sincere efforts on the part of researchers attempting to address significant questions and issues, and practicing specialists being aware of developments in the field.

Conceptual Approaches to Research

Sport and exercise psychology has been advanced considerably by the teachings of cognitive psychology. Major contributions are as follows:

1. The increased understanding of mental processes and operations, as well as cognitive strategies, associated with effective learning and performance.
2. A conceptual framework (the computer metaphor) for studying sequential or parallel stages that are internally activated, ranging from selectively attending to pertinent sources of information (cues) to completing a movement.
3. The formulation of practical guidelines to help individuals use their mental processes to their advantage.
4. The development of self-regulatory strategies to cope with stress and potential performance distractors, thereby enhancing achievement potential.
5. The recognition of expectations and attributions (thought processes) as important factors associated with self-perceptions and achievement motivation.

The counterargument to cognitive psychology models is that traditional research approaches related to this kind of conceptualization are too contrived and do not account for the irregularity and unpredictability of human states and behaviors. One theoretical challenge comes from recent developments associated with theories and models using concepts of ecology, chaos, nonlinear dynamics, self-organizaiton, and perception–action.

Ecological and dynamical concepts (e.g., Cziko, 1992; Turvey, 1990) emphasize the continuing interaction of action and perception and offer alternative approaches to information-processing models for the study and understanding of movement behaviors. Presumably, they are more real-world-oriented and tend to view the larger picture of behavior. Whereas information-processing models depend to a great extent on isolated cognitive processes, perception–action models are linked more closely to the biological sciences. Related to such approaches to understanding human behavior are advances in understanding and applying principles that are based on the concepts of chaos, nonlinear dynamics, and self-organization (Barton, 1994). Although the ideas evolved primarily from the minds of investigators in the physical or natural sciences, these models are now gaining the attention of psychologists. Proponents suggest that the world is not an orderly, predictable place. Things happen and people behave in nondeterministic and nonlinear ways.

It will be of interest to see to what extent cognitive psychology and traditional paradigms will continue to dominate the research directions in SEP and to what degree the alternative models and approaches just described will prevail. There is a concern that there is a need to be liberated from simplistic experimentation and meaningless generalizations. One question is whether this really is the current status of research. Another question is whether alternative models will do a better job. Perhaps different issues and research problems may be accommodated best with different conceptual models and corresponding approaches to research.

Research Themes

Of course, favored conceptual frameworks tend to influence research topics undertaken as well as the methodologies used. As SEP's structure has become more varied and its boundaries extended, themes of research have been expanded considerably. On one hand, SEP draws heavily on the conceptual developments and practical ideas of psychology in general. Yet the analysis of excellence in sport and what contributes to it yields a knowledge base transferable to many other fields. Whereas not too many years ago the study of sport and movement skill and of the athlete's quest for proficiency was perceived as frivolous activity, it is now considered quite significant. Sport is a central fixture and force in society and of interest to many people regardless of occupation and economic level. Furthermore, research conclusions made about striving and achieving provide insights applicable to many endeavors and occupations.

Health promotion also is receiving more and more attention. From the exercise psychologist's perspective, the study of routine exercise involvement as well as factors associated with avoidance or dropping out leads to practical solutions. Researchers have identified potential psychological benefits to exercise, including improved body and self-concept, positive mood shifts, anxiety management, and overall feelings of well-being (e.g., Berger & McInman, 1993; Dishman, 1993). This is encouraging for the average person to know about, as well as for those with psychological disorders.

Considering the breadth of the SEP field and the topics being researched at present, it would be foolish to attempt to identify the most significant ones to be pursued in the future. Figure 1 provides an overview of areas in which sport and exercise psychologists are active.

Researchers concerned with *learning, performance, and skill* focus on how learning processes work, how experts and novices differ in the use of strategies, and how practice conditions might be made most favorable. An interest in *youth sport* participants and programs involves understanding children, capabilities, motives, and the types of support systems that promote beneficial psychological and performance outcomes. *Mental–psychological skills and programs* involves the study of procedures that can best enhance personal resources that contribute to excellence in performance.

Counseling typically applies to those who are trained in clinical or counseling psychology or in psychiatry and are professionally prepared to help athletes with maladaptive behaviors and disorders that can undermine coping with the demands of athletic competition as well as life in general. This general area is more closely associated with the provision of services than with research. Athletes typically compete in some form of team structure, and research in *group dynamics* generally involves

Figure 1

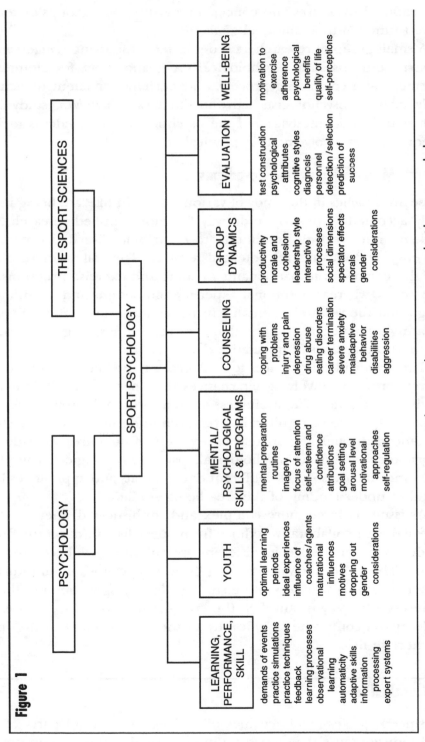

The influence of psychology and the sport sciences on the many dimensions associated with sport psychology.

organizational structures and concepts regarding how groups or teams can best function to attain ideal goals.

A small group of researchers is dedicated to studying *evaluation* for the purpose of assessing psychological states and traits, for aiding the advisement and counseling process, and perhaps for talent detection. Finally, exercise psychologists active in the area of *well-being* study contributors to healthy lifestyles and the psychological antecedents to and consequences of involvement in physical activity.

Research Methodologies and Paradigms

Diverse approaches in the study of various topics in SEP are being more readily accepted. A push is underway for more applied research, undertaken under realistic conditions, to contribute directly to practical knowledge and meaningful potential services. The call is for research to be directly useful to participants in sport and exercise programs. In other words, whereas traditional experimental designs and quantitative data guided the research mentality in the field for a number of years, increasingly popular and acceptable are case studies, single group designs, and the analysis of qualitative data.

The trend in SEP is also toward greater use and acceptance of research protocols involving alternatives to experimental designs and quantitative statistics. The usefulness of an approach, however, depends on the questions to be resolved in a research undertaking. Clearly, study is enhanced through the analysis of a variety of measures, considering performance as well as psychological, psychophysiological, cognitive, and biomechanical sources. Different data formats and approaches lead to a fuller understanding of the area being studied.

As issues become more complex and sophisticated, they are best addressed with collaborative efforts from specialists in different fields. The depth of knowledge in different specializations is becoming impressive. The trend is toward creating "working groups" in an informal manner or through centers and institutes identifying a common theme of interest. One way or another, the cross-fertilization of experts is desirable; it will contribute significantly to the advancement of the sport and exercise field.

Conclusion

The sincere professional activities of colleagues from all parts of the world indicate more than a passing interest in SEP. It is a commitment.

The goals are to establish SEP as a scientifically based specialization, advancing a strong body of knowledge, preparing students with legitimate credentials, and offering valid and effective services. The process is well underway for attaining such goals, as is indicated by the increasing number of graduate students with excellent credentials and enthusiasm, the number of higher education institutions offering specializations, the number and quality of research articles being published, and the commitment by leaders to advance the field. There is still a long road to traverse but in many ways, the process of striving is as exciting as that of realizing.

Differences in backgrounds and opinions are healthy. People challenge each other. They become stronger from mutual stimulation. SEP is growing owing to the increasing numbers of young, talented, and motivated scholars entering the field as well as of mature professionals who can offer guidance. Gaining identity, respect, and recognition does not come easily. SEP is in the process of having its credibility established.

References

American Psychological Association (1992). Ethical principles of psychologists and code of conduct. *American Psychologist, 47,* 1597–1611.

Barton, S. (1994). Chaos, self-organization, and psychology. *American Psychologist, 49,* 5–14.

Berger, B. G., & McInman, A. (1993). Exercise and the quality of life. In R. N. Singer, M. Murphy, & L. K. Tennart (Eds.), *Handbook of research on sport psychology* (pp. 729–760). New York: Macmillan.

Boneau, C. A. (1992). Observations on psychology's past and future. *American Psychologist, 47,* 1586–1596.

Cziko, G. A. (1992). Purposeful behavior as the control of perception: Implications for educational research. *Educational Researcher, 21,* 10–18.

Dishman, R. K. (1993). Exercise adherence. In R. N. Singer, M. Murphy, & R. K. Tennart (Eds.), *Handbook of research on sport psychology* (pp. 779–799). New York: Macmillan.

Howell, W. (1992, December). Field's scientific deficit will have dire effects. *APA Monitor, 23,* 21.

LeUnes, A., & Hayward, S. A. (1990). Sport psychology as viewed by chairpersons of APA-approved clinical psychology programs. *The Sport Psychologist, 4,* 18–24.

Linder, D. E., Brewer, B. W., Van Raalte, J. L., & DeLange, N. (1991). A negative halo for athletes who consult sport psychologists: Replication and extension. *Journal of Sport & Exercise Psychology, 13,* 133–148.

Meade, V. (1994, May). Psychologists forecast future of the profession. *APA Monitor, 25,* p. 14.

Petrie, T. A., & Watkins, C. E. (1994). A survey of counseling psychology programs and exercise/sport science departments: Sport psychology issues and training. *The Sport Psychologist, 8,* 28–36.

Sachs, M. L., Burke, K. L., & Salitsky, P. B. (1992). *Directory of graduate programs in applied sport psychology*. Association for the Advancement of Applied Sport Psychology.

Scott, T. R. (1991). A personal view of psychology departments. *American Psychologist, 46*, 975–976.

Singer, R. N. (1984). What sport psychology can do for the athlete and coach. *International Journal of Sport Psychology, 15*, 52–61.

Singer, R. N. (1986). Current perspectives on motor learning and sport psychology. In L. E. Unestahl (Ed.), *Sport psychology in theory and practice* (pp. 5–19). Orebro, Sweden: VEJE.

Singer, R. N. (1989). Applied sport psychology in the United States. *Journal of Applied Sport Psychology, 1*, 61–80.

Singer, R. N. (1994). Sport psychology: An integrated approach. In S. Serpa, J. Alves, & V. Pataco (Eds.), *International perspectives on sport and exercise psychology* (pp. 1–20). Morgantown, WV: Fitness Information Technology.

Singer, R. N. (in press). Sport psychology: An overview. In K. Henschen (Ed.), *An analysis of athlete behavior*. Ithaca, NY: Mouvement Publications.

Singer, R. N., Murphey, M., & Tennant, L. K. (Eds.). (1993). *Handbook of research on sport psychology*. New York: Macmillan.

Straub, W. F., & Hinman, D. A. (1992). Profiles and professional perspectives of 10 leading sport psychologists, *The Sport Psychologist, 6*, 297–312.

Strean, W. B., & Roberts, G. E. (1992). Future directions in applied sport psychology research. *The Sport Psychologist, 6*, 55–65.

Turvey, M. T. (1990). Coordination. *American Psychologist, 45*, 938–953.

Van Raalte, J. L., Brewer, B. W., Brewer, D. D., & Linder, D. E. (1992). NCAA Division II college football players' perceptions of an athlete who consults a sport psychologist. *Journal of Sport & Exercise Psychology, 14*, 273–282.

Waite, B. T., & Pettit, M. E. (1993). Work experiences of graduates from doctoral programs in sport psychology. *Journal of Applied Sport Psychology, 5*, 234–250.

Index

A

Aaron, Hank, 26

Abstinence violation effect (AVE), 147

Accountability, from certification, 404

Accredited or approved program, 398

Achievement
  exercise as improving, 169–70
  and self-worth, 54–55, 57

Activation level, and self-talk, 60, 68

"Addicted" athlete, 242

Addiction, negative, 265

Adjustment reactions, 263–64

Adolescent development, 206–8

Adolescents, community-based programs for, 205
  and community setting, 216–17
  developing and evaluating of, 218–22
  as psychologists' vocational-avocational combination, 222
  rationale for, 208–10
  and sports-related life skills, 211–13, 218
  SUPER program, 205, 213–16, 218, 220

Advertising, as ethical issue, 443, 445

Affirmation statements, 57

African Americans
  leisure-time exercise participation of, 135
  in sport, 360–62

Aggression, 278–79

Aggression conflicts, posthypnotic suggestion for, 116

Aging (elderly) populations, and exercise, 173–74, 240–41

AIDS
  and exercise, 173
  and health-compromising behaviors, 207

Alcohol and drug use, 238–39
  among college athletes, 321
  as health-compromising behavior, 207

American Alliance for Health, Physical Education, Recreation and Dance (AAHPERD), 390, 391

American Board of Psychological Hypnosis (ABPH), 113

American Coaching Effectiveness Program, 291

American College of Sports Medicine, 238, 390, 391

American Drug Free Power Lifting Association, 244

American Psychological Association (APA), 390
  accreditation program of, 398
  and allegiance issues, 345
  code of ethics of, 431–32, 434–35, 438–39, 442, 456
  competence principle of, 355
  Division 30 (Psychological Hypnosis) of, 112
  Division 38 (Health Psychology) of, 390

About the Editors

Judy L. Van Raalte received her PhD in social psychology from Arizona State University. She is currently associate professor of psychology and head women's tennis coach at Springfield College. Her research interests include professional issues in sport and exercise psychology and social psychological aspects of sport and exercise. She is former editor of the *Exercise and Sport Psychology Newsletter* and is a Certified Consultant, AAASP.

Britton W. Brewer received his PhD in clinical psychology from Arizona State University. He is currently assistant professor of psychology and head men's cross country coach at Springfield College. His research interests include psychological aspects of sport injury rehabilitation and self-identity in sport. He is a Certified Consultant, AAASP and serves on the editorial boards of the *Athletic Academic Journal*, the *Journal of Applied Sport Psychology*, and *The Sport Psychologist*.